The Interpersonal Communication Book

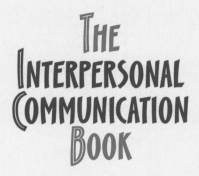

The Interpersonal Communication Book

Ninth Edition

Joseph A. DeVito

Hunter College
of the
City University of New York

Longman

New York San Francisco Boston
London Toronto Sydney Tokyo Singapore Madrid
Mexico City Munich Paris Cape Town Hong Kong Montreal

Publisher: Priscilla McGeehon
Acquisitions Editor: Michael Greer
Development Manager: Lisa Pinto
Development Editor: Nancy Crochiere
Marketing Manager: Megan Galvin-Fak
Supplement Editor: Kristin Muller
Senior Production Manager: Eric Jorgensen
Project Coordination, Text Design, and Electronic Page Makeup: Electronic Publishing Services Inc., NYC
Cover Designer/Manager: Nancy Danahy
Cover Photo: Diana Ong/Superstock
Photo Researcher: Julie Tesser
Manufacturing Buyer: Al Dorsey
Printer and Binder: Quebecor World–Taunton
Cover Printer: The Lehigh Press

For permission to use copyrighted material, grateful acknowledgment is made to the copyright holders on page 398–413, which is hereby made part of this copyright page.

Library of Congress Cataloging-in-Publication Data
DeVito, Joseph A.,
The interpersonal communication book / Joseph A. DeVito.--9th ed.
p. cm.
Includes bibliographical references and index.
ISBN 0-321-05564-0
1. Interpersonal communication. I. Title.
BF637.C45 D49 2001
302.2--dc21 99-087602

Please visit our website at http://www.awl.com/devito

ISBN 0-321-05564-0

12345678910-RNT-03020100

BRIEF CONTENTS

DETAILED CONTENTS

SPECIALIZED CONTENTS

ASK THE **RESEARCHER**

ETHICS IN INTERPERSONAL COMMUNICATION

TEST YOURSELF

PREFACE

Welcome to *The Interpersonal Communication Book*
A GUIDE FOR STUDENTS AND INSTRUCTORS

It's a real privilege to present this ninth edition of *The Interpersonal Communication Book*, a text that has introduced students to interpersonal communication for the last quarter century. Each revision has helped me to improve the presentation of interpersonal communication so that it accurately reflects what we currently know about the subject and is as clear, as interesting, and as involving as it can possibly be.

This ninth edition continues to provide in-depth coverage of interpersonal communication, blending theory and research on the one hand, and practical skills on the other. Its philosophical foundation continues to be the notion of choice. Choice is central to interpersonal communication; as speaker, listener, and communication analyst you are constantly confronted with choice points at every stage of the communication process, choices that will influence the effectiveness of your message and your relationships on which those messages impact. This text provides you with worthwhile options for a vast array of interpersonal situations and discusses the theory, research, and evidence bearing on these communication choices. After completing this text, you should thus be better equipped to make more reasoned, more reasonable, and more effective communication decisions.

THE TEXT

This text is a complete learning package that will provide you with the opportunity to learn about the research and theory in interpersonal communication and to practice the skills necessary for effective interpersonal interaction.

Each **unit opener** contains a photo from a film that serves to visually introduce the topic of the unit. A connecting paragraph then points out the relationship between the film and the contents of the unit. The objective here is to emphasize that interpersonal communication concepts and principles will be found everywhere—in films as well as at the dinner table, in the college cafeteria, and on the telephone and the Internet. After you've read a unit, you may find it interesting to select a topic of the unit that you find especially important, identify a film that would make an appropriate unit opener, and conceptualize a paragraph connecting the film and the concept you're highlighting. If you have the opportunity to share your responses with others, it will be a good way to see how others viewed the unit and to review the unit contents from these different perspectives. In addition, the unit opener contains a list of the major topics covered in the unit along with a brief idea of what each topic entails.

The material continues to be divided into relatively brief units. Students continue to favor their brief length and clear, focused perspective that makes them easier to read and review. Instructors prefer them because they can be more easily rearranged to suit the needs of specific students and courses. As in the previous edition, the units are grouped into three parts: Preliminaries, Messages, and Relationships.

Each unit ends with (1) a **summary,** now in full-sentence outline form; (2) a series of ten **questions** to provide opportunities to apply the material from the unit; and (3) a **guide to the experiential vehicles** that are especially useful in enabling you to work with the unit contents. The **Handbook of Experiential Learning Vehicles**—which may be accessed on the Web—contains 30 exercises that illustrate a wide variety of interpersonal communication concepts and principles. A grid identifying the exercise, and some of the appropriate units to coordinate it with, prefaces the exercises and is also accessed on the Web.

A **Glossary of Concepts and Skills** has been significantly updated and improved. It integrates the concepts and the skills, providing both definitions of key terms and, where appropriate, the corresponding skills *(in italics)*, once again emphasizing the close connection between theoretical concepts and practical skills.

You'll get maximum benefit out of this text if you understand the way the book was written and some of the logic underlying the book's features. Instructors who used the previous edition will find identified here some of the major new and revised features.

Research Q & A

A new feature, **Ask the Researcher,** has been added to this edition to emphasize the close connection between theory and research on the one hand, and practical skills on the other. Nationally and internationally known theorists and researchers were asked to respond to a question typical of those students ask about interpersonal communication. You'll find their responses—26 in all—both provocative and practical. You may find it interesting to read the question and try to answer it yourself. Then you can compare your answer with that provided by the researcher and, in small groups or with the class as a whole, with those that other students came up with. A complete list of these Ask the Researcher items is provided in the Specialized Table of Contents, p. xiii.

Ethics in Interpersonal Communication

New to this edition, 17 **Ethics in Interpersonal Communication** boxes present brief discussions of ethical issues. Early ethics boxes explain the nature of ethics, objective and subjective approaches and a means-ends analysis. Later boxes raise more specific ethical issues, such as the ethics of interpersonal silence, gossiping, lying, revealing secrets, and workplace relationships. In addition to discussing these specific ethical issues, each box contains a related case and asks you to consider how you would respond. A complete list of these Ethics of Interpersonal Communication boxes is provided in the Specialized Table of Contents on pages xiii and xiv.

Workplace Communication and Relationships

A new unit (Unit 22, Interpersonal Communication and Relationships in the Workplace) has been added to this edition to reflect the growing concern students have for insights into interpersonal communication in the business world. This new unit covers using communication to get into the workplace (that is, the employment interview), communication in the workplace (for example, upward, downward, lateral, and grapevine communication), and workplace relationships (for example, romantic, mentoring, and networking relationships).

Cultural Aspects

As our knowledge of culture and its relevance to interpersonal communication grow, so must its presence in an interpersonal communication textbook and course. An entire unit devoted to culture (Unit 3, Culture in Interpersonal Communication) is presented early in the text and as one of the foundation concepts for understanding interpersonal communication. New to this unit is a discussion of masculine and feminine cultures and two new self-tests—one on individual versus collective orientation and one on openness to intercultural communication.

In addition to this separate unit, the importance of culture to all aspects of interpersonal communication is stressed throughout. Here are some of the more important discussions:

- the cultural dimension of context, an introduction to culture and interpersonal communication (the relevance of culture, the aim of a cultural perspective) (Unit 1)
- culture in complementary and symmetrical relationships, in the principle of adjustment, and in objective and subjective views of ethics (Unit 2)
- the role of culture in the development of self-concept and as an influencing factor in self-disclosure (Unit 4)
- culture and communication apprehension and in assertiveness (Unit 5)
- culture and schemata, implicit personality theory, the self-serving bias, uncertainty, and developing cultural sensitivity (Unit 6)
- listening, culture, and gender (Unit 7)
- cultural sensitivity as a skill of interpersonal competence, cultural influences on compliments, equality, immediacy, and expressiveness (Unit 8)
- culture and rules, directness, context, and nonverbal cultural taboos (Unit 9)
- racism, sexism, heterosexism; culture and excluding talk; culture and criticism (Unit 10)
- cultural identifiers, ethnocentrism, lying and cultural differences (Unit 11)
- culture and body gestures, attractiveness and culture, the influence of culture on facial and eye communication, gender and cultural differences in touch, silence in culture and in a socio-political world (Unit 12)
- culture and space expectations, color and culture, gifts and culture, cultural time (displaced-diffused, monochronism-polychronism, the social clock), and time and intercultural communication (Unit 13)
- conversational maxims, culture, and gender (Unit 14)
- relationships in cultural context, cultural differences in dissolving relationships, and relationship length and culture (Unit 15)
- attitude similarity and culture; equity, culture, and gender (Unit 16)
- the cultural dimension of power, Machiavellianism and culture (Unit 18)
- conflict, culture, and gender; culture and face-saving (Unit 19)
- cultural differences in friendship, cultural differences in loving (Unit 20)
- culture and the family (Unit 21)
- cultural rules and the organization, criticism and culture (Unit 22)

Technology

The role of chat groups, e-mail and listservs, and the development of online relationships is fully integrated throughout the text. For example, email, listservs, and chat groups are discussed as forms of interpersonal communication (Unit 1), lurking as a means for uncertainty reduction (Unit 6), conversational maxims and the Internet (Unit 14), online relationships (Unit 15), online conflicts (Unit 19), online interview and online groups (Unit 22).

Self-tests

Self-tests, increased to 27 for this edition, help personalize the material and are presented throughout the text. Self-tests cover such topics as your cultural beliefs and values, your willingness to self-disclose and reveal who you "really" are, your degree of apprehension in various communication situations, and your tendencies to become verbally aggressive or argumentative. New self-tests include: Are You from an Individual or a Collectivist Culture? (Unit 3), How Open Are You Interculturally? (Unit 3), and How Apprehensive Are you in Employment Interviews? (Unit 22). Thirteen of these tests are used regularly in interpersonal communication research, and 14 were developed to highlight and preview some part of the text material. A complete list of self-tests appears in the Specialized Tables of Contents on page xiv.

UNIT-BY-UNIT CHANGES

In addition to the new material in Ask the Researcher and the Ethics of Interpersonal Communication boxes, a variety of new research has been integrated into the text, as have new examples and illustrations. Another general change has been the reduction in the number of brief bulleted items that appeared in previous editions, their combination, and their discussion in paragraphs. Other material has been updated, expanded, or substantially revised; by unit, the most notable are these:

- Unit 1. Universals of Interpersonal Communication. Discussions of e-mail, newsgroups, and chat rooms as forms of interpersonal communication are now included, as is an expansion of noise.
- Unit 2. Axioms of Interpersonal Communication. The theory and research component of interpersonal communication has been more fully integrated into the text and the discussion of symmetrical and complementary relationships has been reduced in length.
- Unit 3. Culture in Interpersonal Communication. The discussion of individual and collective orientation has been expanded to include a new self-test, a consideration of masculine and feminine cultures has been added, the section on uncertainty reduction as a theory of intercultural communication has been revised, and a new self-test on openness to intercultural communication has been added.
- Unit 4. The Self in Interpersonal Communication. New material includes "cultural teachings" in the development of self-concept and a revision of the discussions of the influences on self-disclosure and the rewards of self-disclosure.
- Unit 5. Apprehension and Assertiveness. The section on assertiveness has been substantially revised and includes comparisons of assertive, nonassertive, and aggressive messages and an improved presentation of the guides to communication assertiveness.
- Unit 6. Perception in Interpersonal Communication. This unit has been substantially revised. The interpersonal perception process is now presented in a five-stage model to include rules, schemata, and scripts and the communication implications of such a model. The concepts of schemata and scripts. Attribution is now treated as one of the perceptual processes rather than separately, and over-

attribution has been added as a distortion of perceptual attribution accuracy. In addition, the discussion of reducing uncertainty as a strategy for increasing perceptual accuracy has been substantially revised and cultural sensitivity has been added as a way of increasing perceptual accuracy.

- Unit 7. Listening in Interpersonal Communication. Thinking fallacies have been integrated into critical listening; active listening is presented as one of five styles of listening rather than as a separate section.
- Unit 8. Effectiveness in Interpersonal Communication. The strategies for achieving effectiveness have been recast and regrouped into more general principles and are presented largely in regular text rather than bulleted phrases. A new table, Talking with a Deaf Person, has been added.
- Unit 9. Universals of Verbal and Nonverbal Messages. Discussion of emotions has been integrated into the text, and a new section, Messages Vary in Abstraction, has been added.
- Unit 10. Verbal Messages: Understanding Principles and Pitfalls. The suggestions for talking with the grief stricken and for expressing criticism have been revised.
- Unit 11. Verbal Messages: Reducing Barriers to Interaction. This unit was totally reorganized and recast into five basic principles of language. The discussion of cultural identifiers has been updated. Lying and gossip are included as a barrier concerned with the ethical dimension of messages.
- Unit 12. Nonverbal Messages: Body and Sound. A new section on body appearance has been added to the discussion of body communication.
- Unit 13. Nonverbal Messages: Space and Time. Smell has been placed here with artifactual communication. The discussion of time has been streamlined with subtopics presented in photo captions.
- Unit 14. Messages and Conversation. A new table, Conversationally Difficult People and How Not to Be One of Them, has been added. The discussion of maintaining conversations has been reshaped into Principles and Maxims of Conversation, Netiquette, and Conversational Turns. New material has been added to the discussion of interruptions.
- Unit 15. Universals of Interpersonal Relationships. This unit has been recast to include the cultural dimensions of relationships (so that it appears early in the coverage of relationships rather than at the end of this coverage, as in the previous edition) and also integrates parasocial and online relationships into the text proper.
- Unit 16. Relationship Development and Deterioration. This new unit incorporates material that was formerly in Units 16 and 17 of the previous edition. The section on ending the relationship has been restructured into two parts: strategies of disengagement and what to do if the relationship does end.
- Unit 17. Relationship Maintenance and Repair. The predictions of the theories have been integrated into the text proper rather than appearing as a separate heading.
- Unit 18. Power in Interpersonal Relationships. The unit includes a streamlined discussion of sexual harassment. The discussions of reward and coercive power have been combined to emphasize their similarities and differences. Empowering others and compliance gaining and resisting are now integrated as ways of communicating power.
- Unit 19. Conflict in Interpersonal Relationships. New discussions of gender and online conflicts have been added. The section Before and After the Conflict, from the previous edition, has been integrated into the model of communication resolution.
- Unit 20. Friends and Lovers. The discussions of friends and lovers have been streamlined, with fewer but more meaningful subtopics.

- Unit 21. Primary and Family Relationships. Communication Enhancement, a new approach to improved family communication, incorporates many of the previously discussed principles and so serves a unifying and reviewing function, as well as explaining some of the ways to improve relationship communication.
- Unit 22. Interpersonal Communication and Relationships in the Workplace. This unit is new to this edition and includes three topics: interviewing, workplace communication, and workplace relationships.

THE PEDAGOGY

In this edition, I've increased efforts to make the text even more interactive than it was in the previous editions. Some examples of this emphasis are:

- New to this edition, **thinking ahead** questions introduce each of the major topics in the text, providing a provocative lead-in for the material to be covered. They are designed to help you focus directly on the specific material to be covered and at the same time to personalize the material and make it relevant to your own interpersonal communication experiences. **Thinking back** questions appear at the end of each major topic and are designed to help you reflect upon, review, and in some cases apply what you've just read. When you come upon these "thinking ahead" and "thinking back" questions, pause and try to answer them in terms of your own experiences and newly acquired insights.
- New to this edition, the unit **summaries** (resembling full-sentence outlines) now provide more thorough reviews of the material and also reflect the relationships among the topics of the unit. You may find it helpful to read these both before and after reading the unit. Reading them as a preface to the unit will give you a clear idea of what the unit covers and will help you focus on the major concepts of the unit and on the relationships among the concepts. Reading them as a summary will enable you to review and better remember the unit's content. Key terms covered in the unit appear in the summary in boldface.
- **Questions for thinking critically** about the contents of each unit appear at the end of each unit and will prove useful for stimulating discussion and for extending and applying the principles to other areas.
- **Captions** for photos, tables, and figures have been extended beyond what is customary practice; the captions draw more focused attention to the visuals and better integrate them into the text, making them functional rather than ornamental.
- **Dialogues** to illustrate a wide variety of concepts appear throughout the text and in some of the experiential vehicles. They are designed to invite analysis and argument.
- **Experiential vehicles** on the Web provide opportunities for working actively with the concepts discussed in the text. In all, 30 exercises are provided and cover such topics as assertiveness, listening, facial expressions, and power. New to this edition are No. 14, Must Lie Situations; No. 17, Gender and the Topics of Conversation; No. 18, Formulating Excuses; No. 29, Practicing Interviewing Skills, and No. 30, Confronting Workplace Communication Difficulties. Two experiences integrated into the previous edition text are here presented as experiential vehicles: No. 5, Weighing the Rewards and Costs of Self-Disclosure, and No. 24, Applying the Theories.

Two kinds of web icons in the text margins tie the text and its exciting new Companion Website together:

- **"Try It!" icons** direct students to the Companion Website where they engage in interactive simulations and activities that get them putting principles to practice.
- **"Web Exploration" icons** direct students to the Companion Website where they further explore topics and answer critical thinking questions about what they find.

ACKNOWLEDGMENTS

My primary debt in this revision is to the many researchers who responded to my call for responses to a variety of questions and whose answers appear in the Ask the Researcher feature throughout the text. Without your cooperation, good will, and support, this feature could obviously not have been done. I thank you all (in order of appearance):

Bill Eadie
Howard Giles
Michael L. Hecht
Sandra Petronio
Ruth Ann Clark
Jesse Delia
James C. McCroskey
Charles R. Berger
Andrew D. Wolvin
Matt Martin
Rebecca B. Rubin
Jean Civikly
Ralph Smith
Russel Windes
Thomas M. Steinfatt
Laura Guerrero
Gary Gumpert
Susan Drucker
Marie Radford
Alan Rubin
Steve Duck
Dan Canary
Fred E. Jandt
Andrew S. Rancer
William K. Rawlins
Mary Anne Fitzpatrick
Bernard J. Brommel
Linda L. Putnam
Melanie Booth-Butterfield
Steven Booth-Butterfield

I owe a special debt to Michael Hecht, who consulted with me and advised me on a wide variety of issues and topics.

I want also to express my appreciation to the many specialists who carefully reviewed the eighth edition text and the manuscript for this ninth edition. Your comments resulted in a large number of changes. Thank you:

Dianne L. Blomberg, Metropolitan State College of Denver
William D. Harpine, University of Akron
Sally Henzl, University of Wisconsin, Milwaukee
Susan Kline, Ohio State University
Donald Polzella, University of Dayton
Jacqueline Ralston, Columbia College
Glen Stamp, Ball State University

I want to thank Nancy Crochiere, developmental editor, who offered sound advice and wise counsel throughout the revision process. I also want to thank Michael Greer, communication editor, for taking such good care of this project; Eileen Smith, copy editor, for editing the manuscript with unusual precision and excellent advice; Julie Tesser, photo researcher, for locating the text's many photos; and Brooks Ellis, project editor, who expertly coordinated the process of changing a manuscript into a book.

Joseph A. DeVito
jdevito@shiva.hunter.cuny.edu

UNIT 1

UNIVERSALS OF INTERPERSONAL COMMUNICATION

Alien Nation (1988)

IF YOUR LIPS WOULD KEEP FROM
SLIPS
FIVE THINGS OBSERVE WITH CARE;
TO WHOM YOU SPEAK, OF WHOM YOU
SPEAK,
AND HOW, AND WHEN, AND WHERE.

—W. E. NORRIS

Nature of Interpersonal Communication
Elements of Interpersonal Communication
Culture and Interpersonal Communication

IN THE FILM ALIEN NATION *the literal focus is on alien-human communication; however, in a larger sense the film is about the difficulties in communicating with people from other cultures. Throughout the film, and the television series it gave rise to, you see the same prejudices, biases, and miscommunication that you see today when members of different cultures talk. In this first unit, and throughout the text, we'll examine the role that culture plays in interpersonal communication. First, however, we explain what interpersonal communication is and what its essential parts or elements are.*

Interpersonal communication is something you do every day:

- asking for a date
- applying for a job
- responding to a compliment
- reporting to your supervisor
- asking an instructor about an assignment
- chatting with coworkers
- persuading a friend to go bowling
- developing new relationships
- maintaining and repairing relationships
- dissolving relationships

Understanding these interactions is an essential part of a liberal education. Much as an educated person must know geography, history, science, and mathematics, you need to know the how, why, and what of communication. It's a significant part of the world in which you live and it's becoming more significant daily.

Moreover, interpersonal communication is an extremely practical art, and your effectiveness as a friend, relationship partner, coworker, or manager will depend largely on your interpersonal skills. For example, in a survey of 1,001 people over 18 years of age, 53 percent felt that a lack of effective communication was the major cause of marriage failure, significantly greater than money (38 percent) and in-law interference (14 percent) (How Americans Communicate 1999).

Understanding the theory and research in interpersonal communication and mastering its skills go hand in hand. The more you know about interpersonal communication, the more insight and knowledge you'll gain about what works and what doesn't work. The more skills you have within your arsenal of communication strategies, the greater will be your options for communicating in any situation. In a nutshell, the greater your knowledge and the greater the number of communication options at your disposal, the greater the likelihood that you'll be successful in achieving your interpersonal goals.

The ability to communicate successfully in interpersonal situations gives you the power to achieve a wide variety of goals—to make friends, to establish and maintain successful relationships, to climb the organizational ladder, to interact effectively with people from cultures different from your own, and even to contribute to your own self-esteem (Carlock 1999). So important is this ability that the U.S. Department of Labor identifies interpersonal skills as one of the five essential skills for a nation and an individual to be economically competitive (*New York Times*, 3 July 1991, A17).

In this book, the emphasis is on your understanding of interpersonal communication: its theories and research and its practical skills. Theory-research and skills are considered together as we progress through the elements of interpersonal communication, the ways verbal and nonverbal messages operate in interpersonal encounters, and the ways relationships are developed and maintained, repaired, and even dissolved. As a preface, examine your assumptions about interpersonal communication by taking the accompanying self-test.

TEST YOURSELF *What Do You Believe About Interpersonal Communication?*

Respond to each of the following statements with *true* if you believe the statement is usually true or *false* if you believe the statement is usually false.

_______ 1. Good communicators are born, not made.

_______ 2. The more you communicate, the better at it you will be.

_______ 3. Opening lines such as "Hello, how are you?" or "Fine weather today" or "Have you got the time?" serve no useful interpersonal purpose.

_______ 4. In your interpersonal communications, a good guide to follow is to be as open, empathic, and supportive as you can be.

_______ 5. When verbal and nonverbal messages contradict each other, people believe the verbal message.

_______ 6. The best guide to follow when communicating with people from other cultures is to ignore the differences and treat the other person just as you'd treat members of your own culture.

_______ 7. Effective interpersonal communicators do not rely on "power tactics."

_______ 8. Fear of speaking is detrimental and must be eliminated.

_______ 9. When there is conflict, your relationship is in trouble.

_______ 10. When two people are in a close relationship for a long period of time, one should not have to communicate his or her needs and wants; the other person should know what these are.

As you probably figured out, all 10 statements are generally false. As you read this text, you'll discover not only why these beliefs are false but also the trouble you can get into when you assume they're true. For now, and in brief, here are some of the reasons each of the statements is generally false: (1) Effective communication is a learned skill; although some people are born brighter or more extroverted, all can improve their abilities and become more effective communicators. (2) It's not the amount of communication people engage in but the quality that matters; if you practice bad habits, you're more likely to grow less effective than more effective, so it's important to learn and follow the principles of effectiveness. (3) These kinds of messages actually serve the extremely important purpose of opening the channels of communication and of letting each other know that the normal rules of communication will operate in this conversation. (4) Each interpersonal situation is unique and therefore the type of communication appropriate in one situation may not be appropriate in another. (5) Whether you believe the verbal or the nonverbal messages depends on the total communication context, but generally research does find that people are more likely to believe the nonverbal messages.

(6) This assumption will probably get you into considerable trouble since people from different cultures will often attribute different meanings to a message; members of different cultures also follow different rules for what is and what is not appropriate in interpersonal communication. (7) Power is an inevitable part of all interpersonal interactions, so it really can't be eliminated even if you want it to be. (8) Most speakers are nervous; managing, not eliminating, the fear will enable you to become effective regardless of your current level of fear. (9) All meaningful relationships experience

conflict; relationships are not in trouble when there is conflict, though dealing with conflict ineffectively can often damage the relationship. (10) This assumption is at the heart of many interpersonal difficulties—people aren't mind readers, and to assume they are merely sets up barriers to open and honest communication. ■

THINKING AHEAD ▸▸
How do you communicate differently with, say, a stranger you just met on a bus and a close friend you've known for years?

NATURE OF INTERPERSONAL COMMUNICATION

Interpersonal communication can be defined in a variety of ways. In a dyadic or relational definition, you'd define interpersonal communication by the number of people communicating and by their relationship to each other. In a developmental definition, you'd define interpersonal communication as a process which begins as impersonal and becomes more and more personal as the interactions increase in frequency and intimacy. Explaining these definitions in more detail will help clarify what interpersonal communication is and how it works.

A Dyadic (Relational) Approach to Interpersonal Communication

In a dyadic or relational definition, **interpersonal communication** is the communication that takes place between two persons who have an established relationship; the people are in some way "connected." Interpersonal communication would thus include what takes place between a son and his father, an employer and employee, two sisters, a teacher and a student, two lovers, two friends, and so on.

You could argue that it's impossible to have dyadic (two-person) communication that isn't interpersonal. Invariably, there is some relationship between two people who are interacting. Even the stranger who asks directions of a neighborhood resident has an identifiable relationship with the resident as soon as the first message is sent. This interpersonal (but nonintimate) relationship will then influence how the two individuals interact with each other.

Dyadic Primacy Even when you have triads (groups of three people), dyads (two-person relationships) are still primary; dyads are always central to interpersonal relationships, a process referred to a **dyadic primacy** (Wilmot 1987, 1995). Consider, for example, the following situation: Al and Bob (a dyad) have been roommates for their first two years of college. Expenses have increased, so they ask Carl to join them and become a third roommate. Now a triad exists. But the original dyad has not gone away; in fact, now there are three dyads: Al and Bob, Al and Carl, and Bob and Carl. Al and Bob are ballplayers and interact a lot about sports. Al and Carl are both studying communication and talk about their classes. Bob and Carl belong to the same religious club and frequently discuss the club's activities. At times, of course, all three interact, but even here the topic of conversation will determine who talks primarily to whom. If the topic is sports, Al and Bob will primarily address each other; Carl will be a kind of outsider. When the topic is classes, Bob is the outsider.

If you examine families, workers in a factory, neighbors in an apartment house, or students in class, you'll find that each large group breaks down at times into a series of dyads. The specific dyad formed naturally depends on the situation, and dyads will probably change over time. As in the case of Al, Bob, and Carl, different dyads will form, depending on the nature of the interaction.

TRY IT!
To learn more about dyadic coalitions, go to www.awl.com/devito

Dyadic Coalitions A **dyadic coalition** is a two-person relationship formed by members of a larger group for achieving a mutually desired benefit or goal (Wilmot 1987). Coalitions—whether in the family, among friends, or at work—may be productive or unproductive. Two workers may form a coalition to develop a program for improving worker morale. Two teachers may undertake research together. The result of these coalitions will benefit not only the individuals involved but also, eventually, all members of the group.

At other times, coalitions are unproductive. The grandparent who develops a coalition with the grandchild against the child's parent may cause all sorts of family difficulties; parental resentment and jealousy, as well as guilt for the child, are just a few possibilities. A parent experiencing marital difficulties may form a coalition with one of the children. This often results in alienating the left-out parent and preventing the child from benefiting from a close relationship with that parent.

Dyadic Consciousness In addition to what you do and say, your interpersonal relationships depend on what you think about your relationship. As your relationship develops, a **dyadic consciousness** emerges; you begin to see yourself as part of a pair, a team, a couple. It's almost as if a third party enters the picture. No longer is it just you and the other person; it's now you, the other person, and the relationship. As the relationship becomes more involved, this third party takes on greater importance. Often individuals sacrifice their own desires or needs for the well-being of "the relationship."

A Developmental Approach to Interpersonal Communication

In the developmental approach, communications are viewed as existing on a continuum ranging from impersonal at one end to intimate at the other. Interpersonal communication, which occupies a broad area on this continuum, is distinguished from impersonal communication by three factors: psychological data, explanatory knowledge, and personally established rules (Miller 1978).

Psychological Data In impersonal encounters, people respond to each other chiefly as members of the class or group to which each belongs. For example, initially you respond to a particular college professor as you respond to college professors in general. Similarly, the college professor responds to you as he or she responds to students generally. As your relationship becomes more personal, however, both of you begin to respond to each other not as members of groups but as unique individuals. Put differently, in impersonal encounters, the social or cultural role of the person governs your interaction, while in personal or interpersonal encounters, the psychological uniqueness of the person tells you how to interact.

This general move from social to psychological data is true in the United States and in most European cultures. In many Asian and African cultures, however, the individual's group membership is always important; it never recedes into the background. Thus, in these cultures, one's group membership (one's social data)—even in the closest intimate relationships—is always important, often more important than one's individual or psychological characteristics (Moghaddam, Taylor, and Wright 1993).

Explanatory Knowledge In impersonal relationships, you can do little more than *describe* a person or a person's way of communicating. As you get to know someone a bit better, you can *predict* his or her behavior. If you get to know the person even better, you'll become able to *explain* the behavior. The college professor, in an impersonal relationship, may be able to describe, say, your lateness and perhaps also predict that you'll be five minutes late to class each Friday. In an interpersonal situation, however, the professor can go beyond these levels to explain the behavior—in this case, give reasons why you're late.

WEB EXPLORATION
To learn more about personally established rules, go to www.awl.com/devito.

Personally Established Rules In impersonal situations, the rules of interaction are set down by social norms. Students and professors behave toward one another—in impersonal situations—according to the social norms established by their culture and society. However, as the relationship between student and professor becomes interpersonal, the social rules no longer totally regulate the interaction. Student and professor begin to establish rules of their own largely because they begin to see each other as unique individuals rather than merely as members of the social groups "student" and "professor."

The dyadic and the developmental approaches to interpersonal communication are not as separate as they may at first appear. Both help explain what interpersonal communication is, each giving a different perspective to this important form of human behavior. The dyadic or relational definition presents a broad view of interpersonal communication while emphasizing that the interactants are—in some ways, at least—connected. The developmental definition emphasizes the types of interactions that are most significant to people—the more intimate types of relationships that make a substantial difference in your life.

Often interpersonal communication takes place face-to-face. This is the type of interaction that probably comes to mind when you think of conversation. Because of technological advances, however, much conversation takes place online. Online communication is becoming a part of people's experience throughout the world. Such communications are important personally, socially, and professionally. The three major online types of conversation—e-mail, the mailing list group, and the chat group—differ from each other and from face-to-face interaction.

In *e-mail,* you usually type your letter in an e-mail program and send it (along with other documents you may wish to attach) from your computer via modem to your server (the computer at your school or at some commercial organization like America Online), which relays your message through a series of computer hookups and eventually to the server of the person you're addressing. Unlike face-to-face communication, e-mail does not take place in real time. You may send your message today, but the receiver may not read it for a week and may take another week to respond. Much of the spontaneity created by real-time communication is lost here. You may, for example, be very enthusiastic about a topic when you send your e-mail but practically forget it by the time someone responds.

E-mail is more like a postcard than a letter and so can be read by others along the route. It's also virtually unerasable. Especially in large organizations, employees' e-mails are stored on hard disk or on back-up tapes and may be retrieved for a variety of reasons. Currently, for example, large corporations are being sued because of sexist and racist e-mail that their employees wrote and that plaintiffs' lawyers have retrieved from archives long thought destroyed. Also, your e-mail can be easily forwarded to other people by anyone who has access to your files. Although this practice is considered unethical, it's relatively common.

The *mailing list group* consists of a group of people interested in a particular topic who communicate with each other through e-mail. Generally, you subscribe to a list and communicate with all other members by addressing your mail to the group e-mail address. Any message you send to this address will be sent to each member who subscribes to the list. Your message is sent to all members at the same time; there are no asides to the person sitting next to you (as in face-to-face groups). The accompanying Web site on page 7 will provide you with a list of 1,500 mailing lists categorized by topic.

Chat groups, especially Internet Relay Chat (IRC) groups, have proliferated across the Internet. These groups enable members to converse in real time in discussion

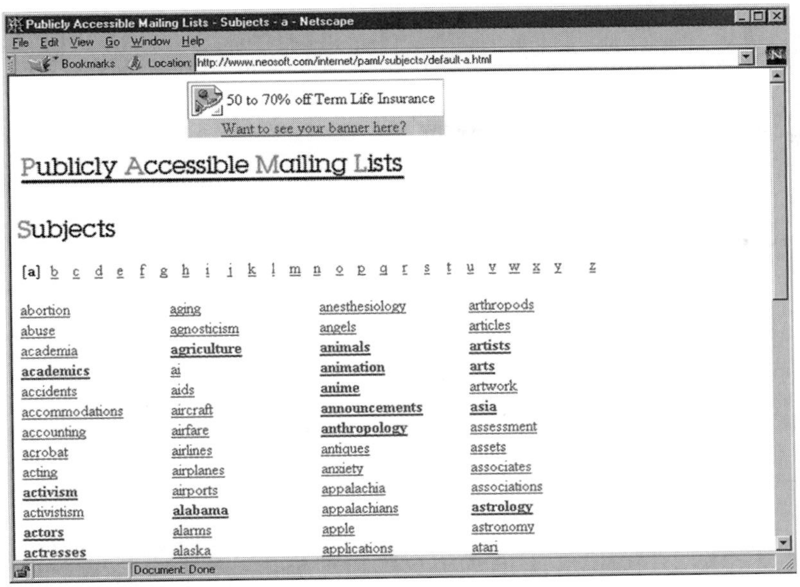

Publicly Accessible Mailing Lists
A useful site for mailing lists is http://www.liszt.com, which contains over 60,000 lists. A list of frequently asked questions and mailing list addresses can be found at http://www.cis.ohiostate.-edu/hypertext/faq/usenet/mail/mailing-lists/top.html. You could also go to one of the search engines and search for mailing lists you might find interesting. To locate a mailing list on a specific topic, you might e-mail your request to listserv@listserv.net. Send the message: *list topic-of-interest*, for example, *list interpersonal communication*. How many mailing lists can you find that might be appropriate to interpersonal communication?

groups. At any one time, there are thousands of groups, so your chances of finding a topic you're interested in are high. Unlike mailing lists, chat communication lets you see a member's message as it's being sent; there's virtually no delay, and recent innovations now enable you to communicate with voice as well as text. Like mailing lists and face-to-face conversation, the purposes of chat groups vary from communication that simply maintains connection with others (what many would call "idle chatter" or "phatic communion") to extremely significant discussions in science, education, health, politics, and just about any field you can name.

Communication chat groups resemble the conversation you'd observe at a large party. The guests divide up into small groups varying from two on up, and each discusses its own topic or version of a general topic. For example, in a group about travel, five people may be discussing the difficulties of traveling to communist countries, three people may be discussing airport security systems, and two people may be discussing bargain rates for cruises to Mexico, all on this one channel dealing with travel. Such groups also allow you to *whisper,* to communicate with just one other person without giving access to your message to other participants. So, although you may be communicating in one primary group (say, dealing with airport security), you also have your eye trained to pick up something particularly interesting in another group (much as you do at a party). Chat groups also notify you when someone new comes into the group and when someone leaves. Like mailing lists, chat groups have the great advantage that they enable you to communicate with people you would never meet and interact with otherwise. Because chat groups are international, they provide excellent exposure to other cultures, other ideas, and other ways of communicating.

In face-to-face conversation you're expected to contribute to the ongoing discussion. In chat groups you can simply observe; in fact, you're encouraged to *lurk*—to observe the participants' interaction before you say anything yourself. In this way, you'll be able to learn the cultural rules and norms of the group.

An additional perspective on interpersonal communication may be gained by looking at the major divisions or areas of the field as identified in Table 1.1.

Can you explain the changes in communication that took place in an interpersonal relationship as it became closer and more intimate? What changes in communication do you see when a relationship deteriorates?

◀◀ THINKING BACK

TABLE 1.1 The Areas of Interpersonal Communication and Relationships

This table is intended as a guide for identifying some of the important areas in the general topic of "interpersonal communication and relationships" and not as a formal outline of the field. The six areas of interpersonal communication interact and overlap; they're not independent. For example, interpersonal interaction is a part of all the other areas; similarly, intercultural communication can exist in any of the other areas. The related academic areas suggest the close ties among fields of study.

General and Related Areas	Selected Topics
Interpersonal interaction: communication between two people *Related areas*: Psychology, Education, Linguistics, Counseling	Characteristics of effectiveness, Conversational processes, Self-disclosure, Active listening, Nonverbal messages in conversation, Online interaction
Health communication: communication between health professional and patient *Related areas*: Medicine, Psychology, Counseling, Health care	Talking about AIDS, Increasing doctor-patient effectiveness, Communication and aging, Therapeutic communication, Communicating safe-sex guidelines
Family communication: communication within the family system *Related areas*: Sociology, Psychology, Family studies, Social Work	Power in the family, Dysfunctional families, Family conflict, Heterosexual and homosexual families, Parent-child communication
Intercultural communication: communication among members of different races, nationalities, religions, genders, and generations *Related areas*: Anthropology, Sociology, Cultural studies, Business	Cross-generational communication, Male-female communication, Black-Hispanic-Asian-Caucasian, communication, Prejudice and stereotypes in communication, Barriers to intercultural communication, The Internet and cultural diversity
Business and organizational communication: communication among workers in an organizational environment *Related areas*: Business, Management, Public relations, Computer science	Interviewing strategies, Sexual harassment, Upward and downward communication, Increasing managerial effectiveness, Leadership in business
Social and personal relationships: communication in close relationships, such as friendship and love *Related areas*: Psychology, Sociology, Anthropology, Family studies	Relationship development, Relationship breakdown, Repairing relationships, Gender differences in relationships, Increasing intimacy, Verbal abuse

THINKING AHEAD ▸▸
What are the essential parts or elements of the interpersonal communication process?

ELEMENTS OF INTERPERSONAL COMMUNICATION

The model presented in Figure 1.1 is designed to reflect the circular nature of interpersonal communication; both persons send messages simultaneously rather than as a linear sequence where communication goes from person 1 to person 2 to person 1 to person 2 and on and on. Each of the concepts identified in the model and discussed here may be thought of as a **universal of interpersonal communication,** in that it's present in all interpersonal interactions.

Source-Receiver

Interpersonal communication involves at least two persons. Each person formulates and sends messages (**source** functions) and also perceives and comprehends messages (**receiver** functions). The hyphenated term *source-receiver* emphasizes that both functions are performed by each individual in interpersonal communication.

Who you are, what you know, what you believe, what you value, what you want, what you have been told, what your attitudes are all influence what you say, how you say it, what messages you receive, and how you receive them. Each person is unique; each person's communications are unique.

Encoding-Decoding

Encoding refers to the act of producing messages—for example, speaking or writing. *Decoding* is the reverse and refers to the act of understanding messages—for example, listening or reading. By sending your ideas via sound waves, you're putting these ideas into a code, hence *en*coding. By translating sound waves into ideas, you're taking them out of a code, hence *de*coding. Thus, speakers and writers are called **encoders,** and listeners and readers **decoders.** The hyphenated term *encoding-decoding* is used to emphasize that the two activities are performed in combination by each participant. For interpersonal communication to occur, messages must be encoded and decoded. For example, when a parent talks to a child whose eyes are closed and whose ears are covered by stereo headphones, interpersonal communication does not occur because the messages sent are not being received.

ASK THE RESEARCHER

Profiting from Interpersonal Communication

I've just returned to college while keeping my job as an assistant buyer for a sports store chain. I'm planning on staying in the sports field as a buyer and I want to use my college education to help me advance. I want this course in interpersonal communication—and every course—to have a practical payoff. Any suggestions?

Congratulations on your decision to advance your career by returning to college. I'm certain that your experience will help you to understand the course material better. Learning is itself inordinately practical. You may not remember all of the content, but you'll see the world in a different way. In ancient Greece, Plato looked around him, saw the populace wanting skills that would allow them to "win at all costs," and decided that it was up to scholars to be the arbiters of truth. His student, Aristotle, took issue, reminding him that truth has to be accepted by all, not just the few. In the process, Aristotle identified communication as the means by which truth comes to be accepted.

In ancient Greece, Plato looked around him, saw the populace wanting skills that would allow them to "win at all costs," and decided that it was up to scholars to be the arbiters of truth. You've probably been to a sales training course and were given specific things to say to customers.

- Observe carefully. Watch individuals' actions, especially those who have recently achieved success. Don't rely so much on verbal reports and "stories" about success. These "stories" may be more myth than reality.
- Talk to as many people as possible at all levels of the organization. Don't rely on a few individuals' opinions/observations.
- Identify sub-goals that will lead to your primary goals and develop plans to reach these goals. However, when the environment is highly dynamic, be prepared to alter goals and plans as the environment changes. Here again, goal setting and planning are ongoing activities, not just one-time events.

You've probably also noticed that sometimes those things worked, and sometimes they didn't. This course will teach you to see your communication differently and to adapt more readily to new truths as they emerge.

—Bill Eadie (Ph.D., Purdue University) is Associate Director at the National Communication Association, the largest scholarly society for the communication discipline, and an adjunct professor of communication at the University of Maryland, College Park. He particularly works with scholars to communicate the results of their research to the general public. weadie@natcom.org

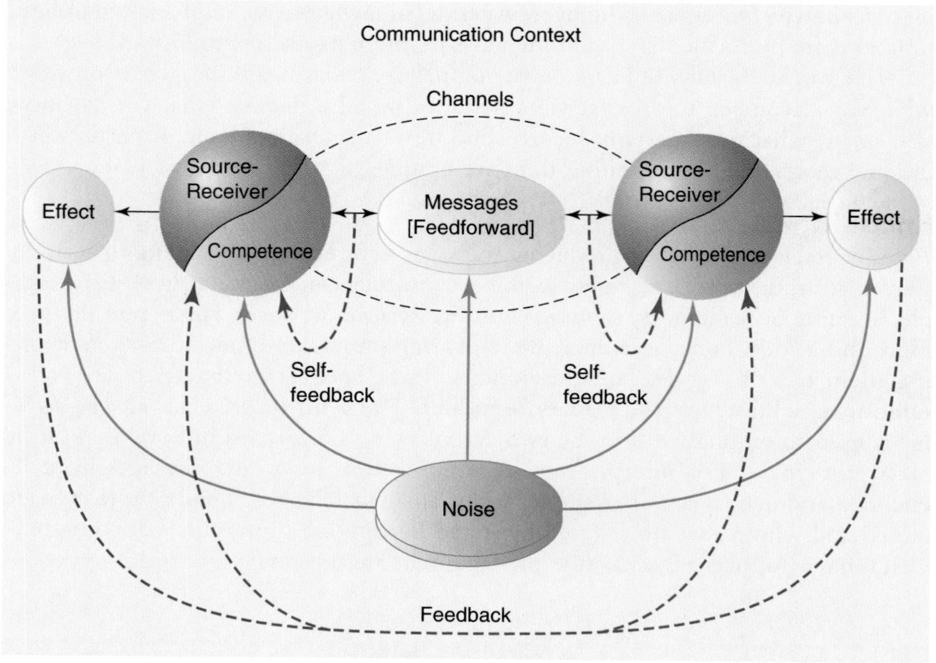

Figure 1.1 A Model of Some Universals of Interpersonal Communication
After you read the section on the elements of interpersonal communication, you may wish to construct your own model of the process. In constructing this model, be careful that you don't fall into the trap of visualizing interpersonal communication as a linear or simple left-to-right, static process. Remember that all elements are interrelated and interdependent. After completing your model, consider, for example: (1) Why is it important to speak of a source-receiver rather than a source and a receiver? (2) Could your model also serve as a model of *intra*personal communication? A model of small-group, public, or mass communication? (3) What elements or concepts other than those noted here might be added to the model?

Competence

Your ability to communicate effectively is your interpersonal **competence** (Spitzberg and Cupach 1989). Your competence includes, for example, the knowledge that in certain contexts and with certain listeners one topic is appropriate and another isn't. Your knowledge about the rules of nonverbal behavior—for example, the appropriateness of touching, vocal volume, and physical closeness—is also part of your competence. In short, interpersonal competence includes knowing how to adjust your communication according to the context of the interaction, the person with whom you're interacting, and a host of other factors discussed throughout this text.

You learn communication competence much as you learn to eat with a knife and fork—by observing others, by explicit instruction, by trial and error. Some have learned better than others, though, and these people are generally the ones with whom you find it interesting and comfortable to talk. They seem to know what to say and how and when to say it.

Not surprisingly there's a positive relationship between interpersonal competence on the one hand and success in college and job satisfaction on the other (Rubin and Graham 1988, Wertz, Sorenson, and Heeren 1988). So much of college and professional life depends on interpersonal competence—meeting and interacting with other students, teachers, or colleagues; asking and answering questions; presenting information or argument—that you should not find this connection surprising. Interpersonal competence also enables you to develop and maintain meaningful relationships in friendship, love, family, and work which, in turn, contribute to the lower levels of anxiety, depression, and loneliness observed in interpersonally competent people (Spitzberg and Cupach 1989).

Messages

Messages—signals that serve as **stimuli** for a receiver—may be auditory (hearing), visual (seeing), tactile (touching), olfactory (smelling), gustatory (tasting), or any combination. You communicate interpersonally by gesture and touch as well as by words and sentences. The clothes you wear communicate to others and, in fact, to yourself as well. The way you walk communicates, as does the way you shake hands, cock your head, comb your hair, sit, smile, or frown. These signals are your interpersonal communication messages. Interpersonal communication can take place by telephone, through prison cell walls, through videophone hookup, or face-to-face. Increasingly, it's taking place through computers.

Messages may be intentional or unintentional. They may result from the most carefully planned strategy as well as from the unintentional slip of the tongue, lingering body odor, or nervous twitch.

Messages may refer to the world, people, and events as well as about other messages. Messages that are about other messages are called **metamessages** and represent many of your everyday messages, for example: "Do you understand?" "Did I say that right?" "What did you say?" "Is it fair to say that . . . ?" "I want to be honest." "That's not logical." Two particularly important types of metamessages are feedback and feedforward.

WEB EXPLORATION
To learn more about feedback messages, go to www.awl.com/devito.

Feedback Messages Throughout the interpersonal communication process, you exchange **feedback**—messages sent back to the speaker concerning reactions

A major goal of this text and your course is to explain the nature of interpersonal competence to improve your own skills. By improving your competence, you'll have a greater number of options available to you. It's much like learning vocabulary: the more words you know, the more ways you have for expressing yourself. What types of interpersonal communication skills would you especially like to develop and improve in this course?

to what is said (Clement and Frandsen 1976). Feedback tells the speaker what effect she or he is having on listeners. On the basis of this feedback, the speaker may adjust, modify, strengthen, de-emphasize, or change the content or form of the messages.

Feedback may come from yourself or from others. In the diagram of the universals of communication (Figure 1.1), the arrows from source-receiver to effect and from one source-receiver to the other source-receiver go in both directions to illustrate the notion of feedback. When you send a message—say, in speaking to another person—you also hear yourself. That is, you get feedback from your own messages: you hear what you say, you feel the way you move, you see what you write. In addition to this self-feedback, you get feedback from others. This feedback can take many forms. A frown or a smile, a yea or a nay, a pat on the back or a punch in the mouth are all types of feedback.

Feedback can be looked upon in terms of five important dimensions: positive-negative, person focused–message focused; immediate-delayed; low monitoring–high monitoring, and supportive-critical. To use feedback effectively, you need to make educated choices along these dimensions (Figure 1.2).

Positive-Negative Feedback may be positive (you compliment or pat someone on the back) or negative (you criticize someone or scowl). **Positive feedback** tells the speaker that he or she is on the right track and should continue communicating in essentially the same way. **Negative feedback** tells the speaker that something is wrong and that some adjustment should be made.

Person Focused–Message Focused Feedback may center on the person ("You're sweet" or "You have a great smile"). Or it may center on the message ("Can you repeat that number?" or "Your argument is a good one").

Immediate-Delayed In interpersonal situations, feedback is often sent immediately after the message is received; you smile or say something in response almost simultaneously with your receiving the message. In other communication situations, however, the feedback may be delayed. Instructor evaluation questionnaires completed at the end of the course provide feedback long after the class began. When you applaud or ask questions of a public speaker at the end of a lecture, the feedback is delayed. In interview situations, the feedback may come weeks afterward. In media situations, some feedback comes immediately through Nielsen ratings, and other feedback comes much later through viewing and buying patterns.

Figure 1.2 Five Dimensions of Feedback
Using these five dimensions of feedback, how would you describe the feedback that longtime and happy lovers would exchange? What kinds of feedback would be exchanged between casual acquaintances? What kinds would be exchanged between two people who disliked each other?

Positive	___:___:___:___:___:___:___	Negative
Person Focused	___:___:___:___:___:___:___	Message Focused
Immediate	___:___:___:___:___:___:___	Delayed
Low Monitoring	___:___:___:___:___:___:___	High Monitoring
Supportive	___:___:___:___:___:___:___	Critical

Low Monitoring–High Monitoring Feedback varies from the spontaneous and totally honest reaction (low-monitored feedback) to the carefully constructed response designed to serve a specific purpose (high-monitored feedback). In most interpersonal situations, you probably give feedback spontaneously; you allow your responses to show without any monitoring. At other times, however, you may be more guarded, as when your boss asks you how you like your job or when your grandfather asks what you think of his new earring.

Supportive-Critical Supportive feedback accepts the speaker and what the speaker says. It occurs, for example, when you console another, encourage him or her to talk, or otherwise confirm the person's definition of self. Critical feedback, on the other hand, is evaluative; it's judgmental. When you give critical feedback (whether positive or negative), you judge another's performance, as in, for example, coaching someone learning a new skill.

Feedforward Messages **Feedforward** is information you provide before sending your primary messages (Richards 1951). Feedforward reveals something about the messages to come. Examples of feedforward include the preface or table of contents of a book, the opening paragraph of a chapter, movie previews, magazine covers, and introductions in public speeches. Feedforward may serve a variety of functions: to open the channels of communication, to preview the message, to disclaim, and to altercast.

To Open the Channels of Communication In his influential essay "The Problem of Meaning in Primitive Languages," anthropologist Bronislaw Malinowski (1923) coined the phrase *phatic communion* to refer to messages that open the channels of communication rather than communicate information. Phatic communion is a perfect example of feedforward. It's information that tells you that the normal, expected, and accepted rules of interaction will be in effect. It tells you another person is willing to communicate.

To Preview the Message Feedforward messages frequently preview other messages. They may, for example, preview the content ("I'm afraid I have bad news for you"), the importance ("Listen to this before you make a move"), the form or style ("I'll tell you all the gory details"), and the positive or negative quality of subsequent messages ("You're not going to like this, but here's what I heard").

To Disclaim The **disclaimer** is a statement that aims to ensure that your message will be understood as you want it to be and that it will not reflect negatively on you. For example, you might use a disclaimer when you think that what you're going to say may be met with opposition. Thus, you say "I'm not against immigration, but . . ." or "Don't think I'm homophobic, but . . ." (Disclaimers, as they function to prevent conversational problems, are discussed in Unit 14.)

To Altercast Feedforward is often used to place the receiver in a specific role and to request responses in terms of this assumed role, a process called **altercasting** (Weinstein and Deutschberger 1963, McLaughlin 1984). For example, you might altercast by asking a friend, "As an advertising executive, what would you think of corrective advertising?" This question casts your friend in the role of advertising executive (rather than parent, Democrat, or Baptist, for example) and asks that she or he answer from a particular perspective.

Channel

The communication **channel** is the medium through which messages pass. It's a kind of bridge connecting source and receiver. Communication rarely takes place over only one channel; two, three, or four channels are often used simultaneously. For example, in face-to-face interaction, you speak and listen (vocal-auditory channel), but you also gesture and receive signals visually (gestural-visual channel), and you emit odors and smell those of others (chemical-olfactory channel). Often you communicate through touch (cutaneous-tactile channel). Another way to think about channels is to consider them as the means of communication: for example, face-to-face contact, telephone, e-mail and snail mail, film, television, radio, smoke signal, fax, or telegraph.

Noise

Noise interferes with your receiving a message someone is sending or with someone receiving your message. Noise may be physical (others talking loudly, cars honking, illegible handwriting, "garbage" on your computer screen), physiological (hearing or visual impairment, articulation disorders), psychological (preconceived ideas, wandering thoughts), or semantic (misunderstood meanings). Technically, noise is anything that distorts the message, anything that prevents the receiver from receiving the message (Table 1.2).

A useful concept in understanding noise and its importance in communication is *signal-to-noise ratio. Signal* refers to information that you'd find useful, and *noise* refers to information that is useless (to you). So, for example, a mailing list or newsgroup that contains lots of useful information would be high on signal and low on noise; those that contain lots of useless information would be high on noise and low on signal.

TABLE 1.2 **Four Types of Noise**

One of the most important skills in communication is to recognize the types of noise and to develop ways to combat them. Consider, for example, what kinds of noise occur in the classroom. What kinds of noise occur in your family communications? What kinds occur at work? What can you do to combat these kinds of noise?

Types of Noise	Definition	Examples
Physical	Interference that is external to both speaker and listener and that prevents accurate transmission of the signal or message	Screeching of passing cars, hum of computer, sunglasses
Physiological	Physical barriers within the speaker or listener	Visual impairments, hearing loss, articulation problems, memory loss
Psychological	Cognitive or mental interference	Biases and prejudices in senders and receivers, closed-mindedness, inaccurate expectations, extreme emotionalism (anger, hate, love, grief)
Semantic	Speaker and listener assigning different meanings	People speaking different languages, use of jargon or overly complex terms not understood by listener, dialectical differences in meaning

Since messages may be visual as well as spoken, noise too may be visual. The sunglasses that prevent someone from seeing the nonverbal messages from your eyes would be considered noise, as would blurred type on a printed page.

All communications contain noise. Noise cannot be totally eliminated, but its effects can be reduced. Making your language more precise, sharpening your skills for sending and receiving nonverbal messages, and improving your listening and feedback skills are some ways to combat the influence of noise.

Context

Communication always takes place in a **context** which influences the form and content of your messages. At times this context isn't obvious or intrusive; it seems so natural that it's ignored—like background music. At other times the context dominates, and the ways in which it restricts or stimulates your messages are obvious. Compare, for example, the differences among communicating in a funeral home, in a football stadium, in a formal restaurant, and at a rock concert. The context of communication has at least four dimensions, all of which interact and influence each other.

The *physical dimension* is the tangible or concrete environment in which communication takes place—the room, hallway, or park, the boardroom or the family dinner table. The size of the space, its temperature, and the number of people present in the physical space would also be part of the physical dimension.

The *temporal dimension* refers not only to the time of day and moment in history but also to where a particular message fits into the sequence of communication events. For example, a joke about illness told immediately after the disclosure of a friend's sickness will be received differently than the same joke told in response to a series of similar jokes.

The *social-psychological dimension* includes, for example, status relationships among the participants, roles and games that people play, norms of the society or group, and the friendliness, formality, or gravity of the situation.

The *cultural context* (Unit 3) refers to the cultural beliefs and customs of the people communicating. When you interact with people from different cultures, you may each follow different rules of communication. This can result in confusion, unintentional insult, inaccurate judgments, and a host of other miscommunications. Similarly, communication strategies or techniques that prove satisfying to members of one culture may prove disturbing or offensive to members of another.

Purpose

Interpersonal communication serves a variety of purposes, for example, to learn, to relate, to influence, to play, and to help. Interpersonal communication enables you to *learn,* to better understand the external world—the world of objects, events, and other people. Although a great deal of information comes from the media, you probably discuss and ultimately learn or internalize information through interpersonal interactions. In fact, your beliefs, attitudes, and values are probably influenced more by interpersonal encounters than by the media or even formal education.

Most important, however, interpersonal communication helps you learn about yourself. By talking about yourself with others, you gain valuable feedback on your feelings, thoughts, and behaviors. Through these communications, you also learn how you appear to others—who likes you, who dislikes you, and why.

Interpersonal communication helps you *relate.* One of the greatest needs people have is to establish and maintain close relationships. You want to feel loved and liked, and in turn you want to love and like others. Such relationships help to alleviate loneliness and depression, enable you to share and heighten your pleasures, and generally make you feel more positive about yourself.

Very likely, you *influence* the attitudes and behaviors of others in your interpersonal encounters. You may wish them to vote a particular way, try a new diet, buy a new book, listen to a record, see a movie, take a specific course, think in a particular way, believe that something is true or false, or value some idea—the list is endless. A good deal of your time is probably spent in interpersonal persuasion.

Talking with friends about your weekend activities, discussing sports or dates, telling stories and jokes, and in general just passing the time are *play* functions. Far from frivolous, this purpose is an extremely important one. It gives your activities a necessary balance and your mind a needed break from all the seriousness around us. Everyone has an inner child, and that child needs time to play.

Therapists of various kinds serve a helping function professionally by offering guidance through interpersonal interaction. But everyone interacts to *help* in everyday interactions: you console a friend who has broken off a love affair, counsel another student about courses to take, or offer advice to a colleague about work. Success in accomplishing this helping function, professionally or otherwise, depends on your knowledge and skill in interpersonal communication.

The purposes of interpersonal communication can also be viewed from two other perspectives (see Figure 1.3). First, purposes may be seen as motives for engaging in interpersonal communication. That is, you engage in interpersonal communication to satisfy your need for knowledge or to form relationships. Second, these purposes may be viewed in terms of the results you want to achieve. That is, you engage in interpersonal communication to increase your knowledge of yourself and others or to exert influence or power over others.

Interpersonal communication is usually motivated by a combination of factors and has a combination of results or effects. Any interpersonal interaction, then, serves a unique combination of purposes, is motivated by a unique combination of factors, and can produce a unique combination of results.

Ethics

Because communication has consequences, interpersonal communication also involves **ethics;** each communication act has a moral dimension, a rightness or wrongness (cf. Jaksa and Pritchard 1994, Johannesen 1990). Communication choices need to be guided by ethical considerations as well as by concerns with effectiveness and satisfaction. The ethical dimension of communication is complicated by the fact that because it's so closely interwoven with your own philosophy of life—heavily influenced by the culture in which you were raised—it's difficult to propose universal guidelines. Notwithstanding this difficulty, ethics is included as a universal of interpersonal communication and is presented in this text in "Ethics in Interpersonal Communication" boxes. These boxes cover such issues as the differences between subjective and objective approaches to ethics, whether the ends justify the means, the ethical obligations of speakers and listeners, lying, gossip, and unethical speech.

Using the elements of message, channel, context, and noise (and any other elements you wish), how would you describe what takes place when you meet a friend and say "Hello" to each other?

◀◀ THINKING BACK

THINKING AHEAD ▶▶

If you could sort your last 100 comments into two categories—one for comments that offered praise and one for comments that offered criticism—how many would be in each category?

CULTURE AND INTERPERSONAL COMMUNICATION

A walk through any large city, many small towns, and through just about any college campus will convince you that the United States is largely a collection of lots of different cultures (see Figure 1.4). These cultures coexist somewhat separately but also with each influencing each other. This coexistence has led some

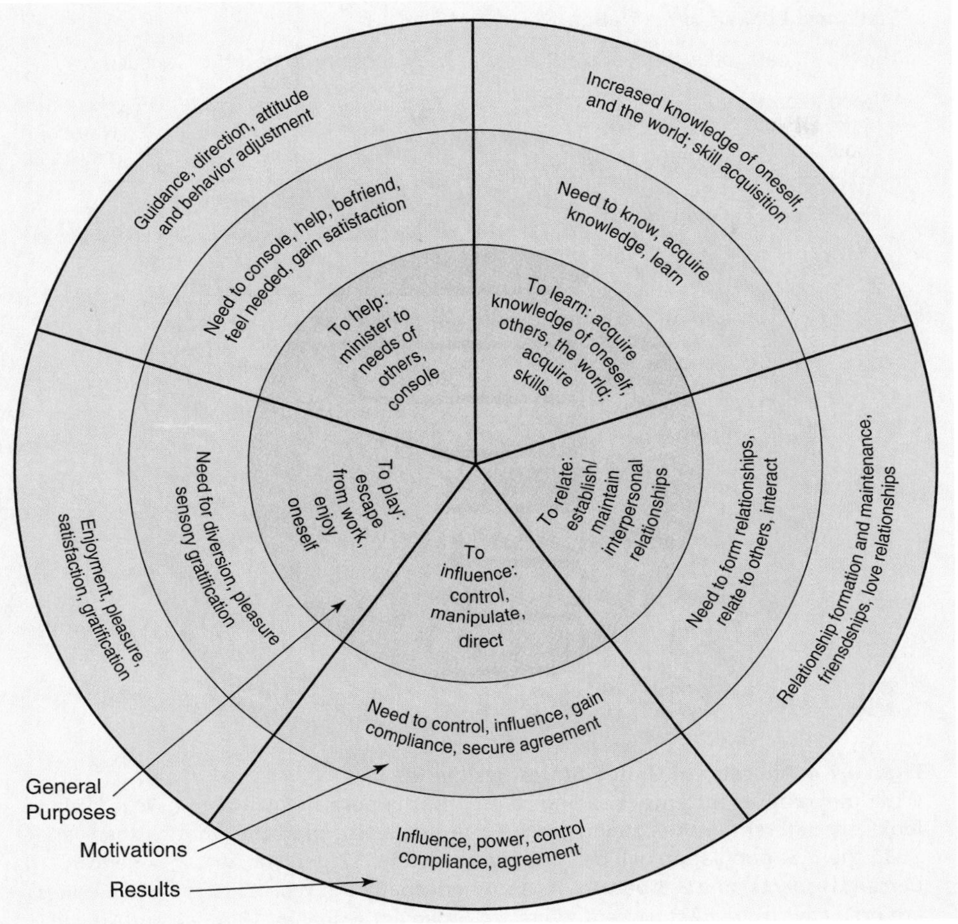

Figure 1.3 Why You Engage in Interpersonal Communication
This figure identifies some of the reasons you listen. The innermost circle contains the general purposes of interpersonal communication. The middle circle contains the motivations that lead you to communicate. The outer circle contains the results that you might hope to achieve by engaging in interpersonal communication. A similar typology of purposes comes from research on motives for communicating. In a series of studies, Rubin and her colleagues (Rubin, Fernandez-Collado, and Hernandez-Sampieri 1992, Rubin and Martin 1994, Rubin, Perse, and Barbato 1988, Rubin and Rubin 1992, Graham 1994, and Graham, Barbato, and Perse 1993) have identified six primary motives for communication: pleasure, affection, inclusion, escape, relaxation, and control. How do these compare to the five purposes discussed here?

researchers to refer to these cultures as co-cultures (Shuter 1990, Samovar and Porter 1991, Jandt 1995). Here are a few random facts to further support the importance of culture generally and of intercultural communication in particular (*Time,* 2 December 1993, 14):

- Over 30 million people in the United States speak languages other than English in their homes.
- In the school systems of New York City, Fairfax County Virginia, Chicago, and Los Angeles over 100 languages are spoken.

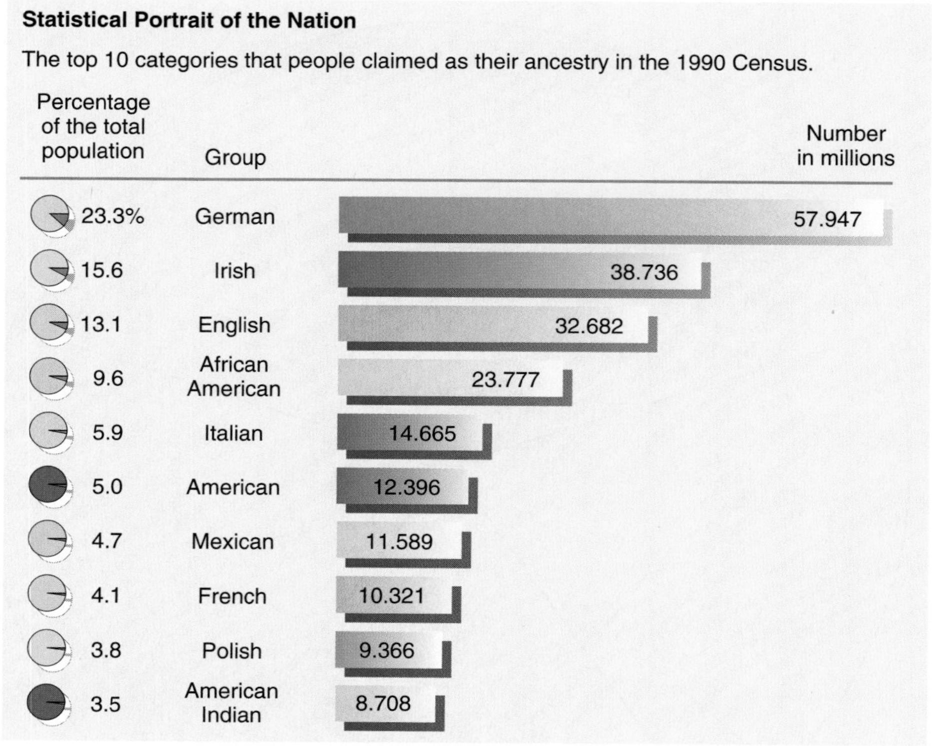

Figure 1.4 Ancestry of United States Residents
With immigration patterns changing so rapidly, the portrait illustrated here is likely to look very different in the coming years. For example, it's predicted that by the year 2030 the U.S. population will be 73.6 percent white, 12 percent African American, 10.2 percent Hispanic, and 3.3 percent Asian American. By the year 2050 the percentages are predicted to be 52.8 percent white, 24.5 percent Hispanic, 13.6 percent African American, and 8.2 percent Asian American (figures projected by the Census Bureau and reported in the *New York Times,* 14 March 1996, A16). To what factors might you attribute these projections? What will your own state, city, or town look like in 2030? In 2050? That is, in what ways will it resemble or differ from the predictions for the nation as a whole?

- Over 50 percent of the residents of such cities as Miami and Hialeah in Florida, Union City in New Jersey, and Huntington Park and Monterey Park in California are foreign born.
- The foreign-born population of the United States in 1990 totaled almost 20 million, approximately 8 percent of the total U.S. population.
- 30 percent of U.S. winners of the Nobel prize (since 1901) were foreign born.

The Relevance of Culture

There are lots of reasons for the cultural emphasis you'll find in this book. Most obviously, perhaps, are the vast demographic changes taking place throughout the United States. Whereas at one time the United States was a country largely populated by Europeans, it's now a country greatly influenced by the enormous number of new citizens from Latin and South America, Africa, and Asia. The demographic shift is even more noticeable on college and university campuses throughout the United States. With these changes have come different interpersonal customs and the need to understand and adapt to new ways of looking at communication.

As a people we've become increasingly sensitive to cultural differences. American society has moved from an assimilationist perspective (people should leave their native culture behind and adapt to their new culture) to one that values cultural diversity (people should retain their native cultural ways). With some notable exceptions—hate speech, racism, sexism, homophobia, and classism come quickly to mind—we are more concerned with saying the right thing and ultimately with developing a society where all cultures can coexist and enrich each other. At the same time, the ability to interact effectively with members of other cultures often translates into financial gain and increased employment opportunities and advancement prospects.

Today, most countries are economically dependent on each other. Our economic lives depend on our ability to communicate effectively across different cultures. Similarly, our political well-being depends in great part on that of other cultures. Political unrest in any part of the world—South Africa, Eastern Europe, Asia, and the Middle East, to take a few examples—affects our own security. Intercultural communication and understanding seem now more crucial than ever.

The rapid spread of technology has made intercultural communication as easy as it is inevitable. News from foreign countries is commonplace. You see nightly—in vivid detail—what is going on in remote countries just as you see what's happening in your own city and state. Of course, the Internet has made intercultural communication as easy as writing a note on your computer. You can now just as easily communicate by e-mail with someone in Asia or Europe, for example, as you can with someone in another U.S. city or state.

Still another reason culture is so important is that interpersonal competence is specific to a given culture; what proves effective in one culture may prove ineffective in another. For example, in the United States corporate executives get down to

Another way of looking at the "interculturalization" of the United States is to look at international visitors. In 1993 for example, 12,029,000 visitors came from ten countries. (That's more people than any state in the United States except for California, New York, Texas, and Florida. It's also more people than the total population of such countries as Cuba, Denmark, Ecuador, Finland, Greece, Haiti, and Israel.) Japanese visitors led the list with over 3 million, followed closely by the United Kingdom, which sent over 3 million. Germany is next with almost 2 million, followed by (in order) France, Italy, Australia, Brazil, Venezuela, Spain, and Argentina. Visitors exert influence on residents, just as residents influence them. Have you ever been a part of this influence process?

business during the first several minutes of a meeting. In Japan, business executives interact socially for an extended period and try to find out something about each other. Thus, the communication principle influenced by U.S. culture would advise participants to get down to the meeting's agenda during the first five minutes. The principle influenced by Japanese culture would advise participants to avoid dealing with business until everyone has socialized sufficiently and feels well enough acquainted to begin negotiations. Giving a birthday gift to a close friend would be appreciated by many, but among Jehovah's Witnesses, for example, this act would be frowned upon since they don't celebrate birthdays (Dresser 1996). Neither principle is right, and neither is wrong. Each is effective within its own culture and ineffective outside its own culture.

The Aim of a Cultural Perspective

Because culture permeates all forms of communication, it's necessary to understand its influences if you're to understand how communication works and master its skills. As illustrated throughout this text, culture influences communications of all types (Moon 1996). It influences what you say to yourself and how you talk with friends, lovers, and family in everyday conversation (for example, Shibazaki and Brennan 1998). It influences how you interact in groups and how much importance you place on the group versus the individual. It influences the topics you talk about and the strategies you use in communicating information or in persuading. It influences how you use the media and the credibility you attribute to them.

A cultural emphasis helps distinguish what is universal (true for all people) from what is relative (true for people in one culture and not true for people in other cultures) (Matsumoto 1994). The principles for communicating information and for changing listeners' attitudes, for example, will vary from one culture to another. If you're to understand communication, then you need to know how its principles vary and how the principles must be qualified and adjusted on the basis of cultural differences.

This cultural understanding is needed to communicate effectively in the wide variety of intercultural situations. Success in interpersonal communication—on your job and in your social and personal life—will depend in great part on your understanding of and your ability to communicate effectively with persons who are culturally different from yourself. Daily the media bombard you with evidence of racial tensions, religious disagreements, sexual bias, and in general, the problems caused when intercultural communication fails.

This emphasis on culture does not imply that you should accept all cultural practices or that all cultural practices are equal (Hatfield and Rapson 1996). Consider this case in point (*Time,* 2 December 1993, 61). Assume you're a judge and the following case is presented to you: A Chinese immigrant killed his wife in New York because he suspected her of cheating. A "cultural defense" was offered, essentially claiming that infidelity so shames a man that he is uncontrollable in his anger. Would this cultural defense have influenced your judgment? In the actual case, influenced by an anthropologist's testimony that infidelity is so serious in Chinese culture that it pushed the defendant to commit the crime, the judge sentenced the defendant to five years' probation.

Further, a cultural emphasis does not imply that you have to accept or follow all of the practices of your own culture. For example, even if the majority in your culture find cockfighting acceptable, you need not agree with or follow the practice. Nor need you consider this practice equal to a cultural practice in which animals are treated kindly. You can reject capitalism or communism or socialism regardless of the culture in which you were raised. Of course, going against your culture's traditions and values is often very difficult. But it's important to realize that culture influences, it does not determine, your values or behavior. Often personality factors (your degree of assertiveness, extroversion, or optimism, for example) will prove more influential than culture (Hatfield and Rapson 1996).

As demonstrated throughout this text, cultural differences exist throughout the interpersonal communication spectrum—from the way you use eye contact to the way you develop or dissolve a relationship (Chang and Holt 1996). But these should not blind you to the great number of similarities existing among even the most widely separated cultures. Further, when discussing differences, remember that these are usually questions of degree rather than all-or-none. Thus, for example, most cultures value honesty, but some cultures give it greater emphasis than others. The advances in media and technology and the widespread use of the Internet, for example, are influencing cultures and cultural change and are perhaps homogenizing the different cultures, lessening the differences and increasing the similarities.

The cultural emphasis in this text will be seen in two ways. First, cultural issues are integrated into the text as they are appropriate. For example, when discussing self-disclosure or the meanings of nonverbal gestures, we also consider how different cultures view these forms of communication. Second, a complete unit (Unit 3) is devoted to the role of culture in interpersonal communication. It introduces intercultural communication and discusses the theories and principles of this rapidly growing area of human communication.

In what ways are interpersonal communication between two persons from the same culture and two persons from widely different cultures the same?

◂◂ THINKING BACK

REVIEWING KEY TERMS AND CONCEPTS IN INTERPERSONAL COMMUNICATION

This unit introduced interpersonal communication, its elements, and the role of culture in understanding and mastering interpersonal communication.

The Nature of Interpersonal Communication

What is interpersonal communication? At what point does communication become interpersonal?

- **A dyadic (relational) definition** defines interpersonal communication as communication between two or a few connected individuals in which there is dyadic primacy (the two-person unit is of central importance), dyadic coalitions (two-person groups form even in larger groups), and dyadic consciousness (the two persons think of themselves as a pair).
- **A developmental definition** defines interpersonal communication as two-person communication in which the persons based their predictions on psychological (rather than sociological) data, explanatory (rather than descriptive) knowledge, and personally established (rather than socially established) rules.

Elements of Interpersonal Communication

What are the essential elements of interpersonal communication?

- **Source-receiver** is the person who sends and receives interpersonal messages simultaneously.
- **Encoding-decoding** refers to the act of putting meaning into verbal and nonverbal messages and deriving meaning from the messages you hear from others.
- **Competence** is the knowledge of and ability to use effectively your own communication system.
- **Messages** are the signals that serve as stimuli for a receiver; **metamessages** are messages that refer to other messages.

  Feedback messages are messages that are sent back by the receiver to the source in response to other messages.

  Feedforward messages are messages that preface other messages and ask that the listener approach future messages in a certain way
- **Channel** is the medium through which messages pass and which acts as a bridge between source and receiver, for example, the vocal-auditory channel used in speaking or cutaneous-tactile used in touch communication.
- **Noise** is the physical, physiological, psychological, and semantic interference that distorts a message and that is inevitable.
- **Context** is the physical, social-psychological, temporal, and cultural environment in which the communication act takes place.
- **Purpose** is the reason for the interpersonal interaction—to learn, relate, influence, play, and help.
- **Ethics** is the moral dimension of communication, the study of what makes behavior moral or good as opposed to immoral and bad.

Culture and Interpersonal Communication

What is culture? What is its relevance to interpersonal communication? What is the aim of a "cultural perspective"?

- **Culture** refers to the specialized lifestyle of a group of people, consisting of their values, beliefs, ways of behaving, and artifacts that are transmitted through communication rather than through genes.
- Culture is an inevitable part of all interpersonal communications and will greatly influence what works and what doesn't work.
- A cultural emphasis argues for an understanding of cultural differences and a sensitivity to them; it does not mean that you have to hold all cultural practices as acceptable or equal.

APPLYING KEY TERMS AND CONCEPTS IN INTERPERSONAL COMMUNICATION

1. Can you identify any primary dyads in your extended family? What functions do these dyads serve?
2. Does the developmental definition of interpersonal communication explain the communication that goes on between, say, you and your best friend or romantic partner? Consider: Do you base your predictions about each other on psychological rather than sociological data? Do you have explanatory (rather than just descriptive or predictive) knowledge of each other? Do your interactions rely on personally established rather than socially established rules?
3. How would you explain interpersonal communication or interpersonal relationships in terms of such metaphors as a seesaw, ball game, flower, ice skates, microscope, television sitcom, work of art, long book, rubber band, or software program?
4. What kinds of feedforward can you find in this book? What additional feedforward messages would you find useful in a textbook? In a lecture?
5. How does feedback work in conversation between persons with impaired hearing? Between a person with impaired hearing and one with normal hearing? Between persons who are blind? Between a person who is blind and one who has normal vision?
6. What characters in television sitcoms or dramas do you think demonstrate superior interpersonal competence? What characters demonstrate obvious interpersonal incompetence?
7. Visit the Web site of a professional communication association (try, for example, the National Communication Association at www.natcom.org, the International Communication Association at www.icahdq.org or the International Listening Association at www.listen.org). What kinds of information do these Web sites provide?
8. Are the media and the Internet—because of their dominance by the United States—fostering an Americanization of different cultures? Do you see this as a loss of valuable diversity? Or do you see it as the result of a democratic process whereby people select the values and customs they wish to adopt? Somewhere in between?
9. In a small group, with the class as a whole, or in a brief paper discuss how your beliefs, attitudes, and values were influenced by the culture in which you were raised. Were you taught that penalties are incurred for going against these beliefs, attitudes, and values?
10. How would you go about finding answers to the following questions:
    - Are interpersonal communication skills related to relationship success, for example, to success as a friend, lover, or parent?
    - Do effective teachers give more feedback and feedforward than less effective teachers?
    - What are the most important interpersonal skills for success in business?
    - Are competent communicators less anxious and less fearful of communication?
    - Does increased knowledge about communication lead to increased ability to communicate effectively?

EXPERIENCING KEY TERMS AND CONCEPTS IN INTERPERSONAL COMMUNICATION

Go to www.awl.com/devito

Exercise No. 2, "Matching Pairs," provides an opportunity to analyze communication and especially intercultural communication. Exercise No. 3, "I'd Prefer to Be," and Exercise No. 12, "Who?" are useful ice breakers and will help you get to know one another in a relatively short time. Exercise No. 16, "Giving and Taking Directions," illustrates the process of interpersonal communication and shows the importance of expressing messages clearly and accurately.

UNIT 2

AXIOMS OF INTERPERSONAL COMMUNICATION

Kiss of the Spider Woman (1985)

IMPORTANT PRINCIPLES MAY AND MUST BE FLEXIBLE.

—ABRAHAM LINCOLN

Interpersonal Communication Is Grounded in Theory and Research

Interpersonal Communication Is a Transactional Process

Interpersonal Relationships May Be Viewed as Symmetrical or Complementary

Interpersonal Communications Have Content and Relationship Dimensions

Interpersonal Communication Is a Process of Adjustment

Interpersonal Communication Is a Series of Punctuated Events

Interpersonal Communication Is Inevitable, Irreversible, and Unrepeatable

Hector Babenco's Kiss of the Spider Woman *focuses on two very different people crammed into a small jail cell—a homosexual, jailed for sex offenses (William Hurt), and a heterosexual, jailed for political reasons (Raul Julia). Throughout the film you see these two extremely different people gradually learn to adjust to and accommodate each other, eventually achieving rare mutual understanding. This process of adjustment represents one of seven axioms (commonly accepted principles) discussed in this unit. Together, these axioms will help further explain what interpersonal communication is and how it works.*

THINKING AHEAD ▸▸

How do we know what we know about communication? How do we collect evidence to help discover how interpersonal communication works and which principles of interpersonal interaction are effective and which aren't?

INTERPERSONAL COMMUNICATION IS GROUNDED IN THEORY AND RESEARCH

Before you begin reading this section, try taking the self-test, "What Do You Know About Research?" It will help clarify some essential concepts in understanding research that you'll encounter in this text as well as in other courses.

TEST YOURSELF *What Do You Know About Research?*

The following statements raise important issues about the research process and particularly how research should be interpreted. Mark each statement T if you think it's generally true and accurate; mark F if you think it's generally false and inaccurate.

______ 1. When one event (B) regularly and consistently follows another event (A), we can say that A causes B or that B results from A.

______ 2. It's important to know the results of research because they will apply to you at some point in your life.

______ 3. Results from research conducted 20 years ago are generally of only historical interest.

______ 4. If the same results emerge from lots of different research studies, we can be pretty sure that the findings are valid.

______ 5. The only really worthwhile research findings are those that are found on the basis of experimental research in which all variables are carefully controlled and which are analyzed with the best statistical techniques.

Statement 1 is False and raises the often confused difference between correlation and causation. When two things occur together (for example, B consistently and reliably accompanies A), it does not mean that one causes the other; in many instances a third variable, C, might be causing both A and B. For example, let's say that fear of communication and low self-disclosure are observed together in a large number of people; those who have great fear of communication also reveal little of themselves and, conversely, those who have little fear of communication reveal a great deal about themselves. Can you conclude that the level of communication fear determines the amount of self-disclosure? The answer is no; a third factor, say self-esteem, may actually cause both the fear of communication and the level of self-disclosure.

Statement 2 is False. Research results, at least in the humanities and social sciences such as communication, are true in a statistical sense; that is, they apply to perhaps 95 percent of the population. You may be in the 5 percent to which the results do not apply. Further, you may be different in crucial respects from the participants sampled in the research study and so the results may not directly apply to you. The vast cultural differences that we're just beginning to understand make it unlikely that research findings obtained from students at a large Midwestern University will apply to the farm workers in Guatemala.

Statement 3 is also False. Although our research methods are a lot better than they were 20 years ago, the time during which a research study was conducted is not sufficient reason to consider one worthless and one worthwhile. There were a lot of worthwhile research studies done 20 years ago and a lot of worthless studies done yesterday. The value of the research depends on the study and on the specific changes that may have taken place over the 20 years. For example, a study conducted on power in the heterosexual relationship 20 years ago would have to be examined in light of the tremendous changes that have taken place in our attitudes toward men and women and in sexual equality generally. Other things being equal (though of course other things are never really equal), the more recent study on this subject will prove the more useful. Similarly, findings on the frequency and causes of divorce, the role of technology in interpersonal relationships, or the reasons relationships are maintained will vary considerably over time, so for these topics recency is important. On the other hand, certain findings reported from experiments in chemistry will probably remain true for many years; the interactions of carbon and hydrogen, for example, are not likely to change over the years.

Statement 4 involves a confusion between validity and reliability—two concepts that are crucial for understanding research findings—and is also False. *Reliability* refers to the consistency of results. It's a measure of how consistently a particular relationship or result is found in research. *Validity,* on the other hand, is a measure of the extent to which an instrument or test measures what it claims to measure. For example, intelligence tests are extremely reliable and you'll obtain essentially the same results on repeated testing. The validity issue, however, is different and asks "Does the intelligence test really measure intelligence?" Similarly, we can measure your degree of romanticism with a simple pencil and paper test and get essentially the same results on repeated testing. But it's quite another issue to claim that the test really measures what we would consider "romanticism." Consistency of findings does not mean that the test is valid, only that it's reliable. Both are important; generally, we want tests and research instruments to be both reliable and valid.

Statement 5 is also False, although not everyone would agree with this. The assumption made in this text is that all research methods are useful for different purposes. Historical research is useful for certain questions, survey research is useful for other questions, and experimental research is useful for still other purposes. ■

Throughout this book and throughout your course you'll encounter a wide variety of theories and research findings on interpersonal communication. These theories and research findings constitute what we know about interpersonal communication. They tell you how interpersonal communication works as well as what works effectively. From these theories and research findings you not only come to understand how interpersonal communication works but you can also derive skills for achieving greater interpersonal effectiveness.

Theory in Interpersonal Communication

A **theory** is a generalization that explains how something works—gravity, DNA identification, interpersonal attraction, or communication, for example. In academic writing the term is usually reserved for a well-established system of knowledge about how something works or how things are related. The theories you'll encounter in this text will vary greatly: communication as a process of adjustment, how we're attracted to some people and not to others, how communication works when relationships deteriorate, or how self-disclosure operates in friendship. In reading about these theories, you may well ask, "Why should I learn this? Of what value is this material to me?" Here are a few answers to these very legitimate questions (Griffin 1999, Infante, Rancer, and Womack 1993, Littlejohn 1996).

Theories help you understand how interpersonal communication works. Theories provide general principles that help you understand a great number of specific events—how and why these events occur and how they're related to each other. One communication theorist argues that a good theory synthesizes data. It focuses your attention on important elements and helps you ignore unimportant elements (Griffin 1999).

Interpersonal communication theories also help you predict future events. The theories summarize what has been discovered in the past and can therefore offer an educated and informed prediction for events in the future. For example, based on the theories of interpersonal conflict resolution, you would be able to predict which conflict strategies will prove effective and which will prove ineffective in resolving differences. Of course, these theories will not provide correct answers 100 percent of the time; but they will offer useful generalizations that are likely to be correct beyond chance.

Interpersonal communication theories also help generate research. For example, if a theory predicts that verbal aggressiveness will lead to physical violence, this suggests to the researcher a variety of important questions that can be subjected to study (Infante, Rancer, and Womack 1993). For example, the research might ask, "What types of verbal aggressiveness lead to physical violence?" "Are men or women more likely to become physically violent after being verbally aggressive?" "Can we reduce the likelihood of physical violence by teaching people to become less verbally aggressive?" In serving this research-generating function, theories add to our knowledge of interpersonal communication.

Theories reveal some degree of accuracy, some degree of truth, not absolute truth. In the natural sciences such as physics and chemistry, theories have extremely high accuracy. If you mix two parts of hydrogen to one part of oxygen, you'll get water—every time you do it. In the social and behavioral sciences (communication, sociology, psychology), the theories are far less accurate in describing the way things work and in predicting how things will work. One communication theorist offers this summary guidance: "[B]ecause a theory does not reveal truth, does not mean that it fails to communicate a kind of truth. An insight or useful way of classifying or explaining events is a kind of truth. Just don't make the mistake of believing too hard in one theory because every theory has its limits" (Littlejohn 1996, p. 361).

Research in Interpersonal Communication

WEB EXPLORATION
To learn more about research in interpersonal communication, go to www.awl.com/devito.

Usually on the basis of some theory and its predictions—though sometimes from a simple desire to answer a question—research is conducted (Clark 1991). It is conducted so that we can learn more about how interpersonal communication works. On the basis of these research findings, we develop the principles for more effective interpersonal interaction. Research, for example, often tells us what interpersonal strategies work and what strategies don't work. Understanding the research process will help you to better appreciate how we learn about communication as well as better understand the findings, conclusions, and principles that are developed on the basis of this research.

Sometimes the research questions are totally theoretical: "How do listeners deal with ambiguous messages?" Sometimes they're extremely practical, even urgent: "How can children best resist drugs?" Often, of course, practical implications are drawn out of "purely theoretical" research, and theoretical insights are drawn out of "purely applied" research.

It is the research, then, that enables you to answer questions about people's interpersonal communication behavior and helps advance truth about an important aspect of human experience. Let's say you find that total honesty in your romantic relationship is effective and that it creates a strong bond between you and your partner. How useful is that "finding" to other couples? On the one hand, it may be very useful because all couples might respond as you and your partner do. Or it may be of limited usefulness if your relationship is unique and unlike those of most other people. Ideally, research provides us with findings that are applicable to a large percentage of the people.

The "Ask the Researcher" boxes that appear throughout the text, and which you've already encountered in Unit 1, are intended to follow up this emphasis on research and its implications for everyday interpersonal communication by asking active researchers and theorists to answer specific questions relating theory to practice.

Now that the nature of theory and research in interpersonal communication is clear, we can explore some of the more specific axioms or principles that are common to all or most interpersonal encounters. These axioms are largely the work of the transactional researchers Paul Watzlawick, Janet Helmick Beavin, and Don D. Jackson, presented in their landmark *Pragmatics of Human Communication* (1967, Watzlawick 1977, 1978). Together with the concepts already presented (Unit 1), these axioms complete the characterization of what interpersonal communication is and how it works.

What one question about interpersonal communication would you like to know the answer to? Can you visualize how you might go about conducting research to answer this question?

◀◀ THINKING BACK

INTERPERSONAL COMMUNICATION IS A TRANSACTIONAL PROCESS

THINKING AHEAD ▶▶

Why is it that when one element in communication changes—say another person enters the conversation—everything else often changes as well?

A transactional perspective views interpersonal communication as (1) a process (2) whose elements are *inter*dependent. Figure 2.1 explains visually this transactional view and distinguishes it from two earlier views of how interpersonal communication works.

Interpersonal Communication Is a Process

Interpersonal communication is best viewed as an ever-changing process. Everything involved in interpersonal communication is in a state of flux: you're changing, the people you communicate with are changing, and your environment is changing. Sometimes these changes go unnoticed, and sometimes they intrude in obvious ways. But they're always occurring.

The process of communication is circular: one person's message serves as the stimulus for another's message, which serves as a stimulus for the other person's message, which serves as a stimulus for the other person's message, and so on. Throughout this circular process, each person serves simultaneously as a speaker *and* a listener, an actor *and* a reactor. Interpersonal communication is a mutually interactive process.

Elements Are Interdependent

The elements in interpersonal communication are *inter*dependent. Each element—each part of interpersonal communication—is intimately connected to the other

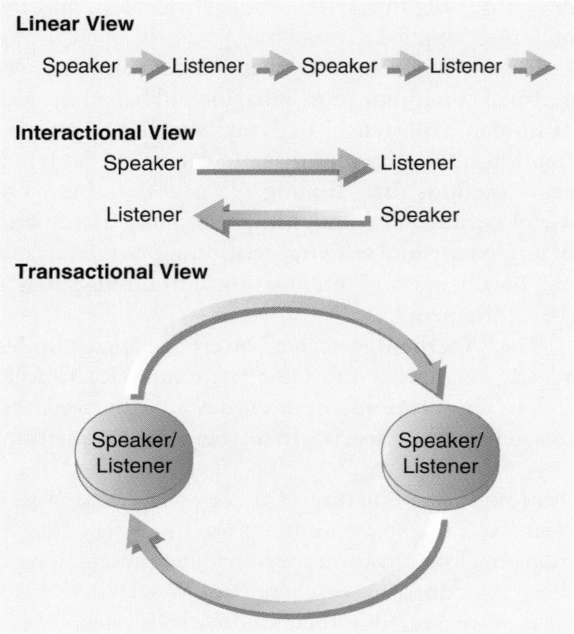

Figure 2.1 The Transactional View of Interpersonal Communication
The top figure represents a linear view of communication, in which the speaker speaks and the listener listens. The middle figure represents an interactional view, in which speaker and listener take turns speaking and listening; A speaks while B listens and then B speaks while A listens. The bottom figure represents a transactional view, in which each person serves simultaneously as speaker and listener; at the same time that you send messages, you also receive messages from your own communications as well as from the reactions of the other person(s).

Can you give a specific example of an interpersonal interaction in which a change in one element led to changes in other elements?

◂◂ THINKING BACK

parts and to the whole. For example, there can be no source without a receiver; there can be no message without a source; there can be no feedback without a receiver. Because of interdependency, a change in any one element causes changes in the others. For example, you're talking with a group of fellow students about a recent examination, and your teacher joins the group. This change in participants will lead to other changes—perhaps in the content of what you say, perhaps in the manner in which you express it. But regardless of what change is introduced, other changes result.

THINKING AHEAD ▸▸

Do you generally mirror the behavior of the person with whom you're interacting? For example, if the other person is aggressive, do you also become aggressive, or are you more apt to become nonaggressive and accepting?

INTERPERSONAL RELATIONSHIPS MAY BE VIEWED AS SYMMETRICAL OR COMPLEMENTARY

Interpersonal relationships can be described as either symmetrical or complementary (Bateson 1972, Watzlawick, Beavin, and Jackson 1967). In a **symmetrical relationship,** the two individuals mirror each other's behavior (Bateson 1972). If one member nags, the other member responds in kind. If one member is passionate, the other member is passionate. If one member expresses jealousy, the other member also expresses jealousy. If one member is passive, so is the other. The relationship is one of equality, with the emphasis on minimizing the differences between the two individuals.

Note, however, the problems that can arise in this type of relationship. Consider the situation of a couple in which both members are very aggressive. The aggressiveness of one person fosters aggressiveness in the other, which fosters increased aggressiveness in the first individual. As this cycle escalates, the aggressiveness can no longer be contained, and the relationship is consumed by the aggression.

In a **complementary relationship,** the two individuals engage in different behaviors. The behavior of one serves as the stimulus for the other's complementary behavior. In complementary relationships, the differences between the parties are maximized. The people occupy different positions, one superior and the other inferior, one passive and the other active, one strong and the other weak. At times, cultures establish such relationships—for example, the complementary relationship between teacher and student or between employer and employee.

Early marriages are likely to be complementary relationships where each person tries to complete himself or herself. When these couples separate and form new relationships, these new ones are more likely to be symmetrical and involve a kind of reconfirmation of their own identity (Prosky 1992). Generally, research finds that complementary couples have a lower marital adjustment level than do symmetrical couples (Main and Oliver 1988, Holden 1991).

Are you more satisfied with your symmetrical or with your complementary relationships?

◀◀ THINKING BACK

INTERPERSONAL COMMUNICATIONS HAVE CONTENT AND RELATIONSHIP DIMENSIONS

THINKING AHEAD ▶▶

When you talk with another person, do your messages also comment on the relationship between you and this other person?

Messages may make reference to the real world, for example, to the events and objects you see before you. At the same time, however, they also refer to the relationship between the people communicating. For example, a judge may say to a lawyer, "See me in my chambers immediately." This simple message has both a content aspect, which refers to the behavioral response expected (namely, that the lawyer will see the judge immediately), and a relationship aspect, which says something about the relationship between the judge and the lawyer and, as a result of this relationship, how the communication is to be dealt with. Even the use of the simple command shows that there is a status difference between the two parties. This difference can perhaps be seen most clearly if you imagine the command being made by the lawyer to the judge. Such a communication appears awkward and out of place because it violates the normal relationship between judge and lawyer.

In any two communications, the content dimension may be the same, but the relationship aspect may be different, or the relationship aspect may be the same and the content dimension different. For example, the judge could say to the lawyer, "You had better see me immediately" or "May I please see you as soon as possible?" In both cases, the content is essentially the same; that is, the message about the expected behavioral response is the same. But the relationship dimension is quite different. The first message signifies a definite superior-inferior relationship; the second signals a more equal relationship, one that shows respect for the lawyer.

Similarly, at times the content may be different but the relationship is essentially the same. For example, a daughter might say to her parents, "May I go away this weekend?" or "May I use the car tonight?" The content of the two questions is clearly very different, but the relationship dimension is essentially the same. It clearly reflects a superior-inferior relationship in which permission to do certain things must be secured.

Implications of Content and Relationship Dimensions

The major implications of these content and relationship dimensions center on conflict and its effective resolution. Many problems between people result from failure to recognize the distinction between the content and the relationship dimensions of communication. For example, consider the couple arguing because Pat made plans to study with friends during the weekend without first asking Chris if that would be all right. Probably both would agree that to study over the weekend is the right decision. Thus, the argument isn't primarily concerned with the content level. It centers on the relationship level; Chris expected to be consulted about plans for the weekend. Pat, in not doing so, rejected this definition of their relationship. Similar situations occur when one member of a couple buys something, makes dinner plans, or invites

WEB EXPLORATION
To learn more about implications of content and relationship dimensions, go to www.awl.com/devito.

a guest to dinner without first asking the other person. Even though the other person might have agreed with the decision, the couple argue because of the message communicated on the relationship level.

Let me give you a personal example. My mother came to stay for a week at a summer place I had. On the first day, she swept the kitchen floor six times, although I repeatedly said that it didn't need sweeping, that I would be tracking in dirt and mud from outside, and that all her effort was just wasted. But she persisted, saying that the floor was dirty and should be swept. On the content level, we were talking about the value of sweeping the kitchen floor, but on the relationship level, we were talking about something quite different: we were each saying, "This is my house." When I realized this (although, I confess, only after considerable argument), I stopped complaining about sweeping a floor that didn't need sweeping. Not surprisingly, she stopped sweeping.

Consider the following interchange:

Dialogue	Comments
HE: I'm going bowling tomorrow. The guys at the plant are starting a team.	He focuses on the content and ignores any relationship implications of the message.
SHE: Why can't we ever do anything together?	She responds primarily on a relationship level, ignores the content implications of the message, and expresses her displeasure at being ignored in his decision.

The axioms discussed in this unit, although significant in terms of explaining theory, also have very practical applications. They provide insight into such day-to-day issues as: Why do disagreements so often center on trivial matters and yet seem so difficult to resolve? Why are you never able to mind read—to know exactly what another person is thinking? How does communication express power relationships? Why do you and your partner often see the causes of arguments very differently?

HE: We can do something together anytime; tomorrow's the day they're organizing the team.	Again, he focuses almost exclusively on the content.

This example reflects research findings that men generally focus more on the content while women focus more on the relationship dimensions of communication (cf. Pearson, West, and Turner 1995, Wood 1994, Ivy and Backlund 2000). Once you recognize this difference, you may be better able to remove a potential barrier to communication between the sexes by being sensitive to the orientation of the opposite sex. Here is essentially the same situation but with the added sensitivity:

Dialogue	Comments
HE: The guys at the plant are organizing a bowling team. I'd sure like to be on the team. Would it be a problem if I went to the organizational meeting tomorrow?	Although focused on content, he is aware of the relationship dimensions of his message and includes both in his comments—by acknowledging their partnership, asking if there would be a problem, and expressing his desire rather than his decision.
SHE: That sounds great, but I was hoping we could do something together.	She focuses on the relationship dimension but also acknowledges his content orientation. Note, too, that she does not respond as though she has to defend her emphasis on relationship aspects.
HE: How about your meeting me at Pizza Hut, and we can have dinner after the organizational meeting?	He responds to the relationship aspect—without abandoning his desire to join the bowling team—and incorporates it
SHE: That sounds great. I'm dying for pizza.	She responds to both messages, approving of his joining the team and their dinner date.

Arguments over the content dimension are relatively easy to resolve. Generally, you can look up something in a book or ask someone what actually took place. It is relatively easy to verify disputed facts. Arguments on the relationship level, however, are much more difficult to resolve, in part because you may not recognize that the argument is in fact a relational one. Once you realize that, you can approach the dispute appropriately and deal with it directly.

> Can you recall an argument that seemed to center on external matters but was really about some unresolved relationship issue?
>
> ◂◂ THINKING BACK

INTERPERSONAL COMMUNICATION IS A PROCESS OF ADJUSTMENT

> THINKING AHEAD ▸▸
>
> How do you manage to communicate effectively with people whose communication styles are so different from each other and from your own?

Interpersonal communication can take place only to the extent that the parties communicating share the same system of symbols. This is obvious when dealing with speakers of two different languages. Your communication with another person will be hindered to the extent that your language systems differ. This principle takes on particular relevance when you realize that no two persons share identical symbol systems. Parents and children, for example, not only have very different vocabularies but also, even more important, have different meanings for some of the terms

ETHICS IN INTERPERSONAL COMMUNICATION Vote online at http://www.awl.com/devito

Objective and Subjective Views

In thinking about the ethics of interpersonal communication, you can take the position that ethics is objective or that it's subjective. In an *objective* view, you'd argue that the morality of an act is absolute and exists apart from the values or beliefs of any individual or culture. With this view, you'd hold that there are standards that apply to all people in all situations at all times. If lying, false advertising, using illegally obtained evidence, or revealing secrets you've promised to keep—to take just a few examples—are considered unethical, then according to the objective view, they would be considered unethical regardless of the circumstances surrounding them or of the values and beliefs of the culture in which they occur.

In a *subjective* view of ethics, you'd argue that absolute statements of morality are too rigid and that the ethics of a message depends on the culture's values and beliefs as well as the particular circumstances. Thus, a subjective position would claim that lying may be wrong to win votes or sell cigarettes, but that it may be quite ethical if good would result from it, for example, making someone feel better by telling them they look great or that they'll get well soon.

What would you do? *You see a student cheating on an examination. After the examination, the instructor accuses the student of cheating and asks you if you witnessed the cheating. Although you believe that both cheating and lying are unethical and you did witness the cheating, you don't want to make trouble for the student—and probably become instantly unpopular with your classmates. Besides, the examination only counted a few points toward the final grade. How would a person who held an objective view of ethics respond to the instructor's query? How would a person who held a subjective view? What would you do in this situation?*

they have in common. Different cultures and social groups, even when they share a common language, often have greatly differing nonverbal communication systems. To the extent that these systems differ, communication will not take place.

Part of the art of interpersonal communication is learning the other person's signals, how they're used, and what they mean. People in close relationships—either as intimate friends or as romantic partners—realize that learning the other person's signals takes a long time and, often, great patience. If you want to understand what another person means—by a smile, by saying "I love you," by arguing about trivial matters, by self-deprecating comments—you have to learn their system of signals. Furthermore, you have to share your own system of signals with others so that they can better understand you. Although some people may know what you mean by your silence or by your avoidance of eye contact, others may not. You cannot expect others to decode your behaviors accurately without help.

This principle is especially important in **intercultural communication**, largely because people from different cultures use different signals and sometimes the same signals to signify quite different things. Focused eye contact means honesty and openness in much of the United States. But that same behavior may signify arrogance or disrespect in Japan and in many Hispanic cultures if engaged in by a youngster with someone significantly older.

Communication Accommodation

An interesting theory largely revolving around adjustment is communication accommodation theory. This theory holds that speakers will adjust to or accommodate to the speaking style of their listeners to gain, for example, social approval and greater communication efficiency (Giles, Mulac, Bradac, and Johnson 1987). For example, when two people have a similar speech rate, they seem to be more attracted to each other than to those with dissimilar rates (Buller, LePoire, Aune, and Eloy 1992). Speech rate similarity has also been associated with greater immediacy, sociability, and intimacy (Buller and Aune 1992). Also, the speaker who uses language intensity similar to that of listeners is judged to have greater credibility than the speaker who uses intensity different from that of listeners (Aune and Kikuchi 1993). Still another study found that roommates who had similar communication **attitudes** (both were high in communication competence and willingness to communicate and low in verbal aggressiveness) were highest in roommate liking and satisfaction (Martin and Anderson 1995).

As illustrated throughout this text, communication characteristics are influenced greatly by culture (Albert and Nelson 1993). Thus, the communication similarities that lead to attraction and more positive perceptions are likely to be present in *intra*cultural communication but absent in many *inter*cultural encounters. This may present an important (but not insurmountable) obstacle to intercultural communication.

How did you accommodate to the communication style of the last few people you spoke with? Did the others accommodate to your style?

◂◂ THINKING BACK

INTERPERSONAL COMMUNICATION IS A SERIES OF PUNCTUATED EVENTS

THINKING AHEAD ▸▸

Why do two people who see the same event or participate in the same conflict see its causes and effects so differently?

Communication events are continuous transactions. There is no clear-cut beginning and no clear-cut end. As participants in or observers of the communication act, you segment this continuous stream of communication into smaller pieces. You label some of these pieces causes or stimuli and others effects or responses.

ASK THE RESEARCHER

Accommodating for Effectiveness

I find your theory of communication accommodation really interesting, but I'm a really practical type of person and I'm taking this course to make myself a more effective communicator. So what I really want to know is how can I use this theory to make myself more effective socially and professionally?

Accommodating to people usually means that you'll be liked and respected. The trick, however, is to get it just right. Don't underaccommodate, yet don't do too much, and especially initially. Don't overaccommodate as that can be seen as patronizing, and be careful you aren't accommodating to what you believe someone should be like (given their social category memberships) rather than what they truly represent. Sometimes people's communicative styles are a core element of their identities and hence accommodating to them is invading their valued distinctiveness (for example, older parents trying to sound "cool" with their teenagers); in other words, nonaccommodating yet being supportive and understanding is the answer. Be wary of misattributing (and then getting upset at) someone's apparent divergence from you as a dissociative message. Someone accentuating their ethnic, for instance, features may be more a statement about how they value their own social identity than any lack of interest in you as a person. Managing the balances of convergence and divergence is a critical element of communicative competence.

For further information see H. Giles, N. Coupland, and J. Coupland (eds.), *The Contexts of Accommodation* (New York: Cambridge University Press, 1991).

—Howard Giles (Ph.D., D.Sc., University of Bristol) is a professor of communication at the University of California, Santa Barbara, and teaches courses in intercultural, intergroup, and intergenerational communication. Giles is also a reserve sergeant with the Santa Barbara Police Department.

Consider an example. A married couple is in a restaurant. The husband is flirting with another woman, and the wife is talking to her sister on her cell phone. Both are scowling at each other and are obviously in a deep nonverbal argument. Recalling the situation later, the husband might observe that the wife talked on the phone, so he innocently flirted with the other woman. The only reason for his behavior (he says) was his anger over her talking on the phone when they were supposed to be having dinner together. Notice that he sees his behavior as a response to her behavior. In recalling the same incident, the wife might say that she phoned her sister when he started flirting. The more he flirted, the longer she talked. She had no intention of calling anyone until he started flirting. To her, his behavior was the stimulus and hers was the response; he caused her behavior. Thus, the husband sees the sequence as going from phoning to flirting, and the wife sees it as going from flirting to phoning. This example is depicted visually in Figure 2.2 and is supported by research which shows that, among marrieds at least, the individuals regularly see their partner's behavior as the cause of conflict (Schutz 1999).

This tendency to divide communication transactions into sequences of stimuli and responses is referred to as **punctuation** (Watzlawick, Beavin, and Jackson 1967). Everyone punctuates the continuous sequences of events into stimuli and responses for convenience. Moreover, as the example of the husband and wife illustrates, punctuation usually is done in ways that benefit the person and are consistent with his or her self-image.

Can you recall a specific episode of a situation comedy in which the plot revolved around two people viewing the same situation in different ways? What happened?

◀◀ THINKING BACK

Understanding how another person interprets a situation, how he or she punctuates, is a crucial step in interpersonal understanding. It is also essential in achieving empathy (feeling what the other person is feeling). In all communication encounters, but especially in conflicts, try to see how others punctuate the situation.

THINKING AHEAD ▶▶

Have you ever tried to "take something back" after you said it? What happened?

INTERPERSONAL COMMUNICATION IS INEVITABLE, IRREVERSIBLE, AND UNREPEATABLE

Interpersonal communication cannot be prevented (is inevitable), cannot be reversed (is irreversible), and cannot be repeated (is unrepeatable). Let's look briefly at each of these qualities and their implications.

Inevitability

Often communication is thought of as intentional, purposeful, and consciously motivated. In many instances it is. But in other instances you're communicating even though you might not think you are or might not even want to communicate. Consider, for example, the new editorial assistant sitting at the desk with an "expressionless" face, perhaps staring out the window. Although this assistant might say that she or he is not communicating with the manager, the manager may derive any of a variety of messages from this behavior—for example, the assistant lacks interest, is bored, or is worried about something. In any event, the manager is receiving messages even though the assistant might not intend to communicate. In an interactional situation, all behavior is potentially communication. Any aspect of your behavior may communicate if the other person gives it message value. On the other hand, if the behavior (for example, the assistant's looking out the window) goes unnoticed, then no communication would have taken place (Watzlawick, Beavin, and Jackson 1967, Motley 1990a, 1990b, Bavelas 1990, Beach 1990).

Further, when in an interactional situation, your responses all have potential message value. For example, if you notice someone winking at you, you must respond in some way. Even if you don't respond openly, that lack of response is itself a response and it communicates (assuming it is perceived by the other person).

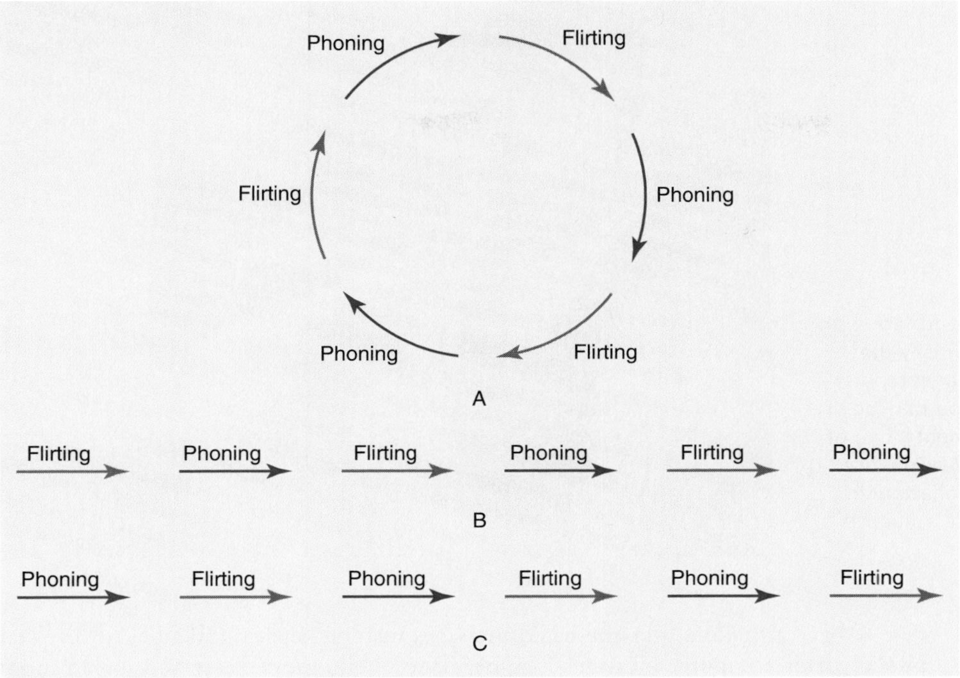

Figure 2.2 Punctuation and the Sequence of Events
In the figure, (A) shows the actual sequence of events as a continuous series of actions with no specific beginning or end. Each action (phoning and flirting) stimulates another action, but no initial cause is identified. (B) shows the same sequence of events as seen by the wife. She sees the sequence as beginning with the husband's flirting and her phoning behavior as a response to that stimulus. (C) shows the same sequence of events from the husband's point of view. He sees the sequence as beginning with the wife's phoning and his flirting as a response to that stimulus. Try using this three-part figure, discussed in the text, to explain what might go on when a supervisor complains that workers are poorly trained for their jobs and when workers complain that supervisors don't know how to supervise.

Irreversibility

The processes of some systems can be reversed. For example, you can turn water into ice and then reverse the process by melting the ice. Moreover, you can repeat this reversal of ice and water for as long as you wish. Other systems, however, are irreversible. In these systems, the process can move in only one direction; it cannot go back again. For example, you can turn grapes into wine, but you cannot reverse the process and turn the wine back into grapes.

TRY IT!
To learn more about irreversibility, go to www.awl.com/devito.

Interpersonal communication is irreversible. What you have communicated remains communicated; you cannot *un*communicate. Although you may try to qualify, negate, or somehow reduce the effects of your message, once it has been sent and received, the message itself cannot be reversed. In interpersonal interactions (especially in conflict), you need to be especially careful that you don't say things you may wish to withdraw later. Similarly, commitment messages, such as "I love you," must be monitored lest you commit yourself to a position you may be uncomfortable with later.

Face-to-face communication is evanescent; it fades after you have spoken. There is no trace of your communications outside of the memories of the parties involved or of those who overheard your conversation. In computer-mediated communication, however, the messages are written and may be saved, stored, and printed. Both

When you communicate face-to-face with a friend, you're both in essentially the same physical environment. In computer-mediated communication, you may be in drastically different environments; one of you may be on a beach in Waikiki while another is in an office in Manhattan. In what ways can this difference influence interpersonal communication?

face-to-face and computer-mediated messages may be kept confidential or revealed publicly. But computer messages may be made public more easily and spread more quickly than face-to-face messages. Written messages provide clear evidence of what you have said and when you said it.

Unrepeatability

In addition to being inevitable and irreversible, interpersonal communication is unrepeatable. The reason is simple: everyone and everything are constantly changing. As a result, you can never recapture the exact same situation, frame of mind, or relationship dynamics that defined a previous interpersonal act. For example, you can never repeat the experience of meeting a particular person for the first time, comforting a grieving friend on the death of his or her mother, or resolving a specific conflict.

You can, of course, try again, as when you say, "I'm sorry I came off so forward; can we try again?" But notice that even when you say this, you don't erase the initial impression. Instead, you try to counteract the initial (and perhaps negative) impression by going through the motions once more. In doing so, you try to create a more positive impression, which you hope will lessen the original negative effect.

On the basis of inevitability, irreversibility, and unrepeatability, what advice would you give someone starting a new job?

◀◀ THINKING BACK

REVIEWING KEY TERMS AND CONCEPTS IN THE AXIOMS OF INTERPERSONAL COMMUNICATION

This unit discussed seven axioms or principles that help explain what interpersonal communication is and how it works.

Interpersonal Communication Is Grounded in Theory and Research

What is a theory? What is research? What functions do theory and research serve in interpersonal communication?

- The theories of interpersonal communication are the organized generalizations about interpersonal communication and the evidence bearing on them.
- Through theory and research you learn how interpersonal communication works and from this can derive principles for achieving more effective interpersonal interaction.

Interpersonal Communication Is a Transactional Process

What is meant by a transactional view of interpersonal communication and how does this differ from a linear and an interactional view?

- Interpersonal communication is a process, an ongoing event, in which the elements are interdependent; communication is constantly occurring and changing.
- Don't expect clear-cut beginnings or endings or sameness from one time to another.

Interpersonal Relationships May Be Viewed as Symmetrical or Complementary

How do symmetrical and complementary relationships differ from each other?

- Interpersonal interactions may stimulate similar or different behavior patterns, and relationships may be described as basically symmetrical or complementary.
- Develop an awareness of symmetrical and complementary relationships. Avoid clinging rigidly to behavioral patterns that are no longer useful and mirroring another's destructive behaviors.

Interpersonal Communications Have Content and Relationship Dimensions

How do content and relationship dimensions of communication differ and what are the implications of these differences?

- All communications refer both to content and to the relationships between the participants.
- Seek out and respond to relationship messages as well as content messages.

Interpersonal Communication Is a Process of Adjustment

How does adjustment (and communication accommodation) operate in interpersonal communication?

- Communication depends on participants sharing the same system of signals and meaning; generally, people move in the direction of imitating or echoing the interpersonal behavior of the other.
- Expand common areas, and learn each other's system of signals to increase interpersonal effectiveness; share your own system of signals with significant others.

Interpersonal Communication Is a Series of Punctuated Events

What role does punctuation play in interpersonal communication?

- Everyone separates communication sequences into stimuli and responses on the basis of his or her own perspective.
- View punctuation as arbitrary, and adopt the other's point of view to increase empathy and understanding.

Interpersonal Communication Is Inevitable, Irreversible, and Unrepeatable

What is meant by interpersonal communication being inevitable, irreversible, and unrepeatable and what are the implications of these qualities?

- When in an interactional situation, you cannot not communicate; you cannot uncommunicate; you cannot repeat exactly a specific message.
- Seek to control as many aspects of your behavior as possible. In listening, seek out nonobvious messages. Beware of messages you may later wish to take back, for example, conflict and commitment messages.

APPLYING KEY TERMS AND CONCEPTS IN THE AXIOMS OF INTERPERSONAL COMMUNICATION

1. Can you describe one of your interpersonal relationships in terms of symmetrical and complementary interactions? For example, is it a relationship defined by the differences or by the similarities between you? Is there equality between you, or is one of you superior? Are you dependent on each other or independent? Is the power shared, or is one person in control?
2. How would you describe a recent argument in terms of relationship and content? How did the argument develop? How was it resolved?
3. A good illustration of double-bind messages is that which takes place between therapist and the client with disabilities; each seems to send contradictory messages that create "double-binds" for each other (Esten and Wilmot 1993). The client communicates both the desire to focus on the disability but also the desire to disregard it. If the therapist focuses on the disability, it's in violation of the client's desire to ignore it; if the therapist ignores it, it's in violation of the client's desire to concentrate on it. What communication guidelines would you offer the therapist and the client?
4. What explanations might you offer to account for someone sending contradictory messages?
5. Do teachers and students or lawyers and witnesses or doctors and patients accommodate to each other's communication style? In what direction is there likely to be greater accommodation? For example, is the teacher or the student more likely to accommodate to the other?
6. Can you recall a recent disagreement in which differences in punctuation figured prominently? What happened? Was the disagreement resolved?
7. How does the principle of inevitability operate in the classroom? In your home? On your job?
8. For what types of messages—in addition to messages of conflict and commitment, noted in the text—is it especially important to remember that communication is irreversible?
9. With very good intentions, you tell your partner: "I guess you'll just never learn how to dress." To your surprise, your partner becomes extremely offended. Although you know you can't take the statement back (communication really is irreversible), you want to lessen its negative tone and its effect on your partner and on your relationship. What can you say?
10. How would you go about finding answers to questions such as these?

- Is there a gender difference in the ability to appreciate the punctuation of another?
- Does the higher adjustment evidenced by symmetrical couples (over complementary couples) hold for all age groups? Does it hold for homosexual, as it seems to hold for heterosexual relationships?
- Are the students in your class who are in symmetrical relationships happier than those who are in complementary relationships?
- Will knowledge of these axioms of interpersonal communication have any impact on the number of conflicts a couple has? On the speed with which the conflicts are resolved?
- How do men and women "take back" something they wished they never said?

EXPERIENCING KEY TERMS AND CONCEPTS IN THE AXIOMS OF INTERPERSONAL COMMUNICATION

Go to www.awl.com/devito

Exercise No. 1, "Analyzing an Interaction," illustrates each of the axioms discussed here and is a useful means for reviewing the major concepts of the unit. Exercise No. 28, "The Television Relationship," can also be used to illustrate these foundation principles.

UNIT 3

CULTURE IN INTERPERSONAL COMMUNICATION

Guess Who's Coming to Dinner? (1967)

WORDS CAN DESTROY. WHAT WE CALL EACH OTHER ULTIMATELY BECOMES WHAT WE THINK OF EACH OTHER, AND IT MATTERS.

--JEANNE J. KIRKPATRICK

In Stanley Kramer's classic Guess Who's Coming to Dinner?, you see the confrontation between the parents of two people who intend to marry—one white (Katharine Houghton) and one African American (Sidney Poitier). Both sets of parents display the prejudices that were common over 30 years ago but that also seem amazingly contemporary. Cultural prejudice has proven extremely resistant to change. In this unit we look at culture from a number of viewpoints and at intercultural communication, its nature and principles.

THINKING AHEAD ▸▸
Why is culture so important in interpersonal communication?

THE NATURE OF CULTURE

Culture refers to the relatively specialized lifestyle of a group of people—consisting of their values, beliefs, artifacts, ways of behaving, and ways of communicating. Included in culture would be all that members of a social group have produced and developed—their language, modes of thinking, art, laws, and religion.

Culture is not synonymous with race or nationality. However, members of a particular race or country are often taught similar beliefs, attitudes, and values. This similarity makes it possible to speak of "Hispanic culture" or "African American culture." But, lest we be guilty of stereotyping, recognize that within any large culture—especially a culture based on race or nationality—there will be enormous differences. The Kansas farmer and the Wall Street executive may both be, say, German American, but they may differ widely in their attitudes and beliefs and in their general lifestyle. In some ways the Kansas farmer may be closer in attitudes and values to the Chinese farmer than to the Philadelphia lawyer.

Culture is passed on from one generation to the next through communication, not through genes. Thus, culture does not refer to color of skin or shape of eyes since these are passed on through genes, not communication. Culture does refer to beliefs in a supreme being, to attitudes toward success and happiness, and to the values placed on friendship, love, family, or money, since these are transmitted through communication.

Culture is transmitted from one generation to another through **enculturation,** a process by which you learn the culture into which you're born (your native culture). Parents, peer groups, schools, religious institutions, and government agencies are the main teachers of culture. One new instrument for spreading culture is the Internet. Because the Internet, although world wide, is so dominated by the United States and by the English language and idiom, the culture of the Internet is dominated by the culture of the United States. "Some countries," notes one media watcher, "already unhappy with the encroachment of American culture—from jeans to Mickey Mouse to movies and TV programs—are worried that their cultures will be further eroded by an American dominance in cyberspace" (Pollack 1995, D1).

A different process of learning culture is **acculturation,** the process by which you learn the rules and norms of a culture different from your native culture. Through acculturation, your original or native culture is modified through direct contact with (or exposure to) a new and different culture. For example, when immigrants settle in the United States, the host country, their own culture becomes influenced by the host culture. Gradually, the values, ways of behaving, and beliefs of the host culture become more and more a part of the immigrants' culture. At the same time, the host culture changes, too, as it interacts with the immigrants' culture. Generally, however, the culture of the immigrant changes more. The reasons for this are that the host country's members far outnumber the immigrant group, and the media are largely dominated by and reflect the values and customs of the host culture.

Before exploring further the role of culture in communication, consider your own cultural values and beliefs by taking the accompanying self-test. This test will suggest how your own cultural values and beliefs might influence the messages you send and the messages you listen to in your interpersonal communication.

TEST YOURSELF *What Are Your Cultural Beliefs and Values?*

Here the extremes of ten cultural differences are identified. For each characteristic indicate your own values: If your values are *very* similar to the extremes, select 1 or 7. If your values are *quite* similar to the extremes, select 2 or 6. If your values are *fairly* similar to the extremes, select 3 or 5. If you're in the middle, select 4.

Men and women are equal and are entitled to equality in all areas	Gender Equality 1 2 3 4 5 6 7	Men and women should stick to their specific and different cultural roles
"Success" is measured by your contribution to the group	Group and Individual Orientation 1 2 3 4 5 6 7	"Success" is measured by how far you out-perform others
You should enjoy yourself as much as possible	Pleasure orientation/Hedonism 1 2 3 4 5 6 7	You should work as much as possible
Religion is the final arbiter of what is right and wrong; your obligation is to abide by your religion's rules	Religion 1 2 3 4 5 6 7	Religion is like any other social institution; it's not inherently moral or right just because it's a religion
Your first obligation is to your family; each person is responsible for the welfare of her or his family	Family 1 2 3 4 5 6 7	Your first obligation is to yourself; each person is responsible for herself or himself
Work hard now for a better future	Time Orientation 1 2 3 4 5 6 7	Live in the present; the future may never come
Marriage, once made, is forever	Marriage 1 2 3 4 5 6 7	Marriage should be maintained as long as it's rewarding and dissolved when it's not
People should express their emotions openly and freely	Emotional Expression 1 2 3 4 5 6 7	People should not reveal their emotions, especially negative ones
Money should be a major consideration in just about any decision you make	Money 1 2 3 4 5 6 7	Money should not enter into life's really important decisions such as what relationship to enter or what career to pursue
The world is just; bad things happen to bad people and good things happen to good people	Belief in a just world 1 2 3 4 5 6 7	The world is random; bad and good things happen to people without reference to whether they're good or bad

This test was designed to help you explore the possible influence of your cultural beliefs and values on communication. Research shows that your cultural values will influence your interpersonal communications (as demonstrated throughout this text) as well as your decision making, assessments of coworkers, teamwork, trust in others, the importance you place on cultural diversity in the workplace, and your attitudes toward the role of women in the workplace (Stephens and Greer 1995, Bochner and Hesketh 1994). For example, your beliefs and values about gender equality will influence the way in which you communicate with and about the opposite sex. Your group and individual orientation will influence how you perform in work teams and how you deal with your peers at school and at work. Your degree of hedonism will influence the kinds of interactions you engage in, the books you read, the television programs you watch. Review the entire list of ten characteristics and try to identify one specific way in which your attitudes on each of the ten characteristics in the self-test influence your communication. ■

How has your culture influenced what you believe?

◀◀ THINKING BACK

THINKING AHEAD ▶▶

How comfortable are you with the beliefs your culture teaches about the importance of the individual versus the group or about the differences between men and women?

HOW CULTURES DIFFER

Cultures differ in at least four major ways that are especially important for communication. Here we discuss power distances, masculine and feminine orientation, collectivism and individualism, and high and low context (Gudykunst 1991, Hall and Hall, 1987, Hofstede 1997). As you review these several differences, recognize that the differences are matters of degree. Characteristics are not in one culture and absent in the other but are present to different degrees in both.

Power Distances

In some cultures power is concentrated in the hands of a few, and there is a great difference in the power held by these people and that held by the ordinary citizen. These are called high power distance cultures; examples are Mexico, Brazil, India, and the Philippines (Hofstede 1983, 1997). In low power distance cultures, power is more evenly distributed throughout the citizenry; examples include Denmark, New Zealand, Sweden, and to a lesser extent the United States. These differences impact on interpersonal communication and relationships in a variety of ways.

Friendship and dating relationships will be influenced by the power distance between groups (Andersen 1991). For example, in India (high power distance), friendships and romantic relationships are expected to take place within your cultural class; in Sweden (low power distance), a person is expected to select friends and romantic partners not on the basis of class or culture, but on individual factors such as personality, appearance, and the like.

In low power distance cultures there is a general feeling of equality which is consistent with acting assertively, and so you're expected to confront a friend, partner, or supervisor assertively (Borden 1991). In high power distance cultures, direct confrontation and assertiveness may be viewed negatively, especially if directed at a superior.

In high power distance cultures you're taught to have great respect for authority; people in these cultures see authority as desirable and beneficial, and challenges to authority are generally not welcomed (Westwood, Tang, and Kirkbride 1992, Bochner and Hesketh 1994). In low power distance cultures, there's a certain distrust for authority; it's seen as a kind of necessary evil that should be limited as much as possible. This difference in attitudes toward authority can be seen right in the classroom. In high power distance cultures there's a great power distance between students and teachers; students are expected to be modest, polite, and totally respectful. In low power distance cultures students are expected to demonstrate their knowledge and command of the subject matter, participate in discussions with the teacher, and even challenge the teacher, something many high power distance culture members wouldn't even think of doing. The same differences can be seen in patient-doctor communication. Patients from high power distance cultures are less likely to challenge their doctor or admit that they don't understand the medical terminology than would patients in low power distance cultures.

High power distance cultures rely more on symbols of power. For example, titles (Dr., Professor, Chef, Inspector) are more important in high power distance cultures. Failure to include these in forms of address is a serious breach of etiquette. Low power distance cultures rely less on symbols of power, and less of a problem is created if you fail to use a respectful title (Victor 1992). But even in low power distance cultures you may create problems if, for example, you call a medical doctor, police captain, military officer, or professor Ms. or Mr.

In the United States, two people quickly move from Title plus Last Name (Mr. or Ms. Smith) to First Name (Pat). Similarly, in low power distance cultures less of a problem is created if you're too informal or if you presume to exchange first names before sufficient interaction has taken place. In high power distance cultures too great an informality—especially between those differing greatly in power—would be a serious breach of etiquette. Again, in even the lowest power distance culture, you may still create problems if you call your English professor Pat.

Masculine and Feminine Cultures

A popular classification of cultures is in terms of their masculinity and femininity (Hofstede 1997). In a highly "masculine" culture men are viewed as assertive, oriented to material success, and strong; women on the other hand are viewed as modest, focused on the quality of life, and tender. In a highly "feminine" culture, both men and women are encouraged to be modest, oriented to maintaining the quality of life, and tender. The ten countries with the highest masculinity score (beginning with the highest) are Japan, Austria, Venezuela, Italy, Switzerland, Mexico, Ireland, Jamaica, Great Britain, and Germany. The ten countries with the highest femininity score (beginning with the highest) are Sweden, Norway, Netherlands, Denmark, Costa Rica, Yugoslavia, Finland, Chile, Portugal, and Thailand. Out of 53 countries ranked, the United States ranks 15th most masculine (Hofstede 1997).

Masculine cultures emphasize success and socialize their people to be assertive, ambitious, and competitive. Members of masculine cultures are thus more likely to confront conflicts directly and to competitively fight out any differences; they're more likely to emphasize win-lose conflict strategies. **Feminine cultures** emphasize the quality of life and socialize their people to be modest and to emphasize close interpersonal relationships. Members of feminine cultures are thus more likely to emphasize compromise and negotiation in resolving conflicts; they're more likely to seek win-win solutions.

Organizations can also be viewed in terms of masculinity or femininity. Masculine organizations emphasize competitiveness and aggressiveness. They emphasize the bottom line and reward their workers on the basis of their contribution to the organization. Feminine organizations are less competitive and less aggressive. They're more likely to emphasize worker satisfaction and reward their workers on the basis of need; those who have large families, for example, may get better raises than the single people, even if the singles have contributed more to the organization.

WEB EXPLORATION
To learn more about individual and collective orientation, go to www.awl.com/devito.

Individual and Collective Orientation

Cultures differ in the extent to which they promote individual values (for example, power, achievement, hedonism, and stimulation) versus collectivist values (for example, benevolence, tradition, and conformity). The countries with the highest individualist orientation (beginning with the highest) are the United States, Australia, Great Britain, Canada, Netherlands, New Zealand, Italy, Belgium, Denmark, Sweden, France, and Ireland. Countries with the highest collectivist orientation (beginning with the highest) are Guatemala, Ecuador, Panama, Venezuela, Colombia, Indonesia, Pakistan, Costa Rica, Peru, Taiwan, and South Korea (Hofstede 1983, 1997, Hatfield and Rapson 1996, Kapoor, Wolfe, and Blue 1995). With a few notable exceptions, the individualist countries are wealthy and the collectivist countries are poor. For example, Japan and Hong Kong—which score in the middle—are wealthier than many of the most individualist countries. The following self-test will help you examine your own orientation toward individualism or collectivism.

TEST YOURSELF *Are You an Individualist or a Collectivist?*

Respond to each of the following statements in terms of how true they are of your behavior and thinking: 1 = almost always true, 2 = more often true than false, 3 = true about half the time and false about half the time, 4 = more often false than true, and 5 = almost always false.

1. My own goals, rather than the goals of my group (for example, my extended family, my organization), are the more important.
2. I feel responsible for myself and to my own conscience rather than for the entire group and to the group's values and rules.
3. Success to me depends on my contribution to the group effort and the group's success rather than to my own individual success or to surpassing others.
4. I make a clear distinction between who is the leader and who are the followers and similarly make a clear distinction between members of my own cultural group and outsiders.
5. In business transactions personal relationships are extremely important, so I would spend considerable time getting to know people with whom I do business.
6. In my communications I prefer a direct and explicit communication style; I believe in "telling it like it is," even if it hurts.

To compute your individualist-collectivist score, follow these steps:

1. Reverse the scores for items 3 and 5 (if your response was 1 reverse it to a 5, if your response was 2 reverse it to a 4, if your response was 3 keep it as 3, if your response was 4 reverse it to a 2, if your response was 5 reverse it to a 1).
2. Add your scores for all 6 items, being sure to use the reverse scores for items 3 and 5 in your calculations. Your score should be between 6 (indicating a highly individualist orientation) to 30 (indicating a highly collectivist orientation).
3. Position your score on the following scale:

6	15	30
highly individualist	about equally individualist and collectivist	highly collectivist

Does this scale and score accurately measure the way in which you see yourself on this dimension? Is this orientation going to help you achieve your personal and professional goals? Might it hinder you? ■

One of the major differences between these two orientations is in the extent to which an individual's goals or the group's goals are given precedence. Individual and collective tendencies are, of course, not mutually exclusive; this is not an all-or-none orientation but rather one of emphasis. You probably have both tendencies. Thus, you may, for example, compete with other members of your basketball team for most baskets or most valuable player award (and thus emphasize individual goals). At the same time, however, you will—in a game—act in a way that will benefit the entire team (and thus emphasize group goals). In actual practice both individual and collective tendencies will help you and your team each achieve your goals. Yet most people and most cultures have a dominant orientation; they're more individually oriented (they see themselves as independent) or more collectively oriented (they see themselves as interdependent) in most situations, most of the time (cf. Singelis 1994).

At some instances, however, these tendencies may come into conflict. For example, do you shoot for the basket and try to raise your own individual score or do you pass the ball to another player who is better positioned to score and thus benefit the team as a whole? You make this distinction in popular talk when you call someone a team player (collectivist orientation) or an individual player (individualist orientation).

In an **individualist culture** members are responsible for themselves and perhaps their immediate family. In a **collectivist culture** members are responsible for the entire group.

In an individualist culture success is measured by the extent to which you surpass other members of your group; you would take pride in standing out from the crowd. Your heroes—in the media, for example—are likely to be those who are unique and who stand apart. In a collectivist culture success is measured by your contribution to the achievements of the group as a whole; you would take pride in your similarity to other members of your group. Your heroes, in contrast, are more likely to be team players who do not stand out from the rest of the group's members. Not surprisingly, advertisements in individualist cultures emphasize individual preferences and benefits, independence, and personal success; advertisements in collectivist cultures emphasize group benefits, family integrity, and group harmony (Han and Shavitt 1994).

In an individualist culture you're responsible to your own conscience, and responsibility is largely an individual matter; in a collectivistic culture you're responsible to the rules of the social group, and responsibility for an accomplishment or a failure is shared by all members. Competition is fostered in individualist cultures while cooperation is promoted in collectivist cultures.

In an individualist culture you might compete for leadership in a small group setting, and there would likely be a very clear distinction between leaders and members. In a collectivist culture leadership would be shared and rotated; there is likely to be little distinction between leader and members. These orientations will also influence the kinds of communication members consider appropriate in an organizational context. For example, individualist members will favor clarity and directness while collectivists will favor "face-saving" and the avoidance of hurting others or arousing negative evaluations (Kim and Sharkey 1995).

Distinctions between in-group members and out-group members are extremely important in collectivist cultures. In individualist cultures, where the person's individuality is prized, the distinction is likely to be less important.

High- and Low-Context Cultures

Cultures also differ in the extent to which information is made explicit or is assumed to be in the context or in the persons communicating. A **high-context culture** is one in which much of the information in communication is in the context or in the person—for example, information that was shared through previous communications, through assumptions about each other, and through shared experiences. The information is thus known by all participants but isn't explicitly stated in the verbal messages. A **low-context culture** is one in which most of the information is explicitly stated in the verbal message. In formal transactions it would be stated in written (or contract) form.

To further appreciate the distinction between high and low context, consider giving directions ("Where's the voter registration center?") to someone who knows the neighborhood and to a newcomer to your city. With someone who knows the neighborhood (a high-context situation), you can assume that she or he knows the local landmarks. So you can give directions such as "next to the laundromat on Main Street" or "the corner of Albany and Elm." With the newcomer (a low-context situation), you can't assume that she or he shares any information with you. So you would have to use only those directions that a stranger would understand, for example, "make a left at the next stop sign" or "go two blocks and then turn right."

High-context cultures are also collectivist cultures (Gudykunst, Ting-Toomey, and Chua 1988; Gudykunst and Kim 1992). These cultures (Japanese, Arabic, Latin American, Thai, Korean, Apache, and Mexican are examples) place great emphasis on personal relationships and oral agreements (Victor 1992). Low-context cultures are also individualist cultures. These cultures (German, Swedish, Norwegian, and American are examples) place less emphasis on personal relationships and more emphasis on verbalized, explicit explanation, and on written contracts in business transactions. The characteristics of individual-collective and high- and low-context cultures discussed here are summarized in Table 3.1.

Members of high-context cultures spend lots of time getting to know each other interpersonally and socially before any important transactions take place. Because of this prior personal knowledge, a great deal of information is shared by the members and therefore does not have to be explicitly stated. Members of low-context cultures spend much less time getting to know each other and hence don't have that shared knowledge. As a result everything has to be stated explicitly.

This difference between high- and low-context orientation is partly responsible for the differences observed in Japanese and American business groups (alluded to in Unit 1). The Japanese spend lots of time getting to know each other before conducting actual business, whereas Americans get down to business very quickly. The Japanese (and other high-context cultures) want to get to know each other because important information isn't made explicit. They have to know you so they can read your nonverbals, for example (Sanders, Wiseman, and Matz 1991). Americans can get right down to business because all important information will be stated explicitly.

To high-context cultural members what is omitted or assumed is a vital part of the communication transaction. Silence, for example, is highly valued (Basso 1972). To low-context cultural members what is omitted creates ambiguity, but this ambiguity is simply something that will be eliminated by explicit and direct communication. To high-context cultural members ambiguity is something to be avoided; it's a sign that the interpersonal and social interactions have not proved sufficient to establish a shared base of information (Gudykunst 1983).

When this simple difference isn't understood, intercultural misunderstandings can easily result. For example, the directness characteristic of the low-context culture may prove insulting, insensitive, or unnecessary to the high-context cultural member. Conversely, to the low-context member, the high-context cultural member may appear vague, underhanded, or dishonest in his or her reluctance to be explicit or engage in communication that a low-context member would consider open and direct.

TABLE 3.1 Differences in Individual (Low-Context) and Collective (High-Context) Cultures

In every culture there will be variations in each of these characteristics. View these, therefore, as general tendencies rather than absolutes. Further, the increased mobility, changing immigration patterns, and the exposure to media from different parts of the world will gradually decrease the differences between these two orientations. This table is based on the work of Hall (1983) and Hall and Hall (1987) and the interpretations by Gudykunst (1991) and Victor (1992).

Individual (Low-Context) Cultures	Collective (High-Context) Cultures
Your own goals are most important	The group's goals are most important
You're responsible for yourself and to your own conscience	You're responsible for the entire group and to the group's values and rules
Success depends on your surpassing others	Success depends on your contribution to the group
Competition is emphasized	Cooperation is emphasized
Clear distinction is made between leaders and members	Little distinction is made between leaders and members; leadership would normally be shared
In-group versus out-group distinctions are of little importance	In-group versus out-group distinctions are of great importance
Information is made explicit; little is left unsaid	Information is often left implicit and much is often omitted from explicit statement
Personal relationships are less important; hence, little time is spent getting to know each other in meetings and conferences	Personal relationships are extremely important; hence, much time is spent getting to know each other in meetings and conferences
Directness is valued; face-saving is seldom thought of	Indirectness is valued and face-saving is a major consideration

Another frequent source of intercultural misunderstanding that can be traced to the differences in high and low context can be seen in face-saving (Hall and Hall 1987). High-context cultures place much more emphasis on face-saving. For example, they're more likely to avoid argument for fear of causing others to lose face; on the other hand, low-context members (with their individualistic orientation) will use argument to win a point. Similarly, in high-context cultures criticism should only take place in private. Low-context cultures may not make this public-private distinction. Low-context managers who criticize high-context workers in public will find that their criticism causes interpersonal problems and does little to resolve the original difficulty that led to the criticism in the first place (Victor 1992).

Members of high-context cultures are reluctant to say no for fear of offending and causing the person to lose face. Thus, it's necessary to be able to read in the Japanese executive's "yes" when it means yes and when it means no. The difference isn't in the words used but in the way in which they're used.

Can you recall an example of how one of these cultural differences (power distance, masculine-feminine, individual-collective, and high-low context) influenced an interpersonal interaction?

◀◀ THINKING BACK

THINKING AHEAD ▶▶

How does your culture influence what you do when you talk with an older and higher status person or with someone with whom you want to establish a romantic relationship?

THEORIES OF CULTURE AND COMMUNICATION

Here are several attempts to explain the interaction of culture and communication, to formulate a theory of culture and communication. Although none provides a

As relationships become more intimate, they come to resemble high-context interactions. The more you and your partner know each other, the less you have to make verbally explicit. Truman Capote once defined love as "never having to finish your sentences," which is an apt description of high-context relationships. Because you know the other person so well, you can make some pretty good guesses as to what the person will say. What other comparisons can you draw between interpersonal relationships and high and low context?

complete explanation, each provides some understanding of how some part of culture interacts with some part of communication.

Language Relativity

The general idea that language influences thought and ultimately behavior got its strongest expression from linguistic anthropologists. In the late 1920s and throughout the 1930s, the view was formulated that the characteristics of language influence the way you think (Carroll 1956, Fishman 1960, Hoijer 1954, Miller and McNeill 1969, Sapir 1929). Since the languages of the world differ greatly in semantics and syntax, it was argued that people speaking widely different languages would also differ in how they viewed and thought about the world. This view became known as the *linguistic relativity hypothesis.*

Subsequent research and theory, however, did not support the extreme claims made by linguistic relativity researchers (Pinker 1994). A more modified hypothesis seems currently supported: The language you speak helps to highlight what you see and how you talk about it. For example, if you speak a language that is rich in color terms (English is a good example), you would find it easier to highlight and talk about nuances of color than would someone from a culture which has fewer color terms (some cultures distinguish only two or three or four parts of the color spectrum). But this does not mean that people see the world differently; only that their language helps (or doesn't help) them to focus on certain variations in nature and makes it easier (or more difficult) to talk about them. Nor does it mean that people speaking widely differing languages are doomed to misunderstanding each other. Translation enables us to understand a great deal of the meaning in a foreign language message. We also have our communication skills; we can ask for clarification, for additional examples, for restatement. We can listen actively, give feedforward and feedback, use perception checking.

Language differences do not make for very important differences in perception, thought, or behavior. Difficulties in intercultural understanding are more often due to ineffective communication than to differences in languages.

Uncertainty Reduction

All communication interactions involve uncertainty and ambiguity. Not surprisingly, uncertainty and ambiguity are greater when there are large cultural differences (Berger and Bradac 1982, Gudykunst 1989, 1994). Because of this greater uncertainty in intercultural communication, time and effort are needed to reduce it and to thus communicate meaningfully. Reducing your uncertainty about another

Is your place of employment basically masculine or feminine? What beliefs, attitudes, and values does it teach? What kinds of rewards or punishments do they administer for following and not following these teachings?

person will not only make your communication more effective, but will also increase your liking for the person (Douglas 1994). In situations of great uncertainty the techniques of effective communication (for example, active listening, perception checking, being specific, and seeking feedback) take on special importance.

Active listening (Unit 7) and perception checking techniques (Unit 6), for example, help you to check on the accuracy of your perceptions and allow you the opportunity to revise and amend any incorrect perceptions. Being specific reduces ambiguity and the chances of misunderstandings. Misunderstanding is a lot more likely when talking about "neglect" (a highly abstract concept) than when talking about "forgetting your last birthday" (a specific event).

Seeking feedback helps you to correct any possible misconceptions almost immediately. Seek feedback on whether you're making yourself clear ("Does that make sense?" "Do you see where to put the widget?") as well as on whether you understand what the other person is saying ("Do you mean that you'll never speak with them again? Do you mean that literally?")

Although you're always in danger of misperceiving and misevaluating another person, you're in special danger in intercultural situations. Therefore, try to resist your natural tendency to judge others quickly and permanently. A judgment made early is likely to be based on too little information. Because of this, flexibility and a willingness to revise opinions are essential intercultural skills.

Maximizing Outcomes

In intercultural communication—as in all communication—you try to maximize the outcomes of your interactions (Sunnafrank 1989). You try to gain the greatest rewards while paying the least costs. For example, you probably interact with those you predict will contribute to positive results, and you seek conversations that will prove satisfying, enjoyable, or exciting. Because intercultural communication is difficult and positive outcomes may seem unlikely (at least at first), you may avoid it. So, for example, you talk with the person in class who is similar to rather than different from you. However, extending and stretching yourself may actually result in greater satisfaction in the long run.

Also, consider that when you have positive outcomes, you continue to engage in communication and increase your communications. When you have negative outcomes, you begin to withdraw and communicate less. The implication here is obvious: Don't give up easily, especially in intercultural settings.

Since intercultural communication may be new or different from your usual communications, you'll probably be more mindful, more consciously aware of it

ASK THE RESEARCHER

Confronting Family Prejudice

My family, I'm embarrassed to say, are really prejudiced against other races and religions. They can't see any value in the contributions of other cultures or the wisdom in other religions. How can I insert a note of reason into their discussions and get them to be less prejudiced?

Deep-seated and strong prejudices are very resistant. They may be based on fear or dislike of any sort of difference—feelings the person may not even admit to himself or herself. Typically, these feelings have been supported by peer groups for a long time and so the prejudiced person sees these opinions as reasonable and natural.

The most realistic goal may be to get them to respect your own feelings. Tell them that you're upset by this type of talk and you don't wish to be around it. Be assertive and consistent. Make it clear that you're upset and that you're asking them to stop telling those types of jokes, using that kind of language, etc. It's your right. If they don't stop, leave the room.

Reducing their prejudice may take a very long time. You can try showing them that the same type of thinking can apply to their own group. You also can try to have them meet members of the group that disconfirm their stereotypes.

For further information see M. L. Hecht (ed.), *Communicating Prejudice* (Newbury Park, CA: Sage, 1998), and B. Lott and D. Maluso (eds.), *The Social Psychology of Interpersonal Discrimination* (New York: Guilford, 1995).

—Michael L. Hecht (Ph.D., University of Illinois) is professor and head of the Department of Speech Communication at Penn State University where he teaches courses and conducts research in inter-ethnic relationships, identity, culture and drug prevention, and interpersonal relationships. He's currently developing a culturally appropriate drug prevention program for middle school students and involved in an international project to improve intergroup relationships. mlh10@psu.edu

(Gudykunst 1989, Langer 1989). This has positive and negative consequences. On the positive side, this increased awareness probably keeps you more alert. It prevents you from saying things that might appear insensitive or inappropriate. On the negative side, it leads to guardedness, lack of spontaneity, and lack of confidence.

In your mindful state you probably make predictions about which types of communication will result in positive outcomes; you try to predict the results of, for example, the choice of topic, the positions you take, the nonverbal behaviors you display, and the amount of talking versus listening that you do. You then do what you think will result in positive outcomes and avoid doing what you think will result in negative outcomes. To do this successfully, however, you'll have to learn as much as you can about the other person's system of communication signals. This will help you predict the outcomes of your behavior more accurately.

Culture Shock

Culture shock refers to the psychological reaction you experience when you're in a culture very different from your own (Furnham and Bochner 1986). Culture shock is normal; most people experience it when entering a new and different culture. Nevertheless, it can be unpleasant and frustrating. Part of this results from the feelings of alienation, conspicuousness, and difference from everyone else. When you lack knowledge of the rules and customs of the new society, you cannot communicate effectively. You're apt to blunder frequently and seriously. In your culture shock you may not know basic things:

- how to ask someone for a favor or pay someone a compliment
- how to extend or accept an invitation for dinner
- how early or how late to arrive for an appointment or how long to stay
- how to distinguish seriousness from playfulness and politeness from indifference

- how to dress for an informal, formal, or business function
- how to order a meal in a restaurant or how to summon a waiter

Anthropologist Kalervo Oberg (1960), who first used the term culture shock, notes that it occurs in stages. These stages are useful for examining many encounters with the new and the different. Going away to college, moving in together, or joining the military, for example, can result in culture shock. To illustrate the four stages of culture shock, we can use the example of moving away from home into your own apartment.

Stage One: The Honeymoon You finally have your own apartment. You're your own boss. Finally, on your own! At this stage you experience fascination, even enchantment, with your new situation and the new people around you. This is similar to the experience of moving to a country with a culture different from your own. This stage is characterized by cordiality and friendship in early and superficial relationships. Many tourists remain at this stage because their stay in foreign countries is so brief.

Stage Two: The Crisis Here, the differences between your own culture and the new one create problems. In your new apartment, for example, no longer do you find dinner ready for you unless you do it yourself. Your clothes are not washed or ironed unless you do them yourself. Feelings of frustration and inadequacy come to the fore. This is the stage at which you experience the actual shock of the new culture. In one study of foreign students coming from over 100 different countries and studying in 11 different countries, it was found that 25 percent of the students experienced depression (Klineberg and Hull 1979).

Stage Three: The Recovery During this period you gain the skills necessary to function effectively. On your own for the first time, you learn how to shop, cook, and plan a meal. You find a local laundry and figure you'll learn how to iron later. You learn the language and ways of the new culture. Your feelings of inadequacy subside.

Stage Four: The Adjustment At this final stage, you adjust to and come to enjoy the new culture and the new experiences. You may still experience periodic difficulties and strains, but on a whole, the experience is pleasant. Actually, now that you've been in your own apartment for a while, you've become a pretty decent cook. You're even coming to enjoy it. You're making a good salary, so why learn to iron?

People may also experience culture shock when they return to their original culture after living in a foreign culture, a kind of reverse culture shock (Jandt 1995). Consider, for example, the Peace Corps volunteers who work in a rural and economically deprived area. Upon returning to Las Vegas or Beverly Hills, they too may experience culture shock. Sailors who serve long periods aboard ship and then return to an isolated farming community might also experience culture shock. In these cases, however, the recovery period is shorter and the sense of inadequacy and frustration is less.

Can you think of one specific practical application that you can derive from these theories of intercultural communication?

◀◀ THINKING BACK

INTERCULTURAL COMMUNICATION

Understanding the role of culture in communication is an essential foundation for understanding intercultural communication as it occurs in an interpersonal context. As a preface to this discussion you may want to take the accompanying self-test to explore your own openness to intercultural communication.

THINKING AHEAD ▶▶

How does intercultural communication differ from communication that is not intercultural? How can you make your own intercultural communication more effective?

ETHICS IN INTERPERSONAL COMMUNICATION

Vote online at http://www.awl.com/devito

Means and Ends

Do the ends justify the means? Would it be ethical for you to say things that would normally be considered unethical (for example, making up statistics), if the end you hoped to achieve was a worthy one (for example, keeping children from using drugs)? Those taking an objective position (see Ethics in Interpersonal Communication box in Unit 2, p. 32) would argue that the ends don't justify the means, that the lie, for example, is always wrong regardless of the specific situation. Those taking a subjective position would argue that at times the end would justify the means and at times it wouldn't; it would depend on the specific means and ends in question.

What would you do? *Your close friend asks for a loan of $100. You can easily afford to lend her the money, but on the basis of past experience you know that you'll never get it back. Would it be ethical to lie and say you don't have the money rather than cause an argument by bringing up the past times when she didn't pay back the loans and perhaps damage an otherwise good friendship? How would a person who believes that the ends justify the means respond to this situation? How would those taking the position that it's wrong to use unethical means even if the ends are good respond? What would you do in this situation?*

TEST YOURSELF *How Open Are You Interculturally?*

Select a specific culture (national, racial, or religious) different from your own, and substitute this culture for the phrase "interculturally different" in each question below. Indicate how open you would be to communicate in each of these situations, using the following scale: 5 = very open and willing, 4 = open and willing, 3 = neutral, 2 = closed and unwilling, and 1 = very closed and unwilling.

_____ 1. Talk with an interculturally different person while alone waiting for a bus.

_____ 2. Talk with an interculturally different person in the presence of those who are interculturally similar to you.

_____ 3. Have a close friendship with an interculturally different person.

_____ 4. Have a long-term romantic relationship with an interculturally different person.

_____ 5. Participate in a problem-solving group that is composed predominantly of interculturally different people.

_____ 6. Openly and fairly observe an information-sharing group consisting predominantly of interculturally different people.

_____ 7. Lead a group of interculturally different people through a problem-solving or information-sharing situation.

_____ 8. Participate in a consciousness-raising group that is composed of one half interculturally different people.

_____ 9. Listen openly and fairly to a conversation by an interculturally different person.

_____ 10. Ascribe a level of credibility for an interculturally different person identical to that ascribed to an interculturally similar person—all other things being equal.

To calculate your total score, simply add your scores for all ten questions. High scores (above 35) indicate considerable openness; low scores (below 20) indicate a lack of openness. Use these numbers for purposes of thinking about your own degree of openness. Not surprisingly, research finds that people who are more willing to communicate interculturally have more friends from foreign countries than do those with less willingness (Kassing 1997). Do you find this generally true? ■

The Nature of Intercultural Communication

Intercultural communication refers to communication between persons who have different cultural beliefs, values, or ways of behaving. The model in Figure 3.1 illustrates this concept. The larger circles represent the culture of the individual communicator. The inner circles identify the communicators (the sources/receivers). In this model each communicator is a member of a different culture. In some instances the cultural differences are relatively slight—say, between persons from Toronto and New York. In other instances the cultural differences are great—say, between persons from Borneo and Germany, or between persons from rural Nigeria and industrialized England.

All messages originate from a specific and unique cultural context, and that context influences their content and form. You communicate as you do largely as a result of your culture. Culture (along with the processes of enculturation and acculturation) influences every aspect of your communication experience.

You receive messages through the filters imposed by your cultural context. That context influences what you receive and how you receive it. For example, some cultures (like the United States) rely heavily on television or newspapers and trust them implicitly. Less media-oriented cultures or cultures in which the media are rigidly controlled by the government are more likely to rely on face-to-face interpersonal interactions, distrusting many of the mass communication systems.

Principles for Improving Intercultural Communication

Murphy's law ("If anything can go wrong, it will") is especially applicable to intercultural communication. Intercultural communication is, of course, subject to all the same barriers and problems as are the other forms of communication that we discuss throughout this text. Drawing on a number of intercultural researchers, we cover here the principles designed to counteract the barriers that are unique to intercultural communication (Barna 1985, Ruben 1985, Spitzberg 1991).

Prepare Yourself There's no better preparation for intercultural communication than learning about the other culture. Fortunately, there are numerous sources to draw

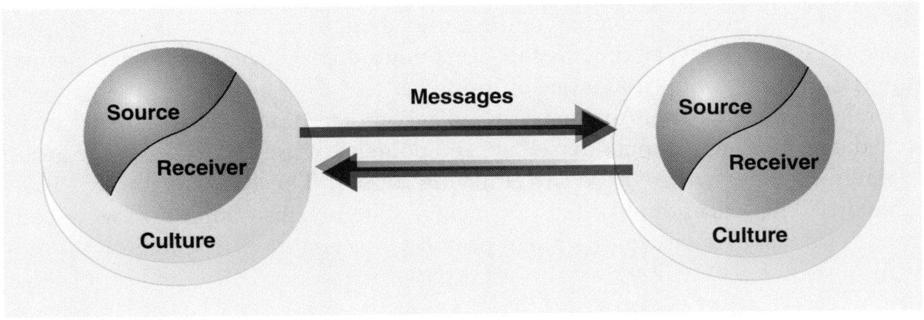

Figure 3.1 A Model of Intercultural Communication This basic model of intercultural communication illustrates that culture is a part of every communication transaction.

on. View a video or film that presents a realistic view of the culture. Read what has been written about the culture by persons from that culture as well as by "outsiders." Scan magazines and Web sites from that culture. Talk with members of that culture. Chat on international IRC channels. Read materials addressed to people who need to communicate with those from other cultures. For example, recent titles include: *Do's and Taboos of Hosting International Visitors* (Axtell 1990), *When In Rome . . . A Business Guide to Cultures and Customs in 12 European Nations* (Mole 1990). *Do's and Taboos Around the World* (Axtell 1993), *The Executive Guide to Asia-Pacific Communications* (James 1995), *How to Negotiate Anything with Anyone Anywhere Around the World* (Acuff 1993), and *Internationally Yours: Writing and Communicating Successfully in Today's Global Marketplace* (DeVries 1994).

Recognize and Face Fears A major factor that stands in the way of effective intercultural communication is fear (Gudykunst and Kim 1992, Stephan and Stephan 1985). For example, you may fear for your self-esteem. You may become anxious about your ability to control the intercultural situation, or you may worry about your own level of discomfort. You may fear saying something that will be considered politically incorrect or culturally insensitive and thereby losing face. You may fear that you'll be taken advantage of by the member of this other culture. Depending upon your own stereotypes, you may fear being lied to, financially duped, or made fun of.

You may fear that members of this other group will react to you negatively. You may fear, for example, that they will not like you or may disapprove of your attitudes or beliefs or perhaps even reject you as a person. Conversely, you may fear negative reactions from members of your own group. They might, for example, disapprove of your socializing with the culturally different.

Some fears, of course, are reasonable. In many cases, however, they're groundless. Either way, they need to be assessed logically and their consequences weighed carefully. Then you'll be able to make informed choices about your communications.

WEB EXPLORATION
To learn more about recognizing the differences between yourself and the culturally different, go to www.awl.com/devito.

Recognize Differences Between Yourself and the Culturally Different A common barrier to intercultural communication occurs when you assume that similarities exist and that differences do not. This is especially true in the area of values, attitudes, and beliefs. You might easily accept different hairstyles, clothing, and foods. In basic values and beliefs, however, you may assume that deep down everyone is really alike. They aren't. When you assume similarities and ignore differences, you'll fail to notice important distinctions and when communicating will convey to others that your ways are the right ways and that their ways are not important to you. Consider this example. An American invites a Filipino coworker to dinner. The Filipino politely refuses. The American is hurt and feels that the Filipino does not want to be friendly. The Filipino is hurt and concludes that the invitation was not extended sincerely. Here, it seems, both the American and the Filipino assume that their customs for inviting people to dinner are the same when, in fact, they aren't. A Filipino expects to be invited several times before accepting a dinner invitation. When an invitation is given only once, it's viewed as insincere.

Here's another example. An American college student hears that her favorite uncle has died. She bites her lip, pulls herself up, and politely excuses herself from the group of foreign students with whom she is having dinner. The Russian thinks: "How unfriendly." The Italian thinks: "How insincere." The Brazilian thinks: "How unconcerned." To many Americans, it's a sign of bravery to endure pain (physical or emotional) in silence and without any outward show of emotion. To members of other groups, such silence is often interpreted negatively to mean that the individual does not consider them friends who can share such sorrow. To members of other cultures, people are expected to reveal to friends how they feel.

Recognize Differences Within the Culturally Different Group Within every cultural group there are wide and important differences. As all Americans are not alike, neither are all Indonesians, Greeks, Mexicans, and so on. When you ignore these differences, when you assume that all persons covered by the same label (in this case a national or racial label) are the same, you're guilty of stereotyping. A good example of this is seen in the use of the term "African American." The term stresses the unity of Africa and those who are of African descent and is analogous to "Asian American" or "European American." At the same time, it ignores the great diversity within the African continent when, for example, it's used as analogous to "German American" or "Japanese American." A more analogous comparison would be "Nigerian American" or "Ethiopian American." Within each culture there are smaller cultures that differ greatly from each other and from the larger culture.

Recognize Differences in Meaning Meaning exists not in words but in people (a principle returned to in Unit 11). Consider, for example, the differences in meaning for such words as *woman* to an American and a Muslim, *religion* to a born-again Christian and an atheist, and *lunch* to a Chinese rice farmer and a Madison Avenue advertising executive. Even though the same word is used, its meanings will vary greatly depending on the listeners' cultural definitions.

A left-handed American who eats with the left hand may be seen by a Muslim as obscene. To the Muslim, the left hand isn't used for eating or for shaking hands but to clean oneself after excretory functions. So using the left hand to eat or to shake hands is considered insulting and obscene.

Follow Cultural Rules and Customs Each culture has its own rules for communicating (Burna 1985, Ruben 1985, Spitzberg 1991). These rules identify what is appropriate and what is inappropriate. Thus, for example, in American culture you would call a person you wish to date three or four days in advance. In certain Asian cultures you might call the person's parents weeks or even months in advance. In American culture you say, as a general friendly gesture and not as a specific invitation, "Come over and pay us a visit." To members of other cultures, this comment is sufficient for the listeners actually to visit at their convenience. In some cultures people show respect by avoiding direct eye contact with the person to whom they're speaking. In other cultures this same eye avoidance would signal disinterest. If a young American girl is talking with an older Indonesian man, for example, she's expected to avoid direct eye contact. To an Indonesian, direct eye contact in this situation would be considered disrespectful. In some southern European cultures men walk arm in arm. Other cultures (the United States, for example) consider this inappropriate.

WEB EXPLORATION
To learn more about following cultural rules and customs, go to www.awl.com/devito.

A good example of a series of rules for an extremely large and important culture that many people don't know appears in Table 3.2, "Ten Commandments for Communicating with People with Disabilities." The suggestions offered here are considered appropriate in the United States but not necessarily in other cultures. For example, although the phrase "person with mental retardation" is accepted in most of the United States, it was considered offensive to many in the United Kingdom (Fernald 1995).

How might you use any of these principles in meeting, say, an exchange student from Nigeria or Korea or Portugal?

◂◂ THINKING BACK

TABLE 3.2 Ten Commandments for Communicating with People with Disabilities

Some research has suggested that able-bodied instructors communicate differently with students who have and students who don't have disabilities (Hart and Williams 1995). Do you communicate differently? Note also that these suggestions are directed at the nondisabled person communicating with the person with disabilities. How would you write "the ten commandments for persons with disabilities communicating with persons without disabilities"? Put differently, what can the person with disabilities do to make communication with those without disabilities easier and more effective?

1. Speak directly rather than through a companion or sign language interpreter who may be present.
2. Offer to shake hands when introduced. People with limited hand use or an artificial limb can usually shake hands and offering the left hand is an acceptable greeting.
3. Always identify yourself and others who may be with you when meeting someone with a visual impairment. When conversing in a group, remember to identify the person to whom you are speaking.
4. If you offer assistance, wait until the offer is accepted. Then listen or ask for instructions.
5. Treat adults as adults. Address people who have disabilities by their first names only when extending that same familiarity to all others. Never patronize people in wheelchairs by patting them on the head or shoulder.
6. Do not lean against or hang on someone's wheelchair. Bear in mind that disabled people treat their chairs as extensions of their bodies.
7. Listen attentively when talking with people who have difficulty speaking and wait for them to finish. If necessary, ask short questions that require short answers, a nod, or shake of the head. Never pretend to understand if you are having difficulty doing so. Instead repeat what you have understood and allow the person to respond.
8. Place yourself at eye level when speaking with someone in a wheelchair or on crutches.
9. Tap a hearing-impaired person on the shoulder or wave your hand to get his or her attention. Look directly at the person and speak clearly, slowly, and expressively to establish if the person can read your lips. If so, try to face the light source and keep hands, cigarettes, and food away from your mouth when speaking.
10. Relax. Don't be embarrassed if you happen to use common expressions such as "See you later," or "Did you hear about this?" that seem to relate to a person's disability.

Source: United Cerebral Palsy Associations, Inc.
"Ten Commandments for Communicating with People with Disabilities," *The New York Times*, June 7, 1992.

REVIEWING KEY TERMS AND CONCEPTS IN CULTURE IN INTERPERSONAL COMMUNICATION

This unit explored the nature of culture and identified some key concepts and principles that explain the role of culture in interpersonal communication.

Nature of Culture

What is culture and how is it transmitted?

- **Culture:** the relatively specialized lifestyle of a group of people (values, beliefs, artifacts, ways of behaving) that are passed from one generation to the next by means of communication (not genes)

- **Enculturation:** the process through which you learn the culture into which you're born
- **Acculturation:** the process by which you learn the rules and norms of a culture different from your native culture and which modifies your original or native culture

How Cultures Differ

How do cultures differ from each other? How do these differences impact on interpersonal communication?

- In **high power distance cultures,** power is concentrated in the hands of a few and there is great difference between those with and those without power. In **low power distance cultures**, the power is more equally shared throughout the citizenry.
- In **highly masculine cultures,** men are viewed as strong, assertive, and focused on being successful, whereas women are viewed as modest, tender, and focused on the quality of life. In highly **feminine cultures,** men and women are viewed more similarly.
- A **collectivist culture** emphasizes the group and subordinates the individual's goals to those of the group. An **individualist culture** emphasizes the individual and subordinates the group's goals to the individual's.
- In **high context cultures**, much of the information is in the context; in **low context cultures,** the information is explicitly stated in the verbal message.

Theories of Culture and Communication

What general principles or theories might help us explain the role of culture in interpersonal communication?

- Language relativity concerns the role of language in influencing what you see and how you see it and assumes those speaking widely differing languages will see the world differently.
- Uncertainty reduction theory holds that the greater the uncertainty and ambiguity, the greater the communication difficulty.
- Maximizing outcomes holds that intercultural communication (or any communication) will be guided by the goal of maximizing positive outcomes.
- Culture shock refers to the psychological reaction to being in a culture different from one's own, often with feelings of alienation and conspicuousness.

Intercultural Communication

What is intercultural communication and what are its central principles?

- Intercultural communication refers to communication between people who have different cultures beliefs, values, or ways of behaving.
- Some intercultural communication principles include: prepare yourself, recognize and face fears, recognize differences between yourself and the culturally different, recognize differences within the culturally different group, recognize meaning differences in verbal and nonverbal messages, and follow cultural rules and customs.

APPLYING KEY TERMS AND CONCEPTS IN CULTURE IN INTERPERSONAL COMMUNICATION

1. In this age of multiculturalism, how do you feel about Article II, Section 1 of the United States Constitution. The relevant section reads: "No person except a natural born citizen, or a citizen of the United States, at the time of the adoption of this Constitution, shall be eligible to the office of President"?
2. Recently, the United States Department of Education issued guidelines (recommendations that are not legally binding on school boards) covering the types of religious communications and activities public schools may permit (*New York Times,* 26 August 1995, 1, 8). Among the permitted activities are student prayer, student-initiated discussions of religion, saying grace, proselytizing that would not be considered harassment, and the wearing of religious symbols and clothing. Among the forbidden activities are prayer endorsed by teachers or administrators, invitations to prayer that could constitute harassment, teaching of a particular religion (rather than about religion), encouraging (officially or through teaching) either religious or antireligious activity, and denying school facilities to religious groups if these same facilities are provided to nonreligious groups. If you were a member of a local school board, would you vote to adopt or reject these guidelines? How do your cultural beliefs influence your view of these guidelines?
3. It's been argued that in the United States women are more likely to view themselves as interdependents, having a more collectivist orientation, while men are more likely to view themselves as independents, having a more individualist orientation (Cross and Madson, 1997). Does your experience support this?
4. Visit one of the numerous travel websites (for example, http://www.globalpassage.com/netstop, http://travel.epicurious.com/travel/g_cnt/home.html, http://www.travelchannel.com/, http://www.lonelyplanet.com/). What can you learn about intercultural communication from such sources?
5. Visit one of the online news organizations (for example, www.pbs.org/, www.npr.org, www.c/net.com, www.reutershealth.com, www.cnnfn.com) for a recent item on culture. Of what value might such information be to someone engaging in intercultural communication?
6. Has anyone ever assumed something about you because you were a member of a particular culture that was not true? Did you find this disturbing?
7. Recently, the Emma Lazarus poem on the Statute of Liberty was changed. The words in brackets were deleted:

   Give me your tired, your poor,
   Your huddled masses yearning to breathe free,
   [the wretched refuse of your teeming shore,]
   Send these, the homeless, tempest-tossed to me:
   I lift my lamp beside the golden door.

Harvard zoologist Stephen Jay Gould, commenting on this change, notes that with the words omitted, the poem no longer has balance or rhyme and, more important, no longer represents what Lazarus wrote (Gould 1995). "The language police triumph," notes Gould, "and integrity bleeds." On the other hand, it can be argued that calling immigrants "wretched refuse" is insulting and degrading and that if Lazarus were writing today, she wouldn't have used that phrase. How do you feel about this? Would you have supported the deletion of this line?

8. A commonly encountered case of culture shock occurs with international students. For example, for the 1993–94 academic year, there were 449,749 international students (*New York Times,* 4 January 1995, A17). These students come to the United States from (in order) China, Japan, Taiwan, India, South Korea, Canada, Hong Kong, Malaysia, Indonesia, and Thailand. If you're an international student, can you describe your culture shock experiences? If you're not an international student, can you visualize the culture shock you might experience if you were to study in another culture?
9. Social Darwinism or cultural evolution holds that much as the human species evolved from lower life forms to homo sapiens, cultures also evolve. Consequently, some cultures may be considered advanced and others primitive. Cultural relativism, on the other hand, holds that all cultures are different but that no culture is either superior or inferior to any other (Berry, Poortinga, Segall, and Dasen 1992). What do you think of these positions?
10. How would you go about finding answers to such questions as these?

- Are couples who are similar in their individual-collective orientation likely to experience less conflict than are couples in which one person is individually orientated and the other collectively?
- Are people living in high and low power distance cultures different in terms of their perceived level of happiness? Their self-esteem?
- Do men and women follow different rules for politeness in conversation? In business?
- Do couples with similar ratings (on the cultural differences scale) stay together longer than couples with dissimilar ratings? Do couples with similar ratings have fewer conflicts than couples with dissimilar ratings?
- Are persons with greater education more likely to enter relationships with dissimilar others than are less educated persons?

EXPERIENCING KEY TERMS AND CONCEPTS IN CULTURE IN INTERPERSONAL COMMUNICATION

Go to www.awl.com/devito

Exercise No. 2, "Matching Pairs," provides an interesting view of intercultural communication and especially of the barriers to it. Exercise No. 22, "Male and Female," offers an opportunity to discuss sexual stereotypes and misconceptions. Exercises No. 20, "Interpersonal Relationships in Songs and Greeting Cards," No. 21, "Mate Preferences," and No. 25, "Power Plays," illustrate the influence of culture in a wide variety of interpersonal communication situations.

UNIT 4

THE SELF IN INTERPERSONAL COMMUNICATION

Marty (1955)

IN ORDER TO HAVE A CONVERSATION WITH SOMEONE YOU MUST REVEAL YOURSELF.

--JAMES BALDWIN

Self-Concept
Self-Awareness
Self-Esteem
Self-Disclosure

MARTY TELLS THE STORY of a lonely Bronx butcher (played by Ernest Borgnine) who has extremely low self-esteem, which contributes to his difficulties with women. Eventually, he meets a teacher (Betsy Blair) who treats him with respect and gives him the self-confidence that he had long ago lost. At the end of the film, Marty—against the negativism of his buddies and his mother—decides to pursue his relationship with the teacher, and we're confident they'll find the happiness that eluded them both for so long. This film is one of many that illustrate the importance of self-esteem in interpersonal communication and relationships, one of the topics of this unit. In addition, we consider self-concept, self-awareness, and self-disclosure.

THINKING AHEAD ▸▸

If someone were to ask you who you are, what would you say? Perhaps equally important, where did you get this self-image?

SELF-CONCEPT

You no doubt have an image of who you are; this is your **self-concept.** It consists of your feelings and thoughts about your strengths and weaknesses, your abilities and limitations. Your self-concept develops from at least four sources: (1) the image of you that others have and that they reveal to you, (2) the comparisons you make between yourself and others, (3) the teachings of your culture, and (4) the way you interpret and evaluate your own thoughts and behaviors (Figure 4.1).

Others' Images of You

If you wished to see the way your hair looked, you would likely look in a mirror. But what would you do if you wanted to see how friendly or how assertive you are? According to Charles Horton Cooley's (1922) concept of the *looking-glass self,* you would look at the image of yourself that others reveal to you through the way they treat you and react to you (Hensley 1996).

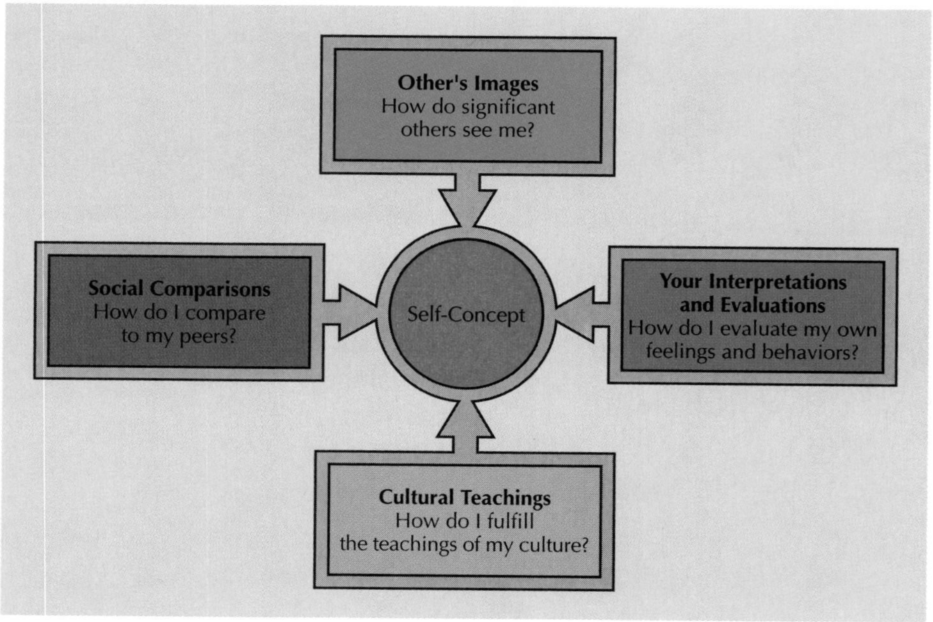

Figure 4.1 The Sources of Self-Concept
This diagram depicts the four sources of self-concept, the four contributors to how you see yourself: other's images of you, social comparisons, cultural teachings, and your own observations, interpretations, and evaluations. As you read about self-concept, consider the influence of each factor throughout your life. Which factor influenced you most as a pre-teen? Which influences you the most now? Which will influence you the most 25 or 30 years from now?

You would look especially to those who are most significant in your life—to your *significant others*. As a child, you would look to your parents and then to your teachers. As an adult, you might look to your friends, romantic partners, and colleagues at work. If these significant others think highly of you, you will see this positive image of yourself reflected in their behaviors; if they think little of you, you will see a more negative image. These reflections that you see in others help you define your self-concept.

Social Comparisons

Another way you develop your self-concept is by comparing yourself with others. When you want to gain insight into who you are and how effective or competent you are, you probably look to your peers. For example, after an examination you probably want to know how you performed relative to the other students in your class. If you play on a baseball team, it's important to know your batting average in comparison with others on the team. You gain an additional perspective when you see your score in comparison with the scores of your peers.

Cultural Teachings

Through your parents, teachers, and the media, your culture instills in you a variety of beliefs, values, and attitudes—about success (how you define it and how you should achieve it); about your religion, race, or nationality; about the ethical principles you should follow in business and in your personal life. These teachings provide benchmarks against which you can measure yourself. Your success in, for example, achieving what your culture defines as success will contribute to a positive self-concept. Your failure to achieve what your culture teaches (for example, not being married by the time you're 30) will contribute to a negative self-concept.

When you demonstrate the qualities that your culture (or your organization) teaches, you'll see yourself as a cultural success and will be rewarded by other members of the culture (or organization). Seeing yourself as culturally successful and getting rewarded by others will contribute positively to your self-concept. When you fail to demonstrate such qualities, you're more likely to see yourself as a cultural failure and to be punished by other members of the culture, contributing to a more negative self-concept.

Your Own Interpretations and Evaluations

Much in the way others form images of you based on what you do, you also react to your own behavior; you interpret and evaluate it. These interpretations and evaluations help to form your self-concept. For example, let us say you believe that lying is wrong. If you lie, you will evaluate this behavior in terms of your internalized beliefs about lying. You will thus react negatively to your own behavior. You may, for example, experience guilt if your behavior contradicts your beliefs. In contrast, let's say you pulled someone out of a burning building at great personal risk. You would probably evaluate this behavior positively; you would feel good about this behavior and, as a result, about yourself.

> Can you identify one specific way in which one or more of these sources influenced your self-concept?
>
> ◀◀ THINKING BACK

SELF-AWARENESS

> THINKING AHEAD ▶▶
>
> Compared to your friends' knowledge of themselves, how well do know yourself?

Your **self-awareness** represents the extent to which you know yourself. Understanding how your self-concept develops is one way to increase your self-awareness: the more you understand about why you view yourself as you do, the more you will understand who you are. Additional insight is gained by looking at self-awareness through the Johari model of the self, or your four selves (Luft 1984).

Your Four Selves

Self-awareness is neatly explained by the model of the four selves, the **Johari window**. This model, presented in Figure 4.2, has four basic areas, or quadrants, each of which represents a somewhat different self. The Johari model emphasizes that the several aspects of the self are not separate pieces but are interactive parts of a whole. Each part is dependent on each other part. Like that of interpersonal communication, this model of the self is a transactional one.

The Open Self The *open self* represents all the information, behaviors, attitudes, feelings, desires, motivations, and ideas that you and others know. The type of information included here might range from your name, skin color, and sex to your age, political and religious affiliations, and financial situation. Your open self will vary in size, depending on the situation you're in and the person with whom you're interacting. Some people, for example, make you feel comfortable and supported; to them, you open yourself wide, but to others you may prefer to leave most of yourself closed.

Communication depends on the degree to which you open yourself to others and to yourself (Luft 1969). If you don't allow other people to know you (thus keeping your open self small), communication between you and others becomes difficult, if not impossible. You can communicate meaningfully only to the extent that you know others and yourself. To improve communication, work first on enlarging the open self.

The Blind Self The *blind self* represents all the things about yourself that others know but of which you're ignorant. These may vary from the relatively insignificant habit of saying "You know," rubbing your nose when you get angry, or having a peculiar body odor, to things as significant as defense mechanisms, fight strategies, or repressed experiences.

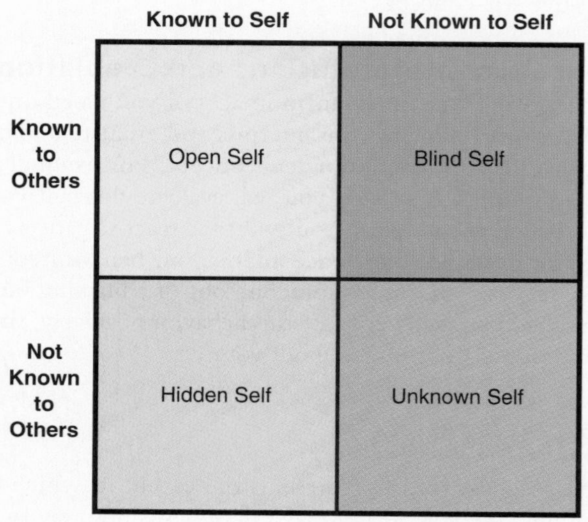

Figure 4.2 The Johari Window
Visualize this model as representing your self. The entire model is of constant size, but each section can vary, from very small to very large. As one section becomes smaller, one or more of the others grow larger. Similarly, as one section grows, one or more of the others must get smaller. For example, if you reveal a secret and thereby enlarge your open self, this shrinks your hidden self. Further, this disclosure may in turn lead to a decrease in the size of your blind self (if your disclosure influences other people to reveal what they know about you but that you have not known). How would you draw your Johari window to show yourself when interacting with your parents? With your friends? With your college instructors? The name Johari, by the way, comes from the first names of the two people who developed the model, Joseph Luft and Harry Ingham.
Source: From Joseph Luft, *Group Processes: An Introduction to Group Dynamics* (Mountain View, CA: Mayfield Publishing, 1984), 60. Reprinted by permission.

Some people have a very large blind self; they seem totally oblivious of their faults and sometimes (though not as often) their virtues. Others seem overly eager to have a small blind self. They seek therapy at every turn and join every self-help group. Some believe they know everything there is to know about themselves, that they have reduced the blind self to zero. Most of us lie between these extremes.

Communication and interpersonal relations are generally enhanced as the blind self becomes smaller. But be careful of trying to help someone else "discover" his or her blind self. This could cause serious problems. Such a revelation might trigger a breakdown in defenses; it might force people to admit their own jealousy or prejudice when they're not psychologically ready to deal with such information. Such revelations are best dealt with cautiously or under the guidance of trained professionals.

The Hidden Self The *hidden self* contains all that you know of yourself and of others that you keep secret. In any interaction, this area includes everything you don't want to reveal, whether it's relevant or irrelevant to the conversation. At the extremes, we have the overdisclosers and the underdisclosers. The overdisclosers tell all. They keep nothing hidden about themselves or others. They tell you their marital difficulties, their children's problems, their financial status, and just about everything else. The underdisclosers tell nothing. They talk about you but not about themselves.

The problem with these extremes is that individuals don't distinguish between those who should and those who shouldn't be privy to such information. They also don't distinguish among the types of information they should or should not disclose. The vast majority of people, however, keep certain things hidden and disclose others; they make disclosures to some people and not to others. They're *selective* disclosers.

The Unknown Self The *unknown self* represents truths about yourself that neither you nor others know. The existence of this self is inferred from a number of sources. Sometimes it's revealed through temporary changes brought about by drugs or through special experimental conditions, such as hypnosis or sensory deprivation. Sometimes this area is revealed by certain projective tests or dreams. Mostly, however, it's revealed by the fact that you're constantly learning things about yourself that you didn't know before (things that were previously in the unknown self)—for example, that you become defensive when someone asks you a question or voices disagreement, or that you compliment others in the hope of being complimented back.

Although you cannot easily manipulate this area, recognize that it does exist and that there are things about yourself and about others that you don't know and may never know.

Increasing Self-Awareness

You can increase your self-awareness in a number of ways: ask yourself about yourself, listen to others, actively seek information about yourself, see your different selves, and increase your open self.

Ask Yourself About Yourself One way to ask yourself about yourself is to take an informal "Who am I?" test (Bugental and Zelen 1950). Head a piece of paper "Who Am I?" and write 10, 15, or 20 times "I am . . ." Then complete each of the sentences. Try not to give only positive or socially acceptable responses; just respond with what comes to mind first. Take another piece of paper and divide it into two columns. Head one column "Strengths" and the other column "Weaknesses." Fill in each column as quickly as possible. Using these first two tests as a base, take a third piece of paper, head it "Self-Improvement Goals," and complete the statement "I want to improve my . . ." as many times as you can in five minutes. Since you're constantly changing, these self-perceptions and goals also change and so must be updated frequently.

Your cultural background will significantly influence your responses to this simple "Who Am I?" test. In one study, for example, participants from Malaysia (a collectivist culture) and from Australia and Great Britain (individualist cultures) completed this test. Malaysians produced significantly more group self-descriptions and fewer idiocentric self-descriptions than did the Australian or British members (Bochner 1994; also see Radford, Mann, Ohta, and Nakane 1993). If you completed the "Who Am I?" test, can you identify responses that were influenced by your individualist or collectivist orientation? Did other cultural factors influence your statements?

Listen to Others You can learn a lot about yourself by seeing yourself as others do. Conveniently, others are constantly giving you the very feedback you need to increase self-awareness. In every interpersonal interaction, people comment on you in some way—on what you do, what you say, how you look. Sometimes these comments are explicit; most often they're discoverable in the way in which others look at you, in what they talk about, in their interest in what you say. Pay close attention to this kind of information (verbal and nonverbal) and use it to increase your own self-awareness.

WEB EXPLORATION
To learn more about actively seeking information about yourself, go to www.awl.com/devito.

Actively Seek Information About Yourself Actively seek out information to reduce your blind self. You need not be so obvious as to say, "Tell me about myself" or "What do you think of me?" But you can use everyday situations to gain self-information: "Do you think I was assertive enough when asking for the raise?" Or "Would I be thought too forward if I invited myself for dinner?" Do not, of course, seek this information constantly; your friends would quickly find others with whom to interact. But you can make use of some situations—perhaps those in which you're particularly unsure of what to do or how you appear—to reduce your blind self and increase self-awareness.

See Your Different Selves Each of your friends and relatives views you differently; to each you're a somewhat different person. Yet you are really all of these selves. Practice seeing yourself as do the people with whom you interact. For starters, visualize how you're seen by your mother, your father, your teachers, your best friend, the stranger you sat next to on the bus, your employer, your neighbor's child. Because you're a composite of all these views, it's important that you periodically see yourself through the eyes of others. The experience will give you new and valuable perspectives on yourself.

Increase Your Open Self When you increase your open self and reveal yourself to others, you also reveal yourself to yourself. At the very least, you bring into clearer focus what you may have buried within. As you discuss yourself, you may see connections that you had previously missed, and with the aid of feedback from others you may gain still more insight. Also, by increasing the open self you increase the likelihood that a meaningful and intimate dialogue will develop; through such interactions you best get to know yourself. Do, however, consider the risks involved in such self-disclosures.

How might you go about increasing your self-awareness?

◀◀ THINKING BACK

SELF-ESTEEM

THINKING AHEAD ▸▸
Generally, would you describe yourself in positive or in negative terms?

How much do you like yourself? How valuable a person do you think you are? How competent do you think you are? The answers to these questions reflect your **self-esteem,** the value you place on yourself. People who have high self-esteem, for example, are going to communicate this throughout their verbal and nonverbal messages. The ways they phrase their ideas and questions or the way they hold their head and maintain eye contact are likely to differ greatly from the way the person with low self-esteem would communicate. Similarly, people with different views of themselves will develop and maintain relationships with friends, lovers, and family differently. As you read this unit, think about your own relationships and how the way you see yourself influences them.

Self-esteem is very important because success breeds success. When you feel good about yourself—about who you are and what you're capable of doing—you will perform better. When you think like a success, you're more likely to act like a success. When you think you're a failure, you're more likely to act like a failure. Increasing self-esteem will, therefore, help you to function more effectively in school, in interpersonal relationships, and in careers. Here are a few suggestions for increasing self-esteem.

Attack Your Self-Destructive Beliefs

Self-destructive beliefs are those that damage your self-esteem and prevent you from building meaningful and productive relationships. They may be about yourself ("I'm not creative"; "I'm boring"), your world ("The world is an unhappy place"; "People are out to get me"), and your relationships ("All the good people are already in relationships"; "If I ever fall in love, I know I'll be hurt"). Identifying these beliefs will help you to examine them critically and to see that they're illogical and self-defeating.

Recognizing that you may have internalized self-destructive beliefs is a first step toward eliminating them. A second step involves recognizing that these beliefs are unrealistic and self-defeating. Psychotherapist Albert Ellis (1988, Ellis and Harper 1975) and other cognitive therapists (for example, Beck 1988) would argue that you can accomplish this by understanding why these beliefs are unrealistic and substituting more realistic ones. For example, following Ellis, you might try replacing an unrealistic desire to please everyone in everything you do with a more realistic belief that it would be nice if others were pleased with you but it certainly is not essential. A third step is giving yourself permission to fail, to be less than perfect, to be normal.

Do recognize that it's the unrealistic nature of these "drivers" that creates problems. Drivers are unrealistic beliefs that may motivate you to act in ways that are self-defeating (Butler 1981). Certainly, trying hard and being strong are not unhealthy when they're realistic. It's only when they become absolute—when you try to be everything to everyone—that they become impossible to achieve and create problems.

Engage in Self-Affirmation

Remind yourself of your successes (Aronson, Cohen, and Nail 1998, Aronson, Wilson, and Akert 1999). There are enough people around who will remind you of your failures. Focus, too, on your good acts, your good deeds. Focus on your positive qualities, your strengths, your virtues. Focus on the good relationships you have with friends and relatives.

The way you talk to yourself about yourself influences what you think of yourself. If you talk positively about yourself, you will come to feel more positive about

Another way of looking at self-destructive beliefs is to identify what Pamela Butler (1981) calls "drivers"—unrealistic beliefs that may motivate you to act in ways that are self-defeating. For example, the drive to be perfect impels you to try to perform at unrealistically high levels in just about everything you do. Whether it's directed toward work, school, athletics, or appearance, this drive tells you that anything short of perfection is unacceptable. The drive to be strong tells you that weakness and any of the more vulnerable emotions, such as sadness, compassion, or loneliness, are wrong. Instead of helping you become successful, these drivers almost ensure your failure. Are you motivated by these unrealistic drivers or, for example, by the drive to hurry up, or to please others, or to try hard?

yourself. If you tell yourself that you're a success, that others like you, that you will succeed on the next test, and that you will be welcomed when asking for a date, you will soon come to feel positive about yourself. Table 4.1 presents a useful list of self-affirming phrases. Reading over the list is sure to stimulate your own self-affirmations.

Seek Out Nourishing People

Psychologist Carl Rogers (1961) drew a distinction between *noxious* and *nourishing* people. Noxious people criticize and find fault with just about everything. Not surprisingly, these people are difficult to be around. More important, however, is that with time you may come to believe that their criticism and fault-finding are justified. When that happens, your self-esteem is likely to diminish.

Nourishing people, on the other hand, are positive. They're optimists. They reward you, they stroke you, they make you feel good about yourself. Here too, with time, you'll come to believe these compliments and positive statements and as a result are likely to raise your self-esteem.

Work on Projects That Will Result in Success

Some people want to fail, or so it seems. Often, they select projects that will result in failure. Perhaps the projects are too large or too difficult. In any event, they're impossible. Instead, select projects that will result in success. Each success helps build self-esteem. Each success makes the next success a little easier.

When a project does fail, recognize that this doesn't mean that you're a failure. Everyone fails somewhere along the line. Failure is something that happens; it's not something inside you. Further, your failing once does not mean that you will fail the next time. So put failure in perspective. Don't make it an excuse for not trying again.

What can you do to increase your self-esteem? What can you do to increase the self-esteem of your best friend, romantic partner, or family member?

◂◂ THINKING BACK

THINKING AHEAD ▸▸

What are some of the advantages of revealing your hidden self to another person? Do you see any disadvantages?

SELF-DISCLOSURE

One of the most important forms of interpersonal communication that you could engage in is talking about yourself, or **self-disclosure.** Self-disclosure refers to your communicating information about yourself to another person. It may involve information about (1) your values, beliefs, and desires ("I believe in reincarnation"), (2) your behavior ("I committed grand larceny but was never caught"), or (3) your self-qualities or characteristics ("I'm dyslexic"). Overt and carefully planned statements about yourself as well as slips of the tongue would be classified as self-disclosing communications. Similarly, you could self-disclose nonverbally by, for example, wearing gang colors, a wedding ring, or a shirt with slogans that reveal your political or social

TABLE 4.1 Self-Affirming Phrases

You may wish to make these general phrases more specific so that they apply more directly to you. What other affirmations would you add? These affirmations are reprinted from *Gathering Power Through Insight and Love* by Ken Keyes Jr. and Penny Keyes. Copyright © 1987 by Living Love Publications.

I am a lovable and worthy person.
I appreciate and love myself!
The love I give to others I also can offer to myself.
I can live a nurturing, exciting, and creative life.
I am creating the experience of love in my life.
My love comes from me.
I can forgive myself.
I am capable and willing to handle my fears as they come up one at a time.
I can accept imperfection.
I can accept the past and welcome the future.
I deserve to feel good.
I am a worthwhile person and there is a place for me.
I am lovable because I'm here.
I am creative, loving, and nurturing.
I can feel good doing the things I'm skilled at.
I can learn to accept and love everyone unconditionally—including myself.
I am learning to support myself with love.
I release the past and now choose a life of love and fulfillment.
I can ask for what I want with love in my heart.
I am the source of my security and self-esteem.
I don't have to be sick to get nurtured.
I am worthy of a loving relationship.
My world is safe and friendly.
I can be gentle with myself.
I can feel supported even when I don't meet my models of perfection.
There is nothing I have to do to feel loved.
My guilt doesn't help anyone.
I am open to new forms of being acknowledged.
I deserve to be healthy.
I can accept praise and attention at any time.

concerns. Self-disclosure may also involve your reactions to the feelings of others: for example, when you tell your friend that you're sorry she was fired.

Self-disclosure occurs in all forms of communication, not just interpersonal. It frequently occurs in small group settings, in public speeches, and the increasingly common television talk show. As these examples make clear, self-disclosure can occur in face-to-face settings as well as through television and the Internet. In chat groups, for example, a great deal of self-disclosure goes on, as it does when people reveal themselves in personal e-mail and in newsgroup and listserv submissions.

You probably self-disclose for a variety of reasons. Perhaps you feel the need for catharsis, to get rid of guilt feelings, or to confess some wrongdoing. Or you might wish to make yourself look good, so you might self-disclose your good qualities by giving examples of your bravery or compassion or determination. You might also disclose to help the listener, to show the listener, for example, how you dealt with an addiction or succeeded in getting a promotion. Of course, you may self-disclose to encourage relationship growth, or to maintain or repair a relationship, or even as a strategy for ending a relationship.

Although self-disclosure may occur as a single message—for example, you tell a stranger on a train that you're thinking about getting a divorce—it's best viewed as a *developing* process in which information is exchanged between people in a relationship over the period of their relationship (Spencer 1993, 1994). If we view it as a developing process, we can then appreciate how self-disclosure changes as the relationship changes, for example, from initial contact through involvement to intimacy and then perhaps to deterioration or dissolution. We can also appreciate how self-disclosure will differ depending on the type of relationship you have with another person, for example, whether the other person is your friend, parent, child, or counselor.

Self-disclosure may involve information that you communicate to others freely or that you normally keep hidden. It may supply information ("I earn $45,000") or reveal feelings ("I'm feeling very depressed").

Self-disclosure involves at least one other individual; it cannot be an *intra*personal communication act. To qualify as self-disclosure, the information must be received and understood by another individual. As you can appreciate, self-disclosure can vary from the relatively insignificant ("I'm a Sagittarius") to the highly revealing and deeply personal ("I'm currently in an abusive relationship" or "I'm almost always depressed"). The remaining discussion of this important concept will be more meaningful if you first take the accompanying self-disclosure test.

TEST YOURSELF *How Willing to Self-Disclose Are You?*

Respond to each of the following questions by indicating the likelihood that you would answer them (and thus disclose such items of information) to, say, other members of this class. Use the following scale: 1 = would definitely self-disclose, 2 = would probably self-disclose, 3 = don't know, 4 = would probably not self-disclose, and 5 = would definitely not self-disclose.

______ 1. What are your hobbies?
______ 2. What are your favorite foods?
______ 3. What is your educational background and how do you feel about it?
______ 4. What are some of your personal characteristics that you are proud of and that give satisfaction?
______ 5. What was the happiest moment of your life?
______ 6. What did your parents do in raising you that you would consider mistakes?
______ 7. Why do some people dislike you?
______ 8. What aspects of your personality do you dislike?
______ 9. With whom have you been sexually intimate?
______ 10. With whom would you most like to have a romantic affair?

Obviously there are no right or wrong answers to these statements. The major purpose of this test is to stimulate you to think about what you would and would not disclose. These questions were drawn from Jourard's (1971a) list of self-disclosure topics and, according to Jourard, illustrate three levels of disclosure; questions 1–3 illustrate low levels of intimacy, questions 4–6 illustrate moderate levels, and questions 7–10 illustrate high levels. Does your own willingness to self-disclose depend on the intimacy of the topic? For example, would you be most willing to answer questions 1–3 and least willing to answer questions 7–10? ■

Influences on Self-Disclosure

A number of factors influence whether or not you disclose, what you disclose, and to whom you disclose. Among the most important factors are who you are, your culture, your gender, who your listeners are, and what your topic is.

WEB EXPLORATION
To learn more about influences on self-disclosure, go to www.awl.com/devito.

Who You Are Highly sociable and extroverted people self-disclose more than those who are less sociable and more introverted. People who are apprehensive about talking in general also self-disclose less than do those who are more comfortable in communicating.

Competent people engage in self-disclosure more than less competent people. Perhaps competent people have greater self-confidence and more positive things to reveal. Similarly, their self-confidence may make them more willing to risk possible negative reactions (McCroskey and Wheeless 1976).

Your Culture Different cultures view self-disclosure differently. People in the United States, for example, disclose more than do those in Great Britain, Germany, Japan, or Puerto Rico (Gudykunst 1983). American students also disclose more than do students from nine different Middle East countries (Jourard, 1971a). Similarly, American students self-disclose more on a variety of controversial issues and also self-disclose more to different types of people than do Chinese students (Chen 1992). Chinese students consider more topics to be taboo and inappropriate for self-disclosure than their British colleagues (Goodwin and Lee 1994). Among the Kabre of Togo, secrecy is a major part of their everyday interaction (Piot 1993).

Some cultures (especially those high in masculinity) view the disclosing of one's inner feelings as a weakness. Among some groups, for example, it would be considered out of place for a man to cry at a happy occasion like a wedding, but that same display of emotion would go unnoticed in some Latin cultures. Similarly, in Japan it's considered undesirable for colleagues to reveal personal information, whereas in much of the United States it's expected (Barnlund 1989, Hall and Hall 1987).

In some cultures—for example, Mexican—there is a strong emphasis on discussing all matters in a positive mode, and this undoubtedly influences the way Mexicans approach self-disclosure as well. Negative self-disclosures, in contrast, are usually made to close intimates and then only after considerable time has elapsed in a relationship. This pattern is consistent with evidence showing that self-disclosure and trust are positively related (Wheeless and Grotz 1977). Additional research finds that the Hispanic reluctance to disclose negative issues such as one's positive HIV status is creating serious problems in preventing and treating HIV infection (Szapocznik 1995).

These differences aside, there are also important similarities across cultures. For example, people from Great Britain, Germany, the United States, and Puerto Rico are all more apt to disclose personal information—hobbies, interests, attitudes, and opinions on politics and religion—than information on finances, sex, personality, and interpersonal relationships (Jourard 1970). Similarly, one study showed self-disclosure patterns between American males to be virtually identical to those between Korean males (Won-Doornink 1991).

Your Gender The popular stereotype of gender differences in self-disclosure emphasizes the male reluctance to speak about himself. For the most part, research supports this view and shows that women disclose more than men. This is especially true in same-sex dyads; women disclose more intimately (and with more emotion) when talking with other women than with men (Shaffer, Pegalis, and Bazzini 1996). Men and women, however, make negative disclosures about equally (Naifeh and Smith 1984).

More specifically, women disclose more than men about their previous romantic relationships, their feelings about their closest same-sex friends, their greatest fears, and what they don't like about their partners (Sprecher 1987). Women also seem to increase the depth of their self-disclosures as the relationship becomes more intimate, whereas men seem not to change their self-disclosure levels. Men, for example, have more taboo topics that they will not disclose to their friends than do women (Goodwin and Lee 1994). Finally, women even self-disclose more to members of the extended family than do men (Komarovsky 1964, Argyle and Henderson 1985, Moghaddam, Taylor, and Wright 1993). One notable exception occurs in initial encounters. Here men will disclose more intimately than women, perhaps "in order to control the relationship's development" (Derlega, Winstead, Wong, and Hunter 1985).

Men and women give different reasons for avoiding self-disclosure (Rosenfeld 1979), but both genders share this reason: "If I disclose, I might project an image I don't want to project." In a society in which image is so important—in which one's image is often the basis for success or failure—this reason is not surprising. Other reasons for avoiding self-disclosure, however, are unique to men or women. Lawrence Rosenfeld (1979) sums up males' reasons for self-disclosure avoidance: "If I disclose to you, I might project an image I don't want to project, which could make me look bad and cause me to lose control over you. This might go so far as to affect relationships I have with people other than you." Men's principal objective in avoiding self-disclosure is to maintain control. The general reason women avoid self-disclosure, says Rosenfeld, is that "if I disclose to you, I might project an image I don't want to project, such as my being emotionally ill, which you might use against me and which might hurt our relationship." Women's principal objective for avoiding self-disclosure is "to avoid personal hurt and problems with the relationship."

Your Listeners Self-disclosure occurs more readily in small groups than in large groups. Dyads or groups of two people are the most hospitable setting for self-disclosure. With one listener, you can attend to the responses carefully. You can monitor the disclosures, continuing if there is support from your listener and stopping if there isn't. With more than one listener, such monitoring becomes difficult since the listeners' responses are sure to vary.

Sometimes self-disclosure takes place in group and public-speaking situations. In consciousness-raising groups and in meetings like those of Alcoholics Anonymous, members may disclose their most intimate problems to ten or perhaps hundreds of people at one time. In these situations, group members are pledged to be totally supportive. These and similar groups are devoted specifically to encouraging self-disclosure and to giving each other support for the disclosures.

Because you disclose, generally at least, on the basis of support you receive, you probably disclose to people you like (Derlega, Winstead, Wong, and Greenspan 1987, Collins and Miller 1994) and to people you trust (Wheeless and Grotz 1977). You probably also come to like those to whom you disclose (Berg and Archer 1983, Collins and Miller 1994). Not surprisingly, you're more likely to disclose to people who are close to you in age (Parker and Parrott 1995).

At times self-disclosure occurs more in temporary than permanent relationships—for example, between strangers on a train or plane, a kind of "in-flight intimacy"

As might be expected, husbands and wives self-disclose to each other more than they do to any other person or group of persons. Marital status, at least for men, even affects self-disclosure to friends. Married men, for example, disclose significantly less to friends than do unmarried men. The marital status of women, however, does not affect the amount of their disclosure to friends. One explanation of this difference may be that women "place a higher value on personal relationships than men do, with the result that women continue friendships even when basic intimacy needs are being met by a spouse, while married men allow friendships to atrophy" (Tschann 1988). What do you think of this explanation?

(McGill 1985). In this situation, two people set up an intimate self-disclosing relationship during a brief travel period, but they don't pursue it beyond that point. In a similar way, you might set up a relationship with one or several people on the Internet and engage in significant disclosure. Perhaps knowing you'll never see these other people and that they will never know where you live or work or what you look like makes it a bit easier.

You're more likely to disclose when the person you're with discloses. This dyadic effect (what one person does, the other person does likewise) probably leads you to feel more secure and reinforces your own self-disclosing behavior. Disclosures are also more intimate when they're made in response to the disclosures of others (Berg and Archer 1983).

Your Topic You're more likely to disclose about some topics than others. For example, you're probably more likely to self-disclose information about your job or hobbies than about your sex life or financial situation (Jourard 1968, 1971a). You're also more likely to disclose favorable information than unfavorable information. Generally, the more personal and negative the topic, the less likely you would be to self-disclose.

Rewards of Self-Disclosure

Research shows that self-disclosure helps to increase self-knowledge, communication and relationship effectiveness, and physiological well-being.

Self-Knowledge One reward of self-disclosure is that you gain a new perspective on yourself, a deeper understanding of your own behavior. Through self-disclosure you may bring to consciousness a great deal that you might otherwise keep from conscious analysis. For example, as Tony talks about the difficulties he had living with an alcoholic father, he may remember details of his early life or entertain new feelings.

Even self-acceptance is difficult without self-disclosure. You accept yourself largely through the eyes of others. Through self-disclosure and subsequent support, you may be in a better position to see the positive responses to you. Thus, you're more likely to respond by developing a more positive self-concept.

Communication and Relationship Effectiveness You understand the messages of another person largely to the extent that you understand the person. For example, you can tell when a friend is serious and when joking, when someone is being sarcastic out of fear and when out of resentment. Self-disclosure is an essential condition for getting to know one another.

Couples who engaged in significant self-disclosure are found to remain together longer than couples who don't (Sprecher 1987). Self-disclosure helps you achieve a closer relationship with the person to whom you self-disclose and increased relationship satisfaction (Schmidt and Cornelius 1987, Meeks, Hendrick, and Hendrick 1998). Without self-disclosure, meaningful relationships seem impossible to develop.

Interestingly enough, you also come to increase your affection for your partner when you self-disclose. Think about your own self-disclosures. Have you come to increase your liking for someone after you disclosed to this person? Do others seem to like you more after they disclose to you?

Physiological Health People who self-disclose are less vulnerable to illnesses (Pennebacker 1991). For example, bereavement over the death of someone very close is linked to physical illness for those who bear this alone and in silence. But it's unrelated to any physical problems for those who share their grief with others. Similarly, women who suffer sexual trauma normally experience a variety of illnesses (among them, headaches and stomach problems). Women who kept these experiences to themselves, however, suffered these illnesses to a much greater extent than did those who talked with others about these traumas. The physiological effort required to keep your burdens to yourself seems to interact with the effects of the trauma to create a combined stress that can lead to a variety of illnesses.

Dangers of Self-Disclosure: Risks Ahead

As is usually the case, when the potential rewards are great so are the risks. Self-disclosure is no exception; the risks can be personal, relational, and professional and

ETHICS IN INTERPERSONAL COMMUNICATION

Vote online at http://www.awl.com/devito

Outing

An interesting variation on self-disclosure occurs when someone else takes information from your hidden self and makes it public. Although this third-party disclosure can concern any aspect of a person's hidden self—for example, an athlete's prison record or drug habit, a movie star's ill-health or alcoholism, or a politician's friends or financial dealings—the media have made a special case out of revealing a person's affectional orientation; the process is called **"outing"** (Gross 1991, Signorile 1993, Johansson and Percy 1994).

Those against outing argue that people have a right to privacy and no one else should take that right from them. Because outing can lead to severe consequences—for example, loss of job, expulsion from the military, or social and physical harassment—no one but the individual himself or herself has the right to reveal such information. Those in favor of outing argue that it's an expedient political and social weapon to silence gay men and lesbians who support homophobic policies.

What would you do? *An excellent staff reporter and regular contributor to the college newspaper brings the editor a story revealing that a particular professor is a lesbian. This professor has repeatedly voted against adding any gay or lesbian courses to the curriculum. She is also an advisor to an exclusive sorority that has repeatedly refused admission to lesbian students. What would be the ethically responsible thing for this editor to do? What would you do in this situation if you were the editor and final judge as to whether this article is published?*

can be considerable. Weigh these potential risks carefully before engaging in significant self-disclosure.

Personal Risks If you self-disclose aspects of your life that are greatly at variance with the values of those to whom you disclose, you may be met by rejection from even the closest friends and family members. Men and women who disclose that they have AIDS, for example, may find their friends and family no longer wanting to be quite as close as before.

Relational Risks Even in close and long-lasting relationships, self-disclosure can cause problems. "Uncensored candor," notes interpersonal researcher Arthur Bochner (1984), "is a bad idea." Total self-disclosure may prove threatening to a relationship by causing a decrease in mutual attraction, trust, or any of the bonds holding the individuals together. Self-disclosures concerning infidelity, romantic fantasies, past indiscretions or crimes, lies, or hidden weaknesses and fears could easily have such negative effects.

Professional Risks The extensive media coverage of gays and lesbians in the military who are coming out in protest of the "don't ask, don't tell" policy amply illustrates the professional dangers that self-disclosure may entail. Openly gay and lesbian personnel in the military, as well as in education, fire departments, law enforcement, or health care agencies—to cite just a few examples—may find themselves confined to desk jobs, prevented from further advancement, or even charged with criminal behavior and fired. Similarly, politicians who disclose that they have been seeing a psychiatrist may later face loss of party and voter support. Teachers who disclose former or current drug use or cohabitation with students may find themselves denied tenure, teaching at undesirable hours, and eventually falling victim to "budget cuts." Further, teachers or students who, in the supportive atmosphere of their interpersonal communication course, disclose details about their sex life or financial condition or reveal self-doubts, anxieties, and fantasies may find some less-than-sympathetic listeners later using that information against them.

In making your choice between disclosing and not disclosing, keep in mind—in addition to the advantages and dangers already noted—the irreversible nature of communication (discussed in Unit 2). Regardless of how many times you may try to qualify something or take it back, once you have said something you cannot withdraw it. You cannot erase the conclusions and inferences listeners have made on the basis of your disclosures. This is not to suggest that you therefore refrain from self-disclosing, but only that it's important to remember that communication is irreversible.

Guidelines for Self-Disclosure

Because self-disclosure is so important and so delicate a matter, guidelines are offered here for (1) deciding whether and how to self-disclose and (2) responding to the disclosures of others.

Guidelines for Making Self-Disclosures In addition to weighing the potential rewards and dangers of self-disclosure already discussed, consider the following guidelines; they will help raise the right questions before you make what must be *your* decision.

Consider the Motivation for the Self-Disclosure Self-disclosure should be motivated by a concern for the relationship, for the others involved, and for oneself. Some people self-disclose out of a desire to hurt the listener. Persons who tell their parents that

ASK THE RESEARCHER

Retaining Privacy

My relational partner and I have just had an argument. I think that she should disclose about her past relationships and she refuses to say a word. I think she is trying to deceive me. What should I do?

She may not be trying to deceive you. Partners often think that certain information, like past histories, belongs to both parties. However, if you consider that your partner may see her relational past as private information she owns alone, it is her right to keep it from you. When we are in a relationship, we like to disclose things about ourselves. It helps to build the relationship. But to keep some autonomy, we don't want to tell absolutely everything. You may define her not telling as deceit, yet she is most likely feeling that the information is hers to control, not yours to know. Respect her privacy and she may reward you with the information you want.

For further information see Sandra Petronio, "Communication Boundary Perspective: A Model of Managing the Disclosure of Private Information Between Marital Couples," *Communication Theory* 4 (1991), 331–332, and Sandra Petronio, "The Boundaries of Privacy: Praxis of Everyday Life," in *Balancing the Secrets of Private Disclosures,* ed. S. Petronio (Mahwah, NJ: LEA Publishers, 2000).

—Sandra Petronio (Ph.D., University of Michigan) is a professor of communication at Arizona State University and teaches classes in interpersonal and family communication. She conducts research in privacy, disclosure, embarrassment, and divorce adjustment.

they never loved them or that the parents hindered rather than helped their emotional development may be disclosing out of a desire to hurt and perhaps punish rather than to improve the relationship. Neither should self-disclosure be used to punish oneself, perhaps because of some guilt feeling or unresolved conflict. Self-disclosure should serve a useful and productive function for all persons involved.

Consider the Appropriateness of the Self-Disclosure Self-disclosure should be appropriate to the context and to the relationship between you and your listener. Before making any significant self-disclosure, ask whether this is the right time and place. Could a better time and place be arranged? Ask, too, whether this self-disclosure is appropriate to the relationship. Generally, the more intimate the disclosures, the closer the relationship should be. It's probably best to resist intimate disclosures (especially negative ones) with nonintimates or casual acquaintances, or in the early stages of a relationship.

Consider the Disclosures of the Other Person During your disclosures, give the other person a chance to reciprocate with his or her own disclosures. If reciprocal disclosures are not made, reassess your own self-disclosures. It may be a signal that for this person at this time and in this context, your disclosures are not welcome or appropriate. It's generally best to disclose gradually and in small increments. When you disclose too rapidly and all at once, you can't monitor your listener's responses and retreat if they're not positive enough. Further, you prevent the listener from responding with his or her own disclosures and thereby upset the natural balance that is so helpful in this kind of communication exchange.

Consider the Possible Burdens Self-Disclosure Might Entail Carefully weigh the potential problems that you may incur as a result of your disclosure. Can you afford to lose your job if you disclose your prison record? Are you willing to risk relational difficulties if you disclose your infidelities? Also, ask yourself whether you're making unreasonable demands on the listener. For example, consider the person who swears his or her mother-in-law to secrecy and then self-discloses having an affair with a neighbor. This disclosure places an unfair burden on the mother-in-law, who is now torn between breaking her promise of secrecy or allowing her child to believe a lie. Parents often place unreasonable burdens on their children by self-disclosing relationship problems, financial difficulties, or self-doubts without realizing that the children may be too young or too emotionally involved to deal effectively with this information.

Guidelines for Responding to Self-Disclosures When someone discloses to you, it's usually a sign of trust and affection. In serving this most important receiver function, keep the following guidelines in mind. These guidelines will help you facilitate the disclosures of another person.

WEB EXPLORATION
To learn more about responding to self-disclosures, go to www.awl.com/devito.

Practice the Skills of Effective and Active Listening The skills of effective listening (Unit 7) are especially important when listening to self-disclosures: listen actively, listen for different levels of meaning, listen with empathy, and listen with an open mind. Paraphrase the speaker so that you can be sure you understand both the thoughts and the feelings communicated. Express an understanding of the speaker's feelings to allow the speaker the opportunity to see them more objectively and through the eyes of another. Ask questions to ensure your own understanding and to signal your interest and attention.

Support and Reinforce the Disclose Express support for the person during and after the disclosures. Try refraining from evaluation. Concentrate on understanding and empathizing with the discloser. Allow the discloser to choose the pace; don't rush the discloser with the too-frequent "So how did it all end?" response. Make your supportiveness clear to the discloser through your verbal and nonverbal responses: maintain eye contact, lean toward the speaker, ask relevant questions, and echo the speaker's thoughts and feelings.

ASK THE RESEARCHER

Listening to Disclosures

For some reason my friends at school tell me a lot of their problems. Often I just don't know what to say in these situations. Have you any suggestions for responding to news of distressing situations?

Although some people begin by offering advice when a friend reveals a problem, it is important to acknowledge their distress and show your concern ("That's really too bad" or "That's so upsetting"). Some people like to talk through their problems, particularly if the discussion shows that the friend didn't bring the problem on himself/herself, that others involved still feel positively about him/her, or that there are good options for dealing with the problem. It's particularly helpful if you can offer solid reasons to believe that the outcome will be favorable, but don't just say "Everything will work out fine," because that remark will seem glib and uncaring. Do remember that some individuals don't like to discuss their problems in depth with others—they consider problems personal and something to be dealt with by themselves—so try to get a sense of how much discussion your friend will welcome.

For further information see R. A. Clark and J. G. Delia, "Individuals' Preferences for Friends' Approaches to Providing Support in Distressing Situations," *Communication Reports* 10 (1997), 115–121, and R. A. Clark, A. J. Pierce, K. Finn, K. Hsu, A. Toosley, and L. Williams, "The Impact of Alternative Approaches to Comforting, Closeness of Relationship, and Gender on Multiple Measures of Effectiveness," *Communication Studies* 49 (1998), 224–239.

—Ruth Anne Clark (Ph.D., University of Wisconsin) is professor of communication, University of Illinois, and Jesse G. Delia (Ph.D., University of Kansas) is dean of liberal arts and sciences, University of Illinois.

Keep the Disclosures Confidential When a person discloses to you, it's because she or he wants you to know the feelings and thoughts that are communicated. If you reveal these disclosures to others, negative effects are inevitable. Revealing what was said will probably inhibit future disclosures by this individual in general and to you in particular, and it's likely that your relationship will suffer considerably. But most important, betraying a confidence is unfair; it debases what could be and should be a meaningful interpersonal experience.

It's interesting to note that one of the netiquette rules of e-mail is that you shouldn't forward mail to third parties without the writer's permission. This rule is a useful one for self-disclosure generally: Maintain confidentiality; don't pass on disclosures made to you to others without the person's permission.

What guidelines would you offer a new employee concerning self-disclosing to workplace associates?

◀◀ THINKING BACK

Don't Use the Disclosures Against the Person Many self-disclosures expose some kind of vulnerability or weakness. If you later turn around and use disclosures against the person, you betray the confidence and trust invested in you. Regardless of how angry you might get, resist the temptation to use the disclosures of others as weapons—the relationship is sure to suffer and may never fully recover.

REVIEWING KEY TERMS AND CONCEPTS OF THE SELF IN INTERPERSONAL COMMUNICATION

This unit looked at the self in interpersonal communication and focused on four basic topics: self-concept, self-awareness, self-esteem, and self-disclosure.

Self-Concept

What is self-concept and how does it develop?

- **Self-concept** is the image you have of who you are.
- Sources of self-concept include: others' images of you, social comparisons, cultural teachings, and your own interpretations and evaluations.

Self-Awareness

What is self-awareness and how might it be increased?

- **Self-awareness** is your knowledge of yourself; the extent to which you know who you are.
- A useful way of looking at self-awareness is with the Johari window which consists of four parts. The *open self:* information known to self and others; the *blind self:* information known only to others; the *hidden self:* information known only to self; and the *unknown self:* information known to neither self nor others.
- To increase self-awareness, ask yourself about yourself, listen to others, actively seek information about yourself, see your different selves, and increase your open self.

Self-Esteem

What is self-esteem and how might it be increased?

- **Self-esteem** is the value you place on yourself; your perceived self-worth.
- To increase self-esteem, try attacking your self-destructive beliefs, engaging in self-affirmation, seeking out nourishing people, and working on projects that will result in success.

Self-Disclosure

What is self-disclosure? What influences self-disclosure? What are its potential rewards and dangers? What guidelines are useful in making decisions to self-disclose and in listening to the disclosures of others?

- **Self-disclosure** is revealing information about yourself to others, usually information normally hidden.
- Self-disclosure is influenced by a variety of factors: who you are, your culture, your gender, your listeners, and your topic.
- Among the rewards of self-disclosure are self-knowledge, ability to cope, communication effectiveness, meaningfulness of relationships, physiological health. Among the dangers are personal risks, relational risks, professional risks, and the fact that communication is irreversible; once something is said, you can't take it back.
- In self-disclosing consider your motivation, the appropriateness of the disclosure to the person and context, the disclosures of others (the dyadic effect), and the possible burdens that the self-disclosure might impose on others and on yourself.
- In responding to the disclosures of others, listen effectively, support and reinforce the discloser, keep disclosures confidential, and don't use disclosures as weapons

APPLYING KEY TERMS AND CONCEPTS OF THE SELF IN INTERPERSONAL COMMUNICATION

1. How satisfied are you with your self-concept? How satisfied are you with your current level of self-esteem? If you're unsatisfied, what are you going to do about it?
2. Do you engage in downward social comparison (comparing yourself to those you know are worse than you are on a particular quality) or upward social comparison (comparing yourself to those who are better than you on a particular quality) (Aspinwall and Taylor 1993)? What purposes do these comparisons serve?
3. Research finds that members of middle-class, two-parent families are reluctant to share financial problems with their children, preferring to shelter them from some of life's harsher realities (McLoyd and Wilson 1992). Low-income, single mothers, however, believe that sharing this with their children will protect them because they will know how difficult life is and what they're up against. (The researchers argue that disclosing such problems actually creates problems for the child such as aggressiveness, difficulties in concentrating, and anxiety disorders.) What would your general advice be to parents about disclosing such matters?
4. Would you consider self-disclosing publicly on a television talk show? What topics would you be willing to discuss? What topics would you be unwilling to discuss in such a public forum?
5. Joseph Luft (1969), one of the developers of the Johari window, argued that "the smaller the first quadrant [the open self], the poorer the communication." Do you agree with this? Can you provide a personal example that supports or contradicts Luft's observation?
6. One research study suggests that gender differences in self-disclosure may be changing. In a study of men and women discussing how their family relationships had changed since they entered college, for example, men disclosed more than women (Leaper, Caron, Baker, Holliday, et al. 1995). What changes in gender differences in self-disclosure do you observe?
7. Focus on one specific thing about yourself that you have not self-disclosed. Why haven't you? What benefits might you derive from self-disclosing? What punishments might you be in line for you if you did disclose?
8. One response that is seldom mentioned in discussions of disclosure is to say that you simply don't want to hear the disclosure. How might you communicate this refusal to listen? Under what conditions would such refusals be appropriate?
9. Access the *New York Times,* the *Washington Post,* the *Wall Street Journal,* or any online newspaper for an article on the self (self-concept, self-awareness, self-esteem, or self-disclosure) that discusses recent research. On the basis of this article, what can you add to this unit?
10. How would you go about seeking answers to the following questions?
    - Do men and women differ in self-awareness? In self-esteem?
    - Do men and women differ in the topics on which they self-disclose to their best friends? Do they differ in disclosures to romantic partners?
    - Can the repetition of self-affirming phrases raise your self-esteem?
    - Are more intelligent people more self-aware than less intelligent people? Does one group have higher self-esteem?
    - Does the physical context influence the amount and type of self-disclosure that takes place between two strangers meeting for the first time?

EXPERIENCING KEY TERMS AND CONCEPTS OF THE SELF IN INTERPERSONAL COMMUNICATION

Go to www.awl.com/devito

Exercise No. 3, "I'd Prefer to Be," offers a means for exploring your self-concept, self-awareness, and self-esteem and also provides the opportunity for self-disclosure. Exercises No. 4, "Disclosing the Hidden Self," and No. 5, "Weighing the Rewards and Costs of Self-Disclosure," allow for the further exploration of the self-disclosure experience and the analysis of the advantages and disadvantages of making specific disclosures. Exercise No. 7, "Perceiving My Selves," stimulates discussion of self concept, self-awareness, and self-esteem.

UNIT 5
APPREHENSION AND ASSERTIVENESS

48 Hours (1982)

THEY CAN CONQUER WHO BELIEVE
THEY CAN.

--VIRGIL

IN 48 HOURS NICK NOLTE teams up with Eddie Murphy, in his screen debut. The character played by Murphy is out of jail for two days to help capture his escaped partner. One of the best scenes occurs when Murphy enters a bar and demands information from its redneck patrons, who are uniformly shocked that an African American would even enter the bar let alone display such assertiveness. As shown in this film, assertiveness can help you achieve your goals, but it can also get you into trouble. In this unit we look at apprehension and assertiveness and the ways to manage both.

COMMUNICATION APPREHENSION

Communication apprehension is one of the most extensively researched variables in the entire field of interpersonal communication, so we know a great deal about this major problem that many people experience. First, we look at the nature of communication apprehension, define it, and consider the factors that influence our level of apprehension. Second, we look at some of the theories of apprehension and how, on the basis of these theories, we can more effectively manage or control it. These discussions will prove more valuable if you first take the brief self-test titled "How Apprehensive Are You?"

THINKING AHEAD ▸▸

In what types of communication situations are you most fearful? In what ways does this fear influence your interactions?

TEST YOURSELF *How Apprehensive Are You?*

This questionnaire is composed of 6 statements concerning your feelings about communicating in interpersonal conversations. Please indicate in the space provided the degree to which each statement applies to you. Use the following scale: 1 = strongly agree, 2 = agree, 3 = undecided, 4 = disagree, 5 = strongly disagree. There are no right or wrong answers. Many of the statements are similar to other statements; do not be concerned about this. Work quickly; record your first impression.

______ 1. While participating in a conversation with a new acquaintance, I feel very nervous.

______ 2. I have no fear of speaking up in conversations.

______ 3. Ordinarily I am very tense and nervous in conversations.

______ 4. Ordinarily I am very calm and relaxed in conversations.

______ 5. While conversing with a new acquaintance, I feel very relaxed.

______ 6. I'm afraid to speak up in conversations.

To compute your score, merely add or subtract your scores for each item as indicated below. Add 18 (this is simply a base used in the formulas so that all scores come out as positive numbers) to the scores for items 2, 4, and 5. Then, from this total, subtract the scores for items 1, 3, and 6. A score above 18 shows some degree of apprehension. Of course, conversations vary widely in the degree to which they may lead to apprehension. For which types do you experience the greatest fear? The least fear? Do others experience apprehension when talking to you?

Source: James C. McCroskey, *Introduction to Rhetorical Communication,* 7th ed. (Englewood Cliffs, NJ: Prentice-Hall, 1997). ■

The Nature of Communication Apprehension

Now that you have a general idea of your own communication apprehension, it might be of interest to note that "communication apprehension is probably the most common handicap . . . suffered by people in contemporary American society" (McCroskey and Wheeless 1976). According to surveys of college students, between 10 percent and 20 percent suffer "severe, debilitating communication apprehension," while another 20 percent suffer from "communication apprehension to a degree substantial enough to interfere to some extent with their normal functioning."

The term **communication apprehension** (and shyness, unwillingness to communicate, stage fright, reticence) refers to a state of fear or anxiety about communication interaction. People develop negative feelings and predict negative results as a function of engaging in communication interactions. They may fear making mistakes and being humiliated (Bippus and Daly 1999). They feel that whatever gain would accrue from engaging in communication would be outweighed by the fear. To those with high communication apprehension, the communication interaction just isn't worth the fear it engenders.

Trait apprehension refers to fear of communication generally, regardless of the specific situation. It appears in dyadic, small-group, public speaking, and mass communication situations. **State apprehension,** in contrast, is specific to a given communication situation. For example, a speaker may fear public speaking but have no difficulty with dyadic communication, or a speaker may fear job interviews but have no fear of public speaking. State apprehension is extremely common; it's experienced by most people in some situations.

Communication apprehension exists on a continuum. People are not either apprehensive or unapprehensive. We all experience some degree of apprehension. Some people are extremely apprehensive and become incapacitated in a communication situation. They suffer a great deal in a society oriented, as our is, around communication and in which one's success depends on the ability to communicate effectively. Others are so mildly apprehensive that they appear to experience no fear at all when confronted by communication situations; they actively seek out communication experiences and rarely feel any significant apprehension. Most of us fall between these two extremes.

Apprehensive Behaviors Generally, apprehension leads to a decrease in the frequency, strength, and likelihood of engaging in communication transactions. High apprehensives avoid communication situations; when forced to participate, they do so as little as possible. This reluctance to communicate shows itself in a variety of forms. For example, those with high apprehension are found to be less willing to communicate, to volunteer, and to work with the terminally ill than were those who were low in apprehension (Ayres and Hopf 1995). In small-group situations, apprehensives not only talk less but also avoid the seats of influence—for example, those in the group leader's direct line of sight. High apprehensives are less likely to be seen as leaders in small-group situations regardless of their actual behaviors. Even in classrooms, they avoid seats where they can be easily called on, and they maintain little direct eye contact with the instructor, especially when a question is likely to be asked. Related to this is that apprehensives have more negative attitudes toward school, earn poorer grades, and are more likely to drop out of college (McCroskey, Booth-Butterfield, and Payne 1989).

Teachers and students consider apprehensives to be less desirable social choices. Apprehensives disclose little and avoid occupations with heavy communication demands (for example, teaching or public relations). Within their occupation, they're less desirous of advancement, largely because of the associated increase in communication. High apprehensives feel less satisfied with their jobs, probably because they're less successful in advancing and in developing interpersonal relationships. High apprehensives are even less likely to get job interviews. In the United States we value "rugged individualism and the conquering of new environments, whether in outer space or in overseas markets. Personal attributes held high in our social esteem are leadership, assertiveness, dominance, independence, and risk taking. Hence a stigma surrounding shyness" (Carducci and Zimbardo 1995, p. 66).

All this does not mean that apprehensives are ineffective or unhappy people. Most apprehensives have learned or can learn to deal with their communication anxiety.

Influences on Communication Apprehension Research has identified several factors that increase communication apprehension (McCroskey and Daly 1987, Beatty 1988, Richmond and McCroskey 1989). A knowledge of these factors will help you to increase your understanding and control of your own apprehension.

- *Degree of Evaluation.* The more you perceive the situation as one in which you will be evaluated, the greater your apprehension is likely to be. Employment interviews, for example, provoke anxiety largely because they're highly evaluative.
- *Subordinate Status.* When you feel that others are better communicators than you are or that they know more than you do, your apprehension increases. For example, shy students report particular difficulty in speaking with authorities (Zimbardo 1977).
- *Degree of Conspicuousness.* The more conspicuous you are, the more likely you are to feel apprehensive. This is why delivering a speech to a large audience is more

Apprehensives are found to engage in more steady dating than those with little apprehension. Why do you think this is so?

anxiety provoking than speaking in a small group; you're more conspicuous before the large group—you stand out, and all attention is on you.

- *Degree of Unpredictability.* The more unpredictable the situation, the greater your apprehension is likely to be. Ambiguous and new situations are unpredictable; you cannot know beforehand what they will be like, hence you become anxious. A similar condition seems to increase your shyness when interacting with strangers; 70 percent of shy students surveyed said they were especially shy with strangers (Zimbardo 1977).
- *Degree of Dissimilarity.* When you feel you have little in common with your listeners, you're likely to feel anxious.
- *Prior Successes and Failures.* Your experience in similar situations greatly influences the way you respond to new ones. Prior success generally (though not always) reduces apprehension, whereas prior failure generally (though not always) increases apprehension. There is no mystery here: prior success says that you can succeed this time as well; prior failure warns that you may fail again.
- *Lack of Communication Skills and Experience.* If you lack skills in typing, you can hardly expect to type very well. If you have never asked for a raise and have no idea how to go about doing it, for example, it's perfectly reasonable that you will feel apprehension.

Culture and Communication Apprehension Apprehension, shyness, and the willingness to communicate generally vary from one culture to another (Breidenstein-Cutspec and Goering 1989). For example, in one study of shyness, Israelis were found to be the least shy; only 24 percent reported they were currently experiencing shyness, compared to Mexicans (39 percent), Americans (42 percent), Germans (50 percent), Taiwanese (55 percent), and Japanese (60 percent) (Carducci and Zimbardo 1995). In a study of the willingness to communicate, American college students indicated the highest willingness to communicate, whereas students from Micronesia indicated the lowest. Micronesian students also indicated the highest degree of shyness while, in this study, Puerto Ricans reported the lowest (McCroskey and Richmond 1990).

When the interpersonal communication is intercultural communication, additional uncertainty, fear, and anxiety, all of which are intimately related to communication apprehension (Stephan and Stephan 1985), may be experienced. When you're in an intercultural situation—say your coworkers are largely people of cultures very different from your own—you're more uncertain about the situation and about their possible responses and you're more likely to experience heightened communication apprehension. Not surprisingly, most people react negatively to high uncertainty and develop a decreased attraction for these other people (Gudykunst and Nishida 1984; Gudykunst, Yang, and Nishida 1985). When you're sure of the situation and can predict what will happen, you're more likely to feel comfortable and at ease. But when the situation is uncertain and you cannot predict what will happen, you become more apprehensive (Gudykunst and Kim 1992).

Intercultural situations can engender fear. You might, for example, fear saying something that will prove offensive or revealing your own prejudices or ethnocentrism. The fear easily translates into apprehension. Intercultural situations can also create anxiety, a feeling very similar to apprehension. Anxiety may be felt for a number of reasons (Stephan and Stephan 1985). For example, your *prior relationships* with members of a culturally different group will influence your apprehension. If your prior relationships were few or if they were unpleasant, then you're likely to experience greater apprehension when dealing with these members than if these prior experiences were numerous and positive.

Your *thoughts and feelings* about the group will also influence your apprehension. For example, if you have little knowledge of the other culture, hold stereotypes and prejudices, are high in ethnocentrism, or if you feel that you're very different from these others, then you're likely to experience more apprehension than if you saw these people as similar to you.

The *situation* you're in can also exert influence. If, for example, you feel that members of another group are competing with you or evaluating you, then you're likely to experience more apprehension than if the situation were more cooperative and equal. Similarly, unstructured and ambiguous situations create more anxiety because you aren't quite sure what is expected of you. Also, your status relative to the others in the group will influence your anxiety; if you're lower in status, you're likely to experience greater anxiety than if you were higher in status.

Theories of Communication Apprehension and Its Management

What causes communication apprehension? Can it be controlled or managed effectively? Following communication researchers Virginia Richmond and James McCroskey (1996), we can distinguish three theoretical (and eminently practical) approaches to understanding communication apprehension and how it may be managed or controlled: cognitive restructuring, systematic desensitization, and skill acquisition.

Cognitive Restructuring The cognitive restructuring theory holds that your own unrealistic beliefs generate a fear of failure. Because you set yourself unachievable goals ("Everyone must love me, I have to be thoroughly competent, I have to be the best in everything"), you logically fear failure. This fear of failure (and the irrational beliefs behind it) are at the foundation of your apprehension (for example, Markway, Carmin, Pollard, and Flynn 1992). Cognitive restructuring, then, advises you to change your irrational beliefs and substitute more rational ones ("It would be nice if everyone loved me but I don't need that to survive. I can fail. Although it would be nice, I don't have to be the best in everything.") Your last step is to practice your new, more rational beliefs (Ellis and Harper 1975, Ellis 1988).

The process may go something like this: unrealistic beliefs give rise to anxiety because you know you can never achieve these unrealistically high goals and that you'll fail at some point. There's not a speaker in the world who wouldn't fail given these unrealistic beliefs. You then focus on the inevitable failure; you can almost see yourself failing. This image leads to a loss of confidence and further visions of failure.

A special type of cognitive restructuring is *performance visualization,* designed specifically to reduce the outward manifestations of communication apprehension and also to reduce negative thinking (Ayres and Hopf 1993, Ayres, Ayres, Grudzinskas, Hopf, et al. 1995). This technique, not surprisingly, has been shown to be significantly more effective with those who can create vivid mental images (Ayres, Hopf, and Ayres 1994). The first part of performance visualization is to develop a positive attitude and a positive self-perception. This involves visualizing yourself in the role of, say, the effective employment interviewee. Visualize yourself walking into the interview—fully and totally confident. You scan the room and sit down. Throughout the interview you're fully in control of the situation. The interviewer is in rapt attention as you ask and respond to questions and, at the end, begs you to take the job. Throughout this visualization, avoid all negative thoughts. As you visualize yourself interviewing effectively, take special note of how you walk, look at the interviewer, respond to questions, and especially how you feel about the whole experience.

The second part of performance visualization is designed to help you model your performance on that of an especially effective communicator. Here you would view a particularly competent interviewee on video and make a mental movie of it. As you review the actual and the mental movie, you begin to shift yourself into the role of the interviewee. You, in effect, become this effective individual.

Systematic Desensitization Systematic desensitization is a technique for dealing with a variety of fears including communication apprehension (Wolpe 1958) and has even been found to reduce dating anxiety (Allen, Bourhis, Emmers-Sommer, and Sahlstein 1998). The general assumption of systematic desensitization is that apprehension was learned, and because it was learned, it can be unlearned. The procedure involves creating a hierarchy of behaviors leading up to the desired but feared behavior (say, asking for a date). One specific hierarchy might look like this:

- Asking for the date.
- Making small talk.
- Introducing yourself to your prospective date.
- Dialing the phone.

You would begin at the bottom of this hierarchy and rehearse this behavior mentally until you can clearly visualize dialing the phone without any uncomfortable anxiety. Once you can accomplish this, you can move to the second level. Here you would visualize the somewhat more threatening, introducing yourself to your prospective date. Once you can do this, you can move to the third level, and so on until you get to the desired behavior.

Skill Acquisition The third general approach to communication apprehension holds that you develop apprehension largely because you see yourself as having inadequate skills. So you logically fear failing. The strategy for managing apprehension, therefore, is to acquire the specific skills involved in any given behavior. For example, the skills for business communication would involve a number of more specific skills. These more specific skills would be mastered individually and then put together into the process of, say, talking with subordinates and supervisors. For example, some such skills would include presenting a positive self-image, complimenting the work of others, and criticizing tactfully another's performance. Other types of skills might be using deep breathing to relax yourself, creative visualization to help you see yourself as successful, or self-affirmation to help you feel better about yourself.

With mastery, the task—in this case business communication, but it could just as logically be any task—becomes less forbidding and hence less anxiety provoking. With mastery also comes successful experiences. These successes help build your confidence and further lessen anxiety. It's probably impossible to eliminate communication apprehension. However, we can manage apprehension effectively so that it does not debilitate us or prevent us from achieving goals that require us to communicate in a variety of situations. Here are some additional suggestions for building skills:

Prepare and Practice The more preparation and practice you put into something, the more comfortable you feel with it and, consequently, the less apprehension you feel. If you're apprehensive telling jokes, then practice the joke you wish to tell. Rehearse it mentally and perhaps aloud until you're comfortable with it. In this way, you'll acquire the very communication skills and experiences you'll need to help you master the tasks at which you want to be effective.

Focus on Success Think positively. Concentrate your energies on doing the very best job you can in whatever situation you are in. Visualize yourself succeeding, and you stand a good chance of doing just that. Remember that having failed in the past does not mean that you must fail again in the future. You now have new skills and new experiences, and they increase your chances for success. But even if you do have a setback, put the setback and the apprehension in perspective; the world will not cave in if you don't succeed in any communication situation.

Familiarize Yourself With the Situation The more familiar you are with the situation, the better. The reason is simple: when you're familiar with the situation and with what will be expected of you, you're better able to predict what will happen. This will reduce ambiguity and make you feel more comfortable.

Try to Relax Apprehension is reduced when you're physically and mentally relaxed. For example, knowing that you have acquired new communication skills and that you have prepared yourself for the task of asking for a raise should help alleviate your normal anxiety.

Empowering Apprehensives

At the same time that you want to manage and perhaps lessen your own apprehension, consider the values and means of empowering others to manage and better control their apprehension or shyness. Here are some suggestions based largely on the insights of shyness and apprehension researchers (Carducci and Zimbardo 1995, McCroskey 1996).

TRY IT!
To learn more about empowering apprehensives, go to www.awl.com/devito.

Don't overprotect the shy person, especially the shy child. If you constantly rush to the child's aid every time he or she experiences social anxiety, the child will never learn how to cope with it. Instead, be supportive (indirectly). Nudge, instead of push, the child (or the adult) to try out new communication situations. In this way, you can help the shy person to interact in small doses and eventually develop the self-confidence needed for more extended interaction.

Demonstrate your understanding and empathy for the other person's shyness. Don't minimize their fear of communication situations, something those with little apprehension often do. Practice active listening, should you sense they wish to discuss their anxiety and shyness.

Shyness researchers Carducci and Zimbardo (1995, p. 66) have observed: "The people given the most attention in our society are expressive, active, and sociable. We single out as heroes actors, athletes, politicians, television personalities, and rock stars—people expert at calling attention to themselves: Madonna, Rosanne, Howard Stern. People who are most likely to be successful are those who are able to obtain attention and feel comfortable with it." What do you think of this observation?

ASK THE RESEARCHER

Meeting New People

Unlike most people, I have very little fear of public speaking. But I do have a great deal of fear in meeting new people in joining a group when I don't know the people well. Is there anything I can do to reduce this type of interpersonal apprehension? I'm starting a new job in September and I want to make the right impression.

A certain amount of nervousness when meeting new people, going to an interview, or starting a new job is normal and may even be somewhat beneficial for most people. You're not sure what you should do or say, and some nervousness is appropriate. It normally will fade after you have interacted for a while. If it does not, or if you can't go to the interview, meet the new person, or move to the new job, that is another matter. Now your CA [communication apprehension] is interfering with your life. Self-help books and other "quick fixes" will not work. You need to seek professional help from someone who can administer therapy (either systematic desensitization or cognitive restructuring). Even then do not expect miracles. CA has a strong genetic base, so only a limited amount of change usually is possible. With professional help, however, most extreme CA conditions can be reduced to a level where the person can function acceptably in everyday life.

—James C. McCroskey (Ed.D., Pennsylvania State University) is a professor of communication at West Virginia University. His teaching and research concentrations are in interpersonal, organizational, nonverbal, and intercultural communication, communication avoidance, and communibiology.

What are some of the things you can do to reduce your own communication apprehension? What might you do to reduce the apprehension of your friends or family members?

◀◀ THINKING BACK

Avoid making the shy person the center of attention. That is exactly what they don't want. Never make their shyness the topic of a group conversation. Saying, "Oh Jane; she's so bright but she's so shy" only makes it more difficult for Jane to even open her mouth. At the same time, make sure that you give the shy person opportunities to speak and that you don't monopolize the conversation. For example, ask their opinions and, when appropriate, try to steer the conversation in the direction of the shy person's expertise and area of competence.

THINKING AHEAD ▶▶

Would your friends or work colleagues describe you as assertive? Aggressive? Nonassertive? How would you describe your own level of assertiveness?

ASSERTIVENESS

If you disagree with other people in a group, do you speak your mind? Do you allow others to take advantage of you because you're reluctant to say what you want? Do you feel uncomfortable when you have to state your opinion in a group? Questions such as these revolve around your degree of **assertiveness.** Before reading further about this type of communication, take the accompanying self-test, "How Assertive Is Your Communication?"

TEST YOURSELF *How Assertive Is Your Communication?*

Indicate how true each of the following statements is about your own communication. Respond instinctively rather than in the way you feel you should respond. Use the following scale: 5 = always or almost always true, 4 = usually true, 3 = sometimes true, sometimes false, 2 = usually false, 1 = always or almost always false.

______ 1. I would express my opinion in a group even if it contradicts the opinions of others.

______ 2. When asked to do something that I really don't want to do, I can say "No" without feeling guilty.

_______ 3. I can express my opinion to my superiors on the job.

_______ 4. I can start up a conversation with a stranger on a bus or at a business gathering without fear.

_______ 5. I voice objection to people's behavior if I feel it infringes on my rights.

_______ 6. I express my feelings directly, using I-messages ("I need you to be more accurate in recording appointments"), rather than you-messages ("Your work is sloppy and inaccurate") or third-person messages ("Everyone says your work isn't up to par").

_______ 7. I use factual and descriptive terms when stating what I object to ("The last three letters you typed contained too many errors"; "You complained about the service in the last seven restaurants we ate at") rather than allness or extreme terms ("You never do the right thing"; "You always complain").

_______ 8. I try to understand and accept the behaviors of others rather than criticize them and label them with such expressions as "That's silly" or "That's insane."

_______ 9. I believe that in most interactions, both people should gain something—rather than one win and one lose.

_______ 10. I believe that my desires are as important as those of others—not more important, but not less important either.

All ten items in this test identified characteristics of assertive communication. So high scores (40 and above) would indicate a high level of assertiveness. Low scores (20 and below) would indicate a low level of assertiveness. The remaining discussion in this unit clarifies the nature of assertive communication and offers guidelines for increasing your own assertiveness. ■

In addition to identifying some specific assertive behaviors (as in the self-test), the nature of assertive communication can be further explained by distinguishing it from nonassertiveness and aggressiveness (Alberti 1977).

Nonassertiveness, Aggressiveness, and Assertiveness

Nonassertiveness refers to a lack of assertiveness in certain types of or in all communication situations. People who are nonassertive fail to assert their rights. In many instances, these people do what others tell them to do—parents, employers, and the like—without questioning and without concern for what is best for them. They operate with a "You win, I lose" philosophy; they give others what they want without concern for themselves (Lloyd 1995). Nonassertive people often ask permission from others to do what is their perfect right. Social situations create anxiety for these individuals, and their self-esteem is generally low.

WEB EXPLORATION
To learn more about nonassertiveness, aggressiveness, and assertiveness, go to www.awl.com/devito.

Aggressiveness is the other extreme. Aggressive people operate with an "I win, you lose" philosophy; they care little for what the other person wants and focus only on their own needs. Some people communicate aggressively only under certain conditions or in certain situations (for example, after being taken advantage of over a long period of time) while others communicate aggressively in all or at least most situations. Aggressive communicators think little of the opinions, values, or beliefs of others and yet are extremely sensitive to others' criticisms of their own behavior. Consequently, they frequently get into arguments with others.

Assertive behavior—behavior that enables you to act in your own best interests without denying or infringing upon the rights of others—is the generally desired alternative to nonassertiveness or aggressiveness. Assertive communication enables you to act in your own best interests without denying or infringing upon the rights of others. Assertive people operate with an "I win, you win" philosophy; they assume that both people can gain something from an interpersonal interaction, even from a confrontation. Assertive people are willing to assert their own rights. Unlike their aggressive counterparts, however, they don't hurt others in the process. Assertive people speak their minds and welcome others' doing likewise.

People who are assertive in interpersonal communication display four major characteristics (Norton and Warnick 1976). Assertive individuals are:

- *open;* they engage in frank and open expressions of their feelings to people in general as well as to those for whom there may be some romantic interest.
- *not anxious;* they readily volunteer opinions and beliefs, deal directly with interpersonal communication situations that may be stressful, and question others without fear. Their communications are dominant, frequent, and of high intensity. They have a positive view of their own communication performance, and others with whom they communicate share this positive view.
- *contentious;* they stand up and argue for their rights, even if this might entail a certain degree of disagreement or conflict with relatives or close friends.
- *not intimidated and not easily persuaded;* they make up their own minds on the basis of evidence and argument.

Do realize that as with communication apprehension, there will be wide cultural differences when it comes to assertiveness. For example, the values of assertiveness are more likely to be extolled in individualistic cultures rather than in collectivist cultures. Assertiveness will be valued more by those cultures that stress competition, individual success, and independence. It will be valued much less by those cultures that stress cooperation, group success, and interdependence of all members on each other. American students, for example, are found to be significantly more assertive than Japanese or Korean students (Thompson, Klopf, and Ishii 1991, Thompson and Klopf 1991). Thus, for some situations assertiveness may be an effective strategy in one culture, but in another culture may create problems. Assertiveness with an elder in many Asian and Hispanic cultures may be seen as insulting and disrespectful.

Principles for Increasing Assertive Communication

Most people are nonassertive in certain situations. If you're one of these people and if you wish to modify your behavior, there are steps you can take to increase your assertiveness. (If you are always and everywhere nonassertive and are unhappy about this, then you may need training with a therapist to change your behavior.)

Analyze Assertive Communications The first step in increasing your assertiveness skills is to understand the nature of these communications. Observe and analyze the messages of others. Learn to distinguish the differences among assertive, aggressive, and nonassertive messages. Focus on what makes one behavior assertive and another behavior nonassertive or aggressive. Table 5.1 reviews some of the verbal and nonverbal messages that distinguish assertive from nonassertive or aggressive communication.

After you've gained some skills in observing the behaviors of others, turn your analysis to yourself. Analyze situations in which you're normally assertive and situations in which you're more likely to act nonassertively or aggressively. What characterizes these situations? What do the situations in which you're normally assertive have in common? How do you speak? How do you communicate nonverbally?

TABLE 5.1 **Assertive and Aggressive Messages**

As you read this table, consider your customary ways of interacting. How often do you use assertive messages? How often do you use aggressive messages?

Assertive messages	Aggressive messages
I-messages, accept responsibility for your own feelings (I feel angry when you…)	You-messages, attribute your feelings to others (You make me angry)
Descriptive and realistic expressions	Allness and extreme expressions
Equality messages (recognizes the essential equality of oneself and others)	Inequality (overly submissive, polite, subservient or overly aggressive, insulting, condescending)
Relaxed and erect body posture	Tense, overly rigid, overly relaxed
Focused but not threatening eye contact	Intense eye contact or excessive eye contact avoidance
Expressive and genuine facial expressions	Unexpressive or overly expressive (and often insincere) facial expressions
Normal vocal volume and rhythm pattern	Overly soft or overly loud and accusatory

Rehearse Assertive Communications Select a situation in which you're normally nonassertive. Build a hierarchy that begins with a relatively nonthreatening message and ends with the desired communication. For example, let us say that you have difficulty voicing your opinion to your supervisor at work. The desired behavior, then, is to tell your supervisor your opinions. You would construct a hierarchy of situations leading up to this desired behavior. Such a hierarchy might begin with visualizing yourself talking with your boss. Visualize this scenario until you can do it without any anxiety or discomfort. Once you have mastered this visualization, visualize a step closer to your goal, such as walking into your boss's office. Again, do this until your visualization creates no discomfort. Continue with these successive visualizations until you can visualize yourself telling your boss your opinion. As with the other visualizations, do this until you can do it while totally relaxed. This is the mental rehearsal.

You might add a vocal dimension to this by actually acting out (with voice and gesture) your telling your boss your opinion. Again, do this until you experience no difficulty or discomfort. Next, try doing this in front of a trusted and supportive friend or group of friends. Ideally this interaction will provide you with useful feedback. After this rehearsal, you're probably ready for the next step.

Communicate Assertively This step is naturally the most difficult but obviously the most important. Here's a generally effective pattern to follow in communicating assertively:

- Describe the problem; don't evaluate or judge it. *We're all working on this advertising project together. You're missing half our meetings and you still haven't produced your first report.* Be sure to use I-messages and to avoid messages that accuse or blame the other person.
- State how this problem affects you. *My job depends on the success of this project and I don't think it's fair that I have to do extra work to make up for what you're not doing.*
- Propose solutions that are workable and that allow the person to save face. *If you can get your report to the group by Tuesday, we'll still be able to meet our deadline. I could give you a call on Monday to remind you.*

- Confirm understanding. *It's clear that we can't produce this project if you're not going to pull your own weight. Will you have the report to us by Tuesday?*
- Reflect on your own assertiveness. Think about what you did. How did you express yourself verbally and nonverbally? What would you do differently next time?

Keep in mind that assertiveness is not always the most desirable response. Assertive people are assertive when they want to be, but they can be nonassertive if the situation seems to call for it. For example, you might wish to be nonassertive in a situation in which assertiveness might emotionally hurt the other person. Let us say that an older relative wishes you to do something for her or him. You could assert your rights and say no, but in doing so you would probably hurt this person; it might be better simply to do as asked. Of course, there are limits that should be observed. You should be careful, in such a situation, that you're not hurt instead. For example, if your parents want you to continue to live at home until marriage, they may be hurt by your assertive behavior in refusing. Yet the alternative is to hurt yourself by living with your parents when you're ready to be on your own.

After communicating, get feedback from others. Start with people who are generally supportive. They should provide you with the social reinforcement so helpful in learning new behavioral patterns. This feedback is particularly important because your intention and the perception of your behavior by an observer may be totally different. For example, you may behave in certain ways with the intention of communicating confidence, but the observer may perceive arrogance. Thus, another person's perception of your behavior can often help you to see yourself as others do.

In all behaviors, but especially with new behaviors, recognize that you may at first fail. You might, for example, try to answer the teacher's question and find that not only do you have the wrong answer but you also don't even understand the question. You might raise your hand and find yourself at a loss for words when you're recognized. Such incidents should not discourage you; realize that in all attempts to change behaviors, you will experience both failure and success.

A note of caution should be added to this discussion. It's easy to visualize a situation in which, for example, people are talking behind you in a movie, and with your newfound enthusiasm for assertiveness, you tell them to be quiet. It's also easy to see yourself getting smashed in the teeth as a result. In applying the principles of assertive communication, be careful that you don't go beyond what you can handle effectively.

If you wanted to increase your interpersonal assertiveness, what would you do? Can you identify situations in which you would like to become less assertive?

◀◀ THINKING BACK

REVIEWING KEY TERMS AND CONCEPTS IN APPREHENSION AND ASSERTIVENESS

In this unit we focused on apprehension and assertiveness and especially on ways to manage and control apprehension and to increase assertiveness when appropriate.

Communication Apprehension

What is communication apprehension? How can you effectively manage your own apprehension? How can you help empower those who are apprehensive?

- **Communication apprehension** is a state of fear or anxiety about communication situations. **Trait apprehension** is a fear of communication generally. **State apprehension** is a fear of communication that is specific to a situation (for example, an interview or public speaking situation).
- Theories and management of communication apprehension include cognitive restructuring, systematic desensitization, and skill acquisition.
- Cognitive restructuring focuses on unrealistic beliefs and seeks to substitute more realistic ones.
- Systematic desensitization attempts to train you to respond without apprehension to increasingly more anxiety-provoking situations.
- Skill acquisition focuses on training you to master the skills involved in situations that normally provoke apprehension.

To build skills: prepare and practice, focus on success, familiarize yourself with the situation, and try to relax.

- Empowering apprehensives involves not overprotecting the person, demonstrating understanding and empathy, and gently encouraging participation rather than making the person the center of attention.

Assertiveness

What is assertiveness? How can you increase your own communication assertiveness?

- **Assertiveness** is a willingness to stand up for your rights but with respect for the rights of others. *Nonassertiveness* refers to an inability to assert oneself or to stand up to defend one's rights in most or all situations (generalized nonassertiveness) or in certain situations (situational nonassertiveness). *Aggressiveness* refers to behavior that serves self-interests without any consideration for the rights of others.
- Principles for increasing assertiveness include:
  Analyze the assertive communications of others.
  Analyze your own communications.
  Rehearse assertive communications.
  Communicate assertively.

APPLYING KEY TERMS AND CONCEPTS IN APPREHENSION AND ASSERTIVENESS

1. How would you characterize your own communication apprehension? In what communication situations are you most apprehensive? Why do you suppose this is so?
2. Research finds that in the classroom, increased instructor clarity and immediacy (language that creates a connection between sender and receiver) helps to reduce receiver apprehension (the fear people have that they won't be able to understand the message they're listening to). What might health care professionals do to help reduce receiver apprehension among patients (Chesebro and McCroskey 1998)?
3. Are you more likely to become apprehensive in an intercultural situation than in a situation in which everyone is culturally similar to you? Why do you think you experience intercultural apprehension?
4. Try creating a hierarchy (as described in the discussion of systematic desensitization) for a communication behavior for which you have apprehension. What insights does creating this hierarchy give you into the causes of your specific apprehension?
5. What do you think has contributed to your current level of communication apprehension? For example, can you identify early childhood influences? Specific communication experiences?
6. How will apprehension affect your professional life? Your relational life?
7. In what situations are you nonassertive? Aggressive? Assertive? What is it about these situations that leads you to behave differently?
8. As noted in the text, attitudes toward assertiveness are influenced by culture. For example, Caucasian Americans endorsed the legitimacy of assertiveness more strongly than did Japanese Americans (Johnson and Marsella 1978). Do you see cultural differences in attitudes toward assertiveness or in actual assertive behaviors?
9. Can you identify at least ten situations in which assertiveness would probably be the wrong response?
10. How would you go about seeking answers to the following questions?
    - Are shyness and apprehension hereditary?
    - In what situations can shyness be an asset?
    - Do preteen boys and girls experience apprehension similarly?
    - Are there points in a person's life when the level of apprehension significantly changes?
    - Are assertive people happier than nonassertive or aggressive people?

EXPERIENCING KEY TERMS AND CONCEPTS IN APPREHENSION AND ASSERTIVENESS

Go to www.awl.com/devito

Exercise No. 8, "Sequential Communication," can be used to illustrate the experience of both speaker and receiver apprehension. Exercise No. 6, "Analyzing Assertiveness," will prove useful for discussing and for role-playing assertiveness.

UNIT 6

PERCEPTION IN INTERPERSONAL COMMUNICATION

Annie Hall (1977)

WE MUST ALWAYS TELL WHAT WE SEE. ABOVE ALL, AND THIS IS MORE DIFFICULT, WE MUST ALWAYS SEE WHAT WE SEE.

--CHARLES PEGUY

The Stages of Perception
Perceptual Processes
Increasing Accuracy in Interpersonal Perception

WOODY ALLEN'S ANNIE HALL tells the story of a relationship between two New York singles (played by Allen and Diane Keaton) and illustrates the near impossibility of meaningful and lasting relationships. Nowhere is this seen more clearly than in their respective perceptions of their relationship. Although both experience the same things, their perceptions of these events differ drastically. Not surprisingly, perceptual differences are one of the major causes of communication problems. Understanding how perception works, the factors that influence it, and how you can make your own perceptions more accurate will help considerably in ensuring more accurate interpersonal communication.

THE STAGES OF PERCEPTION

Perception is the process by which you become aware of objects, events, and especially people through your senses: sight, smell, taste, touch, and hearing. Perception is an active, not a passive process. Your perceptions result from what exists in the outside world and from your own experiences, desires, needs and wants, loves and hatreds. Among the reasons perception is so important in interpersonal communication is that it influences your communication choices. The messages you send and listen to will depend on how you see the world, on how you size up specific situations, on what you think of the people with whom you interact.

THINKING AHEAD ▸▸

What happens when you meet someone for the first time? How objectively do you see this person and how objectively do you recall this person and your meeting at some later date?

Interpersonal perception is a continuous series of processes that blend into one another. For convenience of discussion we can separate them into five stages: (1) you sense, you pick up some kind of stimulation, (2) you organize the stimuli in some way, (3) you interpret and evaluate what you perceive, (4) you store it in memory, and (5) you retrieve it when needed.

Stage One: Stimulation

At this first stage, your sense organs are stimulated—you hear a new CD, see a friend, smell someone's perfume, taste an orange, feel another's sweaty palm. Naturally, you don't perceive everything; rather, you engage in *selective perception,* a general term that includes selective attention and selective exposure. In selective attention, you attend to those things that you anticipate will fulfill your needs or will prove enjoyable. For example, when daydreaming in class, you don't hear what the instructor is saying until your name is called. Your selective attention mechanism focuses your senses on your name.

Through **selective exposure** you expose yourself to people or messages that will confirm your existing beliefs, that will contribute to your objectives, or that will prove satisfying in some way. For example, after you buy a car, you're more apt to read and listen to advertisements for the car you just bought because these messages tell you that you made the right decision. At the same time, you would avoid advertisements for the cars that you considered but eventually rejected because these messages would tell you that you made the wrong decision.

You're also more likely to perceive stimuli that are greater in intensity than surrounding stimuli and those that have novelty value. For example, television commercials normally play at a greater intensity than regular programming to ensure that you take special notice. You're also more likely to notice the coworker who dresses in a novel way than you are to notice the one who dresses like everyone else. You will quickly perceive someone who shows up in class wearing a tuxedo or at a formal party in shorts.

WEB EXPLORATION
To learn more about stage two: organization, go to www.awl.com/devito.

Stage Two: Organization

At the second stage, you organize the information your senses pick up. Three interesting ways in which people organize their perceptions are by rules, by schemata, and by scripts. Let's look at each briefly.

Organization by Rules One frequently used rule of organization is that of **proximity** or physical closeness: things that are physically close together constitute a unit. Thus, using this rule, you would perceive people who are often together, or messages spoken one immediately after the other, as units, as belonging together. You also assume that the verbal and nonverbal signals sent at about the same time are related and constitute a unified whole; you assume they follow a *temporal* rule which says that things occurring together in time belong together.

Another rule is *similarity*: Things that are physically similar, things that look alike, belong together and form a unit. This principle of similarity would lead you to see people who dress alike as belonging together. Similarly, you might assume that people who work at the same jobs, who are of the same religion, who live in the same building, or who talk with the same accent belong together.

The rule of *contrast* is the opposite of similarity: When items (people or messages, for example) are very different from each other, you conclude that they don't belong together; they're too different from each other to be part of the same unit. If you're the only one who shows up at an informal gathering in a tuxedo, you'd be seen as not belonging to the group because you contrast too much with other members.

Schemata Another way you organize material is by creating **schemata,** mental templates or structures that help you organize the millions of items of information you come into contact with every day as well as those you already have in memory. (*Schemata* is the plural of *schema*.) Schemata may thus be viewed as general ideas about people (for Pat and Chris, for Japanese, for Baptists, for New Yorkers), yourself (your qualities, abilities, and even liabilities), or social roles (police officer, professor, or multibillionaire CEO).

You develop schemata from your own experience—actual as well as from television, reading, and hearsay. You might have a schema for college athletes, for example, and this might include that they're strong, ambitious, academically weak, and egocentric. You've probably developed schemata for different religious, racial, and national groups, for men and women, and for people of different affectional orientations. Each group that you have some familiarity with will be represented in your mind in some kind of schema. Schemata help you organize your perceptions by allowing you to classify millions of people into a manageable number of categories or classes. As we'll see below, however, schemata can also create problems and influence you to see what is not there or to miss seeing what is there.

Scripts A **script** is really a type of schema, but because it's a different type, it's given a different name. Like a schema, a script is an organized body of information about some action, event, or procedure. It's a general idea of how some event should play out or unfold; it's the rules governing events and their sequence. For example, you probably have a script for eating in a restaurant, with the actions organized into a pattern something like this: enter, take a seat, review the menu, order from the menu, eat your food, ask for the bill, leave a tip, pay the bill, exit the restaurant. Similarly, you probably have scripts for how you do laundry, how an interview is to be conducted, the stages you go through in introducing someone to someone else, and the way you ask for a date.

Stage Three: Interpretation-Evaluation

The interpretation-evaluation (hyphenated because the two processes cannot be separated) step is inevitably subjective and is greatly influenced by your experiences, needs, wants, values, beliefs about the way things are or should be, expectations, physical and emotional state, and so on. Your interpretation-evaluation will be influenced by your rules, schemata, and scripts as well as by your gender; for example, women have been found to view others more positively than men (Winquist, Mohr, and Kenny 1998).

For example, upon meeting a new person who is introduced to you as a college football player, you would apply your schema to this person and view him as strong, ambitious, academically weak, and egocentric. You would, in other words, see this person through the filter of your schema and evaluate him according to your schema for college athletes. Similarly, when viewing someone performing some series of actions (say, eating in a restaurant), you apply your script to this event and view the event through the script. You would interpret the actions of the diner as appropriate or inappropriate depending on the script you had for this behavior and the ways in which the diner performed the sequence of actions.

Stage Four: Memory

Your perceptions and their interpretations-evaluations are put into memory; they're stored so that you may ultimately retrieve them at some later time. So, for example, you have in memory your schema for college athletes and that Ben Williams is a football player. Ben Williams is then stored in memory with "cognitive tags" that tell you that he's strong, ambitious, academically weak, and egocentric. Despite the fact that you've not witnessed Ben's strength or ambitions and have no idea of his academic record or his psychological profile, you still may store your memory of Ben along with the qualities that make up your script for "college athletes."

Let's say that at different times you hear that Ben failed Spanish I, normally an A or B course at your school, that Ben got an A in Chemistry (normally a tough course), and that Ben is transferring to Harvard as a theoretical physics major. Schemas act as filters or gatekeepers; they allow certain information to get stored in relatively objective form, much as you heard or read it, and may distort or prevent other information from getting stored. As a result, these three items of information about Ben may get stored very differently in your memory along with your schema for college athletes.

For example, you might readily store the information that Ben failed Spanish because it's consistent with your schema; it fits neatly into the template your have of college athletes. Information that's consistent with your schema—such as in this example—will strengthen your schema and make it more resistant to change (Aronson, Wilson, and Akert 1999). Depending on the strength of your schema, you might also store in memory (even though you didn't hear it) that Ben did poorly in other courses as well. The information that Ben got an A in chemistry, because it contradicts your schema (it just doesn't seem right), might easily be distorted or lost. The information that Ben is transferring to Harvard, however, is a bit different. This information is also inconsistent with your schema, but it is so drastically inconsistent that you begin to look at this mindfully and may even begin to question your schema or perhaps view Ben as an exception to the general rule. In either case, you're going to etch Ben's transferring to Harvard very clearly in your mind.

Stage Five: Recall

At some later date, you may want to recall or access the information you have stored in memory. Let's say you want to retrieve your information about Ben because he's the topic of discussion among you and a few friends. As we'll see in our discussion of listening in the next unit, memory isn't reproductive; you don't simply reproduce what you've heard or seen. Rather, you reconstruct what you've heard or seen into a whole that is meaningful to you—depending in great part on your schemata and scripts—and it's this reconstruction that you store in memory. When you want to retrieve this information from memory, you may recall it with a variety of inaccuracies. You're likely to:

- recall information that is consistent with your schema; in fact, you may not even be recalling the specific information (say, about Ben) but may actually just be recalling your schema (which contains the information about college athletes and, because of this, also about Ben)
- fail to recall information that is inconsistent with your schema; you have no place to put that information, so you easily lose it or forget it
- recall information that drastically contradicts your schema because it forces you to think (and perhaps rethink) about your schema and its accuracy; it may even force you to revise your schema for college athletes in general

Before moving on to the more specific processes involved in interpersonal perception, let's spell out some of the implications of this five-stage model for your own interpersonal perceptions:

1. Everyone relies heavily on shortcuts—rules, schemata, and scripts, for example, are all useful shortcuts to simplify your understanding, remembering, and recalling information about people and events. If you didn't have these shortcuts, then you'd have to treat every person, role, or action differently from each other person, role, or action. This would make every experience a new one, totally unrelated to anything you already know. If you didn't use these shortcuts, you'd be unable to generalize, draw connections, and otherwise profit from previously acquired knowledge.
2. Shortcuts, however, may mislead you; they may contribute to your remembering things that are consistent with your schemata (even if they didn't occur) and distorting or forgetting information which is inconsistent.
3. What you remember about a person or an event isn't an objective recollection but is more likely heavily influenced by your preconceptions or your schemata about what belongs and what doesn't belong, what fits neatly into the templates in your brain and what doesn't fit. Your reconstruction of an event or person contains a lot of information that was not in the original sensory experience and may omit a lot that was in this experience.
4. Judgments about others are invariably ethnocentric; because your schemata and scripts are created on the basis of your own cultural experiences, you invariably apply these to members of other cultures. From this it's easy to infer that when members of other cultures do things that conform to your scripts, they're right, and when they do things that contradict your scripts, they're wrong—a classic example of ethnocentric thinking. As you can appreciate, this tendency can easily contribute to intercultural misunderstandings.
5. Memory is especially unreliable when the information can be interpreted in different ways, when it's ambiguous. Thus, for example, consider the statement that "Ben didn't do well in his other courses as he would have liked." If your schema of Ben was "brilliant" then you might "remember" that Ben got Bs. But if, as in our example, your schema was of the academically weak athlete, you might "remember" that Ben got Ds. Conveniently, but unreliably, schemas reduce ambiguity.

Can you recall a specific example of meeting a particular person for the first time and explain how you went through the five stages of perception (stimulation, organization, interpretation-evaluation, memory, and recall)?

◀◀ THINKING BACK

PERCEPTUAL PROCESSES

Before reading about the specific processes that you use in perceiving other people, examine your own perception strategies by taking the self-test, "How Accurate Are You at People Perception?"

THINKING AHEAD ▸▸
Why is it that two people looking at exactly the same thing (seeing the same movie, for example, or watching the same news event on television) come away with totally different ideas of what it meant? Why don't they both perceive the same thing?

TEST YOURSELF *How Accurate Are You at People Perception?*

Respond to each of the following statements with *True* if the statement is usually or generally accurate in describing your behavior or *False* if the statement is usually or generally inaccurate in describing your behavior.

_______ 1. I base most of my impressions of people on the first few minutes of our meeting.

_______ 2. When I know some things about another person, I can fill in what I don't know.

_______ 3. I make predictions about people's behaviors that generally prove to be true.

_______ 4. I have clear ideas of what people of different national, racial, and religious groups are really like.

_______ 5. I generally attribute people's attitudes and behaviors to their most obvious physical or psychological characteristic.

_______ 6. I avoid making assumptions about what is going on in someone else's head on the basis of the person's behaviors.

_______ 7. I pay special attention to behaviors of people that might contradict my initial impressions.

_______ 8. On the basis of my observations of people, I formulate guesses (that I am willing to revise) about them rather than firmly held conclusions.

_______ 9. I reserve making judgments about people until I learn a great deal about them and see them in a variety of situations.

_______ 10. After I formulate an initial impression, I check my perceptions by, for example, asking questions or by gathering more evidence.

This brief perception test is designed to raise issues considered in this unit. The first six questions refer to the tendencies to make judgments of others on the basis of first impressions (question 1), implicit personality theories (question 2), self-fulfilling prophecies (question 3), stereotypes (question 4), attribution (question 5), and mind reading (question 6). Ideally, you would have answered *False* to these six questions. (The tendencies they refer to are covered in the sections titled "Attribution" and "Perceptual Processes.") Questions 7 through 10 refer to specific guidelines for increasing accuracy in people perception: being especially alert to contradictory cues (question 7), formulating hypotheses rather than conclusions (question 8), delaying any conclusions until sufficient evidence is in (question 9), and using perception checking (question 10). Ideally, you would have answered *True* to these four questions. ■

Implicit Personality Theory

Each person has a subconscious or implicit system of rules that says which characteristics of an individual go with other characteristics. Consider, for example, the following brief statements. Note the word in parentheses that you think best completes each sentence:

WEB EXPLORATION
To learn more about implicit personality theory, go to www.awl.com/devito.

In making evaluations, it would seem that you first think about the situation and then make the evaluation. Some research claims, however, that you really don't think before assigning any perception a positive or negative value. This research argues that all perceptions have a positive or negative value attached to them and that these evaluations are most often automatic and involve no conscious thought. Immediately upon perceiving a person, idea, or thing, you attach a positive or negative value (*New York Times,* 8 August 1995, C1, C10). What do you think of this? One bit of evidence against this position would be to identify three or four or five things, ideas, or people about which you feel completely neutral. Can you do it?

Carlo is energetic, eager, and (intelligent, stupid).
Kim is bold, defiant, and (extroverted, introverted).
Joe is bright, lively, and (thin, heavy).
Ava is attractive, intelligent, and (likable, unlikable).
Susan is cheerful, positive, and (outgoing, shy).
Angel is handsome, tall, and (friendly, unfriendly).

What makes some of these choices seem right and others wrong is your **implicit personality theory,** the system of rules that tells you which characteristics go with which other characteristics. Your theory may, for example, have told you that a person who is energetic and eager is also intelligent, not stupid, although there is no logical reason why a stupid person could not be energetic and eager.

The widely documented **halo effect** is a function of the implicit personality theory (Dion, Berscheid, and Walster 1972, Riggio 1987). If you believe a person has some positive qualities, you're likely to infer that she or he also possesses other positive qualities. There is also a *reverse halo effect:* if you know a person possesses several negative qualities, you're more likely to infer that the person also has other negative qualities.

In using implicit personality theories, apply them carefully and critically so as to avoid perceiving qualities in an individual that your theory tells you should be present when they actually are not. For example, you see "goodwill" in a friend's "charitable" acts when a tax deduction may have been the real motive. Similarly, be careful of ignoring or distorting qualities that don't conform to your theory but that are actually present in the individual. For example, you may ignore negative qualities in your friends that you would easily perceive in your enemies.

Cultural Variation in Implicit Personality Theories As might be expected, the implicit personality theories that people hold differ from culture to culture, group to group, and even person to person. For example, the Chinese have the concept *shi gu,* which refers to "someone who is worldly, devoted to his or her family, socially skillful, and somewhat reserved" (Aronson, Wilson, and Akert 1999, p. 117). This concept isn't easily encoded in English, as you can tell by trying to find a general concept that covers this type of person. In English, on the other hand, we have a concept of the "artistic type," a generalization which seems absent in Chinese. Thus, although it is easy for speakers of English or Chinese to refer to specific concepts—such as "socially skilled" or "creative"—each language creates its own generalized categories. Thus, in Chinese the qualities that make up *shi gu* are more easily seen as going together than they might be for an English speaker; they're part of the implicit personality theory of more Chinese speakers than English speakers.

Similarly, consider the different personality theories that "graduate students" and "blue-collar high school dropouts" might have for "college students." Likewise, an individual may have had great experiences with doctors and therefore may have a very positive personality theory of doctors, whereas another person may have had negative experiences with doctors and might thus have developed a very negative personality theory.

Self-Fulfilling Prophecy

A **self-fulfilling prophecy** occurs when you make a prediction that comes true because you act on it as if it were true (Merton 1957). Put differently, a self-fulfilling prophecy occurs when you act on your schema as if it were true and in doing so make it true. There are four basic steps in the self-fulfilling prophecy:

1. You make a prediction or formulate a belief about a person or a situation. For example, you predict that Pat is friendly in interpersonal encounters.
2. You act toward that person or situation as if that prediction or belief were true. For example, you act as if Pat were a friendly person.
3. Because you act as if the belief were true, it becomes true. For example, because of the way you act toward Pat, Pat becomes comfortable and friendly.
4. You observe your effect on the person or the resulting situation, and what you see strengthens your beliefs. For example, you observe Pat's friendliness, and this reinforces your belief that Pat is in fact friendly.

The self-fulfilling prophecy can also be seen when you make predictions about yourself and fulfill them. For example, you might enter a group situation convinced that the other members will dislike you. Almost invariably you'll be proved right; the other members will appear to you to dislike you. What you may be doing is acting in a way that encourages the group to respond to you negatively. In this way, you fulfill your prophecies about yourself.

A widely known example of the self-fulfilling prophecy is the **Pygmalion effect.** In one study, teachers were told that certain pupils were expected to do exceptionally well, that they were late bloomers. The names of these students were actually selected at random by the experimenters. The results, however, were not random. The students whose names were given to the teachers actually performed at a higher level than the others. In fact, these students' IQ scores even improved more than did the other students'. The teachers' expectations probably prompted them to give extra attention to the selected students, thereby positively affecting their performance (Rosenthal and Jacobson 1968, Insel and Jacobson 1975).

Self-fulfilling prophecies can short-circuit critical thinking and influence another's behavior (or your own) so that it conforms to your prophecy. As a result, you may see what you predicted rather than what is really there (for example, to perceive yourself as a failure because you have predicted it rather than because of any actual failures).

Perceptual Accentuation

When poor and rich children were shown pictures of coins and later asked to estimate their size, the poor children's size estimates were much greater than the rich children's. Similarly, hungry people need fewer visual cues to perceive food objects and food terms than do people who are not hungry. This process, called **perceptual accentuation,** leads you to see what you expect or want to see. You see people you like as better looking and smarter than those you don't like. You magnify or accentuate what will satisfy your needs and desires: the thirsty person sees a mirage of water, the sexually deprived person sees a mirage of sexual satisfaction.

Perceptual accentuation can lead you to perceive what you need or want to perceive rather than what is really there, and to fail to perceive what you don't want to perceive. For example, you may not perceive signs of impending problems because you focus on what you want to perceive.

Perceptual accentuation can also lead you to perceive and remember positive qualities more than negative ones (a phenomenon referred to as the *Pollyanna effect*) and thus distort your perceptions of others.

Another interesting distortion created by perceptual accentuation is that you may perceive certain behaviors as indicative that someone likes you simply because you want to be liked. For example, general politeness and friendly behavior used as a persuasive strategy (say, by a salesperson) are frequently seen as indicating a genuine personal liking.

Primacy-Recency

Assume for a moment that you're enrolled in a course in which half the classes are extremely dull and half extremely exciting. At the end of the semester, you evaluate the course and the instructor. Would your evaluation be more favorable if the dull classes occurred in the first half of the semester and the exciting classes in the second? Or would it be more favorable if the order were reversed? If what comes first exerts the most influence, you have a *primacy effect*. If what comes last (or most recently) exerts the most influence, you have a *recency effect*.

In the classic study on the effects of **primacy-recency** in interpersonal perception, college students perceived a person who was described as "intelligent, industrious, impulsive, critical, stubborn, and envious" as more positively than a person described as "envious, stubborn, critical, impulsive, industrious, and intelligent" (Asch 1946). Clearly, there's a tendency to use early information to get a general idea about a person and to use later information to make this impression more specific. The initial information helps you form a schema for the person. Once that schema is formed, you're likely to resist information that contradicts it.

One interesting practical implication of primacy-recency is that the first impression you make is likely to be the most important. The reason for this is that the schema that others form of you functions as a filter to admit or block additional information about you. If the initial impression or schema is positive, others are likely to readily remember additional positive information because it confirms this original positive image or schema and to easily forget or distort negative information because it contradicts this original positive schema, and they are also more likely to interpret ambiguous information as positive. You win in all three ways—if the initial impression is positive.

The tendency to give greater weight to early information and to interpret later information in light of early impressions can lead you to formulate a total picture of an individual on the basis of initial impressions that may not be typical or accurate. For example, if you judge a job applicant as generally nervous when he or she may simply be showing normal nervousness at being interviewed for a much needed job, you will have misperceived this individual.

Similarly, this tendency can lead you to discount or distort subsequent perceptions so as not to disrupt your initial impression or upset your original schema. For example, you may fail to see signs of deceit in someone you like because of your early impressions that this person is a good and honest individual.

Consistency

The tendency to maintain balance among perceptions or attitudes is called **consistency** (McBroom and Reed 1992). You expect certain things to go together and other things not to go together. On a purely intuitive basis, for example, respond to the following sentences by noting your expected response:

1. I expect a person I like to (like, dislike) me.
2. I expect a person I dislike to (like, dislike) me.
3. I expect my friend to (like, dislike) my friend.
4. I expect my friend to (like, dislike) my enemy.
5. I expect my enemy to (like, dislike) my friend.
6. I expect my enemy to (like, dislike) my enemy.

According to most consistency theories, your expectations would be as follows: You would expect a person you liked to like you (1) and one you disliked to dislike you (2). You would expect a friend to like a friend (3) and to dislike an enemy (4). You would expect your enemy to dislike your friend (5) and to like your other enemy (6). All these expectations are intuitively satisfying.

Further, you would expect someone you liked to possess characteristics you like or admire and would expect your enemies not to possess characteristics you like or admire. Conversely, you would expect people you liked to lack unpleasant characteristics and those you disliked to possess unpleasant characteristics.

Uncritically assuming that an individual is consistent can lead you to ignore or distort your perceptions of behaviors that are inconsistent with your picture of the whole person. For example, you may misinterpret Karla's unhappiness because your image of Karla is "happy, controlled, and contented." Consistency can also lead you to see certain behaviors as positive if you interpreted other behaviors positively (the halo effect) or as negative if you interpreted other behaviors negatively (the reverse halo effect).

Stereotyping

One of the most common shortcuts in interpersonal perception is stereotyping. A sociological or psychological **stereotype** is a fixed impression of a group of people; it's a schema. We all have attitudinal stereotypes—of national, religious, sexual, or racial groups, or perhaps of criminals, prostitutes, teachers, or plumbers. If you have these fixed impressions, you will, upon meeting a member of a particular group, often see that person primarily as a member of that group and apply to him or her all the characteristics you assign to that group. If you meet someone who is a prostitute, for example, there is a host of characteristics for prostitutes that you may apply to this one person. To complicate matters further, you will often "see" in this person's behavior the manifestation of characteristics that you would not "see" if you didn't know that this person was a prostitute. Stereotypes can easily distort accurate perception and prevent you from seeing an individual as an individual rather than as a member of a group.

The tendency to group people and to respond to individuals primarily as members of groups can lead you to perceive an individual as possessing those qualities (usually negative) that you believe characterize his or her group (for example, all Mexicans are . . . or all Baptists are . . .) and, therefore, fail to appreciate the multifaceted nature of all individuals and groups. Stereotyping can also lead you to ignore each person's unique characteristics and, therefore, fail to benefit from the special contributions each individual can bring to an encounter.

Attribution

Think about each of the following situations:

1. A woman is begging in the street.
2. A store owner kills a thief.
3. A father leaves his children.

To what do you attribute the causes of these situations? Did the begging, killing, and abandonment result from something within the person or from within the situation? The way you would answer these questions is neatly explained in **attribution** theory. Attribution theory explains the process you go through in trying to understand others' behaviors and your own (in **self-attribution**), particularly the reasons or motivations for these behaviors. Attribution helps you to impose order and logic and to better understand the possible causes of the behaviors you observe.

Attribution also helps you to make predictions about what will happen, what others are likely or unlikely to do. If you can be reasonably sure that Pat gave money out of a desire to help the poor (that is, you can attribute the behavior to a desire to help), then you can make predictions about Pat's future behaviors that are more likely to be correct than predictions made without this initial attribution to guide you.

Attribution Processes In trying to discover the causes of another's behavior, your first step is to determine whether the individual or some outside factor is responsible. That is, you must first determine whether the cause is *internal* (for example, due to some personality trait) or *external* (for example, due to some situational factor). Your assessment of someone's behavior as internally or externally motivated will greatly influence your evaluation of that person. If you judge people's cooperative behavior as internally caused (that is, as motivated by their personality), you're more apt to form a positive evaluation of them and, eventually, to like them. In contrast, if you judge that very same behavior to be externally caused (the watchful eye of the boss is forcing someone to behave cooperatively, for example), you're more apt to form a negative evaluation and, eventually, to dislike the person (because he or she isn't "really" cooperative).

Consider another example. You look at an instructor's grade book and observe that ten Fs were assigned in cultural anthropology. In an attempt to discover what this reveals about the instructor, you first have to discover whether the instructor was in fact responsible for the assignment of the ten Fs or whether the grading could be attributed to external factors. Let's say you discover that the examinations on which the grades were based had been made up by a faculty committee, which also set the standards for passing or failing. In this case, you could not attribute any particular motives to this individual instructor because the behavior was not internally caused.

On the other hand, let's assume the following: this instructor made up the examination without any assistance, no departmental or university standards were used, and the instructor made up a personal set of standards for passing and failing. Now you would be more apt (though perhaps not fully justified) to attribute the ten Fs to internal causes. You would be strengthened in your beliefs that there was something within this instructor, some personality characteristic, for example, that led to this behavior if you discovered that (1) no other instructor in anthropology gave nearly as many Fs, (2) this particular instructor frequently gives Fs in cultural anthropology, (3) this instructor frequently gives Fs in other courses as well, and (4) this instructor is the only one responsible for assigning grades and could have assigned grades other than F. These four bits of added information would lead you to conclude that there was something within this instructor that motivated the behavior. In forming such causal judgments, which you make every day, you use four principles: (1) consensus, (2) consistency, (3) distinctiveness, and (4) controllability.

Consensus: Similarity Others When you use the principle of consensus, you ask, "Do other people behave in the same way as the person on whom I'm focusing?" That is, is the person acting in accordance with the consensus, the majority? If the answer is no, you're more likely to attribute the behavior to some internal cause and conclude: "This person is different." In the instructor example, you would be strengthened in your belief that something internal caused the Fs to be given if you learned that other instructors didn't do this; that is, there was low consensus. When only one person acts contrary to the norm, you're more likely to attribute that person's behavior to internal motivation. If all instructors gave many Fs (that is, if there was high consensus), you'd be more likely to look for causality outside the individual instructor; you might conclude that the anthropology department uses a particular curve in determining grades or that the students were not very bright—or any other reason external to the specific instructor.

Consistency: Similarity Over Time When you use the principle of consistency, you ask if this person repeatedly (consistently) behaves in the same way in similar situations. If the answer is yes, there's high consistency, and you're likely to attribute the behavior to internal motivation. If you knew that this instructor frequently gives Fs in cultural anthropology, it would lead you to attribute the cause to the instructor rather than to outside sources. If, on the other hand, there was low consistency—that is, if this instructor rarely gives Fs—you'd be more likely to look for external reasons. Again, you might conclude, for example, that this specific class was not very bright or that the department required the instructor to start giving out Fs.

Distinctiveness: Similarity in Different Situations When you use the principle of distinctiveness, you ask if this person reacts in similar ways in different situations. If the answer is yes, there is low distinctiveness, and you're likely to conclude that the behavior has an internal cause. If the instructor reacted the same way (gave lots of Fs) in different situations (other courses), it would lead you to conclude that this particular class was not distinctive and that the motivation for the behavior could not be found in the unique situation. You'd further conclude that this behavior is likely due to the instructor's inner motivation. Consider the alternative: if this instructor gave all high grades and no Fs in other courses (that is, if the cultural anthropology class situation was highly distinctive), you'd conclude that the motivation for the failures was to be found in sources outside the instructor and for reasons unique to this class.

Controllability: Was the Person in Control of the Behavior? Let's say your friend is an hour late for a dinner appointment (cf. Weiner, Amirkhan, Folkes, and Verette 1987). How would you feel about the following two possible excuses?

> **Excuse 1:** I was reading this book, and I just couldn't put it down. I had to find out who the killer was.
>
> **Excuse 2:** I was stuck on the subway for two hours; a water main broke, killing all the electricity.

It's likely you'd resent the first and accept the second excuse. The first excuse says that the reason for the lateness was controllable: your friend chose to be late by completing the novel. You'd therefore hold your friend responsible for wasting your time and for a lack of consideration. The second excuse says that the reason was uncontrollable: your friend couldn't help being late. Here you'd not hold your friend responsible. This, by the way, is why excuses involving uncontrollable factors are more effective than those involving controllable factors.

Think about your own tendency to make similar judgments based on controllability. For example, how you would respond to such situations as the following:

- Doris fails her midterm history exam.
- Sidney's car is repossessed because he failed to make the payments.
- Thomas's wife has just filed for divorce and he is feeling depressed.

Very probably you'd be sympathetic to each of these people if you felt they were not in control of what happened—for example, if the examination was unfair, if Sidney lost his job because of employee discrimination, and if Thomas's wife is leaving him for a billionaire. On the other hand, you might blame these people for their problems if you felt that they were in control of the situation—for example, if Doris partied instead of studied, if Sidney gambled his payments away, and if Thomas had been repeatedly unfaithful and his wife finally gave up trying to change him.

In perceiving other people and especially in evaluating their behavior, you frequently ask if the person was in control of the behavior. Generally, research shows that if you feel people are in control of negative behaviors, you'll come to dislike them. But you'll feel sorry for someone you feel isn't in control of negative behaviors, and you won't blame the person for his or her negative circumstances.

Low consensus, high consistency, low distinctiveness, and high controllability lead to an attribution of internal causes. As a result, you praise or blame the person for his or her behaviors. High consensus, low consistency, high distinctiveness, and low controllability lead to an attribution of external causes. Table 6.1 summarizes these four principles of attribution.

Attribution Errors Attribution of causality can lead to several major barriers. Here are three such barriers: the self-serving bias, overattribution, and the fundamental attribution error.

The Self-Serving Bias The **self-serving bias** is a barrier designed to preserve self-esteem. You commit the self-serving bias when you take credit for the positive and deny responsibility for the negative. For example, you're more likely to

TABLE 6.1 A Summary of Causal Attribution

Situation: John was fired from a job he began a few months ago. On what basis will you decide whether this behavior is internally caused (and John is, therefore, responsible) or externally caused (and John isn't responsible)?

Internal if	External if
No one else was fired (low consensus).	Lots of others were fired (high consensus).
John was fired from lots of other jobs (high consistency).	John was never fired from any other job (low consistency).
John has failed at lots of other things (low distinctiveness).	John has always been successful (high distinctiveness).
John could have been retained if he agreed to move to another shop (high controllability).	John was not given any alternatives (low controllability)

attribute your positive behaviors (say, you get an A on an exam) to internal and controllable factors, to your personality, intelligence, or hard work (Bernstein, Stephan, and Davis 1979). You're more likely to attribute your negative behaviors (say, you get a D) to external and uncontrollable factors, to the exam being exceptionally difficult or unfair.

Similarly, the self-serving bias influences the way you view conflict (Schutz 1999). For example, you're more likely to describe your partner's negative behavior as internally motivated and your negative behavior as externally caused ("I couldn't help it" or "They made me do it"). Similarly, you're more likely to make excuses and justify your own behavior rather than your partner's.

There is some evidence (though it's not overwhelming) that we explain the behaviors of ingroup and outgroup members differently (Taylor and Jaggi 1974, Berry, Poortinga, Segall, and Dasen 1992). For example, you're more likely to explain members' positive behavior as internally motivated and nonmembers' positive behaviors as externally motivated . Thus, you would be more apt to explain, say, a high record of charitable contributions for members of your own culture with something like "We're a charitable people; we believe in helping others." If this is shown to be true for members of another culture, you'd be more apt to say something like "They're rich; they need tax deductions."

Alternatively, you're likely to explain the negative behavior of members of your own culture as externally or situationally caused but to explain the very same behavior of members of other cultures as internally motivated. Thus, for example, you would be more apt to attribute a high school dropout rate (a negatively evaluated behavior) to external sources (instructors who were not motivating or irrelevant educational programs) if this was shown to be true of your own cultural group. If, on the other hand, it were shown to be true of another culture, then you'd be more apt to attribute it to internal sources (the people aren't interested in education; they lack motivation).

At times you might construct defensive attributions by which you try to explain behavior in ways that make you seem less vulnerable. One way you might do this is with unrealistic optimism, maintaining the belief that good things are more likely to happen to you than to others. For example, most people think that they will ultimately experience more good things and less bad things than their peers (Aronson, Wilson, and Akert 1999). A similar belief is the *just world* hypothesis, the belief that bad things will happen only to bad people. Since you are a good person, good things will happen to you. Of course, in your mindful state, you know that good things often happen to bad people and that bad things often happen to good people.

Overattribution Overattribution is the tendency to single out one or two obvious characteristics of a person and attribute everything that person does to this one or these two characteristics. For example, if the person had alcoholic parents or is blind or was born into great wealth, there's often a tendency to attribute everything that person does to such factors. So you might say Sally has difficulty forming meaningful relationships because she grew up in a home of alcoholics, Alex overeats because he's blind, and Lillian is irresponsible because she never had to work for her money. To prevent overattribution, recognize that most behaviors and personality characteristics result from lots of factors. You almost always make a mistake when you select one factor and attribute everything to it. When you make a judgment, ask yourself if other factors might be operating here: Are there other factors that might be creating difficulties for Sally to form relationships, for Alex to control his eating habits, and for Lillian to behave irresponsibly?

The Fundamental Attribution Error The fundamental attribution error occurs when you overvalue the contribution of internal factors and undervalue the influence of external factors. It's the tendency to conclude that people do what they do because that's the kind of people they are not because of the situation they're in. When Pat is late for an appointment, you're more likely to conclude that Pat is inconsiderate or irresponsible rather than attribute the lateness to the bus breaking down or to a traffic accident.

When you explain your own behavior, you also favor internal explanations although not to as great an extent as when explaining the behaviors of others. One reason for giving greater weight to external factors in explaining your own behavior than you do in explaining the behavior of others is that you know the situation surrounding your own behavior. You know, for example, what's going on in your love life and you know your financial condition, so you naturally see the influence of these factors. But you rarely know as much about others and, thus, are more likely to give less weight to the external factors in their cases.

This fundamental attribution error is at least in part culturally influenced. For example, in the United States people are more likely to explain behavior by saying that people did what they did because of who they are. But when Hindus in India were asked to explain why their friends behaved as they did, they gave greater weight to external factors than did Americans in the United States (Miller 1984, Aronson, Wilson, and Akert 1999). Further, Americans have little hesitation in offering causal explanations of a person's behavior ("Pat did this because . . . "). Hindus, on the other hand, are generally reluctant to explain a person's behavior in causal terms (Matsumoto 1994).

Let's return to the three examples with which we opened this discussion of attribution as a way of summarizing the principles of consensus, consistency, distinctiveness, and controllability. Generally, you would consider the three actions—begging, killing, and abandonment—to result from something inherent in the begging woman, the store owner, and the father if other people behaved differently in situations similar to these (low consensus), if these people had engaged in these behaviors in the past (high consistency), if these people behaved similarly in other situations (low distinctiveness), and if these people were in control of their own behaviors (high controllability). Under these conditions, you'd probably conclude that the persons bear the responsibility for their behaviors.

Alternatively, you would consider these actions to have resulted from something external to the persons if many other people reacted the same way in similar situations (high consensus), if these people had never behaved in this way before (low consistency), if these people never engaged in these behaviors in different situations (high distinctiveness), and if these people were not in control of their own behavior (low controllability). Under these conditions, you'd probably conclude that these actions resulted from external factors, that these people had little or no control, and that, therefore, they're not personally responsible.

Have you even fallen into one of the traps identified here in making a judgment of another person? What happened?

◀◀ THINKING BACK

THINKING AHEAD ▶▶

Why is it that sometimes you're so accurate about judging another person and at other times so wrong? What makes some perceptions right on target and others drastically off their mark?

INCREASING ACCURACY IN INTERPERSONAL PERCEPTION

Successful interpersonal communication depends largely on the accuracy of your interpersonal perception. We've already identified the potential barriers that can arise with each of the perceptual processes, for example, the self-serving bias, overattribution, and the fundamental attribution error in attribution. There are, however, additional ways to increase your accuracy in interpersonal perception.

ETHICS IN INTERPERSONAL COMMUNICATION

Vote online at http://www.awl.com/devito

Q & A

One of the most difficult conversational situations occurs when you're asked a question and although you want to be truthful you also want to be effective in achieving your communication goal.

What would you do? *Here are a few questions that others might ask you. For each question, there are extenuating circumstances. Consider the mitigating circumstances (these are noted as the Thought you're thinking as you consider your possible answers). What would you do in each of these three situations?*

Question [A romantic partner asks] Do you love me?

Thought I don't want to commit myself, but I don't want to end the relationship, either. I want to allow the relationship to progress further before making any commitment.

Question [An interviewer says] You seem a bit old for this type of job. How old are you?

Thought I am old for this job, but I need it anyway. Further, it's really illegal for the interviewer to ask my age. I don't want to turn the interviewer off, because I really need this job. Yet I don't want to reveal my age either.

Question [A 15-year-old asks] Was I adopted? Who are my real parents?

Thought Yes, you were adopted, but I fear that you will look for your biological parents and will be hurt when you find that they're drug dealers and murderers.

Analyze Your Perceptions

When you become aware of your perceptions, you'll be able to subject them to logical analysis, to critical thinking. Here are a few suggestions.

Recognize your own role in perception. Your emotional and physiological state will influence the meaning you give to your perceptions. A movie may seem hysterically funny when you're in a good mood but just plain stupid when you're in a bad mood or when you're preoccupied with family problems. Beware of your own biases. Know when your perceptual evaluations are unduly influenced by your own biases: for example, perceiving only the positive in people you like and only the negative in people you don't like.

Avoid early conclusions On the basis of your observations of behaviors, formulate hypotheses to test against additional information and evidence rather than drawing conclusions you then look to confirm. Delay formulating conclusions until you have had a chance to process a wide variety of cues. Similarly, avoid the one-cue conclusion. Look for a variety of cues pointing in the same direction. The more cues pointing to the same conclusion, the more likely your conclusion will be correct. Be especially alert to contradictory cues, ones that refute your initial hypotheses. It's relatively easy to perceive cues that confirm your hypotheses but more difficult to acknowledge contradictory evidence. At the same time, seek validation from others. Do others see things in the same way you do? If not, ask yourself if your perceptions may be in some way distorted.

Avoid mind reading Avoid trying to read the thoughts and feelings of another person just from observing their behaviors. Regardless of how many behaviors you observe and how carefully you examine them, you can only guess what is going on in someone's mind. A person's motives are not open to outside inspection; you can only make assumptions based on overt behaviors.

TRY IT!
To learn more about checking your perceptions, go to www.awl.com/devito.

Check Your Perceptions

Perception checking is another way to reduce uncertainty and to make your perceptions more accurate. The goal of perception checking is to explore further the thoughts and feelings of the other person and not to prove that your initial perception is correct. With this simple technique, you lessen your chances of misinterpreting another's feelings. At the same time, you give the other person an opportunity to elaborate on his or her thoughts and feelings. In its most basic form, perception checking consists of two steps:

1. Describe what you see or hear, recognizing that even descriptions are not really objective but are heavily influenced by who you are, your emotional state, and so on. At the same time, you may wish to describe what you think is happening. Again, try to do this as descriptively (not evaluatively) as you can. Sometimes you may wish to offer several possibilities.
   - You've called me from work a lot this week. You seem concerned that everything is all right at home.
   - You've not talked with me all week. You say that my work is fine but you don't seem to want to give me the same responsibilities that other editorial assistants have.
2. Ask the other person for confirmation. Do be careful that your request for confirmation does not sound as though you already know the answer. So avoid phrasing your questions defensively. Avoid saying, for example, "You really don't want to go out, do you? I knew you didn't when you turned on that lousy television." Instead, ask for confirmation in as supportive a way as possible: "Would you rather watch TV?"
   - Are you worried about me or the kids?
   - Are you pleased with my work? Is there anything I can do to improve my job performance?

Reduce Your Uncertainty

We all have a tendency to reduce uncertainty, a process that enables us to achieve greater accuracy in perception. In large part we learned about uncertainty and how to deal with it from our culture.

Culture and Uncertainty People from different cultures differ greatly in their attitudes toward uncertainty and how to deal with it, attitudes that impact on perceptual accuracy. In some cultures people do little to avoid uncertainty and have little anxiety about not knowing what will happen next. Uncertainty to them is a normal part of life and is accepted as it comes. Members of these cultures don't feel threatened by unknown situations. Examples of such low-anxiety cultures include Singapore, Jamaica, Denmark, Sweden, Hong Kong, Ireland, Great Britain, Malaysia, India, Philippines, and the United States. Other cultures do much to avoid uncertainty and have a great deal of anxiety about not knowing what will happen next; uncertainty is seen as threatening and something that must be counteracted. Examples of such high-anxiety cultures include Greece, Portugal, Guatemala, Uruguay, Belgium, El Salvador, Japan, Yugoslavia, Peru, France, Chile, Spain, and Costa Rica (Hofstede 1997).

The potential for communication problems can be great when people come from cultures with different attitudes toward uncertainty. For example, managers from cultures with weak uncertainty avoidance will accept workers who work only when they have to and will not get too upset when workers are late. Managers from cultures with strong uncertainty avoidance will expect workers to be busy at all times and will have little tolerance for lateness.

Because weak uncertainty avoidance cultures have great tolerance for ambiguity and uncertainty, they minimize the rules governing communication and relationships (Hofstede 1997, Lustig and Koester 1999). People who don't follow the same rules as the cultural majority are readily tolerated. Different approaches and perspectives may even be encouraged in cultures with weak uncertainty avoidance. Strong uncertainty avoidance cultures create very clear-cut rules for communication. It's considered unacceptable for people to break these rules.

Students from weak uncertainty avoidance cultures appreciate freedom in education and prefer vague assignments without specific timetables. These students will want to be rewarded for creativity and will easily accept the instructor's (sometimes) lack of knowledge. Students from strong uncertainty avoidance cultures prefer highly structured experiences where there is little ambiguity; they prefer specific objectives, detailed instructions, and definite timetables. These students expect to be judged on the basis of the right answers and expect the instructor to have all the answers all the time (Hofstede 1997).

Strategies for Reducing Uncertainty A variety of strategies can help reduce uncertainty (Berger and Bradac 1982, Gudykunst 1995). Observing another person while he or she is engaged in an active task, preferably interacting with others in more informal social situations, will often reveal a great deal about the person since people are less apt to monitor their behaviors and more likely to reveal their true selves in informal situations.

You can also manipulate the situation in such a way that you observe the person in more specific and more revealing contexts. Employment interviews, theatrical auditions, and student teaching are some of the ways situations can be created to observe how the person might act and react and hence to reduce uncertainty about the person.

When you log on to an Internet chat group for the first time and you lurk, reading the exchanges between the other group members before saying anything yourself, you're learning about the people in the group and about the group itself and thus reducing uncertainty. When uncertainty is reduced, you're more likely to make contributions that will be appropriate to the group and less likely to violate any of the group's norms; in short, you're more likely to communicate effectively.

Another way to reduce uncertainty is to collect information about the person through asking others. You might inquire of a colleague if a third person finds you interesting and might like to have dinner with you.

How does your culture treat uncertainty? How anxious are you about uncertainty? Did you learn this attitude from your culture?

ASK THE RESEARCHER

Learning About Your Workplace

I'm starting a new job this month and want to learn as much as I can about the organization as fast as I can. Put in your academic terms, how can I reduce my uncertainty about my new workplace—its do's and don'ts, its culture, its reward system? I'm planning on going as high as I can as fast as I can.

I think the best way to address your question is simply to provide a list of things you might do:

- Observe carefully. Watch individuals' actions, especially those who have recently achieved success. Don't rely so much on verbal reports and "stories" about success. These "stories" may be more myth than reality.
- Talk to as many people as possible at all levels of the organization. Don't rely on a few individuals' opinions/observations.
- Try to determine what behavior is rewarded by the organization. Most organizations are constantly evolving, so it is vital that information acquisition be an ongoing activity rather than something you do only at the beginning of a career.
- Identify sub-goals that will lead to your primary goals and develop plans to reach these goals. However, when the environment is highly dynamic, be prepared to alter goals and plans as the environment changes. Here again, goal setting and planning are ongoing activities, not just one-time events.

For more information, see C. R. Berger, *Planning Strategic Interaction: Attaining Goals Through Communicative Action* (Mahwah, NJ: Erlbaum, 1997).

—Charles R. Berger (Ph.D., Michigan State University) is a professor and chair of the Department of Communication, University of California, Davis. His teaching concentrations include communication and cognition, interpersonal communication, nonverbal communication, risk communication, and mass media effects; his research focuses on message planning and communication effectiveness and the cognitive processing of risk communication.

Of course, you can interact with the individual. For example, you can ask questions: "Do you enjoy sports?" "What did you think of that computer science course?" "What would you do if you got fired?" You also gain knowledge of another by disclosing information about yourself. Your disclosures will help to create an environment that encourages disclosures from the person about whom you wish to learn more.

Increase Your Cultural Sensitivity

Recognizing and being sensitive to cultural differences will help increase your accuracy in perception. For example, Russian or Chinese artists such as ballet dancers will often applaud their audience by clapping. Americans seeing this may easily interpret this as egotistical. Similarly, a German man will enter a restaurant before the woman in order to see if the place is respectable enough for the woman to enter. This simple custom can easily be interpreted as rude when viewed by members who come from cultures in which it's considered courteous for the woman to enter first (Axtell 1993).

Within every cultural group there are wide and important differences. As all Americans are not alike, neither are all Indonesians, Greeks, Mexicans, and so on. When you make assumptions that all people of a certain culture are alike, you're thinking in stereotypes. Recognizing differences between another culture and your own and recognizing differences among members of a particular culture will help you perceive the situation more accurately.

What do you think is the best way to ensure the accuracy of your perceptions of a new colleague you just met on your job? What about a blind date?

◂◂ THINKING BACK

REVIEWING KEY TERMS AND CONCEPTS IN INTERPERSONAL PERCEPTION

This unit examined perception, a fundamental process in all interpersonal communication encounters, and looked at the stages you go through in perceiving people, the processes that influence your perceptions, and some of the ways in which you can make your perceptions more accurate.

The Stages of Perception

What is perception and how does it work?

- **Perception** is the process by which you become aware of objects and events in the external world.
- Perception occurs in five stages: (1) stimulation, (2) organization, (3) interpretation-evaluation, (4) memory, and (5) recall.

Perceptual Processes

What influences your interpersonal perceptions?

- Your **implicit personality theory** allows you to conclude that certain characteristics go with certain other characteristics.
- Your **self-fulfilling prophecy** may influence the behaviors of others.
- **Perceptual accentuation** may lead you to perceive what you expect to perceive instead of what is really there.
- Perceptions may be affected by **primacy-recency.** Your tendency to give extra importance to what occurs first (a *primacy effect*) may lead you to see what conforms to this judgment and to distort or otherwise misperceive what contradicts it. First impressions often serve as filters, as schemata, for more recent information. In fewer cases, you may give extra weight to what occurs last (a *recency effect*).
- The tendency to seek and expect **consistency** may influence you to see what is consistent and to not see what is inconsistent.
- A **stereotype,** a fixed impression about a group, may influence your perceptions of individual members; you may see individuals only as members of the group instead of as unique individuals.
- Judgments of **attribution,** the process through which you try to understand the behaviors of others (and your own, in **self-attribution**), particularly the reasons or motivations for these behaviors, are made on the basis of consensus, consistency, distinctiveness, and controllability. Errors of attribution include the self-serving bias, overattribution, and the fundamental attribution error.

Increasing Accuracy in Interpersonal Perception

How might you increase your accuracy in perception?

- Perceive critically: for example, recognize your role in perception, avoid early conclusions, and avoid mind reading.
- Check your perceptions; describe what you see or hear and ask for confirmation.
- Reduce uncertainty: for example, by lurking before joining a group, collect information about the person or situation, interact and observe the interaction.
- Be culturally sensitive; recognize the differences between you and others and also the differences among members of the culturally different group.

APPLYING KEY TERMS AND CONCEPTS IN INTERPERSONAL PERCEPTION

1. What role do first impressions play in your perception of other people? Have you ever been wrong? What might you do to make your first impressions more accurate?
2. Although most of the research on the self-fulfilling prophecy illustrates its distorting effect on behavior, consider how you might go about using the self-fulfilling prophecy to encourage behaviors you want to increase in strength and frequency. For example, what might you do to encourage persons who are high in communication apprehension to speak up with greater confidence? What might you do to encourage people who are reluctant to self-disclose to reveal more of their inner selves?
3. What stereotypes do you think men entertain about women? What stereotypes do you think women entertain about men? How might these stereotypes influence their interpersonal communication?
4. Geert Hofstede (1997, p. 119), who conducted much of the cultural research reported in this unit, claims that those cultures which have strong uncertainty avoidance believe "What is different, is dangerous." Weak uncertainty avoidance cultures believe "What is different, is curious." Does your experience support this distinction?
5. Do you engage in selective perception when listening to people talk about you? For example, are you more likely to attend to the positives than the negatives?
6. Has anyone's self-fulfilling prophecy about you ever influenced your behavior? What happened?
7. Can you explain with the concepts of attribution—especially controllability—the attitudes that many people have about homeless people? About drug addicts or alcoholics? About successful politicians, scientists, or millionaires?
8. Writers to advice columnists generally attribute their problems to external sources, whereas the columnists' responses often focus on internal sources, and their advice is therefore directed at the writer (you shouldn't have done that; apologize; get out of the relationship) (Schoeneman and Rubanowitz 1985). Do you find this true when people discuss their problems face-to-face, in letters, in e-mails with you? Do you generally respond as would the columnist?

9. What one suggestion for increasing accuracy do you wish others would use more often when they make judgments about you?
10. How would you go about finding answers to such questions as these:
    - Is the tendency to judge by first impressions universal?
    - In what ways are people with a lot of stereotypes different from people with few stereotypes?
    - Are people who attribute controllability to the homeless more negative in their evaluation of homelessness than those who attribute a lack of controllability?
    - Do different cultures hold different implicit personality theories? Do men and women hold different theories?
    - Does training in perception actually improve perceptual accuracy?

EXPERIENCING KEY TERMS AND CONCEPTS IN INTERPERSONAL PERCEPTION

Go to www.awl.com/devito

Exercises No. 3, "I'd Prefer to Be," No. 7, "Perceiving My Selves," and No. 12, "Who?" will prove useful in illustrating the perception process, how the specific perceptual processes work, and how you can become more accurate in interpersonal perception. Differences in perception and their impact on communication can be illustrated with a variety experiences, for example, Exercises No. 14, "'Must Lie' Situations,"No. 17, Gender and the Topics of Conversation," and No. 21, "Mate Preferences."

UNIT 7
LISTENING IN INTERPERSONAL COMMUNICATION

Ordinary People (1980)

LISTENING, NOT IMITATION, MAY BE
THE SINCEREST FORM OF FLATTERY.
--JOYCE BROTHERS

IN ORDINARY PEOPLE you see a family torn apart by the death of a son and the difficulty each member has in listening to the thoughts and feelings of the others. In watching the movie, we ask ourselves why don't they just listen to each other? Why don't they hear the anguish and fears of those they love? But as we'll see, listening is not an easy task. In this unit we look at listening, discussing what listening is, the functions it serves, and the types of listening that are appropriate for different situations.

If you were to measure importance in terms of time spent, listening would be your most important communication activity because it engages most of your communication time (Figure 7.1). Another way to gauge the importance of listening is to look at the purposes that listening serves and the many benefits that you can derive from listening more effectively. Listening serves the same purposes already noted for interpersonal communication: to learn, to relate, to influence, to play, and to help. Table 7.1 summarizes some of the benefits of effective listening.

There's no denying that you listen a great deal. Whether you listen effectively and efficiently, however, is another matter. In actual practice, most people are relatively poor listeners; their listening behavior could be much improved. Training in listening does increase listening effectiveness (Barker et al. 1992). Given the amount of time spent listening, such improvement seems well worth the required effort. And it does take effort.

Before reading about the principles and techniques of listening, examine your own listening habits by taking the self-test "How Good a Listener Are You?"

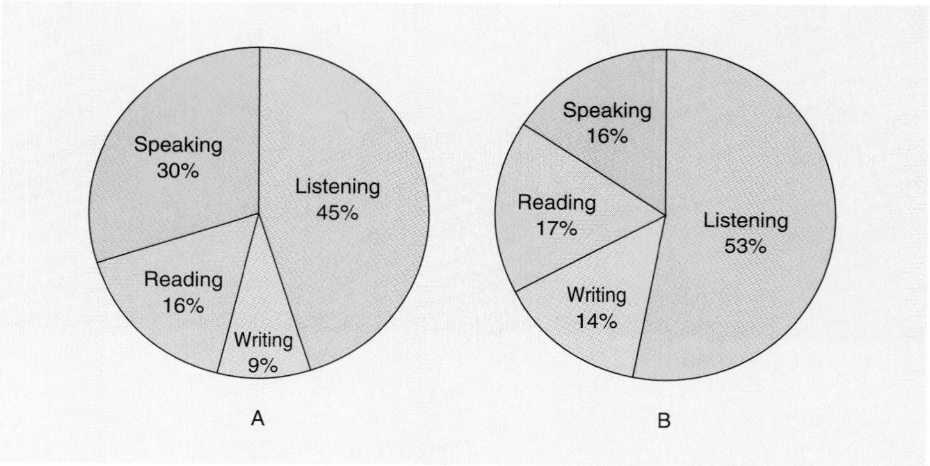

Figure 7.1 The Time Spent in Listening
This figure diagrams the results of two studies and confirms the point that listening occupies an enormous part of our communication life. Note that in both studies, one (Rankin 1929) using adults as subjects (A) and one (Barker et al. 1980) using college students (B), listening occupied more time than any other communication activity. The results of other studies, using people in business, for example, further confirm the importance of listening. What would a pie chart of your communication activities look like? Would listening be the largest area?

TABLE 7.1 **Purposes and Benefits of Effective Listening**

This table identifies the major purposes and benefits of effective listening. Can you identify other purposes and benefits? Under what headings would you explain the purposes and benefits of listening?

Purposes and Benefits	Examples
Learn: to acquire knowledge of others, the world, and yourself, so as to avoid problems and make more reasonable decisions	Listening to Peter about his travels to Cuba will help you understand more about Peter as well as about life in a communist country; listening to the difficulties your sales staff has may help you improve sales training
Relate: form and maintain friendships and love relationships on the basis of social acceptance and popularity because people come to like those who are attentive and supportive	Others will increase their liking for you once they feel you have genuine concern for them
Influence: have an effect on the attitudes and behaviors of others because people are more likely to respect and follow those who they feel have listened to and understood them	Workers are more likely to follow your advice once they feel you have truly listened to and heard their points of view, concerns and insights
Play: know when to suspend critical and evaluative thinking and when simply to engage in passive and accepting listening	Listening to the stories and anecdotes of co-workers will allow you to gain a more comfortable balance between the world of work and the world of play and perhaps to see humor in a world of seriousness
Help: be able to assist other people because you hear more, empathize more, and come to understand others more deeply	Listening to your child's complaints about her teacher (instead of responding "what did you do wrong?") will put you in a better position to help your child cope with school and with her teacher

TEST YOURSELF *How Good a Listener Are You?*

Respond to each question according to the following scale: 1= always, 2 = frequently, 3 = sometimes, 4 = seldom, and 5 = never.

_______ 1. I listen by participating; I interject comments throughout the conversation.

_______ 2. I listen to what the speaker is saying and feeling; I try to feel what the speaker feels.

_______ 3. I listen without judging the speaker.

_______ 4. I listen to the literal meanings that a speaker communicates; I don't look too deeply into hidden meanings.

_______ 5. I listen passively; I generally remain silent and take in what the other person is saying.

_______ 6. I listen objectively; I focus on the logic of the ideas rather than on the emotional meaning of the message.

_______ 7. I listen critically, evaluating the speaker and what the speaker is saying.

_______ 8. I look for the hidden meanings; the meanings that are revealed by subtle verbal or nonverbal cues.

These statements focus on the ways of listening discussed in this unit. All ways are appropriate at times and all ways are inappropriate at times. It depends. The only responses that are really inappropriate are "always" and "never." Effective listening is listening that is appropriate to the specific communication situation. This is, then, a situational view of listening. Review these statements and try to identify situations in which each statement would be appropriate and situations in which each statement would be inappropriate. ■

THINKING AHEAD ▸▸
What do you do when you really want to listen to what someone else is saying?

THE LISTENING PROCESS

Listening is not the same as hearing. Hearing is a physiological process that occurs when you're in the vicinity of vibrations in the air and these vibrations impinge on your eardrum. Hearing is basically a passive process that occurs without any attention or effort on your part. Listening is different.

Listening involves a series of five steps: receiving, understanding, remembering, evaluating, and responding (Figure 7.2). Note that the listening process is a circular one. The responses of one person serve as the stimuli for the other person, whose responses in turn serve as the stimuli for the first person, and so on.

Receiving

Listening begins with receiving the messages the speaker sends. The messages are both verbal and nonverbal; they consist of words as well as gestures, facial expressions, and variations in volume and rate, for example.

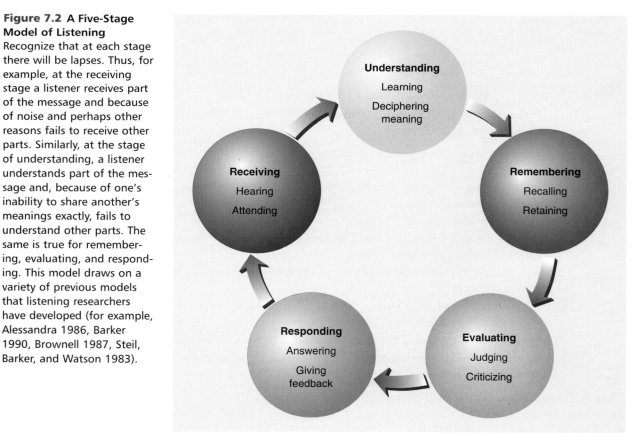

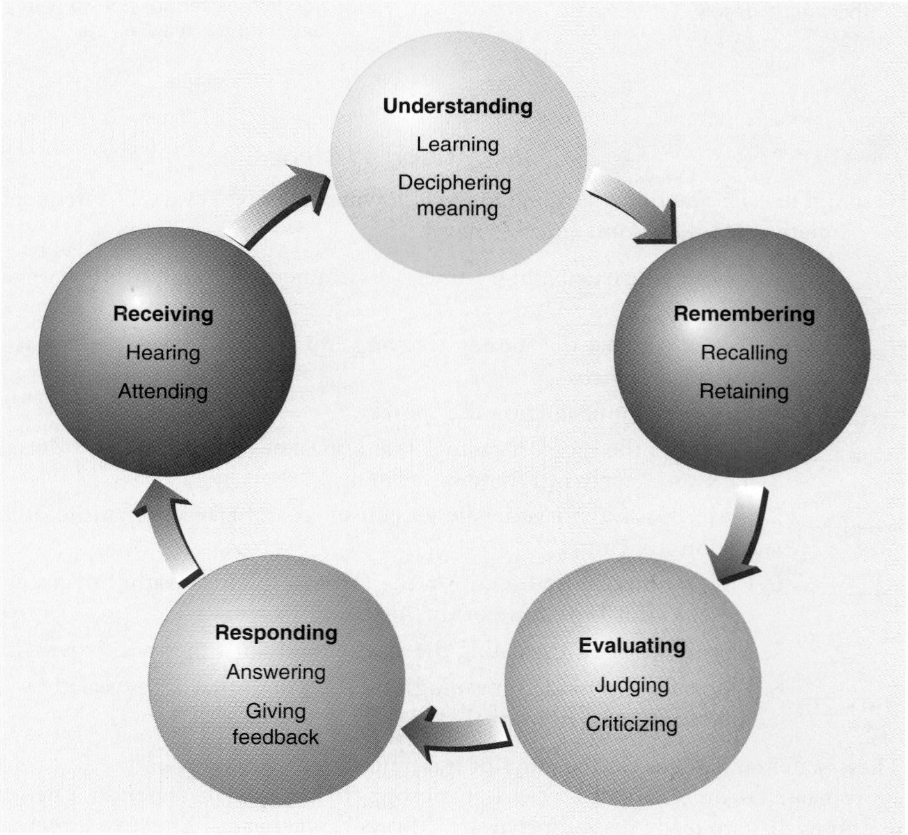

Figure 7.2 A Five-Stage Model of Listening
Recognize that at each stage there will be lapses. Thus, for example, at the receiving stage a listener receives part of the message and because of noise and perhaps other reasons fails to receive other parts. Similarly, at the stage of understanding, a listener understands part of the message and, because of one's inability to share another's meanings exactly, fails to understand other parts. The same is true for remembering, evaluating, and responding. This model draws on a variety of previous models that listening researchers have developed (for example, Alessandra 1986, Barker 1990, Brownell 1987, Steil, Barker, and Watson 1983).

At this stage, you note not only what is said (verbally and nonverbally) but also what is omitted. You receive, for example, your friend's summary of good deeds as well as the omission of all the broken promises. In receiving, try to:

- focus your attention on the speaker's verbal and nonverbal messages, on what is said and on what isn't said.
- avoid distractions in the environment.
- focus your attention on the speaker rather than on what you'll say next.
- maintain your role as listener and avoid interrupting.

Understanding

Understanding is the stage at which you learn what the speaker means—the thoughts and emotional tone. In understanding, try to:

- relate the new information the speaker is giving to what you already know.
- see the speaker's messages from the speaker's point of view; avoid judging the message until you fully understand it as the speaker intended it.
- ask questions for clarification, if necessary; ask for additional details or examples if they're needed.
- rephrase (paraphrase) the speaker's ideas in your own words.

Remembering

For listening to take place, you need to remember the messages. In some small-group and public speaking situations, you can augment your memory by taking notes or by taping the messages. In most interpersonal communication situations, however, note taking is inappropriate, although you often do write down a telephone number, an appointment, or directions.

For example, when Susan says she is planning to buy a new car, the effective listener remembers this and at later meetings asks about the car. When Joe says his mother is ill, the effective listener remembers this and inquires about her health later in the week.

What you remember is actually not what was said but what you think (or remember) was said. Memory for speech isn't reproductive; you don't simply reproduce in your memory what the speaker said. Rather, memory is reconstructive; you actually reconstruct the messages you hear into a system that makes sense to you.

To illustrate this important concept, try to memorize the list of 12 words presented below (Glucksberg and Danks 1975). Don't worry about the order of the words. Only the number remembered counts. Take about 20 seconds to memorize as many words as possible. Don't read any further until you have tried to memorize the list of words.

BED	DREAM	COMFORT
REST	AWAKE	SOUND
WAKE	NIGHT	SLUMBER
TIRED	EAT	SNORE

Now close the book and write down as many of the words from this list as you can remember. Don't read any further until you have tested your own memory.

If you're like my own students, you not only remembered a good number of the words on the list, but you also "remembered" at least one word that was not on the list: "sleep." You didn't simply reproduce the list; you reconstructed it. In this case, you gave the list meaning, and part of that meaning included the word "sleep." You frequently reconstruct messages so they make sense to you. In the process, however, the messages often get distorted. In remembering, try to:

- identify the central ideas and the major support advanced.
- summarize the message in a more easily retained form, but be careful not to ignore crucial details or qualifications.
- repeat names and key concepts to yourself or, if appropriate, aloud.

Evaluating

Evaluating consists of judging the messages in some way. At times, you may try to evaluate the speaker's underlying intentions or motives. Often this evaluation process goes on without much conscious awareness. For example, Elaine tells you that she is up for a promotion and is really excited about it. You may then try to judge her intention: she wants you to use your influence with the company president, or she's preoccupied with the promotion and so tells everyone, or she's looking for a compliment.

In other situations, your evaluation is more in the nature of critical analysis. For example, in listening to proposals advanced in a business meeting, you might ask: Are they practical? Will they increase productivity? What's the evidence? Is there contradictory evidence? In evaluating, try to:

- resist evaluation until you fully understand the speaker's point of view.
- assume that the speaker is a person of goodwill, and give the speaker the benefit of any doubt by asking for clarification on positions to which you feel you might object.
- distinguish facts from inferences (see Unit 11), opinions, and personal interpretations by the speaker.
- identify any biases, self-interests, or prejudices that may lead the speaker to slant unfairly what is presented.

Responding

Responding occurs in two phases: (1) responses you make while the speaker is talking and (2) responses you make after the speaker has stopped talking. These responses are feedback—information that you send back to the speaker; this information tells the speaker how you feel and what you think about his or her messages. Responses made while the speaker is talking should be supportive and should acknowledge that you're listening to the speaker. These responses include what nonverbal researchers call **back-channeling cues,** such as "I see," "yes," "uh-huh," and similar signals that let the speaker know you're listening.

Responses made after the speaker has stopped talking are generally more elaborate and might include expressing empathy ("I know how you must feel"), asking for clarification ("Do you mean that this new health plan is to replace the old one?"), challenging ("I think your evidence is weak here"), and agreeing ("You're absolutely right on this; I'll support your proposal"). In responding, try to:

- be supportive of the speaker throughout the speaker's talk by using and varying your back-channeling cues; using only one back-channeling cue—for example, saying "uh-huh" throughout—will make it appear that you're not listening but are on automatic pilot.
- express support for the speaker in your final responses (especially).
- be honest; the speaker has a right to expect honest responses, even if they express disagreement.

- own your responses; state your thoughts and feelings as your own, and use I-messages (for example, "I think the new proposal will entail greater expense than you outlined" rather than "Everyone will object to the plan for costing too much").
- don't equate (as men are often accused of doing) "responding to another's feelings" with "solving the person's problems" (Tannen 1990); it's usually more productive to view your task in more limited terms: to encourage the person to express and perhaps to clarify his or her feelings and to provide a supportive atmosphere.

Table 7.2 identifies some types of difficult listeners and their problem-causing ways of responding. Review this table and try to see if it includes some of your own listening behaviors.

What one additional suggestion can you offer to make any one of the five stages of listening more effective or more accurate?

◀◀ THINKING BACK

LISTENING, CULTURE, AND GENDER

THINKING AHEAD ▶▶

Do people from different cultures listen differently? Do men and women listen differently?

Listening is difficult, in part, because of the inevitable differences in the communication systems between speaker and listener. Because each person has had a unique set of experiences, each person's meaning system is going to be different from each other person's. When speaker and listener come from different cultures or are of different genders, the differences and their effects are naturally much greater. Consider culture first.

TABLE 7.2 Some Problem-Causing Ways of Responding in Listening

Listener Type	Listening (Responding) Behavior	(Mis)interpreting Thoughts
The static listener	gives no feedback, remains relatively motionless, reveals no expression	Why isn't she reacting? Am I not producing sound?
The monotonous feedback giver	seems responsive but the responses never vary; regardless of what you say, the response is the same	Am I making sense? Why is he still smiling? I'm being dead serious.
The overly expressive listener	reacts to just about everything with extreme responses	Why is she so expressive? I didn't say anything that provocative. She'll have a heart attack when I get to the punchline.
The reader/writer	reads or writes while "listening" and only occasionally glances up	Am I that boring? Is last week's student newspaper more interesting than me?
The eye avoider	looks all around the room and at others but never at you	Why isn't he looking at me? Do I have spinach on my teeth?
The preoccupied listener	listens to other things at the same time, often with headphones with the sound so loud that it interferes with your own thinking	When is she going to shut that music off and really listen? Am I so boring that my talk needs background music?
The waiting listener	listens for a cue to take over the speaking turn	Is he listening to me or rehearsing his next interruption?
The thought completing listener	listens a little and then finishes your thought	Am I that predictable? Why do I bother saying anything? He already knows what I'm going to say.

ETHICS IN INTERPERSONAL COMMUNICATION Vote online at http://www.awl.com/devito

Listening

As a listener you have ethical obligations. First, you owe the speaker an *honest hearing*. Avoid prejudging the speaker. Try to put aside prejudices and preconceptions so you can evaluate the speaker's message fairly. At the same time, try to empathize with the speaker. You don't have to agree with the speaker, but try to understand emotionally as well as intellectually what the speaker means. Then, accept or reject the speaker's ideas on the basis of the information offered, and not on the basis of some bias or incomplete understanding.

Second, you owe the speaker *honest responses*. Just as you should be honest with the listener when speaking, you should be honest with the speaker when listening. This means giving open and honest feedback. It also means reflecting honestly on the questions that the speaker raises. Much as the listener has a right to expect an active speaker, the speaker has the right to expect an active listener. The speaker has a right to expect a listener who will actively deal with, rather than just passively hear, the message.

What would you do? *Your friend seems to have the need to reveal innermost secrets—problems at home, a lack of money, no friends, and on and on. You really don't want to hear all this; in fact, listening to this often depresses you. So you want to ignore these disclosures by making excuses to cut the conversation short or changing the subject. At the same time, however, you wonder about your ethical obligations to your friend and if you should listen openly and respond honestly. What would you do in this situation?*

Culture and Listening

Among the cultural differences we may consider are those concerning language, nonverbal communication, style, story versus evidence, credibility, and feedback. These will give you an idea of some of the many cultural factors that can influence listening.

Speech and Language Even when speaker and listener speak the same language, they speak it with different meanings and different accents. Every speaker speaks an idiolect; a unique variation of the language. Speakers of the same language will, at the very least, have different meanings for the same terms because they have had different experiences.

Speakers and listeners who have different native languages and who may have learned English as a second language will have even greater differences in meaning. Translations are never precise and never fully capture the meaning in the other language. Your meaning for "house" if learned in a culture in which everyone lived in their own house with lots of land around it is going to be very different from someone who learned the word living in a neighborhood of high-rise tenements. Although you will each hear the same word, the meanings you'll each create will be drastically different. In adjusting your listening—especially when in an intercultural setting—understand that the speaker's meanings may be very different from yours even though you're each speaking the same language.

Nonverbal Behavioral Differences Speakers from different cultures have different display rules, cultural rules that govern what nonverbal behaviors are appropriate and which are inappropriate in a public setting. As you listen to another person, you also "listen" to their nonverbals (Units 9, 12, and 13 cover this area). If these are drastically different from what you expect on the basis of the verbal message, you may see them as a kind of interference or perhaps as contradictory messages. Also, different cultures may give very different meanings to the same nonverbal gesture.

In many classrooms throughout the country, there's a wide range of accents. Those whose native language is a tonal one such as Chinese (where differences in pitch signal important meaning differences) may speak English with variations in pitch that may seem puzzling to others. Those whose native language is Japanese may have trouble distinguishing "l" from "r" since Japanese does not make this distinction. The native language acts as a filter and influences the accent given to the second language. Do you have special difficulties when listening to those who speak English with an accent? If so, what can you do about it?

Direct and Indirect Styles Some cultures—Western Europe and the United States, for example—favor **direct speech** in communication; they advise us to "say what you mean and mean what you say." Many Asian cultures, on the other hand, favor **indirect speech;** they emphasize politeness and maintaining a positive public image rather than absolute truth. Listen carefully to persons with different styles of directness. Consider the possibility that the meanings the speaker wishes to communicate with indirectness may be very different from the meanings you would communicate with indirectness.

Credibility What makes a speaker credible or believable will vary from one culture to another. In some cultures, people would claim that competence is the most important factor in, say, choosing a teacher for their pre-school children. In other cultures, the most important factor might be the goodness or morality of the teacher. Similarly, members of different cultures may perceive the **credibility** of the various media very differently. For example, members of a repressive society in which the government controls television news may come to attribute little credibility to such broadcasts. After all, they might reason, television news is simply what the government wants you to know. This may be hard to understand or even recognize by someone raised in the United States, for example, where the media are free of such political control.

Feedback Members of some cultures give very direct and very honest feedback. Speakers from these cultures—the United States is a good example—expect the feedback to be an honest reflection of what their listeners are feeling. In other cultures—Japan and Korea are good examples—it's more important to be positive, so speakers from these cultures may respond with compliments (say, in commenting on a business colleague's proposal) even though they don't feel it. Listen to feedback, as you would all messages, with the recognition that cultures view feedback differently.

Gender and Listening

Men and women learn different styles of listening just as they learn different styles for using verbal and nonverbal messages. Not surprisingly, these different styles can create major difficulties in opposite-sex interpersonal communication. According to Deborah Tannen (1990) in her best-selling *You Just Don't Understand: Women and Men in Conversation*, women seek to build rapport and establish a closer relationship and use listening to achieve these ends. Men, on the other hand, will play up their expertise, emphasize it, and use it in dominating the interaction. Women play down their expertise and are more interested in communicating supportiveness. Tannen argues that the goal of a man in conversation is to be given respect, so he seeks to show his knowledge and expertise. A woman, on the other hand, seeks to be liked, so she expresses agreement.

Men and women also show that they're listening in different ways. In conversation, a woman is more apt to give lots of listening cues such as interjecting "Yeah" or "Uh-uh," nodding in agreement, and smiling. A man is more likely to listen quietly, without giving lots of listening cues as feedback. Subsequent research seems to confirm Tannen's position. For example, an analysis of calls to a crisis center in Finland revealed that calls received by a female counselor were significantly longer for both men and women callers (Salminen and Glad 1992). It's likely that the greater number of listening cues given by the women encouraged the callers to keep talking. This same study also found that male callers were helped by "just listening," whereas women callers were helped by "empathic understanding."

Tannen argues, however, that men listen less to women than women listen to men. The reason, says Tannen, is that listening places the person in an inferior position, whereas speaking places the person in a superior position. Men may seem to assume a more argumentative posture while listening, as if getting ready to argue. They may also appear to ask questions that are more argumentative or that seek to puncture holes in your position as a way to play up their own expertise. Women are more likely to ask supportive questions and perhaps offer criticism that is more positive than men. Women let the speaker see that they're listening. Men, on the other hand, use fewer listening cues in conversation. Men and women act this way to both men and women; their customary ways of talking don't seem to change depending on whether the listener is male or female.

Can you recall a situation in which culture or gender differences in listening patterns created a problem in interpersonal communication?

◀◀ THINKING BACK

There is no evidence to show that these differences represent any negative motives on the part of men to prove themselves superior or of women to ingratiate themselves. Rather, these differences in listening seem largely the result of the way in which men and women have been socialized.

THINKING AHEAD ▶▶

Are there rules that you can follow to make listening more effective and efficient?

STYLES OF EFFECTIVE LISTENING

Because you listen for different purposes, the principles of effective listening should vary from one situation to another. The following five dimensions of listening illustrate the appropriateness of different listening modes for different communication situations.

WEB EXPLORATION
To learn more about styles of effective listening, go to www.awl.com/devito.

Participatory and Passive Listening

The general key to effective listening in interpersonal situations is active participation. Perhaps the best preparation for participatory listening is to act (physically and mentally) like a participant. For many people, this may be the most abused rule of effective listening. Recall, for example, how your body almost automatically reacts to important news: almost immediately, you assume an upright posture, cock your head to the speaker, and remain relatively still and quiet. You do this almost reflexively because this is the way you listen most effectively. Even more important than this physical alertness is mental alertness. As a listener, participate in the communication interaction as an equal partner with the speaker, as one who is emotionally and intellectually ready to engage in the sharing of meaning.

Effective participatory listening is expressive. Let the listener know that you're participating in the communication interaction. Nonverbally, maintain eye contact, focus your concentration on the speaker rather than on others present, and express your feelings facially. Verbally, ask appropriate questions, signal understanding with "I see" or "Yes," and express agreement or disagreement as appropriate.

Passive listening is, however, not without merit, and some recognition of its value is warranted. Passive listening—listening without talking or directing the speaker in any obvious way—is a powerful means of communicating acceptance. This is the kind of listening that people ask for when they say, "Just listen to me." They're essentially asking you to suspend your judgment and "just listen." Passive listening allows the speaker to develop his or her thoughts and ideas in the presence of another person who accepts but does not evaluate, who supports but does not intrude. By listening passively, you provide a supportive and receptive environment. Once that has been established, you may wish to participate in a more active way, verbally and nonverbally.

In regulating participatory and passive listening, realize that all listening is hard work. Unaided, people are likely to follow the law of least effort and do whatever is easiest. Combat this tendency. Avoid, too, "the entertainment syndrome," the expectation to be amused by a speaker (Floyd 1985). Realize, too, that whether participatory or passive, listening will be aided if you combat noise. Remove distractions or other interference (newspapers, magazines, stereos) so that your listening task will have less competition.

Avoid preoccupation with yourself or with external issues. Avoid focusing on your own performance in the interaction or on rehearsing your responses. Avoid, too, focusing on matters that are irrelevant to the interaction—for example, what you did Saturday night or your plans for this evening.

Use the thought-speech time differential effectively. Because you can process information faster than the average rate of speech, there is often a time lag. Use this time to summarize the speaker's thoughts, formulate questions, and draw connections between what the speaker says and what you already know.

Empathic and Objective Listening

If you want to understand what a person means and what a person is feeling, you need to listen empathically: feel with them, see the world as they see it, feel what they feel. Although **empathy** is preferred in most situations, at times you need to go beyond empathy and look at the situation more objectively. It's important to listen to a friend tell you how the entire world hates him or her and to understand how your friend feels and why. But at times you may need to look a bit more objectively at the situation and perhaps see beyond what your friend sees. Sometimes you have to put your empathic responses aside and listen with objectivity and detachment.

In adjusting your empathic and objective listening focus, see the sequence of events as punctuated from the speaker's point of view, and see how this can influence what the speaker says and does (Unit 2). View the speaker as an equal. Seek to understand thoughts and feelings. Don't consider your listening task finished until you have understood what the speaker is feeling as well as thinking.

To encourage openness and empathy, try to eliminate any physical or psychological barriers to equality; for example, step from behind the large desk separating you from your employees. Avoid interrupting, a sign that you feel what you have to say is more important. Avoid "offensive listening," the tendency to listen to bits and pieces of information that will help you attack the speaker or find fault with something the speaker has said.

Beware of the "friend-or-foe" factor that may lead you to distort messages because of your attitudes toward another person. For example, if you think Freddy is stupid, then it will take added effort to listen objectively to Freddy's messages and to hear anything that is clear or insightful.

Nonjudgmental and Critical Listening

Effective listening involves listening nonjudgmentally to help you understand and listening critically to help you make an evaluation or judgment. Listen first with an open mind to help you better understand the messages, and then supplement it with critical listening, which will help you better analyze and evaluate the messages. Effective listening requires that you exercise both levels.

Avoid distorting messages through oversimplification or **leveling**—the tendency to eliminate details and to simplify complex messages so that they're easier to remember. Also avoid filtering out unpleasant or undesirable messages; you may miss the very information you need to change your assumptions or your behaviors.

Recognize your own ethnic, national, or religious biases; everyone has them. They can easily interfere with accurate listening and cause you to distort messages, leading you to hear meanings that conform to your own biases, prejudices, and expectations. They may lead you to give increased importance to something because it confirms your biases or to minimize it because it contradicts them.

In your critical listening, recognize some of the popular fallacies such as the following (Lee and Lee 1972, 1995; Pratkanis and Aronson, 1991).

- *Name-calling* involves giving an idea, a group of people, or a political philosophy a bad name ("atheist," "Neo-Nazi," "cult"). In the opposite of name-calling, the speaker tries to make you accept some idea by associating it with things you value highly ("democracy," "free speech," "academic freedom"). Remember that labels are useful most of the time but can often obscure the actual person or idea. Listen first to evidence and argument; never take labels as evidence or reasons for judgment.
- *Testimonial* involves using the image associated with some person to gain your approval (if you respect the person) or your rejection (if you don't respect the person). This is the technique of advertisers who use people dressed up to look like doctors or plumbers or chefs to sell their products. Listen carefully to the person's credentials; be suspicious when you hear such phrases as "experts agree," "scientists say," "good cooks know," or "dentists advise." Ask yourself exactly who these experts are and what the source of their expertise is.

In Shakespeare's *Julius Caesar,* Marc Antony, delivering Caesar's funeral oration, says: "I come to bury Caesar, not to praise him. . . . The evil that men do lives after them. . . . The good is oft interred with their bones." Later Antony says: "For Brutus is an honorable man. . . . So are they all, all honorable men." But Antony did come to praise Caesar and to convince the crowd that Brutus was not an honorable man. He came to incite the crowd to avenge the death of Caesar. How would you describe the types of listening that Antony hoped the crowd would use?

- *Bandwagon* is a technique that tries to persuade you to accept or reject an idea or proposal because "everybody is doing it," so "jump on the bandwagon." You'll hear this technique used frequently during election time where results of polls are used to get you to join the group and vote for one person or another. Again, listen to the evidence; 50,000 Frenchmen—as the saying goes—can be wrong.
- *Agenda-setting* involves claiming that a particular issue is crucial and all others are unimportant and insignificant. This technique is used frequently in interpersonal conflict situations where each person may claim that her or his objection or need is the important one and that the other person's is unimportant. In almost all situations, and especially in interpersonal conflict situations, there are many issues and many sides to each issue. Often the person proclaiming "X is the issue" really means "I'll be able to get my way if you focus solely on X and ignore the other issues."
- *Attack* involves accusing another person (usually an opponent) of some serious wrong doing so that the issue under discussion never gets examined as in the "argument," "How can I ever believe you after you lied." Although a person's personal reputation and past behavior are often relevant, listen most carefully to the issue at hand. When personal attack draws attention away from other issues, then it becomes fallacious.

Surface and Depth Listening

In most messages, there is an obvious meaning that a literal reading of the words and sentences reveals. But there is often another level of meaning. Sometimes, it's the opposite of the expressed literal meaning; sometimes it seems totally unrelated. In reality, few messages have only one level of meaning. Most function on two or three levels at the same time. Consider some of these frequently heard messages: a friend asks you how you like his new haircut. Another friend asks you how you like her painting. On one level, the meaning is clear: do you like the haircut? Do you like the painting? It's reasonable to assume, however, that on another level your friends are asking you to say something positive—about his appearance, about her artistic ability. The parent who seems at first to be complaining about working hard at the office or in the home may be asking for appreciation. The child who talks about the unfairness of the other children in the playground may be asking for some expression of caring. To appreciate these other meanings, you need to engage in depth listening.

When listening interpersonally, be particularly sensitive to different levels of meaning. If you respond only to the surface-level communication (the literal meaning), you'll miss the opportunity to make meaningful contact with the other person's

ASK THE RESEARCHER

Becoming More Listenable

Although I think of myself as an interesting person, I do notice that I'm not really listened to as carefully or as intently as are my colleagues at work. Is there anything I can do to make people listen to me with greater interest and attention?

Your question is one that many of us face in our professional and personal lives. What we know about listening suggests that speakers need to present "listenable" messages—messages that are easily comprehended and remembered by their listeners. This requires that we engage listeners through our verbal and nonverbal messages alike, and the best way to do that is to be a storyteller. Think of your communication as a story; your task is to visualize your point so that the listener will cut through all the competing stimuli and focus on your message. Since we're bombarded with so much information, the soundbite phrase that visualizes your point quickly and succinctly is probably what will stick with your listener in his or her memory. It's not easy to be "listenable," but it's our only hope in connecting with listeners in today's cluttered, rapid-fire information age.

For further information see Andrew D. Wolvin and Carolyn G. Coakley, *Listening* (New York: McGraw-Hill, 1996), and Andrew D. Wolvin, Roy M. Berko, and Darlyn R. Wolvin, *The Public Speaker/The Public Listener* (Los Angeles: Roxbury, 1999).

—Andrew D. Wolvin (Ph.D., Purdue University) is a professor of communication at the University of Maryland, where he teaches courses in listening, communication management, and speechwriting. He also anchors a cable news show about aging.

feelings and real needs. For example, if you say to your parent, "You're always complaining. I bet you really love working so hard," you may be failing to answer a very real call for understanding and appreciation.

In regulating your surface and depth listening, focus on both verbal and nonverbal messages. Recognize both consistent and inconsistent "packages" of messages, and take these cues as guides to the meaning the speaker is trying to communicate. Ask questions when in doubt. Listen also to what is omitted.

Listen for both content and relational messages. The student who constantly challenges the teacher is on one level communicating disagreement over content. However, on another level—the relationship level—the student may be voicing objections to the instructor's authority or authoritarianism. If the instructor is to deal effectively with the student, he or she must listen and respond to both types of messages.

Don't disregard the literal (surface) meaning of interpersonal messages in your attempt to uncover the more hidden (deep) meanings. If you do, you'll quickly find that your listening problems disappear: no one will talk to you anymore. Balance your attention between the surface and the underlying meanings. Respond to the various levels of meaning in the messages of others as you would like others to respond to yours—sensitively but not obsessively, readily but not overambitiously. One listening expert advises you to use your two ears to hear what the person is saying but use your third ear to listen to why they're saying what they're saying (Rosen 1998).

Active and Inactive Listening

Active listening is one of the most important communication skills you can learn (Gordon 1975). Consider the following brief comment and some possible responses:

APHRODITE: That creep gave me a C on the paper. I really worked on that project, and all I get is a lousy C.

APOLLO: That's not so bad; most people got around the same grade. I got a C, too.

ATHENA: So what? This is your last semester. Who cares about grades anyway?

ACHILLES: You should be pleased with a C. Peggy and Michael both failed, and John and Judy got Ds.

DIANA: You got a C on that paper you were working on for the last three weeks? You sound really angry and hurt.

All four listeners are probably eager to make Aphrodite feel better, but they go about it in very different ways and, you can be sure, with very different outcomes. The first three listeners give fairly typical responses. Apollo and Athena both try to minimize the significance of a C grade, a common response to someone who has expressed displeasure or disappointment. Usually, it's also inappropriate. Although well-intentioned, this response does little to promote meaningful communication and understanding. Achilles tries to give the C grade a more positive meaning. Note, however, that all three listeners also say a great deal more: that Aphrodite should not be feeling unhappy, that these feelings are not legitimate. These responses deny the validity of these feelings and put Aphrodite in the position of having to defend them.

Diana, however, is different. Diana uses **active listening,** a process of sending back to the speaker what the listener thinks the speaker meant, both literally and emotionally. Active listening does not mean simply repeating the speaker's exact words. It's rather a process of putting into some meaningful whole your understanding of the speaker's total message—the verbal and the nonverbal, the content and the feelings.

Purposes of Active Listening Active listening serves a number of important purposes. First, *it shows that you're listening*, and often that is the only thing the speaker really wants—to know that someone cares enough to listen.

Second, it helps you *check how accurately you have understood what the speaker said and meant.* By reflecting back what you perceive to be the speaker's meaning, you give the speaker an opportunity to confirm, clarify, or amend your perceptions. In this way, future messages have a better chance of being relevant and purposeful.

Third, through active listening, *you express acceptance of the speaker's feelings*. Note that in the sample responses given, the first three listeners challenge the speaker; they refuse to give the expressed feelings legitimacy. The active listener accepts the speaker. The speaker's feelings are not challenged; rather, they're echoed in a sympathetic and empathic manner. (Not surprisingly, training in active listening helps to increase a person's empathy [Ikemi and Kubota 1996].) Note, too, that in the first three responses, the feelings of the speaker are denied without ever actually being identified. Diana, however, not only accepts these feelings but also identifies them explicitly, again allowing the opportunity for correction.

Interestingly enough, when confronted by a person in distress, those listeners who try to solve the person's problem or who veer off the issue by engaging in "chitchat" come away significantly more depressed than those listeners who show acceptance of the distressed person's problems or who use supportive listening techniques (Notarius and Herrick 1988).

Fourth, in active listening you *prompt the speaker to further explore his or her feelings and thoughts.* The active listening response gives the speaker the opportunity to elaborate on these feelings without having to defend them. Active listening sets the stage for meaningful dialogue, a dialogue of mutual understanding. In stimulating this further exploration, active listening also encourages the speaker to resolve his or her own conflicts.

TRY IT!
To learn more about techniques of active listening, go to www.awl.com/devito.

Techniques of Active Listening Three techniques will help you master active listening. At first, these principles may seem awkward and unnatural. With practice, however, they will flow and blend into a meaningful and effective dialogue.

1. *Paraphrase the speaker's meaning.* State in your own words what you think the speaker meant. This paraphrase helps to ensure understanding because the speaker can correct or modify your restatement. It also communicates your interest and your attention. Everyone wants to feel attended to, especially when angry or depressed. The active listening paraphrase confirms this.

   When you paraphrase the speaker's meanings, you give the speaker a kind of green light to go into more detail, to elaborate. Thus, when you echo the thought about the C grade, the speaker can elaborate on why that grade was important. Make your paraphrases objective; be careful not to lead the speaker in the direction you think best. Also, be careful that you don't maximize or minimize the speaker's emotions; try to echo these feelings as accurately as you can.
2. *Express understanding of the speaker's feelings.* In addition to paraphrasing the content, echo the feelings you believe the speaker expressed or implied. This enables you to check your perception of the speaker's feelings and provides the speaker with the opportunity to see his or her feelings more objectively. Expressing understanding is especially helpful when someone is angry, hurt, or depressed. Hearing these feelings objectively and seeing them from a less impassioned perspective will help in dealing effectively with them.

   Most of us hold back our feelings until we are certain that others will be accepting. We need to hear statements such as "I understand" and "I see how you feel." When we feel that our emotions are accepted, we then feel free to go into more detail. Active listening provides the speaker with this important opportunity.
3. *Ask questions.* Ask questions to make sure that you understand the speaker's thoughts and feelings and to secure additional helpful information. Design your questions to provide just enough stimulation and support for the speaker to express the thoughts and feelings he or she wants to express. Avoid questions that pry into irrelevant areas or that challenge the speaker in any way.

Consider this dialogue and note the active listening techniques used throughout:

PAT:	That creep demoted me. He told me I wasn't an effective manager. I can't believe he did that, after all I've done for this company.
CHRIS:	I can understand your anger. You've been manager for three or four months now, haven't you?
PAT:	A little over three months. I know I was on trial, but I thought I was doing a good job.
CHRIS:	Can you get another trial?
PAT:	Yes, he said I could try again in a few months. But I feel like a failure.
CHRIS:	I know what you mean. It's not a pleasant feeling. What else did he say?
PAT:	He said I had trouble getting the paperwork done on time.
CHRIS:	You've been late filing the reports?
PAT:	A few times.
CHRIS:	Is there a way to delegate the paperwork?
PAT:	No, but I think I know now what needs to be done.
CHRIS:	You sound as though you're ready to give that manager's position another try.

Participatory	____:____:____:____:____:____:____	Passive
Empathic	____:____:____:____:____:____:____	Objective
Nonjudgmental	____:____:____:____:____:____:____	Critical
Surface	____:____:____:____:____:____:____	Deep
Active	____:____:____:____:____:____:____	Inactive

Figure 7.3 Listening Choices
Effective listening is largely a matter of adjusting your behavior along such dimensions as these. Can you identify an interpersonal situation that would call for listening that is highly participatory, empathic, nonjudgmental, surface, and active and another situation that would call for listening that is passive, objective, critical, in depth, and inactive?

PAT: Yes, I think I am, and I'm going to let him know that I intend to apply in the next few months.

Even in this brief interaction, Pat has moved from unproductive anger with the supervisor as well as a feeling of failure to a determination to correct an unpleasant situation. Note, too, that Chris didn't offer solutions but "simply" listened actively.

As stressed throughout this discussion, listening is situational; the type of listening that is appropriate varies with the situation. You can visualize a listening situation as one in which you have to make choices among at least the five dimensions of listening just discussed (Figure 7.3). Each listening situation should call for a somewhat different configuration of listening responses; the art of effective listening is largely one of making appropriate choices along these five dimensions.

What would be the appropriate listening mode if you wanted to help a friend who wanted to talk about relationship problems? What would be the appropriate mode if you wanted to listen to an instructor explaining the theory of linguistic relativity?

◀◀ THINKING BACK

REVIEWING KEY TERMS AND CONCEPTS IN LISTENING IN INTERPERSONAL COMMUNICATION

This unit focused on the nature of listening, the influence of culture and gender, and the dimensions of listening that you need to consider to listen effectively.

The Listening Process

What is listening? What purposes does listening serve?

- Listening is an active process of receiving, understanding, remembering, evaluating, and responding to communications.
- Listening enables you (1) to learn, to acquire information; (2) to relate, to help form and maintain relationships; (3) to influence, to have an effect on the attitudes and behaviors of others; (4) to play, to enjoy oneself; and (5) to help, to assist others.

Listening, Culture, and Gender

How is listening influenced by culture and gender?

- Members of different cultures vary on a number of communication dimensions that influence listening: speech and language, nonverbal behavioral differences, preferences for direct and indirect styles of communication, the way they evaluate the credibility of the speaker, and the ways they give feedback.
- Men and women may listen differently; generally, women give more specific listening cues to show they're listening than do men.

Styles of Effective Listening

What are your listening options?

- *Participatory-passive listening* refers to the extent to which you participate actively in the interaction
- *Empathic-objective listening* refers to the extent to which you focus on feeling what the speaker is feeling
- *Nonjudgmental-critical listening* refers to the extent to which you accept and support the speaker
- *Surface-depth listening* refers to the extent to which you focus on the obvious surface meanings
- *Active-Inactive listening* refers to the extent to which you reflect back what you think the speaker means in content and feeling

APPLYING KEY TERMS AND CONCEPTS IN LISTENING IN INTERPERSONAL COMMUNICATION

1. Are you satisfied with the level of listening that others give you? How might you go about increasing their level of active and empathic listening?
2. Would it be more difficult to empathize with someone who is overjoyed because of winning the lottery for $7 million or with someone who is overcome with sadness because of the death of a loved one? How easy would it be for you to empathize with someone who was depressed because the expected bonus of $40,000 turned out to be only $25,000?
3. Rob, a server at the Dinner Diner, is efficient in most areas but frequently makes mistakes in taking the customers' orders. This often results in customer dissatisfaction and ruined meals, and it irritates the temperamental cook. Rob's supervisor says that he doesn't listen effectively. What specific advice might his supervisor give Rob to improve his listening effectiveness?
4. Do you engage in much active listening? Do your close friends practice active listening when they listen to you? Can you give a specific example of active listening that you were recently involved in?
5. How would you describe your own culture's teachings and rules as they might influence listening in the classroom or in the workplace?
6. Have you ever "heard" what you hoped or expected to hear, only to find out later that what you heard was different from what was said?
7. Is your classroom listening ever characterized by your filtering out unpleasant or difficult messages or messages that contradict your own deeply held beliefs? What effects might this have?
8. How might sharpening (the process of message distortion in which the details of messages, when repeated, are crystallized and heightened) work in workplace gossip? In campus gossip?
9. What types of listening would you use (and which types would you definitely not use) in each of the following situations: (a) your steady dating partner for the last five years tells you that spells of depression are becoming more frequent and more long lasting; (b) an instructor lectures on the contribution of the Ancient Greeks to modern civilization; (c) a physician discusses your recent physical tests and recommendations; (d) a salesperson tells you the benefits of the new computer; (e) a gossip columnist details the secret life of your favorite movie star.
10. How would you go about finding answers to such questions as these:
    - Are women and men equally effective as listeners?
    - What kinds of listening make health professional-patient communication more effective? More personally satisfying?
    - What attitudes do business executives have toward listening and its importance in the workplace?
    - Do men or women differ in the empathic abilities? In their empathic behaviors?
    - Would some cultures respond negatively to active listening?

EXPERIENCING KEY TERMS AND CONCEPTS IN LISTENING IN INTERPERSONAL COMMUNICATION

Go to www.awl.com/devito

Exercise No. 7, "Sequential Listening," illustrates the difficulties involved in listening and some of the types of errors that occur. Exercise No. 16, "Giving and Taking Directions," will further illustrate the difficulties in listening and the importance of using clear and specific directions.

UNIT 8
EFFECTIVENESS IN INTERPERSONAL COMMUNICATION

As Good as It Gets (1997)

THEIR REMARKS AND RESPONSES WERE LIKE A PING-PONG GAME WITH EACH VOLLEY CLEARING THE NET AND FLYING BACK TO THE OPPOSITION.

--MAYA ANGELOU

In James L. Brooks's As Good as It Gets, Jack Nicholson plays a most ineffective communicator—at least at the beginning—and becomes involved in the lives of a waitress (Helen Hunt) and a neighbor (Greg Kinnear). As these relationships develop, Nicholson's character learns to communicate and in the process becomes more human.

Your interpersonal communication, like any of your behaviors, can vary from extremely effective to extremely ineffective. Still, no interpersonal encounter is ever a total failure or a total success; each could have been worse and each could have been better.

Interpersonal skills exist on two levels. On the specific level, there are the skills of being open or empathic, for example. These skills help you express your openness and empathy when you wish. On a higher level—a metaskill level—there are skills for regulating the specific skills. These metaskills—for example, flexibility and cultural sensitivity—help you regulate your openness and empathy as the specific situation warrants. For example, in being open or empathic, you need to do so with flexibility and with sensitivity to the specific cultural context. Both types of skills are essential to interpersonal effectiveness.

The skills identified here come from research conducted primarily over the last 25 years by a large number of interpersonal communication researchers (Gibb 1961, Hart and Burks 1972, Hart, Carlson, and Eadie 1980, Bochner and Kelly 1974, Wiemann 1977, Spitzberg and Hecht 1984, Rubin and Nevins 1988, Spitzberg and Cupach 1984, 1989, Watzlawick, Beavin, and Jackson 1967, Watzlawick 1977, Lederer 1984, Lederer and Jackson 1968, Kim 1991). What follows is a synthesis.

THINKING AHEAD ▸▸
What general skills should govern your interpersonal communications?

SKILLS ABOUT SKILLS

Four metaskills will help you regulate your use of the more specific skills: mindfulness, flexibility, cultural sensitivity, and metacommunication.

Mindfulness

After you've learned a skill or rule, you may have a tendency to apply it without thinking, or "mindlessly"—without, for example, considering the novel aspects of the situation. For instance, after learning the skills of active listening, many will use them in response to all situations. Some of these responses will be appropriate, but others will be inappropriate and ineffective. In interpersonal and even in small-group communication (Elmes and Gemmill 1990), apply the skills mindfully (Langer 1989). Here are several suggestions for increasing **mindfulness** that will prove useful in most interpersonal situations (Langer 1989). As you read through these suggestions, try to provide a specific example or application for each of these four suggestions.

First, *create and recreate categories*. See an object, event, or person as belonging to a wide variety of categories. For example, learn to see your prospective romantic partner in a variety of roles—child, parent, employee, neighbor, friend, financial contributor, and so on. Avoid storing in memory an image of a person, for example, with only one specific label; it will be difficult to recategorize the image later.

Second, *be open to new information and points of view,* especially if these contradict your most firmly held stereotypes. New information will force you to reconsider what might be outmoded ways of thinking and looking at things. It can help you challenge long-held but now inappropriate beliefs and attitudes. Being open to different points of view will help you avoid the tendency to blame outside forces for your negative behaviors ("That test was unfair") and internal forces for the negative behaviors of others ("Pat didn't study," "Pat isn't very bright"). Be willing to see your own and others' behaviors from a variety of perspectives.

Third, *beware of relying too heavily on first impressions* (Chanowitz and Langer 1981, Langer 1989). Treat your first impressions as tentative, as hypotheses, that you can investigate further. Perhaps most important, be prepared to revise or reject (as well as accept) these initial impressions.

Flexibility

Before reading about **flexibility,** try taking the accompanying self-test, "How Flexible in Communication Are You?"

TEST YOURSELF *How Flexible in Communication Are You?*

Here are some situations that illustrate how people sometimes act when communicating with others. The first part of each situation asks you to imagine that you are in the situation. Then a course of action is identified and you are asked to determine how much your own behavior would be like the action described in the scenario. Respond to each statement according to the following scale: 1 = *not at all* like you, 2 = *not much* like you, 3 = *somewhat* like you, 4 = *a lot* like you, and 5 = *exactly* like you.

Imagine:

______ 1. Last week, as you were discussing your strained finances with your family, family members came up with several possible solutions. Even though you had already decided on one solution, you decided to spend more time considering all the possibilities before making a final decision.

______ 2. You were invited to a Halloween party and, assuming it was a costume party, you dressed as a pumpkin. When you arrived at the party and found everyone else dressed in formal attire, you laughed and joked about the misunderstanding and decided to stay and enjoy the party.

______ 3. You have always enjoyed being with your friend Chris but do not enjoy Chris's habit of always interrupting you. The last time you met, every time Chris interrupted you, you then interrupted Chris to teach Chris a lesson.

______ 4. Your daily schedule is very structured and your calendar is full of appointments and commitments. When asked to make a change in your schedule, you replied that changes are impossible before even considering the change.

______ 5. You went to a party where over 50 people attended. You had a good time but spent most of the evening talking to one close friend rather than meeting new people.

______ 6. When discussing a personal problem with a group of friends, you notice that many different solutions were offered. Although several of the solutions seemed feasible, you already had your opinion and did not listen to any of the alternative solutions.

______ 7. You and a friend are planning a fun evening and you're dressed and ready ahead of time. You find that you are unable to do anything else until your friend arrives.

_______ 8. When you found your seat at the ball game, you realized you did not know anyone sitting nearby. However, you introduced yourself to the people sitting next to you and attempted to strike up a conversation.

_______ 9. You had lunch with your friend Chris, and Chris told you about a too-personal family problem. You quickly finished your lunch and stated that you had to leave because you had a lot to do that afternoon.

_______ 10. You were involved in a discussion about international politics with a group of acquaintances and you assumed that the members of the group were as knowledgeable as you on the topic, but as the discussion progressed, you learned that most of the group knew little about the subject. Instead of explaining your point of view, you decided to withdraw from the discussion.

_______ 11. You and a group of friends got into a discussion about gun control, and after a while, it became obvious that your opinions differed greatly from the rest of the group. You explained your position once again, but you agreed to respect the group's opinion also.

_______ 12. You were asked to speak to a group you belong to, so you worked hard preparing a 30-minute presentation, but at the meeting, the organizer asked you to lead a question and answer session instead of giving your presentation. You agreed and answered the group's questions as candidly and fully as possible.

_______ 13. You were offered a managerial position where every day you would face new tasks and challenges and a changing day-to-day routine. You decided to accept this position instead of one that has a stable daily routine.

_______ 14. You were asked to give a speech at a Chamber of Commerce breakfast. Because you did not know anyone at the breakfast and would feel uncomfortable not knowing anyone in the audience, you declined the invitation.

To compute your score:

1. Reverse the scoring for items 4, 5, 6, 7, 9, 10, and 14. That is, for each of these questions, substitute as follows: If you answered 5, reverse it to 1. If you answered 4, reverse it to 2. If you answered 3, it remains 3. If you answered 2, reverse it to 4. If you answered 1, reverse it to 5.
2. Add the scores for all 14 items. Be sure that you use the reversed scores for items 4, 5, 6, 7, 9, 10, and 14 instead of your original responses. Use your original scores for items 1, 2, 3, 8, 11, 12, and 13.

In general, you can interpret your score as follows:

65–70 = much more flexible than average
57–64 = more flexible than average
44–56 = about average
37–43 = less flexible than average
14–36 = much less flexible than average

Do you agree with the assumption made that flexibility is an essential ingredient in communication effectiveness? What might you do to cultivate greater communication flexibility?

Source: This scale was developed by Matthew M. Martin and Rebecca B. Rubin, "Development of a Communication Flexibility Measure," *Southern Communication Journal* 59 (Winter 1994): 171–178, and is reprinted by permission. ■

Another popular test of flexibility includes statements such as "People should be frank and spontaneous in conversation," "When angry, a person should say nothing rather than say something he or she will be sorry for later," and "It is better to speak your gut feelings than to beat around the bush." The test asks you to indicate how true you believe these statements to be. The "preferred" answer to all such questions, "sometimes true," underscores the importance of flexibility in all interpersonal encounters (Hart and Burks 1972, Hart, Carlson, and Eadie 1980). Although we provide general principles for effective interpersonal communication, be flexible when applying them and be sensitive to the unique factors of every situation. Thus, you may need to be frank and spontaneous when talking with a close friend about your feelings, but you may not want to be so open when talking with your grandmother about the dinner she prepared that you disliked.

Cultural Sensitivity

In applying the skills for interpersonal effectiveness, be sensitive to the cultural differences among people. What may prove effective for high-income people working in the IBM subculture of Boston or New York may prove ineffective for low-income people working as fruit pickers in Florida or California. What works in Japan may not work in Mexico. The close physical distance that is normal in Arab cultures may prove too familiar or too intrusive in much of the United States and Northern Europe. The empathy that most Americans welcome may be uncomfortable for the average Korean (Yun 1976). The specific skills discussed below are considered generally effective in the United States and among most people living in the United States. In Unit 3 we identified several guidelines for more effective intercultural communication; they're the same principles to follow in achieving cultural sensitivity.

- Prepare yourself. Read. Listen. Watch.
- Recognize and face fears.

ASK THE RESEARCHER

Becoming More Flexible

I completed your flexibility scale and, unfortunately, I came out "much less flexible than average." Is there anything I can do to become more flexible in my communications and in general as a person?"

Understanding the importance of being flexible and wanting to be more flexible are important first steps in becoming more flexible. Before you can increase your flexibility, you must (a) become aware that in any given situation there are options and alternative ways of communicating available, (b) be willing to adapt to different people and situations, and (c) have the confidence to adapt and possibly try new behaviors.

One suggestion for improving flexibility would include thinking beforehand of how you could communicate in different ways in a given situation. Flexibility requires that you be able to adapt to the demands of the specific situation; there is no one right or wrong way of communicating. Another suggestion would be to embrace rather than avoid different and new experiences. Talk to people you would normally not talk to, attend events that may not fall under your primary interests, try doing an activity you have not attempted before.

For further information see M. M. Martin and C. M. Anderson, "The Cognitive Flexibility Scale: Three Validity Studies," *Communication Reports* 11 (1998): 1–10, and M. M. Martin and R. B. Rubin, "A New Measure of Cognitive Flexibility," *Psychological Reports* 76 (1995): 623–626.

—Matt Martin (Ph.D., Kent State University) is an associate professor of communication studies at West Virginia University and teaches courses in interpersonal and nonverbal communication and conducts research in communication traits, including flexibility and aggressiveness. mmartin@wvu.edu.

- Recognize differences between yourself and the culturally different.
- Be careful not to ignore differences within the culturally different group.
- Recognize differences in meaning.
- Avoid violating cultural rules and customs.

Metacommunicational Ability

Metacommunication is communication that refers to other communications; it's communication about communication. All behavior, verbal and nonverbal, can be metacommunicational. Verbally, you can say, for example, "This statement is false" or "Do you understand what I am trying to tell you?" Because these sentences refer to communication, they're called metacommunicational statements.

Nonverbal behavior may also be metacommunicational. Obvious examples include crossing one's fingers behind one's back or winking when telling a lie. But the more subtle instances of metacommunication are more interesting: as you say "I had a really nice time" to your blind date, the nonverbal messages—the lack of a smile, the failure to maintain eye contact, the extra-long pauses—contradict the verbal "really nice time" and tell your date that you didn't enjoy the evening.

Nonverbal messages may also metacommunicate about other nonverbal messages. The individual who both smiles and avoids direct eye contact or extends a totally lifeless hand shows how one nonverbal behavior may contradict another. Usually when nonverbal behavior is metacommunicational, it reinforces other verbal or nonverbal behavior. You smile when greeting someone, run to meet the person you say you're eager to see, or arrive early for a party you verbally express pleasure in attending. On the negative—though still consistent—side, you may arrive late for a dental appointment (presumably with a less-than-pleasant facial expression) or frown when telling off your boss.

Your interpersonal effectiveness often hinges on this ability to metacommunicate. Let's say that someone says something positive but in a negative way; for example, the person says, "Yes, I think you did [long pause] a good job," shows no enthusiasm, and avoids eye contact. Here you're faced with several alternatives: (1) You may respond to the message as positive (saying "Thank you" and ignoring the nonverbal negative tone). (2) You may respond to the negative message (saying "What did I do wrong?" and ignoring the verbal message stating that you did a good job. (3) A third alternative, however, is to talk about the message—to metacommunicate—and say something like, "I'm not sure I understand whether you're pleased or displeased with what I did. You said you were pleased, but I detect dissatisfaction in your voice. Am I wrong?" In this way, you may avoid lots of misunderstandings. Here are a few suggestions for increasing your metacommunicational effectiveness:

Give Clear Feedforward This will help the other person get a general picture of the message that will follow; feedforward provides a kind of schema that makes information processing and learning easier.

Confront Contradictory or Inconsistent Messages At the same time, explain messages of your own that may appear inconsistent to your listener.

Explain the Feelings that go with the Thoughts Often people communicate only the thinking part of their message, with the result that listeners aren't able to appreciate the other parts of the meaning.

Paraphrase Your Own Complex Messages Similarly, to check on your understanding of another's message, paraphrase what you think the other person means and ask whether you're accurate.

Negotiate Meanings If you have doubts about another's meaning, don't assume; instead, ask, even in the middle of a conversation (Varonis and Gass 1985, Gudykunst 1991). In intercultural situations, the request for clarification usually comes from the person whose native language is the language being used (Gudykunst 1991).

Talk About Your Talk Only to Gain an Understanding of the Other Person's Thoughts and Feelings Avoid substituting talk about talk for talk about a specific problem. For example, if you're discussing (even arguing) with your partner about what to do with unexpected bonus money, avoid refocusing the discussion on the way the other person is arguing and, instead, focus on what to do with the bonus money.

Which of these four general skills do you find the most important in, say, communicating on your job? In communicating in an intercultural situation?

◂◂ THINKING BACK

A HUMANISTIC MODEL OF INTERPERSONAL EFFECTIVENESS

THINKING AHEAD ▸▸

What is it that makes you want to communicate with some people but not others? What distinguishes the person you want to talk with from the person you don't want to talk with?

In the humanistic (sometimes referred to metaphorically as "soft") approach to interpersonal effectiveness presented here, five general qualities are considered: openness, empathy, supportiveness, positiveness, and equality. In general, these qualities foster meaningful, honest, and satisfying interactions. This approach begins with the qualities that philosophers and humanists feel define superior human relationships,

ETHICS IN INTERPERSONAL COMMUNICATION

Vote online at http://www.awl.com/devito

Speaking

Here are four guidelines that should prove useful in defining the ethical responsibilities of the interpersonal communicator. You may wish to blend these with the discussion of ethical obligations in workplace interactions (see Ethics in Interpersonal Communication box, Ethics on the Job, in Unit 22).

- *Truth.* Present the truth as you understand it; avoid misrepresenting the truth because it might better fit your purpose.
- *Knowledge and Preparation.* If you talk on a specific subject—as a parent advising your children or as a friend giving advice—be so informed, so knowledgeable, that your listeners will be able to get the information they need to make reasoned and reasonable choices.
- *Other Centered.* Have the other person's interests in mind. Communication should not be used to exploit others.
- *Accountability.* Take responsibility for what you say. Communication researcher Jon Hess (1993) suggests that you should tell your listeners if you're not sure of certain information, make clear when you're using facts and when you're using opinions, and avoid misleading your listeners by encouraging them to believe what is not true.

What would you do? *At a job interview, you're asked about your PowerPoint skills. You have a general idea of how to use this program but would have to learn a great deal more to really master the program. You realize that your answer to this question may determine whether or not you get the job and you really want this job. So you want to say that your skills are excellent. Between now and beginning the job, you'd try to learn more about PowerPoint. What would be the most effective thing to say? What would be the ethically responsible thing to say? What would you do in this situation?*

and from these generalizations it derives specific behaviors that should characterize effective interpersonal communication.

TRY IT!
To learn more about openness, go to www.awl.com/devito.

Openness

Openness refers to at least three aspects of interpersonal communication. First, it refers to your willingness to self-disclose—to reveal information about yourself that might normally be kept hidden—provided that such disclosure is appropriate (see Unit 4). Openness shown by only one person is usually insufficient. For interpersonal communication to be effective, it must be *bilateral:* "the exchange of personal, private information must be reciprocal" (Montgomery 1981).

Second, openness refers to a willingness to react honestly to the messages of others. Silent, uncritical, and immovable psychiatrists may be of some help in a clinical situation, but they're generally boring conversationalists. Usually we want people to react openly to what we say, and we feel we have a right to expect this. We demonstrate openness by responding spontaneously and without subterfuge to the communications and the feedback of others.

Third, openness refers to the "owning" of feelings and thoughts. To be open in this sense is to acknowledge that the feelings and thoughts you express are yours and that you bear the responsibility for them; you don't try to shift the responsibility for your feelings to others. For example, consider these comments:

1. Your behavior was grossly inconsiderate.
2. Everyone thought your behavior was grossly inconsiderate.
3. I was really disturbed when you told my father he was an old man.

ASK THE RESEARCHER

Becoming Less Interpersonally Awkward

My roommate is an interpersonal clod. I'm embarrassed at social situations because conversations are awkward and others have to work pretty hard to keep the conversation going. What to do?

Your roommate needs to work on some basic interpersonal skills. For instance, if your roommate is apprehensive about interacting with others, relaxation should be enhanced to allow him/her to feel more comfortable and secure. If there is trouble with interaction management, perhaps the two of you could practice shifting topics smoothly, negotiating which topic gets discussed next, and being perceptive about meanings. If your roommate has difficulty focusing on the other person, perhaps you could practice some techniques to show support, to be more attentive, and to be more responsive. Some people don't understand that both communicators in a dyad are responsible for carrying on the conversation and that sometimes this requires flexibility and adaptability. You can't just tell someone to be more flexible, but you can enlarge the number of strategies that people have by increasing successful experiences. Your roommate may just need more experience, and you can help by offering additional conversation opportunities, even though they may be painful at the beginning.

For more information see R. B. Rubin, "Development of a Measure of Interpersonal Communication Competence," *Communication Research Reports* 11 (1994): 33–44, and R. B. Rubin and R. A. Nevins, *The Road Trip: An Interpersonal Adventure* (Prospect Heights, IL: Waveland, 1988).

—Rebecca B. Rubin (Ph.D., University of Illinois) is a professor of communication studies at Kent State University and teaches courses in interpersonal communication, research methods, and communication competence. She has developed various scales, indexes, and tests of communication skills and has worked with the National Communication Association and U.S. Department of Education on identifying essential skills for college students. rrubin@kent.edu.

Comments 1 and 2 do not demonstrate ownership of feelings. In comment 1, the speaker accuses the listener of being inconsiderate without assuming any responsibility for the judgment. In comment 2, the speaker assigns responsibility to the convenient but vague "everyone" and again assumes none of the responsibility. In comment 3, however, we see a drastic difference. Note that here the speaker is taking responsibility for his or her own feelings ("I was really disturbed").

When you own your messages, you use **I-messages** instead of **you-messages.** Instead of saying, "You make me feel so stupid when you ask what everyone else thinks but don't ask my opinion," you would own your feelings and say, for example, "I feel stupid when you ask everyone else what they think but don't ask me." When you own your feelings and thoughts—when you use I-messages—you say, in effect, "This is how *I* feel," "This is how *I* see the situation," and "This is what *I* think," with the *I* always emphasized. Instead of saying, "This discussion is useless," you would say, "*I'm* bored by this discussion," "*I* want to talk more about myself," or any other such statement that includes a reference to the fact that you're making an evaluation and not describing objective reality. By doing so, you make it explicit that your feelings result from the interaction between what is going on outside your skin (what others say, for example) and what is going on inside your skin (your preconceptions, attitudes, and prejudices, for example).

Empathy

Perhaps the most difficult communication quality to achieve is the ability to empathize with another person. The term **empathy** was derived from Greek to translate the German word *Einfuhlung,* meaning "feeling with." To empathize with someone is to feel as that person feels, to experience what the other is experiencing from that person's point of view without losing your own identity. To sympathize, in contrast, is to feel *for* the person—to feel sorry for the person, for example. To empathize is to feel as the person feels, to walk in the same shoes, to feel the same feelings in the same way. Empathy, then, enables you to understand, emotionally as well as intellectually, what another person is experiencing.

Animal researchers have argued that some animals show empathy. For example, consider the male gorilla who watched a female try in vain to get water that collected in an automobile tire and who then secured the tire and brought it to the female. This gorilla, it has been argued, demonstrated empathy; he felt the other gorilla's thirst (Angier 1995b). Similarly, the animal who cringes when another of its species gets hurt seems also to be showing empathy.

To achieve empathy, try to remain relatively calm, free yourself from your own intense emotions as much as you can (Goleman 1995a). If you're angry, for example, you'll be so caught up in your own anger that you'll be unable to feel or even hear the other person's anger or sadness or fear.

Should you wish to achieve empathy, your first step is to resist evaluating the other person's behaviors. If you evaluate them as right or wrong, good or bad, you will see the behaviors through these labels and will fail to see a great deal more that might not be consistent with them. Therefore, resist the temptation to evaluate, to judge, to interpret, to criticize. Focus, instead, on understanding.

Second, learn as much as you can about the other person's desires, experiences, abilities, fears, and so on. The more you know about a person, the more you'll be able to see what that person sees and feel what that person feels. Try to understand the reasons and the motivations for the person's feelings.

Third, try to experience emotionally what the other person is feeling from his or her point of view. Playing the role of the other person in your mind (or even out loud) can help you see the world a little more as the other person does. This will prove especially difficult in conflict situations where people normally emphasize their own needs and feelings rather than those of the other person (Schutz 1999).

You can communicate empathy nonverbally and verbally (Authier and Gustafson 1982). For example, one way is to focus your concentration; maintain eye contact, an attentive body posture, and physical closeness. Express your active involvement with the other person through appropriate facial expressions and gestures.

Reflect back to the speaker the feelings (and their intensity) that you think are being experienced to help you check on the accuracy of your perceptions and to show your desire to understand the speaker's feelings. In doing so, you may find it helpful to make tentative statements about what you think the person is feeling: for example, "I get the impression you're angry with your father" or "I hear anger in your voice."

When appropriate consider using your own self-disclosures to communicate your understanding of and involvement in what the other is experiencing. Be careful, however, that you don't get so caught up in your own disclosures that you refocus the discussion on yourself.

Still another way is to address mixed messages. This will help to foster more open and honest communication. When your friend verbally expresses contentment but shows nonverbal signs of depression it may be prudent to question the apparent discrepancy.

Although empathy is almost universally considered positive, there is some evidence to show that it has a negative side. For example, people are most empathic with those who are similar—racially and ethnically as well as in appearance and social status. The more empathy one feels toward one's own group, the less empathy—possibly even hostility—one feels toward other groups. The same empathy that increases your understanding of your own group decreases your understanding of other groups. So while empathy may encourage group cohesiveness and identification, it can also create dividing lines between one's own group and "them" (Angier 1995b).

Supportiveness

Supportiveness is fostered by your being (1) descriptive rather than evaluative and (2) provisional rather than certain (cf. Gibb 1961).

Most people find it easier to communicate empathy in response to a person's positive statements (Heiskell and Rychiak 1986). So perhaps we have to exert special effort to communicate empathy for negative statements. In which type of situations do you find it easier to communicate empathy?

Descriptiveness Consider the following sentence sets:

1A. I can't wait to meet him.
1B. He sure is great looking.
1C. His hair is black and his eyes are green.
2A. I'm sure glad we went on strike for this contract.
2B. That contract was ideal for labor but will cripple management.
2C. Workers got a 12 percent raise, more than at any other plant.

Note that the A and C sentences are descriptive. The A sentences describe one's own feelings; the C sentences describe the situation, the "reality." The B sentences, however—which are similar in form to the others—are evaluative. These sentences express the speaker's judgment or evaluation of a person or situation.

An atmosphere that is descriptive rather than evaluative leads to supportiveness. When you perceive a communication as being a request for information or a description of some event, you generally don't perceive it as threatening. You aren't being challenged and have no need to defend yourself. However, a communication that is judgmental or evaluative often leads you to become defensive, to back off, to erect some kind of barrier between yourself and the evaluator.

This does not mean that all evaluative communications elicit a defensive response. People often respond to positive evaluations without **defensiveness.** Even here, however, note that if someone has the power, the knowledge, or the "right" to evaluate you in any way (even positively), it may lead you to feel uneasy and possibly defensive, perhaps anticipating that the next evaluation may not be as favorable.

In a similar way, negative evaluations don't always elicit a defensive response. The would-be actor who wants to improve technique often welcomes negative evaluations. Similarly, many students welcome negative evaluations when they feel they're constructive and lead to improvement in their ability, for example, to communicate or to operate a computer program. Generally, however, an evaluative atmosphere leads people to become more defensive than would a descriptive atmosphere.

In being descriptive (Brougher 1982):

- Describe what happened ("I lost the promotion").
- Describe how you feel ("I feel miserable," "I feel I've failed").
- Explain how this relates to the other person ("Would you mind if we went into the city tonight? I need to forget the job and everything about it").
- Avoid accusations or blame ("I should have stayed with my old job and not listened to your brother's lousy advice").
- Avoid negative evaluative terms ("Didn't your sister look horrible in that red dress?")
- Avoid "preaching" ("Why don't you learn something about word processing before you open your mouth?").

Provisionalism Being provisional means having a tentative, open-minded attitude and a willingness both to hear opposing points of view and to change one's position if warranted. Such **provisionalism,** rather than unwavering **certainty,** helps to create a supportive atmosphere. Compare these two observations:

TRY IT!
To learn more about provisionalism, go to www.awl.com/devito.

1. It's obvious. She just doesn't know the first thing about caring for a relationship. She's so egocentric.
2. It seems to me that she is having trouble in her relationship. Maybe she's too caught up in herself.

Note that sentence 1 claims certainty; it's definite and provides for no other possibility. Sentence 2 expresses essentially the same thought but with a tentativeness, a provisionalism. It's relatively difficult to say anything in response to sentence 1; it appears that everything that needs to be said has already been said. Sentence 2, however, invites comment, involvement, further discussion.

People who "know everything" and who always have a definite answer to any question are rarely appreciated. Such people are set in their ways and seem to tolerate no differences. They have arguments ready for any possible alternative attitude or belief. After a very short time, we become defensive with such people, and we hold back our own opinions rather than subject them to attack. But we open up with people who take a more provisional position, who are willing to change their minds when reasonable arguments are presented. With such people we feel equal.

Positiveness

You can communicate **positiveness** in interpersonal communication in at least two ways: (1) stating positive attitudes and (2) complimenting the person with whom you interact.

Attitudes *Attitudinal positiveness* in interpersonal communication refers to a positive regard for oneself, for the other person, and for the general communication situation. Your feelings (whether positive or negative) become clear during conversation and greatly influence the satisfaction (or dissatisfaction) you derive from the interaction. Negative feelings usually make communication more difficult and can contribute to its eventual breakdown.

Positiveness is seen most clearly in the way you phrase statements. Consider these two sets of sentences:

1A. I wish you wouldn't handle me so roughly.
1B. I really enjoy it when you're especially gentle.
2A. You look horrible in stripes.
2B. You look your best, I think, in solid colors.

The A sentences are negative; they're critical and will almost surely encourage an argument. The B sentences, in contrast, express the speaker's thought clearly but are phrased positively and should encourage cooperative responses.

Compliments Another aspect of positiveness is *complimenting,* behavior that acknowledges the existence of some positive quality in another person or some action that you evaluate positively. Many people, in fact, structure interpersonal encounters almost solely for the purpose of getting complimented. People may buy new clothes to get complimented, compliment associates so that the associates compliment back, do favors for people to receive thanks, associate with certain people because they're generous with their compliments, and so on. Some people even enter relationships because they hold the promise of frequent compliments.

What constitutes an appropriate compliment will naturally vary with the culture (Dresser 1996). For example, in the United States it would be considered appropriate for a teacher to publicly compliment a student on getting the highest grade in an examination or for a supervisor to compliment a worker for doing an exceptional job on some project. But in other cultures (collectivist cultures, for example) this would be considered inappropriate because it singles out the individual and separates that person from the group. Similarly, the responses to compliments will vary from one culture to another (Chen 1992). In the United States, a compliment is generally supposed to be accepted graciously; you did a good job and have a right to have that acknowledged. In more collectivist cultures, however, you're expected to deny your right to the compliment and to instead credit the group or the situation—"It was a very easy thing to do," "I didn't do it by myself," "Others deserve the credit," and so on.

Equality

Equality is a peculiar characteristic. In any situation, there is probably some inequality. One person will be smarter, richer, better looking, or more athletic. No two people are absolutely equal in all respects. Despite this inequality, interpersonal communication is generally considered more effective when the atmosphere is one of equality, at least in the United States. (In other cultures—in Japan, for example—where status differences greatly influence interpersonal interactions, this presumption of equality would not hold.)

Compare these examples:

1A. When will you learn to phone for reservations? Must I do everything?
1B. One of us should phone for reservations. Do you want me to do it, or do you want to do it?
2A. When the hell are you going to fix this wallpaper? It's coming down on my head!
2B. This wallpaper is coming down on my head. How about we stay home tonight and try to fix it together?

The A sentences lack equality; one person demands compliance and the other is ordered to do something. Questions such as these encourage defensiveness, resentment, and hostility. They provoke arguments rather than solve problems. The B sentences express equality—an explicitly stated desire to work together to address a specific problem. As a general rule, requests (especially courteous ones) communicate equality; demands (especially discourteous ones) communicate superiority.

In an equal interpersonal relationship, disagreement and conflict are seen as attempts to understand differences rather than as opportunities to put down the other person. Disagreements are viewed as ways of solving problems rather than of winning points, getting one's way, or proving oneself superior to the other. Equality does not require that you accept and approve of all the other person's behaviors. Some behaviors are self-destructive or have negative consequences for others, and these may, of course, be challenged—again, out of concern for the other person and for the relationship.

In communicating equality, avoid "should" and "ought" statements that signal an unequal relationship (for example, "You really should call your mother more often" or "You should learn to speak up"). These statements put the listener in a one-down position. Similarly, avoid interrupting; this too signals an unequal relationship and says, in effect, that what you have to say is more important than what the other person is saying.

Acknowledge the other person's contributions before expressing your own. Saying "I see," "I understand," or "That's right" lets the other person know you're listening and understanding. Avoid correcting another's messages when the original error is of little consequence. Corrections signal an unequal relationship and often embarrass the other person.

Which of these five skills do you use regularly and effectively? With which skill do you feel you have room for improvement?

◀◀ THINKING BACK

THINKING AHEAD ▶▶

What makes one person effective and another ineffective? What makes one person persuasive and another unconvincing?

A PRAGMATIC MODEL OF INTERPERSONAL EFFECTIVENESS

A **pragmatic** or behavioral (sometimes referred to metaphorically as "hard") approach to interpersonal effectiveness focuses on specific behaviors that a speaker or listener should use to gain his or her desired outcome. This model, too, offers five qualities of effectiveness: confidence, immediacy, interaction management, expressiveness, and other-orientation. This approach starts from specific skills that research finds to be effective in interpersonal communication, then groups these specific skills into general classes of behavior (for example, interaction management skills, other-orientation skills).

Confidence

The effective communicator has social **confidence;** any anxiety that is present is not readily perceived by others. There is instead an ease with the other person and with the communication situation generally. Everyone has some communication apprehension or shyness (see Unit 5), but the effective interpersonal communicator controls it so that it's not a source of discomfort and does not interfere with communication.

The socially confident communicator is relaxed (not rigid), flexible (not locked into one or two vocal ranges or body movements), and controlled (not shaky or awkward). Researchers find that a relaxed posture communicates a sense of control, superior status, and power (Spitzberg and Cupach 1984, 1989). Tenseness, rigidity, and discomfort, on the other hand, signal a lack of self-control, which in turn signals an inability to control one's environment or other people and gives an impression of being under the power and control of an outside force or another person.

In communicating confidence, take the initiative in introducing yourself to others and in introducing topics of conversation. Taking the initiative will help you communicate confidence and control over the situation. Use open-ended questions to involve the other person in the interaction (as opposed to questions that merely ask for a yes or no answer). Use "you-statements"—statements that refer directly to the other person, such as "Do you agree?" or "How do you feel about that?"—to signal your personal attention to the speaker.

Control your emotions. Once your emotions get the best of you, you'll appear to have lost confidence. A confident person approaches situations and makes decisions on the basis of logical and evidence, not on the basis of emotions. If you made a mistake, then admit it. Only a confident person can openly admit mistakes and not worry about what others will think.

Avoid turning normally declarative sentences into questions by a rising intonation, for example, "I'll arrive at nine?" Asking for agreement generally communicates a lack of confidence.

After analyzing the results of a series of five studies, one researcher concluded: "Whether male or female, ex-mental patient, or average person, a nervous and tense individual was disliked and unequivocally rejected by the workers. The consistency and strength of these findings are noteworthy, and we believe they are in keeping with most people's intuition" (Jones et al. 1984, 48). Do these findings accurately describe your reactions to nervous and tense

Immediacy

Immediacy refers to the joining of the speaker and listener, the creation of a sense of togetherness, of oneness. The communicator demonstrating immediacy conveys a sense of interest and attention, a liking for and an attraction to the other person. People respond to language that is immediate more favorably than to language that is not. Immediacy joins speaker and listener; nonimmediacy separates them. For example, students of instructors who used verbal and nonverbal immediacy behaviors felt that the instruction was better and the course more valuable than students of instructors who did not use such behaviors (Moore, Masterson, Christophel, and Shea 1996). Here are a few suggestions for communicating immediacy nonverbally and verbally.

Express psychological closeness and openness by, for example, maintaining physical closeness and arranging your body to exclude third parties. At the same time, maintain appropriate eye contact and limit looking around at others.

Smile and otherwise express your interest in and concern about the other person. Use the other person's name: for example, say, "Joe, what do you think?" instead of "What do you think?" Say "I like that, Mary" instead of "I like that." Use self-references in your evaluative statements rather than depersonalizing them. Say, for example, "I think your report is great" rather than "Your report is great" or "Everyone likes your report."

Focus on the other person's remarks. Make the speaker know that you heard and understood what was said, and give the speaker feedback. For example, use questions that ask for clarification or elaboration ("Do you think the same thing is true of baseball?"). Also, refer to the speaker's previous remarks ("Vermont does sound like a great vacation spot"). In doing so, try to reinforce, reward, or compliment the other person. Make use of such expressions as "I like your new outfit" or "Your comments were really to the point."

In the United States these immediacy behaviors are generally seen as friendly and appropriate. In other cultures, however, the same immediacy behaviors may be viewed as overly familiar, as presuming that a close relationship exists when it's only one of acquaintanceship. In the United States we move quickly from Mr. LastName and Ms. LastName to Fred and Ginger, which signals greater immediacy. In more formal countries (Japan and Germany are two examples), a much longer period of acquaintanceship would be necessary before first names would be considered appropriate (Axtell 1993).

Interaction Management

The effective communicator controls the interaction to the satisfaction of both parties. In effective **interaction management,** neither person feels ignored or on stage; each contributes to the total communication exchange. Maintaining your role as speaker or listener and passing the opportunity to speak back and forth—through appropriate eye movements, vocal expressions, and body and facial gestures—are interaction management skills. Similarly, keeping the conversation fluent without long and awkward pauses is a sign of effective interaction management. For example, it has been found that patients are less satisfied with their interaction with their doctor when the silence between their comments and the doctor's response is overly long (Rowland-Morin and Carroll 1990).

The effective interaction manager presents verbal and nonverbal messages that are consistent and reinforce one another. Contradictory signals—for example, a nonverbal message that contradicts the verbal message—are rarely in evidence. It's relevant to note here that women generally use more positive or pleasant nonverbal expressions than men. For example, they smile more, nod in agreement more, and more openly verbalize positive feelings. When expressing anger or power, however, many (though surely not all) women continue using these positive nonverbal signals, which dilute the verbally expressed anger or power. The net result is that we may see such women as being uncomfortable with strong negative emotions and expressions of power and may therefore be less likely to believe them or to feel threatened by them (Shannon 1987).

Self-Monitoring Integrally related to interpersonal interaction management is **self-monitoring,** the manipulation of the image you present to others in your interpersonal interactions (Snyder 1987). High self-monitors carefully adjust their behaviors according to the feedback they get from others. They manipulate their interpersonal interactions to give the most effective impression and to produce the desired effect. Low self-monitors, in contrast, are not concerned with the image they present. Rather, they communicate their thoughts and feelings openly, without trying to manipulate the impressions they create. Although there seem to be two clear-cut types of persons—high and low self-monitors—we all engage more or less in selective monitoring, depending on the situation. If you go to a job interview, you're likely to monitor your behaviors very carefully. On the other hand, you're less likely to monitor your performance with a group of friends. You may wish to reflect on the situations and the people with whom you are most likely to self-monitor as you take the self test "How Much Do You Self-Monitor?"

TEST YOURSELF *How Much Do You Self-Monitor?*

The following statements concern personal reactions to a number of different situations. No two statements are exactly alike, so consider each statement carefully before answering. If a statement is true or mostly true as applied to you, write *T.* If a statement is false or not usually true as applied to you, write *F.*

______ 1. I find it hard to imitate the behavior of other people.
______ 2. At parties and social gatherings, I do not attempt to do or say things that others will like.
______ 3. I can only argue for ideas which I already believe.
______ 4. I can make impromptu speeches even on topics about which I have almost no information.
______ 5. I guess I put on a show to impress or entertain people.
______ 6. I would probably make a good actor.
______ 7. In a group of people I am rarely the center of attention.
______ 8. In different situations and with different people, I often act like very different persons.
______ 9. I am not particularly good at making other people like me.
______ 10. I'm not always the person I appear to be.
______ 11. I would not change my opinions (or the way I do things) in order to please someone or win their favor.
______ 12. I have considered being an entertainer.
______ 13. I have never been good at games like charades or improvisational acting.
______ 14. I have trouble changing my behavior to suit different people and different situations.
______ 15. At a party I let others keep the jokes and stories going.

_______ 16. I feel a bit awkward in company and do not show up quite as well as I should.

_______ 17. I can look anyone in the eye and tell a lie with a straight face (if for a right end).

_______ 18. I may deceive people by being friendly when I really dislike them.

Give yourself one point for each *true (T)* response you gave to questions 4, 5, 6, 8, 10, 12, 17, and 18, and give yourself one point for each *false (F)* response you gave to questions 1, 2, 3, 7, 9, 11, 13, 14, 15, and 16. According to research (Gangestad and Synder 1985; Snyder 1987), scores may be interpreted roughly as follows: 13 or higher = very high self-monitoring, 11–12 = high self-monitoring, 8–10 = low self-monitoring, and 0–7 = very low self-monitoring.

Does your score correspond to the image you have of yourself in regard to self-monitoring? Do other people see you as a high or a low self-monitor? Does it make a difference to your interpersonal effectiveness? Do you agree with the findings reported in the text about the differences between high and low self-monitors?

When high and low self-monitors are compared, several interesting differences emerge. For example, high self-monitors are more apt to take charge of a situation, more sensitive to the deceptive techniques of others, and better able to detect self-monitoring or impression management techniques being used by others. High self-monitors prefer to interact with low self-monitors. By interacting with low self-monitors, high self-monitors are better able to assume positions of influence and power. They also seem better able to present their true selves than are low self-monitors. For example, if an innocent person is charged with a crime, to use the example cited by Snyder (1987), a high self-monitor would be able to present his or her innocence more effectively than would a low self-monitor.

A careful reading of the research and theory on self-monitoring, openness, and self-disclosure (a topic reviewed in detail in Unit 4) supports the conclusion that we increase our effectiveness if we are selectively self-disclosing, selectively open, and selectively self-monitoring. To be totally open, to disclose everything to everyone, to ignore the feedback of others, and to refuse to engage in any self-monitoring seem effective. The opposite extreme is equally ineffective and should likewise be avoided.

Expressiveness

Expressiveness refers to the skill of communicating genuine involvement in the interpersonal interaction. Similar to openness in its emphasis on involvement, expressiveness includes, for example, taking responsibility for your thoughts and feelings, encouraging expressiveness or openness in others, and providing appropriate feedback. Some cultures (Italian, for example) encourage expressiveness and teach children to be expressive. Other cultures (Japanese and Thai, for example) encourage a more reserved response style (Matsumoto 1996).

In the United States women are expected to participate fully in business discussions, to smile, laugh, and initiate interactions. These behaviors are so expected and seemingly so natural that it seems strange even mentioning them. In many other countries (Arab countries and many Asian countries), however, this expressiveness would be considered inappropriate (Lustig and Koester 1999, Axtell 1993, Hall and Hall 1987).

One obvious way to communicate expressiveness is to use active listening—paraphrase, express understanding of the thoughts and feelings of the other person, and ask relevant questions (as explained in Unit 7). Address **mixed messages**—messages (verbal or nonverbal) that are communicated simultaneously but that contradict each other. Similarly, address messages that seem somehow unrealistic to you (for example, statements claiming that failing a course doesn't mean anything).

Use I-messages to signal personal involvement and a willingness to share your feelings. Instead of saying, "You never give me a chance to make any decisions," say, "I want to contribute to the decisions that affect both of us." Use appropriate variations in vocal rate, pitch, volume, and rhythm to convey involvement and interest. Allow your facial muscles to reflect this inner involvement. These variations will further evidence your personal involvement. Also, avoid cliches and trite expressions; these signal a lack of originality and personal involvement.

Use appropriate gestures, especially gestures that focus on the other person rather than yourself. For example, maintain eye contact and lean toward the person; at the same time, avoid self-touching gestures or directing your eyes to others in the room. Too few gestures may signal disinterest, while too many may communicate discomfort, uneasiness, and awkwardness.

Other-Orientation

WEB EXPLORATION
To learn more about other-orientation, go to www.awl.com/devito.

Some people are self-oriented; they focus almost exclusively on themselves. In interpersonal interaction, this takes the form of doing most of the talking, talking about themselves, and paying no attention to the feedback from others. **Other-orientation** is the opposite; it's the ability to adapt to the other person during the interpersonal encounter. It involves communicating attentiveness and interest in the other person and in what is being said. As you might expect, other-orientation is especially important (and especially difficult) when you're interacting with people who are very different from you as in, for example, talking with people from other cultures.

You can communicate other-orientation by showing consideration and respect—for example, asking if it's all right to dump your troubles on someone before doing so, or asking if your phone call comes at a good time before launching into your conversation. It involves acknowledging the other person's feelings as legitimate: "I can understand why you're so angry; I would be, too."

Acknowledge the presence and the importance of the other person. Ask the other person for suggestions and opinions. Statements such as "How do you feel about it?" or "What do you think?" go a long way toward focusing the communication on the other person. Similarly, ask the other person for clarification as appropriate. This will ensure that you understand what the other person is saying from that person's point of view. Nonverbally, you can communicate other-orientation by focused eye contact, appropriate facial expressions, smiling, nodding, and leaning toward the other person.

You can also express other-orientation by expressing agreement. Comments such as "You're right" or "That's interesting" help to focus the interaction on the other person and assure the person that you're actively listening and understanding.

Grant the other person permission to express feelings. You can do this by talking about your own feelings or perhaps by noting how difficult it is to talk about feelings. Statements such as "I feel especially depressed when I'm alone" or "I know how difficult it is to talk openly about feelings for our parents" open up the topic of feelings and give the necessary permission for such a discussion.

How might you use these skills in going to lunch with new colleagues at a new job?
◂◂ THINKING BACK

Not surprisingly, other-orientation is especially important in communication with a person who has a handicap such as deafness. Table 8.1 offers some useful suggestions for communication with a deaf person.

TABLE 8.1 Talking with a Deaf Person

Get the deaf person's attention before speaking.

Key the deaf person into the topic of discussion.

Speak slowly and clearly, but do not yell, exaggerate, or overpronounce.

Look directly at the deaf person when speaking.

Do not place anything in your mouth when speaking.

Maintain eye contact with the deaf person.

Use the words "I" and "you."

Avoid standing in front of a light source, such as a window or bright light. The glare and shadows created on the face make it almost impossible for the deaf person to speechread.

First, repeat, then try to rephrase a thought if you have problems being understood, rather than repeating the same words again.

Use pantomime, body language, and facial expression to help supplement your communication.

Be courteous to the deaf person during conversation. If the telephone rings or someone knocks at the door, excuse yourself and tell the deaf person that you are answering the phone or responding to the knock.

Use open-ended questions that must be answered by more than "yes" or "no." Do not assume that deaf persons have understood your message if they nod their heads in acknowledgment. A response to an open-ended question ensures that your information has been communicated.

Source: Tips for Communicating with Deaf People (Rochester Institute of Technology, National Technical Institute for the Deaf, Division of Public Affairs, One Lomb Memorial Drive, P.O. Box 9887, Rochester, New York 14623-0887, Phone: 716-475-6824.)

REVIEWING KEY TERMS AND CONCEPTS IN INTERPERSONAL EFFECTIVENESS

This unit explored interpersonal effectiveness and considered general and specific skills.

Skills About Skills

What are the general skills that should regulate the more specific skills making for interpersonal effectiveness?

- **Mindfulness:** Be mindful in applying the principles of interpersonal effectiveness.
- **Flexibility:** Be flexible in applying the principles; each situation requires a slightly different set of interpersonal behaviors.
- **Cultural Sensitivity:** Be careful not to ignore differences between self and other, within the group, or in meaning
- **Metacommunication:** Metacommunicate to ensure understanding of the other person's thoughts and feelings.

A Humanistic Model of Interpersonal Effectiveness

What interpersonal skills are suggested by a humanistic perspective?

- **Openness:** Regulate your self-disclosures, give honest reactions to others, own your thoughts and feelings.
- **Empathy:** Try to feel what the other person is feeling.
- **Supportiveness:** Use descriptions and **provisionalism;** these encourage a supportive atmosphere.
- **Positiveness:** Express positive attitudes toward self, other, and the situation; compliment to acknowledge and reinforce the other person.
- **Equality:** Recognize that both parties are important; strive for an equal sharing of the several communication functions.

A Pragmatic Model of Interpersonal Effectiveness

What interpersonal skills are suggested by a pragmatic perspective?

- **Confidence:** Project a comfortable, at-ease feeling; at the same time, try to control shyness.
- **Immediacy:** Communicate a sense of contact and togetherness, a feeling of interest and liking.
- **Interaction management:** Control the interaction to the satisfaction of both parties; manage conversational turns and self-monitor as appropriate.

- **Expressiveness:** Verbally and nonverbally project genuine involvement in speaking and listening.
- **Other-orientation:** Express attentiveness, interest, and concern for the other.

APPLYING KEY TERMS AND CONCEPTS IN INTERPERSONAL EFFECTIVENESS

1. How flexible are you in your style of communication? Are you basically the same in all situations or does your style change with the situation you're in?
2. Can you give an example of a recent interaction in which the need for cultural sensitivity played an important part?
3. How have you used metalanguage today? What purposes did it serve?
4. Why do you think that men are more reluctant to be open than women? Is this changing?
5. What did you do today to get stroked? Was it effective?
6. In what types of situations do you display confidence? In what situations do you display a lack of confidence? What distinguishes the two types of situations?
7. How important is immediacy in communication between health care providers and patients? What specific recommendations would you offer health care professionals to make their communication with patients more immediate?
8. In what situations are you most likely to self-monitor your behaviors? In what situations are you least likely to self-monitor?
9. Which of the qualities of effectiveness discussed in this unit do you consider most important? Why?
10. How would you go about seeking answers to the following questions?
    - Are people who demonstrate the qualities of effective interpersonal communication better liked than those who don't?
    - In what situations (if any) are people who speak with a superior attitude more effective than those with an equality attitude?
    - Do people become less flexible as they get older (cf. Booth-Butterfield 1998, which found that adults with an average age of 36.6 were less flexible in communication than college students, average age 21)?
    - Are teachers who are expressive more effective in communicating information to students than teachers who are inexpressive?
    - What role does other-orientation play in first dates?

EXPERIENCING KEY TERMS AND CONCEPTS IN INTERPERSONAL EFFECTIVENESS

Go to www.awl.com/devito

Exercise No. 15, "Conversational Analysis," illustrates some of the characteristics making for ineffectiveness. Exercise No. 16, "Giving and Taking Directions," will provide an opportunity to use the characteristics of effectiveness discussed here. Similarly, Exercises No.19, "Analyzing Stage Talk," No. 26, "Analyzing a Conflict Episode," and No. 28, "The Television Relationship," all highlight the principles of interpersonal communication effectiveness.

UNIT 9

UNIVERSALS OF VERBAL AND NONVERBAL MESSAGES

The Miracle Worker (1962)

A WORD IS NOT A CRYSTAL, TRANSPARENT AND UNCHANGED, IT IS THE SKIN OF A LIVING THOUGHT AND MAY VARY GREATLY IN COLOR AND CONTENT ACCORDING TO THE CIRCUMSTANCES AND THE TIME IN WHICH IT IS USED.

--OLIVER WENDELL HOLMES

THE MIRACLE WORKER, an adaptation of William Gibson's Broadway play, tells the true story of how Annie Sullivan (Anne Bancroft) teaches the young deaf and blind Helen Keller (Patty Duke) how to communicate, how to make her thoughts known to others by signing. The dramatic change this brings to Helen Keller shows us the crucial role that communication plays in making us truly functional members of society. This unit introduces the verbal and nonverbal message systems and explains how these work together to enable you to communicate your thoughts and feelings.

THINKING AHEAD ▸▸
How do your verbal and nonverbal messages work together when you talk with someone?

THE INTERACTION OF VERBAL AND NONVERBAL MESSAGES

In face-to-face communication, you blend verbal and nonverbal messages to best convey your meanings. There is also evidence to show that you blend verbal and nonverbal messages to help you think and remember (Iverson and Goldin-Meadow 1999). Enumerating the six major ways in which nonverbal messages are used with verbal messages helps to highlight this important verbal-nonverbal interaction.

Nonverbal communication is often used to *accent,* to emphasize some part of the verbal message. You might, for example, raise your voice to underscore a particular word or phrase, bang your fist on the desk to stress your commitment, or look longingly into someone's eyes when saying "I love you."

Nonverbal communication may be used to *complement,* to add nuances of meaning not communicated by your verbal message. Thus, you might smile when telling a story (to suggest that you find it humorous) or frown and shake your head when recounting someone's deceit (to suggest your disapproval).

You may deliberately *contradict* your verbal messages with nonverbal movements, for example, by crossing your fingers or winking to indicate that you're lying.

Nonverbal movements may be used to *control,* or to indicate your desire to control, the flow of verbal messages, as when you purse your lips, lean forward, or make hand movements to indicate that you want to speak. You might also put up your hand or vocalize your pauses (for example, with "um") to indicate that you have not finished and aren't ready to relinquish the floor to the next speaker.

You can *repeat* or restate the verbal message nonverbally. You can, for example, follow your verbal "Is that all right?" with raised eyebrows and a questioning look, or you can motion with your head or hand to repeat your verbal "Let's go."

You may also use nonverbal communication to take the place of or *substitute* for verbal messages. You can, for example, signal "OK" with a hand gesture. You can nod your head to indicate yes or shake your head to indicate no.

When you communicate electronically, of course, your message is communicated by means of typed letters without facial expressions or gestures that normally accompany face-to-face communication and without the changes in rate and volume that are a part of normal telephone communication. To compensate for this lack of nonverbal behavior, the emoticon was created. Sometimes called a "smiley" after the ever-present :) , the emoticon is a typed symbol that communicates through a keyboard the nuances of the message normally conveyed by nonverbal expression and changes in vocal expression. The absence of the nonverbal channel where you can clarify your message—for example, smiling or winking to communicate sarcasm or humor—make such typed symbols extremely helpful. Here are some of the more popular emoticons used in computer talk. Research is just beginning to look into the factors influencing the use of emoticons and the effects they have (Rezabeck and Cochenour 1995).

: -)	= smile; I'm only kidding
: - (	= frown; I'm feeling sad; this saddens me
★	= kiss
:-	= male
>-	= female
{ }	= hug
{{{★★★}}}	= hugs and kisses
; -)	= sly smile
this is important	= underlining, adds emphasis
★this is important★	= asterisks, adds emphasis
ALL CAPS	= shouting, emphasizing
<G> or <grin>	= grin

Not surprisingly, these symbols aren't used universally (Pollack 1996). For example, because it's considered impolite for a Japanese woman to show her teeth when she smiles, the Japanese emoticon for a woman's smile is (^ . ^) where the dot signifies a closed mouth. A man's smile is written (^ _ ^). Other emoticons popular in Japan but not used in Europe or the United States are (^ ^ ;) for "cold sweat," (^ o ^ ; Ò) for "excuse me," and (^ o ^) for "happy."

Try describing the body and facial gestures you would use in communicating the literal meaning of the following statements: (1) So glad you're on time again. (2) That was great; I really appreciate it. In what ways would these body and facial gestures be different if you were communicating the opposite of the literal meaning?

◀◀ THINKING BACK

MEANINGS AND MESSAGES

Meaning is an active process created in cooperation between source and receiver, speaker and listener, writer and reader. Understanding what meanings are and how they're passed from one person to another will help maximize your own verbal and nonverbal message potential.

THINKING AHEAD ▶▶

Why is it that even when you make yourself "absolutely clear," some people don't understand what you really mean?

? ASK THE RESEARCHER

Becoming a Popular Teacher

I'm planning on becoming a teacher and I want students to like me. Is there anything specific I can do to get them to like me? Is there anything I should be sure to avoid?

First experiences of teaching can be very challenging and are usually very rewarding. Teachers and students have something in common: they want to be liked. Studies about teacher immediacy, affinity-seeking, communication competence, credibility, and classroom management provide very useful suggestions for being viewed positively. Just a few of these are: show you're really listening, use nonverbal immediacy (smile, lean toward the students, use inclusive gestures), offer some self-disclosure to fit the grade level, and be empathic, dynamic, and authentic. A helpful question to ask yourself might be: Did I set up barriers today or did I provide openings for connecting with my students? Another worthwhile practice is to take time to learn specific things about each student and to use their names often.

For further information see J. Civikly-Powell, J. (1999) "How Can We Teach Without Communicating?" in *Teaching and Learning on the Edge of the Millennium: Building on What We Have Learned. New Directions for Teaching and Learning,* no. 80, 61-67, ed. M. Svinicki (San Francisco: Jossey-Bass), and J. M. Civikly, *Classroom Communication: Principles and Practice*, (Dubuque, IA: Wm. C. Brown, 1992).

—Jean Civikly-Powell (Ph.D., Florida State University) is a professor of communication and director of the Teaching Assistant Resource Center and the Faculty Dispute Resolution Program at the University of New Mexico. She teaches courses in conflict resolution, interpersonal communication, and classroom teaching, and is a mediator for the City of Albuquerque's Metropolitan Court. jcivikly@unm.edu.

Meanings Are in People

Meaning depends not only on messages (whether verbal, nonverbal, or both) but also on the interaction of these messages and the receiver's own thoughts and feelings. You don't "receive" meaning; you create meaning. You construct meaning out of the messages you receive combined with your own social and cultural perspectives (beliefs, attitudes, and values, for example) (Berger and Luckmann 1980, Delia 1977, and Delia, O'Keefe, and O'Keefe 1982). Words don't mean; people mean. Consequently, to discover meaning, you need to look into people and not merely into words.

To illustrate the implications of the principle that meanings are in people, record your meanings for the terms listed below on the seven-point scales. Write each term's first letter in the appropriate space for the various dimensions of meaning provided, depending on how close you feel the term's meaning is to the adjectives in the scale. Thus, if you feel that a concept is extremely good or extremely bad, then place the term's first letter on the space closest to good or bad. If you feel that the concept is quite good or quite bad, then place the term's first letter in the second or the seventh position. If you feel that the concept is fairly good or fairly bad, then place the letter in the third or the fifth position. If you feel that the concept is neither good nor bad, then place the letter in the middle position. Do likewise for all six scales and for all five terms.

Terms: (A) abortion, (B) biological warfare, (C) college, (D) death penalty, (E) euthanasia

good	__:__:__:__:__:__:__	bad
ugly	__:__:__:__:__:__:__	beautiful
weak	__:__:__:__:__:__:__	strong
active	__:__:__:__:__:__:__	passive
large	__:__:__:__:__:__:__	small
hot	__:__:__:__:__:__:__	cold

If you have the opportunity, compare your meanings with those of others in small groups or in the class as a whole. Are there large differences between your meanings and those of others? How would you describe these differences in terms of connotation and denotation? What accounts for the differences in meanings? That is, what factors contribute to your meanings for these terms? Put differently, how did you acquire the meanings you indicated on these scales? What does this experience illustrate about the principle that meanings are in people?

Meanings Are More Than Words and Gestures

When you want to communicate a thought or feeling to another person, you do so with relatively few symbols. These symbols represent just a small part of what you're thinking or feeling, much of which remains unspoken. If you were to try to describe every feeling in detail, you would never get on with the job of living. The meanings you seek to communicate are much more than the sum of the words and nonverbal behaviors you use to represent them.

Because of this, you can never fully know what another person is thinking or feeling. You can only approximate it on the basis of the meanings you receive, which, as already noted, are greatly influenced by who you are and what you are feeling. Conversely, others can never fully know you; they, too, can only approximate what you're feeling. Failure to understand another person or to be understood is not an abnormal situation. It's inevitable, although we can always understand each other a little better than we now do.

Meanings Are Unique

Because meanings are derived from both the messages communicated and the receiver's own thoughts and feelings, no two people ever derive the same meanings. Similarly, because people change constantly, no one person can derive the same meanings on two separate occasions. Who you are can never be separated from the meanings you create. As a result, check your perceptions of another's meanings by asking questions, echoing what you perceive to be the other person's feelings or thoughts, seeking elaboration and clarification, and in general practicing the skills identified in the discussion on effective interpersonal perception and listening.

Also recognize that as you change, you also change the meanings you create out of past messages. Thus, although the message sent may not have changed, the meanings you created from it yesterday and the meanings you create today may be quite different. Yesterday, when a special someone said, "I love you," you created certain meanings. But today, when you learn that the same "I love you" was said to three other people or when you fall in love with someone else, you drastically change the meanings you perceive from these words.

Meanings Are Both Denotative and Connotative

WEB EXPLORATION
To learn more about denotation and connotation, go to www.awl.com/devito.

Consider a word such as "death." To a doctor this word might mean, or denote, the point at which the heart stops beating, a rather objective description of an event. To a mother whose son has just died, however, the word means much more. It recalls the son's youth, his ambitions, his family, his illness, and so on. To her, the word is emotional, subjective, and highly personal. These emotional, subjective, and personal associations are the word's connotative meaning. The **denotation** of a word is its objective definition; the **connotation** is its subjective or emotional meaning.

Now consider a simple nod of the head in answer to the question, "Do you agree?" This gesture is largely denotative and simply says yes. What about a wink, a smile, or an overly rapid speech rate? These nonverbal expressions are more connotative; they express your feelings rather than objective information.

The denotative meaning of a message is general or universal; most people would agree with the denotative meanings and would give similar definitions. Connotative meanings, however, are extremely personal, and few people would agree on the precise connotative meaning of a word or nonverbal behavior.

"Snarl words" and "purr words" may further clarify the distinction between denotative and connotative meaning (Hayakawa and Hayakawa 1989). Snarl words are highly negative ("She's an idiot," "He's a pig," "They're a bunch of losers"). Sexist, racist, and heterosexist language and hate speech provide lots of other examples. Purr words are highly positive ("She's a real sweetheart," "He's a dream," "They're the greatest"). Although they may sometimes seem to have denotative meaning and refer to the "real world," snarl and purr words are actually connotative in meaning. They don't describe people or events, but rather, they reveal the speaker's feelings about these people or events.

Meanings Are Context-Based

Verbal and nonverbal communications exist in a context, and that context to a large extent determines the meaning of any verbal or nonverbal behavior. The same words or behaviors may have totally different meanings when they occur in different contexts. For example, the greeting, "How are you?" means "Hello" to someone you pass regularly on the street but means "Is your health improving?" when said to a friend in the hospital. A wink to an attractive person on a bus means something completely different from a wink that signifies a put-on or a lie. Similarly, the meaning of a given signal depends on the other behavior it accompanies or is close to in time. Pounding a fist on the table during a speech in support of a politician means something quite different from that same gesture in response to news of a friend's death. Divorced from the context, it's impossible to tell what meaning was intended from just examining the signals. Of course, even if you know the context in detail, you still might not be able to decipher the meaning of the message.

Can you recall an occasion in which you and another listener understood a message very differently? What caused the difference?

◀◀ THINKING BACK

Especially important is the cultural context, a context emphasized throughout this text. The cultural context will influence not only the meaning assigned to speech and gesture but whether your meaning is friendly, offensive, lacking in respect, condescending, sensitive, and so on.

THINKING AHEAD ▶▶

Why are some messages effective and others ineffective? Why are some people so adept at making their meanings clear and persuasive and others have such difficulty getting their point across?

MESSAGE CHARACTERISTICS

You'll be in a better position to control the message process once you understand the way in which messages work and the principles they follow. Interpersonal communication messages occur in packages, are governed by rules, vary in abstraction, and vary in directness. Reviewing these four characteristics will enable you to understand better how interpersonal messages are transferred and how you can better control your own messages.

Messages Are Packaged

The sounds you make with your mouth or the gestures you make with your hands or eyes usually occur in "packages" where the verbal and nonverbal behaviors reinforce one another. Usually, all parts of the message system work together to communicate a unified meaning. When you speak words of anger, your body and face also communicate anger by tensing, scowling, and perhaps assuming a fighting posture. You often fail to notice this because it seems so natural, so expected. But when the nonverbal messages of someone's posture or face contradict what is said verbally, you take special notice. For example, the person who says, "I'm so glad to see you," but avoids direct eye contact and looks around to see who else is present is sending contradictory messages. You also see contradictory messages (mixed messages) when couples say they love each other but seem to go out of their way to hurt each other nonverbally—for example, being late for important dates, flirting with others, or not touching each other.

In the packaged nature of communication, then, is a warning against the too easy interpretation of another's meaning, especially as revealed in nonverbal behaviors. Before you identify or guess the meaning of any bit of behavior, look at the entire package or cluster of which it's a part, the way in which the cluster is a response to its context, and the role of the specific nonverbal behavior within that cluster. That attractive person winking in your direction may be giving you the come-on; however, don't rule out the possibility of ill-fitting contact lenses.

Messages Are Rule-Governed

TRY IT!
To learn more about rule-governed messages, go to www.awl.com/devito.

The rule-governed nature of verbal communication is well known. These are the rules of a language (the rules of grammar) that native speakers follow in producing and in understanding sentences, although they may be unable to state such rules explicitly. You learned these rules from observing the behaviors of the adult community. For example, you learned how to express sympathy along with the rules that your culture has established for expressing it appropriately. You learned that touch is permissible under certain circumstances but not under others and which types of touching are permissible and which aren't.

Generally, you don't pay much attention to the packaged nature of communication unless there is an incongruity. When you spot a contradiction between the verbal and the nonverbal message, you begin to wonder if something is wrong. In the classic film *The Graduate,* there's a particularly good example of such contradictory messages. Benjamin, the graduate (played by Dustin Hoffman), and Mrs. Robinson (Anne Bancroft) are having an affair , which under normal circumstances would indicate a high degree of intimacy. But Benjamin repeatedly and consistently calls his partner "Mrs. Robinson," which shows that he is uncomfortable with the relationship and that he feels unequal in this partnership with a mature woman. Can you give a similar example of contradictory messages from film, television, or literature?

You learned that women may touch each other in public; for example, they may hold hands, walk arm in arm, engage in prolonged hugging, and even dance together. You also learned that men may not do these things, at least not without inviting social criticism. Further, perhaps most obvious, you learned that certain parts of the body may not be touched and others may. As a relationship changes, so do the rules for touching. As you become more intimate, the rules for touching become less restrictive.

Nonverbal communication is also regulated by a system of rules or norms that state what is and what is not appropriate, expected, and permissible in specific social situations. Of course, these rules vary greatly from one culture to another. Rules are cultural (and relative) institutions; they're not universal laws. In the United States, for example, direct eye contact usually signals openness and honesty. Among some Latin Americans and Native Americans, however, direct eye contact between, say, a teacher and a student is considered inappropriate, perhaps aggressive; appropriate student behavior is to avoid eye contact with the teacher. From even this simple example it's easy to see how miscommunication can take place. To a teacher in the United States, avoidance of eye contact by a Latin American or Native American could signify guilt, lack of interest, or disrespect when in fact the child was following her or his own culturally established rules. Table 9.1, drawn from Axtell (1993) and Sabath (1999), gives you an idea of the problems that can arise when you assume that the rules governing message behavior in one culture are the same rules used in other cultures.

A somewhat different system of verbal and nonverbal rules governs communication between sighted and blind or visually impaired persons. The Lighthouse, an organization devoted to enabling blind and partially sighted people to lead independent lives, offers suggestions in the accompanying "What Do You Do When You Meet a Blind Person?" (see p.160)

Messages Vary in Abstraction

Consider the following list of terms:

entertainment
film
American film
recent American film
Titanic

TABLE 9.1 Some Nonverbal Taboos

These are only a small number of the nonverbal taboos that exist throughout the world. Can you add any nonverbal taboos to this list?

Nonverbal Behavior	Taboo
Blinking your eyes	Considered impolite in Taiwan
Folding your arms over your chest	Considered disrespectful in Fiji
Putting your hands in your pockets	Considered impolite in Malaysia
Waving your hand	Insulting in Nigeria and Greece
Gesturing with the thumb up	Considered rude in Australia
Tapping your two index fingers together	In Egypt this means that a couple is sleeping together or the request that we sleep together
Pointing with the index finger	Considered impolite in many Middle-Eastern countries, China, and Indonesia
Bowing to a lesser degree than your host	Implies that you're superior in Japan
With a clenched fist, inserting your thumb between your index and middle finger (called the *fig*)	Considered obscene in some southern European countries
Using your left hand to eat or shake hands	Considered impolite in a wide variety of cultures, for example, Malaysia, Indonesia, and Arab countries
Pointing at someone with your index and third fingers	Means you're wishing evil on the person in some African countries
Resting your feet on a table or chair	Insulting in some Middle-Eastern countries

At the top is the general or abstract category of entertainment. Note that entertainment includes all the other items on the list plus various other items—television, novels, drama, comics, and so on. Film is more specific and concrete. It includes all of the items below it as well as various other items such as Indian film or Russian film. It excludes, however, all entertainment that is not film. "American film" is again more specific than film and excludes all films that aren't American. "Recent American film" further limits American film to a time period. "*Titanic*" specifies concretely the one item to which reference is made.

The more general term—in this case, entertainment—conjures up a number of different images. One person in the audience may focus on television, another on music, another on comic books, and still another on radio. To some, "film" may bring to mind the early silent films. To others, it brings to mind high-tech special effects. To still others, it recalls Disney's animated cartoons. "*Titanic*" guides the listener still further—in this case to one film. But note that even though "*Titanic*" identifies one film, different listeners are likely to focus on different aspects of the film, perhaps its special effects, perhaps its love story, perhaps its historical accuracy, perhaps its financial success.

Effective verbal messages include words from a wide range of abstractions. At times a general term may suit your needs best; at other times a more specific term may serve better. Generally, however, the specific term will prove the better choice. As you get more specific—less abstract—you more effectively guide the images that come to your listeners' minds.

Messages Vary in Directness

Think about how you would respond to someone saying the following sentences.

1A. I'm so bored; I have nothing to do tonight.
2A. I'd like to go to the movies. Would you like to come?
1B. Do you feel like hamburgers tonight?
2B. I'd like hamburgers tonight. How about you?

WEB EXPLORATION
To learn more about indirect messages, go to www.awl.com/devito.

The statements numbered 1 are relatively indirect; they're attempts to get the listener to say or do something without committing the speaker. The statements numbered 2 are more direct—they state more clearly the speaker's preferences and then ask the listeners if they agree. A more obvious example of an indirect message occurs when you glance at your watch to communicate that it's late and that you had better be going. Indirect messages have both advantages and disadvantages.

Advantages of Indirect Messages Indirect messages allow you to express a desire without insulting or offending anyone; they allow you to observe the rules of polite interaction. So instead of saying, "I'm bored with this group," you say, "It's getting late and I have to get up early tomorrow," or you look at your watch and pretend to be surprised by the time. Instead of saying, "This food tastes like cardboard," you say, "I just started my diet" or "I just ate." In each instance you're stating a preference but are saying it indirectly so as to avoid offending someone.

Sometimes indirect messages allow you to ask for compliments in a socially acceptable manner, such as saying, "I was thinking of getting a nose job." You hope to get the desired compliment: "A nose job? You? Your nose is perfect."

Disadvantages of Indirect Messages Indirect messages can create problems. Consider the following dialogue in which an indirect request is made:

PAT: You wouldn't like to have my parents over for dinner this weekend, would you?
CHRIS: I really wanted to go to the shore and just relax.
PAT: Well, if you feel you have to go to the shore, I'll make the dinner myself. You go to the shore. I really hate having them over and doing all the work myself. It's such a drag shopping, cooking, and cleaning all by myself.

Given this situation, Chris has two basic alternatives. One is to stick with the plans to go to the shore and relax. In this case Pat is going to be upset and Chris is going to be made to feel guilty for not helping with the dinner. A second alternative is to give in to Pat, help with the dinner, and not go to the shore. In this case Chris is going to have to give up a much desired plan and is likely to resent Pat's "manipulative" tactics. Regardless of which decision is made, one person wins and one person loses. This win-lose situation creates resentment, competition, and often an "I'll get even" attitude. With direct requests, this type of situation is much less likely to develop. Consider:

PAT: I'd like to have my parents over for dinner this weekend. What do you think?
CHRIS: Well, I really wanted to go to the shore and just relax.

Regardless of what develops next, both individuals are starting out on relatively equal footing. Each has clearly and directly stated a preference. Although at first these preferences seem mutually exclusive, it might be possible to meet both persons' needs. For example, Chris might say, "How about going to the shore this weekend and having your parents over next weekend? I'm really exhausted; I could use the rest." Here is a direct response to a direct request. Unless there is some pressing need to have Pat's parents over for dinner this weekend, this response may enable each to meet the other's needs.

Gender and Cultural Differences in Directness The popular stereotype in much of the United States holds that women are indirect in making requests and in giving orders. This indirectness communicates powerlessness, discomfort with their own authority. Men, the stereotype continues, are direct, sometimes to the point of being blunt or rude. This directness communicates power and comfort with one's own authority.

Deborah Tannen (1994b) provides an interesting perspective on these stereotypes. Women are, it seems, more indirect in giving orders and are more likely to say, for example, "It would be great if these letters could go out today" than "Have these letters out by three." But Tannen (1994b, p. 84) argues that "issuing orders indirectly can be the prerogative of those in power" and does in no way show powerlessness. Power, to Tannen, is the ability to chose your own style of communication.

Men, however, are also indirect but in different situations (Rundquist 1992). According to Tannen, men are more likely to use indirectness when they express weakness, reveal a problem, or admit an error. Men are more likely to speak indirectly

What Do You Do When You Meet a Blind Person?

On the Street—Ask if assistance would be helpful. Sometimes a blind person prefers to proceed unaided. If the person wants your help, offer your elbow. You should walk a half-step ahead so that your body movements will indicate when to change direction, stop and start, and step up or down at curbside.

Giving Directions—Verbal directions should have the blind person as the reference point. Example: "You are facing Lexington Avenue and you will have to cross it as you continue east on 59th Street."

Handling Money—When giving out bills, indicate the denomination of each so that the blind person can identify it and put it away. Coins are identified by touch.

Safety—Half-open doors are a hazard to everyone, particularly to a blind person. Keep doors closed or wide open.

Dining Out—Guide blind people to the table by offering your arm. Then place their hand on the chair back so they can seat themselves. Read the menu aloud and encourage the waiter to speak directly to the blind person rather than to you. Describe placement of food, using an imaginary clock face (e.g., vegetables are at 2 o'clock, salad plate is at 11 o'clock).

Traveling—Just as a sighted person enjoys hearing a tour guide describe unfamiliar scenery, a blind person likes to hear about indoor and outdoor sights.

Guide Dogs—These are working animals, not pets. Do not distract a guide dog by petting it or by seeking its attention.

Remember—Talk with a blind person as you would with a sighted one, in a normal tone. You may use such expressions as "See you later" and "Did you see that?"

If you enter a room in which a blind person is alone, announce your presence by speaking or introducing yourself. In a group, address blind people by name if they are expected to reply. Excuse yourself when you are leaving.

Source: "What Do You Do When You Meet a Blind Person?" published by the Lighthouse, Inc. Reprinted by permission of the Lighthouse, Inc.

ETHICS IN INTERPERSONAL COMMUNICATION

Vote online at http://www.awl.com/devito

Lying

One deception researcher says lying occurs when "one person intends to mislead another, doing so deliberately, without prior notification of this purpose, and without having been explicitly asked to do so by the target [the person the liar intends to mislead]" (Ekman 1985, p. 28). As this definition implies, lying may be overt and covert. Although it usually involves overt statements, lying may also be committed by omission. When you omit something relevant, leading others to draw incorrect inferences, you're lying just as surely as if you stated an untruth. Similarly, although most lies are verbal, some are nonverbal; in fact, most lies involve at least some nonverbal elements. The innocent facial expression despite the commission of some wrong and the knowing nod instead of the honest expression of ignorance are common examples of nonverbal lying (O'Hair, Cody, and McLaughlin 1981). Lies may range from the "white lie" and truth stretching to lies that form the basis of infidelity in a relationship, libel, and perjury. Not surprisingly, lies have ethical implications.

Some lies are considered innocent, acceptable, and generally ethical (for example, lying to a child to protect a fantasy belief in Santa Claus or the Tooth Fairy, telling someone who looks terrible that he or she looks great, or publicly agreeing with someone to enable the person to save face). Other lies are considered unacceptable and generally unethical (for example, lying to defraud investors, to falsely accuse someone of a crime, or to get out of paying your fair share of income tax). Other lies, however, aren't so easy to classify as ethical or unethical.

What would you do? *You've been called for jury duty and really don't want to serve. You've served before and never get put on a case because, you suspect, you teach critical thinking courses. So rather than spend two weeks in a jury room for no reason, you wonder if it would be ethical to lie and say that your invalid mother can't do without you (actually your sister could easily fill in for you). Would it be ethical to lie under these circumstances? What would you do in this situation?*

in expressing emotions other than anger. Men are also more indirect when they refuse expressions of increased romantic intimacy. Men are thus indirect, the theory goes, when they're saying something that goes against the masculine stereotype.

Many Asian and Latin American cultures stress the values of indirectness largely because it enables a person to avoid appearing criticized or contradicted and thereby losing face. A somewhat different kind of indirectness is seen in the greater use of intermediaries to resolve conflict among the Chinese than among North Americans, for example (Ma 1992). In most of the United States, however, directness is preferred. "Be up front" and "tell it like it is" are commonly heard communication

When asked what they would like to change about the communication of the opposite sex, men said they wanted women to be more direct and women said they wanted men to stop interrupting and offering advice (Noble 1994). What one change would you like to see in the communication style of the opposite sex? Of your own sex? How would you describe your own relational communication in terms of direct versus indirect messages? In what specific ways would you want your present communication patterns to change?

guidelines. Contrast these with the following two principles of indirectness found in the Japanese language (Tannen 1994b):

> *omoiyari,* close to empathy, says that listeners need to understand the speaker without the speaker being specific or direct. This style obviously places a much greater demand on the listener than would a direct speaking style.
>
> *sassuru* advises listeners to anticipate a speaker's meanings and use subtle cues from the speaker to infer his or her total meaning.

Can you recall an instance when you used an indirect message? Why did you use it? For example, did you assume that it would be more effective than a direct message? What happened?

◀◀ THINKING BACK

In thinking about direct and indirect messages, it's important to realize the ease with which misunderstandings can occur. For example, a person who uses an indirect style of speech may be doing so to be polite and may have been taught this style by his or her culture. If you assume, instead, that the person is using indirectness to be manipulative, because your culture regards it so, then miscommunication is inevitable.

REVIEWING KEY TERMS AND CONCEPTS IN VERBAL AND NONVERBAL MESSAGES

This unit introduced the message system and examined some of the similarities and differences in verbal and nonverbal messages.

The Interaction of Verbal and Nonverbal Messages

How do verbal and nonverbal messages interact?

- Nonverbal messages often **accent** or emphasize some part of the verbal message.
- Nonverbal messages often **complement,** add to, or supplement the verbal message.
- Nonverbal messages often **contradict** or deny the meaning of the verbal message.
- Nonverbal messages often regulate or **control** the flow of the verbal message.
- Nonverbal messages often **repeat** or restate the meaning of the verbal message.
- Nonverbal messages often **substitute** or take the place of verbal messages.

Meanings and Messages

What is meaning and what are the principles that regulate the communication of meaning from one person to another?

- *Meaning* is an active process created by cooperation between source and receiver; it's a function of the interaction of messages and the receiver's previous experiences, expectations, attitudes, and so forth.
- Meanings are *in people* rather than in just the words themselves.
- Meanings are *more than words and gestures;* meanings include what speaker and listener bring to the interpersonal interaction.
- Meanings are *unique;* no two people will have the same exact meaning for any term or gesture.
- Meanings have *denotative* (objective, dictionary-like) and *connotative* (subjective, personal) dimensions.
- Meanings are *context-based;* the context heavily influences the meanings words and gestures are given.

Message Characteristics

What are the major characteristics of verbal and nonverbal messages?

- Communication behaviors occur in clusters; they're *packaged*.
- Verbal and nonverbal messages are *rule governed*.
- Messages vary in *abstraction*.
- Messages may vary in *directness,* ranging from extremely direct to extremely indirect.

APPLYING KEY TERMS AND CONCEPTS IN VERBAL AND NONVERBAL MESSAGES

1. How many examples of the six ways in which verbal and nonverbal messages interact can you find in a half-hour situation comedy?
2. The National Easter Seal Society offers a number of suggestions for communicating with people with disabilities. (Also see "Ten Commandments for Communicating with People with Disabilities" in Unit 3, page 56, and "What Do You Do When You Meet a Blind Person?" in this unit on page 161.) Among their recommendations are: (a) Don't use the word *handicap;* instead us the word *disability*. (b) Don't emphasize the disability; emphasize the person. For example, don't label a person as an epileptic; instead, refer to someone who has epilepsy. How would you explain these suggestions in terms of denotation and connotation?

3. How would you state the rules for the appropriateness of such common nonverbal messages as (a) smiling, (b) winking, and (c) shaking hands?
4. Many people who communicate directly see those who communicate indirectly as being manipulative. According to Tannen (1994b, p. 92), however, "'manipulative' is often just a way of blaming others for our discomfort with their styles." Do you agree with Tannen? Or do you think that indirectness is often intentionally manipulative?
5. Why is it relatively easy for two people to agree on a word's denotative meaning and so difficult for the same two people to agree on its connotative meaning? How difficult would it be to secure agreement on the connotative meaning of *religion, democracy, wealth,* and *freedom* from members of this class?
6. Consider the differences in meaning for such words as *woman* to an American and an Iranian, *religion* to a born-again Christian and an atheist, and *lunch* to a Chinese rice farmer and a Wall Street executive. What principles might help such diverse groups understand the meanings of the other?
7. Visit http://www.ccil.org/jargon/ or any electronic dictionary and browse through the terms and definitions. How is an online dictionary different from a print one?
8. Have others ever misinterpreted the meaning you wanted to communicate because they failed to look for meaning in you?
9. A weasel is a slippery rodent; just when you're going to catch it, it slips away. Weasel words are words whose meanings are difficult to pin down. For example, the medicine that claims to work better than Brand X doesn't specify how much better or in what respect it performs better. It's possible that it performs better in one respect and less effective on the other nine measures. "Better" is a weasel word. "Like" is another word often used for weaseling, as when a claim is made that "Brand X will make you feel like a new man." Other weasel words are "helped," "virtually," "as much as," and "more economical." How many weasel words can you identify in a half-hour television show's commercials?
10. How would you go about finding answers to questions such as these:
    - Are men or women more effective liars? More effective lie detectors?
    - What rules do you follow when you introduce two people to each other?
    - Do men and women have similar connotative meanings for such terms as *relationships, love, friendship,* and *family*?
    - Do couples who talk about their talk (that is, who metacommunicate) argue less than couples who don't metacommunicate? Are teachers who metacommunicate more effective than teachers who don't?
    - Are close relationship partners better at detecting their partners' lies than are casual acquaintances? For an interesting investigation of this question see Metts (1989).

EXPERIENCING KEY TERMS AND CONCEPTS IN VERBAL AND NONVERBAL MESSAGES

Go to www.awl.com/devito

Exercises No. 9, "Facial Expressions," No. 10, "Eye Contact," No. 11, "Interpersonal Interactions and Space," and No. 13, "The Meanings of Color," illustrate various dimensions of nonverbal communication.

UNIT 10
VERBAL MESSAGES: UNDERSTANDING PRINCIPLES AND PITFALLS

Philadelphia (1993)

IF WOMEN SPEAK AND HEAR A LANGUAGE OF CONNECTION AND INTIMACY, WHILE MEN SPEAK AND HEAR A LANGUAGE OF STATUS AND INDEPENDENCE... INSTEAD OF DIFFERENT DIALECTS, IT HAS BEEN SAID THEY SPEAK DIFFERENT GENDERLECTS.

--DEBORAH TANNEN

JONATHAN DEMME'S PHILADELPHIA *focuses on a lawyer (Tom Hanks) stricken with AIDS who is fired from his prestigious law position because of the firm's homophobia. Another lawyer (Denzel Washington) undertakes to handle the case to sue the law firm, but he does so reluctantly because of his own homophobia. This film illustrates the illogic of homophobia and how interpersonal interactions are influenced in so many ways by homophobia. In this unit we consider some of the principles and pitfalls of verbal messages—disconfirmation (including homophobia, racism, and sexism), excluding talk, self-talk, and criticism and praise.*

DISCONFIRMATION AND CONFIRMATION

Before reading about these important concepts, take the self-test "How Confirming Are You?" to examine your own message behavior.

THINKING AHEAD ▸▸

Have you ever felt ignored, as if your presence or your opinions didn't matter? What gave you that feeling?

TEST YOURSELF *How Confirming Are You?*

In your typical communications, how likely are you to display the following behaviors? Use the accompanying scale in responding to each statement: 5 = always, 4 = often, 3 = sometimes, 2 = rarely, 1 = never.

_______ 1. I acknowledge the presence of another person both verbally and nonverbally.

_______ 2. I acknowledge the contributions of the other person—for example, by supporting or taking issue with what the person says.

_______ 3. During the conversation, I make nonverbal contact by maintaining direct eye contact, touching, hugging, kissing, and otherwise demonstrating acknowledgment of the other person.

_______ 4. I communicate as both speaker and listener with involvement, and with a concern and respect for the other person.

_______ 5. I signal my understanding of the other person both verbally and nonverbally.

_______ 6. I reflect the other person's feelings as a way of showing that I understand these feelings.

_______ 7. I ask questions when appropriate concerning the other person's thoughts and feelings.

_______ 8. I respond to the other person's requests, for example, by returning phone calls and answering letters within a reasonable time.

_______ 9. I encourage the other person to express his or her thoughts and feelings.

_______ 10. I respond directly and exclusively to what the other person says.

All ten statements express confirming behaviors. Therefore, high scores (above 35) reflect a strong tendency to engage in confirmation. Low scores (below 25) reflect a strong tendency to engage in disconfirmation. Can you provide at least one specific message to illustrate how you might express confirmation in each of the ten situations identified in the self-test. For example, for the first statement, you might say: "Hi, Pat, come over and join us" or simply smile and wave Pat to join your group. ■

Confirmation and disconfirmation—as illustrated in the self-test—refer to the extent to which you acknowledge another person. Consider this situation. Pat arrives home late one night. Chris is angry and complains about Pat's coming home so late. Consider some responses Pat might make:

1. Stop screaming. I'm not interested in what you're babbling about. I'll do what I want, when I want. I'm going to bed.
2. What are you so angry about? Didn't you get in three hours late last Thursday when you went to that office party? So knock it off.
3. You have a right to be angry. I should have called to tell you I was going to be late, but I got involved in an argument at work, and I couldn't leave until it was resolved.

In response 1, Pat dismisses Chris's anger and even indicates dismissal of Chris as a person. In response 2, Pat rejects the validity of Chris's reasons for being angry but does not dismiss either Chris's feelings of anger or Chris as a person. In response 3, Pat acknowledges Chris's anger and the reasons for being angry. In addition, Pat provides some kind of explanation and, in doing so, shows that both Chris's feelings and Chris as a person are important and that Chris deserves to know what happened. The first response is an example of disconfirmation, the second of rejection, and the third of confirmation.

Psychologist William James once observed that "no more fiendish punishment could be devised, even were such a thing physically possible, than that one should be turned loose in society and remain absolutely unnoticed by all the members thereof." In this often-quoted observation, James identifies the essence of disconfirmation (Watzlawick, Beavin, and Jackson 1967, Veenendall and Feinstein 1995).

Disconfirmation is a communication pattern in which you ignore a person's presence as well as that person's communications. You say, in effect, that the person and what she or he has to say aren't worth serious attention. Disconfirming responses often lead to loss of self-esteem.

Note that disconfirmation is not the same as **rejection.** In rejection, you disagree with the person; you indicate your unwillingness to accept something the other person says or does. In disconfirming someone, however, you deny that person's significance; you claim that what this person says or does simply does not count.

Confirmation is the opposite communication pattern. In confirmation, you not only acknowledge the presence of the other person but also indicate your acceptance of this person, of this person's definition of self, and of your relationship as defined or viewed by this other person. Confirming responses often lead to gains in self-esteem. You can communicate confirmation (and disconfirmation) in a wide variety of ways. Table 10.1 shows just a few.

Talking with the Grief Stricken

TRY IT!
To learn more about talking with the grief stricken, go to www.awl.com/devito.

Talking with the grief stricken provides an interesting perspective on confirmation. Grief is something everyone experiences at some time. It may be experienced because of illness or death, the loss of a highly valued relationship (for example, a romantic breakup), the loss of certain physical or mental abilities, or the loss of material possessions (your house burning down or stock market losses). Consider the following example of one attempt to talk with a grief stricken individual.

> I just heard that Harry died—I mean—passed away. I'm so sorry. I know exactly how you feel. But you know, it's for the best. I mean the man was suffering. I remember seeing him last month; he was so weak he could hardly stand. And he looked so sad. He must have been in constant pain. It's better this way. He's at peace. You'll get over it. You'll see. Time heals all wounds. It was the same way with me, and you know how close we were. I mean we were devoted to each other. Everyone said we were the clos-

TABLE 10.1 Confirmation and Disconfirmation

This table parallels the self-test presented earlier in this unit so that you can see clearly not only the confirming but also the opposite, disconfirming behaviors. As you review this table, try to imagine a specific illustration for each of the ways of communicating disconfirmation and confirmation (Pearson 1993; Galvin and Brommel 1996).

Confirmation	Disconfirmation
1. Acknowledge the presence of the other verbally or nonverbally	1. Ignore the presence of the other person
2. Acknowledge the contributions of the other by either supporting or taking issue with what the other says	2. Ignore what the other says; express (nonverbally and verbally) indifference to anything the other says
3. Make nonverbal contact by maintaining direct eye contact, touching, hugging, kissing, and otherwise demonstrating acknowledgment of the other	3. Make no nonverbal contact; avoid direct eye contact; avoid touching other person
4. Engage in dialogue—communication in which both persons are speakers and listeners, both are involved, and both are concerned with and have respect for each other	4. Engage in monologue—communication in which one person speaks and one person listens, there is no real interaction, and there is no real concern or respect for each other
5. Demonstrate understanding of what the other says and means	5. Jump to interpretation or evaluation rather than working at understanding what the other means
6. Reflect the other's feelings to demonstrate your understanding of these feelings	6. Express your own feelings, ignore feelings of the other, or give abstract intellectualized responses
7. Ask questions of the other concerning both his or her thoughts and feelings	7. Make statements about yourself; ignore any lack of clarity in the other's remarks
8. Acknowledge the other's requests; answer the other's questions, return phone calls, and answer letters	8. Ignore the other's requests; fail to answer questions, return phone calls, and answer letters
9. Encourage the other to express thoughts and feelings	9. Interrupt or otherwise make it difficult for the other to express himself or herself
10. Respond directly and exclusively to what the other says	10. Respond tangentially by acknowledging the other's comment but then shifting the focus of the message in another direction

est pair they had ever seen. And I got over it. So how about we go to dinner tonight? We'll talk about old times. Come on. Come on. Don't be a spoilsport. I really need to get out. I've been in the house all week. Come on, do it for me. After all, you have to forget; you have to get on with your own life. I won't take no for an answer. I'll pick you up at seven.

To avoid the kind of communication illustrated above and to make this often difficult form of communication easier, confirm the other person and the person's feelings. "You must miss him a great deal" confirms the person's feelings, for example. Avoid expressions that are disconfirming: "You'll see, things will be better tomorrow." At the same time, give the grieving person permission to grieve. Let the person know that it's acceptable for him or her to grieve in the ways that feel most comfortable—for example, crying or talking about old times.

Encourage the grieving person to express feelings and talk about the loss. Most people who experience grief welcome the opportunity to talk about it. However, don't try to force the person to talk about experiences or feelings she or he may not be ready to share. At the same time, avoid trying to force the grief-stricken individual to focus on the bright side; she or he may not be ready. Avoid expressions such as "You're so lucky you still have some vision left" or "It's better this way; Pat was suffering so much."

Empathize with the grief-stricken person and communicate this empathic understanding. Let the person know that you can understand what he or she is feeling. Don't assume, though, that your feelings (however empathic) are the same in depth or in kind. If, having never experienced this tragedy, you say to a parent who has lost a child, "I know exactly what you're feeling," you risk arousing resentment. (See Unit 8 for more on empathy.)

Be especially sensitive to leave-taking cues. Don't try to force your presence on someone who is grief stricken or press the person to stay with you or a group of people. When in doubt, ask.

These concepts of confirmation and disconfirmation also give unique insight into a wide variety of offensive language practices, language that alienates and separates, language that disconfirms. The three obvious practices are racism, sexism, and heterosexism.

Racism

According to Andrea Rich (1974), "any language that, through a conscious or unconscious attempt by the user, places a particular racial or ethnic group in an inferior position is racist." **Racist language** expresses racist attitudes. It also contributes to the development of racist attitudes in those who use or hear such language.

Racist terms are used by members of one culture to disparage members of other cultures—their customs or their accomplishments. Racist language emphasizes differences rather than similarities and separates rather than unites members of different cultures. Traditionally, racist language has been used by the dominant group to establish and maintain power over other groups. Today, however, it is used by racists (or the racist-talking) in all groups. The social consequences of racist language in terms of employment, education, housing opportunities, and general community acceptance are well known.

It's interesting to note that the terms denoting some of the major movements in art—for example, "impressionism" and "cubism"—were originally applied negatively. The terms were adopted by the artists themselves and eventually became positive. A parallel can be seen in the use of the word "queer" by some lesbian and gay organizations. Their purpose in using the term is to cause it to lose its negative connotation.

It has often been pointed out (Davis 1973, Bosmajian 1974, Purnell 1982) that some aspects of language may be inherently racist. For example, Davis's examination of English found 134 synonyms for "white." Of these, 44 have positive connotations (for example, "clean," "chaste," and "unblemished") and only 10 have negative connotations (for example, "whitewash" and "pale"); the remaining synonyms are relatively neutral. Of the 120 synonyms for "black," 60 were found to have unfavorable connotations ("unclean," "foreboding," and "deadly") and none to have positive connotations.

Consider such phrases as the following:

the Korean doctor
the Latino prodigy
the African American mathematician
the white nurse
the Indian physicist

In some cases, of course, the racial identifier may be relevant, as in "The Korean doctor argued for hours with the French doctor while the Swiss tried to secure a com-

Many people feel that it's permissible for members of a culture to refer to themselves with the terms that, if said by outsiders, would normally be considered racist. That is, Chinese may use the negative terms referring to Chinese, Italians may use the negative terms referring to Italians, and so on. This issue is seen clearly in rap music where performers use such racial terms. The reasoning seems to be that groups should be able to laugh at themselves. One possible problem, though, is that these terms may reinforce the negative stereotypes that society has already assigned this group. By using these terms, members may come to accept these labels with their negative connotations and thus contribute to their own stereotyping. Others would argue that by using such terms, they're making them less negative. The use of the word *queer,* for example, by militant gay and lesbian groups is designed to give a negatively evaluated term a positive spin. What are your feelings about this issue?

promise." Here the aim might be to identify the nationality of the doctor as you would if you had forgotten her or his name. Often, however, such identifiers are used to emphasize that the combination of race and occupation (or talent or accomplishment) is rare and unexpected, that this member of the race is an exception. It also implies that racial factors are somehow important in the context. As noted, at times this may be true, but most often race would be irrelevant.

Sexism

The National Council of Teachers of English has proposed guidelines for nonsexist (gender-free, gender-neutral, or sex-fair) language. These concern the use of generic *man,* the use of generic *he* and *his,* and sex-role stereotyping (Penfield 1987).

WEB EXPLORATION
To learn more about sexism and language, go to www.awl.com/devito.

Generic Man The word *man* refers most clearly to an adult male. To use the term to refer to both men and women emphasizes "maleness" at the expense of "femaleness". Similarly the terms *mankind* or *the common man* or even *cavemen* imply a primary focus on adult males. Gender-neutral terms can easily be substituted. Instead of *mankind,* you can say *humanity, people,* or *human beings*. Instead of *the common man,* you can say *the average person* or *ordinary people*. Instead of *cavemen,* you can say *prehistoric people* or *cave dwellers*.

Similarly, the use of such terms as *policeman* or *fireman* and other terms that presume maleness as the norm and femaleness as a deviation from this norm are clear and common examples of **sexist language.** Consider using nonsexist alternatives for these and similar terms; make these alternatives (for example, *police officer* and *firefighter*) a part of your active vocabulary. What alternatives can you offer for each of these terms: chairman, the common man, countryman, doorman, man, mankind, manmade, mailman, manpower, repairman, fireman, freshman, salesman, stewardess, waitress, web master, and womanizer?

Generic He and His The use of the masculine pronoun to refer to any individual regardless of sex is certainly declining. But it was only as far back as 1975 that all college textbooks, for example, used the masculine pronoun as generic. There seems to be no legitimate reason the feminine pronoun could not alternate with the masculine pronoun in referring to hypothetical individuals, or why such terms as he and she or her and him could not be used instead of just he or him. Alternatively, you can restructure your sentences to eliminate any reference to gender. For example, the NCTE Guidelines (Penfield 1987) suggest that instead of saying, "The average student is worried about his grades," say, "The average student is worried about grades." Instead of saying, "Ask the student to hand in his work as soon as he is finished," say, "Ask students to hand in their work as soon as they're finished."

Sex-Role Stereotyping The words you use often reflect a sex-role bias, the assumption that certain roles or professions belong to men and others belong to women. In eliminating sex-role stereotyping, avoid, for example, making the hypothetical elementary school teacher female and the college professor male. Avoid referring to doctors as male and nurses as female. Avoid noting the sex of a professional with terms such as "female doctor" or "male nurse." When you're referring to a specific doctor or nurse, the person's sex will become clear when you use the appropriate pronoun: "Dr. Smith wrote the prescription for her new patient" or "The nurse recorded the patient's temperature himself." Here are a few additional examples. How would you rephrase these?

1. You really should get a second doctor's opinion. Just see what he says.
2. Johnny went to school today and met his kindergarten teacher. I wonder who she is?
3. Everyone needs to examine his own conscience.
4. The effective communicator is a selective self-discloser; he discloses to some people about some things some of the time.
5. The effective waitress knows when her customers need her.
6. The history of man is largely one of technology replacing his manual labor.

Heterosexism

A close relative of sexism is heterosexism. The term is a relatively new addition to our list of linguistic prejudices. **Heterosexist language** refers to language used to disparage lesbians and gay men (Rothblum and Bond 1996). As in the case of racist and sexist language, we see heterosexism in the derogatory terms used for lesbians and gay men and in more subtle forms. For example, when we qualify a description of a profession—as in "gay athlete" or "lesbian doctor"—we are in effect stating that athletes and doctors are not normally gay or lesbian. Further, we are highlighting the affectional orientation of the athlete and the doctor in a context in which it may have no relevance. This practice is, of course, the same as qualifying by race or gender, as already noted.

Still another instance of heterosexism—and perhaps the most difficult to deal with—is the presumption of heterosexuality. Usually, people assume that the person they're talking to or about is heterosexual. Usually, they're correct, because the majority of the population is heterosexual. At the same time, however, note that heterosexism denies lesbians and gay males their true identity. The practice of assuming that a person is heterosexual is very similar to the presumption of whiteness and maleness that we have made significant progress toward eliminating.

In eliminating heterosexism from your own language, perhaps the most important step is to avoid any offensive nonverbal mannerisms that parody stereotypes when talking about gays and lesbians. At the same time, avoid "complimenting" gay men and lesbians by saying they "don't look it." To gays and lesbians, that is not a compliment. Similarly, expressing disappointment that a person is gay—for example, saying "What a waste!" and meaning it as a compliment is not really a compliment.

Avoid, too, the assumption that every gay or lesbian knows what every other gay or lesbian is thinking. To do so is very similar to asking someone from Japan why Sony is investing heavily in the United States, or as one comic put it, asking an African American, "What do you think Jesse Jackson meant by that last speech?" Similarly, saying things like "Lesbians are so loyal" or "Gay men are so open with their feelings"—statements that ignore the reality of wide differences within any group—are potentially insulting to all groups and deny the vast individual differences existing within any large group of people.

Avoid *overattribution,* the tendency to attribute just about everything a person does, says, and believes to being gay or lesbian. This tendency helps to recall and perpetuate stereotypes.

Remember that relationship milestones are important to all people. Ignoring the anniversary of your uncle and his same-sex partner or that partner's birthday while remembering and celebrating similar milestones of another uncle and his opposite-sex partner is unfair and will be resented.

Racist, Sexist, and Heterosexist Listening

Just as racist, sexist, and heterosexist attitudes will influence your language , they also influence your listening. In this type of listening you only hear what the speaker is saying through your stereotypes. You assume that what the speaker is saying is unfairly influenced by the speaker's sex, race, or affectional orientation.

Sexist, racist, and heterosexist listening occur in a wide variety of situations. For example, when you dismiss a valid argument or attribute validity to an invalid argument, when you refuse to give someone a fair hearing, or when you give less credibility (or more credibility) to a speaker because the speaker is of a particular sex, race, or affectional orientation, you're practicing sexist, racist, or heterosexist listening. Put differently, sexist, racist, or heterosexist listening occurs when you listen differently to a person because of his or her sex, race, or affectional orientation when these characteristics are irrelevant to the message.

But in many instances these characteristics are relevant and pertinent to your evaluation of the message. For example, the sex of the speaker talking on pregnancy, fathering a child, birth control, or surrogate motherhood or fatherhood is, most would agree, probably relevant to the message. It's not sexist listening to take the sex of the speaker into account when listening to such messages. However, it is sexist listening to assume that only one sex has anything to say that's worth hearing or that what one sex says can be discounted without a fair hearing. The same is true when your listening is filtered through your schemata or stereotypes of race, gender, or affectional orientation.

What kinds of sexist, heterosexist, and racist comments have you heard from your peers? Did you respond with a message that was confirming, rejecting, disconfirming?

◄◄ THINKING BACK

ASK THE RESEARCHER

Confronting Homophobia

A lot of homophobic language is used around the office and I'd like to know what I can do to respond effectively to such homophobic statements. I don't want to be a language cop, ready to pounce on every politically incorrect word, yet I don't want to remain silent and thereby imply agreement with what's being said. Any suggestions?

Homophobic language perpetuates cruel images of inadequacy and marginality which rob all sexual nonconformists of human dignity. Moreover, employing homophobic language "erases" gay and lesbian people by presuming, contrary to fact, that nearly everyone is heterosexual. Choosing what to say in this situation depends, of course, on your relationship with the other individual, the organizational culture in which you work, and the motive which you perceive behind the remark.

Generally, your response to such remarks can be either distant or personal. A distant response would stress the social effects of antigay language, perhaps equating hostile words with gay bashing. Depending on the context, you might also stress the effect of antigay remarks on organizational morale and image. The use of a personal voice might include objections on grounds of a commitment to inclusiveness, concern for the sensitivities of other people who might well be gay men or lesbians, and, if you are a gay or lesbian person, disclosure of your own identity.

For further information see Richard D. Mohr, *Gay Ideas: Outing and Other Controversies* (Boston: Beacon Press, 1992), and Brian McNaught, *Gay Issues in the Workplace* (New York: St. Martin's Press, 1993).

—Ralph Smith (Ph.D., University of Southern California) is a professor of communication at Southwest Missouri State University, where he teaches courses in public relations and the rhetoric of social movements. Russel Windes (Ph.D., Northwestern University) is a professor emeritus of the City University of New York, where he taught courses in argumentation, persuasion, and political communication.

THINKING AHEAD ▸▸
What makes you feel included in a conversation? What makes you feel excluded?

EXCLUDING TALK AND INCLUSION

Excluding talk is used here as a general term to refer to communication that excludes certain people, though on the surface it may appear to apply to everyone. You see this, for example, in the use of in-group language in the presence of an out-group member. When doctors get together and discuss medicine, there is no problem. But when they get together with someone who isn't a doctor, they often fail to adjust to this new person. Instead, they simply continue with discussions of prescriptions, symptoms, medication, and all the talk that excludes others present.

Excluding talk also occurs when people of the same nationality get together within a larger, more heterogeneous group and use the language of their nationality, sometimes just isolated words, sometimes sentences, and sometimes even entire conversations. Similarly, the use of experiences not shared by all (common topics include having children, exotic vacations, and people we know) can serve to include some and exclude others. The use of these terms and experiences in the presence of nonmembers emphasizes their status as outsiders and excludes these people from full participation in the communication act.

Another form of excluding talk is the use of the terms of one's own cultural group as universal, as applying to everyone. In using such terms, you exclude others. For example, *church* refers to the place of worship for specific religions, not all religions. Similarly, *Bible* refers to the Christian religious scriptures and is not a general term for *religious scriptures*. Nor does *Judeo-Christian tradition* include the religious traditions of everyone. Similarly, the terms *marriage, husband,* and *wife* refer to some heterosexual relationships and exclude others; they also exclude gay and lesbian relationships.

Instead of trying to emphasize the exclusion of one or more members, consider the principle of **inclusion.** Regardless of the type of communication situation we are in, everyone needs to be included in the interaction. Even if job-related issues have to be discussed in the presence of a nonmember, that person can be included in a variety of ways, for example, by seeking the nonmember's perspective or drawing an analogy from his or her field.

Another way to practice inclusion is to fill in relevant details discussed by the group for those who may be unaware. For example, when people, places, or events are mentioned in a group discussion, briefly identify them for those to whom they may be unfamiliar. Brief parenthetical identifying phrases are usually sufficient: "Margo—she's Jeff's daughter—loved San Francisco State."

When someone asks a question or makes a comment requiring a response, be sure to respond in some way. Even if you're talking, attending to someone else, or otherwise engaged, respond in some way to indicate your acknowledgment of the comment—verbally, if possible, or nonverbally with a nod or smile, for example. Practicing inclusion is so easy that it's surprising that it's violated so blatantly and so often. When inclusion is practiced, everyone gains a great deal more satisfaction from the interaction.

Also, consider the vast array of alternative terms that are inclusive rather than exclusive. For example, the Association of American University Presses (Schwartz et al. 1995) recommends using *place of worship* instead of *church* when you wish to include the religious houses of worship of all people. Similarly, *committed relationship* is more inclusive than *marriage, couple's therapy* is more inclusive than *marriage counseling,* and *life partner* is more inclusive than *husband* or *wife. Religious scriptures* is more inclusive than *Bible.* Of course, if you're referring to, say, a specific Baptist church or married heterosexual couples. then the terms *church* and *marriage* are perfectly appropriate.

Some people would consider the above suggestions for inclusion controversial. How do you see them?

◀◀ THINKING BACK

SELF-TALK, OTHER-TALK, AND BALANCE

THINKING AHEAD ▶▶

On a ten-point scale (with 1 being all self-talk and 10 being all other-talk), how would you describe your last few days of conversation?

Many people—friends and family members are surely among them—act and talk as if they were the center of the universe. They talk constantly about themselves—about their jobs, their accomplishments, their plans, their families, their love lives, their problems, their successes, and sometimes even their failures. Rarely do they ask how

Do men and women use excluding talk equally, or do you find that one sex uses it more often than the other?

you are, what you think (except perhaps about them), or what your plans are. Other people go to the other extreme and never talk about themselves. They're the underdisclosers discussed in Unit 8, the people who want to learn everything about you but aren't willing (or perhaps unable) to share anything about themselves that might make them vulnerable. As a result, you come away from the interaction with the feeling that they either did not like you very much or did not trust you. Otherwise, you feel, they would have revealed something of themselves.

Admittedly, it's not easy to steer a comfortable course between too much and too little **self-talk.** Moreover, there are certainly times when we just cannot stop talking about a new job or new romantic partner. Under most circumstances, however, we should strive for interactions governed by the principle of balance—some self-talk, some **other-talk,** never all of either one. Communication is a two-way process: each person needs to function as source and as receiver, and each person should have a chance to function as subject. Balanced communication interactions are more satisfying and more interesting. We all get bored with too much talk about the other person, and, let's face it, others get bored with too much talk about us. The principle of balance is a guide to protect both us and others.

How satisfied are you with the relative balance between self and other that characterizes your own style of speaking? If you're unsatisfied, what do you intend to do about it?

◀◀ THINKING BACK

THINKING AHEAD ▶▶

If you could sort your last 100 comments into two categories—one for comments that offered praise and one for comments that offered criticism—how many would be in each category?

CRITICISM, PRAISE, AND HONEST APPRAISAL

Throughout your communication experiences, you're expected to criticize, to evaluate, and otherwise to render judgment on some person or on something someone did or created. Especially in helping professions, such as teaching, nursing, or counseling, criticism is an important and frequently used skill. The problem arises when criticism is used outside of its helping function, when it's inappropriate or excessive. An important interpersonal skill is to develop a facility for detecting when a person is asking for criticism and when that person is simply asking for a compliment. For example, when a friend asks how you like the new apartment, he or she may be searching for a compliment rather than wanting you to itemize all the things wrong with it. Similarly, the person who says, "Do I look okay?" may be asking for a compliment.

Sometimes the desire to be liked (or perhaps the need to be appreciated) is so strong that we go to the other extreme and paint everything with praise. The most ordinary jacket, the most common thought, the most average meal are given extraordinary praise, way beyond their merits. The overly critical and the overly complimentary soon find that their comments are no longer met with concern or interest.

As an alternative to excessive criticism or praise, consider the principle of honest appraisal. Tell the truth, but note that there is an art to truth telling, just as there is an art to all other forms of effective communication. First, distinguish between instances in which an honest appraisal is sought and those in which the individual needs a compliment. Respond to the appropriate level of meaning. Second, if an honest appraisal is desired and if yours is a negative one, give some consideration to how you should phrase your criticism.

In giving criticism focus on the event or the behavior rather than on personality; for example, say "This paper has four errors and needs retyping" rather than "You're a lousy typist; do this over." In offering such criticism, be specific. Instead of saying "This paper is weak," as some English teachers might, say "I think the introduction wasn't clear enough. Perhaps a more specific statement of purpose would have worked better."

Try to state criticism positively, if at all possible. Rather than saying "You look terrible in black," it might be more helpful to say "You look much better in bright colors." In this way, you're also being constructive; you're explaining what could be done to make the situation better. If you do express criticism that seems to prove destructive, it may be helpful to offer a direct apology or to disclaim any harmful intentions (Baron 1990). In your positive statement of criticism, try to state your concern for the other person along with your criticism, if appropriate. Instead of saying "The introduction to your report is boring," say "I really want your report to be great; I'd open with some humor to get the group's attention." Say "I want you to make a good impression. I think the dark suit would work better."

Own your thoughts and feelings. Instead of saying "Your report was unintelligible," say "I had difficulty following your ideas." At the same time, avoid mind reading. Instead of saying "Don't you care about the impression you make? This report is terrible," say "I think I would use a stronger introduction and a friendlier writing style."

Avoid ordering or directing the other person to change; try identifying possible alternatives. Instead of saying "Don't be so forward when you're first introduced to someone," say "I think they might respond better to a less forward approach."

Consider the context of the criticism. Generally, it's best to express criticism in situations where you can interact with the person and express your attitudes in dialogue rather than monologue. By this principle, then, your first choice would be to express criticism face-to-face, your second choice would be by telephone, and a distant third choice by letter, memo, or e-mail. Also, try to express your criticism in private. This is especially important when dealing with members from cultures where public criticism could result in a serious loss of face.

In expressing praise, keep the following in mind:

- Use I-messages. Instead of saying "That report was good," say "I thought that report was good" or "I liked your report."
- Make sure your affect (facial movement) communicates your positive feelings. Often when people praise others simply because it's the socially correct response, they may betray their lack of conviction with too little or inappropriate affect.
- Name the behavior you're praising. Instead of saying "That was good," say "I enjoyed your speech" or "I thought your introduction was great."
- Take culture into consideration. Many Asians, for example, feel uncomfortable when praised because it's often taken as a sign of veiled criticism (Dresser 1996).

What do you think of the relative emphases on criticism and praise in your typical style of speaking? Are you satisfied?

◀◀ THINKING BACK

REVIEWING KEY TERMS AND CONCEPTS IN VERBAL MESSAGE PRINCIPLES AND PITFALLS

This unit covered a variety of principles that will prove generally useful in interpersonal communication; when conscientiously applied, they should go a long way toward both reducing the frequency of some annoying and destructive habits and making verbal interaction more pleasant and productive.

Disconfirmation and Confirmation

What is disconfirmation and confirmation (and the related sexist, racist, and heterosexist communications)?

- **Disconfirmation** is communication that ignores another, that denies the other person's definition of self.
- **Confirmation** expresses acknowledgment and acceptance of others and avoids racist, sexist, and heterosexist expressions that are disconfirming.

Excluding Talk and Inclusion

What is excluding and inclusive talk and how can these be managed more effectively?

- Excluding or in-group talk is talk that includes some and excludes others and is generally resented especially by those who are excluded.
- **Inclusion** seeks to make everyone present a significant part of the interpersonal interaction.

Self-Talk, Other-Talk, and Balance

What is the difference between self-talk and other-talk, and how can you more effectively balance these?

- Excessive **self-talk** or excessive **other-talk** is communication that is unbalanced in terms of self and other and generally is not as effective as talk that is more balanced.
- Balanced talk involves a reasonable mixture of self-talk and other-talk.

Criticism, Praise, and Honest Appraisal

How can you more effectively communicate criticism and praise?

- Excessive criticism or praise is talk that is basically dishonest and in many instances manipulative.
- The principle of honest appraisal calls for saying what you feel, but gently and kindly.

APPLYING KEY TERMS AND CONCEPTS IN VERBAL MESSAGE PRINCIPLES AND PITFALLS

1. How would you describe your own behavior in terms of confirmation and disconfirmation? In which specific situations are you most likely to be confirming? Most likely to be disconfirming?
2. Visit and lurk a while at one of the Internet sites devoted to grief (for example, http://www.yahoo-.com/Society_and_Culture/death, and http://www.katsden.com/-death/index.html). What kinds of information do these sites provide?
3. What would you say to Doris, whose fiancé (their wedding was scheduled for next week) was in a car accident and will have to lose both his legs? You see her walking to the hospital.
4. Do you find sexist, racist, and heterosexist listening on your campus, in your family, or at your place of work?
5. How does racist, sexist, and heterosexist language in interpersonal interactions differ from such language in more public situations (for example, in print, on television, or in public speeches)? Is your own language sexist, racist, or heterosexist?
6. One study found that seventh-grade science textbooks contained sexist language and failed to integrate the achievements of women scientists and to provide the necessary information on women's health (Potter and Rosser 1992). Do you find sexism in your college textbooks? Do you find racism and heterosexism?
7. On your college campus, which would be considered the most offensive: sexist, racist, or heterosexist language? Least offensive? What is your ethical obligation when you encounter racist, sexist, and heterosexist talk?
8. If you asked your friends how often you talk about yourself versus how often you talk about them, what do you think they would say? Use a ten-point scale with 1 being exclusively "self-talk" and 10 being exclusively "other-talk." Now ask a few friends. How accurate were you?
9. What guidelines would you like others to observe when they offer criticism of you or your behavior?
10. How would you go about finding answers to the following questions?
    - Is the tendency to confirm others related to one's own level of self-esteem?
    - What are the effects of using racist, sexist, and heterosexist language on campus?
    - Does using derogatory language about your own group influence your self-esteem?
    - How is disconfirmation used in Internet communication?
    - How important is face-saving in the United States compared with Asian countries such as China, Japan, and Korea?

EXPERIENCING KEY TERMS AND CONCEPTS IN VERBAL MESSAGE PRINCIPLES AND PITFALLS

Go to www.awl.com/devito

Exercises No. 15, "Conversational Analysis: A Chance Meeting," and No. 16, "Giving and Taking Directions," will prove useful for illustrating verbal message principles.

UNIT 11

VERBAL MESSAGES: REDUCING BARRIERS TO INTERACTION

Flower Drum Song (1961)

IT IS NOT ONLY TRUE THAT THE LANGUAGE WE USE PUTS WORDS IN OUR MOUTHS; IT ALSO PUTS NOTIONS IN OUR HEADS.

--WENDELL JOHNSON

In Flower Drum Song, a Chinese woman (Myoshi Umeki) comes to America to wed a nightclub owner (Jack Soo) who really doesn't want this marriage (arranged by his mother through an exchange of photos). The film depicts the communication barriers created by the cultural differences between those raised on traditional Chinese values and those raised on American values as well as between the generations. In this unit we consider a wide variety of communication barriers, visible not only in this film but in just about any film where there are interpersonal differences and conflict.

Interpersonal communication is fragile—in part because of its complexity and in part because it's a human process, subject to all the failings and problems of fallible people. Chief among these problems are what are called **barriers** or cognitive distortions. All barriers discussed here are ways in which your verbal messages describe the world in illogical, distorted, or unscientific ways (Burns 1980, Beck 1988).

The term *barriers* is used not to convey the idea that communicators function as machines or that communication is a mechanical process. Rather it emphasizes that meaningful interpersonal communication may lose some of its effectiveness when communicators think or behave in certain ways. Recognize that these barriers are of human origin and development; it's the communicators who, for one reason or another, create and maintain them.

Consider an analogy between verbal messages and geographic maps. Maps that accurately portray the world assist you in getting from one place to another. To the extent that such maps inaccurately portray the world, they hinder you. Verbal messages are like maps. When they accurately represent reality, they aid effective and meaningful interpersonal communication; when they distort reality, they hinder effective and meaningful interpersonal communication. These barriers may all be understood and examined in light of five general principles of language: language symbolizes reality (partially), language expresses both facts and inferences, language is relatively static, language can obscure distinctions, and language can be used unethically as well as ethically.

THINKING AHEAD ▸▸

Do you ever treat the word as if it's the thing? Do you treat what you say as if it's all that could or need be said?

LANGUAGE SYMBOLIZES REALITY (PARTIALLY)

Language symbolizes reality; it's not the reality itself. Of course, this is obvious. But consider: have you ever reacted to the way something was labeled or described rather than to the actual item? Have you ever bought something because of its name rather than because of the actual object? If so, you were probably responding as if language was the reality, a distortion called intensional orientation.

Intensional Orientation

Intensional orientation refers to the tendency to view people, objects, and events in terms of how they're talked about or labeled rather than in terms of how they actually exist. **Extensional orientation** is the opposite, the tendency to look first at the actual people, objects, and events and only then at the labels. It's the tendency to be guided by what you see happening rather than by the way something or someone is talked about or labeled.

Intensional orientation occurs when you act as if the words and labels are more important than the things they represent—as if the map is more important than the territory. In its extreme form, intensional orientation is seen in the person who is afraid of dogs and who begins to sweat when shown a picture of a dog or when hearing people talk about dogs. Here the person is responding to a label as if it were the actual thing. In its more common form it occurs when you see people through your schemata instead of on the basis of their specific behaviors. It occurs when you think of a supermodel as vain and superficial before getting to know the specific supermodel.

The corrective to intensional orientation is to focus first on the object, person, or event and then on the way in which the object, person, or event is talked about. Labels are certainly helpful guides, but don't allow them to obscure what they're meant to symbolize.

Cultural Identifiers Having said that the word is not the thing does not mean that words may be chosen at random or that all words are equal. This is seen most clearly in the preferences people have for identifying their cultural origins. As always, when in doubt, find out. The preferences and many of the specific examples identified here are drawn largely from the findings of the Task Force on Bias-Free Language of the Association of American University Presses. Do realize that not everyone would agree with these recommendations; they're presented here—in the words of the Task Force—"to encourage sensitivity to usages that may be imprecise, misleading, and needlessly offensive" (Schwartz et al. 1995, p. ix).

WEB EXPLORATION
To learn more about cultural identifiers, go to www.awl.com/devito.

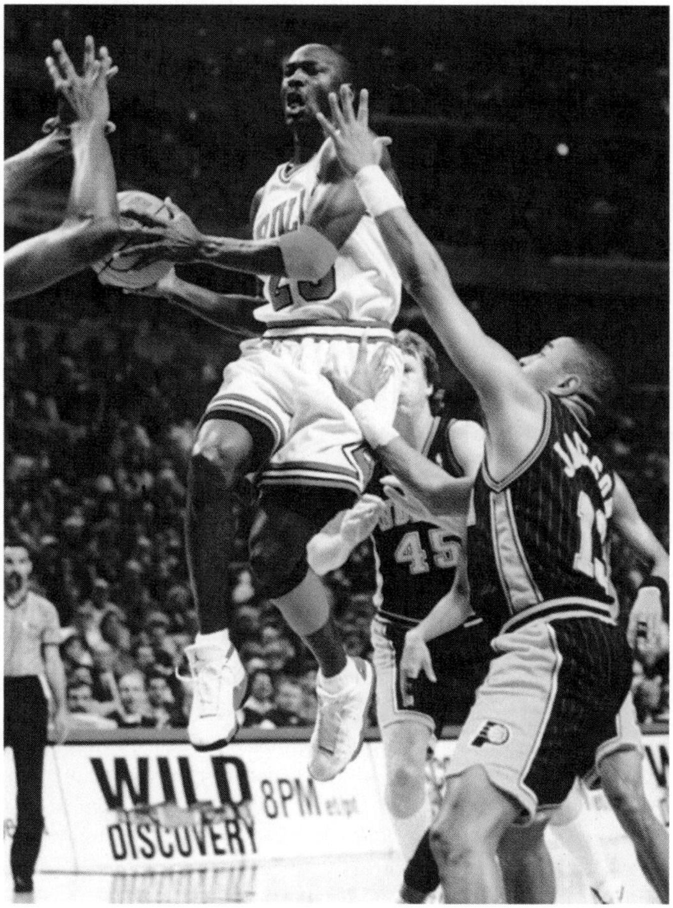

Intensional orientation is seen in the numerous studies on credibility (Riggio 1987). These studies demonstrate that you're influenced more when you assume that the message comes from a highly credible source than when you assume it comes from an average individual. Such studies have shown, for example, that you'll evaluate a painting highly if you think it was painted by a famous artist, but you'll give it a low evaluation if you think it was produced by a little-known artist. In all such credibility studies, the influencing factor was not the message itself—the painting or the speech, for example—but the name attached to it. Advertisers have long known the value of this type of appeal and have capitalized on it by using popular figures from sports or music to endorse sneakers, soft drinks, and underwear. Do these celebrity endorsements influence your buying behavior?

Generally, the term *girl* should only be used to refer to very young females and is equivalent to *boy*. Neither term should be used for people older than, say, 13 or 14, though some popular uses extend the terms through high school age. *Girl* is never used to refer to a grown woman, nor is *boy* used to refer to persons in blue-collar positions, as it once was. *Lady* is negatively evaluated by many because it connotes the stereotype of the prim and proper woman. *Woman* or *young woman* is preferred. *Older person* is preferred to *elder, elderly, senior,* or *senior citizen* (which technically refers to someone older than 65).

Generally, *gay* is the preferred term to refer to a man who has an affectional preference for another man and *lesbian* is the preferred term for a woman who has an affectional preference for another woman. (*Lesbian* means "homosexual woman" so the phrase *lesbian woman* is redundant.) This preference for the term *lesbian* is not universal among homosexual women; in one survey, for example, 58 percent preferred *lesbian;* 34 percent preferred *gay* (Lever 1995). *Homosexual* refers to both gay men and lesbians but more often to a sexual orientation to members of one's own sex. *Gay* and *lesbian* refer to a lifestyle and not just to sexual orientation. *Gay* as a noun, although widely used, may prove offensive in some contexts, for example, "We have two gays on the team." Although used within the gay community in an effort to remove the negative stigma through frequent usage, the term *queer*—as in *queer power*—is often resented when used by outsiders. Because most scientific thinking holds that one's sexuality is genetically determined rather than being a matter of choice, the term *sexual orientation* rather than *sexual preference* or *sexual status* (which is also vague) is preferred.

Generally, most African Americans prefer *African American* to *black* (Hecht, Collier, and Ribeau 1993) though *black* is often used with *white* and is used in a variety of other contexts (for example, Department of Black and Puerto Rican Studies, the *Journal of Black History,* and Black History Month). The American Psychological Association recommends that both terms be capitalized, but *The Chicago Manual of Style* (the manual used by most publishing houses) recommends using lowercase. The terms *negro* and *colored,* although used in the names of some organizations (for example, the United Negro College Fund and the National Association for the Advancement of Colored People) aren't used outside of these contexts.

White is generally used to refer to those whose roots are in European cultures and usually does not include Hispanics. On the analogy of *African American* comes the phrase *European American*. Few European Americans, however, would want to be called that; most would prefer their national origins emphasized, for example, *German American* or *Greek American*. This preference may well change as Europe moves into a more cohesive and united entity. *People of color*—a more literary-sounding term appropriate perhaps to public speaking but awkward in most conversations—is preferred to *nonwhite*, which implies that whiteness is the norm and nonwhiteness is a deviation from that norm. The same is true of the term *non-Christian*.

Generally, *Hispanic* is used to refer to anyone who identifies himself or herself as belonging to a Spanish-speaking culture. *Latina* (female) and *Latino* (male) refer to those whose roots are in one of the Latin American countries, for example, Dominican Republic, Nicaragua, or Guatemala. *Hispanic American* refers to those United States residents whose ancestry is a Spanish culture and includes Mexican, Caribbean, and Central and South Americans. In emphasizing a Spanish heritage, the term is really inadequate in referring to those large numbers in the Caribbean and in South America whose origins are French or Portuguese. *Chicana* (female) and *Chicano* (male) refer to those with roots in Mexico, though it often connotes a nationalist attitude

(Jandt 1995) and is considered offensive by many Mexican Americans. *Mexican American* is preferred.

Inuk (pl. *Inuit*) was officially adopted at the Inuit Circumpolar Conference to refer to the group of indigenous people of Alaska, Northern Canada, Greenland, and Eastern Siberia. This term is preferred to *Eskimo* (a term the United States Census Bureau uses), which was applied to the indigenous peoples of Alaska by Europeans and derives from a term that means "raw meat eaters" (Maggio 1997).

Indian refers only to someone from India and is incorrectly used when applied to members of other Asian countries or to the indigenous peoples of North America. *American Indian* or *Native American* are preferred, even though many Native Americans refer to themselves as *Indians* and *Indian people*. The term *native American* (with a lowercase *n*) is most often used to refer to persons born in the United States. Although the term technically could refer to anyone born in North or South America, people outside the United States generally prefer more specific designations such as *Argentinean, Cuban,* or *Canadian*. The term *native* means an indigenous inhabitant; it's not used to mean "someone having a less developed culture."

Muslim is the preferred form (rather than the older *Moslem*) to refer to a person who adheres to the religious teachings of Islam. *Quran* (rather than *Koran*) is the preferred term for the scriptures of Islam. The terms *Mohammedan* or *Mohammedanism* aren't considered appropriate since they imply worship of Muhammad, the prophet, "considered by Muslims to be a blasphemy against the absolute oneness of God" (Maggio 1997, p. 277).

Although there is no universal agreement, generally *Jewish people* is preferred to *Jews,* and *Jewess* (a Jewish female) is considered derogatory. *Jew* should only be used as a noun and is never correctly used as a verb or an adjective (Maggio 1997).

When history was being written with a European perspective, it was taken as the focal point and the rest of the world was defined in terms of its location from Europe. Thus, Asia became the *east* or the *orient* and Asians became *Orientals*—a term that is today considered inappropriate or Eurocentric. Thus, people from Asia are *Asians* just as people from Africa are *Africans* and people from Europe are *Europeans*.

Allness

Another way in which your messages fail to recognize that language symbolizes reality only partially is with **allness.** The world is infinitely complex, and because of this you can never say all there is to say about anything—at least not logically. This is particularly true in dealing with people. You may think you know all there is to know about certain individuals or about why they did what they did, yet clearly you don't know all. You can never know all the reasons you yourself do something, so there is no way you can know all the reasons your parents, friends, or enemies did something.

You may, for example, be assigned to read a textbook, and because previous texts have been dull and because perhaps the first chapter of this one is dull, you might infer that all the rest of the book will likewise be dull. Of course, the rest of a book is often even worse than its beginning. Yet it could be that the rest of the book would prove exciting were it read with an open mind. The problem here is that you run the risk of judging an entire text in such a way as to preclude any other possibilities. If you tell yourself that the book is dull, it will probably seem dull; if you say a required course will be useless, it will be extremely difficult for the instructor to make the course anything but what you have defined it to be. Only occasionally do people allow themselves to be proven wrong.

The parable of the six blind men and the elephant is an excellent example of an "allness orientation"—the tendency to judge the whole on the basis of experience with only some part of the whole—and its attendant problems. You may recall from elementary school the poem by John Saxe that concerns six blind men of Indostan who came to examine an elephant, an animal they had only heard about. The first blind man touched the elephant's side and concluded that the elephant was like a wall. The second felt the tusk and said the elephant must be like a spear. The third held the trunk and concluded that the elephant was much like a snake. The fourth touched the knee and knew the elephant was like a tree. The fifth felt the ear and said the elephant was like a fan. The sixth grabbed the tail and concluded that the elephant was like a rope. Each of these learned men reached his own conclusion regarding what the elephant was really like. Each argued that he was correct and that the others were wrong.

Each, of course, was correct; at the same time, however, all were wrong. The point this parable illustrates is that you can never see all of anything; you can never experience anything fully. You see part of an object, event, or person—and on that limited basis, you conclude what the whole is like. This procedure is universal, and you follow it because you cannot possibly observe everything. Yet recognize that when making judgments of the whole based on only a part, you're actually making inferences that can later be proved wrong. If you assume that you know everything there is to know about something or someone, you fall into the pattern of misevaluation called allness.

Famed British prime minister Disraeli once said that "to be conscious that you are ignorant is a great step toward knowledge." This observation is an excellent example of a **nonallness** attitude. If you recognize that there is more to learn, more to see, more to hear, you leave yourself open to this additional information, and you're better prepared to assimilate it.

A useful device to help remember to avoid allness is to end each statement, sometimes verbally but always mentally, with an **"etc."** (et cetera), a reminder that there is more to learn, more to know, more to say—a reminder that every statement is inevitably incomplete. Some people, however, overuse the et cetera. They use it as a substitute for being specific, which really defeats its purpose. Instead, it should be used to mentally remind yourself that there is more to know and more to say.

Have you ever assumed you knew everything about a person and then learned something completely surprising about him or her? What did this experience teach you about allness?

◀◀ THINKING BACK

THINKING AHEAD ▶▶

How do you distinguish between statements that are factual and statements that are inferences or assumptions?

LANGUAGE EXPRESSES BOTH FACTS AND INFERENCES

Language enables you to form statements of facts and inferences without making any linguistic distinction between the two. Similarly, when you speak or listen to such statements you often don't make a clear distinction between statements of facts and statements of inference. Yet there are great differences between the two. Barriers to clear thinking can be created when inferences are treated as facts, a tendency called **fact-inference confusion.**

For example, you can make statements about the world that you observe, and you can make statements about what you have not observed. In form or structure, these statements are similar and cannot be distinguished from each other by any grammatical analysis. For example, you can say, "She is wearing a blue jacket" as well as "She is harboring an illogical hatred." If you diagramed these sentences, they would yield identical structures, and yet you know that they're different types of statements. In the first one, you can observe the jacket and the blue color. But how do you observe "illogical hatred"? Obviously, this is not a descriptive statement but an

inferential statement, a statement that you make not solely on the basis of what you observe but on the basis of what you observe plus your own conclusions.

There's no problem with making inferential statements; you must make them if you're to talk about much that is meaningful. The problem arises when you act as though those inferential statements are factual statements. Consider, for example, the following anecdote (Maynard 1963):

> A woman went for a walk one day and met her friend, whom she had not seen, heard from, or heard of in ten years. After an exchange of greetings, the woman said, "Is this your little boy?" and her friend replied, "Yes. I got married about six years ago." The woman then asked the child, "What is your name?" and the little boy replied, "Same as my father's." "Oh," said the woman, "then it must be Peter."

The question, of course, is how did the woman know the boy's father's name? The answer is obvious, but only after you recognize that in reading this short passage you have, quite unconsciously, made an inference that is preventing you from arriving at the answer. You have inferred that the woman's friend is a woman. Actually, the friend is a man named Peter.

Perhaps the classic example of this type of fact-inference confusion concerns the case of the "empty" gun that unfortunately proves to be loaded. With amazing frequency, we find in the newspapers examples of people being so sure that the guns are empty that they point them at someone else and fire. Often, of course, they're empty. But unfortunately, often they're not. Here one draws the inference that the gun is empty but acts as if it were a fact and fires the gun.

You may wish to test your ability to distinguish facts from inferences by taking the self-test "Can You Distinguish Facts from Inferences?"

TEST YOURSELF *Can You Distinguish Facts from Inferences?*

Carefully read the following report, modeled on that developed by William Haney (1973), and the observations based on it. Indicate whether you think the observations are true, false, or doubtful on the basis of the information presented in the report. Circle *T* if the observation is definitely true, *F* if the observation is definitely false, and *?* if the observation may be either true or false. Judge each observation in order. Don't reread the observations after you have indicated your judgment, and don't change any of your answers.

A well-liked college teacher had just completed making up the final examinations and had turned off the lights in the office. Just then a tall, broad figure appeared and demanded the examination. The professor opened the drawer. Everything in the drawer was picked up and the individual ran down the corridor. The dean was notified immediately.

T F ? 1. The thief was tall and broad.
T F ? 2. The professor turned off the lights.
T F ? 3. A tall figure demanded the examination.
T F ? 4. The examination was picked up by someone.
T F ? 5. The examination was picked up by the professor.
T F ? 6. A tall figure appeared after the professor turned off the lights in the office.
T F ? 7. The man who opened the drawer was the professor.
T F ? 8. The professor ran down the corridor.
T F ? 9. The drawer was never actually opened.
T F ? 10. Three persons are referred to in this report.

This test is designed to trap you into making inferences and treating them as facts. Statement 3 is true (it's in the report), Statement 9 is false (the drawer was opened), but all other statements are inferences and should have been marked ?. Review the remaining eight statements to see why you cannot be certain that any of them are either true or false. ■

A related communication barrier is raised by what linguistic philosophers call **pragmatic implication.** Consider the following: the sales manager has been replaced. You know that this manager was not doing a particularly good job and that many sales representatives complained about poor leadership. On the basis of this knowledge, you draw a pragmatic implication, an inference that is probably but not necessarily true. In this example, you infer that the sales manager was fired. Now, there is nothing wrong with drawing such inferences; we all do it. The problem comes in when we forget or disregard that they're inferences and not facts. This type of situation occurs every day. You see your supervisor in a romantic restaurant with the new sales manager. You make the pragmatic implication that they're having an affair. You might further infer that the reason the old sales manager was fired was because of the supervisor's affair with the new manager. When inferences are made on top of inferences, it often becomes difficult to distinguish exactly where the facts stopped and the inferences began.

Have you ever mistaken another person's inferences as if they were facts? Did you then act on them as if they were facts? What happened?

◀◀ THINKING BACK

Some of the essential differences between factual and inferential statements are summarized in Table 11.1. Distinguishing between these two types of statements does not imply that one type is better than the other. Both types of statements are useful; both are important. The problem arises when you treat an inferential statement as if it were fact. Phrase your inferential statements as tentative. Recognize that such statements may prove to be wrong. Leave open the possibility of other alternatives.

Can you recall an example where you made a pragmatic implication that proved to be incorrect? What happened?

TABLE 11.1 Differences Between Factual and Inferential Statements

These differences highlight the important distinctions between factual and inferential statements and are based on the discussions of Haney (1973) and Weinberg (1959). As you go through this table, consider how you would classify such statements as: "God exists," "Democracy is the best form of government," "This paper is white," "The Internet will grow in size and importance over the next ten years," and "This table is based on Haney and Weinberg."

Factual Statements	Inferential Statements
May be made only after observation	May be made at any time
Are limited to what has been observed	Go beyond what has been observed
May be made only by the observer	May be made by anyone
May be about only the past or the present	May be about any time—past, present, or future
Approach certainty	Involve varying degrees of probability
Are subject to verifiable standards	Are not subject to verifiable standards

LANGUAGE IS RELATIVELY STATIC

Language changes only very slowly, especially when compared to the rapid change in people and things. **Static evaluation** is the tendency to retain evaluations without change, even though the reality to which they refer is constantly changing. A verbal statement about an event or person remains static and unchanging, while the object or person to whom it refers may change enormously. Alfred Korzybski (1933) used an interesting illustration in this connection: In a tank there is a large fish and many small fish that are its natural food source. Given freedom in the tank, the large fish will eat the small fish. After some time, the tank is partitioned, with the large fish on one side and the small fish on the other, divided only by glass. For a time, the large fish will try to eat the small fish but will fail; each time it tries, it will knock into the glass partition. After some time, it will "learn" that trying to eat the small fish means difficulty, and it will no longer go after them. Now, however, the partition is removed and the small fish swim all around the big fish. But the big fish does not eat them and in fact will die of starvation while its natural food swims all around. The large fish has learned a pattern of behavior, and even though the actual territory has changed, the map remains static.

THINKING AHEAD ▸▸
Do you maintain evaluations—opinions of others, say—as unchanging and permanent or do you revise them regularly?

TRY IT!
To learn more about static language, go to www.awl.com/devito.

While you would probably agree that everything is in a constant state of flux, the relevant question is whether you act as if you know this. Do you act in accordance with the notion of change, instead of just accepting it intellectually? Do you treat your little sister as if she were ten years old, or do you treat her like the 20-year-old woman she has become? Your evaluations of yourself and others must keep pace with the rapidly changing real world. Otherwise you'll be left with attitudes and beliefs—static evaluations—about a world that no longer exists.

To guard against static evaluation, date your statements and especially your evaluations. Remember that Gerry Smith$_{1994}$ is not Gerry Smith$_{2001}$; academic abilities$_{1995}$ are not academic abilities$_{2001}$. T. S. Eliot, in *The Cocktail Party,* said that "what we know of other people is only our memory of the moments during which we knew them. And they have changed since then . . . at every meeting we are meeting a stranger."

Has another person ever failed to take change into consideration with the result that her or his evaluations of you no longer corresponded to the person you were at the time?
◂◂ THINKING BACK

ETHICS IN INTERPERSONAL COMMUNICATION

Vote online at http://www.awl.com/devito

Libel, Slander, and More

The First Amendment to the United States Constitution states: *Congress shall make no law . . . abridging the freedom of speech, or of the press; or the right of the people peaceably to assemble and to petition the Government for a redress of grievances.*

But speech is not always free and, in fact, it becomes unlawful and unethical in a variety of ways. For example, it's considered unethical (and it's illegal as well) to defame another person, to falsely attack his or her reputation, causing damage to it. When this attack is done in print or in pictures, it's called *libel;* when done through speech, it's called *slander*.

People are becoming increasingly sensitive to and accepting of cultural differences. Whereas just decades ago it would have been considered quite respectable to use racial, sexist, or homophobic terms in conversation or tell jokes at the expense of various cultural groups, today it's considered inappropriate. Today it would be considered unethical to demean another person because of that person's sex, age, race, nationality, affectional orientation, or religion or to speak in cultural stereotypes—fixed images of groups that promote generally negative pictures.

Sexual harassment is unethical and a form of speech that would not be protected by the First Amendment. Recently, the courts have ruled that sexual harassment can take place by either sex against either sex.

Verbal abuse of people because of their position on a particular issue, because of their cultural identification, or because they've done something you disapprove of is considered unethical.

What would you do? *At the water cooler in the office, you join two of your colleagues only to discover that they're exchanging racist jokes. You don't want to criticize them for fear that you'll become unpopular, with the likelihood that these colleagues will make it harder for you to get ahead. At the same time, you don't want to remain silent for fear it would imply that you're accepting of this type of talk. What would you do in this situation?*

THINKING AHEAD ▸▸
Do you react to people as individuals, or do you lump them together into a group without recognizing the individual nature of each? Do you have a tendency to talk in opposites—black and white, good and bad, young and old? Does this influence the way you think?

LANGUAGE CAN OBSCURE DISTINCTIONS

Language can obscure distinctions among people or events that are covered by the same label but are really quite different (indiscrimination) and by making it easy to focus on extremes rather than on the vast middle ground between opposites (polarization).

Indiscrimination

Nature seems to abhor sameness at least as much as vacuums, for nowhere in the universe can you find identical entities. Everything is unique. Language, however, provides common nouns, such as *teacher, student, friend, enemy, war, politician, liberal,* and the like, which may lead you to focus on similarities. Such nouns can lead you to group together all teachers, all students, and all friends and perhaps divert attention from the uniqueness of each individual, object, and event.

The misevaluation of **indiscrimination,** then, occurs when you focus on classes of individuals, objects, or events and fail to see that each is unique and needs to be looked at individually. Indiscrimination can be seen in such statements as these:

- He's just like the rest of them: lazy, stupid, a real slob.
- I really don't want another Martian on the board of directors. One is enough for me.
- Read a romance novel? I read one when I was 16. That was enough to convince me.

A useful antidote to indiscrimination is the **index,** a verbal or mental subscript that identifies each individual in a group as an individual even though all members of the group may be covered by the same label: politician_1 is not politician_2; teacher_1 is not teacher_2.

Ethnocentrism An interesting perspective can be gained on indiscrimination by looking briefly at **ethnocentrism,** the tendency to evaluate the values, beliefs, and behaviors of your own culture as being more positive, logical, and natural than those of other cultures. Although normally thought of negatively, there are positive aspects to ethnocentrism. For example, if a group is under attack, ethnocentrism will help create cohesiveness. It has also been argued that it forms the basis of patriotism and a willingness to sacrifice for the benefit of the group (Neuliep and McCroskey 1997).

But ethnocentrism can also create considerable problems. For example, it can set up obstacles to communication with those who are culturally different from you. It can also lead to hostility to outside groups and may blind you to seeing other perspectives, other values, other ways of doing things (Neuliep and McCroskey 1997).

Ethnocentrism exists on a continuum (see Table 11.2). People aren't either ethnocentric or not ethnocentric; rather, most are somewhere between these polar opposites. Of course, your degree of ethnocentrism varies, depending on the group on which you focus. For example, if you're Greek American, you may have a low degree of ethnocentrism when dealing with Italian Americans but a high degree when dealing with Turkish Americans or Japanese Americans. Most important for our purposes is that your degree of ethnocentrism (and we are all ethnocentric to at least some degree) will influence your interpersonal interactions.

TABLE 11.2 The Ethnocentrism Continuum

This table summarizes some of the interconnections between ethnocentrism and communication. In this table, five degrees of ethnocentrism are identified; in reality, there are as many degrees as there are people. The "communication distances" are general terms that highlight the attitude that dominates that level of ethnocentrism. Under "communications" are some of the major ways people might interact given their particular degree of ethnocentrism. Can you identify your own ethnocentrism on this table? For example, are there groups to which you have low ethnocentrism? Middle? High? What accounts for these differences? This table draws on the work of a number of intercultural researchers (Lukens 1978; Gudykunst and Kim 1984; Gudykunst 1991).

Degree of Ethnocentrism	Communication Distance	Communications
Low	Equality	Treats others as equals; views different customs and ways of behaving as equal to one's own
↑	Sensitivity	Wants to decrease distance between self and others
	Indifference	Lacks concern for others; prefers to interact in a world of similar others
↓	Avoidance	Avoids and limits communications, especially intimate ones with interculturally different others
High	Disparagement	Engages in hostile behavior; belittles others; views different cultures and ways of behaving as inferior to one's own

Ethnocentric thinking is at the heart of the common practice of stereotyping national, sexual, racial, and religious groups. A **stereotype** is a relatively fixed mental picture of some group that is applied to each individual of the group without regard to his or her unique qualities. It's important to note that although stereotypes are usually thought of as negative, they may also be positive. You can, for example, consider certain national groups as lazy, superstitious, mercenary, or criminal, but you can also consider them as intelligent, progressive, honest, or hardworking. Regardless of whether such stereotypes are positive or negative, however, the problems they create are the same. They provide shortcuts that are usually inappropriate. For example, when you see someone through a stereotype, you invariably fail to devote sufficient attention to his or her unique characteristics.

There is nothing wrong with classifying. In fact, it's an extremely useful method of dealing with any complex matter; it puts order into thinking. The problem arises not from classification itself but from the application of an evaluative label to that class and the use of that label as an "adequate" map for each and every individual in the group.

Polarization

Polarization, often referred to as the fallacy of "either-or," is the tendency to look at the world and to describe it in terms of extremes—good or bad, positive or negative, healthy or sick, brilliant or stupid, rich or poor, and so on. Polarized statements come in many forms, for example:

- After listening to the evidence, I'm still not clear who the good guys are and who the bad guys are.
- Well, are you for us or against us?
- College had better get me a good job. Otherwise, this has been a big waste of time.

ASK THE RESEARCHER

Becoming Less Ethnocentric

Intellectually I understand that ethnocentrism often has negative effects and is limiting. Emotionally, however, I'm highly ethnocentric and down deep I wonder why members of other cultures don't see the superiority of my culture. Is there anything I can do to become less ethnocentric and more open to other cultures?

Recognize that seeing your culture as "the best" is quite normal in all cultures; that feeling is not necessarily harmful. For example, the "black pride" movement is aimed specifically at promoting feelings of being "the best" within black culture. What is harmful in ethnocentrism is when we treat emotional statements as though they were logical statements. If the University of Miami is playing Florida State in football, fans from both teams engage in yelling and "chest pounding" behaviors fully believing that "they" are "the best." The problem occurs when the emotional attitude "We're the best" is translated into the cognitive belief "We're the best" and treated as a logical statement. Logically, if I am the best, you must be less than I am. But emotionally and psychologically, we can both be the best at the same time. Be proud of your culture. But be open to and proud of other cultures at the same time.

For further information see Everett M. Rogers and Thomas M. Steinfatt, *Intercultural Communication* (Prospect Heights, IL: Waveland, 1999).

—Thomas M. Steinfatt (Ph.D., Michigan State University) is a professor and director of communication, University of Miami, where he teaches courses in intercultural communication, organizational communication, and persuasion and propaganda. Dr. Steinfatt also works as a consultant in diversity training and executive communication, and as an expert witness in persuasion/propaganda and organizational communication. tms@Miami.edu.

Most people exist somewhere between the extremes of good and bad, healthy and sick, brilliant and stupid, rich and poor. Yet there seems to be a strong tendency to view only the extremes and to categorize people, objects, and events in terms of these polar opposites. You can easily demonstrate this tendency by filling in the opposites for each of the following words:

		Opposite
tall	__:__:__:__:__:__	________
heavy	__:__:__:__:__:__	________
strong	__:__:__:__:__:__	________
happy	__:__:__:__:__:__	________
legal	__:__:__:__:__:__	________

Filling in the opposites should have been relatively easy and quick. The words should also have been fairly short. Further, if a number of people supplied opposites, there should be a high degree of agreement among them.

Now try to fill in the middle positions with words meaning, for example, "midway between tall and short," "midway between heavy and light," and so on. Do this before reading any further.

The midway responses (compared to the opposites) were probably more difficult to think of and took you more time. The responses should also have been either fairly long words or phrases of several words. Further, you would probably find little agreement among different people completing this same task.

Consider the familiar bell-shaped curve. If you selected 100 people at random, you would find that their intelligence, height, weight, income, age, health, and so on would fall into a bell-shaped or "normal" distribution. Few items exist at either of the two extremes, but as you move closer to the center, more and more items are included. This is true of any random sample. Yet many people tend to concentrate on the ends of this curve and ignore the middle, which contains the vast majority of cases.

It's legitimate to phrase certain statements in terms of two values. For example, this thing you're holding is either a book or it isn't. Clearly, the classes "book" and "not book" include all possibilities. There is no problem with this kind of statement. Similarly, you may say that a student will either pass this course or will not, as these two categories include all the possibilities.

You create problems when you use polarization, "either-or," in situations where it's inappropriate: for example, "The politician is either for us or against us." Note that these two choices don't include all possibilities; the politician may be for us in some things and against us in others, or may be neutral. During the Vietnam War, there was a tendency to categorize people as either "hawk" or "dove," but clearly many people were neither and many were probably both—hawks on certain issues and doves on others.

Recognize that the vast majority of cases exist between extremes. Don't allow the ready availability of extreme terms to obscure the reality of what lies in between.

How does the index help you to discriminate *among* without discriminating *against*? Can you identify a specific occasion when thinking in opposites got you into trouble or caused you to misevaluate a situation?

◂◂ THINKING BACK

THINKING AHEAD ▸▸

Is it ethical to lie and tell a friend he looks good when he really doesn't? Is it ethical to lie to get a promotion you really deserve? What types of things might you say about someone not present that might be ethically questionable?

LANGUAGE CAN BE USED UNETHICALLY AS WELL AS ETHICALLY

As mentioned in Unit 1, the messages you formulate and send to others have ethical implications. They may often be judged as moral or immoral, just or unjust, fair or unfair. Two obvious types of messages suggest attention: lying and gossip.

Lying

According to deception researcher Paul Ekman (1985, p. 28), *lying* occurs when "one person intends to mislead another, doing so deliberately, without prior notification of this purpose, and without having been explicitly asked to do so by the target [the person the liar intends to mislead]." Lying may be committed by omission as well as commission. When you omit something relevant, and this omission leads others to be misled, you've lied just as surely as if you had made a false statement (Bok 1978).

Most lies are verbal, but some are nonverbal, and most seem to involve at least some nonverbal elements—for example, an innocent facial expression while denying the commission of some unethical act. Most lies are told to benefit the liar, generally (1) to gain some reward (to increase desirable relationships, to protect one's self-esteem, to obtain money) or (2) to avoid some punishment. In an analysis of 322 lies, researchers found that 75.8 percent benefited the liar, 21.7 percent benefited the person who was told the lie, and 2.5 percent benefited some third party (Camden, Motley, and Wilson 1984).

You may wish to examine your own beliefs about the ethics of lying by taking the accompanying self-test.

TEST YOURSELF *Is Lying Unethical?*

Each of the situations below presents an occasion for a lie. For purposes of this exercise, let's define a lie as a deliberate misstatement intended to mislead another person. How would you rate each in terms of its ethicality, using the scale presented below? Note that many of the situations will lead you to look for more specific information before making your decision. For example, you may want to know how old the child in No. 1 is before making your decision, or you may want to know what kind of lie will be used in the employment interview in No. 3. Because of this you might want to give more than one response for each statement, depending on the specifics of the situation: 1 = definitely ethical, 2 = probably ethical, 3 = not sure, need to think more about this one, 4 = probably unethical, 5 = definitely unethical.

______ 1. to lie to a child to protect a fantasy belief, for example, to protect the child's belief in Santa Claus or the Tooth Fairy

______ 2. to lie to achieve some greater good, for example, to prevent someone from committing suicide or getting depressed, or to prevent a burglary or theft

______ 3. to lie in an employment interview in answer to a question that is overly personal (and irrelevant) or illegal

______ 4. to lie to protect the reputation of your family, some specific family member, or some third party

______ 5. to lie to make another person feel good, for example, to tell someone that he or she looks great or has a great sense of humor

______ 6. to lie to enable the other person to save face, for example, to voice agreement with an idea you find foolish, to say you enjoyed meeting the person when you didn't, or to compliment the other person when it's totally undeserved

______ 7. to lie to get what you deserve but can't get any other way, for example, a well-earned promotion or raise or another chance with your relationship partner

______ 8. to lie to get out of jury duty or to the Internal Revenue Service in order to pay less income tax in April

_______ 9. to lie to keep hidden information about yourself that you simply don't want to reveal to anyone, for example, your religious beliefs, affectional orientation, or financial situation

_______ 10. to lie to your relationship partner to avoid a fight

_______ 11. to lie to get elected to some office since you believe everyone else does it and if you don't, you'll never get elected

_______ 12. to lie to get yourself out of an unpleasant situation, for example, to get out of a date, an extra office chore, or a boring conversation

Each of these situations will be responded to differently by different people, depending on the culture in which they were raised, their beliefs about lying, and their own ethical codes. What cultural beliefs influence the ways in which lying and ethics are looked at? Can you identify situations for which a lie is always unethical? Are there situations in which truth-telling would be unethical and lying would be ethical? ■

Gossip

There can be no doubt that everyone spends a great deal of time gossiping. In fact, gossip seems universal among all cultures (Laing 1993), and among some it's a commonly accepted ritual (Hall 1993). Gossip refers to third party talk about another person; the word **gossip** "now embraces both the talker and the talk, the tattler and the tattle, the newsmonger and the newsmongering" (Bremner 1980, p. 178). Gossip is an inevitable part of daily interactions; to advise anyone not to gossip would be absurd. Not gossiping would eliminate one of the most frequent and enjoyable forms of communication.

In some instances, however, gossip is unethical (Bok 1983). First, it's unethical to reveal information that you've promised to keep secret. Although this principle may seem too obvious to even mention, it seems violated in many cases. For example, in a study of 133 school executives, board presidents, and superintendents, the majority received communications that violated an employee's right to confidentiality (Wilson and Bishard 1994). When it is impossible to keep something secret (Bok offers the example of the teenager who confides a suicide plan), the information should be revealed only to those who must know it, not to the world at large. Second, gossip is unethical when it invades the privacy that everyone has a right to, for example, when it concerns matters that are properly considered private and when the gossip can hurt the individuals involved. Third, gossip is unethical when it's known to be false and is nevertheless passed on to others.

WEB EXPLORATION
To learn more about gossip, go to www.awl.com/devito.

Can you identify recent lies you've heard or used that you consider unethical? Did you participate in any gossip that you consider unethical?

◀◀ THINKING BACK

REVIEWING KEY TERMS AND CONCEPTS IN MESSAGE BARRIERS

This unit covered some of the barriers to interpersonal communication, some of the obstacles to effectively communicating your meaning to another person.

Language Symbolizes Reality (Partially)

What is intensional orientation and how can it be combated? What is allness and how can it be corrected?

- **Intensional orientation** is the tendency to view the world in the way it's talked about or labeled. To combat intensional orientation, respond to things first; look for the labels second.
- **Allness** is the tendency to describe the world in extreme terms that imply one knows all or is saying all there is to say. To combat allness, recognize that one can never know all or say all about anything; use a mental and sometimes verbal "etc."

Language Expresses Both Facts and Inferences

How do facts and inferences differ, and how can they better be distinguished?

- **Fact-inference confusion** is the tendency to confuse factual and inferential statements and to respond to inferences as if they were facts. To combat such confusions, distinguish facts from inferences and respond to inferences as inferences, not as facts.

Language Is Relatively Static

What is static evaluation, and how can a process orientation be integrated into our talk?

- **Static evaluation** is the tendency to describe the world in static terms, denying constant change. To combat static evaluation, recognize the inevitability of change; date statements and especially evaluations.

Language Can Obscure Distinctions

What are indiscrimination and ethnocentrism, and how can they be reduced? What is polarization and what can be done to eliminate it?

- **Indiscrimination** is the tendency to group unique individuals or items because they're covered by the same term or phrase. To combat indiscrimination, recognize that sameness does not exist; index terms and statements.
- **Polarization** is the tendency to describe the world in terms of extremes or polar opposites. To combat polarization use middle terms and qualifiers.

Language Can Be Used Unethically as Well as Ethically

What is lying and when might it be considered unethical? What is gossip and when might it be considered unethical?

- **Lying,** deliberately misleading another person, is viewed by many as unethical under some circumstances and not under others. Its ethical dimension is also heavily influenced by culture.
- **Gossip,** communication about someone not present, is viewed by many as unethical when it violates a confidentiality agreement, when it invades a person's privacy, and when it's known to be false.

APPLYING KEY TERMS AND CONCEPTS IN MESSAGE BARRIERS

1. Do you accept the assumptions about language that are discussed throughout this unit? Can you think of reasons to reject any of these assumptions?
2. Do the media give greater attention to ideas phrased in the extreme than to ideas phrased more logically as somewhere between the extremes?
3. Visualize yourself seated with a packet of photographs of strangers before you. You're asked to scratch out the eyes in each photograph. As you progress scratching out the eyes, you come upon a photograph of your mother. Are you able to scratch out the eyes as you have done with the pictures of the strangers? Are you responding intensionally or extensionally?
4. What cultural identifiers do you prefer? How can you let other people know the cultural descriptions that you want to be used to refer to you?
5. Watch a few television situation comedies. How many plots revolving around fact-inference confusion can you identify?
6. Do you ever commit the fallacy of allness? Do you, for example, group all teachers together? All gay people? All politicians? All born-again Christians? All atheists? All African Americans? All European Americans? All Jews? All Hispanics?
7. Would it be possible to have ethnocentric thinking without indiscrimination? Does prejudice depend on indiscrimination?
8. Look up your own city and the cities you've visited or hope to visit and examine their cultural makeup (try http://tiger.census.gov/cgi-bin/gazetteer). Are the labels used for cultural groups consistent with those cultural identifiers suggested in this chapter?
9. Have people ever committed indiscrimination against you by assuming that you believed something or behaved in a particular way because of your sex, race, nationality, religion, or affectional orientation?
10. How would you go about finding answers to the following questions?
    - Do people become less intensionally oriented with education?
    - What other qualities do ethnocentric individuals possess? That is, are people high in ethnocentrism different in other ways from people who are low in ethnocentrism?
    - Is there a sex difference in the ability to distinguish facts from inferences?
    - Are these barriers related to a person's interpersonal popularity?
    - Are people who differ widely in their tendencies toward static evaluation equally satisfied in their interpersonal relationships?

EXPERIENCING KEY TERMS AND CONCEPTS IN MESSAGE BARRIERS

Go to www.awl.com/devito

Exercises No. 15, "Conversational Analysis: A Chance Meeting," No. 16, "Giving and Taking Directions," and No. 26, "Analyzing a Conflict Episode," will provide different perspectives on verbal messages and especially barriers to interaction.

UNIT 12

NONVERBAL MESSAGES: BODY AND SOUND

Pumping Iron (1977)

THE BODY SAYS WHAT WORDS CANNOT.

--MARTHA GRAHAM

The documentary Pumping Iron *and its sequel* Pumping Iron II: The Women *(1985) renewed interest in body building and made Arnold Schwarzenegger a film star. There's no doubt that your body—its shape, size, muscle tone, skin color—communicates messages and tells others something about who you are. In this unit we look at body communication—body type as well as body movement, facial and eye communication, touch, vocal quality, and silence as they communicate messages in interpersonal interactions.*

THINKING AHEAD ▸▸
What types of messages can you communicate with your body?

BODY COMMUNICATION

Generally, we can consider body communication in two parts—the gestures you make with your body and your body's appearance.

Body Gestures

An especially useful classification of body movement (sometimes called **kinesics**) identifies five types: emblems, illustrators, affect displays, regulators, and adaptors (Ekman and Friesen 1969). Table 12.1 summarizes and provides examples of these five movements.

Can you identify similar gestures that mean different things in different cultures and that might create interpersonal misunderstandings?

WEB EXPLORATION
To learn more about emblems, go to www.awl.com/devito.

Emblems Emblems substitute for words. **Emblems** are body movements that have rather specific verbal translations. Emblems are nonverbal substitutes for specific words or phrases: for example, the nonverbal signs for "OK," "peace," "come here," "go away," "who me?" "be quiet," "I'm warning you," "I'm tired," and "it's cold." Emblems are as arbitrary as any words in any language. Consequently, your present culture's emblems are not necessarily the same as your culture's emblems of 300 years ago or the same as the emblems of other cultures. For example, the sign made by forming a circle with the

TABLE 12.1 The Five Body Movements

Can you identify similar gestures that mean different things in different cultures and that might create interpersonal misunderstandings?

	Name and Function	Examples
	**Emblems** directly translate words or phrases.	"OK" sign, "come here" wave, hitchhiker's sign
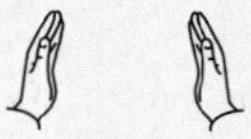	**Illustrators** accompany and literally "illustrate" verbal messages.	Circular hand movements when talking of a circle, hands far apart when talking of something large.
	**Affect displays** communicate emotional meaning.	Expressions of happiness, surprise, fear, anger, sadness, disgust/contempt.
	**Regulators** monitor, maintain, or control the speaking of another.	Facial expressions and hand gestures indicating "keep going," "slow down," or "what else happened?"
	**Adaptors** satisfy some need.	Scratching one's head.

thumb and index finger may mean "nothing" or "zero" in France, "money" in Japan, and something sexual in certain southern European cultures. But just as the English language is spreading throughout the world, so, too, is the English nonverbal language. The American use of this emblem to mean "OK" is spreading just as fast, for example, as English technical and scientific terms.

Illustrators **Illustrators** accompany and literally illustrate the verbal messages. Illustrators make your communications more vivid and help to maintain your listener's attention. They also help to clarify and make more intense your verbal messages. In saying, "Let's go up," for example, you probably move your head and perhaps your finger in an upward direction. In describing a circle or a square, you more than likely make circular or square movements with your hands.

We are aware of illustrators only part of the time; at times, they may have to be brought to our attention. Illustrators are more universal than emblems; illustrators will be recognized and understood by members of more different cultures than will emblems.

Affect Displays **Affect displays** are the movements of the face that convey emotional meaning—the expressions that show anger and fear, happiness and surprise, eagerness and fatigue. They're the facial expressions that give you away when you try to present a false image and that lead people to say, "You look angry. What's wrong?" We can, however, consciously control affect displays, as actors do when they play a role. Affect displays may be unintentional (as when they give you away) or intentional (as when you want to show anger, love, or surprise).

Regulators **Regulators** monitor, maintain, or control the speaking of another individual. When you listen to another, you're not passive; you nod your head, purse your lips, adjust your eye focus, and make various paralinguistic sounds such as "mm-mm" or "tsk." Regulators are culture-bound: each culture develops its own rules for the regulation of conversation. Regulators also include such broad movements as shaking your head to show disbelief or leaning forward in your chair to show that you want to hear more.

Regulators communicate what you expect or want speakers to do as they're talking: for example, "Keep going," "Tell me what else happened," "I don't believe that. Are you sure?" "Speed up," and "Slow down." Speakers often receive these nonverbal signals without being consciously aware of them. Depending on their degree of sensitivity, they modify their speaking behavior in accordance with these regulators.

Adaptors **Adaptors** satisfy some need and usually occur without conscious awareness; they're unintentional movements that usually go unnoticed. Nonverbal researchers identify three types of adaptors based on their focus, direction, or target: self-adaptors, alter-adaptors, and object-adaptors (Burgoon, Buller, and Woodall 1995).

Self-adaptors usually satisfy a physical need, especially to make you more comfortable, for example, scratching your head to relieve an itch, moistening your lips because they feel dry, or pushing your hair out of your eyes. When these adaptors occur in private, they occur in their entirety: you scratch until the itch is gone. But in public, these adaptors usually occur in abbreviated form. When people are watching you, for example, you might put your fingers to your head and move them around a bit but probably not scratch with the same vigor as when in private.

Alter-adaptors are the body movements you make in response to your current interactions. Examples would include crossing your arms over your chest when someone unpleasant approaches or moving closer to someone you like.

Object-adaptors are those that involve your manipulation of some object. Frequently observed examples include punching holes in or drawing on a styrofoam coffee cup, clicking a ball point pen, or chewing on a pencil. Object adaptors are usually signs of negative feelings; for example, you emit more adaptors when feeling hostile than when feeling friendly. Further, as anxiety and uneasiness increase, so does the frequency of adaptors (Burgoon, Buller, and Woodall 1995).

Body Appearance

Of course, the body communicates even without movement. For example, others may form impressions of you from your general body build, from your height and weight, and from your skin, eye, and hair color. Assessments of your power, your attractiveness, and your suitability as a friend or romantic partner are often made on the basis of your physical body (Sheppard and Strathman 1989).

Height, for example, has been shown to be significant in a wide variety of situations. Tall presidential candidates have a much better record of winning the election than do their shorter opponents. Tall people seem to be paid more and are favored by interviewers over shorter applicants (Keyes 1980, Guerrero, DeVito, and Hecht 1999, Knapp and Hall 1992, Jackson and Ervin 1992).

Your body also reveals your race through skin color and tone and may also give clues as to your more specific nationality. Your weight in proportion to your height will also communicate messages to others, as will the length, color, and style of your hair.

Your general attractiveness is also a part of body communication. Attractive people have the advantage in just about every activity you can name. They get better grades in school, are more valued as friends and lovers, and are preferred as coworkers (Burgoon, Buller, and Woodall 1995). Although we normally think that attractiveness is culturally determined—and to some degree it is—recent research seems to be showing that definitions of attractiveness are becoming universal (Brody 1994). A person rated as attractive in one culture is likely to be rated as attractive in other cultures—even cultures that are widely different in appearance.

In what ways can you make your body communication more effective?

◀◀ THINKING BACK

THINKING AHEAD ▶▶

What messages do you communicate with your face?

FACIAL COMMUNICATION

Throughout your interpersonal interactions, your face communicates, especially your emotions. In fact, facial movements alone seem to communicate the degree of pleasantness, agreement, and sympathy felt; the rest of the body doesn't provide any additional information. For other aspects, however—for example, the intensity with which an emotion is felt—both facial and bodily cues are used (Graham, Bitti, and Argyle 1975, Graham and Argyle 1975).

Some nonverbal communication researchers claim that facial movements may communicate at least the following eight emotions: happiness, surprise, fear, anger, sadness, disgust, contempt, and interest (Ekman, Friesen, and Ellsworth 1972). Others propose that, in addition, facial movements may communicate bewilderment and determination (Leathers 1992).

Try to communicate surprise using only facial movements. Do this in front of a mirror, and try to describe in as much detail as possible the specific movements of the face that make up surprise. If you signal surprise as most people do, you probably exhibit raised and curved eyebrows, long horizontal forehead wrinkles, wide-open eyes, dropped-open mouth, and lips parted with no tension. Even if there were differences—and clearly there would be from one person to another—you could probably recognize the movements listed here as indicative of surprise.

Of course, some emotions are easier to communicate and to decode than others. For example, in one study, happiness was judged with an accuracy ranging from 55 percent to 100 percent, surprise from 38 percent to 86 percent, and sadness from 19 percent to 88 percent (Ekman, Friesen, and Ellsworth 1972). Research finds that women and girls are more accurate judges of facial emotional expression than men and boys (Hall 1984, Argyle 1988).

Facial Management

As you learned the nonverbal system of communication, you also learned certain **facial management techniques**: for example, to hide certain emotions and to emphasize others. Table 12.2 identifies four types of facial management techniques that you'll quickly recognize from their frequent use (Ekman and Friesen 1978, Malandro, Barker, and Barker 1989).

These facial management techniques tell you what emotions to express when. For example, when someone gets bad news in which you may secretly take pleasure, the display rule dictates that you frown and otherwise nonverbally signal your displeasure. If you place first in a race and your best friend barely finishes, the display rule requires that you minimize your expression of pleasure in winning and certainly avoid any signs of gloating. If you violate these display rules, you'll be judged insensitive.

Facial Feedback

In one interesting study, participants held a pen in their teeth to simulate a sad expression. They then rated photographs. Results showed that mimicking sad expressions actually increased the degree of sadness the subjects reported feeling when viewing the photographs (Larsen, Kasimatis, and Frey 1992). This finding is an example of the facial feedback hypothesis that holds that your facial expression influences physiological arousal (Lanzetta, Cartwright-Smith, and Kleck 1976, Zuckerman, Klorman, Larrance, and Spiegel 1981).

Further support for this hypothesis comes from a study which compared participants who (1) feel emotions such as happiness and anger with those who (2) both feel and express these emotions. In support of the **facial feedback hypothesis,** subjects

TABLE 12.2 Facial Management Techniques

These techniques may be thought of as rules for appropriate facial expression. Have you ever violated one of these display rules? What happened?

Technique	Function	Example
Intensifying	To exaggerate a feeling	Exaggerating surprise when friends throw you a party, to make your friends feel better
Deintensifying	To underplay a feeling	To cover up your own joy in the presence of a friend who didn't receive such good news
Neutralizing	To hide a feeling	To cover up your sadness so as not to depress others
Masking	To replace or substitute the expression of one emotion for another	To express happiness in order to cover up your disappointment at not receiving the gift you had expected

who felt and expressed the emotions became emotionally aroused faster than did those who only felt the emotion (Hess, Kappas, McHugo, and Lanzetta 1992). So not only does your facial expression influence the judgments and impressions that others have of you; it also influences your level of emotional arousal (Cappella 1993).

Context and Culture

The same facial expressions are seen differently if people are given different contexts. For example, when a smiling face was presented looking at a glum face, the smiling face was judged to be vicious and taunting. But when the same smiling face is presented looking at a frowning face, it's judged peaceful and friendly (Cline 1956).

The wide variations in facial communication that we observe in different cultures seem to reflect which reactions are publicly permissible, rather than a difference in the way emotions are facially expressed. For example, Japanese and American students watched a film of an operation (Ekman 1985). The students were videotaped in both an interview situation about the film and alone while watching the film. When alone, the students showed very similar reactions, but in the interview, the American students displayed facial expressions indicating displeasure, whereas the Japanese students didn't show any great emotion. Similarly, Japanese women aren't supposed to reveal broad smiles and so will hide their smile, sometimes with their hands (cf. Ma 1996). Women in the United States, on the other hand, have no such restrictions and so are more likely to smile openly. Thus, the difference may not be in the way different cultures express emotions but rather in the cultural rules for displaying emotions in public (cf. Matsumoto 1991).

Can you recall an instance in which a friend tried using a facial management technique but you saw through it? What gave it away?

◀◀ THINKING BACK

Similarly, cultural differences exist in decoding the meaning of a facial expression. For example, American and Japanese students judged the meaning of a smiling and a neutral facial expression. The Americans rated the smiling face as more attractive, more intelligent, and displaying greater sociability than the neutral face. The Japanese, however, rated the smiling face as more sociable but not as more attractive. The Japanese, in fact, rated the neutral face as the more intelligent (Matsumoto and Kudoh 1993).

THINKING AHEAD ▶▶

What types of messages can you communicate by just moving your eyes?

EYE COMMUNICATION

The messages communicated by the eyes vary depending on the duration, direction, and quality of the eye behavior. For example, in every culture there are rather strict, though unstated, rules for the proper duration for eye contact. In much of England and the United States, for example, the average length of gaze is 2.95 seconds. The average length of mutual gaze (two persons gazing at each other) is 1.18 seconds (Argyle 1988, Argyle and Ingham 1972). When eye contact falls short of this amount, you may think the person is uninterested, shy, or preoccupied. When the appropriate amount of time is exceeded, you may perceive this as showing high interest.

In much of the United States direct eye contact is considered an expression of honesty and forthrightness. But the Japanese often view this as a lack of respect. The Japanese will glance at the other person's face rarely and then only for very short periods (Axtell 1993). In many Hispanic cultures, direct eye contact signifies a certain equality and so should be avoided by, say, children when speaking to a person in authority. Try visualizing the potential misunderstandings that eye communication alone could create when people from Tokyo, San Francisco, and San Juan try to communicate.

The direction of the eye also communicates. Generally, in communicating with another person, you would glance alternatively at the other person's face, then away, then again at the face, and so on. When these directional rules are broken, different meanings are communicated—abnormally high or low interest, self-consciousness, nervousness over the interaction, and so on. The quality—how wide or how narrow your eyes get during interaction—also communicates meaning, especially interest level and such emotions as surprise, fear, and disgust.

Eye Contact

You use eye contact to serve several important functions (Knapp and Hall 1992, Malandro, Barker, and Barker 1989, Marshall 1983, Marsh 1988). You can use eye contact to *monitor feedback*. For example, when you talk with someone, you look at the person intently, as if to say, "Well, what do you think?" or "React to what I've just said." You also look at speakers to let them know that you're listening. Studies show that listeners gaze at speakers more than speakers gaze at listeners (Knapp and Hall 1992). The percentage of interaction time spent gazing while listening, for example, ranges from 62 percent to 75 percent; the percentage of time spent gazing while talking, however, ranges from 38 percent and 41 percent. When these percentages are reversed—when a speaker gazes at the listener for longer than "normal" periods or when a listener gazes at the speaker for shorter than "normal" periods—the conversational interaction becomes awkward. You may wish to try this with a friend. Even with mutual awareness, you'll notice the discomfort caused by this seemingly minor communication change.

When you speak with two or three other people, you maintain eye contact to *secure the attention and interest* of your listeners. When someone fails to pay the attention you want, you probably increase your eye contact, hoping your focus on this person will increase attention. When making an especially important point, you would look intently at your listeners—assuming what nonverbal researchers call "visual dominance behavior"—almost as a way of preventing them from devoting any attention to anything but what you're saying.

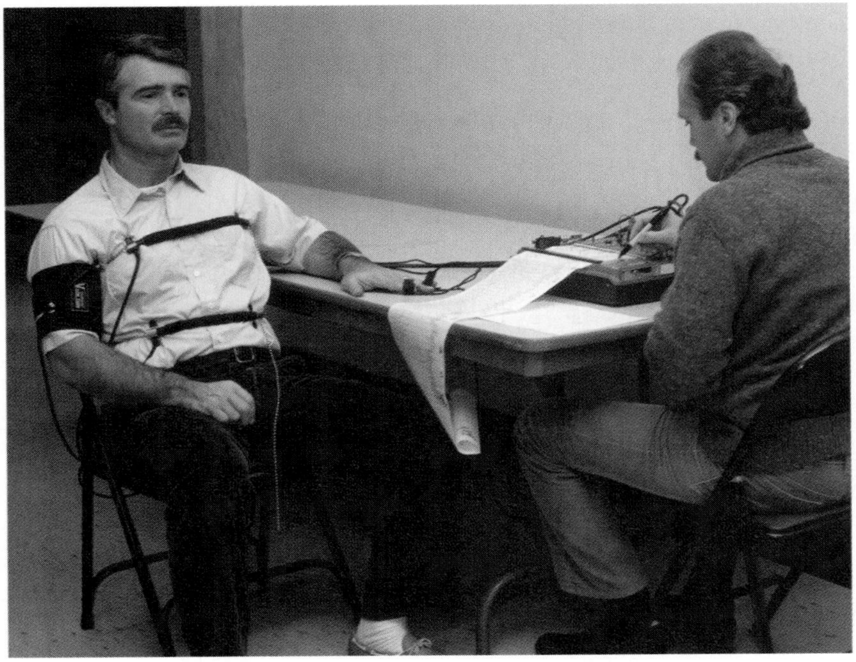

On average we blink about 15 times a minute, in part to lubricate and protect the eye. Increases in blinking, however, often accompany psychological and physical stress (Stern 1988). For example, you would probably increase your blinking rate if you were being interrogated by the police. Excess blinking, one of the cues people use to detect lying, may communicate a kind of nervousness over telling a lie. In actual fact, however, it may be due to dry eyes. Have you ever drawn conclusions about another person on the basis of eye blinking behavior? Were your conclusions accurate?

Eye communication can also *regulate or control the conversation*. For example, with eye movements you can inform the other person that the channel of communication is open and that she or he should now speak. A clear example of this occurs in the college classroom, where the instructor asks a question and then locks eyes with a student. Without any verbal message, it's assumed that the student should answer the question. Similarly, when you're nearing the end of what you want to say, you'll probably focus eye contact on the person you think wants to speak next and then turn over the conversation to that person.

Eye communication also helps *signal the nature of the relationship* between two people—for example, one of positive or negative regard. In the United States when you like someone, you increase your eye contact. When eye contact exceeds 60 percent in an interaction, the people are probably more interested in each other than in the verbal messages being exchanged (Argyle 1988).

Eye contact in the higher primates is often used to signal status and aggression. Among many younger people, prolonged eye contact from a stranger is taken to signify aggressiveness and has frequently prompted physical violence, just because one person looked perhaps a little longer than is considered normal in that specific culture (Matsumoto 1996). A less extreme way to assert one's position is with **visual dominance** behavior (Exline, Ellyson, and Long 1975). The average person maintains a higher level of eye contact while listening and a lower level while speaking. When people want to signal dominance, they may reverse this pattern and maintain a high level of eye contact while talking but a much lower level while listening. Another way people try to signal dominance is to lower their eyebrows. Research does support this general interpretation of the behavior. For example, faces with lowered eyebrows, in both cartoons and photographs, were judged to communicate greater dominance than raised eyebrows (Keating, Mazur, and Segall 1977). Eye movements may also signal whether the relationship between two people is amorous, hostile, or indifferent.

Eye movements are often used to *compensate for increased physical distance*. By making eye contact, we overcome psychologically the physical distance between us. When we catch someone's eye at a party, for example, we become psychologically close even though we may be separated by considerable physical distance. Eye contact and other expressions of psychological closeness, such as self-disclosure and intimacy, have been found to vary in proportion to each other.

Eye Avoidance

The eyes, sociologist Erving Goffman observed in *Interaction Ritual* (1967), are "great intruders." When you avoid eye contact or avert your glance, you allow others to maintain their privacy. You probably do this when you see a couple arguing in the street or on a bus. You turn your eyes away as if to say, "I don't mean to intrude; I respect your privacy." Goffman refers to this behavior as **civil inattention.**

Eye avoidance can also signal lack of interest—in a person, a conversation, or some visual stimulus. At times, like the ostrich, we hide our eyes to try to cut off unpleasant stimuli. Notice, for example, how quickly people close their eyes in the face of some extreme unpleasantness. Interestingly enough, even if the unpleasantness is auditory, we tend to shut it out by closing our eyes. At other times, we close our eyes to block out visual stimuli and thus heighten our other senses; for example, we often listen to music with our eyes closed. Lovers often close their eyes while kissing, and many prefer to make love in a dark or dimly lit room.

Pupil Dilation

In the fifteenth and sixteenth centuries, Italian women used to put drops of belladonna (which literally means "beautiful woman") into their eyes to enlarge the pupils so that they would look more attractive. Contemporary research supports the intuitive logic of these women: dilated pupils are in fact judged more attractive than constricted ones (Hess 1975, Marshall 1983).

In one study, photographs of women were retouched (Hess 1975). In one set of photographs, the pupils were enlarged, and in the other they were made smaller. Men were then asked to judge the women's personalities from the photographs. The photos of women with small pupils drew responses such as cold, hard, and selfish; those with dilated pupils drew responses such as feminine and soft. However, the male observers could not verbalize the reasons for the different perceptions. **Pupil dilation** and reactions to changes in the pupil size of others both seem to function below the level of conscious awareness.

Pupil size also reveals your interest and level of emotional arousal. Your pupils enlarge when you're interested in something or when you're emotionally aroused. When homosexuals and heterosexuals were shown pictures of nude bodies, the homosexuals' pupils dilated more when viewing same-sex bodies, whereas the heterosexuals' pupils dilated more when viewing opposite-sex bodies (Hess, Seltzer, and Schlien 1965). These pupillary responses are unconscious and are even observed in persons with profound mental retardation (Chaney, Givens, Aoki, and Gombiner 1989). Perhaps we judge dilated pupils more attractive because we judge them as indicative of a person's interest in us. That may be why models, Beanie Babies, and Teletubbies have exceptionally large pupils.

Although belladonna is no longer used, the cosmetics industry has made millions selling eye enhancers—eye shadow, eyeliner, false eyelashes, and tinted contact lenses that change eye color. These items function (ideally, at least) to draw attention to these most powerful communicators.

How effectively do you use eye communication? How effectively do you read the eye messages of others?

◀◀ THINKING BACK

TOUCH COMMUNICATION

THINKING AHEAD ▶▶

What meanings can you communicate with touch?

Touch communication, also referred to as **haptics,** is perhaps the most primitive form of communication. Developmentally, touch is probably the first sense to be used; even in the womb, the child is stimulated by touch. Soon after birth, the child is fondled, caressed, patted, and stroked. In turn, the child explores its world through touch. In a very short time, the child learns to communicate a wide variety of meanings through touch.

The Meanings of Touch

Touch may communicate five major meanings (Jones and Yarbrough 1985). *Positive emotions* may be communicated by touch, mainly between intimates or others who have a relatively close relationship. Among the most important of these positive emotions are support, appreciation, inclusion, sexual interest or intent, and affection. It's interesting to note that people in relationships touch each other more during the intermediate stage than in either the beginning or firmly established relationship stages (Guerrero and Andersen 1991). Additional research found that touch communicated such positive feelings as composure, immediacy, affection, trust, similarity and quality, and informality (Burgoon 1991). Touch has also been found to facilitate self-disclosure (Rabinowitz 1991).

Touch often communicates *playfulness,* either affectionately or aggressively. When touch is used in this manner, the playfulness deemphasizes the emotion and tells the other person that it's not to be taken seriously. Playful touches lighten an interaction.

Touch may also *control* the behaviors, attitudes, or feelings of the other person. Such control may communicate a number of messages. To ask for compliance, for example, we touch the other person to communicate "Move over," "Hurry," "Stay here," or "Do it." Touching to control may also communicate dominance (Henley 1977). The higher-status and dominant person, for example, initiates touch. In fact, it would be a breach of etiquette for the lower-status person to touch the person of higher status.

Ritualistic touching centers on greetings and departures. Shaking hands to say hello or goodbye is perhaps the clearest example of ritualistic touching, but we might also hug, kiss, or put an arm around another's shoulder.

Task-related touching is associated with the performance of some function. This includes removing a speck of dust from another person's face, helping someone out of a car, or checking someone's forehead for fever. Task-related touching seems generally to be regarded positively. For example, book borrowers had a more positive attitude toward the library and the librarian when touched lightly, and customers gave larger tips when lightly touched by the waitress (Marsh 1988). Similarly, diners who were touched on the shoulder or hand when being given their change in a restaurant tipped more than diners who were not touched (Crusco and Wetzel 1984).

Touch Avoidance

Much as we have a need and desire to touch and be touched by others, we also have a tendency to avoid touch from certain people or in certain circumstances (Andersen and Leibowitz 1978). Before reading about the research findings on **touch avoidance,** you may wish to take the accompanying touch avoidance self-test.

Consider, as Nancy Henley suggests in *Body Politics* (1977), who would touch whom—say, by putting an arm on the other person's shoulder or by putting a hand on the other person's back—in the following dyads: teacher and student, doctor and patient, master and servant, manager and worker, minister and parishioner, police officer and accused, business executive and secretary. Most people would say that the first person in each dyad would be more likely to touch the second person than the other way around. It's the higher-status person who is permitted to touch the lower-status person. What implications does this have for your own touching and being touched?

TEST YOURSELF *Do You Avoid Touch?*

This instrument is composed of 18 statements concerning how you feel about touching other people and being touched. Please indicate the degree to which each statement applies to you by indicating whether you: 1 = strongly agree, 2 = agree, 3 = are undecided, 4 = disagree, 5 = strongly disagree.

_______ 1. A hug from a same-sex friend is a true sign of friendship.
_______ 2. Opposite-sex friends enjoy it when I touch them.
_______ 3. I often put my arm around friends of the same sex.
_______ 4. When I see two friends of the same sex hugging, it revolts me.
_______ 5. I like it when members of the opposite sex touch me.
_______ 6. People shouldn't be so uptight about touching persons of the same sex.
_______ 7. I think it is vulgar when members of the opposite sex touch me.
_______ 8. When a member of the opposite sex touches me, I find it unpleasant.
_______ 9. I wish I were free to show emotions by touching members of same sex.
_______ 10. I'd enjoy giving a massage to an opposite-sex friend.
_______ 11. I enjoy kissing a person of the same sex.
_______ 12. I like to touch friends that are the same sex as I am.
_______ 13. Touching a friend of the same sex does not make me uncomfortable.
_______ 14. I find it enjoyable when my date and I embrace.
_______ 15. I enjoy getting a back rub from a member of the opposite sex.
_______ 16. I dislike kissing relatives of the same sex.
_______ 17. Intimate touching with members of the opposite sex is pleasurable.
_______ 18. I find it difficult to be touched by a member of my own sex.

To score your Touch Avoidance Questionnaire:

1. Reverse your scores for items 4, 7, 8, 16, and 18. Use these reversed scores in all future calculations.
2. To obtain your same-sex touch avoidance score (the extent to which you avoid touching members of your sex), total the scores for items 1, 3, 4, 6, 9, 11, 12, 13, 16, and 18.
3. To obtain your opposite-sex touch avoidance score (the extent to which you avoid touching members of the opposite sex), total the scores for items 2, 5, 7, 8, 10, 14, 15, and 17.
4. To obtain your total touch avoidance score, add the subtotals from steps 2 and 3.

The higher the score, the higher the touch avoidance—that is, the greater your tendency to avoid touch. In studies by Andersen and Liebowitz (1978), who constructed this test, average opposite-sex touch avoidance scores for males were 12.9 and for females 14.85. Average same-sex touch avoidance scores were 26.43 for males and 21.70 for females. How close are you to these averages? Can you identify the influences that have led you to have the touch avoidance tendencies you now have?

Adapted from Peter Andersen and Ken Liebowitz, "The Development and Nature of the Construct Touch Avoidance," *Environmental Psychology and Nonverbal Behavior* 3 (1978): 89–106. Reprinted by permission of Plenum Publishing Corporation. ■

Among the important findings is the observation that touch avoidance is positively related to communication apprehension. Those who fear oral communication also seem to score high on touch avoidance. (You may wish to compare your scores on this touch avoidance test with your scores on the communication apprehension test presented in Unit 5.) Touch avoidance is also high among those who self-disclose little; touch and self-disclosure are intimate forms of communication, and people who are reluctant to get close to another person by self-disclosure also seem reluctant to get close through touch. The tendency to avoid communication seems a general one that applies to all forms of communication.

Older people have higher touch avoidance scores for opposite-sex persons than do younger people. Apparently, as we get older we are touched less by members of the opposite sex, and this decreased frequency of touching may lead us to avoid touching. Males score higher than females on same-sex touch avoidance. This accords well with our stereotypes: men avoid touching other men, but women may and do touch other women. Women, it was also found, have higher touch avoidance scores for opposite-sex touching than do men.

Gender and Cultural Differences

A great deal of research has been directed at the question of who touches whom where. Most of it has attempted to address two basic questions: (1) Are there gender differences? Do men and women communicate through touch in the same way? Are men and women touched in the same way? (2) Are there cultural differences? Do people in widely different cultures communicate through touch in the same way?

Gender Differences and Touch Early research reported that touching and being touched differ little between men and women (Jourard 1968). Men touch and are touched as often and in the same places as women. The major exception to this finding

ASK THE RESEARCHER

Reading Nonverbal Cues

A good friend recently told me that I'm becoming insensitive to what others are saying and feeling. Maybe I am becoming more absorbed with myself and my own problems. Is there anything I can do to pick up on people's nonverbal cues that reveal how they feel and what they expect from the person they're talking with?

Before trying to read your partner's nonverbal cues, evaluate your own communication skill. Do you look attentive and give positive feedback through eye contact, head nods, and backchannelling cues such as "uh-huh" and "oh, really?" If not, your behavior could be signaling that you're not partner-focused. Even if you do use these nonverbal cues, you may be a pseudo listener rather than an active listener—one who acts like a listener but is actually thinking about other things. Active listeners, in contrast, concentrate on what their partners are saying to achieve understanding. Unfortunately, there is no tell-tale nonverbal sign that will clue you into a person's feelings. Instead, consider whether your partner's behavior is different from her or his normal behavior. For example, if your partner's face and posture are more tense than usual, you might ask if something is wrong. Thus, three keys to becoming a more sensitive communicator are to display attentive nonverbal behavior, be an active listener, and look for atypical partner behavior. Good luck!

—Laura Guerrero (Ph.D., University of Arizona) is an associate professor in the Hugh Downs School of Human Communication at Arizona State University, where she teaches courses on relational and nonverbal communication. The majority of her research examines how emotion and nonverbal messages function within the context of close relationships.

is the touching behavior of mothers and fathers. Mothers touch children of both sexes and of all ages more than do fathers. In fact, many fathers go no further than touching the hands of their children. More recent research has found differences.

Contrary to popular stereotype, research shows that females initiate more opposite-sex touching (especially more opposite-sex touching designed to control) than do men (Jones 1986). In another study, women were found to initiate touch more in married relationships and less in casual romantic relationships than did men (Guerrero and Andersen 1994).

Opposite-sex friends report more touching than do same-sex friends. Male and female college students report that they touch and are touched more by their opposite-sex friends than by their same-sex friends. No doubt the strong societal bias against same-sex touching accounts for these generalizations.

Cultural Differences and Touch The several functions and examples of touching discussed here have been based on studies in North America; in other cultures these functions might not be served in the same way. In some cultures, for example, some task-related touching is viewed negatively and is to be avoided. Among Koreans, it's considered disrespectful for a store owner to touch a customer in, say, handing back change; it's considered too intimate a gesture. Members of other cultures, expecting such touching, may consider the Korean's behavior cold and insulting. Muslim children are not supposed to touch members of the opposite sex, which can easily be interpreted as unfriendly by American children who are used to touching each other (Dresser 1996).

In one study on touch, college students in Japan and in the United States were surveyed (Barnlund 1975). Students from the United States reported being touched twice as much as did the Japanese students. In Japan, there is a strong taboo against strangers touching, and the Japanese are therefore especially careful to maintain sufficient distance.

Some cultures are contact cultures and others are noncontact cultures. Members of contact cultures (for example, Southern European) maintain close distances, touch each other in conversation, face each other more directly, and maintain longer and more focused eye contact. Members of noncontact cultures (for example, Northern European or Japan) maintain greater distance in their interactions, touch each other only rarely if at all, avoid facing each other directly, and maintain much less direct eye contact. As a result, northern Europeans and Japanese may be perceived as cold, distant, and uninvolved by southern Europeans, who may in turn be perceived as pushy, aggressive, and inappropriately intimate.

Can you identify specific rules for touching and not touching that you were taught by your culture?

◀◀ THINKING BACK

PARALANGUAGE AND SILENCE

THINKING AHEAD ▶▶

What kinds of messages can you send by saying nothing?

Two aspects of nonverbal communication, often considered together because they involve manipulating sound, are paralanguage and silence. Let's consider paralanguage first.

Paralanguage

An old exercise used to increase a student's ability to express different emotions, feelings, and attitudes was to have the student say the following sentence while accenting or stressing different words: "Is this the face that launched a thousand ships?" Significant differences in meaning are easily communicated, depending on where the stress is placed. Consider, for example, the following variations:

1. *Is* this the face that launched a thousand ships?
2. Is *this* the face that launched a thousand ships?

3. Is this the *face* that launched a thousand ships?
4. Is this the face that *launched* a thousand ships?
5. Is this the face that launched a *thousand ships*?

Each of these five sentences communicates something different. Each, in fact, asks a totally different question, even though the words used are identical. All that distinguishes the sentences is stress, one of the aspects of what is called paralanguage. **Paralanguage** is the vocal (but nonverbal) dimension of speech. It refers to the manner in which you say something rather than to what you say.

In addition to stress, paralanguage includes such vocal characteristics as **rate** and **volume**. Paralanguage also includes the vocalizations we make when laughing, yelling, moaning, whining, and belching; vocal segregates—sound combinations that aren't words—such as "uh-uh" and "shh"; and **pitch,** the highness or lowness of vocal tone (Argyle 1988, Trager 1958, 1961).

A good way to appreciate the workings of paralanguage is to examine your own vocal behavior when communicating different meanings. Try reading each of the sentences below first to communicate praise and then to communicate criticism. What changes in your vocal expression communicates the differences in meaning:

Now that looks good on you.
That was some meal.
You're an expert.
You're so sensitive.
Are you ready?

People Perception and Paralanguage It does seem that certain voices are symptomatic of certain personality types or certain problems and, specifically, that the personality orientation gives rise to the vocal qualities. When listening to people—regardless of what they're saying—we form impressions based on their paralanguage as to what kind of people they are. Our impressions from paralanguage cues span a broad range and consist of physical impressions (perhaps about body type and certainly about sex and age), personality impressions (they sound shy, they appear aggressive), and evaluative impressions (they sound like good people, they sound evil and menacing, they have vicious laughs).

One of the most interesting findings on voice and personal characteristics is that listeners can accurately judge the status (high, middle, or low) of speakers after hearing a 60-second voice sample. In fact, many listeners reported that they made their judgments in less than 15 seconds. It has also been found that the speakers judged to be of high status were rated as being of higher credibility than those rated of middle or low status.

It's interesting to note that listeners agree with each other about the personality of the speaker even when their judgments are in error. Listeners seem to have stereotyped ideas about the way vocal characteristics and personality characteristics are related, and they use these stereotypes in their judgments.

Persuasion and Paralanguage The rate of speech is the aspect of paralanguage that has received the most attention. It's of interest to the advertiser, the politician, and, in fact, anyone who tries to convey information or to influence others orally, especially when time is limited or expensive. The research on rate of speech shows that in one-way communication situations, persons who talk fast are more persuasive and are evaluated more highly than those who talk at or below normal speeds

(MacLachlan 1979). This greater persuasiveness and higher regard holds true whether the person talks fast naturally or the speech is sped up electronically (as in time-compressed speech).

In one experiment, subjects were asked to listen to taped messages and then to indicate both the degree to which they agreed with the message and their opinions as to how intelligent and objective they thought the speaker was (MacLachlan 1979). Rates of 111, 140, and 191 words per minute were used. (The average speaking rate is about 130 to 150 words per minute.) Subjects agreed most with the fastest speech and least with the slowest speech. Further, they rated the fastest speaker as the most intelligent and objective and the slowest speaker as the least intelligent and objective. Even in experiments in which the speaker was known to have something to gain personally from persuasion (as would, say, a used-car dealer), the speaker who spoke at the fastest rate was the most persuasive. More recent research finds that faster speech rates increase speaker competence and dominance (Buller, LePoire, Aune, and Eloy 1992).

Rapid speech also has the advantage in comprehension. Subjects who listened to speeches at 201 words per minute (about 140 is average) comprehended 95 percent of the message, and those who listened to speeches at 282 words per minute (that is, double the normal rate) comprehended 90 percent. Even though the rates increased dramatically, the comprehension rates fell only slightly. These 5 percent and 10 percent losses are more than offset by the increased speed and thus make the faster rates much more efficient in communicating information. If the speech speeds are increased more than 100 percent, however, comprehension falls dramatically.

Exercise caution in applying this research to your own interpersonal interactions (MacLachlan 1979). Realize that during the time the speaker is speaking, the listener is generating and framing a reply. If the speaker talks too rapidly, there may not be enough time to compose this reply, and resentment may therefore be generated. Furthermore, the increased rate may seem so unnatural that the listener may come to focus on the speed of speech rather than the thought expressed.

Silence

"Speech," wrote Thomas Mann, "is civilization itself. The word, even the most contradictory word, preserves contact; it's silence which isolates." Philosopher Karl Jaspers, on the other hand, observed that "the ultimate in thinking as in communication is silence," and philosopher Max Picard noted that "silence is nothing merely negative; it's not the mere absence of speech. It's a positive, a complete world in itself." The one thing on which these contradictory observations agree is that silence communicates. Your silence communicates just as intensely as anything you verbalize (see Jaworski 1993).

Functions of Silence Like words and gestures, **silence,** too, serves important communication functions. Silence allows the speaker *time to think,* time to formulate and organize his or her verbal communications. Before messages of intense conflict, as well as those confessing undying love, there is often silence. Again, silence seems to prepare the receiver for the importance of these future messages.

TRY IT!
To learn more about silence in a socio-political world, go to www.awl.com/devito.

Some people use silence as a weapon *to hurt* others. We often speak of giving someone "the silent treatment." After a conflict, for example, one or both individuals might remain silent as a kind of punishment. Silence used to hurt others may also take the form of refusing to acknowledge the presence of another person, as in disconfirmation (see Unit 10); here silence is a dramatic demonstration of the total indifference one person feels toward the other.

Sometimes silence is used as a *response to personal anxiety,* shyness, or threats. You may feel anxious or shy among new people and prefer to remain silent. By remaining silent you preclude the chance of rejection. Only when the silence is broken and an attempt to communicate with another person is made do you risk rejection.

Silence may be used to *prevent communication* of certain messages. In conflict situations, silence is sometimes used to prevent certain topics from surfacing and to prevent one or both parties from saying things they may later regret. In such situations, silence often allows us time to cool off before expressing hatred, severe criticism, or personal attacks which we know are irreversible.

Like the eyes, face, or hands, silence can also be used to *communicate emotional responses* (Ehrenhaus 1988). Sometimes silence communicates a determination to be uncooperative or defiant; by refusing to engage in verbal communication, you defy the authority or the legitimacy of the other person's position. Silence is often used to communicate annoyance, usually accompanied by a pouting expression, arms crossed in front of the chest, and nostrils flared. Silence may express affection or love, especially when coupled with long and longing stares into each other's eyes.

Silence may also be used strategically, to *achieve specific effects.* The pause before what you feel is an important comment or after hearing about some mishap may be strategically positioned to communicate a desired impression—to make your idea stand out among others or perhaps to give others the impression that you care a lot more than you really do. Generally, research finds that people use silence strategically more with strangers than they do with close friends (Hasegawa and Gudykunst 1998).

Of course, you may also use silence when you simply have *nothing to say,* when nothing occurs to you, or when you don't want to say anything. James Russell Lowell expressed this well: "Blessed are they who have nothing to say, and who cannot be persuaded to say it."

Cultural Differences and Silence The communicative functions of silence in the situations just cited are not universal; each culture seems to view silence very differently (cf. Kivik 1998, Jaworski 1993). In the United States, for example, silence is often taken as negative. At a business meeting or even in informal social groups, silence may often be interpreted negatively—perhaps the silent member wasn't listening, has nothing interesting to add, doesn't understand the issues, is insensitive, is too self-absorbed to focus on the messages of others, or isn't interested in and isn't paying attention to the conversation. Other cultures, however, view silence more positively. In many situations in Japan, for example, silence is preferred to speech (Haga 1988). Among first-generation Japanese women, silence is used as a means of maintaining power, though in the process it often alienates their daughters, who feel they know little of their mothers (Von Hassell 1993).

The traditional Apache regard silence very differently (Basso 1972). Among the Apache, mutual friends don't feel the need to introduce strangers who may be working in the same area or on the same project. The strangers may remain silent for several days. During this time they're looking each other over, trying to determine if the other person is all right. Only after this period do the individuals talk. When courting, especially during the initial stages, the Apache remain silent for hours; if they do talk, they generally talk very little. Only after a couple has been dating for several months will they have lengthy conversations. These periods of silence are generally attributed to shyness or self-consciousness. The use of silence is explicitly taught to Apache women, who are especially discouraged from engaging in long discussions with their dates. Silence during courtship is a sign of modesty to many Apache.

Silence in a Socio-Political World Silence can be viewed in the broader social and political context with an interesting theory known as the spiral of silence. Consider your own tendency to discuss or remain silent about your attitudes and beliefs when interacting with others. Are you equally likely to voice opinions that agree with others as those that disagree? The spiral of silence theory claims that you're more likely to voice agreement positions than disagreement ones (Noelle-Neumann 1973, 1980, 1991, Becker and Roberts 1992, Windahl, Signitzer, and Olson 1992).

TRY IT!
To learn more about silence in a socio-political world, go to www.awl.com/devito.

The spiral of silence theory argues that when a controversial issue arises, you estimate the opinions of others; you try to estimate public opinion on the issue. You estimate which views are popular and which are not, and you also estimate how popular these positions are. At the same time, you also judge the likelihood of being punished for expressing minority opinions and the severity of that punishment. You do this largely by attending to the media. Once these assumptions about the popularity of an issue are formed, you use these to regulate your willingness to express your own opinions on that issue or remain silent.

When you feel your opinions are in agreement with the majority, you're more likely to voice them than if you feel they're in disagreement. Of course, there are many reasons you might be reluctant to voice minority opinions. After all, you probably want to be one of the crowd, so you resist any possible isolation that unpopular opinions might impose on you. Another reason is that disagreement often means confrontation with the possibility of being proven wrong, both unpleasant results. You may assume that the majority, because they're a majority, must be right, and you of course want to be right, not wrong.

Not all people seem equally affected by this spiral (Noelle-Neumann 1991). For example, younger people and men are more likely to express minority opinions than are older people and women. Educated people are more likely to express minority opinions than are those who are less educated. This isn't surprising, since the expression of a minority opinion often requires some defense which the educated feel competent to present but the uneducated don't. As these people remain silent, the media position gets stronger (because those who agree with it are the only ones who are speaking). As the media's position grows stronger, the silence of the opposition also grows. The silence becomes an ever widening spiral.

One of the problems this situation creates is that the media are likely to express the same general opinions, values, and beliefs and thus present a false picture of the extent to which people are in agreement. Those who take their cues from the media are therefore likely to estimate incorrectly the real degree of agreement and disagreement.

How effective are you in using and in responding to silence?

THINKING BACK

ETHICS IN INTERPERSONAL COMMUNICATION

Vote online at http://www.awl.com/devito

Interpersonal Silence

Often, but not always, you have the right to remain silent and to not incriminate yourself. You have a right to privacy, to withhold information that has no bearing on the matter at hand. Thus, for example, your previous relationship history, affectional orientation, or religion is usually irrelevant to your ability to function as a doctor or police officer and may thus be kept private in most job-related situations. If these issues become relevant—say, you're about to enter a new relationship—then there may be an obligation to reveal your relationship history, affectional orientation, or religion.

In a court, of course, you have the right to refuse to incriminate yourself, to reveal information about yourself that could be used against you. But you don't have the right to refuse to reveal information about the criminal activities of others. Psychiatrists, clergy, and lawyers are often exempt from this general rule.

What would you do? *As you walk by a house, you witness a mother shaking and hitting her three-year-old child in the backyard. You worry that the mother might physically harm the child, and your first impulse is to report the incident to the police. At the same time, you don't want to interfere with a mother's right to discipline her child or to make trouble for someone who may be an excellent parent generally but is perhaps having a particularly bad time today. What is your ethical obligation in this case? What would you do in this situation?*

REVIEWING KEY TERMS AND CONCEPTS IN BODY AND SOUND COMMUNICATION

In this unit we introduced six types or channels of nonverbal communication: body movements, facial communication, eye communication, touch, paralanguage, and silence.

Body Communication

What meanings are communicated with body movements? What meanings can your general body appearance communicate?

- Among the body gestures identified are **emblems** (translate words and phrases rather directly), **illustrators** (accompany and literally illustrate the verbal messages), **affect displays** (convey emotional meaning), **regulators** (monitor or control the speaking of the other person), and **adaptors** (serve some need and are usually performed only partially in public).
- General body appearance (height, weight, level of attractiveness, and skin color, for example) can communicate about your power, your attractiveness, and your suitability as a friend or romantic partner.

Facial Communication

What meanings do facial movements communicate?

- To express emotions: happiness, surprise, fear, anger, sadness, disgust/contempt, interest, bewilderment, determination
- To manage meanings communicated: intensifying, deintensifying, neutralizing, masking

Eye Communication

What messages do eye contact, eye avoidance, and pupil dilation communicate?

- Eye gaze: monitor feedback, maintain interest/attention, signal conversational turns, signal nature of relationship, compensate for physical distance
- Eye avoidance: give others privacy, signal disinterest, cut off unpleasant stimuli, heighten other senses
- Pupil dilation: indicate interest/arousal, increase attractiveness

Touch Communication

What meanings can you communicate by touching?

- Among the meanings touch can communicate are positive affect, playfulness, control, ritual, and task-relatedness.
- Significant gender and cultural differences are found in touching behavior and in the tendencies to avoid touch.

Paralanguage and Silence

What meanings do variations in paralanguage and silence communicate?

- Paralanguage cues are used for forming impressions, for identifying emotional states, and for making judgments of credibility, intelligence, and objectivity.
- Silence is used in widely different ways: to provide thinking time, to inflict hurt, to hide anxiety, to prevent communication, to communicate feelings, to communicate "nothing."

APPLYING KEY TERMS AND CONCEPTS IN BODY AND SOUND COMMUNICATION

1. What messages does your general physical appearance communicate about you? Check your theories with those who know you.
2. What implications does the finding that women smile more than men, even when making negative comments or expressing negative feelings, for male-female communication, child rearing, or teaching (Shannon 1987)?
3. Research shows that women are perceived to be and are in reality more skilled at both encoding and decoding nonverbal messages (Briton and Hall 1995). Do you notice this in your own interactions? Do these differences give women an advantage in conversation? In negotiation? In conflict resolution?
4. On the basis of your observations for a period of one day (admittedly, much too short a time), what general conclusions can you draw about the following: Whom do you touch the most? Who touches you the most? What meanings do you use touch to communicate? What meanings do you derive from being touched by others?
5. Take a close look at popular plush toy animals and Beanie Babies. Are their pupils larger than normal? What do the pupils on these toys communicate?
6. A popular defense tactic in sex crimes against women, gay men, and lesbians is to blame the victim by referring to the way the victim was dressed and to imply that the victim's clothing provoked the attack. What do you think of this tactic?
7. How do you use **civil inattention?** In what situations might civil inattention be inappropriate?
8. What nonverbal cues do you look for in judging whether someone likes you? Do men and women indicate liking with the same cues?
9. Can you think of an instance when "reading" nonverbal messages through your own cultural and gender rules prevented you from accurately assessing another person or another's meaning?
10. How would you go about seeking answers to questions such as these:
    - Do high-status people touch each other more than lower-status people?
    - Do children born blind express emotions with the same facial expressions that sighted children use?
    - How do men and women in different cultures express romantic interest?
    - Are concepts of body attractiveness universal across all cultures?
    - Are men and women equally adept at sending and receiving messages from eye movements?

EXPERIENCING KEY TERMS AND CONCEPTS IN BODY AND SOUND COMMUNICATION

Go to www.awl.com/devito

Exercises No. 9, "Facial Expressions," No. 10, "Eye Contact," and No. 12, "Who?" will all prove useful in illustrating the role of nonverbal messages in interpersonal communication.

UNIT 13
NONVERBAL MESSAGES: SPACE AND TIME

A Passage to India (1984)

I THINK THAT I SHALL NEVER SEE
A BILLBOARD LOVELY AS A TREE.
INDEED, UNLESS THE BILLBOARDS FALL
I'LL NEVER SEE A TREE AT ALL.

--OGDEN NASH

Spatial Messages
Territoriality
Artifactual Communication
Temporal Communication

Director David Lean's last film, A Passage to India, *set in the India of the 1920s when Britain ruled, and based on E. M. Forster's novel, shows you the clash of East-West cultures. Although British and Indian people understand each other on the verbal level (they speak the same language), they fail to understand each other on the nonverbal level. Their customs, ways of doing things, and ways of looking at the world are so drastically different, it's not surprising that real understanding, at least among Foster's players, is never really achieved. In this unit we continue our exploration of nonverbal communication, focusing here on space and time, and the vast cultural differences that exist at every turn.*

SPATIAL MESSAGES

Space is an especially important factor in interpersonal communication, although we seldom think about it. Edward T. Hall (1959, 1963, 1966), who has pioneered the study of spatial communication (sometimes called **proxemics**), distinguishes four distances that correspond closely to the major types of relationships: intimate, personal, social, and public (see Figure 13.1).

THINKING AHEAD ▸▸
What kinds of messages can you communicate by the space you maintain between yourself and the person with whom you're talking?

Intimate Distance Within **intimate distance,** ranging from the close phase of actual touching to the far phase of 6 to 18 inches, the presence of the other person is unmistakable. You experience the sound, smell, and feel of the other's breath. The close phase is used for lovemaking and wrestling, for comforting and protecting. In the close phase, the muscles and the skin communicate, while actual words play a minor role. The far phase allows people to touch each other by extending their hands. The individuals are so close that this distance is not considered proper for strangers in

WEB EXPLORATION
To learn more about spatial messages, go to www.awl.com/devito.

Figure 13.1 Four Spatial Distances
Most people would agree that our relationships determine our proxemic distances; intimate relationships create intimate distances and public relationships create public distances, for example. Could you make a case for the reverse assumption, namely that our proxemic distances influence (even determine) our relationships?

public. Because of the feeling of inappropriateness and discomfort (at least for some Americans) if strangers are this close (say, on a crowded bus), their eyes seldom meet but remain fixed on some remote object.

Personal Distance You carry a protective bubble defining your **personal distance,** which allows you to stay protected and untouched by others and ranges from 18 inches to about 4 feet. In the close phase, people can still hold or grasp each other but only by extending their arms. You can then take into your protective bubble certain individuals—for example, loved ones. In the far phase, you can touch another person only if you both extend your arms. This far phase is the extent to which you can physically get your hands on things; hence, it defines, in one sense, the limits of your physical control over others. At times, you may detect breath odor, but generally at this distance etiquette demands that you direct your breath to some neutral area.

Social Distance At the **social distance,** ranging from 4 to 12 feet, you lose the visual detail you had at the personal distance. The close phase is the distance at which you conduct impersonal business or interact at a social gathering. The far phase is the distance at which you stand when someone says, "Stand away so I can look at you." At this distance, business transactions have a more formal tone than they do when conducted in the close phase. In the offices of high officials, the desks are often positioned so that clients are kept at least this distance away. Unlike the intimate distance, where eye contact is awkward, the far phase of the social distance makes eye contact essential—otherwise, communication is lost. The voice is generally louder than normal at this level. This distance frees you from constant interaction with those with whom you work without seeming rude.

Public Distance **Public distance** ranges from 12 to more than 25 feet. In the close phase, a person seems protected by space. At this distance, you're able to take defensive action should you feel threatened. On a public bus or train, for example, you might keep at least this distance from a drunkard. Although you lose the fine details of the face and eyes, you're still close enough to see what is happening.

At the far phase, you see others not as separate individuals but as part of the whole setting. People automatically establish a space of approximately 30 feet around important public figures, and they seem to do this whether or not there are guards preventing their coming closer. The far phase is the distance by which actors on stage are separated from their audience; consequently, their actions and voices have to be somewhat exaggerated.

The specific distances you would maintain between yourself and another person depend on a wide variety of factors. Some of the factors are presented in Table 13.1.

Theories About Space

A number of nonverbal communication researchers have offered explanations as to why people maintain the distances they do. Prominent among these explanations are protection theory, equilibrium theory, and expectancy violation theory—rather complex names for simple and interesting concepts.

Protection Theory **Protection theory** holds that you establish a body buffer zone around yourself as protection against unwanted touching or attack (Dosey and Meisels 1976). When you feel that you may be attacked, your body buffer zone increases; you want more space around you. For example, if you found yourself in a dangerous neighborhood at night, your body buffer zone would probably expand well

TABLE 13.1 Factors Influencing Dyadic Distance

As you read through this table, consider your own spatial behavior. For example, do you approach a woman more closely than you approach a man? Do you stand farther away from others than do members of other cultures? Do you stand closer to people you like than to people you don't like? This table is based on the extensive research summary of Burgoon, Buller, and Woodall (1995).

Influencing Factors	Sample Research Findings
Communication characteristics:	
Gender	• women sit and stand closer to each other than do men in same-sex dyads • people approach women more closely than they approach men
Age	• distance increases with age • people maintain closer distances with peers than with persons much older or younger
Race/ethnicity	• Mexican Americans maintain closer distances than do either blacks or whites
Personality	• introverts and highly anxious people maintain greater distances than do extroverts
Relationship characteristics:	
Familiarity	• persons familiar with each other maintain shorter distances
Liking	• persons maintain shorter distances with those they like
Status	• the greater the status difference, the greater the space
Context characteristics:	
Formality	• the more formal the situation, the greater the space
Purpose of interaction	• shorter distances are maintained for cooperative tasks than for competitive tasks
Space availability	• the greater the space, the shorter the distance

beyond what it would be if you were in familiar and safe surroundings. If someone entered this buffer zone, you would probably feel threatened and seek to expand that distance by walking faster or crossing the street.

In contrast, when you're feeling secure and protected, your buffer zone becomes much smaller. For example, if you're with a group of close friends and feel secure, your buffer zone shrinks, and you may welcome the close proximity and mutual touching.

Equilibrium Theory **Equilibrium theory** holds that intimacy and distance vary together: the greater the intimacy, the closer the distance; the lower the intimacy, the greater the distance. This theory says that you maintain close distances with those with whom you have close interpersonal relationships and that you maintain greater distances with those with whom you do not have close relationships (Argyle and Dean 1965).

At times, of course, your interpersonal distance does not accurately reflect your level of intimacy. When this happens, you make adjustments. For example, let's say that you have an intimate relationship with someone, but for some reason you're separated—perhaps because you could not get concert seats next to each other or you're at a party and have each been led to different parts of a large banquet hall. When this happens, you probably try to preserve your psychological closeness by maintaining frequent eye contact or perhaps by facing each other.

At other times, however, you're forced into close distances with someone with whom you're not intimate (or may even dislike)—for example, on a crowded bus or perhaps in the dentist's chair. In these situations, you also compensate, but in such cases you seek to make the psychological distance greater. Consequently, you might avoid eye contact and turn in an opposite direction. In the dentist's chair, you probably close your eyes to decrease this normally intimate distance. If seated to the right of a stranger, you might cross your legs and turn your torso to the left.

Expectancy Violations Theory **Expectancy violations theory** explains what happens when you increase or decrease the distance between yourself and another in an interpersonal interaction (Burgoon and Hale 1988; Burgoon, Buller, and Woodall 1995). Each culture has certain expectancies for the distance people are to maintain in their conversations. Of course, each person has certain idiosyncrasies. Together, these determine "expected distance." What happens when these expectations are violated?

If you violate the expected distance to a great extent—small violations most often go unnoticed—then the relationship itself comes into focus. The other person begins to turn attention away from the topic of conversation and toward you and your relationship with him or her. It's also interesting to note that those who violate normal expected spatial relationships are judged to be less truthful than those who didn't commit such violations (Feeley and deTurck 1995).

If this other person perceives you positively—for example, you're a high-status person or you're particularly attractive—then you'll be perceived even more positively if you violate the norm. If, however, you're perceived negatively and you violate the norm, you'll be perceived even more negatively. Thus, the positively evaluated person will be perceived more positively if he or she violates the norm, whereas the negatively evaluated person will be more positively perceived if the distance norm is not violated.

Can you recall an instance in which someone violated the expected distance between you? How did you react?

◀◀ THINKING BACK

THINKING AHEAD ▶▶

What do you consider your territory? Do you get annoyed when another student sits in a seat that you normally sit in even if the seats weren't assigned?

TERRITORIALITY

Another type of communication having to do with space is **territoriality,** the possessive reaction to an area or to particular objects. Of course, not all territories are the same (Altman 1975). **Primary territories** are yours and yours alone. **Secondary territories** are associated with you but aren't owned by you. **Public territories** belong to or are used by all people. Table 13.2 summarizes these three types. Through territorial behavior, you signal ownership and status.

Ownership

Many male animals stake out a particular territory and signal their ownership to all others. They allow prospective mates to enter but defend the territory against other males of the same species. Among deer, for example, the size of the territory signifies the power of the buck, which in turn determines how many females he will mate with. Less powerful bucks will be able to control only small territories and consequently will mate with only one or two females. This adaptive measure ensures that the strongest members of the species produce most of the offspring.

ASK THE RESEARCHER

Building for Interaction

I'm an urban planning and design student, and for my senior project I have to design a suburban community for 2,000 people. Since I'm also taking a course in interpersonal communication, I'm wondering what I can do to incorporate the interpersonal communication needs of the residents into my design. Any suggestions?

Your challenge is to design a neighborhood encouraging intended and serendipitous contact with neighbors taking into account that media technology has privatized relationships once experienced in public. Designing such a community begins with the creation of mixed use zones that encourage individuals to leave their homes for nearby activities such as shopping and work. Mixed use zones incorporating local shopping within easy walking distance to residential areas provide reason for people to leave their home thereby creating opportunities for unplanned interaction with neighbors along the way. Narrow sidewalks incorporated in the plan would likewise provide potential sites of interaction. Residential streets would be placed in a pattern leading to nodes of activity every few blocks in which parks, benches, shops or cafes/pubs would be located. Street lights and street furniture such as benches, ledges, and public phones would be incorporated. Balancing face-to-face contact with mediated communication would round out the plan with community access cable television, community based Web sites and an Intranet system supplementing community information and interaction.

For further information see S. Drucker and G. Gumpert, "Public Space and Communication: The Zoning of Public Interaction," *Communication Theory* 1(4) (1991): 296–310, and S. Drucker and G. Gumpert, eds., *Voices in the Street: Explorations in Gender, Media and Public Space* (Hampton Press, 1997).

—Gary Gumpert (Ph.D., Wayne State University) is a professor emeritus of Queens College, CUNY, and Susan Drucker (J.D., St. John's University School of Law) is an associate professor in Hofstra University School of Communication. Their current research focuses on the relationship of new communication technologies and the use of public spaces, social cohesion, and planning and architecture. They are cofounders of Communication Landscapers, a communication consulting firm specializing in designing for the human factor in a technological environment. ggumpert@ix.netcom.com; druckers@ix.netcom.com.

These same general patterns are believed by many ethologists—scientists who study animal behavior in the animals' natural surroundings—to be integral to human behavior. Some researchers claim that this form of behavior is instinctive and is a symptom of the innate aggressiveness of humans. Others claim that territoriality is learned and is culturally based. Most, however, seem to agree that a great deal of human behavior can be understood and described as territoriality regardless of its possible origin or development (Ardrey 1966).

When you operate in your own territory, you have an interpersonal advantage, what's called the **home field advantage.** In their own home or office, people take on a kind of leadership role: they initiate conversations, fill in silences, assume relaxed and comfortable postures, and maintain their positions with greater conviction. Because the territorial owner is dominant, you stand a better chance of getting your raise, your point accepted, and the contract resolved in your favor if you're in your territory (your office, your home) rather than in someone else's (your supervisor's office, for example) (Marsh 1988).

To help signal ownership, humans, like animals, mark their territory, using three types of **markers:** central, boundary, and ear markers (Goffman 1971). **Central markers** are items you place in a territory to reserve it for you—for example, a drink at the bar, books on your desk, or a sweater over a library chair.

Boundary markers set boundaries that divide your territory from that of others. In the supermarket checkout line, the bar that is placed between your groceries

TABLE 13.2 Three Types of Territory

Can you identify specific kinds of primary, secondary, and public territories that you interacted in today? How did the type of territory you were in influence your communications?

Territory	Definition	Example
Primary	areas you might call your own; your exclusive preserve	your room, your desk, your office
Secondary	areas that don't belong to you but which you have occupied and with which you're associated	a table in the cafeteria that you sit at regularly; your neighborhood turf
Public	areas that are open to all people	a movie house, a restaurant, a shopping mall

and those of the person behind you is a boundary marker, as are a fence, the armrests separating your chair from those on either side, and the contours of the molded plastic seats on a bus or train.

Ear markers—a term taken from the practice of branding animals on their ears—are identifying marks that indicate your possession of a territory or object. Trademarks, nameplates, and initials on a shirt or briefcase are all examples of ear markers.

Markers are also important in giving you a feeling of belonging and ownership. For example, students in college dormitories who marked their rooms by displaying personal items stayed in school longer than did those who didn't personalize their spaces (Marsh 1988).

Status

Like animals' territory, the territory of humans communicates status. Clearly, the size and location of the territory indicates something about status. Status is also signaled by the unwritten law granting the right of invasion. Higher-status individuals have a "right" to invade the territory of lower-status persons, but the reverse is not true. The boss of a large company, for example, can barge into the office of a junior executive, but the reverse would be unthinkable. Similarly, a teacher may invade a student's personal space by looking over her or his shoulder as the student writes, but the student cannot do the same to the teacher.

In what ways have your marked your territories today?

◀◀ THINKING BACK

THINKING AHEAD ▶▶

Do you use clothing, jewelry, or cologne to communicate? What meanings do you try to send?

ARTIFACTUAL COMMUNICATION

Artifactual communication concerns the messages conveyed by objects that are made by human hands. Thus, aesthetics, color, clothing, jewelry, hairstyle, or scents such as perfume, cologne, or incense are considered artifactual. We look at each of these briefly.

Space Decoration

That the decoration or surroundings of a place exert influence on perceptions should be obvious to anyone who has ever entered a hospital, with its sterile walls and furniture, or a museum, with its imposing columns, glass-encased exhibits, and brass plaques. Even the way a room is furnished exerts influence on us. In a classic study, researchers attempted to determine if the aesthetic conditions of a room would influence the judgments people made in it (Maslow and Mintz 1956, Mintz 1956). Three rooms were used: one was beautiful, one average, and one ugly. The beautiful room had large windows, beige walls, indirect lighting, and attractive, comfortable furnishings. The average room was a professor's office with mahogany desks and chairs, metal bookcases and filing cabinets, and window shades. The ugly room was painted battleship gray; lighting was provided by an overhead bulb with a dirty, torn shade. The room was furnished to give the impression of a janitor's storeroom in horrible condition. The ashtrays were filled and the window shades torn.

In the three different rooms, students rated art prints in terms of the fatigue/energy and displeasure/well-being depicted in them. As predicted, the students in the beautiful room rated the prints as more energetic and as displaying well-being; the prints judged in the ugly room were rated as displaying fatigue and displeasure, while those judged in the average room were perceived as somewhere between these two extremes.

The way you decorate your private spaces communicates something about who you are. The office with a mahogany desk, bookcases, and oriental rugs communicates importance and status within the organization, just as the metal desk and bare floors communicate a status much further down in the hierarchy. At home, the cost of the furnishings may communicate your status and wealth, and their coordination may communicate your sense of style. The magazines may communicate your interests. The arrangement of chairs around a television set may reveal how important watching television is. Bookcases lining the walls reveal the importance of reading. In fact, there is probably little in your home that would not send messages to others and that others would not use for making inferences about you. Computers, wide-screen televisions, well-equipped kitchens, and oil paintings of great grandparents, for example, all say something about the people who own them. Likewise, the lack of certain items will communicate something about you. Consider, for example, what messages you would get from a home in which there was no television, telephone, or books.

Color Communication

When you're in debt, you speak of being "in the red"; when you make a profit, you're "in the black." When you're sad, you're "blue"; when you're healthy, you're "in the pink"; when you're jealous, you're "green with envy." To be a coward is to be "yellow" and to be inexperienced is to be "green." When you talk a great deal, you talk "a blue streak"; when you're angry, you "see red." As revealed through these time-worn cliches, language abounds in color symbolism.

Colors vary greatly in their meanings from one culture to another. Some of these cultural differences are illustrated in Table 13.3, but before looking at the table, think about the meanings your own culture gives to such colors as red, green, black, white, blue, yellow, and purpose.

There is some evidence that colors affect us physiologically. For example, respiratory movements increase in the presence of red light and decrease in the presence of blue light. Similarly, eye blinks increase in frequency when eyes are exposed to red light and decrease when exposed to blue. This seems consistent with our intuitive feelings that blue is more soothing and red more provocative. After changing a school's walls from orange and white to blue, the students' blood pressure decreased and their academic performance improved.

Colors surely influence our perceptions and behaviors (Kanner 1989). People's acceptance of a product, for example, is largely determined by its package. For example, the very same coffee taken from a yellow can was described as weak, from a dark brown can as too strong, from a red can as rich, and from a blue can as mild. Even our acceptance of a person may depend on the colors worn. Consider, for

TABLE 13.3 Some Cultural Meanings of Color

This table, constructed from the research reported by Henry Dreyfuss (1971), Nancy Hoft (1995), and Norine Dresser (1996), illustrates only some of the different meanings that colors may communicate and especially how they're viewed in different cultures. As you read this table, consider the meanings you give to these colors and where your meanings came from.

Color	Cultural Meanings and Comments
Red	In China red signifies prosperity and rebirth and is used for festive and joyous occasions, in France and the United Kingdom masculinity, in many African countries blasphemy or death, and in Japan, anger and danger. Red ink, especially among Korean Buddhists, is used only to write a person's name at the time of death or on the anniversary of the person's death and creates lots of problems when American teachers use red ink to mark homework.
Green	In the United States green signifies capitalism, go ahead, and envy; in Ireland patriotism; among some Native Americans femininity; to the Egyptians fertility and strength; and to the Japanese youth and energy.
Black	In Thailand black signifies old age, in parts of Malaysia courage, and in much of Europe death.
White	In Thailand white signifies purity, in many Muslim and Hindu cultures purity and peace, and in Japan and other Asian countries death and mourning.
Blue	In Iran blue signifies something negative, in Ghana joy; among the Cherokee it signifies defeat and for the Egyptian virtue and truth.
Yellow	In China yellow signifies wealth and authority, in the United States caution and cowardice, in Egypt happiness and prosperity, and in many countries throughout the world femininity.
Purple	In Latin America purple signifies death, in Europe royalty, in Egypt virtue and faith, in Japan grace and nobility, and in China barbarism.

example, the comments of one color expert (Kanner 1989): "If you have to pick the wardrobe for your defense lawyer heading into court and choose anything but blue, you deserve to lose the case." Black is so powerful that it can work against the lawyer with the jury. Brown lacks sufficient authority. Green will probably elicit a negative response.

Clothing and Body Adornment

Clothing serves a variety of functions. It protects you from the weather and, in sports like football, from injury. It helps you conceal parts of your body and so serves a modesty function. Clothing also serves as a cultural display (Morris 1977). It communicates your cultural and subcultural affiliations. In the United States, where there are so many different ethnic groups, you regularly see examples of dress that tell you from what country the wearers have come.

The very poor and the very rich don't dress in the same way, nor do white- and blue-collar workers or the young and the old (Lurie 1983). People dress, in part at least, to identify with the groups of which they are or want to be members.

Similarly, college students will perceive an instructor dressed informally as friendly, fair, enthusiastic, and flexible, and the same instructor dressed formally as prepared, knowledgeable, and organized (Malandro, Barker, and Barker 1989).

People infer who you are, in part, by the way you dress. Whether these inferences prove to be accurate or inaccurate, they will nevertheless influence what people think of you and how they react to you. Your social class, your seriousness, your attitudes (for example, whether you're conservative or liberal), your concern for convention, your sense of style, and perhaps even your creativity will all be judged—in part at least—from the way you dress. In fact, the very popular *Dress for Success* (1975) and *The Woman's Dress for Success Book* by John Molloy (1977) instructed men and women in how to dress so that they could communicate the image they wanted: for example, efficient, reliable, or authoritative. What do you think the clothes you are wearing right now would communicate about you to

Your jewelry likewise communicates messages about you. Wedding and engagement rings are obvious examples of jewelry that communicates very specific messages. College rings and political buttons also communicate specific messages. If you wear a Rolex watch or large precious stones, others are likely to infer that you're rich. Men with earrings will be judged differently from men without earrings.

The way you wear your hair communicates who you are. Your hair may communicate a concern for being up-to-date, a desire to shock, or perhaps a lack of concern for appearances. Men with long hair will generally be judged as less conservative than men with shorter hair.

In a study on interpersonal attraction, slides of male and female models were shown with and without glasses and were evaluated by men and women. Results indicated that persons with glasses were rated more negatively than the very same persons without glasses (Hasart and Hutchinson 1993).

Clothing also seems to influence your own behavior and the behavior of groups. For example, it has been argued that people who dress casually act more informally (Morand, cited in *Psychology Today,* March/April 1995, p. 16). Therefore, meetings with such casually dressed people are more likely to involve a freer exchange of thoughts and ideas which stimulates creativity. This casual attire seems to work well in companies that must rely heavily on creative developments, such as a computer software company. I.B.M., for example, relaxed its conservative dress code and allowed some measure of informal dress among its workers (*New York Times,* 7 February 1995, p. B1). But banks and insurance companies, which traditionally have resisted change, may prefer a more formal attire that creates distance between workers as well as between employees and customers.

Scent

Smell is a peculiar aspect of nonverbal communication and is discussed in widely different ways by different writers. Here, because the emphasis is on using scents (for example, perfume or cologne), it's grouped with artifactual communication. But recognize that body odor also communicates, and perhaps that part of smell is best thought of as a form of body communication (see Unit 12). You also use odors to make yourself feel better; after all, you also smell yourself. When the smells are pleasant, you feel better about yourself; when the smells are unpleasant, you feel less good about yourself.

Olfactory communication, or olfactics, is extremely important in a wide variety of situations. Scientists estimate that you can smell some 10,000 different odors (Angier 1995a). Smell is now big business (Kleinfield, 1992). There is some, though not conclusive, evidence showing that the smell of lemon contributes to a perception of heath, the smell of lavender and eucalyptus seems to increase alertness, and the smell of rose oil seems to reduce blood pressure. Findings such as these have contributed to the growth of aromatherapy and to a new profession of aromatherapist (Furlow 1996). Because humans possess "denser skin concentrations of scent glands than almost any other mammal," it has been argued that it only remains for us to discover how we use scent to communicate a wide variety of messages (Furlow 1996, p. 41). Some of the most important messages scent seems to communicate are attraction, taste, memory, and identification.

In many animal species the female gives off a scent that *draws* males, often from far distances, and thus ensures the continuation of the species. Humans, too, emit sexual *attractants,* called sex pheromones, body secretions that arouse sexual desire. Humans, of course, supplement that with perfumes, colognes, after-shave lotions, powders, and the like to further enhance attractiveness and sexuality. Not surprisingly, biotechnology companies are busily at work with the aim of bottling human sex pheromones (Bishop 1993).

Without smell, *taste* would be severely impaired. For example, it would be extremely difficult to taste the difference between a raw potato and an apple without the sense of smell. Street vendors selling hot dogs, sausages, and similar foods are aided greatly by the smells that stimulate the appetites of passersby.

Smell is a powerful *memory* aid; you can often recall situations from months and even years ago when you happen upon a similar smell. One reason smell can so effectively recall a previous situation is that it's often associated with significant emotional experiences (Rubin, Groth, and Goldsmith 1984, Malandro, Barker, and Barker 1989).

Smell is often used to create an image or an *identity* for a product. Advertisers and manufacturers spend millions of dollars each year creating scents for cleaning products and toothpastes, for example, which have nothing to do with their cleaning power. Instead, they function solely to help create an image for the product. There is also evidence that we can identify specific significant others by smell. For example, infants find their mothers' breasts through smell, mothers can identify their newborn solely through smell, and young children were able to identify the t-shirts of their brothers and sisters solely on the basis of smell (Porter and Moore 1981, Angier 1995a). One researcher goes so far as to advise: "If your man's odor reminds you of Dad or your brother, you may want genetic tests before trying to conceive a child" (Furlow 1996, p. 41).

Gifts and Culture

An aspect of artifactual communication that is frequently overlooked is the giving of gifts, a practice in which rules and customs vary according to each culture. Here are a few situations where gift giving backfired and created barriers rather than bonds. These examples are designed to heighten your awareness of both the importance of gift giving and of recognizing intercultural differences. What might have gone wrong in each of these situations? These few examples should serve to illustrate the wide variations that exist among cultures in the meaning given to artifacts and in the seemingly simple process of giving gifts (Axtell 1993, Dresser 1996).

WEB EXPLORATION
To learn more about gifts and culture, go to www.awl.com/devito.

1. You bring chrysanthemums to a Belgian colleague and a clock to a Chinese colleague. Both react negatively.
2. Upon meeting an Arab businessman for the first time—someone with whom you wish to do considerable business—you present him with a gift. He seems disturbed. To smooth things over, when you go to visit him and his family in Oman, you bring a bottle of your favorite brandy for after dinner. Your host seems even more disturbed now.
3. Arriving for dinner at the home of a Kenya colleague, you present flowers as a dinner gift. Your host accepts them politely but looks puzzled. The next evening you visit your Swiss colleague and bring 14 red roses. Your host accepts them politely but looks strangely at you. Figuring that the red got you in trouble, on your third evening out you bring yellow roses to your Iranian friend. Again, there was a similar reaction.
4. You give your Chinese friend a set of dinner knives as a gift but she doesn't open it in front of you; you get offended. After she opens it, she gets offended.
5. You bring your Mexican friend a statue of an elephant drinking water from a lake. Your friend says he cannot accept it; his expressions tell you he really doesn't want it.

Possible reasons for the negative responses to your gifts: (1) Chrysanthemums in Belgium and clocks in China are both reminders of death and that time is running out. (2) Gifts given at the first meeting may be interpreted as a bribe and thus should be avoided. Further, alcohol is prohibited by Islamic law, so it should be avoided as a gift for most Arabs. (3) In Kenya flowers are only brought to express condolence. In Switzerland red roses are a sign of romantic interest. Also, an even number of flowers (or 13) is generally considered bad luck and should be avoided. Yellow flowers to Iranians signify the enemy and means that you dislike them. (4) The custom in China is simply not to open gifts in front of the donor. Knives (and scissors) symbolize the severing of a relationship. (5) Among many Latin Americans the elephant's upward trunk symbolizes a holding of good luck; an elephant's downward trunk symbolizes luck slipping away.

How effective are you in communicating the messages you want to send through artifacts, especially your clothing and scent?

THINKING BACK

THINKING AHEAD ▸▸
How would you describe your view of time? Would you consider yourself one who uses time wisely? One who wastes a great deal of time?

TEMPORAL COMMUNICATION

The study of **temporal communication,** or **chronemics,** focuses on the use of time—how you organize it, how you react to it, and the messages it communicates. Time can be viewed from two major perspectives: cultural and psychological.

Cultural Time

Generally, three types of cultural time are identified (Hall 1959). *Technical time* is precise, scientific time. Milliseconds and atomic years are examples of units of technical or scientific time. This time system is used only in the laboratory, so it seems to have little relevance to our daily lives.

Formal time refers to the manner in which a culture defines time. In the United States, time is divided into seconds, minutes, hours, days, weeks, months, and years. Other cultures use phases of the moon or the seasons to delineate time periods. College courses are divided into 50- or 75-minute periods that meet at various times each week for 10- or 14-week periods called quarters or semesters. A certain number of quarters or semesters equal a college education. Formal time units are arbitrary and have been established by the culture for reasons of convenience.

Informal time refers to a rather loose use of time terms—for example, words such as "forever," "immediately," "soon," "right away," and "as soon as possible." This is the aspect of time that creates the most communication problems because the terms have different meanings for different people.

Displaced and Diffused Time Orientations An important distinction can be drawn between displaced and diffused time orientations (Hall 1959). In a *displaced time orientation,* time is viewed exactly. Persons with this orientation will be exactly on time. In a *diffused time orientation,* time is seen as approximate rather than exact. People with this orientation are usually late for appointments because they understand, for example, a scheduled time of 8:00 as meaning anywhere from 7:45 to 8:15 or 8:30.

Even the accuracy of clocks varies in different cultures and probably reflects each culture's time orientation. In one study (LeVine and Bartlett 1984), clocks in Japan were found to be the most accurate, while clocks in Indonesia were least accurate. Clocks in England, Italy, Taiwan, and the United States fell between these two extremes in accuracy. Not surprisingly, when the speed of pedestrians in these countries was measured, the Japanese were found to walk the fastest and the Indonesians the slowest. Such differences reflect the different ways in which cultures treat time and their general attitude toward the importance of time in everyday life.

TRY IT!
To learn more about monochronism and polychronism , go to www.awl.com/devito.

Monochronism and Polychronism Another important distinction is that between monochronic and polychronic time orientations (Hall 1959, 1976, Hall and Hall 1987). **Monochronic** people or cultures (the United States, Germany, Scandinavia, and Switzerland are good examples) schedule one thing at a time. Time is compartmentalized; there is a time for everything, and everything has its own time. **Polychronic** people or cultures (Latin Americans, Mediterranean people, and Arabs are good examples) schedule a number of things at the same time. Eating, conducting business with several different people, and taking care of family matters may all be conducted at the same time. No culture is entirely monochronic or polychronic; rather, these are general tendencies that are found across a large part of the culture. Some cultures combine both time orientations; in Japanese and parts of American culture, both orientations are found. Table 13.4, based on Hall and Hall (1987), identifies some of the distinctions between these two time orientations.

TABLE 13.4 Monochronic and Polychronic Time

As you read down this table, note the potential for miscommunication that these differences might create when M-time and P-time people interact. Has this difference ever created interpersonal misunderstandings for you?

The Monochronic Person	The Polychronic Person
does one thing at a time	does several things at one time
treats time schedules and plans very seriously; they may only be broken for the most serious of reasons	treats time schedules and plans as useful (not sacred); they may be broken for a variety of causes
considers the job the most important part of one's life, ahead of even family	considers the family and interpersonal relationships more important than the job
considers privacy extremely important, seldom borrows or lends to others, works independently	is actively involved with others, works in the presence of and with lots of people at the same time

Psychological Time

Psychological time refers to the importance placed on the past, present, or future. In a *past orientation,* you give particular reverence to the past; you might relive old times and regard the old methods as the best. Events are seen as circular and recurring, so that the wisdom of yesterday is applicable also to today and tomorrow. In a *present orientation,* you live in the present for the present. Present activities command your attention; you engage in them not for their future rewards or their past significance but because they're happening now. In its extreme form, this orientation is hedonistic. In a *future orientation,* you give primary attention to the future. You save today, work hard in college, and deny yourself certain enjoyments and luxuries, all because you're preparing for the future.

An especially interesting aspect of cultural time is your "social clock" (Neugarten 1979). Your culture and your more specific society maintain a time schedule for the right time to do a variety of important things, for example, the right time to start dating, to finish college, to buy your own home, to have a child. You no doubt learned about this clock as you were growing up. On the basis of this social clock you evaluate your own social and professional development. If you're on time with the rest of your peers—for example, you all started dating at around the same age or you're all finishing college at around the same age—then you'll feel well adjusted, competent, and a part of the group. If you're late, you'll probably experience feelings of dissatisfaction. Are you on time generally?

Researchers have provided some interesting correlations to these different time orientations (Gonzalez and Zimbardo 1985, Rappaport, Enrich, and Wilson 1985). Before reading their conclusions, you may wish to take the following self-test "What Time Do You Have?"

TEST YOURSELF *What Time Do You Have?*

For each statement, indicate whether the statement is true (T) of your general attitude and behavior, or untrue (F) of your general attitude and behavior. (A few statements are purposely repeated to facilitate scoring and analyzing your responses.)

_______ 1. Meeting tomorrow's deadlines and doing other necessary work comes before tonight's partying.
_______ 2. I meet my obligations to friends and authorities on time.
_______ 3. I complete projects on time by making steady progress.
_______ 4. I am able to resist temptations when I know there is work to be done.
_______ 5. I keep working at a difficult, uninteresting task if it will help me get ahead.
_______ 6. If things don't get done on time, I don't worry about it.
_______ 7. I think that it's useless to plan too far ahead because things hardly ever come out the way you planned anyway.
_______ 8. I try to live one day at a time.
_______ 9. I live to make better what is rather than to be concerned about what will be.
_______ 10. It seems to me that it doesn't make sense to worry about the future, since fate determines that whatever will be, will be.
_______ 11. I believe that getting together with friends to party is one of life's important pleasures.
_______ 12. I do things impulsively, making decisions on the spur of the moment.
_______ 13. I take risks to put excitement in my life.
_______ 14. I get drunk at parties.
_______ 15. It's fun to gamble.
_______ 16. Thinking about the future is pleasant to me.
_______ 17. When I want to achieve something, I set subgoals and consider specific means for reaching these goals.
_______ 18. It seems to me that my career path is pretty well laid out.
_______ 19. It upsets me to be late for appointments.
_______ 20. I meet my obligations to friends and authorities on time.
_______ 21. I get irritated at people who keep me waiting when we've agreed to meet at a given time.
_______ 22. It makes sense to invest a substantial part of my income in insurance premiums.
_______ 23. I believe that "a stitch in time saves nine."
_______ 24. I believe that "a bird in the hand is worth two in the bush."
_______ 25. I believe it is important to save for a rainy day.
_______ 26. I believe a person's day should be planned each morning.

_______ 27. I make lists of things I must do.

_______ 28. When I want to achieve something, I set subgoals and consider specific means for reaching those goals.

_______ 29. I believe that "a stitch in time saves nine."

This psychological time test measures seven different factors. If you scored True for all or most of the questions within any given factor, then you're probably high on that factor. If you scored False for all or most of the questions within any given factor, then you're probably low on that factor.

The first factor, measured by questions 1–5, is a future, work-motivation, perseverance orientation. People with this orientation have a strong work ethic and are committed to completing a task despite difficulties and temptations.

The second factor, measured by questions 6–10, is a present, fatalistic, worry-free orientation. People who score high on this factor live one day at a time, not necessarily to enjoy the day but to avoid planning for the next day and to avoid the anxiety about a future that seems determined by fate rather than by anything they can do themselves.

The third factor, measured by questions 11–15, is a present, hedonistic, pleasure-seeking, partying orientation. People with this orientation seek to enjoy the present, take risks, and engage in a variety of impulsive actions. Teenagers score particularly high on this factor.

The fourth factor, measured by questions 16–18, is a future, goal-seeking and planning orientation. People with this orientation derive special pleasure from planning and achieving a variety of goals.

The fifth factor, measured by questions 19–21, is a time-sensitivity orientation. People who score high on this factor are especially sensitive to time and its role in social obligations.

The sixth factor, measured by questions 22–25, is a future, pragmatic-action orientation. People with this orientation do what they have to do to achieve the future they want. They take practical actions for future gain.

The seventh factor, measured by questions 26–29, is a future, somewhat obsessive daily-planning orientation. People who score high on this factor make daily "to do" lists and devote great attention to specific details and subordinate goals.

From A. Gonzalez and P. Zimbardo, "Time in Perspective," *Psychology Today,* March 1985. Copyright 1985 by Sussex Publishers, Inc. Reprinted by permission of *Psychology Today*. ■

One of the findings of this time study is that future income is positively related to future orientation. The more future oriented a person is, the greater that person's income is likely to be. Present orientation is strongest among lowest-income males.

The time orientation that people develop depends a great deal on their socioeconomic class and personal experiences. Gonzalez and Zimbardo (1985) observe: "A child with parents in unskilled and semi-skilled occupations is usually socialized in a way that promotes a present-oriented fatalism and hedonism. A child of parents who are managers, teachers, or other professionals learns future-oriented values and strategies designed to promote achievement."

Different time perspectives also account for much intercultural misunderstanding, because different cultures often teach their members drastically different time orientations. The future-oriented person who works for tomorrow's goals will frequently look down on the present-oriented person who focuses on enjoying today as being lazy and poorly motivated. In turn, the present-oriented person may see those with strong future orientations as obsessed with accumulating wealth or rising in status.

What would you advise someone about to take a job with a conservative brokerage firm about time and time orientation?

◀◀ THINKING BACK

Time is especially linked to status considerations. For example, the importance of being on time varies with the status of the individual you're visiting. If the person is extremely important, you had better be there on time or even early, just in case he or she is able to see you before schedule. As the person's status decreases, so does the importance of being on time. Can you see this principle operate in your own life? For example, is this "rule" part of the culture of your organization?

REVIEWING KEY TERMS AND CONCEPTS IN SPATIAL AND TEMPORAL COMMUNICATION

In this unit we continued our study of nonverbal communication and considered several additional types of nonverbal messages: space, territory, artifactual, and time.

Spacial Messages

How do you communicate by space?

- The major types of distance that correspond to types of relationships are **intimate distance** (touching to 18 inches), **personal distance** (18 inches to 4 feet), **social distance** (4 to 12 feet), and **public distance** (12 or more feet).
- Theories about space include **protection theory,** which claims you maintain spatial distance to protect yourself; **equilibrium theory,** which claims that you regulate distance according to the intimacy level of your relationship; and **expectancy violations theory,** which explains what happens when you increase or decrease the distance between yourself and another in an interpersonal interaction.

Territoriality

What messages does territoriality communicate?

- Your territorial behavior signals ownership of specific spaces and objects which you often mark (with **central, boundary,** and **ear markers**) as proof of ownership.
- Your territorial behavior also communicates status relationships.

Artifactual Communication

How do you communicate with artifacts, for example, with space decoration, color, clothing and body adornment, and scents?

- Space decoration influences perceptions of energy, time, status, and personal characteristics.
- Colors communicate different meanings depending on the culture.
- Clothing and body adornment serve especially as cultural display and communicate messages about status and perhaps social thinking.
- Scents can communicate messages of attraction, taste, memory, and identification.

Temporal Communication

How does time vary between cultures and people?

- Cultural time consists of technical time (for example, the milliseconds of the researcher), formal time (the 50-minute class period) and informal time ("soon," "later," "early").
- Displaced and diffused time orientations identify how accurately and specifically time is viewed and defined.
- **Monochronic** people do one thing at a time, and **polychronic** people do several things at the same time.
- **Psychological time** is the personal orientation of a person to time and is generally divided into three orientations: past, present, and future.

APPLYING KEY TERMS AND CONCEPTS IN SPATIAL AND TEMPORAL COMMUNICATION

1. How do protection, equilibrium, and expectancy violations theories explain your own spatial behavior?
2. Why do you suppose people who are angry or tense need greater space around them? Do you find this true from your personal experience?
3. What factors other than those listed in Table 13.1 might influence the distances you maintain in your conversations?
4. Can you recall a situation in which your territory was violated? Invaded? Contaminated? How did you respond to these encroachments?
5. Look around your home and at your belongings. Can you identify examples of central, boundary, and ear markers?
6. What messages does your clothing (including your jewelry, hairstyle, makeup, and the colors you're wearing) communicate? Does it communicate different messages to different (types of) people?
7. The "Pygmalion gift" is one that is designed to change the person into what the donor wants that person to become; for example, the parent who gives a child books or science equipment may be asking the child to be a scholar. What messages have you recently communicated in your gift-giving behavior? What messages do you think others communicated to you by the gifts they gave you?
8. How do you feel about gang clothing being worn in elementary or high school or college? Do you think it contributes to violence in the schools? Do you think it should be covered by the right to freedom of expression?
9. Another type of time is biological time, which refers to your body clock, the ways your body functions differently at different times. Your intellectual, physical, and emotional lives, according to theories of biorhythms, are lived in cycles which influence your effectiveness. Detailed explanations and instructions for calculating your own intellectual, physical, and emotional cycles can be found in DeVito (1989), or even better, you can visit a Web site that will compute your biorhythms (www.kfu.com/~nsayer/compat.html).
10. How would you go about finding answers to the following questions?
    - What is the ideal outfit for a college teacher to wear on the first day of class?
    - What types of uniforms command the greatest respect? Have the highest credibility?
    - Do family photographs on an executive's desk contribute to credibility?
    - Do markers contribute to students' staying in school, or are the students who are committed to staying in school more likely to personalize their spaces with markers?
    - What kinds of relationship problems can be created when people have widely different perceptions about time and how it should be used?

EXPERIENCING KEY TERMS AND CONCEPTS IN SPATIAL AND TEMPORAL COMMUNICATION

Go to www.awl.com/devito

Exercises No. 11, "Interpersonal Interactions and Space," and No. 13, "The Meanings of Color," illustrate the role of space and color in interpersonal communication. Exercise No. 12, "Who?" will help illustrate and personalize the nature of nonverbal messages and summarize the vast number of nonverbal cues people use in making judgments of others.

UNIT 14

MESSAGES AND CONVERSATION

In the Heat of the Night (1967)

> CONVERSATION IS THE SOCIALIZING INSTRUMENT PAR EXCELLENCE, AND IN ITS STYLE ONE CAN SEE REFLECTED THE CAPACITIES OF A RACE.
>
> --JOSE ORTEGA Y GASSET

The Conversation Process
Conversational Management
Conversational Problems: Prevention and Repair

IN THE HEAT OF THE NIGHT tells the story of a Philadelphia detective (Sidney Poitier) and a small-town Mississippi sheriff (Rod Steiger) who have to work together to solve a murder. Despite their prejudices and limiting preconceptions of each other, they eventually learn to communicate and solve the crime. The film illustrates how difficult the seemingly simple process of conversation can be when cultural prejudice dominates. In this unit we look at conversation from a variety of perspectives and ask how conversation works; how a conversation is opened, maintained, and closed; and how conversational problems may be prevented or repaired.

Conversation can be defined as "relatively informal social interaction in which the roles of speaker and hearer are exchanged in a nonautomatic fashion under the collaborative management of all parties"(McLaughlin 1984). Examining conversation provides an excellent opportunity to look at verbal and nonverbal messages as they're used in day-to-day communications and thus serves as a useful culmination for this second part of the text.

Before reading about the process of conversation, think of your own conversations, the ones that were satisfactory and the ones that were unsatisfactory. Think of a specific recent conversation as you respond to the accompanying self-test, "How Satisfactory Is Your Conversation?" Taking this test now will help highlight the characteristics of conversational behavior and what makes some conversations satisfying and others unsatisfying.

TEST YOURSELF *How Satisfying Is Your Conversation?*

Respond to each of the following statements by recording the number best representing your feelings, using this scale: 1 = strongly agree, 2 = moderately agree, 3 = slightly agree, 4 = neutral, 5 = slightly disagree, 6 = moderately disagree, 7 = strongly disagree.

______ 1. The other person let me know that I was communicating effectively.
______ 2. Nothing was accomplished.
______ 3. I would like to have another conversation like this one.
______ 4. The other person genuinely wanted to get to know me.
______ 5. I was very dissatisfied with the conversation.
______ 6. I felt that during the conversation I was able to present myself as I wanted the other person to view me.
______ 7. I was very satisfied with the conversation.
______ 8. The other person expressed a lot of interest in what I had to say.
______ 9. I did *not* enjoy the conversation.
______ 10. The other person did *not* provide support for what he or she was saying.
______ 11. I felt I could talk about anything with the other person.
______ 12. We each got to say what we wanted.
______ 13. I felt that we could laugh easily together.
______ 14. The conversation flowed smoothly.
______ 15. The other person frequently said things which added little to the conversation.
______ 16. We talked about something I was *not* interested in.

To compute your score, follow these steps:

1. Add the scores for items 1, 3, 4, 6, 7, 8, 11, 12, 13, and 14.
2. Reverse the scores for items 2, 5, 9, 10, 15, and 16 such that 7 becomes 1, 6 becomes 2, 5 becomes 3, 4 remains 4, 3 becomes 5, 2 becomes 6, and 1 becomes 7.
3. Add the reversed scores for items 2, 5, 9, 10, 15, and 16.
4. Add the totals from Steps 1 and 3 to yield your communication satisfaction score.

You may interpret your score along the following scale: 16 = extremely satisfying, 32 = quite satisfying, 48 = fairly satisfying, 64 = average, 80 = fairly unsatisfying, 96 = quite unsatisfying, 112 = extremely unsatisfying.

How accurately do you think this scale captures conversational satisfaction? Before reading the remainder of this unit, try to identify those qualities that make a conversation satisfying for you. What interpersonal qualities are most important to making a person a satisfying conversational partner? Table 14.1 identifies some types of unsatisfying conversationalists.

From Michael Hecht, "The Conceptualization and Measurement of Interpersonal Communication Satisfaction," *Human Communication Research* 4 (1978): 253–264; reprinted by permission of the author. ■

THINKING AHEAD ▸▸
How would you describe what happens when you have a conversation?

THE CONVERSATION PROCESS

It's convenient to divide up **conversation** into chunks or stages and view each stage as requiring a choice as to what you'll say and how you'll say it. Here we divided up the sequence into five steps: opening, feedforward, business, feedback, and closing (see Figure 14.1). These stages and the way people follow them will vary depending on the personalities of the communicators, their culture, the context in which the conversation occurs, the purpose of the conversation, and the entire host of factors considered throughout this text.

WEB EXPLORATION
To learn more about opening a conversation, go to www.awl.com/devito.

Opening

The first step is to open the conversation, usually with some kind of greeting: "Hi. How are you?" "Hello, this is Joe." The greeting is a good example of **phatic communion.** It's a message that establishes a connection between two people and opens up the channels for more meaningful interaction. Openings, of course, may be nonverbal as well as verbal. A smile, kiss, or handshake may be as clear an opening as "Hello." Greetings are so common that they often go unnoticed. But when they're omitted—as when the doctor begins the conversation by saying, "What's wrong?"—you may feel uncomfortable and thrown off guard.

In normal conversation, the greeting is reciprocated with a greeting similar in degree of formality and intensity. When it isn't—when the other person turns away or responds coldly to your friendly "Good morning"—you know that something is wrong.

Openings are also generally consistent in tone with the main part of the conversation; a cheery "How ya doing today, bud?" is not normally followed by news of a family death, and a friendly conversation is not begun with insensitive openers: "Wow, you've gained a few pounds haven't you?"

Feedforward

At the second step, you usually provide some kind of feedforward (see Unit 1), which gives the other person a general idea of the conversation's focus: "I've got to tell you about Jack," "Did you hear what happened in class yesterday?" or "We need to

TABLE 14.1 Conversationally Difficult People and How Not to Become One of Them

As you read this table, consider your own conversations. Have you met any of these people? Have you ever been one of these people?

Conversationally Difficult People	How Not to Become One of Them
The Detour Taker begins to talk about the topic and then a key word or idea suggests another topic and off this person goes pursuing this other topic.	Follow a logical pattern in conversation and avoid frequent and long detours.
The Complainer complains. Family, friends, job, and school all create problems and this person never tires of listing each of them.	Be positive; emphasize what's good before what's bad.
The Moralist evaluates and judges and frequently interjects such judgments into even the most mundane conversations.	Avoid evaluation and judgment; see the world through the eyes of the other person and (perhaps) the other culture.
The Inactive Responder makes no reactions; whether you talk of winning the lottery or the death of a loved one, this person remains expressionless.	Respond overtly with verbal and nonverbal messages.
The Story Teller may have difficulty talking about the here-and-now and so tells stories. Often the stories get in the way of two-way conversation.	Talk about yourself in moderation; be other oriented.
The Interrogator asks questions. No sooner have you answered one question than you're shot with another and another and another.	Ask questions in moderation—to secure needed information and not to get every detail imaginable.
The Egotist talks only about topics that are self-related and can connect even the most unusual topics to self-concerns.	Be other oriented; focus on the other person as an individual; listen as much as you speak and speak about the listener at least as much as you speak about yourself.
The Doomsayer is the ultimate negative thinker; the past was a problem, the present is unsatisfying, and the future is bleak.	Be positive.
The Arguer listens only to find something to take issue with. Like some people play cards or watch television, this person argues.	Be supportive but argue when it's appropriate; focus arguments on issues and behaviors rather than on personalities.
The Thought Completer "knows" exactly what you're going to say and so says it for you.	Don't interrupt; assume that the speaker wants to finish her or his own thoughts.
The Self-Discloser discloses more than you want to hear; often the disclosures are so personal that they make you feel uncomfortable.	Disclose selectively, in ways appropriate to your relationship with the listener.
The Advisor assumes whenever you talk of a decision that you want advice and proceeds to analyze your "problem" and solve it for you.	Don't assume that the expression of a problem is a request for a solution.
The Psychiatrist analyzes everything you say—traces the origin of your behaviors and mind reads your motives.	Avoid playing the therapist; be a friend, lover, or parent, for example, rather than psychological counselor.

talk about our vacation plans." Feedforward may also identify the tone of the conversation ("I'm really depressed and need to talk with you") or the time required ("This will just take a minute") (Frentz 1976, Reardon 1987).

Conversational awkwardness often occurs when feedforwards are used inappropriately. For example, using overly long feedforwards may make the listener wonder whether you'll ever get to the business at hand and may make you seem

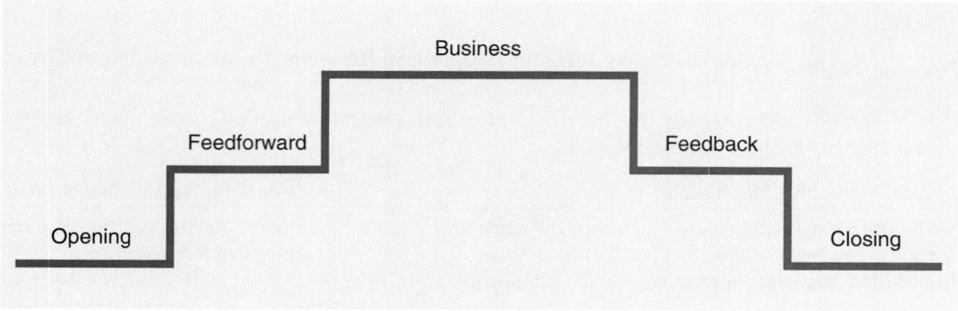

Figure 14.1 A Five-Step Model of Conversation
This model of the stages of conversation is best seen as a way of talking about conversation and not as the unvarying stages all conversations follow. As you review the model, consider how accurately it depicts conversation as you experience it. Can you develop a more accurate and more revealing model?

disorganized and lacking in focus. Omitting feedforward before a truly shocking message (for example, the death or illness of a friend or relative) can make you seem insensitive or uncaring.

Often the feedforward is combined with the opening, as when you see someone on campus, for example, and say, "Hey, listen to this" or when, in a work situation, someone says, "Well, folks, let's get the meeting going."

Business

At the third step, you talk "business," the substance or focus of the conversation. The term "business" is used to emphasize that most conversations are goal directed; you converse to fulfill one or several of the general purposes of interpersonal communication: to learn, relate, influence, play, or help (see Unit 1). The term is also sufficiently general to incorporate all kinds of interactions. The business is conducted through an exchange of speaker and listener roles. Brief, rather than long, speaking turns characterize most satisfying conversations.

In the business stage, you talk about Jack, what happened in class, or your vacation plans. This is obviously the longest part of the conversation and the reason for the opening and the feedforward.

Feedback

The fourth step is feedback (see Unit 1), the reverse of the second step. Here you reflect back on the conversation to signal that, as far as you're concerned, the business is completed: "So you want to send Jack a get-well card," "Wasn't that the craziest class you ever heard of?" or "I'll call for reservations, and you'll shop for what we need."

Of course, the other person may not agree that the business has been completed and may therefore counter with, for example, "But what hospital is he in?" When this happens, you normally go back a step and complete the business.

Closing

The fifth and last step, the opposite of the first step, is the closing, the good-bye, which often reveals how satisfied the persons were with the conversation: "I hope you'll call soon" or "Don't call us, we'll call you." The closing may also be used to schedule future conversations: "Give me a call tomorrow night" or "Let's meet for lunch at twelve." When closings are indefinite or vague, conversation often becomes awk-

ASK THE RESEARCHER

Seeking Library Assistance

I'm a returning student, and today's college library is frightening to me. On top of this I have great difficulty in asking for assistance. Can you give me any advice for approaching a librarian and learning what I have to learn?

Today's computerized libraries can be intimidating, especially to returning students who discover familiar card catalogs and paper indexes are gone, replaced by sophisticated online catalogs and electronic indexes. Approach librarians with a positive attitude and warm nonverbal behaviors like direct eye contact and a smile. Librarians are professionals, with master's degrees in library science, and want to help you. They do, however, expect you to be prepared. Librarians are not receptive to those with bad attitudes or those who are impatient. Take time to think about your assignment and your goals. Don't procrastinate, for although many resources are available in full text (in paper, on the Internet, or on electronic databases), it will probably take more time than you estimate to locate needed information. Be open to the librarian's advice as to whether paper or electronic sources are best suited to your purposes. By cultivating positive relationships with librarians, you'll find the library will become much less intimidating.

For further information see M. L. Radford, *The Reference Encounter: Interpersonal Communication in the Academic Library* (Chicago: Association of College and Research Libraries, American Library Association, 1999).

—Marie L. Radford (Ph.D., Rutgers University) is an associate professor at the Pratt Institute, School of Information and Library Science. She teaches courses in interpersonal communication, reference, and electronic information retrieval and conducts research on interpersonal communication, especially in library settings, and in media images of librarians. radford@sils.pratt.edu.

ward; you're not quite sure if you should say goodbye or if you should wait for something else to be said.

In a way similar to the opening and the feedforward being combined, the closing and the feedback might be combined, as when you say: "Look, I've got to think more about this commitment, okay?"

Is there one particular stage of the conversation process that you have more difficulty with than others? What can you do to make that stage more comfortable and more effective?

◀◀ THINKING BACK

CONVERSATIONAL MANAGEMENT

Speakers and listeners have to work together to make conversation an effective and satisfying experience. **Conversational management** includes initiating, maintaining, and closing conversations.

THINKING AHEAD ▶▶

Do others enjoy talking with you? How do they reveal their enjoyment?

Initiating Conversations

Several approaches to opening a conversation can be derived from the elements of the interpersonal communication process discussed in Unit 1:

- *Self-references* say something about yourself. Such references may be of the "name, rank, and serial number" type—for example: "My name is Joe. I'm from Omaha." On the first day of class, students might say, "I'm worried about this class" or "I took this instructor last semester; she was excellent."
- *Other-references* say something about the other person or ask a question: "I like that sweater." "Didn't we meet at Charlie's?" Of course, there are pitfalls here. Generally, it's best not to comment on the person's race ("My uncle married a Korean"), the person's affectional orientation ("Nice to meet you; I have a gay brother"), or physical disability ("It must be awful to be confined to a wheelchair").

Not surprisingly, each culture has its own conversational taboos, topics that should be avoided, especially by visitors from other cultures. For example, in Belgium avoid politics, language differences between French and Flemish, and religion. In Norway avoid talk of salaries and social status. In Spain avoid the topics of family, religion, jobs, and negative comments on bullfighting. In Egypt avoid talk of Middle-Eastern politics. In Nigeria avoid talk of religion. In Iraq avoid talk of religion and Middle-Eastern politics. In Japan avoid talking about World War II. In the Philippines avoid talk of politics, religion, corruption, and foreign aid. In South Korea avoid talking about internal politics, criticism of the government, socialism or communism. In Mexico avoid talking about the Mexican-American war and illegal aliens. In the Caribbean avoid discussing race, local politics, and religion (Axtell 1993.) Have you ever broken conversational taboos? What happened?

- *Relational references* say something about the two of you: for example, "May I buy you a drink?" "Would you like to dance?" or simply "May I join you?"
- *Context references* say something about the physical, social-psychological, cultural, or temporal context. The familiar "Do you have the time?" is a reference of this type. But you can be more creative and say, for example, "This place seems very friendly" or "That painting is just great."

As you know from experience, conversations are most satisfying when they're upbeat and positive. So it's generally best to lead off with something positive rather than something negative. Say, for example, "I like the music here" instead of "Don't you just hate this place?" Also, it's best not to be too revealing, disclosing too much too early in an interaction. It can make the other person feel uncomfortable.

Another way of looking at the process of initiating conversations is to examine the infamous "opening line," the opener designed to begin a romantic relationship. Several types are identified in Table 14.2.

Maintaining Conversations

In maintaining conversations you follow a variety of principles and rules. Here we discuss, first, the principles and maxims you follow in conversation and, second, the ways in which the speaker and listener exchange turns in conversation.

TRY IT!
To learn more about principles and maxims of conversation, go to www.awl.com/devito.

Principles and Maxims of Conversation During conversation you probably follow the principle of cooperation, implicitly agreeing with the other person

TABLE 14.2 Opening Lines

This table is based on the research of Chris Kleinke (1986), who finds that opening lines are of three basic types. As you review this list, try to classify the opening lines you use or that have been used on you. What's the best opening line you ever heard? The worst?

Opening Line Type	Examples	Comments
Cute-flippant openers are humorous, indirect, and ambiguous as to whether the one opening the conversation actually wants an extended encounter.	"Is that really your hair?" "Bet I can out drink you." "I bet the cherry jubilee isn't as sweet as you are."	One advantage of these opening lines is that they're indirect enough to cushion any rejection. These are also, however, the lines least preferred by men and women.
Innocuous openers are highly ambiguous as to whether they're simple comments that might be made to just anyone or whether they're in fact openers designed to initiate an extended encounter.	"What do you think of the band?" "I haven't been here before. What's good on the menu?" "Could you show me how to work this machine?"	Men and women generally like these openers; they are indirect enough to allow for an easy out if the other person doesn't want to talk.
Direct openers clearly demonstrate the speaker's interest in meeting the other person.	"I feel a little embarrassed about this, but I'd like to meet you." "Would you like to have a drink after dinner? "Since we're both eating alone, would you like to join me?"	Men like direct openers that are very clear in meaning, possibly because men are not used to having a woman initiate a meeting. Women prefer openers that aren't too strong and that are relatively modest.

to cooperate in trying to understand what each is saying (Grice 1975). You cooperate largely by using four **conversational maxims**—principles that speakers and listeners in the United States and in many other cultures follow in conversation. Although the names for these maxims may be new, the principles themselves will be easily recognized from your own experiences.

The Maxim of Quantity Be as informative as necessary to communicate the intended meaning. Thus, you include information that makes the meaning clear but omit what does not. In following this principle, you give neither too little nor too much information. You see people violate this maxim when they try to relate an incident and digress to give unnecessary information. You find yourself thinking or saying, "Get to the point; so what happened?" This maxim is also violated when necessary information is omitted. In this situation, you find yourself constantly interrupting to ask questions: "Where were they?" "When did this happen?" "Who else was there?"

The Maxim of Quality Say what you know or assume to be true, and do not say what you know to be false. When you're in conversation, you assume that the other person's information is true—at least as far as he or she knows. When you speak with people who frequently violate this principle by lying, exaggerating, or minimizing major problems, you come to distrust what the person is saying and wonder what is true and what is fabricated.

The Maxim of Relation Talk about what is relevant to the conversation. Thus, if you're talking about Pat and Chris and say, for example, "Money causes all sorts of relationship problems," it's assumed by others that your comment is somehow related to Pat and Chris. This principle is frequently violated by speakers who digress widely or frequently interject irrelevant comments and you wonder how these comments are related to what you're discussing.

The Maxim of Manner Be clear, avoid ambiguities, be relatively brief, and organize your thoughts into a meaningful sequence. Thus, you use terms that the listener understands and clarify terms that you suspect the listener will not understand. When talking with a child, for example, you would simplify your vocabulary. Similarly, you adjust your manner of speaking on the basis of the information you and the listener share. When talking to a close friend, for example, you can refer to mutual acquaintances and to experiences you've had together. When talking to a stranger, however, you'd either omit such references or explain them.

The four maxims just discussed aptly describe most conversations as they take place in much of the United States. Recognize, however, that maxims will vary from one culture to another. Here are a few maxims appropriate in cultures other than the culture of the United States, but also appropriate to some degree throughout the United States.

In Japanese conversations and group discussions, a maxim of *preserving peaceful relationships* with others may be observed (Midooka 1990). Thus, for example, it would be considered inappropriate to argue and to directly demonstrate that another person is wrong. It would be inappropriate to contribute to another person's embarrassment or, worse, loss of face.

The maxim of *self-denigration,* observed in the conversations of Chinese speakers, may require that you avoid taking credit for some accomplishment or make less of some ability or talent you have (Gu 1990). To put yourself down in this way is a form of politeness that seeks to elevate the person to whom you're speaking.

The maxim of *politeness* is probably universal across all cultures (Brown and Levinson 1987). Cultures differ, however, in how they define politeness and in how important politeness is compared with, say, openness or honesty. Cultures also differ in the rules for expressing politeness or impoliteness and in the punishments for violating the accepted rules of politeness (Mao 1994, Strecker 1993). Asian cultures, especially Chinese and

In New York City, to take one example, politeness between cab drivers and riders has never been especially high and has prompted a great deal of criticism. In an attempt to combat this negative attitude, cab drivers have been given 50 polite phrases and are instructed to use these frequently: "May I open (close) the window for you?" "Madam (Sir), is the temperature okay for you?" "I'm sorry, I made a wrong turn. I'll take care of it, and we can deduct if from the fare" (*New York Times*, 6 May 1996, p. B1). How can you, in turn, be more polite to cab drivers?

Japanese, are often singled out because they emphasize politeness more and mete out harsher social punishments for violations than would most people in, say, the United States or Western Europe. This has led some to propose that a maxim of politeness operates in Asian cultures (Fraser 1990).

There are large gender differences (and some similarities) in the expression of politeness (Holmes 1995). Generally, studies from a number of different cultures show that women's speech is more polite than men's speech (Brown 1980, Wetzel 1988, Holmes 1995). Women more often seek areas of agreement in conversation and conflict situations than do men. Similarly, young girls are more apt to try to modify disagreements while young boys are more apt to express "bald disagreements" (Holmes 1995). But men and women in the United States and New Zealand seem to pay compliments in similar ways (Manes and Wolfson 1981, Holmes 1986, 1995). Similarly, men and women use politeness strategies when communicating bad news in an organization (Lee 1993).

Politeness also varies with the type of relationship. One researcher, for example, has proposed that politeness is greatest with friends and considerably less with strangers and intimates, as depicted in Figure 14.2 (Wolfson 1988, Holmes 1995).

Netiquette The Internet has very specific rules for politeness, called netiquette. Much as the rules of etiquette provide guidance in communicating in social situations, the rules of netiquette provide guidance in communicating over the Net. These rules are helpful for making Internet communication more pleasant and easier and also for achieving greater personal efficiency. They also help to lessen the strain on the system and on other users. Here are several of these netiquette guidelines:

WEB EXPLORATION
To learn more about "Netiquette", go to www.awl.com/devito.

- Read the FAQs. Before asking questions about the system, read the Frequently Asked Questions. Your question has probably been asked before, and you'll put less strain on the system.
- Don't shout. WRITING IN CAPS IS PERCEIVED AS SHOUTING. It's okay to use caps occasionally to achieve emphasis. If you wish to give emphasis, underline _like this_ or *like this*
- Lurk before speaking. Lurking refers to reading the posted notices and reading the conversations without contributing anything. In computer communication,

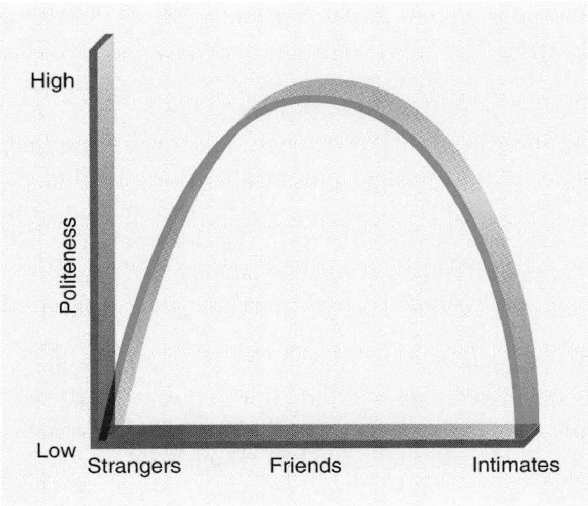

Figure 14.2 Wolfson's Bulge Model of Politeness
Do you find this model a generally accurate representation of your own level of politeness in different types of relationships? Can you build a case for an inverted U theory (where politeness would be high for both strangers and intimates and low for friends)?

lurking is good, not bad. Lurking will help you learn the rules of the particular group and will help you avoid saying things you'd like to take back.

- Don't contribute to traffic jams. Try connecting during off hours whenever possible. If you're unable to connect, try later, not immediately. It only puts added strain on the system and you're likely to still be unable to connect. In securing information, try local information sources before trying more distant sources; it requires fewer connections and less time. Be economical in using files (for example, photographs) that may tie up lines for long periods of time.
- Be brief. Follow the maxim of quantity by communicating only the information that is needed; follow the maxim of manner by communicating clearly, briefly, and in an organized way.
- Treat newbies kindly; you were one once yourself.
- Don't send commercial messages to those who didn't request them. Junk mail is junk mail; but on the Internet, the receiver has to pay for the time it takes to read and delete these unwanted messages.
- Don't spam. Spamming occurs when you send someone unsolicited mail, repeatedly sending the same mail, or posting the same message on lots of bulletin boards, even when the message is irrelevant to the focus of the group One of the very practical reasons spamming is frowned upon is that it often costs you money to maintain the Internet connection needed to download the e-mail you didn't want in the first place. Also, it costs you time. Another reason, of course, is that it clogs the system, slowing it down for everyone.
- Don't flame. Flaming refers to using personal attacks on another user. As in face-to-face conflict, personal attacks are best avoided on the Internet. So avoid flaming and participating in flame wars.

Conversational Turns The defining feature of conversation is that the speaker and listener exchange roles throughout the interaction. You accomplish this through a wide variety of verbal and nonverbal cues that signal **conversational turns**—the changing (or maintaining) of the speaker or listener role during the conversation. Combining the insights of a variety of communication researchers (Duncan 1972, Burgoon, Buller, and Woodall 1995, Pearson and Spitzberg 1990), we can look at conversational turns in terms of cues that speakers use and cues that listeners use.

Speaker Cues As a speaker, you regulate conversation through two major types of cues: turn-maintaining and turn-yielding cues. *Turn-maintaining cues* are designed to help you maintain the speaker's role. You can do this with a variety of cues, for example, audibly inhaling to show that you have more to say, continuing a gesture or gestures to show that you have not completed the thought, avoiding eye contact with the listener so there's no indication that you're passing the speaking turn to him or her, sustaining your intonation pattern to indicate that you intend to say more, or vocalizing pauses ("er," "umm") to prevent the listener from speaking and to show that you're still talking (Duncan 1972, Burgoon, Buller, and Woodall 1995). In most cases, speakers are expected to maintain relatively brief speaking turns and to turn over the speaking role willingly to the listener (when so signaled by the listener).

With *turn-yielding cues* you tell the listener that you're finished and wish to exchange the role of speaker for that of listener. These cues tell the listener (sometimes a specific listener) to take over the role of speaker. For example, at the end of a statement you might add some paralinguistic cue such as "eh?" which asks one of the listeners to assume the role of speaker. You can also indicate that you've finished speaking by dropping your intonation, by prolonged silence, by making direct eye contact with a listener, by asking some general question, or by nodding in the direction of a particular listener.

In much the same way that you expect a speaker to yield the role of speaker, you also expect the listener to willingly assume the speaking role. Those who don't may be regarded as reticent or unwilling to involve themselves and take equal responsibility for the conversation. For example, in an analysis of turn-taking violations in the conversations of marrieds, the most common violation found was that of no response. Forty-five percent of the 540 violations identified involved a lack of response to an invitation to assume the speaker role Of these "no response" violations, 68 percent were committed by men and 32 percent by women. Other turn-taking violations include interruptions, delayed responses, and inappropriately brief responses. From this it's been argued that with these violations, all of which are committed more frequently by men, men silence women in marital interactions (DeFrancisco 1991).

Listener Cues As a listener, you can regulate the conversation by using a variety of cues. *Turn-requesting cues* let the speaker know that you'd like to take a turn as speaker. Sometimes you can do this by simply saying, "I'd like to say something," but often you do it more subtly through some vocalized "er" or "um" that tells the mindful speaker that you'd now like to speak. This request to speak is also often made with facial and mouth gestures. You can, for example, indicate a desire to speak by opening your eyes and mouth widely as if to say something, by beginning to gesture with your hand, or by leaning forward.

You can also indicate your reluctance to assume the role of speaker by using *turn-denying cues*. For example, intoning a slurred "I don't know" or a brief grunt signals you have nothing to say. Turn-denying is often accomplished by avoiding eye contact with the speaker who wishes you to take on the role of speaker or by engaging in some behavior that is incompatible with speaking—for example, coughing or blowing your nose.

Back-channeling cues are used to communicate various types of information back to the speaker without your assuming the role of speaker. Some researchers call these "acknowledgment tokens"—brief utterances such as "mm-hm," "uh-huh," and "yeah," the three most often used such tokens—that tell the speaker you're listening (Schegloff 1982, Drummond and Hopper 1993). You can communicate quite a variety of messages with these back-channeling cues; four such types are included in Table 14.3.

Some back-channeling cues are actually *interruptions*. These interruptions, however, are generally confirming rather than disconfirming. They tell the speaker that you're listening and are involved (Kennedy and Camden 1988). Other interruptions are not as confirming and simply take the speaking turn away from the speaker, either temporarily or permanently. Sometimes the interrupter may apologize for breaking in and at other times may not even seem aware of interrupting.

Interruptions can serve a variety of specific functions. For example, interruptions may be used to change the topic ("I gotta tell you this story before I bust"), to correct the speaker ("You mean four months, not years, don't you?"), to seek information and perhaps interject a question of clarification ("Do you mean Jeff's cousin?"), or to introduce essential information ("Your car's on fire"). Of course, you can interrupt to end the conversation ("I hate to interrupt, but I really have to get back to the office").

Not surprisingly, research finds that superiors (bosses, supervisors) and those in positions of authority (police officers, interviewers) interrupt those in inferior positions more than the other way around (Carroll 1994, Ashcraft 1998). In fact, it would

TABLE 14.3 Functions of Backchanneling Cues

Although we're seldom mindful of using backchanneling cues, we would miss them sorely if our own listeners didn't use them. As you read through this table, consider how you communicate these various functions and how responsive you are to the backchanneling cues of others. This table is based on the excellent research summaries of Burgoon, Buller, and Woodall (1995) and Pearson and Spitzberg (1990).

Functions	Examples
To indicate agreement or disagreement	Smiles, nods of approval, brief comments such as "Right" and "Of course," or a vocalization like "hu-hah" signal agreement. Frowning, shaking your head, or making comments such as "No" or "Never" signal disagreement.
To indicate degree of involvement	An attentive posture, forward leaning, and focused eye contact tell the speaker that you're involved in the conversation. An inattentive posture, backward leaning, and avoidance of eye contact communicate a lack of involvement.
To pace the speaker	Ask the speaker to slow down by raising your hand near your ear and leaning forward or to speed up by continued nodding of your head. Cue the speaker verbally by simply asking the speaker to slow down or to speed up.
To ask for clarification	Puzzled facial expressions, perhaps coupled with a forward lean, signal your need for clarification. Directly interjecting "Who?," "When?," or "Where?"

probably strike you as strange to see a worker repeatedly interrupting a supervisor or a student repeatedly interrupting a professor.

Another and even more often studied aspect of interruption is that of gender difference. Do men or women interrupt more? Research here is conflicting. These few research findings will give you an idea of the differing results (Pearson, West, and Turner 1995):

- The more malelike the person's gender identity—regardless of the person's biological sex—the more likely it is that the person will interrupt (Drass 1986).
- There are no significant differences between boys and girls (ages 2–5) in interrupting behavior (Greif 1980).
- Fathers interrupt their children more than mothers do (Greif 1980).
- Women more so than men judge "simultaneous talk" as being interruptions (Bresnahan and Cai 1996).
- Men interrupt more than women do (Zimmerman and West 1975, West and Zimmerman 1977).
- Men and women do not differ in their interrupting behavior (Roger and Nesshoever 1987).
- No single linguistic feature has been found that definitely identifies a message as an interruption (Coon and Schwanenflugel 1996).

The various turn-taking cues and how they correspond to the conversational wants of speaker and listener are summarized in Figure 14.3.

Closing Conversations

Closing a conversation is often a difficult task. It can be an awkward and uncomfortable part of interpersonal interaction. Here are a few suggestions you might consider:

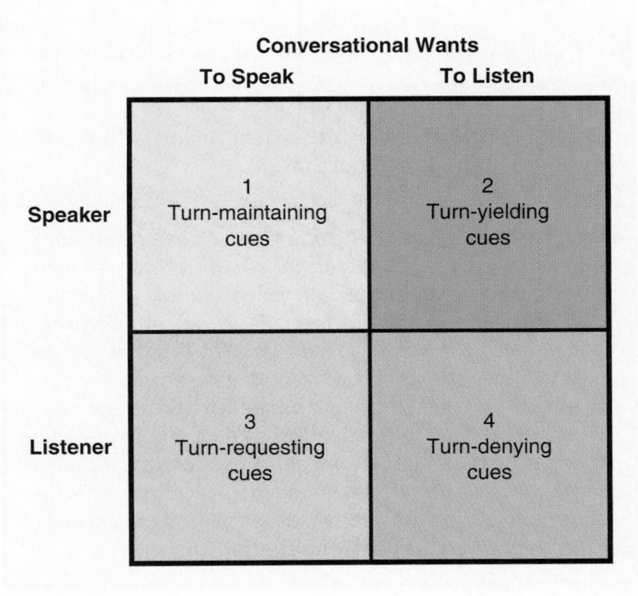

Conversational Wants
To Speak
To Listen
Speaker
Listener
1
Turn-maintaining cues
2
Turn-yielding cues
3
Turn-requesting cues
4
Turn-denying cues

Figure 14.3 Turn-Taking and Conversational Wants Quadrant 1 represents the speaker who wishes to speak (continue to speak) and uses turn-maintaining cues; Quadrant 2 the speaker who wishes to listen and uses turn-yielding cues; Quadrant 3 the listener who wishes to speak and uses turn-requesting cues; and Quadrant 4 the listener who wishes to listen (continue listening) and uses turn-denying cues. Back-channeling cues would appear in Quadrant 4, since they're cues that listeners use while they continue to listen. Interruptions would appear in Quadrant 3, though they're not so much cues that request a turn but are actual takeovers of the speaker's position. Does this system allow for the representation of all conversational cues? Are there other types of cues that are not represented here?

- Reflect back on the conversation and briefly summarize it so as to bring it to a close. For example: "I'm glad I ran into you and found out what happened at that union meeting. I'll probably be seeing you at the meetings next week."
- Directly state the desire to end the conversation and to get on with other things. For example: "I'd like to continue talking, but I really have to run. I'll see you around."
- Refer to future interaction. For example: "Why don't we get together next week sometime and continue this discussion?"
- Ask for closure. For example: "Have I explained what you wanted to know?"
- State that you enjoyed the interaction. For example: "I really enjoyed talking with you."

With any of these closings, it should be clear to the other person that you're attempting to end the conversation. Obviously, you will have to use more direct methods with those who don't take these subtle hints or don't realize that both persons are responsible for the interpersonal interaction and for bringing it to a satisfactory close.

How do the conversations with your best friend differ from those you have with casual acquaintances?

◀◀ THINKING BACK

CONVERSATIONAL PROBLEMS: PREVENTION AND REPAIR

THINKING AHEAD ▶▶

Have you ever said something that you wished you could take back? What happened?

In conversation, you may anticipate a problem and seek to prevent it. Or you may discover that you said or did something that will lead to disapproval, and you may seek to excuse yourself. Here we give just one example of a device to prevent potential conversational problems (the disclaimer) and one example of a device to repair conversational problems (the excuse). Our purpose is simply to illustrate the complexity of these processes, not to present you with an exhaustive list of the ways conversational problems may be prevented or repaired.

Preventing Conversational Problems: The Disclaimer

Let's say, for example, that you fear your listeners will at first think a comment you're about to make is inappropriate, that they may rush to judge you without hearing your full account, or will think that you're not in full possession of your

ETHICS IN INTERPERSONAL COMMUNICATION

Vote online at http://www.awl.com/devito

Motivational Appeals

Appeals to motives are commonplace. For example, if you want a friend to take a vacation with you, you're likely to appeal to such motives as the desire for fun and excitement, the financial advantage of taking the trip now rather than at the height of the season, and perhaps the possibility of meeting one's true love. If you look at the advertisements for cruises and vacation packages, you'll see very similar motives being appealed to. There can be no doubt that such motivational appeals are effective. But are they ethical? Are motivational appeals ethical under certain conditions and unethical under other conditions? For example, is it ethical to appeal to peoples' vanity and desire for status to get them to buy cosmetics and expensive clothing which they really can't afford and often go into debt to purchase?

What would you do? *You're a car dealer and your job is to sell cars. A potential customer comes into the showroom, and after a brief interview, you know that this person should logically buy a moderately priced car rather than go into debt to buy the higher priced, fancy sports model. Would it be ethical for you to appeal to the customer's desire for status and sexual gratification to ensure the sale of the expensive sports car? Would it be ethical for you to appeal to the same status and sex motives with a customer who could easily afford the most expensive car on the lot? What would you do in this situation?*

faculties. In these cases, you may use some form of disclaimer. A **disclaimer** is a statement that aims to ensure that your message will be understood and will not reflect negatively on you (Hewitt and Stokes 1975, McLaughlin 1984). There are several types of disclaimer.

Hedging helps you to separate yourself from the message, so that if your listeners reject your message, they need not reject you (for example, "I may be wrong here, but . . ."). If the hedges are seen as indicating a lack of certainty or conviction because of some inadequacy, they decrease the attractiveness of both women and men (Wright and Hosman 1983). However, they'll be more positively received if they're seen as indicating a lack of belief in allness (as indicating that no one can know all about any subject), as well as a belief that tentative statements are all one can reasonably make (Hosman 1989, Pearson, Turner, and Todd-Mancillas 1991).

Credentialing helps you establish your special qualifications for saying what you're about to say ("Don't get me wrong, I'm not homophobic"). *Sin licenses* ask listeners for permission to deviate in some way from some normally accepted convention ("I know this may not be the place to discuss business, but . . ."). *Cognitive disclaimers* help you make the case that you're in full possession of your faculties ("I know you'll think I'm crazy, but let me explain the logic of the case"). *Appeals for the suspension of judgment* ask listeners to hear you out before making a judgment ("Don't hang up on me until you hear my side of the story").

Generally, disclaimers are effective when you think you might offend listeners in telling a joke ("I don't usually like these types of jokes, but . . ."). In one study, for example, 11-year-old children were read a story about someone whose actions created negative effects. Some children heard the story with a disclaimer, and others heard the same story without the disclaimer. When the children were asked to indicate how the person should be punished, those who heard the story with the disclaimer recommended significantly lower punishments (Bennett 1990).

Disclaimers, however, can also get you into trouble. For example, to preface remarks with "I'm no liar" may well lead listeners to think that perhaps you are lying. Also, if you use too many disclaimers, you may be perceived as someone who doesn't have any strong convictions or as one who wants to avoid responsibility for just about everything. This seems especially true of hedges.

In responding to statements containing disclaimers, it's often necessary to respond to both the disclaimer and to the statement. By doing so, you let the speaker know that you heard the disclaimer and that you aren't going to view this communication negatively. Appropriate responses might be: "I know you're no sexist, but I don't agree that . . ." or "Well, perhaps we should discuss the money now even if it doesn't seem right."

Repairing Conversational Problems: The Excuse

At times you may say the wrong thing, but because you can't erase the message (communication really is irreversible), you may try to account for it. Perhaps the most common method for doing so is the excuse. You learn early in life that when you do something that others will view negatively, an excuse is in order to justify your performance. **Excuses,** central to all forms of communication and interaction, are "explanations or actions that lessen the negative implications of an actor's performance, thereby maintaining a positive image for oneself and others" (Snyder 1984, Snyder, Higgins, and Stucky 1983).

Excuses seem especially in order when you say or are accused of saying something that runs counter to what is expected, sanctioned, or considered "right" by the people with whom you're talking. Ideally, the excuse lessens the negative impact of the message.

Some Motives for Excuse Making The major motive for excuse making seems to be to maintain your self-esteem, to project a positive image to yourself and to others. Excuses are also offered to reduce the stress that may be created by a bad performance. You may feel that if you can offer an excuse—especially a good one that is accepted by those around you—it will reduce the negative reaction and the subsequent stress that accompanies a poor performance.

Excuses also enable you to maintain effective interpersonal relationships even after some negative behavior. For example, after criticizing a friend's behavior and observing the negative reaction to your criticism, you might offer an excuse such as, "Please forgive me; I'm really exhausted. I'm just not thinking straight." Excuses enable you to place your messages—even your possible failures—in a more favorable light.

Good and Bad Excuses The most important question for most people is what makes a good excuse and what makes a bad excuse (Snyder 1984, Slade 1995). How can you make good excuses and thus get out of problems, and how can you avoid bad excuses and thus only make matters worse? Good excuse makers use excuses in moderation; bad excuse makers rely on excuses too often. Good excuse makers avoid using excuses in the presence of those who know what really happened; bad excuse makers will make excuses even in these inappropriate situations. Good excuse makers avoid blaming others, especially those they work with; bad excuse makers blame even their work colleagues. In a similar way, good excuse makers don't attribute their failure to others or to the company; bad excuse makers do. Good excuse makers acknowledge their own responsibility for the failure by noting that they did something wrong (not that they lack competence); bad excuse makers refuse to accept any responsibility for their failure.

The best excuses are apologies because they contain three essential elements for a good excuse (Slade 1995):

- an acknowledgement of the responsibility
- a request for forgiveness
- the suggestion that things will be done better in the future

How effective are you in preventing and in correcting conversational problems? What's your most effective strategy?

◀◀ THINKING BACK

The worst excuse is the falsely proclaimed "I didn't do it." This fails to acknowledge responsibility and offers no assurance that the failure will not happen again.

In his introduction to Margaret McLaughlin's insightful *Conversation* (1984), Mark Knapp observes, "While there is something inherently fascinating about discovering the anatomy of behaviors we habitually (and sometimes unthinkingly) perform, the real significance of understanding the structure of conversations is its centrality for understanding human interaction in general." The intention of this unit has been to help you approach this understanding.

REVIEWING KEY TERMS AND CONCEPTS IN CONVERSATION

This unit reviewed the process of conversation and focused on its stages, principles, rules for effective management, and conversational problems.

The Conversation Process

What are the major stages in conversation?

- The *opening* initiates and begins the conversation.
- The *feedforward* previews or prefaces the major part of the conversation which is to follow.
- The *business* is the major part of the conversation; it's the reason for the conversation.
- The *feedback* summarizes or reflecting back on the conversation.
- The *closing* brings the conversation to an end.

Conversational Management

How do you go about initiating, maintaining, and closing conversations so that they're effective and satisfying?

- Initiating conversations is often accomplished with self-references, other-references, relational references, and context references.
- Maintaining conversations depends on the principle of cooperation and the maxims of quantity, quality, relation, and manner. Speakers and listeners also take turns, using maintaining, yielding, requesting, denying, and backchanneling cues).
- Closing conversations is often accomplished by reflecting back on the conversation, directly stating the desire to end conversation, referring to future interactions, asking for closure, and expressing pleasure with interaction.

Conversational Problems: Prevention and Repair

How might conversational problems be prevented and repaired?

- Preventing conversational problems may be aided by the disclaimer, a statement that helps to ensure that your message will be understood and will not reflect negatively on the speaker. Disclaimer types includes hedging, credentialing, sin licenses, cognitive disclaimers, and appeals for the suspension of judgment.
- Conversational repair is often accomplished with the excuse, an explanation designed to lessen the negative impact of a speaker's messages.

APPLYING KEY TERMS AND CONCEPTS IN CONVERSATION

1. How would your conversational openers differ if you wanted to establish a friendship and if you wanted to establish a romantic relationship?
2. Does your experience agree with or disagree with Chris Kleinke's conclusions (in Table 14.2) about how men and women use and respond to opening lines?
3. Can you give examples to illustrate the importance of the general skills of mindfulness, flexibility, cultural sensitivity, and metacommunication from your own conversation experiences?
4. After reviewing the research on the empathic and listening abilities of men and women, Pearson, West, and Turner (1995) conclude: "Men and women do not differ as much as conventional wisdom would have us believe. In many instances, she thinks like a man, and he thinks like a woman because they both think alike." Does your experience support this observation?
5. Visit one of the IRCs and lurk for 5 to 10 minutes. What characterizes the conversation on the channel you observed? What is the topic of conversation? What is the most obvious purpose of the group?
6. Access ERIC, Medline, Psychlit, or Sociofile (databases of citations and abstracts of thousands of articles on communication and education, medicine, psychology, and sociology) and locate an article dealing with some aspect of conversation. What can you learn about conversation and interpersonal communication from this article?
7. If you were compiling excuses for a book called *The World's Worst Excuses*, which ones would you include? Which would you include in *The World's Best Excuses*?

8. How sensitive are you to the back-channeling cues of others? How sensitive are others to your back-channeling cues?
9. Blind and sighted people make use of the same vocal and verbal cues in managing a conversation, but the blind make little use of touch cues, postural shifts, and gestures (Sharkey and Stafford 1990). What implications can be drawn from this finding for improving communication between blind and sighted persons?
10. How would you go about finding answers to the following questions?
    - How are people who violate conversational maxims perceived?
    - Are people who give lots of back-channeling cues perceived in the same way as people who give few or no back-channeling cues?
    - Can disclaimers increase the perception of the user's credibility?
    - Do men and women use the same kinds of excuses?
    - Do happy and unhappy couples use the same kinds of disclaimers and excuses?

EXPERIENCING KEY TERMS AND CONCEPTS IN CONVERSATION

Go to www.awl.com/devito

Exercise No 15, Conversational Analysis: A Chance Meeting," can be used to illustrate the process of conversation and conversational management. Exercise No. 16, Giving and Taking Directions," is useful in illustrating some of the difficulties experienced in conversation. Exercise No. 17, "Gender and the Topics of Conversation," illustrates the role of gender in conversation. Exercise No. 18, "Formulating Excuses," will enable you to explore the uses of excuses and the qualities of effective and ineffective excuses.

UNIT 15
UNIVERSALS OF INTERPERSONAL RELATIONSHIPS

Regarding Henry (1991)

COMMUNICATION IS TO A RELATIONSHIP WHAT BREATHING IS TO MAINTAINING LIFE.

--VIRGINIA SATIR

Advantages and Disadvantages of Interpersonal Relationships

Stages in Interpersonal Relationships: Development to Dissolution

Relationships in Cultural Context

IN MIKE NICHOLS'S REGARDING HENRY you see the transformation of a one-time reprehensible lawyer who gets shot and suffers brain damage. As a result he must begin life and his relationships over again and in the process of recovery becomes a totally changed person. Especially interesting is how the relationships between Henry (Harrison Ford) and his wife (Annette Bening) and daughter as well as those with his friends and colleagues change, echoing the stages of interpersonal relationships we discuss in this unit (Bell 1996).

So important is contact with other human beings that when you're deprived of it for long periods, depression sets in, self-doubt surfaces, and you may find it difficult to manage even the basics of daily life. Research shows clearly that the most important contributor to happiness—outranking money, job, and sex—is a close relationship with one other person (Freedman 1978, Laroche and deGrace 1997, Lu and Shih 1997). The desire for relationships is universal; they're important to men and to women, to homosexuals and to heterosexuals (Huston and Schwartz 1995).

ADVANTAGES AND DISADVANTAGES OF INTERPERSONAL RELATIONSHIPS

THINKING AHEAD ▶▶
Why do you develop interpersonal relationships?

All relationships have the potential for increasing or decreasing your happiness and satisfaction. There are, potentially, advantages and disadvantages to all interpersonal relationships.

Advantages of Interpersonal Relationships

Interpersonal relationships lessen loneliness, help you secure stimulation, enable you to gain in self-knowledge and self-esteem, enhance your physical and emotional well-being, and most generally, maximize your pleasures and minimize your pains. Since you anticipate that your relationship will bring advantages, you can look at these advantages as the reasons you develop relationships in the first place.

To Lessen Loneliness Relationships often lessen loneliness (Rokach 1998, Rokach and Brock 1995). They make you feel that someone cares, that someone likes you, that someone will protect you, that someone ultimately will love you. Close relationships assure you that someone cares and will be there when you need them. Sometimes surrounding yourself with lots of people helps; often, however, a crowd only serves to underscore loneliness. One close relationship usually works a lot better.

To Secure Stimulation Human beings need stimulation; without it, they withdraw—sometimes they die. As plants are heliotropic and orient themselves to light, humans are stimulotropic and orient themselves to sources of stimulation (M. Davis 1973). Human contact is one of the best ways to secure this stimulation—intellectual, physical, and emotional.

To Gain in Self-Knowledge and Self-Esteem Through contact with others you learn about yourself. Your self-perceptions are greatly influenced by what you think others think of you; if your friends see you as warm and generous, you probably will, too. Contact with others allows you to see yourself from different perspectives and in different roles, as a child or parent, as a coworker, as a manager, as a best friend. You also gain self-knowledge by getting to know others and comparing yourself to them. In fact, social comparison theory holds that you evaluate yourself—your attitudes, talents, values, accomplishments, abilities—primarily by comparing yourself with others.

Healthy interpersonal relationships help enhance self-esteem and self-worth. Simply having a friend or romantic partner (at least most of the time) makes you feel desirable and worthy. When you're fortunate enough to have a supportive partner, the relationship can enhance self-esteem even more.

To Enhance Physical and Emotional Health Research consistently shows that interpersonal relationships contribute significantly to physical and emotional health (Goleman 1995a, Rosengren et al. 1993, Pennebacker 1991) and to personal happiness (Berscheid and Reis 1998). For example, without close interpersonal relationships you're more likely to become depressed, and this depression, in turn, contributes significantly to physical illness. Isolation, in fact, contributes as much to mortality as high blood pressure, high cholesterol, obesity, smoking, or lack of physical exercise (Goleman 1995a). One psychiatrist has argued that the most important indicator of a person's emotional health is "how long-lived and committed are their current intimate relationships" (Rosen 1998, p. 56).

To Maximize Pleasure and Minimize Pain The most general function served by interpersonal relationships, and one that encompasses all the others, is that of maximizing pleasure and minimizing pain. You have a need to share good fortune as well as your emotional and physical pain. Perhaps this goes back to childhood, when you ran to mother to have your wounds kissed or to be told everything is all right. You now find it difficult to run to mother, so you go to others, generally to friends who will provide the same consolation mother did.

Disadvantages of Interpersonal Relationships

Although seldom discussed in most presentations of interpersonal relationships, there are potential disadvantages or costs. Four may be mentioned here: pressure for revealing who you really are, increased obligations to share and care for the other person, increased isolation from other generally rewarding relationships, and the difficulties involved in breaking up.

Pressure for Exposure Close relationships put pressure on you to reveal yourself and to expose your vulnerabilities. While this is generally worthwhile in the context of a supporting and caring relationship, it may backfire if the relationship deteriorates and these weaknesses are used against you. Furthermore, many find no satisfaction in revealing themselves and no advantage in exposing weaknesses.

Increased Obligations In close relationships one person's behavior influences the other person's, sometimes to great extents. Your time is no longer entirely your own. Although you enter a relationship to spend more time with this special person, you also incur time obligations with which you may not be happy. Similarly, if your money is pooled (as it is in many close relationships), then your financial successes have to be shared, as do your partner's losses. On the positive side, of course, your partner shares your losses, and you share in your partner's gains. Perhaps the obligation that creates the most difficulty is an emotional one. To be emotionally responsive and sensitive—all the time—isn't always easy.

Increased Isolation Close relationships can result in abandoning other relationships. You may like someone your partner can't stand, so you may give up this person or see him or her less often. More often, however, it's simply a matter of time and energy; relationships take a lot of both. You consequently have less to give to these other and less intimate relationships.

Difficulty in Dissolving Once entered into, a relationship may prove difficult to get out of. In some cultures, for example, religious pressures may prevent married couples from separating. If children are part of the relationship, it may be emotionally difficult to exit. If lots of money is involved, dissolving a relationship can often mean giving up the fortune you have spent your life accumulating.

Also, of course, your partner may break your heart. Your partner may leave you—against all your pleading and promises. Your hurt will be in proportion to how much you care and need your partner. The person who cares a lot is hurt a lot; the person who cares little is hurt little.

Parasocial and Online Relationships

Although we often think of relationships—especially intimacy ones—as taking place face-to-face, it's important to recognize that other types of relationships play significant roles in our lives. Two drastically different kinds of relationships should be mentioned within this context of relationship advantages and disadvantages: parasocial and online relationships.

Parasocial Relationships Some people develop and maintain relationships that are less than real, that are with, for example, media personalities or a fictional character in a soap opera or television drama (Rubin and McHugh 1987, Rubin, Perse, and Powell 1985). At times viewers develop these parasocial relationships with real media personalities—Kathy Lee Gifford, Geraldo Rivera, or even Charles Manson, for example. As a result they may watch these personalities faithfully and communicate with the individual in their own imaginations. At other times, the relationship is with the fictional character—like Frasier, Ally McBeal, or a doctor on the series *ER*. In fact, those who play doctors frequently get mail asking their medical advice. Soap opera stars who are about to be "killed" may get warning letters from their parasocial relationship partners. Most people obviously don't go quite this far. Yet many viewers consider the role real enough to make that actor in that role a bankable spokesperson for a product. For example, actor Susan Sullivan, who played a nurse on television some ten years ago, is still a spokesperson for a particular medication.

WEB EXPLORATION
To learn more about parasocial relationships, go to www.awl.com/devito.

In the talk shows where viewers can often write in to meet the guests from the show, the relationships may begin as parasocial but quickly move to real. For example, a *Sally Jesse Raphael* show in early 1995 was devoted to viewers who had crushes on former guests and whom the show got together for another show. Viewers can see the characters on television—and in some ways talk-show panelists are very much like dramatic characters in a play—as potential relationship partners. Even though such occurrences are infrequent, they seem to happen often enough for people to write in with the possibility of meeting a guest. On home-shopping programs, you may develop a parasocial relationship with the host (Grant and Guthrie 1991). On some shows you can often talk with the host or with a product's spokesperson. You can, for example, call the number on the screen and talk to minor and sometimes major celebrities. As the ability to interact with the television programs increases, the distinction between real and parasocial relationships will become increasingly blurred (cf. Auter and Moore 1993).

Online Relationships Online interpersonal relationships are on the increase. The number of Internet users is rapidly increasing, and commercial Web sites devoted to meeting other people are proliferating, making it especially easy to develop online relationships. Books such as Phyllis Phlegar's (1995) *Love Online: A Practical Guide to Digital Dating* and Linda K. Fuller's (1996) *Media-Mediated Relationships: Straight and Gay, Mainstream and Alternative Perspectives* attest to the growing importance of online relationships. The afternoon television talk shows frequently focus on computer relationships, especially getting people together who have established a relationship online but who have never met. Clearly, many are turning to the Internet to find a friend or romantic partner. Some are using the Internet as their only means of interaction; others are using it as a way of beginning a relationship and intend to later supplement computer talk with photographs, phone calls, and face-to-face meetings.

Almost two-thirds of newsgroup users had formed new acquaintances, friendships, or other personal relationships with someone they met on the Internet. Almost one-third said that they communicated with their partner at least three or four times a week; more than half communicated on a weekly basis (Parks and Floyd 1996).

Women, it seems, are more likely to form relationships on the Internet than men. About 72 percent of women and 55 percent of men had formed personal relationships online (Parks and Floyd 1996). Not surprisingly, those who communicated more frequently formed more relationships.

ASK THE RESEARCHER

Interacting with Media Personalities

I have a friend who watches a lot of television and seems to develop almost real relationships with the characters from a variety of shows. Is this typical behavior? Is it dangerous for interpersonal relationships?

We often experience a sense of friendship, or *parasocial interaction,* with TV characters. Parasocial interaction is a normal response to media exposure, providing we realize these are one-sided relationships that don't replace interpersonal interaction. It's an emotional tie with media personalities, which reminds us of face-to-face interaction. It's based on feelings of similarity, attraction, and empathy. We may seek guidance from what that TV personality says, see her as a friend, imagine being part of his social world, and feel that we want to meet or be like that person. Media performers even use informal gestures and a conversational style that mirrors interpersonal communication to invite this interaction. Similar to reducing uncertainty in interpersonal communication, we may attribute motives to the behavior of the characters, predict their attitudes, and develop expectations about their behavior. By involving the audience in the news, the program, or the story, TV producers are able to retain audience members as continuing viewers.

For further information see D. Horton and R. R. Wohl, "Mass Communication and Parasocial Interaction: Observations on Intimacy at a Distance," *Psychiatry* 19 (1956): 215–229, and A. M. Rubin, E. M. Perse, and R. A. Powell, "Loneliness, Parasocial Interaction, and Local Television News Viewing," *Human Communication Research* 12 (1985): 155–180.

—Alan M. Rubin (Ph.D., University of Illinois) is a professor of communication studies at Kent State University. He teaches courses in and conducts research about the uses and effects of the media and the links between personal and mediated communication. arubin@kent.edu.

As relationships develop on the Internet, network convergence occurs; that is, as a relationship between two people develops, they begin to share their network of other communicators with each other (Parks 1995, Parks and Floyd 1996). This, of course, is similar to relationships formed through face-to-face contact.

There are lots of advantages to establishing relationships online. For example, it's safe in terms of avoiding the potential for physical violence or sexually transmitted diseases. Unlike relationships established in face-to-face encounters where physical appearance tends to outweigh personality, on the Internet your inner qualities are communicated first. Friendship and romantic interaction on the Internet are a natural boon to shut-ins and the extremely shy for whom traditional ways of meeting someone are often difficult. Computer talk is more empowering for those with "physical disabilities or disfigurements" where face-to-face interactions are often superficial and often end with withdrawal (Lea and Spears 1995, Bull and Rumsey 1988). By eliminating the physical cues, computer talk equalizes the interaction and doesn't put the disfigured person, for example, at an immediate disadvantage in a society where physical attractiveness is so highly valued. You're then free to reveal as much or as little about your physical self as you wish, when you wish.

Another obvious advantage is that the number of people you can reach is so vast that it's relatively easy to find someone who matches what you're looking for. The situation is like finding a book that covers just what you need from a library of millions of volumes rather than from one of only several thousand. Still another advantage for many is that the socioeconomic and educational status of people on the Net is significantly higher than you're likely to find in a bar or singles group.

Of course, there are also disadvantages. For one thing, you can't see the person. Unless you exchange photos or meet face-to-face, you won't know what the person looks like. Even if photos are exchanged, how certain can you be that the photos are of the person or that they were taken recently? In addition, you can't hear the person's voice, and this too hinders you in formulating a total picture of the other person. Of course, you can always add an occasional phone call to give you this added information.

Online, people can present a false self with little chance of detection. For example, minors may present themselves as adults, and adults may present themselves as children for illicit and illegal sexual communications and, perhaps, meetings. Similarly, people can present themselves as poor when they're rich, as mature when they're immature, as serious and committed when they're just enjoying the experience.

Another potential disadvantage—though some might argue it is actually an advantage—is that computer interactions may become all consuming and may substitute for face-to-face interpersonal relationships.

All relationships (including parasocial and online relationships) will bring advantages and disadvantages; in an imperfect world, that's to be expected. The insights and skills of interpersonal communication and relationships, however, should stack the odds in favor of greater and longer lived advantages and fewer and shorter lived disadvantages.

Do your friendships provide a different group of advantages and disadvantages than do your romantic relationships? Do your face-to-face relationships provide different advantages and disadvantages from your online relationships?

◂◂ THINKING BACK

STAGES IN INTERPERSONAL RELATIONSHIPS: DEVELOPMENT TO DISSOLUTION

THINKING AHEAD ▸▸

How would you describe the stages you go through in forming a relationship? Are you generally in sync with the other person, or do you move more slowly or more rapidly?

You and another person don't become intimate friends immediately upon meeting. Rather, you build an intimate relationship gradually, through a series of steps

ETHICS IN INTERPERSONAL COMMUNICATION

Vote online at http://www.awl.com/devito

Your Right to Know

At some point in a relationship, you may feel that the other person—because he or she is so close to you—has an ethical obligation to reveal certain information to you. Conversely, you may feel that you have an ethical obligation to reveal certain information about yourself to this lover or friend.

What would you do? *At what point—if any—do you feel you have the right to know each of the ten items of information listed here? Record your feelings for romantic relationships in the first column and for friendship relationships in the second column. Use numbers from 1 to 10 to indicate at what point you would feel you have a right to know this information by visualizing a relationship as existing on a continuum from initial contact at 1 and extreme intimacy at 10. If you feel you would never have the right to know this information use 0. [As you complete these items, consider in which type of relationship does the ethical obligation to reveal certain information come earlier? What is it that gives one person the right to know personal information about another person? Conversely, what imposes an ethical obligation on a friend or lover to reveal such information?] What would you do in each of these situations?*

Initial Contact • *1* ◄——► Extreme Intimacy • *10*

Romantic Partner	Close Friend	Information you feel you have the right to know and that you feel your romantic partner or close friend has an ethical obligation to reveal:
______	______	1. HIV status
______	______	2. History of family genetic disorders
______	______	3. The existence and number of children the person has
______	______	4. Past sexual experiences
______	______	5. Marital history
______	______	6. Annual salary, net financial worth
______	______	7. Affectional orientation
______	______	8. Race and nationality
______	______	9. Religion and religious beliefs
______	______	10. Social and political beliefs and attitudes

TRY IT!
To learn more about stages in interpersonal relationships, go to www.awl.com/devito.

or stages. The same is true of most relationships. The "love at first sight" phenomenon creates a problem for a stage model of relationships. So rather than argue that such love cannot occur (my own feeling is that it can and frequently does), it seems wiser to claim that the stage model characterizes most relationships for most people most of the time.

Within each relationship and within each relationship stage, there are dynamic tensions between several opposites. The assumption made by this theory—called **relationship dialectics theory**—is that all relationships can be defined by a series of opposites. For example, some research has found three such opposites (Baxter 1988, 1990, Baxter and Simon 1993). The tension between *autonomy and connection* expresses your desire to remain an individual but also to intimately connect to another person and to a relationship. This theme appears in women's magazines and seems to teach readers to want both autonomy and connection (Prusank, Duran, and DeLillo 1993). The tension between *novelty and predictability* centers on the dual desires for newness and adventure on the one hand and sameness and comfortableness on the other. The tension between *closedness and openness* relates to the desires to be in an exclusive relationship and one that is open to different people. The closedness-openness tension is more in evidence during the early stages of relationship development. Autonomy-connection and novelty-predictability are more a factor as the relationship progresses.

The six-stage model in Figure 15.1 describes the main stages in most relationships. For a particular relationship, you might wish to modify the basic model. But as a general description of relationship development, the stages seem fairly standard. Do realize, of course, that both partners may not perceive their relationship in the same way; one person, for example, may see the relationship as an intimate one but the other may not.

The six stages of relationships are contact, involvement, intimacy, deterioration, repair, and dissolution. Each stage has an early and a late phase. These stages describe relationships as they are; they don't evaluate or prescribe how relationships should be.

Contact

At the initial phase of the contact stage, there is some kind of *perceptual contact*—you see, hear, and perhaps smell the person. From this you get a physical picture—sex, approximate age, height, and so on. After this perception, there is usually *interactional contact*. Here the contact is superficial and relatively impersonal. This is the stage at which you exchange basic information that is preliminary to any more intense involvement ("Hello, my name is Joe"). Here you initiate interaction ("May I join you?") and engage in invitational communication ("May I buy you a drink?"). According to some researchers, it's at this stage—within the first four minutes of initial interaction—that you decide whether you want to pursue the relationship (Zunin and Zunin 1972).

At the contact stage, physical appearance is especially important because it's the most readily seen. Yet through verbal and nonverbal behaviors, qualities such as friendliness, warmth, openness, and dynamism are also revealed.

Involvement

At the involvement stage, a sense of mutuality, of being connected develops. Here you experiment and try to learn more about the other person. At the initial phase

Research shows that the closedness-openness tension is more in evidence during the early stages of development and that autonomy-connection and novelty-predictability were more frequent as the relationship progressed (Baxter 1988, 1990, Baxter and Simon 1993). Why do you suppose this is true?

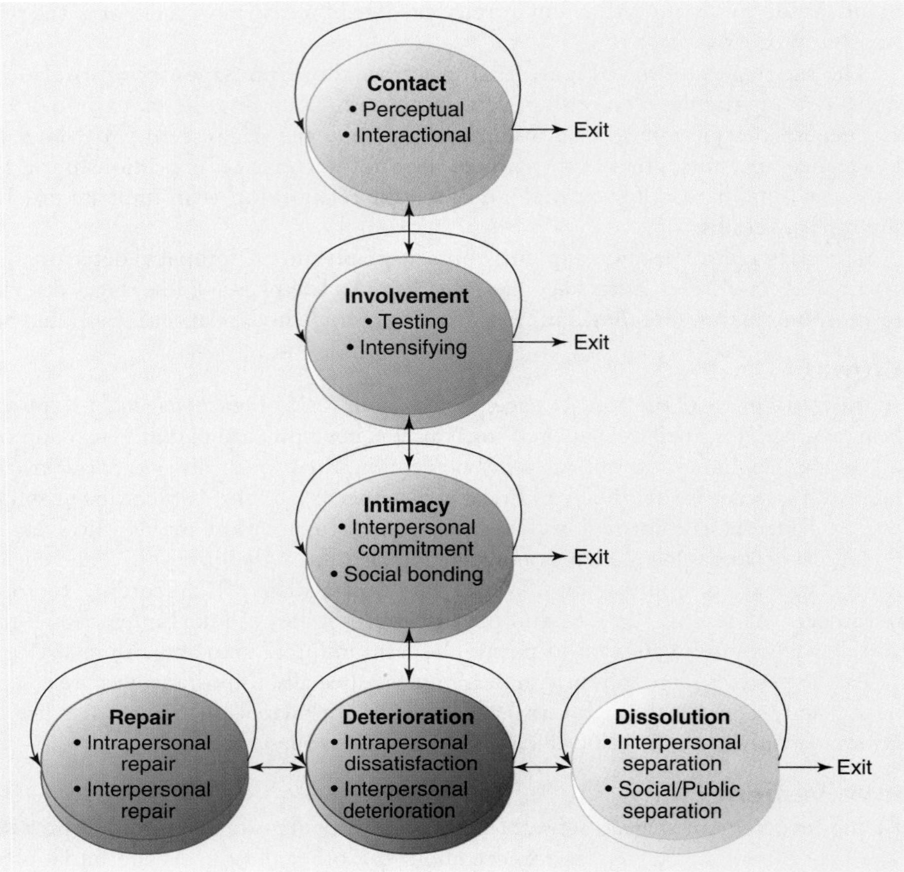

Figure 15.1 Because relationships differ so widely, it's best to think of any relationship model as a tool for talking about relationships rather than as a specific map that indicates how you move from one relationship position to another. Can you identify other steps or stages that would further explain what goes on in relationship development? What happens when the two people in a relationship experience the stages differently? Can you provide an example from literature or from your own experience?

of involvement, a kind of *testing* goes on. You want to see whether your initial judgment proves reasonable. So you may ask questions: "Where do you work?" "What are you majoring in?" If you want to get to know the person even better, you might continue your involvement by intensifying your interaction. Here you not only try to get to know the other person better but also begin to reveal yourself, though in a preliminary way. If in a dating relationship, you might, for example, use a variety of strategies to help you move to the next stage and perhaps to intimacy. For example, you might increase contact with your partner; give your partner tokens of affection such as gifts, cards, or flowers; increase your own personal attractiveness; do things that suggest intensifying the relationship, such as flirting or making your partner jealous; and become more sexually intimate (Tolhuizen 1989).

Throughout the relationship process, but especially during the involvement and early intimacy stages, you test your partner; you try to find out how your partner feels about the relationship. Among the strategies you might use are these (Baxter and Wilmot 1984, Bell and Buerkel-Rothfuss 1990):

- *Directness.* You ask your partner directly how he or she feels, or you disclose your own feelings on the assumption that your partner will also self-disclose.
- *Endurance.* You subject your partner to various negative behaviors (for example, you behave badly or make inconvenient requests) on the assumption that if your partner endures them, he or she is serious about the relationship.

- *Indirect suggestion.* For example, you joke about a shared future together, touch more intimately, or hint that you're serious about the relationship. Similar responses from your partner will mean that he or she wishes to increase the intimacy of the relationship.
- *Public presentation.* For example, you introduce your partner as your "boyfriend" or "girlfriend" and see how your partner responds.
- *Separation.* You separate yourself physically to see how the other person responds. If your partner calls, then you know he or she is interested in the relationship.
- *Third party.* You ask mutual friends about your partner's feelings and intentions.
- *Triangle.* You set up a triangle and tell your partner that, for example, another person is interested in him or her; then you see how your partner reacts. If your partner shows no interest, it indicates a stronger commitment to you.

Intimacy

At the **intimacy** stage, you commit yourself still further to the other person and establish a relationship in which this individual becomes your best or closest friend, lover, or companion. You also come to share each other's social networks, a practice followed by members of widely different cultures (Gao and Gudykunst 1995). Not surprisingly, your relationship satisfaction also increases with the move to this stage (Siavelis and Lamke 1992).

The intimacy stage usually divides itself into two phases. In the *interpersonal commitment* phase the two people commit themselves to each other in a private way. In the *social bonding* phase the commitment is made public—perhaps to family and friends, perhaps to the public at large. Here you and your partner become a unit, an identifiable pair.

When the intimacy stage involves a life-time partnership, you face three main anxieties (Zimmer 1986). A *security anxiety* leads you to worry that your partner may leave you for someone else or that he or she will be sexually unfaithful. A *fulfillment anxiety* leads to concerns that you may not be able to achieve a close, warm, and special rapport or that you won't be able to have an equal relationship. An *excitement anxiety* makes you worry that boredom and routine may set in or that you'll lose your freedom and become trapped.

Of course, not everyone strives for intimacy (Bartholomew 1990, Thelen, Sherman, and Brost 1998, Bumby and Hansen 1997). Some are so fearful of the consequences of intimacy that they actively avoid it. Others dismiss intimacy and defensively deny their need for more and deeper interpersonal contact.

Intimacy and Risk To some people, relational intimacy is extremely risky. To others, it involves only low risk. For example, how true of your attitudes are the following statements?

- It is dangerous to get really close to people.
- I'm afraid to get really close to someone because I might get hurt.
- I find it difficult to trust other people.
- The most important thing to consider in a relationship is whether I might get hurt.

People who agree with these and similar statements see intimacy as involving great risk (Pilkington and Richardson 1988). Such people have fewer close friends, are less likely to have a romantic relationship, have less trust in others, have a low level of dating assertiveness, have lower self-esteem, are more possessive and jealous in their love, and are generally less sociable and extraverted than those who see intimacy as involving little risk (Pilkington and Woods 1999).

Intimacy and Social Penetration As you progress from contact through involvement to intimacy, you can see that the number of topics you talk about ***(breadth)*** and the degree of "personalness" with which you pursue them ***(depth)*** increase (Altman and Taylor 1973, Hensley 1996). Visualize an individual as a circle divided into various parts (to represent the topics of interpersonal communication or the breadth of the relationship) and into layers (to represent the degree of personalness with which you talk or the depth of the relationship). For illustration, see Figure 15.2. Each circle in the figure contains eight topic areas to depict breadth (identified A through H) and five levels of intimacy to depict depth (represented by the concentric circles). Note that in circle 1, only three topic areas are penetrated. Of these, two are penetrated only to the first level and one to the second. In this type of interaction, three topic areas are discussed, and only at rather superficial levels. This is the type of relationship you might have with an acquaintance. Circle 2 represents a more intense relationship, one that has greater breadth and depth; more topics are discussed and to deeper levels of penetration. This is the type of relationship you might have with a friend. Circle 3 represents a still more intense relationship. Here there is considerable breadth (seven of the eight areas are penetrated) and depth (most of the areas are penetrated to the deepest levels). This is the type of relationship you might have with a lover or a parent.

All relationships—friendships, loves, families—may be described in terms of breadth and depth, concepts that are central to the **social penetration theory** (Altman and Taylor 1973). In its initial stage, a relationship is normally characterized by narrow breadth (few topics are discussed) and shallow depth (the topics are discussed only superficially). As the relationship grows in intensity and intimacy, breadth and depth increase. Equally important, these increases are seen as comfortable, normal, and natural progressions.

Deterioration

The **relationship deterioration** stage is characterized by a weakening of the bonds between the friends or lovers. The first phase of deterioration is usually *intrapersonal dissatisfaction:* you begin to experience personal dissatisfaction with everyday interactions and begin to view the future with your partner more negatively. If this dis-

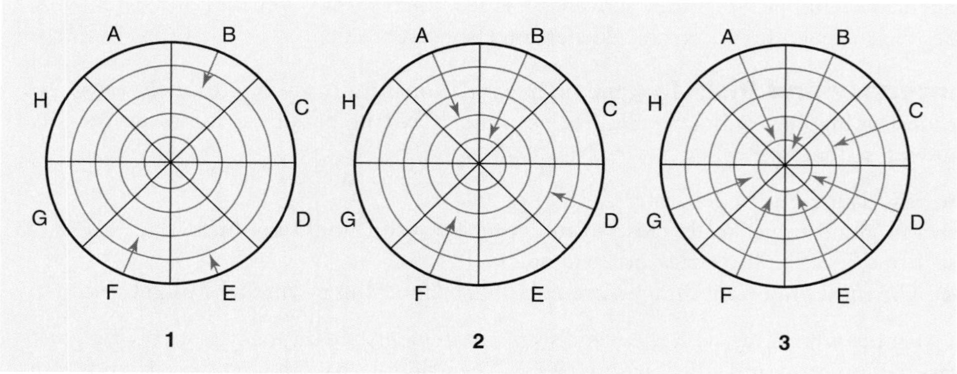

Figure 15.2 How accurately do the concepts of breadth and depth express your communication in relationships of different intensities? Can you identify other aspects of messages that change as you go from talking to an acquaintance, to a friend, or to an intimate?

satisfaction grows, you pass to the second phase, *interpersonal deterioration*. You withdraw and grow further and further apart. You share less of your free time. When you're together, there are awkward silences, fewer disclosures, less physical contact, and a lack of psychological closeness. Conflicts become more common and their resolution more difficult.

When a relationship begins to deteriorate, the breadth and depth (which increase as the relationship becomes more intimate) will often reverse themselves—a process of **depenetration,** sometimes referred to as the *reversal hypothesis*. For example, in the process of terminating a relationship, you might eliminate certain topics from your interpersonal interactions and at the same time discuss acceptable topics in less depth. You might reduce the level of your disclosure, revealing less and less of your inner feelings. This reversal does not always occur (Baxter 1983). There is some evidence to show, for example, that, among friends, although depth decreases in the early stages of deterioration, it may later increase (Tolhuizen 1986).

Repair

The **relationship repair** stage is optional and so is indicated in Figure 15.1 by a broken circle. Some relational partners may pause during deterioration and try to repair their relationship. Others, however, may progress—without stopping, without thinking—to dissolution.

At the first repair phase, *intrapersonal repair,* you analyze what went wrong and consider ways of solving your relational difficulties. You might at this stage consider changing your behaviors or perhaps changing your expectations of your partner. You might also evaluate the rewards of your relationship as it is now and the rewards to be gained if your relationship ended.

Should you decide that you want to repair your relationship, you might discuss this with your partner at the *interpersonal repair* phase—the problems in the relationship, the changes you want to see, and perhaps what you'd be willing to do and what you'd want your partner to do. This is the stage of negotiating new agreements and new behaviors. You and your partner might try to repair your relationship by yourselves, by seeking the advice of friends or family, or perhaps going for professional counseling.

Dissolution

At the **relationship dissolution** stage, the bonds between the individuals are broken. In the beginning, it usually takes the form of *interpersonal separation,* in which you might move into separate apartments and begin to lead lives apart from each other. If this separation proves acceptable and if the original relationship isn't repaired, you enter the phase of *social or public separation*. If the relationship is a marriage, this phase corresponds to divorce. In some cases, the former partners change the definition of their relationship, and, for example, the "ex-lovers" become "friends" or "business partners." Avoidance of each other and a return to being "single" are among the primary characteristics of dissolution.

Dissolution is also the stage during which the ex-partners begin to look upon themselves as individuals rather than halves of a pair. They try to establish a new and different life, either alone or with another person. Some people, it's true, continue to live psychologically with a relationship that has already been dissolved; they frequent old meeting places, reread old love letters, daydream about all the good times, and fail to extricate themselves from a relationship that has died in every way except in their memory.

In cultures that emphasize continuity from one generation to the next and where being "old-fashioned" is evaluated positively—as in, say, China—interpersonal relationships are likely to be long lasting and permanent. Those who maintain long-term relationships will be rewarded and those who break relationships will be punished. But in cultures where change is seen as positive and being old-fashioned as negative—as in, say, the United States—interpersonal relationships are likely to be more temporary (Moghaddam, Taylor, and Wright 1993). Here the rewards for long-term relationships and the punishments for broken relationships will be significantly less.

Movement Among the Stages

Notice that Figure 15.1 contains three different types of arrows. The exit arrows indicate that each stage offers the opportunity to exit the relationship. After saying hello, you can say good-bye and exit. The vertical or movement arrows between stages represent the fact that you can move to another stage, either a more intense one (say, from involvement to intimacy) or a less intense one (say, from intimacy to deterioration). You can also go back to a previously established stage. For example, you may have established an intimate relationship with someone but don't want to maintain it at that level. You want it to be less intense. So you may go back to the involvement stage and reestablish the relationship at that more comfortable level (Masheter and Harris 1986). The self-reflexive arrows—the arrows that loop back to the beginning of the same level or stage—signify that any relationship may become stabilized at any point. You may, for example, maintain a relationship at the intimate level without its deteriorating or returning to the less intense stage of involvement. Or you might remain at the "Hello, how are you?" stage—the contact stage—without ever getting any further involved.

Movement through the various stages is usually a gradual process; you don't jump from contact to involvement to intimacy. Rather, you progress gradually, a few degrees at a time. Yet there are leaps that must and do take place. For example, during the involvement stage of a romantic relationship, the first kiss or the first sexual encounter requires a leap. It requires a change in the kind of communication and in the kind of intimacy experienced by the two people. Before you take these leaps, you probably first test the waters. Before the first kiss, for example, you may hold each other, look longingly into each other's eyes, and perhaps caress each other's face. You might do this (in part) to discover if the leap—the kiss, for example—will be met with a favorable response. No one wants rejection—especially of romantic advances. These major jumps or turning points provide an interesting perspective on how relationships develop. Table 15.1 presents the five most frequently reported turning points in romantic relationships among college students (Baxter and Bullis 1986).

Have your relationships generally followed the pattern described here? If not, how did they differ?

◀◀ THINKING BACK

THINKING AHEAD ▶▶

How does culture influence what you believe about relationships?

RELATIONSHIPS IN CULTURAL CONTEXT

The research and theory discussed here and in the next two units derive in great part from research conducted in the United States and on heterosexual couples. This research and the corresponding theory reflect the way most heterosexual relationships are viewed in the United States. Although we paused periodically to note cultural differences, it's helpful to bring the influence of culture together now that we've covered a major part of our relationship discussion.

For example, it's assumed in the model and in the discussion of relationship development that you voluntarily choose your relationship partners. You consciously choose to pursue certain relationships and not others. In some cultures, however, your

TABLE 15.1 **Turning Points in Romantic Relationships**

Can you identify similar turning points in your own relationships? What turning points were most important to you? If you're in a close relationship now, ask your partner to identify the five most important turning points as he or she sees them and see if these match your own. Don't give any hints or examples (other than those from this study); don't let your partner know what you expect or would like to hear. This table is based on research by Baxter and Bullis (1986).

Turning Point	Examples
Getting-to-know time	The first meeting, the time spent together studying, the first date
Quality time that enables the couple to appreciate one another and their relationship	Meeting the family or getting away together
Physical separation	Separations due to vacations or trips (not to breakups)
External competition	The presence of a new or old rival and demands that compete for relationship time
Reunion	Getting back together after physical separation

romantic partner is chosen for you by your parents. In some cases, your husband or wife is chosen to solidify two families or to bring some financial advantage to your family or village. An arrangement such as this may have been entered into by your parents when you were an infant or even before you were born. In most cultures, of course, there's pressure to marry "the right" person and to be friends with certain people and not others.

In the United States, researchers study and textbook authors write about dissolving relationships and how to survive relationship breakups. It's assumed that you have the right to exit an undesirable relationship. But in some cultures, you simply cannot dissolve a relationship once it's formed or once there are children. In the practice of Roman Catholicism, once people are validly married, they're always married and cannot dissolve that relationship. More important to such cultures may be such issues as "How do you maintain a relationship that has problems?" "What can you do to survive in this unpleasant relationship?" "How can you repair a troubled relationship?" (Moghaddam, Taylor, and Wright 1993).

Further, the culture will influence the difficulty that you go through when relationships break up. For example, married persons whose religion forbids divorce and remarriage will experience religious disapproval and condemnation as well as the same economic and social difficulties everyone else goes through. In the United States, child custody almost invariably goes to the woman, and this presents an added emotional burden for the man. In Iran, child custody goes to the man, which presents added emotional burdens for the woman. In India, women experience greater difficulty than men in divorce because of their economic dependence on men, the cultural beliefs about women, and the patriarchal order of the family (Amato 1994).

In most of the United States, interpersonal friendships are drawn from a relatively large pool. Out of all the people you come into regular contact with, you choose relatively few of these as friends. With computer chat groups, the number of friends you can have has increased enormously, as has the range from which these friends can be chosen. In rural areas and in small villages throughout the world, however, you would have very few choices. The two or three other children your age become your friends; there's no real choice because these are the only possible friends you could make.

Most cultures assume that relationships should be permanent or at least long lasting. Consequently, it's assumed that people want to keep relationships together and will exert considerable energy to maintain relationships. Because of this bias, little research has studied how to move effortlessly from one intimate relationship to another, or advises you how to do this more effectively and efficiently.

Culture influences heterosexual relationships by assigning different roles to men and women. In the United States, men and women are supposed to be equal; at least that is the stated ideal. As a result, either a man or a woman can initiate a relationship, and either can dissolve it. Men and women are equally expected to derive satisfaction from their interpersonal relationships, and when that satisfaction isn't present, either may seek to exit the relationship. In Iran, on the other hand, only the man has the right to dissolve a marriage without giving reasons.

How has your culture influenced your own views on who should initiate a romantic relationship and how long it should last?

◀◀ THINKING BACK

In some cultures, gay and lesbian relationships are accepted, but in others they are condemned. In some areas of the United States "domestic partnerships" may be registered, and these grant gay men, lesbians, and (in some cases) unmarried heterosexuals rights that were formerly only reserved for married couples, for example, health insurance benefits and the right to make decisions when one member is incapacitated. In Norway, Sweden, and Denmark, same-sex relationship partners have the same rights as married partners.

Some cultures consider sexual relationships to be undesirable outside of a formally sanctioned marriage, whereas others consider it a normal part of relationships and view chastity as undesirable. Intercultural researchers Elaine Hatfield and Richard Rapson (1996, p. 36) recall a meeting of the International Academy of Sex Research at which colleagues from Sweden and the United States were discussing ways of preventing AIDS. When members from the United States suggested teaching abstinence as a way of preventing AIDS, Swedish members asked, "How will teenagers ever learn to become loving, considerate sexual partners if they don't practice?" "The silence that greeted the question," note Hatfield and Rapson, "was the sound of two cultures clashing." Have you ever witnessed a similar "culture clash"?

REVIEWING KEY TERMS AND CONCEPTS IN INTERPERSONAL RELATIONSHIPS

This unit introduced interpersonal relationships and focused on three areas: the advantages and disadvantages of relationships, the stages you go through in developing and perhaps dissolving relationships, and the influence of culture on interpersonal relationships.

Advantages and Disadvantages of Interpersonal Relationships

What are the advantages and disadvantages of interpersonal relationships?

- *Advantages:* interpersonal relationships help alleviate loneliness, enable you to secure stimulation, help you to gain self-knowledge and enhance your self-esteem, and enable you to maximize pleasure and minimize pain.
- *Disadvantages:* interpersonal relationships put pressure on you to reveal yourself to others; impose significant financial, emotional, and temporal obligations; may lead to increased isolation from former friends; present difficulties in dissolving.

Stages in Interpersonal Relationships

What are the stages that a relationship goes through?

- At the *contact* stage you make perceptual contact and later interact with the person.
- At the *involvement* stage you test your potential partner, and if this proves satisfactory, you move on to intensifying your relationship.
- At the *intimacy* stage you may make an interpersonal commitment and later enter the stage of social bonding, where you publicly reveal your relationship status.
- At the *deterioration* stage the bonds holding you together begin to weaken. Intrapersonal dissatisfaction is experienced and later becomes interpersonal when you discuss it with your partner and perhaps others.
- At the *repair* stage you first engage in intrapersonal repair, analyzing what went wrong and perhaps what you can do to set things right; later you may engage in interpersonal repair, where you and your partner consider ways to mend your deteriorating relationships.
- At the *dissolution* stage you separate yourself from your partner and later perhaps separate socially and publicly.

Relationships in Cultural Context

In what ways does culture influence interpersonal relationships?

- Culture influences the beliefs you have about relationships, the purposes and values you feel they should serve, the choices involved in developing and in dissolving relationships, the rules that relationships should follow, and the roles that are considered appropriate in relationships.
- Culture also influences what researchers consider important and therefore influences the type and extent of the information that we have about relationships.

APPLYING KEY TERMS AND CONCEPTS IN INTERPERSONAL RELATIONSHIPS

1. What reasons motivated you to develop the relationships you did? What maintains them?
2. What advantages and disadvantages do you see in the relationships existing among the characters in any specific television situation comedy or drama.
3. How do your interpersonal relationships help to lessen loneliness? Do they ever increase loneliness?
4. Do any of your relationships involve tension between such opposites as autonomy-connection, novelty-predictability, and closedness-openness? How do you deal with them?
5. Can you supply personal examples that illustrate the three types of movement among the relationship stages—one that moved from one stage to another, one that remained at one stage for a long period, and one that ended?
6. What strategies have you used in testing your friendship or romantic relationships? Can you identify strategies that others have used on you?
7. How do you know when you have reached "relational intimacy"?
8. Have you ever experienced anxieties concerning security, fulfillment, and excitement as you considered entering a relationship (Zimmer 1986)? What happened?
9. Is the six-stage model presented here an adequate way to describe most interpersonal relationships as you understand them? How would you describe the stages of interpersonal relationships?
10. How would you design a research study to answer any one of the following questions?
    - Do the perceived advantages and disadvantages of relationships change with age?
    - Do men and women see relationship advantages and disadvantages in the same way?
    - Do the tensions in interpersonal relationships (for example, autonomy versus connection) vary from one culture to another?
    - Do men and women perceive their relationship stage similarly?
    - Is there a difference in what people talk about with their acquaintances, friends, and intimates?

EXPERIENCING KEY TERMS AND CONCEPTS IN INTERPERSONAL RELATIONSHIPS

Go to www.awl.com/devito

Exercise No. 19, "Analyzing Stage Talk," is useful for illustrating and analyzing the different messages that are appropriate at each relationship stage. Exercises No. 21, "Mate Preferences," No. 22, "Male and Female," No. 23, "Relationship Repair from Advice Columnists," and No. 28, "The Television Relationship," can all be used to gain additional perspectives on interpersonal relationships.

UNIT 16
RELATIONSHIP DEVELOPMENT AND DETERIORATION

Cyrano De Bergerac (1950)

AFTER ALL, MY ERSTWHILE DEAR,
MY NO LONGER CHERISHED,
NEED WE SAY IT WAS NOT LOVE,
JUST BECAUSE IT PERISHED?

--EDNA ST. VINCENT MILLAY

In the film Cyrano De Bergerac, *based on Edmond Rostand's classic love triangle, we see Cyrano (Jose Ferrer) deeply in love with Roxanne. But his own negative self-image—caused largely by his concern for his enormous nose—prevents him from speaking for himself. Instead he writes the love letters and speeches for his friend Christian, who is in love with Roxanne. Moved by the sentiments of Cyrano, Roxanne falls in love with her suitor. Eventually, of course, Roxanne realizes that the thoughts and emotions she fell in love with were actually Cyrano's. In this unit we look at how and why intimate relationships development and how and why some of these deteriorate.*

Now that we have a general idea of the functions that relationships serve and the various stages relationships go through, we can explore relationship development and relationship deterioration in greater detail. The next unit focuses on maintenance and repair, and later units cover relationships as they're maintained in friendship, love, family, and workplace situations.

RELATIONSHIP DEVELOPMENT

A number of theories offer insight into why you develop your relationships. Several theories bearing directly on relationship development have already been discussed.

THINKING AHEAD ▸▸
Why do you develop the relationships you do? What qualities do you look for in a friend or romantic partner?

Uncertainty reduction theory (Unit 6) describes relationship development as a process of reducing uncertainty about one another (Berger and Calabrese 1975). For example, the theory predicts that high uncertainty prevents intimacy, whereas low uncertainty creates intimacy. Similarly, high uncertainty decreases liking for another person, whereas low uncertainty increases liking.

Social penetration theory (Unit 15) describes the progression of a relationship along the communication dimensions of breadth and depth. As a relationship moves to greater intimacy, relationship depth and breadth increase; as a relationship moves away from intimacy, relationship depth and breadth decrease (usually).

Relationship dialectics theory (Unit 15) describes relationships along a series of opposites representing competing desires or motivations, such as the desire for autonomy and the desire to belong to someone, for novelty and predictability, and for closedness and openness.

Rules theory (to be discussed in Unit 17) describes relationships as interactions governed by a series of rules that a couple agrees to follow. When the rules are followed, the relationship is maintained; when they're broken, the relationship experiences difficulty and perhaps deteriorates or even dissolves.

In this unit, three additional theories are singled out: attraction theory, social exchange theory, and equity theory. The theories offer interesting perspectives on relationships. They help explain what happens in interpersonal relationships (and in interpersonal communication generally) during the stages of development, maintenance, deterioration, and repair. They shed light on important interpersonal processes—for example, power and conflict—and on significant interpersonal relationships, such as friendship, love, and family.

Attraction Theory

You're no doubt attracted to some people and not attracted to others. In a similar way, some people are attracted to you and some aren't. If you were to examine the people to whom you're attracted and those to whom you're not attracted, you would probably see patterns in your judgments, even though many of them seem unconsciously motivated. **Attraction theory** holds that you develop relationships with others on the basis of three major factors: attractiveness (physical appearance and personality), proximity, and similarity.

Physical Appearance and Personality When you say, "I find that person attractive," you probably mean either that (1) you find that person physically attractive or that (2) you find that person's personality or behavior attractive. For the most part, you probably like physically attractive rather than physically unattractive people, and you probably like people who possess a pleasant rather than an unpleasant personality. Generally, you attribute positive characteristics to people you find attractive and negative characteristics to people you find unattractive.

Supporting the popular belief, research—in Bulgaria, Nigeria, Indonesia, Germany, and the United States—finds that men consider physical attractiveness in their partner more important than do women (Buss and Schmitt 1993). Similarly, in a study of gay male dating behavior, the physical attractiveness of the partner was the most important factor in influencing how much the person enjoyed his date and how much he wished to date that person again (Sergios and Cody 1985). The more attractive you find someone, the more you are apt to exaggerate your good qualities in order to get a date with that person (Rowatt, Cunningham, and Druen 1999). Apparently, lying is seen as more acceptable when the goal is a date with an exceptionally attractive person but less acceptable when the prospective date is relatively less attractive.

Note that the importance of physical attractiveness enters the face-to-face relationship immediately, whereas it's only revealed after considerable communication via computer. Information conveyed by computer or mail often comes gradually: first some general verbal descriptions ("I'm 6 feet tall, brown hair, brown eyes"), then perhaps a photo, and then perhaps a face-to-face meeting. It seems reasonable to assume that physical attractiveness will prove most important when it's immediate and less important when it's revealed after a period of acquaintanceship.

Those who are perceived as attractive are also seen as competent, and conversely, those who are perceived as competent—say, as a team member working on a project or in social situations—are also seen as more attractive (Duran and Kelly 1988).

Proximity If you look around at people you find attractive, you'll probably notice that they're the ones who live or work close to you. For example, in a study of friendships in a student housing development, researchers found that the closer the students' rooms were to each other, the better the chances that the occupants would become friends (Festinger, Schachter, and Back 1950). The people who became friends were those who had the greatest opportunity to interact. One reason proximity influences attraction is that it allows you to get to know the other person. You come to like people you know because you can better predict their behavior, and perhaps because of this they seem less frightening than complete strangers do (Berger and Bradac 1982).

Another approach argues that "mere exposure" to others leads you to develop positive feelings for them (Zajonc 1968). In one study a female stranger attended some classes 5 times, some classes 10 times, some classes 15 times, and some classes not at all (Moreland and Beach 1992). At the end of the semester the students in the classes rated this woman (who never spoke but just sat where people could see her) in terms of how attractive they felt she was and how much they liked her. Consistent with the mere exposure hypothesis, the woman was least liked and considered least attractive in the class in which she never appeared, more liked and more attractive in the class in which she appeared 5 times, still more in the class in which she appeared 10 times, and most in the class in which she appeared 15 times. How can you account for these results except by "mere exposure"? Exposure increases attraction when the initial interaction is favorable or neutral. When the initial interaction is negative, repeated exposure may actually decrease attraction.

Similarity If you could construct your mate, he or she would probably look, act, and think very much like you. By being attracted to people like yourself, you validate yourself; you tell yourself that you're worthy of being liked. Although there are exceptions, you probably are attracted to your own mirror image, to people who are similar to you in nationality, race, ability, physical characteristics, intelligence, attitudes, and so on.

WEB EXPLORATION To learn more about similarity in relationship development, go to www.awl.com/devito.

If you were to ask a group of friends, "To whom are you attracted?" they would probably name very attractive people; in fact, they would probably name the most attractive people they know. But if you were to observe these friends, you would find that they go out with and establish relationships with people who are quite similar to themselves in physical attractiveness. This tendency, known as the **matching hypothesis**, predicts that although you may be attracted to the most physically attractive people, you will date and mate with people who are similar to yourself in physical attractiveness (Walster, Walster, and Berscheid 1978). Intuitively, this seems satisfying. In some cases, however, you notice discrepancies: for example, an attractive person dating someone much less attractive. In cases such as these, you would probably look for compensating factors, for qualities that compensate for the lack of physical attractiveness. Prestige, money, power, intelligence, and various personality characteristics are obvious factors that compensate for a lack of attractiveness.

Similarity in attitudes has been found to be an important element in attraction in such diverse cultures as the United States, India, Japan, and Mexico (Hatfield and Rapson 1992). Not surprisingly, people who are similar in attitudes grow in attraction for each other over time. People who are dissimilar in attitudes, on the other hand, grow less attracted to each other (Neimeyer and Mitchell 1988, Honeycutt

It has been argued that you don't actually develop an attraction for those who are similar to you but rather develop a repulsion for those who are dissimilar (Rosenbaum 1986). For example, you may be repulsed by those who disagree with you and therefore exclude them from those with whom you might develop a relationship. You're therefore left with a pool of possible partners who are similar to you. What do you think of this repulsion hypothesis?

1986). You're probably attracted to people who have attitudes similar to your own, who like what you like and who dislike what you dislike. The more significant the attitude, the more important the similarity. Marriages between people with great and salient dissimilarities are more likely to end in divorce than marriages between people who are very much alike (Blumstein and Schwartz 1983).

Attitude similarity is especially significant in initial attraction. It also seems to predict relationship success. People who are similar in attitude become more attracted to each other over time, whereas people who are dissimilar in attitude become less attracted to each other over time (Neimeyer and Mitchell 1988). Also, the more intellectually similar people are, the more they're alike in the way they see the world, the greater their interpersonal attraction to each other (Neimeyer and Neimeyer 1983).

Although many people would argue that "birds of a feather flock together" (the similarity position), others argue that "opposites attract." This latter concept is the principle of **complementarity.** People are attracted to dissimilar others only in certain situations. For example, the submissive student may get along especially well with an assertive teacher but may not get along with an assertive romantic partner. In *A Psychologist Looks at Love* (1944), Theodore Reik argues that you fall in love with people who possess characteristics that you do not possess and actually envy. The introvert, for example, if displeased with being shy, might be attracted to an extrovert.

Affinity-Seeking Strategies Attractiveness, proximity, and similarity are factors that influence interpersonal attraction apart from anything you may do or say. In addition, however, you can increase your attractiveness by using **affinity-seeking strategies,** which are listed in Table 16.1. These strategies were derived from studies in which people were asked to "produce a list of things people can say or do to get others to like them"; other subjects were asked to identify those things that lead others to dislike them. Thus, the strategies represent what people think makes them attractive to others, what people think makes people like them, what people think makes others feel positive toward them.

Social Exchange Theory

Social exchange theory, based on an economic model of profits and losses, claims that you develop relationships that enable you to maximize your profits (Chadwick-Jones 1976, Gergen, Greenberg, and Willis 1980, Thibaut and Kelley 1959).

TRY IT!
To learn more about profits, rewards, and costs, go to www.awl.com/devito.

Profits, Rewards, and Costs The theory begins with the following equation:

Profits = Rewards - Costs

Rewards are anything that you want, that you enjoy, and that you'd be willing to incur costs to obtain. For example, to acquire the reward of financial gain, you might have to work rather than play. To earn an A in an interpersonal communication course, you might have to write a term paper or study more than you want to. To gain a promotion, you might have to do unpleasant tasks or work overtime. Love, affection, status, money, gifts, security, social acceptance, companionship, friendship, and intimacy are just a few examples of rewards for which you would be willing to work (that is, incur costs).

Costs are those things that you normally try to avoid—things you consider unpleasant or difficult. Working overtime, washing dishes and ironing clothes, watching a television show that your partner enjoys but you find boring, dressing in ways that are physically uncomfortable, and doing favors for people you dislike might all be considered costs.

Using this basic economic model, social exchange theory claims that you seek to develop relationships (friendship and romantic) that will give you the greatest profit,

TABLE 16.1 Affinity-Seeking Strategies: How to Get People to Like Us and Feel Positive Toward Us

Are there any affinity-seeking strategies that you observe regularly that aren't included in this table? Are strategies included that you find ineffective? Which strategies work best *for* you? Which strategies work best *on* you? In these definitions, the term "Other" is used as shorthand for "other person or persons." This table is based on the research of Bell and Daly (1984).

Altruism. Be of help to Other.

Assumption of control. Appear in control, as a leader, as one who takes charge.

Assumption of equality. Present yourself as socially equal to Other.

Comfort. Present yourself as comfortable and relaxed when with Other.

Concession of control. Allow Other to assume control over relational activities.

Conversational rule keeping. Follow the cultural rules for polite, cooperative conversation with Other.

Dynamism. Appear active, enthusiastic, and dynamic.

Drawing out Other's disclosures. Stimulate and encourage Other to talk about himself or herself; reinforce disclosures and contributions of Other.

Facilitation of enjoyment. Ensure that activities with Other are enjoyable and positive.

Inclusion of Other. Include Other in your social activities and groupings.

Perceptions of closeness. Create the impression that your relationship with Other is closer than it really is.

Listening. Listen to Other attentively and actively.

Nonverbal immediacy. Communicate interest in Other.

Openness. Engage in self-disclosure with Other.

Optimism. Appear optimistic and positive rather than pessimistic and negative.

Personal autonomy. Appear to Other as an independent and freethinking individual.

Physical attractiveness. Appear to Other as physically attractive as possible.

Presentation of interesting self. Appear to Other as an interesting person to get to know.

Reward association. Appear as one who is able to administer rewards to Other for associating with you.

Self-concept confirmation. Show respect for Other and help Other to feel positive about himself or herself.

Self-inclusion. Arrange circumstances so that you and Other come into frequent contact.

Sensitivity. Communicate warmth and empathy to Other.

Similarity. Demonstrate that you share significant attitudes and values with Other.

Supportiveness. Communicate supportiveness in Other's interpersonal interactions.

Trustworthiness. Appear to Other as honest and reliable.

relationships in which the rewards are greater than the costs. The preferred relationships, according to this theory, are those that are most profitable and thus give you the greatest rewards with the least costs.

Comparison Levels You enter a relationship with a general idea of the kinds of profit you ought to get out of it. This is your *comparison level,* your realistic expectations of what you feel you deserve from a relationship. For example, in a study of couples, it was found that most people expect reasonably high levels of trust, mutual respect, love, and commitment. Their expectations are significantly lower for time spent together, privacy, sexual activity, and communication (Sabatelli and Pearce 1986). When the rewards you get equal or surpass this comparison level, you feel satisfied with your relationship.

You also have a *comparison level for alternatives.* That is, you probably compare the profits you get from your current relationships with the ones you think you can get from alternative relationships. For example, if you believe you'll not be able to find another suitable partner, you're more likely to stay in your relationship, even if it's an abusive one (Berscheid 1985). If you see that the profits from your present relationship are less than the profits you could get from an alternative relationship, you might decide to leave your current relationship and enter this new and potentially more profitable one.

Equity Theory

Equity theory uses the concepts of social exchange but goes a step further. It claims that you develop and maintain relationships in which your ratio of rewards to costs is approximately equal to your partner's (Walster, Walster, and Berscheid 1978, Messick and Cook 1983). An equitable relationship, then, is one in which participants derive rewards that are proportional to their costs. If you work harder for the relationship than your partner does, then equity demands that you should get greater rewards than your partner. If you work equally hard, then equity demands that each of you should get approximately equal rewards. Much research finds that people want equity and feel that relationships should be characterized by equity (Ueleke et al. 1983). The idea behind this is that if you're underbenefited (you get less than you put in), you'll be angry. If, on the other hand, you're overbenefited (you get more than you put in), you'll feel guilty (Walster, Walster, and Traupman 1978). However, some research has questioned this rather neat but intuitively unsatisfying assumption and finds that the overbenefited person is often quite happy and contented; guilt deriving from getting more than you deserve seems easily forgotten (Noller and Fitzpatrick 1993, Sprecher and Schwartz 1994).

Relationship Satisfaction and Equity Equity theory puts into clear focus the sources of relational dissatisfaction you see every day. For example, in a traditional marriage, husband and wife may have full-time jobs, but the wife may also do the major share of the household chores. Thus, although both may be deriving equal rewards—they have equally good cars, they live in the same three-bedroom house, and so on—the wife is paying more of the costs. According to equity theory, she will be dissatisfied because of this lack of equity. In a work situation, you see the same dynamic with two management trainees: each does an equal amount of work but one gets a bonus of $2,000 and the other a bonus of $5,000. Clearly, there is inequity, and there will be dissatisfaction.

Equity, Culture, and Gender Equity is consistent with the capitalistic orientation of Western culture, where each person is paid, for example, according to his or her contributions. The more you contribute to the organization or the relationship, the more rewards you should get out of it. In other cultures, a principle of equality or need might operate. According to the principle of equality, each person would get equal rewards, regardless of their individual contribution. According to the principle of need, each person would get rewards according to individual need (Moghaddam, Taylor, and Wright 1993). People from India are, for example, more likely to distribute rewards on the basis of need than are Americans, who would distribute rewards on the basis of equity, on the basis of the costs paid into the relationship

(Berman, Murphy-Erman, and Singh 1985, Moghaddam, Taylor, and Wright 1993). It's not surprising to find that in the United States equity is highly correlated with relationship satisfaction and with relationship endurance (Schafer and Keith 1980). In much of Europe, on the other hand, equity seems to be unrelated to satisfaction or endurance (Lujansky and Mikula 1983).

Women are more likely to engage in extramarital affairs when they perceive their relationship as inequitable (Prins, Buunk, and Van Yperen 1993). Perceptions of inequity by men, however, did not influence their likelihood of engaging in extramarital affairs. Further, women are more likely than men to break up a relationship as a result of their own extrarelational affair (Janus and Janus 1993).

Do these theories help explain what goes on in your own relationships?

◀◀ THINKING BACK

RELATIONSHIP DETERIORATION

THINKING AHEAD ▶▶

Using social exchange theory, can you do a rewards-costs analysis of a relationship you're in or observe?

Relationship deterioration refers to the weakening of the bonds that hold people together. The process of deterioration may be gradual or sudden. Gradual deterioration might occur in a situation in which one of the parties in a relationship develops close ties with a new intimate, and this new relationship gradually pushes out the old. Sudden deterioration might occur when a rule that was essential to the relationship (for example, the rule of complete fidelity) is broken and both realize that the relationship cannot be sustained.

In terms of the theories introduced earlier, relationship deterioration would occur when you no longer find your partner attractive physically and in personality, when you no longer experience closeness, or when the differences become more important than the similarities. When relationships break up, it's the more attractive person who leaves (Blumstein and Schwartz 1983). There is no denying the power of attractiveness in the development of relationships and the influence of its loss to the deterioration of relationships. According to social exchange, deterioration would set in when the costs begin to exceed the rewards. Similarly, a relationship may deteriorate when you feel that you could do better with someone else. Even if your relationship is less than you expected it to be, you would probably not dissolve it unless you perceived that another relationship (or being alone) will provide a greater profit. In terms of equity, deterioration would occur when you feel that you're putting more into the relationship than you're getting out of it or that your partner is benefiting from the relationship disproportionately.

When relationships deteriorate or break up, a number of things happen. Although we're conditioned to view relationship breakup as something negative, it's certainly not always negative and, in fact, may bring a variety of positive benefits as well. On the negative side, perhaps the most obvious is a loss of all the positives you enjoyed as a result of the relationship. Regardless of how unsatisfying the relationship might ultimately have been, it probably also had many good aspects. These are now lost.

There is also, generally, a loss of self-esteem. You may feel unworthy or perhaps guilty. You may blame yourself for doing the wrong things, not doing the right things, or being responsible for the losses you now confront. Of course, there are likely to be friends and family members who will give you a hard time, often implying that you're to blame.

There are also practical issues. Most relationship breakups have financial implications, and you may now encounter money problems. Paying the rent, tuition, or outstanding loans by yourself may prove difficult. If the relationship is a marriage, then there are legal and perhaps religious implications of the breakup. If there are children, the situation becomes even more complicated.

Nevertheless, not all relationships should be sustained. Not all breakups are bad, and few, if any, bad breakups are entirely bad. In the midst of a breakup, this may be difficult to appreciate. In retrospect, it's almost always true.

Some relationships are unproductive for one or both parties, and a breakup is often the best alternative. A breakup may provide an opportunity for the individuals to regain their independence and to become self-reliant again. Some relationships are so absorbing that there is little time for reflection on oneself, on others, and on the relationship. Sometimes distance helps. A breakup may also allow you to develop new associations and to explore different types of relationships with different types of people. So relational deterioration need not have only negative consequences. For the most part, it's up to you to draw out of any decaying relationship the positive and productive lessons.

The Stages of Relationship Deterioration

One research study, based on responses from 1,480 men and women, found that you go through 16 steps (several of which repeat) in breaking up a romantic relationship (Battaglia, Richard, Datteri, and Lord 1998):

1. you lose interest
2. you notice other people
3. you act distant
4. you try to work things out
5. you put distance between yourself and your partner
6. you lose interest
7. you consider breaking up
8. you talk about your feelings
9. you try to work things out
10. you notice other people
11. you act distant
12. you date other people
13. you go back together
14. you consider breaking up
15. you move on and recover
16. you break up

Another approach argues that relationship breakups can be explained in four stages, identified in the Ask the Researcher box on page 273.

Causes of Relationship Deterioration

There are as many reasons for relationship deterioration as there are people in relationships. It is, therefore, extremely difficult to identify specific causes for any specific relationship deterioration. Still, some general causes—applicable to a wide variety of relationship breakups—may be identified.

All these "causes" can also be effects of relationship deterioration. For example, when things start to go sour, you may remove yourself physically from your partner. This physical separation in turn causes further deterioration by driving you farther apart emotionally and psychologically. Similarly, the degree of mutual commitment between you may lessen as other signs of deterioration appear.

As a preface, recall that the factors that are important in establishing relationships (discussed in Unit 15) may, when no longer present, contribute to deterioration. For example, when loneliness is no longer reduced by the relationship (when one or both individuals feel lonely frequently or for prolonged periods), the relationship may well be on the road to decay because it's not serving a function it was entered

ASK THE RESEARCHER

Breaking Up

I've been really unlucky in my romantic relationships; all of them have broken up, leaving me in severe depression for long periods. Since I seem doomed to relationships that will break up, I'm wondering if there's an easier way of dissolving relationships that won't cause me so many problems. Any suggestions?

Most romantic relationships *do* break up—especially during college years and ages 16–26, when you find "what works for you." Remember, you learn from these relationships. Breakups may be stressful and depressing, and you feel "doomed" to failure, but changing attitudes is a good first step! Relationships break up for many reasons, because of one partner (poor social skills), processes between partners (mismatched personalities, different interests, inability to handle conflicts), and chance (relocation, different career needs). Breakups involve phases: Intrapsychic (thinking/reflection), Dyadic (discussion with partner), Social (talking to other people), and Grave Dressing (constructing accounts). To break up more easily/less hurtfully, recognize that process rather than blaming yourself. To prevent breakup in the first place you need different communication strategies for the different stages—Intrapsychic: reflect on partner's good qualities; Dyadic: talk the difficulties out with partner; Social: enlist help from your network of friends; Grave Dressing: create a relational account that stresses the positives and goodwill of both people.

For further information see S. W. Duck, "A Topography of Relationship Disengagement and Dissolution," in *Personal Relationships 4: Dissolving Personal Relationships,* ed. S. W. Duck (London: Academic Press, 1982), pp. 1–30.

—Steve Duck (Ph.D., University of Sheffield, UK) is Daniel and Amy Starch Distinguished Professor, University of Iowa, Departments of Communication Studies and Psychology (adjunct). His main research and teaching interests are in various aspects of personal relationships, especially the management of "good" and "bad" aspects of relating as this concerns everyday life communication. He is editor or author of 34 books, the founding editor of the *Journal of Social and Personal Relationships,* and a former president of the International Network on Personal Relationships.

into to serve. Similarly, when relationships no longer provide stimulation, gains in knowledge and esteem, enhancement of physical and emotional health, and maximizing of pleasures and minimizing of pain, they are likely to be in trouble.

Unrealistic Beliefs About Relationships The way in which you think about relationships can influence the course of a relationship and is well illustrated in the accompanying self-test, "What Do You Believe About Relationships?"

TEST YOURSELF *What Do You Believe About Relationships?*

On the line next to each statement, enter the number that best fits how much you agree or disagree. Use the following scale: agree completely = 7, agree a good deal = 6, agree somewhat = 5, neither agree nor disagree = 4, disagree somewhat = 3, disagree a good deal = 2, disagree completely = 1.

______ 1. If a person has any questions about the relationship, then it means there is something wrong with it.

______ 2. If my partner truly loved me, we would not have any quarrels.

______ 3. If my partner really cared, he or she would always feel affection for me.

______ 4. If my partner gets angry at me or is critical in public, this indicates he or she doesn't really love me.

______ 5. My partner should know what is important to me without my having to tell him or her.

______ 6. If I have to ask for something that I really want, it spoils it.

_______ 7. If my partner really cared, he or she would do what I ask.

_______ 8. A good relationship should not have any problems.

_______ 9. If people really love each other, they should not have to work on their relationship.

_______ 10. If my partner does something that upsets me, I think it is because he or she deliberately wants to hurt me.

_______ 11. When my partner disagrees with me in public, I think it is a sign that he or she doesn't care for me very much.

_______ 12. If my partner contradicts me, I think that he or she doesn't have much respect for me.

_______ 13. If my partner hurts my feelings, I think that it is because he or she is mean.

_______ 14. My partner always tries to get his or her own way.

_______ 15. My partner doesn't listen to what I have to say.

Aaron Beck, one of the leading theorists in cognitive therapy and the author of the popular *Love Is Never Enough,* claims that all of these beliefs are unrealistic and may well create problems in your interpersonal relationships. The test was developed to help people identify potential sources of difficulty for relationship development and maintenance. The more statements that you indicated you believe in, the more unrealistic your expectations are.

Do you agree with Beck that these beliefs are unrealistic and that they will cause problems? Which belief is the most dangerous to the development and maintenance of an interpersonal relationship?

This test was taken from Aaron Beck, *Love Is Never Enough* (New York: Harper and Row, 1988), pp. 67–68. Beck notes that this test was adapted in part from the Relationship Belief Inventory of N. Epstein, J. L. Pretzer, and B. Fleming, "The Role of Cognitive Appraisal in Self-Reports of Marital Communication," *Behavior Therapy* 18 (1987): 51–69. ■

Excessive Intimacy Claims In most relationships—especially intense ones—the members make intimacy claims on each other (Blood 1973). Such claims may include expectations that the partner will sympathize and empathize, attend to self-disclosures with total absorption, or share the other's preferences with equal intensity. These intimacy claims often restrict personal freedom and may take the form of possessiveness. To be always responsive, always sympathetic, always loving, always attentive is more than many can manage. In some relationships, the intimacy claims and demands are so great that the partners' individual identities may be in danger of being absorbed or destroyed.

Third-Party Relationships You establish and maintain relationships to maximize your pleasure and minimize your pain. When this ceases to be the case, the relationship stands little chance of survival. These needs are so great that when they're not met within the existing relationship, their fulfillment will be sought elsewhere. When a new relationship serves these needs better, the old relationship may deteriorate. At times, this may be a romantic interest; at other times, the new relationship may be with a parent or, frequently, a child. When your need for affection or attention, once supplied by the other person, is now supplied by a friend or a child, the primary relationship may be in trouble.

Relationship Changes The development of incompatible attitudes, vastly different intellectual interests and abilities, and major goal changes may contribute to relationship deterioration. Similarly, changes in behavior may create difficulties. For example, if you once devoted lots of time to your partner and to the relationship and now are totally absorbed with business or school, your relationship is going to face significant repercussions. The person who develops an addiction (to drugs, alcohol, or even stamp collecting) will likewise present the relationship with a serious problem.

Undefined Expectations Unresolved expectations over who is in charge are a frequent cause of relationship difficulties (Lederer 1984). Often, conflicts over such trivial issues as who does the dishes or who walks the dog mask resentment and hostility concerning some more significant unresolved expectation.

At times, the expectations each person has of the other may be unrealistic, and when reality enters the relationship, difficulties arise. This type of situation often occurs early in a relationship when, for example, the individuals think they will want to spend all their time together. When it's discovered that neither one does, each resents this "lessening" of feeling in the other. The resolution of such problems lies in demonstrating that the original expectations are unrealistic and that realistic and satisfying ones can be substituted.

Another kind of undefined expectation may involve sex-role stereotypes. One person, for example, might hold very traditional views about the role of the man and the role of the woman, whereas the other person may hold very liberal views, rejecting the more conservative sex-role assignments. With this type of difference, conflicts over who puts the children to sleep or who works a second job are easy to imagine.

Sex-Related Problems Few relationships are free of sexual differences and problems. In fact, sexual problems rank among the top three problems in almost all studies of newlyweds (Blumstein and Schwartz 1983). When these same couples are surveyed later in their relationship, the sexual problems have not gone away; they're just discussed less. Apparently, people resign themselves to living with the problems. In one survey, for example, 80 percent of the respondents identified their marriages as either "very happy" or "happy," but some 90 percent said they had sexual problems (Freedman 1978).

Although sexual frequency isn't related to relationship breakdown, sexual satisfaction is. It's the quality, not the quantity, of a sexual relationship that is crucial (Blumstein and Schwartz 1983). When the quality is poor, outside affairs may be sought, and these contribute significantly to breakups for all couples, whether married or cohabiting (Blumstein and Schwartz 1983).

Work-Related Problems Problems associated with either partner's job often lead to difficulties within the relationship. This is true for all types of couples. With heterosexual couples (both marrieds and cohabitants), if the man is disturbed about the woman's job—for example, if she earns a great deal more than he does or devotes a great deal of time to the job—the relationship is in considerable trouble. This is true whether the relationship is in its early stages or is well established (Blumstein and Schwartz 1983). One research study found that husbands whose wives worked were less satisfied with their own jobs and lives than were men whose wives didn't work (Staines, Pottick, and Fudge 1986). This personal dissatisfaction will naturally have negative effects on the relationship.

With homosexual relationships the situation is a bit different. Gay men, like heterosexual men, are career oriented. Because of this, work-related problems may be magnified, since both devote considerable time to work with less time available for the more relational concerns. Lesbians, on the other hand, are less career oriented than gay men and are more relationship oriented. This may be one reason lesbian relationships seem to last longer than gay male relationships (Blumstein and Schwartz 1983, Huston and Schwartz 1995).

Financial Difficulties In surveys of problems among couples, financial difficulties loom large. Money is a major taboo topic for couples beginning a relationship, yet it proves to be the cause of major problems as people settle into their relationship. One-fourth to one-third of all couples rank money as their primary problem; almost all rank it as one of their major problems (Blumstein and Schwartz 1983).

Money is so important in relationships because of its close connection with power. Money brings power in relationships, as it does in business. The person bringing in the most money wields the most power. This person has the final say, for example, on the purchase of expensive items as well as on decisions having nothing to do with money. The power that money brings quickly spreads to nonfinancial issues as well.

Money also creates problems because men and women view it differently (Blumstein and Schwartz 1983). To many men, money is power. To many women, it's security and independence. To men, money is accumulated to exert power and influence. To women, money is accumulated to achieve security and reduce dependence on others. Conflicts over the way the couple's money is to be spent or invested can easily result from such different views. Further, when the wife earns a high income, marital conflict increases and the husband's satisfaction with the relationship decreases (Harrell 1990).

Dissatisfaction with money creates relationship problems for married and cohabiting couples and gay male couples but not for lesbian couples, who seem to care a great deal less about financial matters (Blumstein and Schwartz 1983). This difference has led some researchers to postulate (though without conclusive evidence) that the concern over money and its equation with power and relational satisfaction are largely male attitudes.

A *New York Times* survey (24 February 1988), based on interviews with 1,870 people throughout the United States, found that "even though more women are in the work force and have less time at home, they're still the primary care-givers and the people who pay attention to how, when, what, and where their families eat. . . . The idea of equality at home," the report concludes, "is an illusion." Too often the man expects the woman to work but neither reduces his expectations concerning her household responsibilities nor agrees to assume any of them himself. The man becomes resentful if the woman does not fulfill these expectations, and the woman becomes resentful if she takes on both outside work and full household duties. It's a no-win situation, and the relationship suffers as a result. How do you feel about the gender-gap in the division of labor?

Communication in Relationship Deterioration

Relationship deterioration involves special communication patterns. These patterns are in part a response to the deterioration; you communicate the way you do because you feel that your relationship is in trouble. However, these patterns are also causative: the communication patterns you use largely determine the fate of your relationship. As a general pattern, recall the discussion of social penetration in Unit 15; deterioration will generally foster a decrease in both the breadth of issues discussed and in the depth to which they're pursued—a pattern termed **depenetration.**

Withdrawal The easiest communication pattern to see is that of withdrawal (Miller and Parks 1982). Nonverbally, this withdrawal is seen in the greater space you need and the speed with which tempers and other signs of disturbance arise when that space is invaded. Other nonverbal signs of withdrawal include a decrease in eye contact, touching, similarities in clothing, and displays of items associated with the other person, for example, bracelets, photographs, and rings (Knapp and Vangelisti 1992).

Verbally, withdrawal is marked by decreased desire to talk and listen. At times, phatic communication (or something resembling it) is used not as a preliminary to serious conversation but as an alternative, perhaps to avoid confronting the serious issues.

Decline in Self-Disclosure Self-disclosing communications decline significantly. If the relationship is dying, you may think it not worth the effort. Or you might limit your self-disclosures because you feel that the other person may not accept them or can no longer be trusted to be supportive and empathic.

Deception Deception increases as relationships break down. Sometimes this takes the form of clear-cut lies that may be used to avoid arguments over such things as staying out all night, not calling, or being seen in the wrong place with the wrong person. At other times, lies may be used because of a feeling of shame; you might not want the other person to think less of you. Perhaps you want to save the relationship and don't want to add another obstacle. One of the problems with deception is that it has a way of escalating. Eventually, a climate of distrust and disbelief comes to characterize the relationship.

Evaluative Behaviors During deterioration, there is likely to be an increase in negative and a decrease in positive evaluation. Where once you may have praised the other's behaviors or ideas, you now criticize them. Often the behaviors have not changed significantly; what has changed is your way of looking at them. What was once a cute habit now becomes annoying; what was once seen as "different" now becomes inconsiderate. This negative evaluation frequently leads to outright fighting and conflict. Although conflict isn't necessarily bad, in deteriorating relationships the conflict is often left unresolved.

During relational deterioration, there is also a marked change in the types of requests made (Lederer 1984). When a relationship is deteriorating, requests for pleasurable behaviors decrease ("Will you fix me my favorite dessert?"). At the same time, requests to stop unpleasant or negative behaviors increase ("Will you stop monopolizing the phone every evening?").

Another symptom is the sometimes gradual, sometimes sudden decrease in the social niceties that accompany requests, a progression from "Would you please make me a cup of coffee, honey?" to "Get me some coffee, will you?" to "Where's my coffee?"

Figure 16.1 summarizes the changes in communication (discussed in this unit and the previous one) that take place as you move toward or away from intimacy. The general and most important point this figure makes is that communication effectiveness and satisfaction increase as you move toward intimacy and decrease as you move away from intimacy.

Ending the Relationship

Some relationships, of course, do end. Sometimes there is simply not enough to hold the couple together. Sometimes there are problems that cannot be resolved. Sometimes the costs are too high and the rewards too few, or the relationship is recognized as destructive and escape is the only alternative. As a relationship ends, you're confronted with two general issues: (1) how to end the relationship, and (2) how to deal with the inevitable problems that relationship endings cause.

The Strategies of Disengagement When you wish to exit a relationship, you need some way of explaining this—to yourself as well as to your partner. You develop a strategy for getting out of a relationship that you no longer find satisfying or profitable. Table 16.2 identifies five major disengagement strategies (Cody 1982). As you read down the table, note that the strategies depend on your goal. For example, you're more likely to remain friends if you use de-escalation than if you use justification or avoidance (Banks, Altendorf, Greene, and Cody 1987). You may find it interesting to identify the disengagement strategies you have heard of or used yourself and see how they fit in with these five types.

Dealing With a Breakup Regardless of the specific reason, relationship breakups are difficult to deal with; invariably they cause stress. You're likely to experience high levels of distress over the breakup of a relationship in which you were satisfied, were close to your partner, had dated your partner for a long time, and felt it would not be easy to replace the relationship with another one (Simpson 1987, Frazier and Cook 1993).

Given both the inevitability that some relationships will break up and the importance of such breakups, here are some suggestions to ease the difficulty that is sure to be experienced. These suggestions apply to the termination of any type of relationship—between friends or lovers, through death, separation, or breakup.

Break the Loneliness-Depression Cycle The two most common feelings following the end of a relationship are loneliness and depression. These feelings are significant; treat them seriously. Realize that depression often leads to serious illness. In most cases, fortunately, loneliness and depression are temporary. Depression, for example, usually does not last longer than three or four days. Similarly, the loneliness that follows a breakup is generally linked to this specific situation and will fade when the situation changes. When depression does last, is especially deep, or disturbs your normal functioning, it's time for professional help.

Take Time Out Resist the temptation to jump into a new relationship while the old one is still warm or before a new one can be assessed with some objectivity. At the same time, resist swearing off all relationships. Neither extreme works well.

Take time out for yourself. Renew your relationship with yourself. If you were in a long-term relationship, you probably saw yourself as part of a team, as part of a couple. Now get to know yourself as a unique individual, standing alone at present but fully capable of entering a meaningful relationship in the near future.

Bolster Self-Esteem When relationships fail, self-esteem often declines. This seems especially true for those who did not initiate the breakup (Collins and Clark 1989).

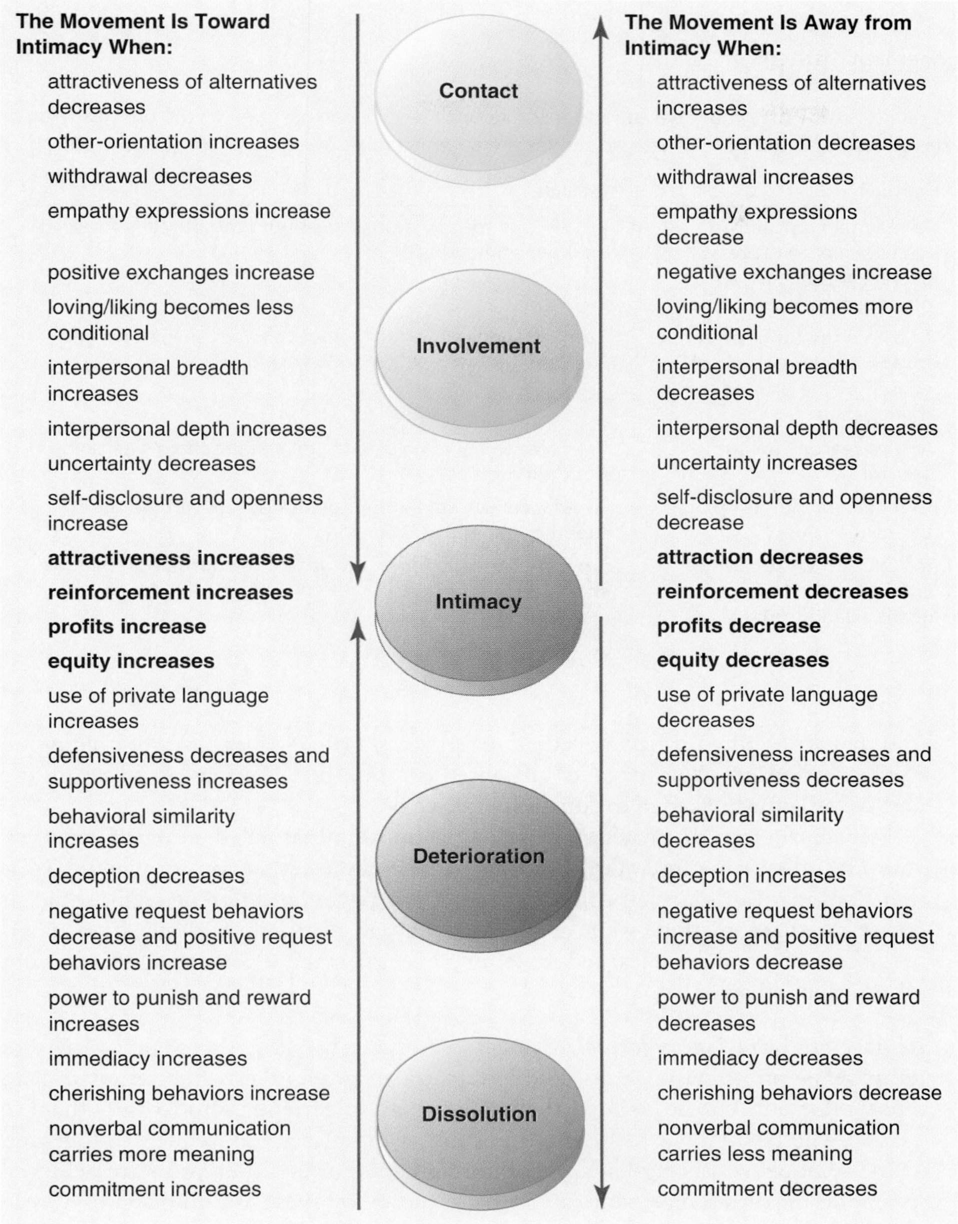

The Movement Is Toward Intimacy When:
attractiveness of alternatives decreases
other-orientation increases
withdrawal decreases
empathy expressions increase
positive exchanges increase
loving/liking becomes less conditional
interpersonal breadth increases
interpersonal depth increases
uncertainty decreases
self-disclosure and openness increase
attractiveness increases
reinforcement increases
profits increase
equity increases
use of private language increases
defensiveness decreases and supportiveness increases
behavioral similarity increases
deception decreases
negative request behaviors decrease and positive request behaviors increase
power to punish and reward increases
immediacy increases
cherishing behaviors increase
nonverbal communication carries more meaning
commitment increases
Contact
Involvement
Intimacy
Deterioration
Dissolution
The Movement Is Away from Intimacy When:
attractiveness of alternatives increases
other-orientation decreases
withdrawal increases
empathy expressions decrease
negative exchanges increase
loving/liking becomes more conditional
interpersonal breadth decreases
interpersonal depth decreases
uncertainty increases
self-disclosure and openness decrease
attraction decreases
reinforcement decreases
profits decrease
equity decreases
use of private language decreases
defensiveness increases and supportiveness decreases
behavioral similarity decreases
deception increases
negative request behaviors increase and positive request behaviors decrease
power to punish and reward decreases
immediacy decreases
cherishing behaviors decrease
nonverbal communication carries less meaning
commitment decreases

Figure 16.1 Communication in Relationships
This summary of some of the changes that accompany increased intimacy and some that accompany decreased intimacy contains many of the findings discussed here and in Unit 15. The major theories discussed in this unit are noted here in boldface. As you read down the list, try to identify examples that influenced your own relationships. Did any factors listed here produce effects on your relationships different from that predicted here? For example, did one of the factors listed here as leading to greater intimacy actually result in decreased intimacy? What else happens as a relationship moves toward intimacy? Toward deterioration? How would you go about testing the validity of these movement predictions?

TABLE 16.2 Five Disengagement Strategies

Think back to relationships that you have tried to dissolve or that your partner tried to dissolve. Did you or your partner use any of the strategies listed here? These strategies are taken from research by Michael Cody (1982).

Strategy	Function	Examples
Positive tone	To maintain a positive relationship; to express positive feelings for the other person	I really care for you a great deal but I'm not ready for such an intense relationship.
Negative identity management	To blame the other person for the breakup; to absolve oneself of the blame for the breakup	I can't stand your jealousy, your constant suspicions, your checking up on me. I need my freedom.
Justification	To give reasons for the breakup	I'm going away to college for four years; there's no point in not dating others.
Behavioral de-escalation	To reduce the intensity of the relationship	Avoidance; cut down on phone calls; reduce time spent together, especially time alone.
De-escalation	To reduce the exclusivity and hence the intensity of the relationship	I'm just not ready for so exclusive a relationship. I think we should see other people.

You may feel guilty for having caused the breakup or inadequate for not holding on to the relationship. You may feel unwanted and unloved. Your task is to regain the positive self-image needed to function effectively.

Recognize, too, that having been in a relationship that failed—even if you view yourself as the main cause of the breakup—does not mean that you are a failure. Neither does it mean that you cannot succeed in a new and different relationship. It does mean that something went wrong with this one relationship. Ideally, it was a failure from which you have learned something important about yourself and about your relationship behavior.

Remove or Avoid Uncomfortable Symbols After any breakup, there are a variety of reminders—photographs, gifts, and letters, for example. Resist the temptation to throw these out. Instead, remove them. Give them to a friend to hold or put them in a closet where you'll not see them. If possible, avoid places you frequented together. These symbols will bring back uncomfortable memories. After you have achieved some emotional distance, you can go back and enjoy these as reminders of a once pleasant relationship. Support for this suggestion comes from research showing that the more vivid your memory of a broken love affair—a memory greatly aided by these relationship symbols—the greater your depression is likely to be (Harvey, Flanary, and Morgan 1986).

Seek Support Many people feel they should bear their burdens alone. Men, in particular, have been taught that this is the only "manly" way to handle things. But seeking the support of others is one of the best antidotes to the unhappiness caused when a relationship ends. Tell your friends and family of your situation—in only general terms, if you prefer—and make it clear that you want support. Seek out people who are positive and nurturing. Avoid negative individuals who will paint the world in even darker tones. Make the distinction between seeking support and seeking advice. If you feel you need advice, seek out a professional.

Avoid Repeating Negative Patterns Many people repeat their mistakes. They enter second and third relationships with the same blinders, faulty preconceptions, and unrealistic expectations with which they entered earlier ones. Instead, use the knowledge gained from your failed relationships to prevent repeating the same patterns.

At the same time, don't become a prophet of doom. Don't see in every relationship vestiges of the old. Don't jump at the first conflict and say, "Here it goes all over again." Treat the new relationship as the unique relationship it is. Don't evaluate it through past experiences. Use past relationships and experiences as guides, not filters.

What advice, if any, would you give someone who was recently dumped by his or her partner after a long-time relationship and is having a difficult time emotionally?

◀◀ THINKING BACK

REVIEWING KEY TERMS AND CONCEPTS IN RELATIONSHIP DEVELOPMENT AND DETERIORATION

This unit focused on relationship development and relationship deterioration.

Relationship Development

What are some of the major theories that explain why you develop the relationships you do?

- **Attraction theory** holds that you develop relationships with those you consider attractive (physically and in personality), who are physically close to you, and who are similar to you.
- **Social exchange theory** holds that you develop relationships that enable you to maximize profits, relationships from which you derive more rewards than costs.
- **Equity theory** holds that you develop and maintain relationships in which the ratio of rewards compared to costs is approximately equal to your partner's.

Relationship Deterioration

Why do relationships deteriorate? How do you communicate during relationship deterioration? What can you do if the relationship does end?

- Among the causes of relationship deterioration are maintaining unrealistic beliefs about relationships, excessive intimacy claims, third-party relationships, relationship changes, undefined expectations, sex-related problems, work-related problems, and financial difficulties.
- Among the important communication patterns observable in deteriorating relationships are withdrawal, a decline in self-disclosure, increased deception, and a change in evaluations from positive to negative.
- Strategies for ending the relationship include, for example, maintaining a positive tone, negative identity management, justification, behavioral de-escalation, and de-escalation.
- In managing relationship dissolution, try to break the loneliness-depression cycle, take time out, bolster self-esteem, remove or avoid uncomfortable symbols, seek support (of friends or professionals as appropriate), and avoid repeating negative patterns.

APPLYING KEY TERMS AND CONCEPTS IN RELATIONSHIP DEVELOPMENT AND DETERIORATION

1. What has to be going on in a relationship for you to say that it's "developing" or that it's "deteriorating?"
2. Research shows that teachers' affinity-seeking strategies influence classroom climate. For example, if the teacher is supportive, the students are more likely to view the classroom environment as supportive (Cabello and Terrell 1994, Myers 1995). Given this finding, what suggestions would you offer a new instructor about affinity seeking?
3. What ethical guidelines for using affinity-seeking strategies would you suggest?
4. Do you "comparison shop" (compare your own relationship against potential alternative relationships) regardless of the type of relationship you're in, or do you stop "shopping" when the relationship reaches a certain level of commitment?
5. Do a cost-benefit analysis of any one of your current relationships. In one column, identify all the costs, and in the other column identify all the benefits you get from the relationship. Next, altercast, playing the role of the person you just did an analysis of and do a cost-benefit analysis of yourself (as you think you might be seen by this person). What can you learn from this type of analysis?
6. How would you feel if you were in a relationship in which you and your partner contributed an equal share of the costs (that is, you each worked equally hard) but your partner derived significantly greater rewards?

7. How do your communication patterns change during relationship deterioration? What effects do these changed patterns have?
8. Do the theories of attraction, social exchange, and equity offer any practical suggestions for dealing with relationship deterioration and dissolution?
9. How would you explain the finding that when relationships break up, it's the more attractive person who leaves first? What other factors might account for who leaves first?
10. How would you design a research study to seek answers to the following questions?
    - Which personality characteristics are especially attractive to men and which are especially attractive to women?
    - Which affinity-seeking strategies are especially important during the early stages of a relationship, say, at the contact and the involvement stages?
    - Can social exchange theory account for the relationships (past and present) of those in this class?
    - When a relationship isn't equitable, which person is more likely to leave first—the one who is getting more profit than deserved or the one getting less profit?
    - Do men and women differ in the satisfaction they derive from their current romantic, friendship, or workplace relationships?

EXPERIENCING KEY TERMS AND CONCEPTS IN RELATIONSHIP DEVELOPMENT AND DETERIORATION

Go to www.awl.com/devito

Exercise No. 24, "Applying the Theories," allows for the exploration of the theories of relationship development, and Exercise No. 20, "Interpersonal Relationships in Songs and Greeting Cards," offers a way to explore the theories and principles of interpersonal relationships as they appear in songs and cards. Exercise No. 21, "Mate Preferences," provides an opportunity to explore the ideal mate in terms of the theories of relationship development.

UNIT 17
RELATIONSHIP MAINTENANCE AND REPAIR

84 Charing Cross Road (1987)

THE MAGIC OF FIRST LOVE IS OUR IGNORANCE THAT IT CAN NEVER END.
--BENJAMIN DISRAELI

84 Charing Cross Road tells the story of a relationship that was begun and maintained solely through an exchange of letters between a New York proofreader (Anne Bancroft) and a London bookseller (Anthony Hopkins). They never actually meet or even talk by telephone, but their relationship is no less real and is actually immensely fulfilling. Although this relationship is set in the 1940s to the 1960s, it's amazingly contemporary and resembles the many online relationships we see today. In this unit we look at the maintenance of interpersonal relationships and the strategies that people use to keep their relationship intact and to repair it when things go wrong.

After a relationship is established, it needs to be maintained and sometimes repaired—two topics we cover in this unit.

THINKING AHEAD ▸▸
If you're in a relationship now, what specifically do you do to keep it intact? What does your partner do?

RELATIONSHIP MAINTENANCE

Relationship maintenance concerns what you do to continue (maintain, retain) your relationship. Of course, maintenance behaviors can serve a variety of functions, for example:

- to keep the relationship intact, to retain the semblance of a relationship, to prevent dissolution of the relationship
- to keep the relationship at its present stage, to prevent it from moving too far toward either less or greater intimacy
- to keep the relationship satisfying, to maintain an appropriate balance between rewards and penalties

Some people, after entering a relationship, assume that it will continue unless something catastrophic happens. Consequently, while they may seek to prevent any major mishaps, they're unlikely to engage in much maintenance behavior. Others will be ever on the lookout for something wrong and will seek to patch it up as quickly and as effectively as possible. In between lie most people, who will engage in maintenance behaviors when things are going wrong and when there is the possibility that the relationship can be improved. Behaviors directed at improving badly damaged or even broken relationships are considered under the topic of repair, in the second half of this unit.

Reasons for Maintaining Relationships

The reasons for maintaining relationships are as numerous and varied as the reasons for beginning them. Before looking at the specific reasons, let's look at what the theories predict. Attraction theory holds that relationships are maintained when there is significant attraction, generally of the kind that led to the development of the relationship. Although both individuals, as well as their definitions of what constitutes attractiveness, may have changed, the importance of attraction—however defined—is likely to continue throughout the life of the relationship.

Social exchange theory holds that relationships will be maintained as long as the relationship is profitable, as long as the rewards exceed the costs. Note, of course, that what constitutes a reward and how significant that reward is can only be defined by the individual. More specifically, you're likely to maintain a relationship when it's more rewarding than what you expected (your comparison level) or better than what you feel you could get elsewhere (your comparison level for alternatives). You're also likely to maintain your present relationship even when it falls short of your comparison level as long as it's still higher than what you could get elsewhere (your comparison level for alternatives). So even though you may think you deserve more, if you can't get more, then you're likely to stay put.

Equity theory holds that you maintain a relationship when you perceive relative equity. If you feel that you're getting rewards from the relationship proportional to the costs you're paying, then you're likely to maintain the relationship. If either person—but especially the person who is being shortchanged—perceives a lack of equity, the relationship may experience difficulty.

In addition to these theoretical predictions, let's look at some of the more popular and frequently cited reasons for relationship maintenance.

- *Emotional Attachment.* Often you maintain a relationship because you love each other and want to preserve your relationship and you don't find alternative couplings as inviting or as potentially enjoyable.
- *Convenience.* The difficulties involved in finding another person to live with, another business partner, or another social escort may make it more convenient to stay together than to break up.
- *Children.* A couple may stay together because they feel, rightly or wrongly, that it's in the best interests of the children, or the children may provide a socially acceptable excuse to mask the real reason—convenience, financial advantage, fear of being alone, and so on.
- *Fear.* People may fear the outside world, being alone, facing others as "single," or even of making it on one paycheck and so may elect to preserve their current relationship as the better alternative.
- *Inertia.* Some relationships are maintained because of inertia, the tendency for a body at rest to remain at rest and a body in motion to remain in motion; change seems too much trouble.
- *Commitment.* People may have a strong commitment to each other or to the relationship (Knapp and Taylor 1994, Kurdek 1995).

You may find the accompanying self-test, "How Committed Are You?" interesting at this point.

TEST YOURSELF *How Committed Are You?*

Think about a current romantic relationship—long-term and serious or short-term and casual—and respond to each of the following questions according to the following scale: 1 = the statement is "absolutely" true, 7 = the statement is "absolutely not" true, and numbers 2–6 for statements that are sometimes true and sometimes not true.

______ 1. I am likely to pursue another relationship or a single lifestyle.

______ 2. I believe there will be a lot of future rewards associated with the relationship.

______ 3. I feel a strong sense of "we" when thinking of my partner and me.

______ 4. I am willing to exert a great deal of effort on behalf of this relationship.

______ 5. I have a lot invested in this relationship.

______ 6. I can imagine having an affair with another person and not having it affect my relationship with ______________.

______ 7. I expect to be with ______________ for the rest of my life.

______ 8. There is nothing holding me in this relationship except my own free choice.

To compute your score follow these steps:

1. Add your scores from questions 2, 3, 4, 5, 7, and 8.
2. Add your score from items 1 and 6, and subtract this sum from 16 (the number 16 is chosen simply to eliminate negative numbers).
3. Add the totals from steps 1 and 2.

Your score should range somewhere between 8 and 56. Low scores indicate great commitment and high scores indicate less commitment. One of the purposes of including this self-test here is that it encourages you to look at your own commitment in very specific terms; it stimulates you to ask yourself the reasons for your own relationship commitment. Did it achieve this purpose, or did you already have a good idea of the extent and reasons for your commitment in a relationship? Are there other items that you would add to this test? That is, are there other aspects of commitment that this test does not tap?

From Mark L. Knapp and Eric H. Taylor, "Commitment and Its Communication in Romantic Relationships," in *Perspectives on Close Relationships,* ed. Ann L. Weber and John H. Harvey (Boston: Allyn and Bacon, 1994), pp. 153–175. Reprinted by permission of Mark Knapp. ■

Interpersonal Maintenance and Rules

You gain an interesting perspective by looking at interpersonal relationships in terms of the rules that govern them. The general assumption of this perspective is that relationships—friendship and love in particular—are held together by mutual adherence to certain rules. When those rules are broken, the relationships may deteriorate and eventually dissolve.

Relationship rules help distinguish successful from destructive relationship behavior. They help pinpoint why relationships break up and how they may be repaired. Further, if you know what the rules are, you'll be better able to learn (and teach) the social skills involved in relationship development and maintenance.

Can you identify any rules that help maintain one or more of your friendships? Your romantic relationships? How would you react if your friend or romantic partner broke these rules? How would your friend or romantic partner react if you broke these rules?

ETHICS IN INTERPERSONAL COMMUNICATION Vote online at http://www.awl.com/devito

Preserving Relationships

In our culture, it's generally thought worthwhile to preserve relationships, especially romantic relationships of long standing. If the relationship is a marriage or a domestic partnership or if it involves children, for example, then it seems that most people would advise you to do what you have to do to maintain the relationship. But at what point does "doing what you have to do" become unethical?

What would you do? *Jim and Patsy have been married for 12 years and have three adopted preteen children. Recently, Jim has begun to have an affair with someone at work. Patsy has heard about the affair and wants a divorce unless Jim promises to end it immediately. Jim definitely does not want to end his relationship with Patsy—he loves her and the children very much— but wonders if he really can end this affair as quickly as Patsy demands. Jim's decision is to promise to end the affair but actually to continue it until it dies a natural death, which he honestly feels it will. Jim also feels that to end the relationship so quickly would hurt his colleague and would cause problems at work, since this person is also Jim's supervisor. What would be the ethical course for Jim? If you were Jim what would you do in this situation?*

Friendship Rules The left half of Table 17.1 presents some of the most important rules of friendship (Argyle and Henderson 1984). When these rules are followed, the friendship is strong and mutually satisfying. When these rules are broken, interpersonal conflict is likely to occur (Samter and Cupach 1998). Sometimes rule breaking creates problems that cannot be fixed, and so the friendship dies. The right half of Table 17.1 presents the abuses that are most significant in breaking up a friendship (Argyle and Henderson 1984). Note that some of the rules for maintaining a friendship directly correspond to the abuses that break up friendships. For example, it's important to "demonstrate emotional support" to maintain a friendship; when emotional support is not shown, the friendship will prove less satisfying and may well break up. The general assumption here is that friendships break down when a significant friendship rule is violated. The maintenance strategy depends on your knowing the rules and having the ability to apply the appropriate skills (Trower 1981, Blieszner and Adams 1992).

Romantic Rules Other research has identified the rules that romantic relationships establish and follow. For example, here are rules that both keep the relationship together and, when broken, lead to deterioration and eventually to dissolution (Baxter 1986).

TRY IT! To learn more about romantic rules, go to www.awl.com/devito.

The general form for each rule, as Baxter phrases it, is "If parties are in a close relationship, they should ________________"

- acknowledge one another's individual identities and lives beyond the relationship.
- express similar attitudes, beliefs, values, and interests.
- enhance one another's self-worth and self-esteem.
- be open, genuine, and authentic with one another.
- remain loyal and faithful to one another.
- have substantial shared time together.
- reap rewards commensurate with their investments relative to the other party.
- experience a mysterious and inexplicable "magic" in one another's presence.

TABLE 17.1 Maintaining and Breaking Up a Friendship

Have you seen these rules in operation in your own friendships? Are there other important rules that you would add to the list presented here?

Maintaining a Friendship	Breaking Up a Friendship
Stand up for the friend in his or her absence.	Be intolerant of the friend's friends.
Share information and feelings about successes.	Criticize the friend in public.
Demonstrate emotional support.	Discuss confidences between yourself and the friend with others.
Trust each other; confide in each other.	Don't display any positive regard for the friend.
Offer to help the friend in time of need.	Don't demonstrate any positive support for the friend.
Try to make the friend happy when the two of you are together.	Nag the friend.
Don't criticize in public.	Don't trust or confide in the friend.
Keep confidences.	Don't volunteer to help the friend in time of need.
Don't be jealous or negative about other relationships.	Be jealous or critical of the friend's other relationships.
Respect the friend's privacy.	Feel free to take up as much of the friend's time as you want.

Maintenance Behaviors

One reason relationships last is that you try to make them work. Interestingly enough, among married couples, the wives' use of maintenance strategies have a more significant effect on the satisfaction, love, and commitment the couple experiences than do the husband's use of such strategies (Weigel and Ballard-Reisch 1999). This is not to say that the man's maintenance strategies are ineffective, just that in heterosexual married relationships the couple is more influenced by the wives' maintenance behaviors.

A number of researchers have focused on the maintenance strategies people use in their various relationships (Ayres 1983, Dindia and Baxter 1987, Dainton and Stafford 1993, Guerrero, Eloy, and Wabnik 1993, Canary, Stafford, Hause, and Wallace 1993, Canary and Stafford 1994). Here are some examples of how people maintain their relationships, presented in the form of suggestions for maintaining relationships.

- *Be nice.* Researchers call this *prosocial behavior.* It includes being polite, cheerful, and friendly; avoiding criticism; and compromising even when it involves self-sacrifice. Prosocial behaviors also include talking about a shared future, for example, talking about a future vacation or buying a house together. It also includes acting affectionately and romantically.
- *Communicate,* including, for example, calling just to say, "How are you?" or sending cards or letters. Sometimes it's just "small talk" that is in itself insignificant but is engaged in because it preserves contact. Also included would be talking about the honesty and openness in the relationship and talking about shared feelings. Responding constructively in a conflict (even when your partner may act in ways harmful to the relationship) is another type of communicative maintenance strategy (Rusbult and Buunk 1993).
- *Be open.* You engage in direct discussion and listen to the other—for example, you self-disclose, talk about what you want from the relationship, give advice, and express empathy.

- *Give assurances.* You assure the other person of the significance of the relationship—for example, you comfort the other, put your partner first, and express love.
- *Share joint activities.* You spend time with the other—for example, playing ball, visiting mutual friends, doing specific things as a couple (even cleaning the house), and sometimes just being together and talking with no concern for what is done. Controlling (eliminating or reducing) extrarelational activities would be another type of togetherness behavior (Rusbult and Buunk 1993). Also included here would be ceremonial behaviors, for example, celebrating birthdays and anniversaries, discussing past pleasurable times, and eating at a favorite restaurant.
- *Be positive.* You try to make interactions pleasant and upbeat—for example, holding hands, giving in to make your partner happy, and doing favors. At the same time, you would avoid certain issues that might cause arguments.
- *Focus on improving yourself,* for example, making yourself look especially good and attractive to the other person.

Why do you maintain your current relationships? How do you maintain them?

◀◀ THINKING BACK

RELATIONSHIP REPAIR

THINKING AHEAD ▶▶

Did you ever try to patch up a damaged relationship? What did you do?

If you wish to save a relationship, you may try to do so by changing your communication patterns and, in effect, putting into practice the insights and skills learned in this course. First, let's look at some general ways to repair a relationship, and second we can examine ways to deal with repair when you're the only one who wants to change the relationship.

General Relationship Repair Strategies

We can look at the strategies for repairing a relationship in terms of the following six suggestions, which conveniently spell out the word REPAIR, a useful reminder that repair is not a one-step but a multistep process (Figure 17.1).

WEB EXPLORATION
To learn more about relationship repair, go to www.awl.com/devito.

ASK THE RESEARCHER

Keeping Relationships Exciting

I've been dating this woman for two years now, and we're planning to get married in about a year. But I'm worried because our relationship has become routine and stale; it's comfortable but there's little excitement—it's all very predictable. Is there anything I can do to make our relationship more exciting, more unpredictable?

It's probably not possible to keep any relationship exciting all the time. Indeed, one of the major goals of developing relationships is to make them more stable and predictable. It appears that you've achieved that goal. However, you can add variety to the predictability of a close relationship. Look at the activities that make your relationship predictable. Do you watch TV every night? Do you eat the same meal a lot? Do you stay at home over the weekends? Of course, these are common patterns that can be easily detected and changed. Instead of watching a video, try going to a live performance of a play. Instead of cooking the same meals, buy a cookbook and learn some new recipes. If you stay home all weekend, try getting out of the house (if only for a couple of hours). On the other hand, if you've been on the go for a long period of time, then relaxing at home might be the most exciting thing you want to do!

—Dan Canary (Ph.D., University of Southern California) is a professor at the Hugh Downs School of Human Communication, Arizona State University, where he teaches courses in interpersonal communication at the undergraduate and graduate levels and writes books and articles about interpersonal communication, conflict management, and sex differences and similarities.

Karen Ma (1996, p. 18), in *The Modern Madam Butterfly: Fantasy and Reality in Japanese Cross-Cultural Relationships,* tells the story of a recently divorced Australian man who confided that the next time he married it would be to a Japanese woman. "This man," notes Ma, "had no prior experience in Japan nor did he speak a word of Japanese. Yet he presumed he would have a better marriage with a woman from a country he knew nothing about after failing in a relationship with someone from his own culture." If this man said this to you, what would you say to him?

Recognize the Problem Your first step is to identify the problem and to recognize it both intellectually and emotionally. Specify what is wrong with your present relationship (in concrete terms) and what changes would be needed to make it better (again, in specific terms). Create a picture of your relationship as you would want it to be, and compare that picture to the way the relationship looks now. Specify the changes that would have to take place if the ideal picture were to replace the present picture.

Try also to see the problem from your partner's point of view and to have your partner see the problem from yours. Exchange these perspectives, empathically and with open minds. Try, too, to be descriptive when discussing grievances, taking special care to avoid such troublesome terms as "always" and "never." Own your feelings and thoughts; use I-messages and take responsibility for your feelings instead of blaming your partner.

Engage in Productive Communication and Conflict Resolution Interpersonal communication skills (such as openness, empathy, and other-orientation) are especially important during repair and are an essential part of any repair strategy. These skills were considered in detail in Unit 8 but appear throughout the text. Here is just a handful of suggestions designed to refresh your memory:

- Look closely for relational messages that will help clarify motivations and needs. Respond to these messages as well as to the content messages.
- Exchange perspectives with your partner, and see the situation as your partner does.
- Practice empathic and positive responses, even in conflict situations.
- Own your feelings and thoughts. Use I-messages and take responsibility for these feelings.
- Use active listening techniques to help your partner explore and express relevant thoughts and feelings.

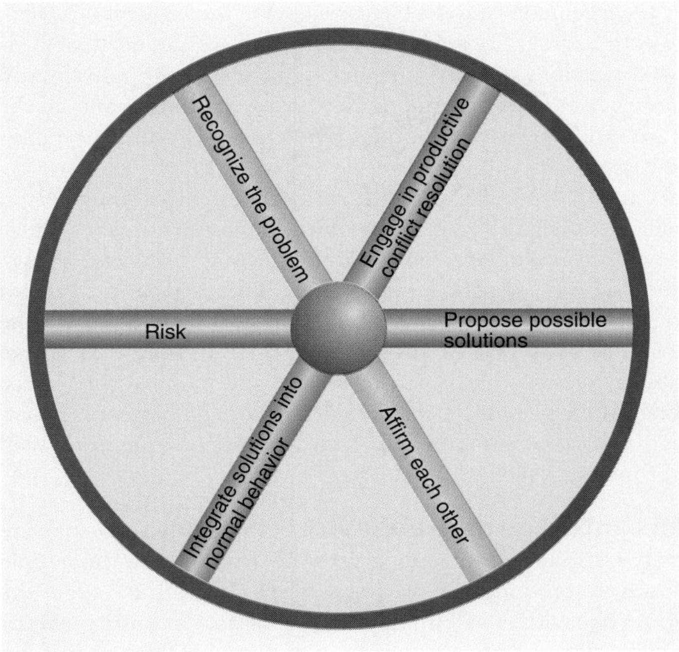

Figure 17.1 The Relationship Repair Wheel
The wheel seems an apt metaphor for the repair process; the specific repair strategies—the spokes—all work together in constant process. The wheel is difficult to get moving, but once in motion it becomes easier to turn. Also, it's easier to start when two people are pushing but not impossible for one to move it in the right direction. What metaphor do you find helpful in thinking about relationship repair?

- Remember the principle of irreversibility. Think carefully before saying things you may later regret.
- Keep the channels of communication open. Be available to discuss problems, to negotiate solutions, and to practice new and more productive communication patterns.

Similarly, the skills of effective interpersonal conflict resolution are crucial in any attempt at relationship repair. If relationship problems are confronted with productive conflict resolution strategies, the difficulties may be resolved, and the relationship may actually emerge stronger and healthier. If, however, unproductive and destructive strategies are used, then the relationship may well deteriorate further. The nature and skills of conflict resolution are considered in depth in Unit 19.

Pose Possible Solutions After the problem is identified, you discuss solutions, the ways to lessen or eliminate the difficulty. Look for solutions that will enable both of you to win. Try to avoid "solutions" in which one person wins and the other loses. With such win-lose solutions, resentment and hostility are likely to fester.

WEB EXPLORATION
To learn more about posing possible solutions, go to www.awl.com/devito.

Affirm Each Other Any strategy of relationship repair should incorporate supportiveness and positive evaluations. For example, happy couples engage in greater positive behavior exchange; they communicate more agreement, approval, and positive affect than do unhappy couples (Dindia and Fitzpatrick 1985). Clearly, these behaviors result from the positive feelings the partners have for each other. However, it can also be argued that these expressions help to increase the positive regard each person has for the other.

One way to affirm another is to talk positively. Reverse negative communication patterns. For example, instead of withdrawing, talk about the causes of and the possible cures for your disagreements and problems. Reverse the tendency to hide your inner self. Disclose your feelings. Increase positive evaluations and decrease negative evaluations. Positive expressions and behaviors help to increase the positive regard each person has for his or her partner. Compliments, positive stroking, and all the nonverbals that say "I care" are especially important when you wish to reverse negative communication patterns.

Cherishing behaviors are an especially insightful way to affirm another person and to increase favor exchange (Lederer 1984). **Cherishing behaviors** are those small gestures you enjoy receiving from your partner (a smile, a wink, a squeeze, a kiss). Cherishing behaviors should be (1) specific and positive, (2) focused on the present and future rather than related to issues about which the partners have argued in the past, (3) capable of being performed daily, and (4) easily executed. People can make a list of the cherishing behaviors they each wish to receive and then exchange lists. Each person then performs the cherishing behaviors desired by the partner. At first, these behaviors may seem self-conscious and awkward. In time, however, they will become a normal part of interaction.

Integrate Solutions into Normal Behavior Often solutions that are reached after an argument are followed for only a very short time; then the couple goes back to their previous, unproductive behavior patterns. Instead, integrate the solutions into your normal behavior; make them an integral part of your everyday relationship behavior. Make the exchange of favors, compliments, and cherishing behaviors a part of your normal relationship behavior.

Risk Take risks in trying to improve your relationship. Risk giving favors without any certainty of reciprocity. Risk rejection by making the first move to make up or saying you're sorry. Be willing to change, to adapt, to take on new tasks and responsibilities.

Risk the possibility that a significant part of the problem is you, that you're being unreasonable or unduly controlling or stingy and that this is causing problems and needs to be changed.

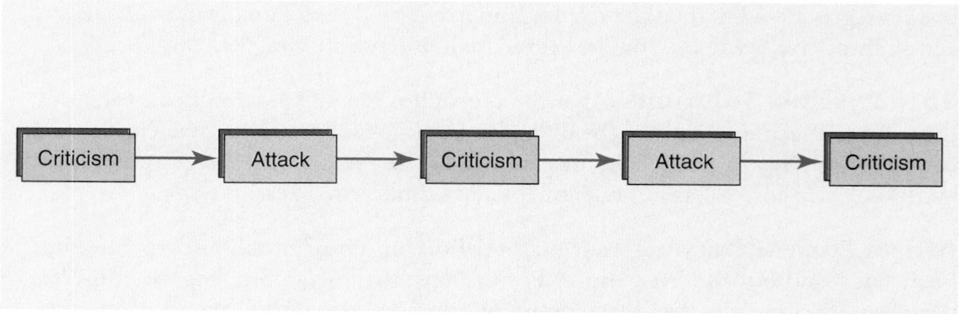

Figure 17.2 A Stimulus-Response View of Relationship Problems
This view of the relationship process implies that one behavior is the stimulus and one behavior is the response. It implies that a pattern of behavior can only be modified if you change the stimulus, which will produce a different (more desirable) response.

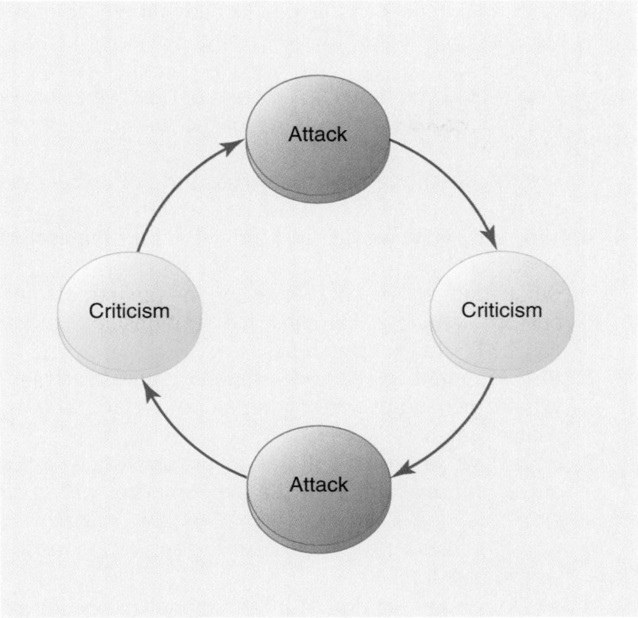

Figure 17.3 A Circular View of Relationship Problems Note that in this view of relationships, as distinguished from that depicted in Figure 17.2, relationship behaviors are seen in a circular pattern where no specific behavior is singled out as a stimulus and none as a response. The pattern can thus be broken by interference anywhere along the circle.

Solo Relationship Repair

One of the most important implications for repair comes from the principle of punctuation (see Unit 2) and the idea that communication is circular rather than linear (see Unit 1; Duncan and Rock 1991). Let's consider an example involving Pat and Chris: Pat is highly critical of Chris; Chris is defensive and attacks Pat for being insensitive, overly negative, and unsupportive. If you view the communication process as beginning with Pat's being critical (that is, the stimulus) and with Chris's attacks being the response, you have a pattern such as occurs in Figure 17.2.

With this view, the only way to stop the unproductive communication pattern is for Pat to stop criticizing. But what if you are Chris and can't get Pat to stop being critical? What if Pat doesn't want to stop being critical?

You get a different view of the problem when you see communication as circular and apply the principle of punctuation. The result is a pattern such as appears in Figure 17.3.

Note that no assumptions are made about causes. Instead, the only assumption is that each response triggers another response; each response depends in part on the previous response. Therefore, the pattern can be broken at any point: Pat's criticism, for example, may be stopped by Chris not responding with attacks. Similarly, Pat can stop Chris's attacks by not responding with criticism.

In this view, either person can break an unproductive circle. Clearly, relationship communication can be most effectively improved when both parties change their unproductive patterns. Nevertheless, communication can be improved even if only one person changes and begins to use a more productive pattern. This is true to the extent that Pat's criticism depends on Chris's attacks and to the extent that Chris's attacks depend on Pat's criticism.

Can you think of a current relationship problem that could be alleviated with solo repair? How would you go about it?

◂◂ THINKING BACK

REVIEWING KEY TERMS AND CONCEPTS IN RELATIONSHIP MAINTENANCE AND REPAIR

This unit examined the processes of relationship maintenance and relationship repair.

Relationship Maintenance

What are the reasons for relationship maintenance? What behaviors do people use to maintain their relationships?

- Reasons for maintaining a relationship include emotional attachment, convenience, children, fear, inertia, and commitment.
- Maintenance behaviors include being nice, communicating, being open, giving assurances, sharing joint activities, being positive, and improving yourself.
- Relationship maintenance can be achieved by following the rules for keeping the relationship, whether friendship or romance, together.

Relationship Repair

What is relationship repair? What strategies can you use to repair a relationship?

- General repair strategies include: recognizing the problem, engaging in productive communication and conflict resolution, posing possible solutions, affirming each other, integrating solutions into normal behavior, and risking.
- Repair isn't necessarily a two-person process; one person can break unproductive and destructive cycles.

APPLYING KEY TERMS AND CONCEPTS IN RELATIONSHIP MAINTENANCE AND REPAIR

1. What maintains your own friendship or romantic relationships?
2. How would you describe your current friendship or romantic relationships in terms of need satisfaction? Can you distinguish close friends and acquaintances on the basis of need satisfaction?
3. The more friends women (married, over the age of 50) had, the less content they were with life in general. The number of friends men have, however, is unrelated to how satisfied they are with their lives in general (findings cited in *Psychology Today,* March/April 1998). How would you account for this?
4. What maintenance strategies would you feel comfortable using? What strategies would make you uncomfortable?
5. How would you describe a current or past friendship or romantic relationship in terms of the rules discussed in this unit?
6. Are the descriptions of the verbal and nonverbal indicators of love given here consistent with what you've observed? How would you modify the list of indicators given here?
7. What additional practical advice do the theories of interpersonal relationships offer for relationship maintenance? For relationship repair?
8. Can you identify additional general repair strategies? What other suggestions for repairing a relationship by yourself might you offer?
9. How have your own cultural beliefs and values influenced your evaluation of the maintenance and repair processes?
10. How would you go about researching answers to the following questions?
    - Does a knowledge of interpersonal communication really help in dealing with relationship problems?
    - Do men and women use the same or different repair strategies?
    - Are certain repair strategies more effective than others?
    - Do men and women see relationship commitment in the same way?
    - How do romantic and friendship rules vary between two cultures?

EXPERIENCING KEY TERMS AND CONCEPTS IN RELATIONSHIP MAINTENANCE AND REPAIR

Go to www.awl.com/devito

Exercise No. 23, "Relationship Repair from Advice Columnists," may be used to stimulate discussion on interpersonal relationship repair. Exercise No. 28, "The Television Relationship," may be focused on maintenance and repair. Exercise No. 20, "Interpersonal Relationships in Songs and Greeting Cards," will help illustrate the use of songs and cards as relational maintenance and relationship repair devices.

UNIT 18

POWER IN INTERPERSONAL RELATIONSHIPS

Citizen Kane (1941)

COMMUNICATION IS POWER. THOSE WHO HAVE MASTERED ITS EFFECTIVE USE CAN CHANGE THEIR OWN EXPERIENCE OF THE WORLD, AND THE WORLD'S EXPERIENCE OF THEM.

--ANTHONY ROBBINS

Principles of Power
Bases of Power
Communicating Power

ORSON WELLES'S CITIZEN KANE—almost universally regarded as one of the greatest films of all time—tells the story of a powerful tycoon, Charles Foster Kane (played by Welles), who sacrifices his own interpersonal relationships and happiness for power and for the newspapers he controlled that gave him that power. But power is not limited to such extreme situations; rather, it's a part of all and every interpersonal relationship you have. In this unit we look at how power operates in interpersonal relationships, the types of power you can hold, and how you can increase your own interpersonal power.

THINKING AHEAD ▸▸
Who maintains the power in your own friendship, romantic, and work relationships? Why?

PRINCIPLES OF POWER

Power influences what you do, when you do it, and with whom. It influences your choice of friends, your romantic and your family relationships—and how successful you feel they are. Interpersonal power is what enables one person to control the behavior of the other. Thus, if A has power over B, then A, by virtue of this power—through either its exercise or the threat of its being exercised—can control B's behaviors. Power in interpersonal relationships may best be introduced by a discussion of some of its most important principles. These principles explain how power operates interpersonally and offer suggestions on how you can more effectively manage power.

Some People Are More Powerful Than Others

In the United States, all people are considered equal under the law and therefore equal in their entitlement to education, legal protection, and freedom of speech. But all people are not equal when it comes to just about everything else. Some are born into wealth, others into poverty. Some are born physically strong, good-looking, and healthy; others are born weak, less attractive, and with a variety of inherited illnesses.

Some people are born into power, and some of those who are not born powerful learn to be so. In short, some people control and others are controlled. Of course, the world is not quite that simple; some exert power in certain areas, some in others. Some exert power in many areas, some in just a few.

WEB EXPLORATION
To learn more about Machiavellian behavior, go to www.awl.com/devito.

Some People Are More Machiavellian Than Others

Before reading about this fascinating concept, take the accompanying self-test, "How Machiavellian Are You?" It focuses on your beliefs about how easily you think people can be manipulated.

TEST YOURSELF *How Machiavellian Are You?*

For each statement, record the number on the following scale which most closely represents your attitude: 1 = disagree a lot, 2 = disagree a little, 3 = neutral, 4 = agree a bit, 5 = agree a lot.

______ 1. The best way to handle people is to tell them what they want to hear.
______ 2. When you ask someone to do something for you, it is best to give the real reasons rather than giving reasons that might carry more weight.
______ 3. Anyone who completely trusts anyone else is asking for trouble.
______ 4. It is hard to get ahead without cutting corners here and there.
______ 5. It is safest to assume that all people have a vicious streak and it will come out when they are given a chance.

______ 6. One should take action only when sure it is morally right.

______ 7. Most people are basically good and kind.

______ 8. There is no excuse for lying to someone.

______ 9. Most people forget more easily the death of their parents than the loss of their property.

______ 10. Generally speaking, people won't work hard unless they're forced to.

To compute your Mach score follow these steps:

1. Reverse the scores on items 2, 6, 7, and 8: If you responded with 5 change it to 1; if you responded with 4, change it to 2; if you responded with 3, it remains 3; if you responded with 2, change it to 4; if you responded with 5, change it to 1.
2. Add all ten scores, being sure to use the reversed numbers for 2, 6, 7, and 8.

Your Mach score is a measure of the degree to which you believe that people in general are manipulable and not necessarily that you would or do manipulate others. If you scored somewhere between 35 and 50, you would be considered a high Mach; if you scored between 10 and 15, you would be considered a low Mach. Most of us would score in between these extremes.

The concept of Machiavellianism is explained in the text. As you read the discussion, try to visualize what you would do in the various situations described. See if your score on this test is a generally accurate description of your own Machiavellianism. You'll also note a similarity between this concept and self-monitoring (discussed in Unit 8). High self-monitors and high Machs try to manipulate others and get their own way. The difference is that self-monitors change their own behaviors as a way of pleasing and manipulating others; Machiavellians try to change the behaviors of others to get what they want.

From Richard Christie, "The Machiavellis Among Us," *Psychology Today* 4 (November 1970): 82–86. ■

Niccolo Machiavelli (1469–1527) was a political philosopher and advisor who wrote his theory of political control in *The Prince*. Machiavelli argued that the prince must do whatever is necessary to rule the people; the ends justified the means. The ruler was in fact obligated to use power to gain more power and thus better achieve the desired goals (Steinfatt 1987). The term *Machiavellian* has thus come to refer to the techniques or tactics one person uses to control another person. Research finds significant differences between those who score high and those who score low on the Mach scale. Low Machs are more easily persuaded; high Machs are more resistant to persuasion. Low Machs are more empathic; high Machs are more logical. Low Machs are more interpersonally oriented and involved with other people; high Machs are more assertive and more controlling. Business students (especially marketing students) score higher in Machiavellianism than do nonbusiness majors (McLean and Jones 1992).

Machiavellianism seems, in part at least, to be culturally conditioned. Individualist orientation, which favors competition and being Number One, seems more conducive to the development of Machiavellianism. Collectivist orientation, which favors cooperation and being one of a group, seems a less friendly environment for the development of Machiavellianism in its members. Some evidence of this comes from research showing that Chinese students attending a traditional Chinese (Confucian) school rated lower in Machiavellianism than similar Chinese students attending a Western-style school (Christie 1970).

Your level of Machiavellianism will influence the communication choices you make. For example, if you were a high Mach, you would be more strategic and manipulative in your self-disclosures and in your conflict-solving strategies than you would be if you were a low Mach. High Machs are generally more effective in just about all aspects studied—they even earn higher grades in communication courses that involve face-to-face interaction (Burgoon 1971). Low Mach women, however, are preferred as dating partners by both high and low Mach men (Steinfatt 1987).

Power Can Be Increased or Decreased

Although people differ greatly in the amount of power they wield at any time and in any specific area, everyone can increase their power in some ways. You can lift weights and increase your physical power. You can learn the techniques of negotiation and increase your power in group situations. You can learn the principles of communication and increase your persuasive power.

Power can also be decreased. Probably the most common way to lose power is by unsuccessfully trying to control another's behavior. For example, the person who threatens you with punishment and then fails to carry out the threat loses power. Another way to lose power is to allow others to control you, for example, to take unfair advantage of you. When you don't confront these power tactics of others, you lose power yourself.

Power Follows the Principle of Less Interest

In any interpersonal relationship, the person who holds the power is the one less interested in and less dependent on the rewards and punishments controlled by the other person. If, for example, Pat can walk away from the rewards Chris controls or can suffer the punishments Chris can mete out, Pat controls the relationship. If, on the other hand, Pat needs the rewards Chris controls or is unable or unwilling to suffer the punishments Chris can administer, Chris maintains the power and controls the relationship. Put differently, Chris holds the relationship power to the degree that Chris is not dependent upon the rewards and punishments under Pat's control.

The more a person needs a relationship, the less power that person has in it. The less a person needs a relationship, the greater that person's power. In a love relationship, for example, the person who maintains greater power is the one who would find it easier to break up the relationship. The person who is unwilling (or unable) to break up has little power, precisely because he or she is dependent upon the relationship and the rewards provided by the other person.

Not surprisingly, if you perceive your partner as having greater power than you, you would probably be more likely to avoid confrontation and to be less expressive in your criticism (Solomon and Samp 1998).

Power Has a Cultural Dimension

Recall the concept of power distance discussed earlier (Unit 3). There it was pointed out that cultures differ in the amount of power that exists between people and in the attitudes that people have about power, its legitimacy, and its desirability (Hofstede 1983). In many Asian, African, and Arab cultures (as well as in many European cultures such as Italian and Greek), for example, there is a great power distance between men and women. Men have the greater power and women are expected to recognize this and abide by its implications. Men, for example, make the important decisions and have the final word in any difference of opinion (Hatfield and Rapson 1996).

In the United States the power structure is undergoing considerable changes. In many families men still have the greater power. Partly because they earn more money,

Another way of looking at power following the principle of less interest is in terms of social exchange theory (see Unit 16). From this perspective, power may be viewed as control of the significant rewards and costs in the relationship. The person who controls the rewards and punishments controls the relationship. The person who needs to receive the rewards and to avoid the costs or punishments controlled by the other person is less powerful. Alternatively, the person who can effectively ignore both the rewards and the costs is the less interested party and therefore possesses the controlling power in the relationship. Is this general description supported by the relationships with which you're familiar? Does it describe the power in your own relationships?

they also make the more important decisions. As economic equality becomes more a reality than an ideal, this power difference may also change. In Arab cultures the man makes the more important decisions not because he earns more money, but because he is the man and men are simply given greater power.

In some of these cultures, the power difference is perpetuated by granting men greater educational opportunities. For example, although college education for women is taken for granted in most of the United States, it's the exception in many other cultures throughout the world.

In some Asian cultures, persons in positions of authority—for example, teachers—have unquestioned power. Students do not contradict, criticize, or challenge teachers. This can easily create problems in the typical multicultural classroom. Those students from cultures which teach that the teacher has unquestioned authority may have difficulty meeting the United States teacher expectation that students interact critically with the material and develop interpretations of their own.

Power Is Frequently Used Unfairly

Although it would be nice to believe that power is wielded for the good of all, it's often used selfishly and unfairly. Here are two examples: sexual harassment and the use of power plays.

Sexual Harassment One type of unfair use of power is **sexual harassment.** Sexual harassment may be defined as "bothering someone in a sexual way" (Bravo and Cassedy 1992). "Sexual harassment," note another team of researchers, refers to conduct, typically experienced as offensive in nature, in which unwanted sexual advances are made in the context of a relationship of unequal power or authority. The victims are subjected to verbal comments of a sexual nature, unconsented touching and requests for sexual favors" (Friedman, Boumil, and Taylor 1992).

WEB EXPLORATION
To learn more about sexual harassment, go to www.awl.com/devito.

Attorneys note that under the law "sexual harassment is any unwelcome sexual advance or conduct on the job that creates an intimidating, hostile or offensive working environment" (Petrocelli and Repa 1992).

The Equal Employment Opportunity Commission (EEOC) has defined sexual harassment as follows:

> Unwelcome sexual advances, requests for sexual favors and other verbal or physical conduct of a sexual nature constitute sexual harassment when (1) submission to such conduct is made either explicitly or implicitly a term or condition of an individual's employment, (2) submission to or rejection of such conduct by an individual is used as the basis for employment decisions affecting such individual, or (3) such conduct has the purpose or effect of unreasonably interfering with an individual's work performance or creating an intimidating, hostile, or offensive working environment. (Friedman, Boumil, and Taylor 1992)

To determine whether behavior constitutes sexual harassment, ask yourself the following questions to help you assess your own situation objectively rather than emotionally (VanHyning 1993):

1. Is it real? Does this behavior have the meaning it seems to have?
2. Is it job related? Does this behavior have something to do with or will it influence the way you do your job?
3. Did you reject this behavior? Did you make your rejection of unwanted messages clear to the other person?
4. Have these types of messages persisted? Is there a pattern, a consistency to these messages?

"Yes" answers to all four questions define the behavior as sexual harassment (VanHyning 1993).

How Can You Avoid Sexual Harassment Behaviors? Three suggestions for avoiding behaviors that might be considered sexual harassment will help to clarify the concept further and to prevent the occurrence of harassment (Bravo and Cassedy 1992). First, begin with the assumption that others at work aren't interested in your sexual advances, sexual stories and jokes, or sexual gestures. Second, listen and watch for negative reactions to any sex-related discussion. Use the suggestions and techniques discussed throughout this book (for example, perception checking, critical listening) to become aware of such reactions. When in doubt, find out; ask questions, for example. Third, avoid saying or doing what you think your parent, partner, or child would find offensive in the behavior of someone with whom she or he worked.

What Can You do About Sexual Harassment? What should you do if you believe you're being sexually harassed and feel a need to do something about it? Here are a few suggestions recommended by workers in the field (Petrocelli and Repa 1992, Bravo and Cassedy 1992, Rubenstein 1993):

1. Talk to the harasser. Tell this person, assertively, that you do not welcome the behavior and that you find it offensive. Simply informing Fred that his sexual jokes aren't appreciated and are seen as offensive may be sufficient to make him stop this joke telling. In some instances, unfortunately, such criticism goes unheeded, and the offensive behavior continues.
2. Collect evidence—perhaps corroboration from others who have experienced similar harassment at the hands of the same individual, perhaps a log of the offensive behaviors.
3. Use appropriate channels within the organization. Most organizations have established channels to deal with such grievances. This step will, in most cases, eliminate any further harassment. In the event that it doesn't, you may consider going further.

4. File a complaint with an organization or governmental agency or perhaps take legal action.
5. Don't blame yourself. Like many who are abused, you may tend to blame yourself, feeling that you're responsible for being harassed. You aren't; however, you may need to secure emotional support from friends or perhaps from trained professionals.

Power Plays Power plays are patterns (not isolated instances) of behavior that take unfair advantage of another person (Steiner 1981). Put in terms of the notion of choice (Unit 1), power plays aim to rob us of our right to make our own choices, free of harassment or intimidation.

For example, in the "nobody upstairs" power play, the individual refuses to acknowledge your request, regardless of how or how many times you make it. One common form is the refusal to take no for an answer. Sometimes "nobody upstairs" takes the form of pleading ignorance of common socially accepted (but unspoken) rules, such as knocking when you enter someone's room or refraining from opening another person's mail or wallet: "I didn't know you didn't want me to look in your wallet," or "Do you want me to knock the next time I come into your room?"

Another power play is "you owe me." Here others do something for you and then demand something in return. They remind you of what they did for you and use this to get you to do what they want.

In "yougottobekidding," one person attacks the other by saying "You've got to be kidding" or some similar phrase, not out of surprise (which is fine) but out of a desire to put your ideas down: "You can't be serious." "You can't mean that." "You didn't say what I thought you said, did you?" The intention here is to express utter disbelief in the other's statement so as to make the statement and the person seem inadequate or stupid.

These power plays are just examples. There are, of course, many others that you have no doubt met on occasion. What do you do when you recognize such a power play? One commonly employed response is to ignore the power play and allow the other person to take control. Another response is to treat the power play as an isolated instance (rather than as a pattern of behavior) and object to it. For example, you might say quite simply, "Please don't come into my room without knocking first," or "Please don't look in my wallet without permission."

A third response is a cooperative one (Steiner 1981). In this response, you do the following:

- Express your feelings. Tell the person that you're angry, annoyed, or disturbed by his or her behavior.
- Describe the behavior to which you object. Tell the person—in language that describes rather than evaluates—the specific behavior you object to: for example, reading your mail, saying I owe you something, or responding to everything you say with disbelief.
- State a cooperative response you both can live with comfortably. Tell the person—in a cooperative tone—what you want: for example: "I want you to knock before coming into my room." "I want you to stop telling me I owe you things." "I want you to stop ridiculing my ideas."

A cooperative response to "nobody upstairs" might go something like this: "I'm angry (*statement of feelings*) that you persist in opening my mail. You have opened my mail four times this past week alone (*description of the behavior to which you object*). I want you to allow me to open my own mail. If there is anything in it that concerns you, I will let you know immediately" (*statement of cooperative response*).

What forms of sexual harassment or types of power plays have you observed lately? What happened?

THINKING BACK

ETHICS IN INTERPERSONAL COMMUNICATION

Vote online at http://www.awl.com/devito

Censoring Messages and Interactions

A gatekeeper is a person or institution that regulates what information gets through from a source to a receiver. Television programmers, for example, are gatekeepers in determining which programs people will see. Teachers, authors, newsgroup moderators, and parents are also gatekeepers—passing on certain information and preventing other information from getting through.

Similarly, relational gatekeepers encourage certain relationships and discourage or even prevent other relationships. Parents, for example, often encourage their children to play with and become friends with children from the same racial or national group and religion and discourage friendships with children from different cultures. Your friends might also exert pressure on you to date one person and not other, to associate with some people but not others.

What would you do? *Jennifer and Colleen have been friends all through college. Recently, John has been interested in Colleen and approaches Jennifer to ask what his chances are, if Colleen likes him, and so on. John's been charged with physically abusing a former girlfriend and rumor has it that he's still married. Colleen, on the other hand, is extremely vulnerable and would probably be tempted by John's fast talk. Jennifer is convinced that John would be bad for Colleen, so she tells John that Colleen is not interested in him. Jennifer also decides not to tell Colleen anything about John's interest. Was Jennifer ethical in lying to John? Was she ethical in concealing John's expression of interest from Colleen? If you were Colleen's best friend, what would you do in this situation?*

THINKING AHEAD ▸▸
How would you describe your own interpersonal power?

BASES OF POWER

Power is present in all relationships and in all communication interchanges. But the type of power varies greatly from one situation to another and from one person to another. Here we identify six types of power: referent, legitimate, expert, information or persuasion, reward, and coercive power (French and Raven 1968, Raven, Centers, and Rodrigues 1975).

Referent Power

You have *referent power* over others when they wish to be like you or be identified with you. For example, an older brother may have power over a younger brother because the younger brother wants to be like the older one. The assumption made by the younger brother is that he will be more like his older brother if he behaves and believes as his brother does. Once he decides to do so, it takes little effort for the older brother to exert influence or power over the younger. Referent power depends greatly on attractiveness and prestige; as they increase, so does identification and, consequently, power. When you're well liked and well respected, of the same sex as the other person, and have the same attitudes and experiences as the other person, your referent power is especially great.

Legitimate Power

You have *legitimate power* over others when they believe you have the right—by virtue of your position—to influence or control their behavior. Legitimate power stems from our belief that certain people should have power over us, that they have a right to influence us because of who they are. Legitimate power usually derives from the roles people occupy. Teachers are often perceived to have legitimate power, and this is doubly true for religious teachers. Parents are seen as having legitimate power over their children. Employers, judges, managers, doctors, and police officers are others who hold legitimate power in different areas.

Expert Power

You have *expert power* over others when they see you as having expertise or knowledge. Your knowledge—as seen by others—gives you expert power. Usually expert power is subject specific. For example, when you're ill, you're influenced by the recommendation of someone with expert power related to your illness—say, a doctor. But you would not be influenced by the recommendation of someone to whom you don't attribute illness-related expert power—say, the mail carrier or a plumber. You give the lawyer expert power in matters of law and psychiatrists expert power in matters of the mind, but, ideally, you don't interchange them.

Your expert power increases when you're seen as unbiased and as having nothing to gain personally from influencing others. It decreases when you're seen as biased or as having something to gain from influencing others.

Information or Persuasion Power

You have *information or persuasion power* over others when they see you as having the ability to communicate logically and persuasively. If others believe that you have persuasive ability, then you have persuasion power. If you're seen as possessing significant information and the ability to use that information in presenting a well-reasoned argument, then you have information power.

Reward and Coercive Powers

You have *reward power* over others if you have the ability to reward them. Rewards may be material (money, promotion, jewelry) or social (love, friendship, respect). If you're able to grant others some kind of reward, you have control over them to the extent that they want what you can give them. The degree of power you have is directly related to the desirability of the reward as seen by others. Teachers have reward power over students because they control grades, letters of recommendation, social approval, and so on. Students, in turn, have reward power over teachers because they control social approval, student evaluations of faculty, and various other rewards. Parents control rewards for children—food, television privileges, rights to the car, curfew times, and the like—and thus possess reward power.

You have *coercive power* over others when you have the ability to administer punishments or remove rewards should they not yield to your influence. Usually, if you have reward power, you also have coercive power. Teachers not only may reward with high grades, favorable letters of recommendation, and social approval but also may punish with low grades, unfavorable letters, and social disapproval. Parents may deny as well as grant privileges to their children, and hence they possess coercive as well as reward power.

The strength of coercive power depends on two factors: (1) the magnitude of the punishment that can be administered and (2) the likelihood that it will be administered as a result of noncompliance. When threatened by mild punishment or by punishment you think will not be administered, you're not as likely to do as directed as you would if the threatened punishment were severe and highly likely to be administered.

Reward and coercive power are opposite sides of a coin, and the consequences of using them are quite different. First, if you have reward power, you're likely to be seen as more attractive. People like those who have the power to reward them and who do in fact reward them. Coercive power, on the other hand, decreases attractiveness;

people dislike those who have the power to punish them or who threaten them with punishment, whether they actually follow through or not.

Second, when you use rewards to exert power, you don't incur the same costs as when you use punishment. When you exert reward power, you're dealing with a contented and happy individual. When you use coercive punishments, however, you must be prepared to incur anger and hostility, which may well be turned against you in the future.

Third, when you give a reward, it signals that you effectively exercised power and that you gained the compliance of the other person. You give the reward because the person did as you wanted. In the exercise of coercive power, however, the reverse is true. When you administer punishment, it shows that you have been ineffective in using the threat of coercive power and that there has been no compliance.

Fourth, when you exert coercive power, other bases of power frequently are diminished. There seems to be a boomerang effect in operation. People who exercise coercive power are seen as possessing less expert, legitimate, and referent power. Alternatively, when reward power is exerted, other bases of power increase.

You rarely find only one base of power used to influence another person. Usually, a number of power bases are used in concert. If you possess expert power, it's likely that you also possess information power and perhaps legitimate power as well.

It's interesting to note that the use of coercive power in the classroom leads to a decrease in cognitive learning and hinders effective learning generally (Richmond and McCroskey 1984, Kearney, Plax, Richmond, and McCroskey 1984, 1985). In classrooms where the teacher is seen by the students to exercise coercive (and legitimate) power, students learn less effectively; have more negative attitudes toward the course, the course content, and the teacher; are less likely to take similar courses; and are less likely to perform the behaviors taught in the course. Coercive power and legitimate power also have a negative impact when used by supervisors on subordinates in business settings (Richmond, Davis, Saylor, and McCroskey 1984). All in all, coercive power seems a last resort, one whose potential negative consequences should be carefully weighed before it's used. Are these results consistent with your own experience?

If you want to control the behavior of another person, you would probably use all three bases of power rather than rely on just one. As you can appreciate, certain individuals have a number of power bases at their disposal, whereas others seem to have few to none. This point brings us back to our first principle: some people are more powerful than others.

Also, recognize that attempts to influence others may backfire. At times, negative power operates. Each of the six power bases may, at times, have such negative influence. For example, negative referent power occurs when a son rejects his father and wants to be his exact opposite. Negative coercive power may be seen when a child is warned against doing something under threat of punishment and then does exactly what he or she was told not to do; the threat of punishment may have made the forbidden behavior seem exciting or challenging.

What types of power do you possess in abundance? What types do you lack?

◀◀ THINKING BACK

COMMUNICATING POWER

THINKING AHEAD ▶▶

How can you establish your power when communicating interpersonally?

You can communicate power much as you communicate any other message. Here we consider how you can communicate power through speaking, nonverbal communication, and listening as well as suggestions for gaining and resisting compliance and for empowering others.

Speaking Power

The ways in which powerfulness and powerlessness are communicated through speech have received lots of research attention. A summary of some of the major characteristics of powerful and powerless speech is presented in Table 18.1 (Molloy 1981, Kleinke 1986, Johnson 1987).

TABLE 18.1 Toward More Powerful Speech

As you read this table, think of your own speech and the kind of power it communicates. Are you satisfied with the level of power your speech communicates?

Suggestions	Examples	Reasons
Avoid hesitations.	I *er* want to say that *ah* this one is *er* the best, *you know.*	Hesitations make a person sound unprepared and uncertain.
Avoid too many intensifiers.	*Really,* this was *the greatest;* it was *truly phenomenal.*	Too many intensifiers make speech sound the same and don't allow for intensifying what should be emphasized.
Avoid disqualifiers.	*I didn't read the entire article,* but... *I didn't actually see the accident,* but....	Disqualifiers signal a lack of competence and a feeling of uncertainty.
Avoid tag questions.	That was a great movie, *wasn't it?* She's brilliant, *don't you think?*	Tag questions ask for another's agreement and therefore signal the speaker's uncertainty.
Avoid self-critical statements.	*I'm not very good at this. This is my first public speech.*	Self-critical statements signal a lack of confidence and make public the speaker's inadequacies.
Avoid slang and vulgar expressions.	##!!!///****! *No shit!*	Slang and vulgarity signal low social class and hence little power.

Nonverbal Power

Much nonverbal research has focused on the factors related to your ability to persuade and influence others (Burgoon, Buller, and Woodall 1995). For example, clothing and other artifactual symbols of authority help you to influence others. Research shows you would be more easily influenced by people in, for example, a respected uniform than in civilian clothes.

Affirmative nodding, facial expressions, and gestures help you express your concern for the other person and for the interaction and help you establish your charisma, an essential component of credibility. Self-manipulations (playing with your hair or touching your face, for example) and backward leaning will damage your persuasiveness.

Here are some popular suggestions for communicating power nonverbally in a business situation, most of which come from Lewis (1989). As you read this list, try to provide specific examples of these suggestions and how they might work in business, at home, or at school. Are there situations in which these suggestions would have negative effects? How would you go about testing the validity of these suggestions?

- Be sure to respond in kind to another's eyebrow flash (raising the eyebrow as a way of acknowledging another person).
- Avoid adaptors—self, other, and object—especially when you wish to communicate confidence and control.
- Use consistent packaging; be especially careful that your verbal and nonverbal messages don't contradict each other.
- When sitting, select chairs you can get in and out of easily; avoid deep plush chairs which you sink into and have trouble getting out of.
- To communicate dominance with your handshake, exert more pressure than usual and hold the grip a bit longer than normal.
- Walk slowly and deliberately. To appear hurried is to appear as without power, as if you were rushing to meet the expectations of another person who had power over you.
- Maintain eye contact. People who maintain eye contact are judged to be more at ease and less afraid to engage in meaningful interaction than those who avoid eye contact. When you break eye contact, direct your gaze downward; otherwise you'll communicate a lack of interest in the other person.
- Avoid vocalized pauses—the "ers" and "ahs"—that frequently punctuate conversations when you're not quite sure of what to say next.
- Maintain reasonably close distances between yourself and those with whom you interact. If the distance is too far, you may be seen as fearful or uninvolved. If the distance is too close, you may be seen as pushy or overly aggressive.

Listening Power

Much as you can communicate power and authority with words and nonverbal expression, you also communicate power through listening. Throughout your listening, you're communicating messages to others, and these messages comment in some way on your power.

Powerful listeners listen actively. They focus and concentrate (with no real effort) on what is being said, especially on what people say they want or need (Fisher 1995). Listen to phrases such as "I want," "It would help if I had," or "I'm looking for." Too, respond to what others have said. For example, preface comments with "In light of what you said about," or "If you feel strongly about." Powerless listeners, on the other hand, listen passively, appear to be thinking about something else and only pretending to listen, and rarely refer to what the other person has said when they do respond.

Powerful listeners respond visibly but in moderation; an occasional nod of agreement or a facial expression that says "that's interesting" are usually sufficient. Responding with too little or too much reaction is likely to be perceived as powerless. Too little response says you aren't listening, and too much response says you aren't listening critically. Powerful listeners also use back-channeling cues—head nods and brief oral responses that say "I'm listening, I'm following you"—when appropriate. When no back-channeling cues are given, the speaker comes to wonder if the other person is really listening.

Powerful listeners maintain more focused eye contact than do those seen to have less power. In conversation, normal eye contact is intermittent—you glance at the speaker's face, then away, then back again, and so on. In a small-group or public-speaking situation, eye contact with the speaker is normally greater.

Adaptors—playing with your hair or a pencil—give the appearance of discomfort. Because of this, adaptors communicate a lack of power. These body movements show the listener to be more concerned with himself or herself than with the speaker. The absence of adaptors, on the other hand, makes the listener appear in control of the situation and comfortable in the role of listener.

Powerful listeners are more likely to maintain an open posture. When around a table or in an audience, they resist covering their stomach or face with their hands. Persons who maintain a defensive posture with, for example, arms crossed around their stomach may communicate a feeling of vulnerability and, hence, powerlessness.

Powerful listeners avoid interrupting the speaker in conversations or in small-group situations. The reason is simple: not interrupting is one of the rules of business communication that powerful people follow and powerless people don't. Completing the speaker's thoughts (or what the listener thinks is the speaker's thought) has a similar powerless effect.

You can also signal power through visual dominance behavior (Exline, Ellyson, and Long 1975), a consideration mentioned in the discussion of eye communication in Unit 12. For example, the average speaker maintains a high level of eye contact while listening and a lower level while speaking. When powerful individuals want to signal dominance, they may reverse this pattern. They may, for example, maintain a high level of eye contact while talking but a much lower level while listening.

Compliance Gaining and Compliance Resisting

The use of compliance strategies clearly illustrates the way power is exercised. **Compliance-gaining strategies** are the tactics that influence others to do what you want them to do. **Compliance-resisting strategies** are the tactics that enable you to say no and to resist another person's attempts to influence you.

Compliance-Gaining Strategies Sixteen compliance-gaining are presented in Table 18.2. In reviewing these strategies, keep in mind that compliance gaining, like all interpersonal processes, involves two people in a transaction. Reading down the list may give the impression that these strategies are one-shot affairs, with one person using the strategy and the other person complying. Actually, compliance gaining is best viewed as a transactional, back-and-forth process. Conflict, compromise, renegotiation of the goal, rejection of the strategy, and a host of other responses—in addition to simple compliance—are possible.

Compliance-Resisting Strategies Let's say that someone you know asks you to do something you don't want to do, such as lend your term paper so this person can copy it and turn it in to another teacher. Research with college students shows

TABLE 18.2 Compliance-Gaining Strategies

As you read this table, realize that these strategies and the responses to them depend both on the personalities of the individuals and on their unique relationship. Which strategies you use, which strategies will work for you, and which strategies will backfire all depend on who you are, who the other person is, and the interpersonal relationship between you. These compliance-gaining strategies come from the research of Marwell and Schmitt (1967, 1990; also see Miller and Parks 1982, Dillard 1990).

Compliance Strategy	Example
Pregiving. Pat rewards Chris and then requests compliance.	**Pat:** I'm glad you enjoyed dinner. This really is the best restaurant in the city. How about going back to my place for a nightcap and whatever?
Liking. Pat is helpful and friendly in order to get Chris in a good mood so that Chris will be more likely to comply with Pat's request.	**Pat:** [After cleaning up the living room and bedroom] I'd really like to relax and bowl a few games with Terry. Okay?
Promise. Pat promises to reward Chris if Chris complies with Pat's request.	**Pat:** I'll give you anything you want if you will just give me a divorce. You can have the house, the car, the stocks, the three kids; just give me my freedom.
Threat. Pat threatens to punish Chris for noncompliance.	**Pat:** If you don't give me a divorce, you'll never see the kids again.
Aversive stimulation. Pat continuously punishes Chris and makes cessation of the punishment contingent upon compliance.	**Pat:** demonstrates hysterical reactions (for example, screaming and crying) and stops only when Chris agrees to comply.
Positive expertise. Pat promises that Chris will be rewarded for compliance because of "the nature of things."	**Pat:** If you follow the doctor's advice, you'll be fine.
Negative expertise. Pat promises that Chris will be punished for noncompliance because of "the nature of things."	**Pat:** If you don't listen to the doctor, you're going to wind up back in the hospital.
Positive self-feelings. Pat promises that Chris will feel better if Chris complies with Pat's request.	**Pat:** You'll see. You'll be a lot better off without me; you'll feel a lot better after the divorce.
Negative self-feelings. Pat promises that Chris will feel worse if Chris does not comply with Pat's request.	**Pat:** Only a selfish creep would force another person to stay in a relationship. You'll hate yourself if you don't give me this divorce.
Positive altercasting. Pat casts Chris in the role of the "good" person and argues that Chris should comply because a person with "good" qualities would comply.	**Pat:** Any intelligent person would grant their partner a divorce when the relationship had died.
Negative altercasting. Pat casts Chris in the role of the "bad" person and argues that Chris should comply because only a person with "bad" qualities would not comply.	**Pat:** Only a cruel and selfish neurotic could stand in the way of another's happiness.
Positive esteem. Pat tells Chris that people will think more highly of Chris (relying on our need for the approval of others) if Chris complies with Pat's request.	**Pat:** Everyone will respect your decision to place your parents in an assisted living community.
Negative esteem. Pat tells Chris that people will think poorly of Chris if Chris does not comply with Pat's request.	**Pat:** Everyone will think that you're paranoid if you don't join the club.
Moral appeals. Pat argues that Chris should comply because it's moral to comply and immoral not to comply.	**Pat:** Any ethical person would return the mistaken overpayment.
Altruism. Pat asks Chris to comply because Pat needs this compliance (relying on Chris's desire to help and be of assistance).	**Pat:** I would feel so disappointed if you quit college now. Don't hurt me by quitting.
Debt. Pat asks Chris to comply because of the past favors given to Chris.	**Pat:** Look at how we sacrificed to send you to college.

that there are four principal ways of responding (McLaughlin, Cody, and Robey 1980, O'Hair, Cody, and O'Hair 1991).

In *identity management,* you resist by trying to manipulate the image of the person making the request. You might do this negatively or positively. In negative identity management, you might portray the person as unreasonable or unfair and say, for example, "That's really unfair of you to ask me to compromise my ethics." Or you might tell the person that it hurts that he or she would even think you would do such a thing.

You might also use positive identity management. Here you resist complying by making the other person feel good about himself or herself. For example, you might say, "You know this material much better than I do; you can easily do a much better paper yourself."

Another way to resist compliance is to use *nonnegotiation,* a direct refusal to do as asked. You might simply say, "No, I don't lend my papers out."

In *negotiation,* you resist compliance by, for example, offering a compromise ("I'll let you read my paper but not copy it") or by offering to help the person in some other way ("If you write a first draft, I'll go over it and try to make some comments"). If the request is a romantic one—for example, a request to go away for a ski weekend—you might resist by discussing your feelings and proposing an alternative: for example, "Let's double date first."

Another way to resist compliance is through *justification.* Here you justify your refusal by citing possible consequences of compliance or noncompliance. For example, you might cite a negative consequence if you complied ("I'm afraid that I'd get caught, and then I'd fail the course"). Or you might cite a positive consequence of your not complying ("You'll really enjoy writing this paper; it's a lot of fun").

Remember that compliance gaining and resisting—like all interpersonal communication—are transactional processes in which all elements are interdependent; each element influences each other. Your attempts to gain compliance, for example, will be influenced by the responses of the person you wish to influence. These responses in turn will influence your responses, and so on. Also, just as your relationship (its type, length, intimacy, for example) will influence the strategies you use, so will the strategies you use influence your relationship. Inappropriate strategies will have negative effects, just as positive strategies will have positive effects.

Empowering Others

Empowerment involves helping others (your relational partner, an employee, another student, a sibling) to gain increased power over themselves and their environment. Empowerment is not just an altruistic gesture on the part of one relationship partner or of management; for many, it is a basic philosophy. The reason empowerment is so much discussed and so much a part of modern business practices is that it provides lots of benefits. Empowered people are more likely to take a more personal interest in the job or in the relationship. Empowered people will be proactive; they will act and not just react. They're more likely to take on decision-making responsibilities, are willing to take risks, and are willing to take responsibility for their actions, qualities that make relationships and business exciting. In an interpersonal relationship (though the same would apply to a multinational organization), two empowered partners are more likely to effectively meet the challenges and difficulties most relationships will encounter.

TRY IT!
To learn more about empowering others, go to www.awl.com/devito.

In empowering others, try to raise their self-esteem. Resist fault-finding. It doesn't really benefit the fault-finder and certainly doesn't benefit the other person. Fault-finding disempowers others. Any criticism that is offered should be constructive.

Be willing to offer your perspective, to lend an ear to a first-try singing effort, or to read a new poem. Also, avoid verbal aggressiveness and abusiveness. Resist the temptation to win an argument with unfair tactics, tactics that are going to hurt the other person.

Be open, positive, empathic, and supportive and treat the other person with an equality of respect. These, of course, are the humanistic qualities of effectiveness that were identified in Unit 8. Similarly, be attentive and listen actively. Attentiveness and active listening tell the other person that he or she is important. After all, what greater praise could you pay than to give another person your time and energy?

Share skills and share decision making. Be willing to relinquish control and allow the other person the freedom to make decisions. Encourage growth in all forms, academic and relational. Growth, like empowerment, is not something that a relationship has a limited supply of and that has to be parceled out. Both persons can grow and develop and both persons can be empowered. The growth and empowerment of one person enhances the growth and power of the other.

What's the single best idea you can think of for communicating your own power interpersonally? What's the single best idea you can think of for empowering others?

◀◀ THINKING BACK

REVIEWING KEY TERMS AND CONCEPTS OF POWER IN INTERPERSONAL RELATIONSHIPS

This unit discussed the importance of power in interpersonal relationships, emphasizing the nature of power and its principles, its types, and the ways to communicate power.

Principles of Power

What is power? What principles govern the operation of power in interpersonal relationships?

- Some people are more powerful than others; some are born to power, others learn it.
- Some people are more Machiavellian than others; people differ in their beliefs about the extent to which people can be controlled by others.
- Power can be increased or decreased; power is never static.
- Power follows the principle of less interest; generally, the less interest, the greater the power.
- Power has a cultural dimension; power is distributed differently in different cultures.
- Power is often used unfairly, as in sexual harassment and power plays.

Bases of Power

In what ways can one person have power over another?

- *Referent:* B wants to be like A.
- *Legitimate:* B believes that A has a right to influence or control B's behavior.
- *Reward:* A has the ability to reward B.
- *Coercive:* A has the ability to punish B.
- *Expert:* B regards A as having knowledge.
- *Information or Persuasion:* B attributes to A the ability to communicate effectively.

Communicating Power

How can you communicate power?

- *Speaking power* includes, for example, avoiding hesitations, disqualifiers, and self-critical statements.
- *Nonverbal power* includes avoiding adaptors, using consistent packaging, and avoiding excessive movements.
- *Listening power* includes responding visibly, maintaining eye contact and an open posture, and avoiding interrupting.
- Compliance-gaining and compliance-resisting tactics enable you to influence others to do as you want or enable you to resist compliance attempts of others. Compliance-gaining tactics include expressing liking, making promises, and threatening. Compliance-resisting tactics include using identity management and negotiation.
- Empowering others enables the others to gain in power and control over themselves and over the environment. Empowering others has numerous advantages, for example, empowered people are more proactive and more responsible. Empowering others involves such strategies as being positive, avoiding verbal aggressiveness and abusiveness, encouraging growth.

APPLYING KEY TERMS AND CONCEPTS OF POWER IN INTERPERSONAL RELATIONSHIPS

1. Whom do you consider the three most interpersonally powerful people you have ever known? Which types of power did they possess?
2. What has your culture taught you about power? When is power good? When is it bad?

3. What would you add to the discussion of sexual harassment presented here?
4. In what kinds of situations do you think it might be best to (1) ignore the power play, (2) neutralize it, and (3) employ a cooperative response?
5. Will the discussion of reward and coercive power influence your own exercise of these types of power? In what ways?
6. How satisfied are you with your command of each of these six bases of power? What might you do to increase those bases with which you're not satisfied?
7. How would you evaluate your own speaking, nonverbal, and listening power? What might you do to increase your power in these areas?
8. Which of the compliance-gaining strategies do you find most effective? Which strategies work best on you?
9. How would you use compliance-gaining strategies to influence someone to go on a date with you? How would you use compliance-resisting strategies to resist someone's persistent attempts to have you go on a date?
10. How would you go about designing a study to investigate each of the following questions?
    - What bases of power work best in the elementary or high school classroom? Which work best in the college classroom?
    - What effects does the recommended management strategy for power plays have on friendship relationships? On romantic relationships?
    - Which compliance-gaining strategies work best in same-sex and opposite-sex interactions? Which are least effective?
    - Which compliance-resisting strategies work best for teenagers resisting drugs? Which are least effective?
    - Do the women and the men at your school differ in Machiavellianism?

EXPERIENCING KEY TERMS AND CONCEPTS OF POWER IN INTERPERSONAL RELATIONSHIPS

Go to www.awl.com/devito

Exercise No. 25, "Power Plays," explores several types of power plays and appropriate responses to them. Exercise No. 28, "The Television Relationship," can be used to identify the principles of power.

UNIT 19
CONFLICT IN INTERPERSONAL RELATIONSHIPS

Who's Afraid of Virginia Woolf? (1966)

IN A QUARREL, EACH SIDE IS RIGHT.

--YIDDISH PROVERB

WHEN TWO QUARREL, BOTH ARE IN THE WRONG.

--DUTCH PROVERB

Nature of Conflict
Conflict Resolution Stages
Conflict Management Strategies

Mike Nichols's Who's Afraid of Virginia Woolf?—based on the Edward Albee play—is perhaps the classic film of interpersonal conflict. Here we see husband George (Richard Burton), a mediocre college professor, and wife Martha (Elizabeth Taylor) in a love-hate relationship, constantly in conflict. The ways they fight and the strategies they use provide a virtual manual of how to fight dirty and hurt your partner. The film provides vivid testimony to the importance of learning to engage in conflict fairly and constructively and the consequences of not doing so.

Interpersonal conflict refers to a disagreement between or among connected individuals: close friends, lovers, or family members. The word "connected" emphasizes the fact that each person's position and each person's actions affect the other person.

Conflict is a part of every interpersonal relationship, between parents and children, brothers and sisters, friends, lovers, coworkers. As Louis Nizer put it, "Where there is no difference, there is only indifference."

NATURE OF CONFLICT

THINKING AHEAD ▸▸
What do you fight about with your friends or romantic partners? How are these conflicts usually resolved?

Consider the following statements. Do you think they're true or false?

1. If two people engage in relationship conflict, it means their relationship is in trouble.
2. Conflict hurts an interpersonal relationship.
3. Conflict is bad because it reveals our negative selves—for example, our pettiness, our need to be in control, our unreasonable expectations.

As with most things, simple answers are usually wrong. The three statements may all be true or may all be false; it depends. (1) Conflict is inevitable, so the fact that a relationship experiences it merely means the relationship is typical. (2) If the conflict is approached properly, the relationship may not only not be hurt but may be improved as a result of the conflict's resolution. (3) Similarly, it's not the conflict that reveals your negative side but the fight strategies you use. Thus, if you attack the other person personally or use force, you do reveal a negative side. But you can also reveal a positive self, as when you show your willingness to listen to opposing points of view, to change unpleasant behaviors, and to accept imperfection in others.

Negative and Positive Effects of Conflict

Because people are different and will necessarily see things differently, interpersonal conflict is inevitable. The way you deal with conflict, however, can have both negative and positive effects.

Negative Effects Among the disadvantages of conflict is that it often leads to increased negative feelings. Many conflicts involve unfair fighting methods and focus largely on hurting the other person. If this happens, negative feelings are sure to increase. Conflict may also deplete energy better spent on other areas, especially when unproductive conflict strategies are used.

At times, conflict may lead you to close yourself off from the other individual. When you hide your feelings from your partner, you prevent meaningful communication and interaction; this, in turn, creates barriers to intimacy. Because the need for intimacy is so strong, one possible outcome is that one or both parties may seek intimacy elsewhere. This often leads to further conflict, mutual hurt, and resentment—qualities that add heavily to the costs carried by the relationship. As these costs increase, the rewards may become more difficult to exchange. Here, then, is a situation in which costs increase and rewards decrease, one that often results in relationship deterioration and eventual dissolution.

Positive Effects Among the advantages of conflict is that it forces you to examine a problem and work toward a potential solution. If you use productive conflict strategies, your relationship is likely to become stronger, healthier, and more satisfying than it was before.

Conflict often prevents hostilities and resentments from festering. Say you're annoyed at your partner, who comes home from work and then talks on the phone with colleagues for two hours instead of giving that time to you. If you say nothing, your annoyance is likely to grow. Further, by saying nothing you implicitly approve of such behavior, so it's likely that such phone calls will continue. Through your conflict and its resolution, you each let your needs be known: your partner needs to review the day's work to gain assurance that it's been properly completed, and you have a need for your partner's attention. If you both can appreciate the legitimacy of these needs, then you stand a good chance of finding workable solutions. Perhaps you partner can make the phone call after your attention needs are met. Perhaps you can delay your need for attention until your partner gets closure about work. Perhaps you can learn to provide for your partner's closure needs and in doing so get your own attention needs met. Again, you have win-win solutions; each of you gets your needs met.

Conflict also enables you to state what you each want and perhaps to get it. For example, let's say that you want to spend your money on a new car because your old one is unreliable. Your partner, on the other hand, wants to spend it on a vacation, feeling the need for a change of pace. Through your conflict and its resolution, you learn what each wants; from this you may then be able to figure how each of you can get what you want. You might accept a used car and your partner might accept a shorter vacation. Or you might buy a used car and take an inexpensive motor trip. Each of these solutions may prove satisfying. They're win-win solutions—each of you wins, each of you gets what you want.

Consider, too, that when you try to resolve conflict within an interpersonal relationship, you're saying that the relationship is worth the effort; otherwise, you'd walk away. Although there may be exceptions—as when you confront conflict to save face or to gratify some ego need—confronting a conflict often indicates concern, commitment, and a desire to protect and preserve the relationship.

Content and Relationship Conflicts

Using concepts developed earlier (Unit 2), you can distinguish between content and relationship conflicts. *Content conflict* centers on objects, events, and persons in the world that are usually external to the people involved in the conflict. These include the millions of issues that you argue and fight about every day—the value of a particular movie, what to watch on television, the fairness of the last examination, who should get promoted, and the way to spend your savings.

Relationship conflicts are equally numerous and include conflicts concerned with the relationships between the individuals, with such issues as who's in charge, the equality or lack of it in the relationship, and who has the right to establish rules of behavior. Relationship conflicts include such examples as a younger brother who does not obey his older brother, two partners who each want an equal say in making vacation plans, and the mother and daughter who each want to have the final word concerning the daughter's lifestyle.

Relationship conflicts are often hidden and are often disguised as content conflicts. Thus, a conflict over where you should vacation may, on the content level, center on the advantages and disadvantages of Mexico versus Hawaii. On a relationship level, however, it may center on who has the greater right to select the place to vacation, who should win the argument, or who is the decision maker in the relationship.

Interpersonal conflicts involve a variety of issues. For example, in one study gay, lesbian, and heterosexual couples were surveyed on the issues they argued about most. The six major issues were virtually identical for all couples (from those most often mentioned to the least often): (1) intimacy issues such as affection and sex, (2) power issues such as excessive demands or possessiveness, lack of equality in the relationship, friends, and leisure time, (3) personal flaws issues such as drinking or smoking, personal grooming, and driving style, (4) personal distance issues such as frequently being absent and school or job commitments, (5) social issues such as politics and social concerns, parents, and personal values, and (6) distrust issues such as previous lovers and lying (Kurdek 1994).

Another study found that four conditions led up to a couple's "first big fight": uncertainty over commitment, jealousy, violation of expectations, and personality differences (Siegert and Stamp 1994).

Among top managers, the major source of conflict revolved around the issue of executive responsibility and coordination. Other conflicts focused on differences in organizational objectives, in how resources are to be allocated, and in what constitutes an appropriate management style (Morrill 1992).

In a study of same-sex and opposite-sex friends, the four issues most often argued about were: sharing living space or possessions, violating friendship rules, sharing activities, and disagreement about ideas (Samter and Cupach 1998).

ASK THE RESEARCHER

Arguing Productively

My life partner and I seem to argue about the least little things, and all these little arguments are causing major dissatisfaction, at least on my part. What can I do to put an end to these petty arguments?

Sometimes people in a relationship don't know how to discuss things that upset them or they're afraid to raise those issues because they fear doing so would end their relationship. Often people who can't or won't express these feelings openly express them indirectly in what is called a passive-aggressive communication style. Petty arguments can then arise over spending, driving skills, anything but the real feelings.

If this is your situation, first assure your partner of your commitment to the relationship and then model constructive conflict resolution behaviors by sharing your emotions and asking to discuss relationship issues. Consider saying, "I value our relationship. When you criticize my driving I really worry that our relationship is in jeopardy. Even though it's hard to do, I want to work on any relationship issues that we might have because I love you. Is there anything on your mind about us that's worrying you?"

—Fred E. Jandt (Ph.D., Bowling Green State University) is a professor of communication at California State University, San Bernardino, where he teaches courses in mediation and conflict and in intercultural communication. He is the author of *Win-Win Negotiating: Turning Conflict into Agreement.* fjandt@csusb.edu.

Culture and Conflict

Culture influences the topics people fight about as well as what are considered appropriate and inappropriate ways of dealing with conflict. For example, cohabitating 18-year-olds are more likely to have conflict with their parents over their living style if they live in the United States than if they live in Sweden, where cohabitation is much more accepted. Similarly, male infidelity is more likely to cause conflict among American couples than among Southern European couples. Students from the United States are more likely to pursue a conflict with another United States student than with someone from another culture. Chinese students, on the other hand, are more likely to pursue a conflict with a non-Chinese than with another Chinese student (Leung 1988).

The topics of conflicts will also depend on whether the culture is high or low context. In high-context cultures, conflicts are more likely to center on violating collective or group norms and values. Conversely, in low-context cultures, conflicts are more likely to come up when individual norms are violated (Ting-Toomey 1985).

Cultures also differ in how they define and evaluate a conflict strategy. For example, in some cultures it's quite common for women to be referred to negatively and as less than equal. To most people in the United States, this would constitute verbal abuse. To some Japanese women, however, this isn't uncommon and isn't perceived as abusive (*New York Times*, 11 February 1996, pp. 1, 12).

Cultures vary widely in their responses to physical and verbal abuse. In some Asian and Hispanic cultures, for example, the fear of losing face or embarrassing the family is so great that people prefer not to report or reveal abuses. When looking over statistics, it may at first appear that little violence occurs in the families of certain cultures. Yet we know from research that wife beating is quite common in India, Taiwan, and Iran, for example (Counts, Brown, and Campbell 1992, Hatfield and Rapson 1996). In much of the United States, and in many other cultures as well, such abuse would not be tolerated no matter who was embarrassed or insulted.

African Americans and European Americans engage in conflict in very different ways (Kochman 1981, Hecht, Collier, and Ribeau 1993). The issues that cause and aggravate conflict, the conflict strategies that are expected and accepted, and the attitude toward conflict vary from one group to the other.

Different cultures also view conflict management techniques differently. In one study, African American females were found to use more direct controlling strategies (for example, assuming control over the conflict and arguing persistently for their point of view) than did white females. White females, on the other hand, used more solution-oriented conflict styles than did African American females. African American and white men were similar in their conflict strategies; both avoided or withdrew from relationship conflict, preferring to keep quiet about their differences or make them seem insignificant (Ting-Toomey 1986).

The following brief dialogue (modeled on an idea by Crohn 1995) is designed to illustrate the issue of cultural differences in conflict and some of the problems these may create. As you read it, try to explain what is possibly going on interculturally.

PAT: Why did you tell her I was home? I told you an hour ago that I didn't want to speak with her. You just don't listen.

CHRIS: I'm sorry. I completely forgot. But you seemed to have a nice talk. So no harm done—right?

PAT: Wrong. You just don't understand. I didn't want to talk with her.

CHRIS: Okay. Sorry.

Chris withdraws to next room and remains silent, saying nothing to Pat's repeated comments and criticisms. After about two hours:

PAT: I can't stand your silent treatment. You're making me the villain. You're the one who screwed up.
CHRIS: I'm sorry. [Walks away]

Communication continues in this way for the rest of the evening—with Pat ranting and raving every several minutes and with Chris saying hardly anything and always trying to walk away. Pat comes from a culture where anger is regularly and expectedly expressed. Yelling and screaming are customary ways of dealing with conflict. Chris comes from a culture where anger is expressed by silence. The extent to which you remain silent is a measure of how angry you are.

Their different cultural beliefs about conflict can lead each to draw incorrect conclusions about the other. For example, from Chris's silence it's easy for Pat to conclude that Chris doesn't care about what happened and is indifferent to Pat's anger. From Pat's outburst Chris may easily conclude that Pat is unhappy in their relationship.

If Pat and Chris came from the same culture—with the same rules for expressing anger—or if they had sufficient intercultural awareness, their argument would have been no less real. Don't let us fool ourselves into thinking that cultural awareness will resolve all conflicts or that culture is the only factor that can cause such differences; it won't and it isn't. However, it would have prevented a large part of the conflict—for example, the anger over the way the other person expressed anger—and would have prevented each from making inaccurate assumptions about the other.

Gender and Conflict

One of the few stereotypes that is supported by research is that of the withdrawing and sometime aggressive male. Men are more apt to withdraw from a conflict situation, often coupled with a denial that anything is wrong, than are women (Haferkamp 1991/1992). Women, on the other hand, want to get closer to the conflict; they want to talk about it and resolve it. One theory accounting for this tendency to withdraw is that men experience *flooding* (a sense of being out of control, of extreme negative feelings of anger or rage, for example) more easily and with less provocation than women (Gottman 1993, 1994, Goleman 1995a, Gottman and Carrere 1994, Canary, Cupach, and Messman 1995). Physiologically, flooding occurs at 10 heartbeats per minute more than normal; when the heart rate increases to about 100, the distress level—because of the extra adrenaline pumped in—will remain high for some time, even after the conflict is "settled." The tendency to withdraw from an argument or to say nothing in response to a woman's desire to discuss the conflict may be due to a desire to avoid or reduce the effects of flooding.

Even adolescents reveal differences in avoidance. In a study of boys and girls ages 11 to 17, boys withdrew more than girls but were more aggressive when they didn't withdraw (Lindeman, Harakka, and Keltikangas-Jarvinen 1997). Similarly, in a study of offensive language, girls were found to be more easily offended by language than were boys, but boys were more apt to fight when they were offended by the words used (Heasley, Babbitt, and Burbach 1995).

One study found that African American men preferred clear arguments and a focus on problem-solving, whereas African American women preferred assertiveness and respect (Collier 1991). Other research has found that women are more emotional and men are more logical when they argue (Schaap, Buunk, and Kerkstra 1988, Canary, Cupach, and Messman 1995). Women have been defined as conflict "feelers" and men as conflict "thinkers" (Sorenson, Hawkins, and Sorenson 1995). Another difference found is that women are more apt to reveal their negative feelings than are men (Schaap, Buunk, and Kerkstra 1988, Canary, Cupach, and Messman 1995).

Of course, many cultures have different rules for men and women. These rules don't seem to vary on the basis of affectional orientation; gay and lesbian couples use essentially the same conflict resolution strategies as do heterosexual couples (Metz, Rosser, and Strapko 1994). For example, one study found that in the United States when men argue with other men, they both use assertiveness and reason throughout. When women argue with women, they begin with assertiveness, then reasoning, and then move to bargaining. When women and men argue, they both use reason and bargaining throughout the discussion (Papa and Natalle 1989).

Asian cultures are more strongly prohibitive of women's conflict strategies. Asian women are expected to be exceptionally polite; this is even more important when women are in conflict with men and when the conflict is public (Tannen 1994b). In the United States, there is a verbalized equality; men and women have equal rights when it comes to permissible conflict strategies. In reality, many expect women to be more polite and to pursue conflict in a nonargumentative way, whereas men are expected to argue forcefully and logically.

Despite these gender differences, there are also great similarities in the ways men and women approach and deal with conflict. Much research fails to find the gender differences that cartoons, situation comedies, novels, and films portray so readily and so clearly. For example, in a number of studies, dealing with college students and men and women in business, no significant differences were found in the way men and women engage in conflict (Wilkins and Andersen 1991, Canary and Hause 1993, Canary, Cupach, and Messman 1995).

Online Conflicts

Just as you experience conflict in face-to-face communication, you can experience the same conflicts online. A few conflict situations that are unique to online communication may be noted here.

Sending commercial messages to those who didn't request them often creates conflict. Junk mail is junk mail; but on the Internet, the receiver often has to pay for the time it takes to read and delete these unwanted messages. Even if there is no financial cost, there is still a loss of time.

Sending messages to an entire listserv when they're only relevant to one member may annoy members who expect to receive only messages relevant to the entire group and not personal exchanges between two people. This often occurs when someone sends a message seeking specific information, and then individual members reply, not just to the person seeking the information, but to the entire listserv. Sometimes the reply is simply, "I can't help you with that question," a message relevant only to the person asking the question and not to the entire listserv.

Spamming often causes conflict. Spamming is sending someone unsolicited mail, repeatedly sending the same mail, or posting the same message in lots of newsgroups, even when the message is irrelevant to the focus of the group. Like commercial messages, these unwanted messages absorb your valuable time and energy. Another reason, of course, is that spamming clogs the system, slowing it down for everyone.

Flaming, especially common in newsgroups, refers to sending messages that personally attack another user. Frequently, flaming leads to flame wars where everyone in the group gets into the act and attacks each other. Generally, flaming and flame wars prevent you from achieving your goals and are counterproductive.

Trolling, putting out purposely incorrect information or outrageous viewpoints to watch other people correct you or get emotionally upset by your message, can obviously lead to conflict, though some see it as fun.

Have you changed any of your preconceptions about interpersonal conflict after reading this section? If so, which ones?

◀◀ THINKING BACK

CONFLICT RESOLUTION STAGES

THINKING AHEAD ▸▸
You want to spend a tax refund on new clothes, but your partner wants to spend it on a vacation. How would you go about resolving this conflict?

Before trying to resolve a conflict, you need to prepare. Conflict resolution is an extremely important communication experience, and you don't want to enter it without adequate thought. Here are a few suggestions for preparing for resolving conflict.

Try to fight in private. When you air your conflicts in front of others, you create a variety of other problems. You may not be willing to be totally honest when third parties are present; you may feel you have to save face and therefore must win the fight at all costs. This may lead you to use strategies to win the argument rather than to resolve the conflict. You may become so absorbed by the image that others will have of you that you forget you have a relationship problem that needs to be resolved. Also, you run the risk of embarrassing your partner in front of others, and this embarrassment may create resentment and hostility.

Be sure you're each ready to fight. Although conflicts arise at the most inopportune times, you can choose the time to resolve them. Confronting your partner when she or he comes home after a hard day of work may not be the right time for resolving a conflict. Make sure you're both relatively free of other problems and ready to deal with the conflict at hand.

Know what you're fighting about. Sometimes people in a relationship become so hurt and angry that they lash out at the other person just to vent their own frustration. The problem at the center of the conflict (for example, the uncapped toothpaste tube) is merely an excuse to express anger. Any attempt to resolve this "problem" will be doomed to failure because the problem addressed is not what is causing the conflict. Instead, the underlying hostility, anger, and frustration need to be addressed.

Fight about problems that can be solved. Fighting about past behaviors or about family members or situations over which you have no control solves nothing; instead, it creates additional difficulties. Any attempt at resolution will fail because the problems are incapable of being solved. Often such conflicts are concealed attempts at expressing one's frustration or dissatisfaction.

Now that you're prepared for the conflict resolution interaction, refer to the model in Figure 19.1. It identifies the steps that will help you navigate through this process.

Define the Conflict

TRY IT!
To learn more about defining the conflict, go to www.awl.com/devito.

Your first and most essential step is to define the conflict. Here are several techniques to keep in mind.

Define the content and relationship issues Define the obvious content issues (who should do the dishes, who should take the kids to school, who should take out the dog) as well as the underlying relationship issues (who has been avoiding household responsibilities, who has been neglecting responsibility toward the kids, whose time is more valuable).

Define the problem in specific terms Conflict defined in the abstract is difficult to deal with and resolve. It's one thing for a husband to say that his wife is "cold and unfeeling" and quite another to say that she doesn't call him at the office, kiss him when he comes home, or hold his hand when they're at a party. These behaviors can be agreed upon and dealt with, but the abstract "cold and unfeeling" remains elusive.

Focus on the present Avoid **gunnysacking**—a term derived from the large burlap bag called a gunnysack—the practice of storing up grievances so they may be unloaded at another time. The immediate occasion may be relatively simple (or so

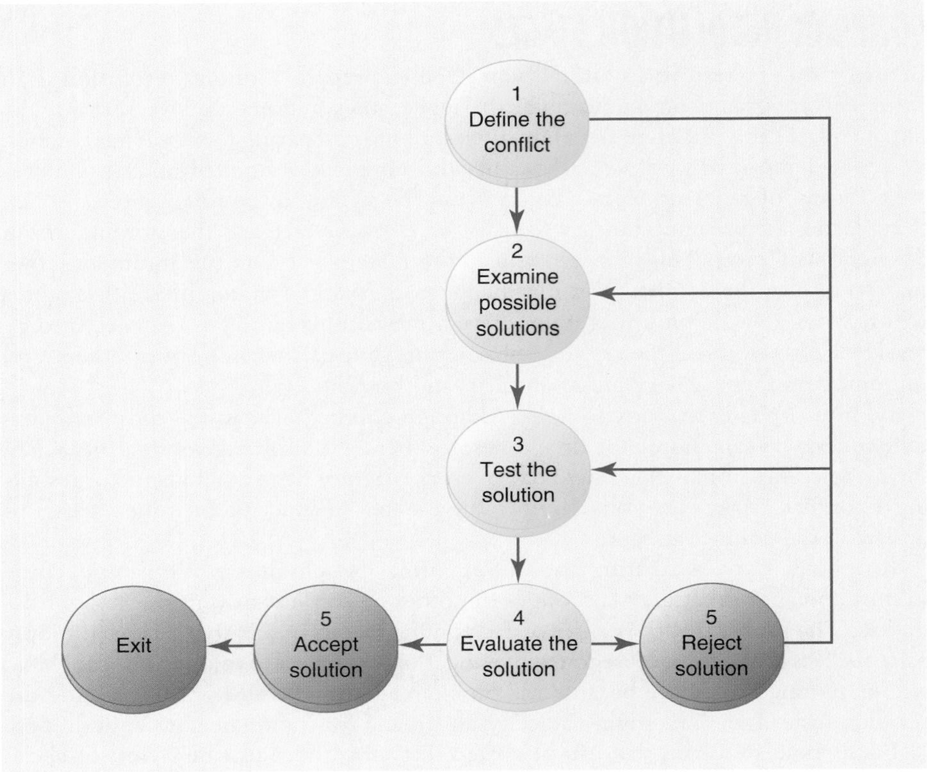

Figure 19.1 Stages in Conflict Resolution
This model of conflict resolution is essentially John Dewey's problem-solving sequence. The assumption made here is that a conflict to be resolved is essentially a problem to be solved and follows the same general sequence. As you read about this problem/conflict-solving sequence, try visualizing a specific conflict and how these several steps might help to resolve it.

it might seem at first), such as someone's coming home late without calling. Instead of arguing about this, the gunnysacker unloads all past grievances. The birthday you forgot, the time you arrived late for dinner, the hotel reservations you forgot to make are all thrown at you. As you may know from experience, gunnysacking begets gunnysacking. When one person gunnysacks, the other person gunnysacks. The result is two people dumping their stored-up grievances on one another. Frequently, the original problem never gets addressed. Instead, resentment and hostility escalate. So focus your conflict on the here-and-now rather than on issues that occurred two months ago.

Empathize Throughout this process, try to understand the nature of the conflict from the other person's point of view. Use your perspective-taking skills to achieve this empathy. Why is your partner disturbed that you're not doing the dishes? Why is your neighbor complaining about taking the kids to school? Why is your mother insisting you take out the dog?

Be especially careful to avoid blame Because most relationship conflicts are caused by a wide variety of factors, any attempt to single out one or two for blame is sure to fail. Yet a frequently used fight strategy is to blame someone. Often when you blame someone, you attribute motives to the person. Thus, if the person forgot your birthday and this oversight disturbs you, fight about the forgetting of the birthday (the actual behavior). Try not to mind read the motives of another person: "Well, it's obvious you just don't care about me. If you really cared, you could never have forgotten my birthday!"

Demonstrate empathic understanding Once you have empathically understood your opponent's feelings, validate those feelings when appropriate. If your partner is hurt or angry and you believe such feelings are legitimate and justified, say so: "You have a right to be angry. I shouldn't have called your mother a slob. I'm sorry. But I still don't want to go on vacation with her." In expressing validation, you're not necessarily expressing agreement on the issue in conflict; you're merely stating that your partner has feelings that you recognize as legitimate.

Avoid mindreading Don't try to read the other person's mind. Ask questions to make sure you understand the problem as the other person is experiencing it. Ask directly and simply: for example, "Why are you insisting that I take the dog out now when I have to call three clients before nine o'clock?"

Let's select an example and work with it through the remaining steps. This conflict revolves around Pat's not wanting to socialize with Chris's friends. Chris is devoted to them, but Pat actively dislikes them. Chris thinks they're wonderful and exciting; Pat thinks they're unpleasant and boring.

Examine Possible Solutions

Most conflicts can probably be resolved through a variety of solutions. Here are a few suggestions.

WEB EXPLORATION
To learn more about examining possible solutions, go to www.awl.com/devito.

Try to identify as many solutions as possible Brainstorm by yourself or with your partner. Try not to inhibit or censor yourself or your partner as you generate these potential solutions.

Look for win-win solutions Once you have proposed a variety of solutions, look especially for solutions that will enable both parties to win—to get something each wants. Avoid win-lose solutions, in which one wins and one loses. They will cause difficulty for the relationship by engendering frustration and resentment.

Carefully weigh the costs and the rewards that each solution entails. Most solutions will involve costs to one or both parties (after all, someone has to take the dog out). Seek solutions in which the costs and the rewards will be evenly shared. For example, among the solutions that Pat and Chris might identify are these:

1. Chris should not interact with these friends anymore.
2. Pat should interact with Chris's friends.
3. Chris should see these friends without Pat.

Clearly solutions 1 and 2 are win-lose solutions. In solution 1, Pat wins and Chris loses; in 2, Chris wins and Pat loses. Solution 3 has some possibilities. Both might win and neither must necessarily lose. This potential solution, then, needs to be looked at more closely.

Test the Solution

Test the solution mentally How does it feel now? How will it feel tomorrow? Are you comfortable with it? Would Pat be comfortable with Chris's socializing with these friends alone? Some of Chris's friends are attractive; would this cause difficulty for Pat and Chris's relationship? Will Chris give people too much to gossip about? Will Chris feel guilty? Will Chris enjoy these friends without Pat?

Test the solution in practice Put the solution into operation. How does it work? If it doesn't work, then discard it and try another solution. Give each solution a fair chance, but don't hang on to a solution when it's clear that it won't resolve the conflict.

Perhaps Chris might go out without Pat once to test this solution. How was it? Did these friends think there was something wrong with Chris's relationship with Pat? Did Chris feel guilty? Did Chris enjoy this new experience? How did Pat feel? Did Pat feel jealous? Lonely? Abandoned?

Evaluate the Solution

Did the solution help resolve the conflict? Is the situation better now than it was before the solution was tried? Share your feelings and evaluations of the solution.

Pat and Chris now need to share their perceptions of this possible solution. Would they be comfortable with this solution on a monthly basis? Is the solution worth the costs each will pay? Are the costs and rewards evenly distributed? Might other solutions be more effective?

Critical-thinking pioneer Edward deBono (1987) suggests that in analyzing problems, you use six "thinking hats" as a way of seeking different perspectives. With each hat you look at the problem from a different angle.

- *The fact hat* focuses attention on the facts and figures that bear on the problem. For example, how can Pat learn more about the rewards that Chris gets from friends? How can Chris learn why Pat doesn't like these great friends?
- *The feeling hat* focuses attention on the emotional responses to the problem. How does Pat feel when Chris goes out with these friends? How does Chris feel when Pat refuses to meet them?
- *The negative argument hat* asks you to become the devil's advocate. How might this relationship deteriorate if Chris continues seeing these friends without Pat or if Pat resists interacting with Chris's friends?
- *The positive benefits hat* asks you to look at the up side. What are the opportunities that Chris's seeing friends without Pat might yield? What benefits might Pat and Chris get from this new arrangement?
- *The creative new idea hat* focuses on new ways of looking at the problem. In what other ways can Pat and Chris look at this problem? What other possible solutions might they consider?
- *The control of thinking hat* helps you analyze what you're doing; it asks you to reflect on your own thinking. Have Pat and Chris adequately defined the problem? Are they focusing too much on insignificant issues? Have they given enough attention to possible negative effects?

Accept or Reject the Solution

If you accept the solution, you're ready to put it into more permanent operation. Let's say that Pat is actually quite happy with the solution. Pat was able to use that time to visit college friends. The next time Chris goes out with the friends Pat doesn't like, Pat intends to go out with some friends from college. Chris feels pretty good about seeing friends without Pat. Chris explains that they have both decided to see their friends separately and both are comfortable with this decision. If, however, either Pat or Chris felt unhappy with this solution, they would have to try out another solution or perhaps go back and redefine the problem and seek other ways to resolve it.

Even after the conflict is resolved, there is still work to be done. Often after one conflict is supposedly settled, another conflict will emerge because, for example, one person feels that harm was done to them and they need to retaliate and take revenge in order to restore their own self-worth (Kim and Smith 1993). So it's especially important that the conflict be resolved and not allowed to generate other, perhaps more significant conflicts.

Learn from the conflict and from the process you went through in trying to resolve it. For example, can you identify the fight strategies that merely aggravated the situation? Do you or your partner need a cooling-off period? Can you tell when minor issues are going to escalate into major arguments? Does avoidance make matters worse? What issues are particularly disturbing and likely to cause difficulties? Can they be avoided?

Keep the conflict in perspective. Be careful not to blow it out of proportion to the extent that you begin to define your relationship in terms of conflict. Avoid the tendency to see disagreement as inevitably leading to major blowups. Conflicts in most relationships actually occupy a very small percentage of the couple's time, and yet, in recollection, they often loom extremely large. Also, don't allow the conflict to undermine your own or your partner's self-esteem. Don't view yourself, your partner, or your relationship as failures just because you had an argument or even lots of arguments.

Attack your negative feelings. Negative feelings frequently arise after an interpersonal conflict. Most often they arise because unfair fight strategies were used to undermine the other person—for example, personal rejection, manipulation, or force. Resolve to avoid such unfair tactics in the future, but at the same time let go of guilt, of blame, for yourself and your partner. If you think it would help, discuss these feelings with your partner or even a therapist.

Increase the exchange of rewards and cherishing behaviors to demonstrate your positive feelings and to show you're over the conflict and want the relationship to survive and flourish.

Which of the steps just discussed do you regularly follow in trying to resolve a conflict? Do you omit any steps?

◀◀ THINKING BACK

CONFLICT MANAGEMENT STRATEGIES

THINKING AHEAD ▶▶

How effective are you in dealing with interpersonal conflict? Generally, is your relationship stronger or weaker after a conflict episode?

Your conflict management strategies will be influenced by a variety of considerations. For example, the short- and long-term goals you wish to achieve will influence what strategies seem appropriate. If you just want to save the date you are on, you might want to simply give in and ignore any difficulty. On the other hand, if you want to build a long-term relationship, you might want to fully analyze the cause of the problem and look for win-win strategies.

Similarly, your cognitive assessment of the situation will exert powerful influence. For example, your attitudes and beliefs about what is fair and equitable will influence your readiness to acknowledge the fairness in the other person's position. Your assessment of the likely effects of various strategies will influence the ones you select to argue with your supervisor.

A wide variety of conflict resolution skills has already been covered. For example, active listening is a skill that has wide application in conflict situations (see Unit 7). Similarly, using I-messages rather than accusatory you-messages (see Unit 8) will contribute to effective interpersonal conflict resolution (Noller and Fitzpatrick 1993). Of course, the characteristics of interpersonal competence (Unit 8) are clear and effective conflict resolution techniques. The following discussion identifies additional strategies, the unproductive strategies that should be avoided as well as their productive counterparts.

Avoidance and Fighting Actively

Avoidance may involve actual physical flight: for example, leaving the scene of the conflict (walking out of the apartment or going to another part of the office), falling asleep, or blasting the stereo to drown out all conversation. It may also take the form

ETHICS IN INTERPERSONAL COMMUNICATION

Vote online at http://www.awl.com/devito

A Question of Choice

One way of looking at interpersonal communication ethics is from the perspective of choice. The assumption made in this view is that people have a right to make their own choices. Interpersonal communications are ethical to the extent that they facilitate a person's freedom of choice by presenting that person with accurate information. Communications are unethical to the extent that they interfere with the individual's freedom of choice by preventing the person from securing information relevant to the choices he or she will make. The ethical communicator provides others with the kind of information that is helpful in making their choices.

You have the right to information about yourself that others possess and that influences the choices you'll make. Thus, for example, you have the right to face your accusers, to know the witnesses who will be called to testify against you, to see your credit ratings, and to know what Social Security benefits you'll receive. On the other hand, you don't have the right to information about others, for example, information about whether your neighbors are happy, what they argue about, or how much money they have.

At the same time, you also have the obligation to reveal information that you possess that bears on the choices of your society. Thus, for example, you have an obligation to identify wrongdoing that you witness, to identify someone in a police lineup, to report criminal activity, and to testify at a trial when you possess pertinent information. This information is essential for society to accomplish its purposes and to make its legitimate choices.

What would you do? *Pat and Chris are weekend pot smokers and only smoke when the children are out of the house. Their teenager, however, has heard rumors about the smoking and asks them if they smoke pot. Would it be ethical for Pat and Chris to lie and say they don't smoke? Would it be ethical for them to tell the truth and say they do smoke? If you were one of the parents, what would you do in this situation?*

of emotional or intellectual avoidance, whereby you leave the conflict psychologically by not dealing with the issues raised. Not surprisingly, as avoidance increases, relationship satisfaction decreases (Meeks, Hendrick, and Hendrick 1998).

Nonnegotiation is a special type of avoidance. Here you refuse to discuss the conflict or to listen to the other person's argument. At times, this nonnegotiation takes the form of hammering away at one's own point of view until the other person gives in.

Instead of avoiding the issues, consider taking an active role in your interpersonal conflicts. This is not to say that a cooling-off period isn't at times desirable. It is to say, instead, that if you wish to resolve conflicts, you need to confront them actively. Involve yourself on both sides of the communication exchange. Be an active participant as a speaker and as a listener; voice your own feelings and listen carefully to your partner's feelings.

Another part of active fighting involves the avoidance of silencers. **Silencers** are conflict techniques that literally silence the other individual. Among the wide variety that exists, one frequently used silencer is crying. When a person is unable to deal with a conflict or when winning seems unlikely, he or she may cry and thus silence the other person. Another silencer is to feign extreme emotionalism—to yell and scream and pretend to be losing control of oneself. Still another is to develop some physical reaction—headaches and shortness of breath are probably the most popular. One of the major problems with silencers is that you can never be certain whether they're strategies to win the argument or real physical reactions to which you should pay attention. Regardless of what we do, however, the conflict remains unexamined and unresolved.

Still another part of active fighting involves taking responsibility for your thoughts and feelings. For example, when you disagree with your partner or find fault with her or his behavior, take responsibility for these feelings. Say, for example, "I disagree with . . ." or "I don't like it when you . . ." Avoid statements that deny your responsibility, such as "Everybody thinks you're wrong about . . ." or "Chris thinks you shouldn't . . ."

Force and Talk

When confronted with conflict, many people prefer not to deal with the issues but rather to force their position on the other person. The **force** may be emotional or physical. In either case, however, the issues are avoided, and the person who "wins" is the one who exerts the most force. This is the technique of warring nations, children, and even some normally sensible adults.

More than 50 percent of single and married couples reported that they had experienced physical violence in their relationship. If we add symbolic violence (for example, threatening to hit the other person or throwing something), the percentages are above 60 percent for singles and above 70 percent for marrieds (Marshall and Rose 1987). In another study, 47 percent of a sample of 410 college students reported some experience with violence in a dating relationship (Deal and Wampler 1986). In most cases, the violence was reciprocal—each person in the relationship used violence.

The only real alternative to force is talk. Instead of using force, talk. The qualities of openness, empathy, and positiveness (see Unit 8), for example, are suitable starting points. In addition, be sure to listen actively and openly. This may be especially difficult in conflict situations where tempers may run high and where you may find yourself attacked or at least disagreed with. Here are some suggestions for talking and listening more effectively in the conflict situation.

Act the role of the listener. Also, think as a listener. Turn off the television, stereo, or computer; face the other person. Devote your total attention to what the other person is saying. Make sure you understand what the person is saying and feeling. One way to make sure is obviously to ask questions. Another way is to paraphrase what the other person is saying and ask for confirmation: "You feel that if we pooled our money and didn't have separate savings accounts that you'd feel the relationship would be a more equitable one. Is that the way you feel?"

Express your support or empathy for what the other person is saying and feeling: "I can understand how you feel. I know I control the finances and that can create a feeling of inequality." If appropriate, indicate your agreement: "You're right to be disturbed."

State your thoughts and feelings on the issue as objectively as you can; if you disagree with what the other person said, then say so: "My problem is that when we did have equal access to the finances, you ran up so many bills that we still haven't recovered. To be honest with you, I'm worried the same thing will happen again."

Face-Detracting and Face-Enhancing Strategies

Face-detracting or face-attacking orientation involves treating the other person as incompetent or untrustworthy, as unable or bad (Donahue and Kolt 1992). Such attacks can vary from mildly embarrassing the other person to severely damaging his or her ego or reputation. When such attacks become extreme, they may be similar to verbal aggressiveness—a tactic explained in the next section.

Face-enhancing techniques involve helping the other person to maintain a positive image, an image as competent and trustworthy, able and good. Even when you

One of the most puzzling findings on violence is that many victims interpret it as a sign of love. For some reason, they see being beaten or verbally abused as a sign that their partner is fully in love with them. Also, many victims blame themselves for the violence instead of blaming their partners (Gelles and Cornell 1985). Why do you think this is so? What part does force or violence play in your own interpersonal relationship conflicts?

get what you want, say at bargaining, it's wise to help the other person retain positive face because it makes it less likely that future conflicts will arise (Donahue and Kolt 1992). Not surprisingly, people are more likely to make a greater effort to support the listener's "face" if they like the listener than if they don't (Meyer 1994).

Generally, collectivist cultures place great emphasis on face, especially on maintaining a positive image in public. Face is generally less crucial in individualist cultures such as the United States. Consequently, collectivist peoples are less likely to use conflict strategies such as blame and personal rejection, since these are likely to result in a loss of face. Many collectivists are more likely to use strategies that preserve and enhance one's public image. Those from individualist cultures which favor more open discussion of conflict might be more apt to use argumentativeness and to fight actively. If you're from a collective culture, you're more likely to prefer mediation and bargaining as conflict resolution strategies than would those from individualist cultures who prefer a more adversarial and confrontational conflict style (Leung 1987, Berry, Poortinga, Segall, and Dasen 1992).

Confirming the other person's definition of self (Unit 4), avoiding attack and blame, and using excuses and apologies as appropriate are some generally useful face-enhancing strategies.

Verbal Aggressiveness and Argumentativeness

An especially interesting perspective on conflict is emerging from the work on verbal aggressiveness and argumentativeness (Infante and Rancer 1982, Infante and Wigley 1986, Infante 1988, Rancer 1998). Understanding these concepts will help in understanding some of the reasons things go wrong and some of the ways in which you can use conflict to actually improve your relationships.

TRY IT!
To learn more about verbal aggressiveness, go to www.awl.com/devito.

Verbal Aggressiveness **Verbal aggressiveness** is a method of winning an argument by inflicting psychological pain, by attacking the other person's self-concept. It's a type of disconfirmation (and the opposite of confirmation) in that it seeks to discredit the individual's view of self (see Unit 10). To explore this tendency further, take the accompanying self-test of verbal aggressiveness.

TEST YOURSELF *How Verbally Aggressive Are You?*

This scale is designed to measure how people try to obtain compliance from others. For each statement, indicate the extent to which you feel it's true for you in your attempts to influence others. Use the following scale: 1 = almost never true, 2 = rarely true, 3 = occasionally true, 4 = often true, and 5 = almost always true.

_______ 1. I am extremely careful to avoid attacking individuals' intelligence when I attack their ideas.

_______ 2. When individuals are very stubborn, I use insults to soften the stubbornness.

_______ 3. I try very hard to avoid having other people feel bad about themselves when I try to influence them.

_______ 4. When people refuse to do a task I know is important, without good reason, I tell them they are unreasonable.

_______ 5. When others do things I regard as stupid, I try to be extremely gentle with them.

_______ 6. If individuals I am trying to influence really deserve it, I attack their character.

_______ 7. When people behave in ways that are in very poor taste, I insult them in order to shock them into proper behavior.

_______ 8. I try to make people feel good about themselves even when their ideas are stupid.

_______ 9. When people simply will not budge on a matter of importance, I lose my temper and say rather strong things to them.

_______ 10. When people criticize my shortcomings, I take it in good humor and do not try to get back at them.

_______ 11. When individuals insult me, I get a lot of pleasure out of really telling them off.

_______ 12. When I dislike individuals greatly, I try not to show it in what I say or how I say it.

_______ 13. I like poking fun at people who do things which are very stupid in order to stimulate their intelligence.

_______ 14. When I attack a person's ideas, I try not to damage their self-concepts.

_______ 15. When I try to influence people, I make a great effort not to offend them.

_______ 16. When people do things which are mean or cruel, I attack their character in order to help correct their behavior.

_______ 17. I refuse to participate in arguments when they involve personal attacks.

_______ 18. When nothing seems to work in trying to influence others, I yell and scream in order to get some movement from them.

_______ 19. When I am not able to refute others' positions, I try to make them feel defensive in order to weaken their positions.

______ 20. When an argument shifts to personal attacks, I try very hard to change the subject.

To compute your verbal aggressiveness score, follow these steps:

1. Add the scores on items 2, 4, 6, 7, 9, 11, 13, 16, 18, 19.
2. Add the scores on items 1, 3, 5, 8, 10, 12, 14, 15, 17, 20.
3. Subtract the sum obtained in step 2 from 60.
4. Add the total obtained in step 1 to the result obtained in step 3.

If you scored between 59 and 100, you're high in verbal aggressiveness; if you scored between 39 and 58, you're moderate in verbal aggressiveness; if you scored between 20 and 38, you're low in verbal aggressiveness.

In computing your score, make special note of the characteristics the statements identify in connection with the tendency to act verbally aggressive. Note those inappropriate behaviors you're especially prone to commit. High agreement (4 or 5 on the scale) with statements 2, 4, 6, 7, 9, 11, 13, 16, 18, and 19 and low agreement (1 and 2 on the scale) with statements 1, 3, 5, 8, 10, 12, 14, 15, 17, and 20 will help you highlight any significant verbal aggressiveness you might have. Review previous encounters when you acted verbally aggressive. What effect did such action have on your subsequent interaction? What effect did it have on your relationship with the other person? What alternative ways of getting your point across might you have used? Might these have proved more effective?

From Dominic Infante and C. J. Wrigley, "Verbal Aggressiveness: An Interpersonal Model and Measure" *Communication Monographs* 53 (1986): 61–69. Reprinted by permission of the Speech Communication Association. ■

Character attack, perhaps because it's extremely effective in inflicting psychological pain, is the most popular tactic of verbal aggressiveness. Other tactics include attacking the person's abilities, background, and physical appearance; cursing; teasing; ridiculing; threatening; swearing; and using various nonverbal emblems (Infante, Sabourin, Rudd, and Shannon 1990).

Some researchers have argued that "unless aroused by verbal aggression, a hostile disposition remains latent in the form of unexpressed anger" (Infante, Chandler, and Rudd 1989). There is some evidence to show that people in violent relationships are more often verbally aggressive than people in nonviolent relationships (Sutter and Martin 1998).

Because verbal aggressiveness does not help to resolve conflicts, results in loss of credibility for the person using it, and actually increases the credibility of the target of the aggressiveness, you may wonder why people act aggressively (Infante, Hartley, Martin, Higgins, et al. 1992, Infante, Riddle, Horvath, and Tumlin 1992).

Communicating with an affirming style (for example, smiling, pleasant facial expression, touching, physical closeness, eye contact, nodding, warm and sincere voice, vocal variety) leads others to perceive less verbal aggression in an interaction than when communicating with a nonaffirming style. The assumption people seem to make is that if your actions are affirming, then your messages are also, and if your actions are nonaffirming, then your messages are also (Infante, Rancer, and Jordan 1996).

Argumentativeness Contrary to popular usage, the term **argumentativeness** refers to a quality to be cultivated rather than avoided. Argumentativeness is your willingness to argue for a point of view, your tendency to speak your mind on significant issues. It's the preferred alternative to verbal aggressiveness. Before reading about ways to increase your argumentativeness, take the accompanying self-test, "How Argumentative Are You?"

Persons with disabilities are often singled out for verbal abuse and physical violence. Among the types of violence and verbal abuse identified in one study are physical attacks, denying persons of their rights and opportunities, verbal abuse, and failure to respond to complaints about abuse (Roeher Institute 1995). What do you think contributes to abuse against persons with disabilities? Are these the same factors that contribute to abuse against women, against newly arrived immigrants, and against gay men and lesbians?

TEST YOURSELF *How Argumentative Are You?*

This questionnaire contains statements about controversial issues. Indicate how often each statement is true for you personally according to the following scale: 1 = almost never true, 2 = rarely true, 3 = occasionally true, 4 = often true, and 5 = almost always true.

______ 1. While in an argument, I worry that the person I am arguing with will form a negative impression of me.

______ 2. Arguing over controversial issues improves my intelligence.

______ 3. I enjoy avoiding arguments.

______ 4. I am energetic and enthusiastic when I argue.

______ 5. Once I finish an argument, I promise myself that I will not get into another.

______ 6. Arguing with a person creates more problems for me than it solves.

______ 7. I have a pleasant, good feeling when I win a point in an argument.

______ 8. When I finish arguing with someone, I feel nervous and upset.

_______ 9. I enjoy a good argument over a controversial issue.
_______ 10. I get an unpleasant feeling when I realize I am about to get into an argument.
_______ 11. I enjoy defending my point of view on an issue.
_______ 12. I am happy when I keep an argument from happening.
_______ 13. I do not like to miss the opportunity to argue a controversial issue.
_______ 14. I prefer being with people who rarely disagree with me.
_______ 15. I consider an argument an exciting intellectual challenge.
_______ 16. I find myself unable to think of effective points during an argument.
_______ 17. I feel refreshed and satisfied after an argument on a controversial issue.
_______ 18. I have the ability to do well in an argument.
_______ 19. I try to avoid getting into arguments.
_______ 20. I feel excitement when I expect that a conversation I am in is leading to an argument.

To compute your score, follow these steps:

1. Add your scores on items 2, 4, 7, 9, 11, 13, 15, 17, 18, and 20.
2. Add 60 to the sum obtained in step 1.
3. Add your scores on items 1, 3, 5, 6, 8, 10, 12, 14, 16, and 19.
4. Subtract the total obtained in step 3 from the total obtained in step 2.

Scores between 73 and 100 indicate high argumentativeness. Scores between 56 and 72 indicate moderate argumentativeness. Scores between 20 and 55 indicate low argumentativeness.

How accurately does your score reflect your self-image concerning your tendency to speak up?

From Dominic Infante and Andrew Rancer, "A Conceptualization and Measure of Argumentativeness" *Journal of Personality Assessment* 46 (1982): 72–80. Copyright 1982 Lawrence Erlbaum Associates, Inc. Reprinted by permission of Lawrence Erlbaum Associates, Inc., and the authors. ■

Generally, those who score high in argumentativeness have a strong tendency to state their position on controversial issues and argue against the positions of others. High scorers see arguing as exciting, intellectually challenging, and as an opportunity to win a kind of contest. For them, arguing has a positive impact on their self-concept, has functional outcomes, and is highly ego-involving. They find arguing enjoyable and practical (Rancer, Kosberg, and Baukus 1992).

The low argumentative sees arguing as unpleasant and unsatisfying. Not surprisingly, low argumentatives have little confidence in their ability to argue effectively. They believe that arguing has a negative impact on their self-concept, that it has dysfunctional outcomes, and that it's not very ego-involving. They see arguing as having little enjoyment or practical outcomes. Low argumentatives try to prevent arguments and experience satisfaction not from arguing, but from avoiding arguments.

Both high and low argumentatives may experience communication difficulties. The high argumentative, for example, may argue needlessly, too often, and too forcefully. The low argumentative, on the other hand, may avoid taking a stand even when it seems necessary. Persons scoring somewhere in the middle are probably the most interpersonally skilled and adaptable, arguing when it's necessary but avoiding the many arguments that are needless and repetitive.

Here are some suggestions for cultivating argumentativeness and for preventing it from degenerating into aggressiveness (Infante 1988):

ASK THE RESEARCHER

Bridging the Gap

I'm a police officer charged with the responsibility of improving relationships between the police department and the community. Are there any insights you can offer from your work on argumentativeness and verbal aggressiveness that may help me create a more comfortable and more cordial atmosphere between these two groups?

Argumentativeness involves defending positions on controversial issues, while attacking the positions that other people take on the issues. Verbal aggressiveness involves attacking the self-concept of others, instead of or in addition to their position on controversial issues, in order to inflict psychological pain, humiliation, embarrassment, and other negative feelings. Some recommendations which may prevent or reduce verbal aggression include making people aware of situations and behaviors which are likely to stimulate verbal aggression, such as personal rejection, "hitting below the belt," nonnegotiation, and gunnysacking.

Teach people to deal with conflict through argumentativeness, helping them to argue in a relaxed, friendly, and attentive way. Teach people that if the verbal aggression continues, they can stop communicating. Make sure that people understand exactly what they're arguing about. Allow the other person to speak without interruption, try to use a calm delivery, allow the opponent to save face, and reaffirm the adversary's sense of competence.

—Andrew S. Rancer (Ph.D., Kent State University) is a professor of communication in the School of Communication at the University of Akron, where he teaches courses in interpersonal communication, communication theory, research methods, and training methods in communication. His research centers on the aggressive communication traits of argumentativeness and verbal aggressiveness. He also acts as a consultant to business and industry.

- Treat disagreements as objectively as possible; avoid assuming that because someone takes issue with your position or your interpretation he or she is attacking you as a person.
- Avoid attacking the other person (rather than the person's arguments) even if this would give you a tactical advantage—it will probably backfire at some later time and make your relationship more difficult. Center your arguments on issues rather than personalities.
- Reaffirm the other person's sense of competence; compliment the other person as appropriate.
- Avoid interrupting; allow the other person to state her or his position fully before you respond.
- Stress equality (see Unit 8) and stress the similarities that you have with the other person; stress your areas of agreement before attacking the disagreements.
- Express interest in the other person's position, attitude, and point of view.
- Avoid presenting your arguments too emotionally; using an overly loud voice or interjecting vulgar expressions will prove offensive and eventually ineffective.
- Allow the other person to save face; never humiliate the other person.

Do you use any of the unproductive strategies discussed here in your own interpersonal conflicts? What can you do to improve the way you engage in interpersonal conflict?

◄◄ THINKING BACK

REVIEWING KEY TERMS AND CONCEPTS IN INTERPERSONAL CONFLICT

This unit examined interpersonal conflict, one possible model to follow in trying to resolve conflicts, and some of the popular productive and unproductive conflict strategies.

Nature of Conflict

What is interpersonal conflict?

- Interpersonal conflict is a disagreement between or among connected individuals who each want something that is incompatible with what the other wants.
- Interpersonal conflict is neither good nor bad, but depending on how the disagreements are resolved, the conflict can strengthen or weaken a relationship.
- Conflict can center on disagreements on matters external to the relationship and also on relationship issues such as who's the boss.

- Conflict and the strategies used to resolve it are heavily influenced by culture.
- Before the conflict: try to fight in private, fight when you're ready, know what you're fighting about, and fight about problems that can be solved.
- After the conflict: learn something from the conflict, keep the conflict in perspective, attack your negative feelings, and increase the exchange of rewards.

Conflict Resolution Stages

How do you go about resolving a conflict or solving a problem?

- Define the conflict; define the content and relationship issues in specific terms, avoiding gunnysacking and mind reading, and empathizing with the other person.
- Examine the possible solutions; try to identify as many as possible, look for win-win solutions, and carefully weigh the costs and rewards of each solution.
- Test the solution mentally and in practice to see if it works.
- Evaluate the tested solution from a variety of perspectives.
- Accept the solution and integrate it into your behavior. Or reject the solution and begin again, for example, defining the problem differently or looking in other directions for possible solutions.

Conflict Management Strategies

What are some of the strategies that people use that help and that hinder resolving the conflict?

- Become an active participant in the conflict; don't avoid the issues or the arguments of the other person.
- Use talk to discuss the issues rather than trying to force the other person to accept your position.
- Try to enhance the self-esteem, the face, of the person you're arguing with; avoid strategies that may cause the other person to lose face.
- Argue the issues, focusing as objectively as possible on the points of disagreement; avoid being verbally aggressive or attacking the other person.

APPLYING KEY TERMS AND CONCEPTS IN INTERPERSONAL CONFLICT

1. What characters in television series can you identify who frequently demonstrate verbal aggressiveness? Which characters frequently demonstrate argumentativeness? What distinguishes these types of characters?
2. Recall a recent conflict that you tried to resolve. Did you follow (at least generally) the five stages identified in the model presented in this unit? If not, can you identify the steps you did follow?
3. Men generally score higher in argumentativeness (and in verbal aggressiveness) than women. Men are also more apt to be perceived (by both men and women) as more argumentative and verbally aggressive than women (Nicotera and Rancer 1994). Why do you think this is so?
4. What changes would you like to see your relational partners (friends, family members, romantic partners) make in their own verbal aggressiveness and argumentativeness? What might you do to more effectively regulate your own verbal aggressiveness and argumentativeness?
5. Access ERIC, Medline, Psychlit, or Sociofile and locate an article dealing with interpersonal conflict. What can you learn about conflict and interpersonal communication from this article?
6. Visit some game Web sites (for example, http://www.games-domain.co.uk or http://www.gamepen.com/yellowpages/) and examine the rules of the games. What kinds of conflict strategies do these game rules embody?
7. A variation on face-detracting strategies is to hit the other person below the belt, a technique referred to as **beltlining** (Bach and Wyden 1968). Much like prize fighters in a ring, each of us has a "belt line." When you hit someone below it, you can seriously damage the relationship. Have you ever witnessed beltlining? What happened?
8. Have you ever been accused of failing to see what the "real" conflict is about? Were you accused of misunderstanding the content conflict or the relationship conflict?
9. How might failing to appreciate gender and cultural variations in approaches to conflict lead you to misread the verbal and nonverbal cues of the other person? Can you imagine an experience where this could happen?
10. How would you go about finding answers to the following questions?
    - Are men or women more likely to use avoidance (or blame, force, manipulation, ridicule, silencers, beltlining, gunnysacking, or personal rejection) as a romantic conflict strategy?

- Are people with high self-esteem likely to have more or fewer interpersonal conflicts than those with low self-esteem?
- Are high argumentatives more satisfied with their communication than are those who are high in verbal aggressiveness?
- Are highly educated people more likely to use argumentativeness than are less educated people?
- How do man-to-man and woman-to-woman friendship, romantic, family, or business conflicts differ from each other?

EXPERIENCING KEY TERMS AND CONCEPTS IN INTERPERSONAL CONFLICT

Go to www.awl.com/devito

Exercise No. 22, "Male and Female," will illustrate some of the causes of communication difficulties between men and women. Exercise No. 26, "Analyzing a Conflict Episode," provides a script appropriate for analyzing productive and unproductive conflict strategies. Exercise No. 28, "The Television Relationship," is useful for analyzing the numerous conflict episodes as they're developed and resolved on television.

UNIT 20
FRIENDS AND LOVERS

Waiting to Exhale (1995)

TRUE LOVE COMES QUIETLY, WITHOUT BANNERS OR FLASHING LIGHTS. IF YOU HEAR BELLS, GET YOUR EARS CHECKED.

--ERICH SEGAL

Friends
Lovers

IN WAITING TO EXHALE, based on Terry McMillan's best-selling novel and directed by Forest Whitaker, four women in Arizona (Whitney Houston, Angela Bassett, Loretta Devine, and Lela Rochon) reveal the difficulties in finding suitable relationship partners. At the same time that the film depicts the difficulties in finding romantic love, it illustrates how friendships are developed, maintained, and strengthened. In this unit we also look at friendship and love, inquiring into some of the types of love and friendship you may encounter and some of the ways in which you may nurture such relationships.

FRIENDS

THINKING AHEAD ▸▸
What's a friend? What distinguishes a friend from someone who is just an acquaintance?

Friendship has engaged the attention and imagination of poets, novelists, and artists of all kinds. In television, our most influential mass medium, friendships have become almost as important as romantic pairings. Friendship now engages the attention of a range of interpersonal communication researchers. Here are a selection of findings to illustrate the range of topics addressed, taken from an extensive literature review (Blieszner and Adams 1992). In reviewing this list, consider the possible reasons the results were obtained and what implications they may have for developing, maintaining, and repairing friendship relationships.

- Young single men see their friends more often than young married men do (Farrell and Rosenberg 1981).
- Women are more expressive in their friendships than are men. Men talk about business, politics, and sports, whereas women talk about feelings and relationship issues (Fox, Gibbs, and Auerbach 1985).
- When women were asked about the most important benefit they derive from their friendships, conversation was highlighted and included listening in a supportive way, enhancing feelings of self-esteem, and validating their experiences (Johnson and Aries 1983).
- Men and women did not differ in what they saw as the most important characteristics of their friendships (Albert and Moss 1990).
- Similarity in personality was not found to be a strong basis for selecting friends, but similarity of needs and beliefs was (Henderson and Furnham 1982). Conversely, another study found that friends with dissimilar attitudes were preferred in recent friendships, whereas in established friendships similar attitudes were preferred (McCarthy and Duck 1976).
- The average number of friends of college students varies from 2.88 to 9.1 (Blieszner and Adams 1992); for older persons, the average varies between 1 and 12.2 (Adams 1987).

Throughout your life you'll meet many people, but out of this wide array you'll develop relatively few relationships you would call friendships. Yet despite the low number of friendships you may form, their importance is great.

The Nature of Friendship

Friendship is an interpersonal relationship between two persons that is mutually productive and characterized by mutual positive regard.

Friendship is an interpersonal relationship; communication interactions must have taken place between the people. Further, the interpersonal relationship involves a "personalistic focus" (Wright 1978, 1984). Friends react to each other as complete persons, as unique, genuine, and irreplaceable individuals.

Friendships must be mutually productive; this qualifier emphasizes that, by definition, they cannot be destructive either to oneself or to the other person. Once destructiveness enters into a relationship, it can no longer be characterized as friendship. Lover relationships, marriage relationships, parent-child relationships, and just about any other possible relationship can be either destructive or productive. But friendship must enhance the potential of each person and can only be productive.

Friendships are characterized by mutual positive regard. Liking people is essential if we are to call them friends. Three major characteristics of friends—trust, emotional support, and sharing of interests (Blieszner and Adams 1992)—testify to this positive regard.

The closer friends are the more *interdependent* they become; that is, when friends are especially close, the actions of one will impact more significantly on the other than they would if the friends were just casual acquaintances. At the same time, however, the closer friends are the more *independent* they are of, for example, the attitudes and behaviors of others. Also, they're less influenced by the societal rules that govern more casual relationships (see Unit 1 on the developmental definition of interpersonal communication). Close friends are likely to make up their own rules for interacting with each other; they decide what they will talk about and when, what they can say to each other without offending and what they can't, when and for what reasons they can call each other, and so on.

In North America, friendships clearly are a matter of choice; you choose—within limits—who your friends will be. The density of the cities and the ease of communication and relocation makes friendships voluntary, a matter of choice. But in many parts of the world—small villages miles away from urban centers, where people are born, live, and die without venturing much beyond this small village, for example—relationships aren't voluntary. In these cases, you simply form relationships with those in your village. Here you don't have the luxury of selecting certain people to interact with and others to ignore. You must interact with and form relationships with members of the community simply because these people are the only ones you come into contact with on a regular basis (Moghaddam, Taylor, and Wright 1993).

Three Types of Friendships Not all friendships are the same. But how do they differ? One way of answering this question is by distinguishing among the three major types of friendship: reciprocity, receptivity, and association (Reisman 1979, 1981).

The friendship of *reciprocity* is the ideal type, characterized by loyalty, self-sacrifice, mutual affection, and generosity. A friendship of reciprocity is based on equality: each individual shares equally in giving and receiving the benefits and rewards of the relationship. In the friendship of *receptivity,* in contrast, there is an imbalance in giving and receiving; one person is the primary giver and one the primary receiver. This imbalance, however, is a positive one because each person gains something from the relationship. The different needs of both the person who receives and the person who gives affection are satisfied. This is the friendship that may develop between a teacher and a student or between a doctor and a patient. In fact, a difference in status is essential for the friendship of receptivity to develop.

The friendship of *association* is a transitory one. It might be described as a friendly relationship rather than a true friendship. Associative friendships are the kind we often have with classmates, neighbors, or coworkers. There is no great loyalty, no great trust, no great giving or receiving. The association is cordial but not intense.

TRY IT!
To learn more about the needs that friendships serve, go to www.awl.com/devito.

The Needs Friendships Serve You develop and maintain friendships to satisfy those needs that can only be satisfied by certain people. On the basis of your experiences or your predictions, you select as friends those who will help to satisfy your basic growth needs. Selecting friends on the basis of need satisfaction is similar to choosing a marriage partner, an employee, or any person who may be in a position to satisfy your needs. Thus, for example, if you need to be the center of attention or to be popular, you might select friends who allow you, and even encourage you, to be the center of attention or who tell you, verbally and nonverbally, that you're popular.

As your needs change, the qualities you look for in friendships also change. In many instances, old friends are dropped from your close circle to be replaced by new friends who better serve these new needs. We can also look at needs in terms of the five values or rewards we seek to gain through our friendships: utility, affirmation, ego support, stimulation, and security (Wright 1978, 1984).

Utility Value A friend may have special talents, skills, or resources that prove useful to us in achieving our specific goals and needs. We may, for example, become friends with someone who is particularly bright because such a person might assist us in getting better grades, in solving our personal problems, or in getting a better job.

Affirmation Value A friend's behavior toward us acts as a mirror that affirms our personal value and helps us to recognize our attributes. A friend may, for example, help us to see more clearly our leadership abilities, athletic prowess, or sense of humor.

Ego-Support Value By behaving in a supportive, encouraging, and helpful manner, friends help us to view ourselves as worthy and competent individuals.

Stimulation Value A friend introduces us to new ideas and new ways of seeing the world and helps us to expand our worldview. A friend brings us into contact with previously unfamiliar issues, concepts, and experiences—for example, modern art, foreign cultures, new foods.

Security Value A friend does nothing to hurt us or to emphasize or call attention to our inadequacies or weaknesses. Because of this security value, friends can interact freely and openly without having to worry about betrayal or negative responses.

Stages and Communication in Friendship Development

Friendships develop over time in stages. At one end of the friendship continuum are strangers, or two persons who have just met, and at the other end are intimate friends. What happens between these two extremes?

As you progress from the initial contact stage to intimate friendship, the depth and breadth of communications increase (see Unit 16). You talk about issues that are closer and closer to your inner core. Similarly, the number of communication topics increases as your friendship becomes closer. As depth and breadth increase, so does the satisfaction you derive from the friendship.

Earlier (Unit 15), the concept of dynamic tension in relationships was discussed. It was pointed out that there is a tension between, for example, autonomy and connection—the desire to be an individual but also to be connected to another person. Friendships are also defined by dynamic tensions (Rawlins 1983). One tension is between the impulse to be open and to reveal personal thoughts and feelings on the one hand, and the impulse to protect oneself by not revealing personal information on the other. Also, there is the tension between being open and candid with your friend and being discreet. These contradictory impulses make it clear that friendships don't follow a straight path of always increasing openness, for example, or candor. This is not

Consider the activities you share with friends. How similar are the activities you engage in with those identified here in research conducted some 20 years ago (Parlee 1979)? Beginning with the most frequent, the ten most frequently identified activities shared with friends were: had an intimate talk, had a friend ask you to do something for him or her, went to dinner in a restaurant, asked your friend to do something for you, had a meal together at home or at your friend's home, went to a movie, play, or concert, went drinking together, went shopping, participated in sports, and watched a sporting event. How do you think this list would differ from one compiled today?

to say that openness and candor don't increase as you progress from initial to casual to close friendships; they do. But the pattern does not follow a straight line; throughout the friendship development process, there are tensions that periodically restrict openness and candor.

Similarly, there are regressions that may temporarily pull the friendship back to a less intimate stage. Friendships stabilize at a level that is, ideally at least, comfortable to both persons; some friendships will remain casual and others will remain close. Keep in mind that although friendship is presented in stages, the progression is not always a straight line to ever increasing intimacy.

With these qualifications in mind, we can discuss three stages of friendship development and integrate the ten characteristics of effective interpersonal communication identified earlier (Unit 8). The assumption made here is that as the friendship progresses from initial contact and acquaintanceship through casual friendship to close and intimate friendship, the qualities of effective interpersonal communication increase. However, there is no assumption made that close relationships are necessarily the preferred type or that they're better than casual or temporary relationships. We need all types.

Initial Contact and Acquaintanceship The first stage of friendship development is obviously an initial meeting of some kind. This does not mean that what has happened prior to the encounter is unimportant—quite the contrary. In fact, your prior history of friendships, your personal needs, and your readiness for friendship development are extremely important in determining whether the relationship will develop.

At the initial stage, the characteristics of effective interpersonal communication are usually present to only a small degree. You're guarded rather than open or expressive, lest you reveal aspects of yourself that might be viewed negatively. Because you don't yet know the other person, your ability to empathize with or to orient your-

ASK THE RESEARCHER

Building Friendships

I don't seem to have as many friends as others in my class say they have and I'm wondering if there's anything I can do to make myself more desirable as a friend?

Making new friends and sustaining old friendships are challenges most people face throughout their lives. So it's important to have realistic expectations about how friendships develop. Friendships don't occur overnight; they take time and effort. Seek out situations where you're likely to encounter persons who are similar to you in important ways—for example, they also might be students, have small children, or enjoy sports or music. Allow time in your schedule for conversation with persons you want to know better. Getting to class or to meetings early and lingering afterward allows for "small talk" which lets you learn things about each other while speaking about unthreatening topics. If you enjoy talking with each other, small talk can grow into more involving conversation. A next step in making friends involves inviting the person to do something together that you feel you both would enjoy apart from where you routinely see each other. Find the time, make the effort, and don't rush things in making friends.

For further information see W. K. Rawlins, *Friendship Matters: Communication, Dialectics, and the Life Course* (Hawthorne, NY: Aldine de Gruyter, 1992), and W. K. Rawlins, "Being There and Growing Apart: Sustaining Friendships During Adulthood," in *Communication and Relational Maintenance,* ed. D. J. Canary and L. Stafford (San Diego: Academic Press, 1994), pp. 275–294.

—William K. Rawlins (Ph.D., Temple University) is a professor of communication at Purdue University and teaches courses in interpersonal and relational communication, dialogue and experience, communication theory, and qualitative/interpretive research methods. He has published extensively about the unique challenges and dialectical tensions of communicating in friendships. wrawlins@purdue.edu.

self significantly to the other is limited, and the relationship—at this stage, at least—is probably viewed as too temporary to be worth the effort. Because the other person is not well known to you, supportiveness, positiveness, and equality would all be difficult to manifest in any meaningful sense. The characteristics demonstrated are probably more the result of politeness than any genuine expression of positive regard.

At this stage, there is little genuine immediacy; the people see themselves as separate and distinct rather than as a unit. The confidence that is demonstrated is probably more a function of the individual personalities than of the relationship. Because the relationship is so new and because the people don't know each other very well, the interaction is often characterized by awkwardness—for example, overlong pauses, uncertainty over the topics to be discussed, and ineffective exchanges of speaker and listener roles.

Casual Friendship In this second stage, there is a dyadic consciousness, a clear sense of "we-ness," of togetherness; communication demonstrates a sense of immediacy. At this stage, you participate in activities as a unit rather than as separate individuals. A casual friend is one we would go with to the movies, sit with in the cafeteria or in class, or ride home with from school.

At this casual-friendship stage, the qualities of effective interpersonal interaction begin to be seen more clearly. You start to express yourself openly and become interested in the other person's disclosures. You begin to own your feelings and thoughts and respond openly to his or her communications. Because you're beginning to understand this person, you empathize and demonstrate significant other-orientation. You also demonstrate supportiveness and develop a genuinely positive attitude toward both the other person and mutual communication situations. As you learn this person's needs and wants, you can stroke more effectively.

There is an ease at this stage, a coordination in the interaction between the two persons. You communicate with confidence, maintain appropriate eye contact and flexibility in body posture and gesturing, and use few adaptors signaling discomfort.

Close and Intimate Friendship At the stage of close and intimate friendship, there is an intensification of the casual friendship; you and your friend see yourselves more as an exclusive unit, and each of you derives greater benefits (for example, emotional support) from intimate friendship than from casual friendship (Hays 1989).

Because you know each other well (for example, you know one another's values, opinions, attitudes), your uncertainty about each other has been significantly reduced—you're able to predict each other's behaviors with considerable accuracy. This knowledge makes possible significant interaction management. Similarly, you can read the other's nonverbal signals more accurately and can use these signals as guides to your interactions—avoiding certain topics at certain times or offering consolation on the basis of facial expressions. At this stage, you exchange significant messages of affection, messages that express fondness, liking, loving, and caring for the other person. Openness and expressiveness are more clearly in evidence.

You become more other-oriented and willing to make significant sacrifices for the other person. You'll go far out of your way for the benefit of this friend, and the friend does the same for you. You empathize and exchange perspectives a great deal more, and you expect in return that your friend will also empathize with you. With a genuinely positive feeling for this individual, your supportiveness and positive stroking become spontaneous. Because you see yourselves as an exclusive unit, equality and immediacy are in clear evidence. You view this friend as one who is important in your life; as a result, conflicts—inevitable in all close relationships—become important to work out and resolve through compromise and empathic understanding rather than through, for example, refusal to negotiate or a show of force.

You're willing to respond openly, confidently, and expressively to this person and to own your feelings and thoughts. Your supportiveness and positiveness are genuine expressions of the closeness you feel for this person. Each person in an intimate friendship is truly equal; each can initiate and each can respond; each can be active and each can be passive; each speaks and each listens.

Culture and Friendship

Your friendships and the way you look at friendships will be influenced by your culture. In the United States you can be friends with someone yet never really be expected to go much out of your way for this person. Many Middle Easterners, Asians, and Latin Americans would consider going significantly out of their way an absolutely essential ingredient in friendship; if you're not willing to sacrifice for your friend, then this person is really not your friend (Dresser 1996).

Generally, friendships are closer in collectivist cultures than in individualist cultures (see Unit 3). In their emphasis on the group and on cooperating, collectivist cultures foster the development of close friendship bonds. Members of a collectivist culture are expected to help others in the group. When you help or do things for someone else, you increase your own attraction for this person (recall our discussion in Unit 16 on attraction and reinforcement), and this is certainly a good start for a friendship. Of course, the culture continues to reward these close associations.

Members of individualist cultures, on the other hand, are expected to look out for Number One, themselves. Consequently, they're more likely to compete and to try to do better than each other—conditions that don't support, generally at least, the development of friendships.

Do recall as we noted earlier (Unit 3) that these characteristics are extremes; most people have both collectivist and individualist values but have them to different degrees, and that is what we are talking about here—differences in degree of collectivist and individualist orientation.

Gender and Friendship

Gender influences your friendships and the way you look at friendships. Perhaps the best-documented finding—already noted in our discussion of self-disclosure—is that women self-disclose more than do men (for example, Dolgin, Meyer, and Schwartz 1991). This difference holds throughout male and female friendships. Male friends self-disclose less often and with less intimate details than female friends do. Men generally don't view intimacy as a necessary quality of their friendships (Hart 1990).

WEB EXPLORATION
To learn more about gender and friendship, go to www.awl.com/devito.

Women engage in significantly more affectional behaviors with their friends than do males; this difference may account for the greater difficulty men experience in beginning and maintaining close friendships (Hays 1989). Women engage in more casual communication; they also share greater intimacy and more confidences with their friends than do men. Communication, in all its forms and functions, seems a much more important dimension of women's friendships.

When women and men were asked to evaluate their friendships, women rated their same-sex friendships higher in general quality, intimacy, enjoyment, and nurturance than did men (Sapadin 1988). Men, in contrast, rated their opposite-sex friendships higher in quality, enjoyment, and nurturance than did women. Both men and women rated their opposite-sex friendships similarly in intimacy. These differences may be due, in part, to our society's suspicion of male friendships; as a result, a man may be reluctant to admit to having close relationship bonds with another man.

Men's friendships are often built around shared activities—attending a ball game, playing cards, working on a project at the office. Women's friendships, on the other hand, are built more around a sharing of feelings, support, and "personalism." Similarity in status, in willingness to protect one's friend in uncomfortable situations, in academic major, and even in proficiency in playing the game Password were significantly related to the relationship closeness of male-male friends but not of female-female or female-male friends (Griffin and Sparks 1990). Perhaps similarity is a criterion for male friendships but not for female or mixed-sex friendships.

The ways in which men and women develop and maintain their friendships will undoubtedly change considerably—as will all sex-related variables—in the next several years. Perhaps there will be a further differentiation or perhaps an increase in similarities. In the meantime, given the present state of research in gender differences, we need to be careful not to exaggerate and to treat small differences as if they were highly significant. We need to avoid stereotypes and the stress on opposites to the neglect of the huge number of similarities in men and women (Wright 1988, Deaux and LaFrance 1998).

Further, friendship researchers warn that even when we find differences, the reasons for them aren't always clear (Blieszner and Adams 1992). An interesting example is the finding that middle-aged men have more friends than middle-aged women and that women have more intimate friendships (Fischer and Oliker 1983). But why is this so? Do men have more friends because they're friendlier than women or because

ETHICS IN INTERPERSONAL COMMUNICATION

Vote online at http://www.awl.com/devito

Gossip

There can be no doubt that we spend a great deal of time gossiping. In fact, gossiping seems universal among all cultures (Laing 1993), and among some it's a commonly accepted ritual (Hall 1993). Gossip may be defined as social evaluations about a person who is not a party to or present during the conversation (Eder and Enke 1991). Gossip generally occurs when two people talk about a third party and profit in some way—for example, to hear more gossip, gain social status or control, have fun, cement social bonds (Rosnow 1977, Miller and Wilcox 1986), or make social comparisons (Leaper and Holliday 1995).

What would you do? *Pete and Paul, who have been friends ever since high school, are now competing for the position of regional manager. Pete intends to stay with the company and hopefully move up the hierarchy. Paul wants the job as a bargaining chip for a job he wants with a rival organization. If this were known, Paul would never be considered for the job because it involves a lot of in-house training. Would Pete be ethical in letting this information be more widely known? If you were Pete what would you do in this situation?*

How would you describe your female friends? Your male friends?

◀◀ THINKING BACK

THINKING AHEAD ▶▶

What is love? How would you describe yourself as a lover?

they have more opportunities to develop such friendships? Do women have more intimate friends because they have more opportunities to pursue such friendships or because they have a greater psychological capacity for intimacy?

LOVERS

Of all the qualities of interpersonal relationships, none seems as important as love. "We are all born for love," noted famed British prime minister Disraeli; "It is the principle of existence and its only end." It's also an interpersonal relationship developed, maintained, and sometimes destroyed through communication.

WEB EXPLORATION
To learn more about types of love, go to www.awl.com/devito.

Types of Love

Although there are many theories about love, the one that has captured the attention of interpersonal researchers was one proposing that there is not one but six types of love (Lee 1976). View the descriptions of each type as broad characterizations that are generally but not always true. As a preface to this discussion of the types of love, you may wish to respond to the self-test "What Kind of Lover Are You?"

TEST YOURSELF *What Kind of Lover Are You?*

Respond to each of the following statements with *T* for true (if you believe the statement to be a generally accurate representation of your attitudes about love) or *F* for false (if you believe the statement does not adequately represent your attitudes about love).

______ 1. My lover and I have the right physical "chemistry" between us.
______ 2. I feel that my lover and I were meant for each other.
______ 3. My lover and I really understand each other.
______ 4. I believe that what my lover doesn't know about me won't hurt him or her.
______ 5. My lover would get upset if he or she knew of some of the things I've done with other people.

One research program has identified love as a combination of intimacy, passion, and commitment (Sternberg 1986, 1988). Intimacy is the emotional aspect of love and includes sharing, communicating, and mutual support; it's a sense of closeness and connection. Passion is the motivational aspect and consists of physical attraction and romantic passion. Commitment is the cognitive aspect and consists of the decisions you make concerning your lover. When you have a relationship characterized by intimacy only, you have essentially a liking relationship. When you have only passion, you have a relationship of infatuation. When you have only commitment, you have empty love. When you have all three components to about equal degrees, you have complete or consummate love. What do you think of this position?

_______ 6. When my lover gets too dependent on me, I want to back off a little.
_______ 7. I expect to always be friends with my lover.
_______ 8. Our love is really a deep friendship, not a mysterious, mystical emotion.
_______ 9. Our love relationship is the most satisfying because it developed from a good friendship.
_______ 10. In choosing my lover, I believed it was best to love someone with a similar background.
_______ 11. An important factor in choosing a partner is whether or not he or she would be a good parent.
_______ 12. One consideration in choosing my lover was how he or she would reflect on my career.
_______ 13. Sometimes I get so excited about being in love with my lover that I can't sleep.
_______ 14. When my lover doesn't pay attention to me, I feel sick all over.
_______ 15. I cannot relax if I suspect that my lover is with someone else.
_______ 16. I would rather suffer myself than let my lover suffer.

_______ 17. When my lover gets angry with me, I still love him or her fully and unconditionally.

_______ 18. I would endure all things for the sake of my lover.

This scale, from Hendrick and Hendrick (1990), is based on the work of Lee (1976), as is the following discussion of the six types of love. The scale is designed to enable you to identify those styles that best reflect your own beliefs about love. The statements refer to the six types of love that we discuss below: eros, ludus, storge, pragma, mania, and agape. "True" answers represent your agreement and "false" answers represent your disagreement with the type of love to which the statements refer. Statements 1–3 are characteristic of the eros lover. If you answered "true" to these statements, you have a strong eros component to your love style. If you answered "false," you have a weak eros component. Statements 4–6 refer to ludus love, 7–9 refer to storge love, 10–12 to pragma love, 13–15 to manic love, and 16–18 to agapic love. ■

Eros: Beauty and Sexuality Like Narcissus, who fell in love with the beauty of his own image, the erotic lover focuses on beauty and physical attractiveness, sometimes to the exclusion of qualities you might consider more important and more lasting. Also like Narcissus, the erotic lover has an idealized image of beauty that is unattainable in reality. Consequently, the erotic lover often feels unfulfilled. Not surprisingly, erotic lovers are particularly sensitive to physical imperfections in the ones they love.

Ludus: Entertainment and Excitement Ludus love is experienced as a game, as fun. The better he or she can play the game, the greater the enjoyment. Love is not to be taken too seriously; emotions are to be held in check lest they get out of hand and make trouble; passions never rise to the point where they get out of control. A ludic lover is self-controlled, always aware of the need to manage love rather than allow it to be in control. Perhaps because of this need to control love, some researchers have proposed that ludic love tendencies may reveal tendencies to sexual aggression (Sarwer, Kalichman, Johnson, Early, et al. 1993). Not surprisingly, the ludic lover retains a partner only as long as the partner is interesting and amusing. When interest fades, it's time to change partners. Perhaps because love is a game, sexual fidelity is of little importance. In fact, recent research shows that people who score high on ludic love are more likely to engage in "extradyadic" dating and sex than those who score low on ludus (Wiederman and Hurd 1999).

Storge: Peaceful and Slow Storge love lacks passion and intensity. Storgic lovers don't set out to find lovers but to establish a companionable relationship with someone they know and with whom they can share interests and activities. Storgic love is a gradual process of unfolding thoughts and feelings; the changes seem to come so slowly and so gradually that it's often difficult to define exactly where the relationship is at any point in time. Sex in storgic relationships comes late, and when it comes, it assumes no great importance.

Pragma: Practical and Traditional The pragma lover is practical and seeks a relationship that will work. Pragma lovers want compatibility and a relationship in which their important needs and desires will be satisfied. They're concerned with the social qualifications of a potential mate even more than with personal qualities; family and background are extremely important to the pragma lover, who relies not so much on feelings as on logic. The pragma lover views love as a useful relationship, one that makes the rest of life easier. So the pragma lover asks such questions of a potential mate as "Will this person earn a good living?" "Can this person cook?" "Will this person help me advance in my career?" Pragma lovers' relationships rarely deteriorate. This is partly because pragma lovers choose their mates carefully and emphasize similarities. Another reason is that they have realistic romantic expectations.

Mania: Elation and Depression Mania is characterized by extreme highs and extreme lows. The manic lover loves intensely and at the same time intensely worries about the loss of the love. This fear often prevents the manic lover from deriving as much pleasure as possible from the relationship. With little provocation, the manic lover may experience extreme jealousy. Manic love is obsessive; the manic lover has to possess the beloved completely. In return, the manic lover wishes to be possessed, to be loved intensely. The manic lover's poor self-image seems capable of being improved only by love; self-worth comes from being loved rather than from any sense of inner satisfaction. Because love is so important, danger signs in a relationship are often ignored; the manic lover believes that if there is love, then nothing else matters.

Agape: Compassionate and Selfless Agape is a compassionate, egoless, self-giving love. The agapic lover loves even people with whom he or she has no close ties. This lover loves the stranger on the road even though they will probably never meet again. Agape is a spiritual love, offered without concern for personal reward or gain. This lover loves without expecting that the love will be reciprocated. Jesus, Buddha, and Gandhi practiced and preached this unqualified love, agape (Lee 1976). In one sense, agape is more a philosophical kind of love than a love that most people have the strength to achieve.

Love Styles and Personality In reading about the love styles, you may have felt that certain personality types are likely to favor one type of love over another. Here are personality traits that research finds people assign to each love style. Try identifying which personality traits people think go with each of the six love styles: eros, ludus, storge, pragma, mania, and agape.

______ 1. inconsiderate, secretive, dishonest, selfish, and dangerous
______ 2. honest, loyal, mature, caring, loving, and understanding
______ 3. jealous, possessive, obsessed, emotional, and dependent
______ 4. sexual, exciting, loving, happy, optimistic
______ 5. committed, giving, caring, self-sacrificing, and loving
______ 6. family-oriented, planning, careful, hard-working, and concerned

Very likely you perceived these personality factors in the same way as did the participants in research from which these traits were drawn (Taraban and Hendrick 1995): 1 = ludus, 2 = storge, 3 = mania, 4 = eros, 5 = agape, and 6 = pragma. Do note, of course, that these results do not imply that ludus lovers are inconsiderate, secretive, and dishonest. They merely mean that people think of ludus lovers as inconsiderate, secretive, and dishonest.

Love Styles in Combination Each of these varieties of love can combine with others to form new and different patterns (for example, manic and ludic or storge and pragma). These six, however, identify the major types of love and illustrate the complexity of any love relationship. The six styles should also make it clear that different people want different things, that each person seeks satisfaction in a unique way. The love that may seem lifeless or crazy or boring to you may be ideal for someone else.

At the same time, another person may see these very same negative qualities in the love you're seeking.

Love changes. A relationship that began as pragma may develop into ludus or eros. A relationship that began as erotic may develop into mania or storge. One approach sees this as a developmental process having three major stages (Duck 1986):

First stage	Initial attraction: eros, mania, and ludus
Second stage	Storge (as the relationship develops)
Third stage	Pragma (as relationship bonds develop)

Love and Communication

How do you communicate when you're in love? What do you say? What do you do nonverbally? According to research, you exaggerate your beloved's virtues and minimize his or her faults. You share emotions and experiences and speak tenderly, with an extra degree of courtesy, to each other; "please," "thank you," and similar politenesses abound. You frequently use "personalized communication." This type of communication includes secrets you keep from other people and messages that have meaning only within your specific relationship (Knapp, Ellis, and Williams 1980). You also create and use personal idioms, those words, phrases, and gestures that carry meaning only for the particular relationship and that say you have a special language that signifies your special bond (Hopper, Knapp, and Scott 1981). When outsiders try to use personal idioms—as they sometimes do—the expressions seem inappropriate, at times even an invasion of privacy.

You engage in significant self-disclosure. There is more confirmation and less disconfirmation among lovers than among either nonlovers or those who are going through romantic breakups. You're also highly aware of what is and is not appropriate to the one you love. You know how to reward, but also how to punish, each other. In short, you know what to do to obtain the reaction you want.

Among your most often used means for communicating love are telling the person face to face or by telephone (in one survey 79 percent indicated they did it this way), expressing supportiveness, and talking things out and cooperating (Marston, Hecht, and Robers 1987).

Nonverbally, you also communicate your love. Prolonged and focused eye contact is perhaps the clearest nonverbal indicator of love. So important is eye contact that its avoidance almost always triggers a "what's wrong?" response. You also have longer periods of silence than you do with friends (Guerrero 1997).

You grow more aware not only of your loved one but also of your own physical self. Your muscle tone is heightened, for example. When you're in love you engage in preening gestures, especially immediately prior to meeting your lover, and you position your body attractively—stomach pulled in, shoulders square, legs arranged in appropriate masculine or feminine positions. Your speech may even have a somewhat different vocal quality. There is some evidence to show that sexual excitement enlarges the nasal membranes, which introduces a certain nasal quality into the voice (M. Davis 1973).

You eliminate socially taboo adaptors, at least in the presence of the loved one. You would curtail, for example, scratching your head, picking your teeth, cleaning your ears, and passing wind. Interestingly enough, these adaptors often return after the lovers have achieved a permanent relationship.

You touch more frequently and more intimately (Guerrero 1997). You also use more "tie signs," nonverbal gestures that show that you're together, such as holding hands, walking with arms entwined, kissing, and the like. You may even dress alike. The styles of clothes and even the colors selected by lovers are more similar than those worn by nonlovers.

Culture and Love

Like friendship, love is heavily influenced by culture (Dion and Dion 1996). Let's consider some of the cultural influences on the way you look at love and perhaps on the love you're seeking or maintaining. Although most of the research on these love styles has been done in the United States, some research has been conducted in other cultures (Bierhoff and Klein 1991). Here is just a sampling of the research findings—just enough to illustrate that culture is an important factor in love. Asians have been found to be more friendship oriented in their love style than are Europeans (Dion and Dion 1993b). Members of individualist cultures (for example, Europeans) are likely to place greater emphasis on romantic love and on individual fulfillment. Members of collectivist cultures are likely to spread their love over a large network of relatives (Dion and Dion 1993a).

One study finds a love style among Mexicans characterized as calm, compassionate, and deliberate (Leon, Philbrick, Parra, Escobedo, et al. 1994). In comparisons between loves styles in the United States and France, it was found that subjects from the United States scored higher on storge and mania than the French; in contrast, the French scored higher on agape (Murstein, Merighi, and Vyse 1991). Caucasian women, compared to African American women, scored higher on mania, whereas African American women scored higher on agape. Caucasian and African American men, however, scored very similarly; no statistically significant differences have been found (Morrow, Clark, and Brock 1995).

Gender and Love

Gender is another factor that influences love (Dion and Dion 1996). In the United States, the differences between men and women in love are considered great. In poetry, novels, and the mass media, women and men are depicted as acting very differently when falling in love, being in love, and ending a love relationship. As Lord Byron put it in *Don Juan,* "Man's love is of man's life a thing apart, / 'Tis woman's whole existence." Women are portrayed as emotional, men as logical. Women are supposed to love intensely; men are supposed to love with detachment.

Women and men seem to experience love to a similar degree (Rubin 1973). However, women indicate greater love than men do for their same-sex friends. This may reflect a real difference between the sexes, or it may be a function of the greater social restrictions on men. A man is not supposed to admit his love for another man. Women are permitted greater freedom to communicate their love for other women.

Men and women also differ in the types of love they prefer (Hendrick, Hendrick, Foote, and Slapion-Foote 1984). For example, on one version of the love self-test presented earlier, men have been found to score higher on erotic and ludic love, whereas women score higher on manic, pragmatic, and storgic love. No difference has been found for agapic love.

Another gender difference frequently noted is that of romanticism. Before reading about this topic, you may wish to take the accompanying self-test, "How Romantic Are You?"

TEST YOURSELF *How Romantic Are You?*

Indicate the extent to which you agree or disagree with each of the following beliefs. Use the following scale: agree strongly = 7, agree a good deal = 6, agree somewhat = 5, neither agree nor disagree = 4, disagree somewhat = 3, disagree a good deal = 2, disagree strongly = 1.

______ 1. I don't need to know someone for a period of time before I fall in love with him or her.

_______ 2. If I were in love with someone, I would commit myself to him or her even if my parents and friends disapproved of the relationship.

_______ 3. Once I experience "true love," I could never experience it again, to the same degree, with another person.

_______ 4. I believe that to be truly in love is to be in love forever.

_______ 5. If I love someone, I know I can make the relationship work, despite any obstacles.

_______ 6. When I find my "true love," I will probably know it soon after we meet.

_______ 7. I'm sure that every new thing I learn about the person I choose for a long-term commitment will please me.

_______ 8. The relationship I will have with my "true love" will be nearly perfect.

_______ 9. If I love someone, I will find a way for us to be together regardless of the opposition to the relationship, physical distance between us, or any other barrier.

_______ 10. There will be only one real love for me.

_______ 11. If a relationship I have was meant to be, any obstacles (for example, lack of money, physical distance, career conflicts) can be overcome.

_______ 12. I am likely to fall in love almost immediately if I meet the right person.

_______ 13. I expect that in my relationship, romantic love will really last; it won't fade with time.

_______ 14. The person I love will make a perfect romantic partner; for example, he or she will be completely accepting, loving, and understanding.

_______ 15. I believe if another person and I love each other, we can overcome any differences and problems that may arise.

To compute your romanticism score, add your scores for all 15 items. The higher your score, the stronger your romantic beliefs are. In research by Sprecher and Metts (1989), the mean score for this test was 60.45 for males and females taken together. The mean score for males was 62.55 and for females 59.10. How romantic are your beliefs compared to this research sample?

From Susan Sprecher and Sandra Metts, "Development of the 'Romantic Beliefs Scale' and Examination of the Effects of Gender and Gender-Role Orientation," *Journal of Social and Personal Relationships* 6 (1989): 387–411. Copyright 1989 Sage Publications Ltd. Reprinted by permission of Sage Publications Ltd. ■

Women have their first romantic experiences earlier than men. The median age of first infatuation for women is 13 and for men 13.6; the median age for first time in love for women is 17.1 and for men 17.6 (Kirkpatrick and Caplow 1945, Hendrick, Hendrick, Foote, and Slapion-Foote 1984).

In much research, men are found to place more emphasis on romance than women. For example, when college students were asked the question "If a man (woman) has all the other qualities you desired, would you marry this person if you were not in love with him (her)?" approximately two-thirds of the men responded no, which seems to indicate that a high percentage were concerned with love and romance. However, less than one-third of the women responded no (LeVine, Sato, Hashimoto, and Verma 1994). Further, when men and women were surveyed concerning their view on love—whether it's basically realistic or basically romantic—it was found that married women had a more realistic (less romantic) conception of love than did married men (Knapp and Vangelisti 1992).

Additional research (based on the romanticism questionnaire presented here) also supports the view that men are more romantic. For example, "Men are more likely than women to believe in love at first sight, in love as the basis for marriage and for overcoming obstacles, and to believe that their partner and relationship will be perfect" (Sprecher and Metts 1989). This difference seems to increase as the romantic relationship develops: men become more romantic and women less romantic (Fengler 1974).

One further gender difference may be noted, and that is differences between men and women in breaking up a relationship (Blumstein and Schwartz 1983, cf. Janus and Janus 1993). Popular myth would have us believe that love affairs break up as a result of the man's outside affair. But the research does not support this. When surveyed as to the reason for breaking up, only 15 percent of the men indicated that it was their interest in another partner, whereas 32 percent of the women noted this as a cause of the breakup. These findings are consistent with their partners' perceptions as well: 30 percent of the men (but only 15 percent of the women) noted that their partner's interest in another person was the reason for the breakup.

In their reactions to broken romantic affairs, women and men exhibit similarities and differences. For example, the tendency for women and men to recall only pleasant memories and to revisit places with past associations was about equal. However, men engaged in more dreaming about the lost partner and in more daydreaming generally as a reaction to the breakup than did women.

How would you describe your ideal love relationship in terms of the styles of love introduced here?

◂◂ THINKING BACK

REVIEWING KEY TERMS AND CONCEPTS IN FRIENDSHIP AND LOVE RELATIONSHIPS

This unit explored friendship and love, two of our most important interpersonal relationships.

Friends

What is friendship? What are the types of friendship? What purposes does it serve? How does friendship differ in different cultures and between men and women?

- **Friendship** is an interpersonal relationship between two persons that is mutually productive, and characterized by mutual positive regard.
- The types of friendships are:
  Reciprocity, characterized by loyalty, self-sacrifice, mutual affection, and generosity.
  Receptivity, characterized by a comfortable and positive imbalance in the giving and receiving of rewards; each person's needs are satisfied by the exchange.
  Association, a transitory relationship, more like a friendly relationship than a true friendship.
- Friendships serve a variety of needs and give us a variety of values, among which are the values of utility, affirmation, ego-support, stimulation, and security.
- Friendship demands vary between collectivist and individualist cultures.
- Women share more and are more intimate with same-sex friends than are men. Men's friendships are often built around shared activities rather than shared intimacies.

Lovers

What is love? What are the major kinds of love? What is the effect of love on communication? How does love vary in different cultures and between men and women?

- Love is a feeling that may be characterized by passion and caring and by intimacy, passion, and commitment.
- Types of love:
  Eros love focuses on beauty and sexuality, sometimes to the exclusion of other qualities.
  Ludus love is seen as a game and focuses on entertainment and excitement.
  Storge love is a kind of companionship, peaceful and slow.
  Pragma love is practical and traditional.
  Mania love is obsessive and possessive, characterized by elation and depression.
  Agape love is compassionate and selfless, characterized as self-giving and altruistic.
- Verbal and nonverbal messages echo the intimacy of a love relationship. With increased intimacy, you share more, speak in a more personalized style, engage in prolonged eye contact, and touch each other more often.
- Members of individualist cultures are likely to place greater emphasis on romantic love than are members of collectivist cultures.
- Men generally score higher on erotic and ludic love, whereas women score higher on manic, pragmatic, and storgic love. Men generally score higher on romanticism than women.

APPLYING KEY TERMS AND CONCEPTS IN FRIENDSHIP AND LOVE RELATIONSHIPS

1. Try formulating "findings" on friendship (similar to those cited in the opening paragraphs of this unit) based on your own observations. Do others also find these reasonable conclusions about friendship?
2. Of the three types of friendship discussed in this unit—reciprocity, receptivity, and association—which type characterizes most of your friendships?
3. After meeting someone for the first time, how long (on average) does it take you to decide whether this person will become a friend? What specific qualities do you look for?
4. In what ways do you find men and women different in their friendship behaviors? In what ways are they the same?
5. In an interesting study on love, men and women from different cultures were asked the following question: "If a man (woman) has all the other qualities you desired, would you marry this person if you were not in love with him (her)?" Results varied greatly from one culture to another (LeVine, Sato, Hashimoto, and Verma 1994). For example, 50.4 percent of the respondents from Pakistan said yes, as did 49 percent from India and 18.8 percent from Thailand. At the other extreme were those from Japan (only 2.3 percent said yes), the United States (3.5 percent said yes), and Brazil (4.3 percent said yes). How would you answer this question? Is your answer influenced by your culture?
6. When college students were asked to identify the features that characterize romantic love, the five most frequently noted qualities were trust, sexual attraction, acceptance and tolerance, spending time together, and sharing thoughts and secrets (Regan, Kocan, and Whitlock 1998). What additional qualities do you think characterize love?
7. Do you think that love develops in essentially the same way in men and women? In a heterosexual relationship and in a homosexual relationship?
8. Do you have difficulty saying "I love you" to a romantic partner? To a family member? To a same-sex friend? To an opposite-sex friend? Do you find that one sex has greater difficulty saying "I love you," or are men and women equally willing or unwilling?
9. Psychotherapist Albert Ellis has argued that love and infatuation are actually the same emotion; he claims that we use the term "infatuation" to describe relationships that didn't work out and "love" to describe our current romantic relationships. How would you compare infatuation and love?
10. How would you go about finding answers to the following questions?
    - Why are women's friendships considered more intimate than men's?
    - Why do men's friendships seem to revolve around doing something while women's friendships seem to revolve around talking and relating?
    - How is friendship related to loneliness? To self-esteem? To having successful romantic relationships?
    - What types of lovers (eros, ludus, storge, pragma, mania, agape) were the great lovers of history and literature?
    - What are the major ways in which men differ from women in the way they communicate when in love?

EXPERIENCING KEY TERMS AND CONCEPTS IN FRIENDSHIP AND LOVE RELATIONSHIPS

Go to www.awl.com/devito

Exercises No. 27, "Friendship Behaviors," and No. 28, "The Television Relationship," are useful for illustrating the role of interpersonal communication in friendship and love. Exercises No. 20, "Interpersonal Relationships in Songs and Greeting Cards," and No. 21, "Mate Preferences," will prove useful in exploring the qualities we look for in friends and lovers.

UNIT 21

PRIMARY AND FAMILY RELATIONSHIPS

Moonstruck (1987)

FAMILY IS A MIXED BLESSING. YOU'RE GLAD TO HAVE ONE, BUT IT'S ALSO LIKE RECEIVING A SENTENCE FOR A CRIME YOU DIDN'T COMMIT.

--RICHARD PRYOR

In Moonstruck, *you see family communication in a variety of forms and functions. The interpersonal relationships are influenced by the moon in ways that are crazy and yet highly romantic—finding true love, repairing a damaged relationship, or finding renewed energy and satisfaction. Even more interesting is how all the players interact as a family, and how the behavior of one member impacts on all the other members. In this unit we also look at the family—the nature of family and primary relationships, the types of primary relationships, and communication in primary relationships and families and especially how it can be improved.*

THINKING AHEAD ▸▸

What makes a group of people a family?

PRIMARY RELATIONSHIPS AND FAMILIES: NATURE AND CHARACTERISTICS

If you had to define "family," you might reply that a family consists of a husband, a wife, and one or more children. When pressed, you might add that some of these families also consist of other relatives-in-law, brothers and sisters, grandparents, aunts and uncles, and so on. But other types of relationships are, to their own members, "families."

One obvious example is the family with one parent. There are now over 10 million single-family households in the United States (Wright 1995). If current trends continue, notes *American Demographic* magazine (July 1992), 61 percent of all children (up to age 18) will spend part of their time in a single-parent home (Wright 1995).

Another obvious example is people living together in an exclusive relationship who are not married. For the most part, these cohabitants live as if they were married: there is an exclusive sexual commitment; there may be children; there are shared financial responsibilities, shared time, and shared space. These relationships mirror traditional marriages, except that in marriage the union is recognized by a religious body, the state, or both, whereas in a relationship of cohabitants it generally is not. In their comprehensive study *American Couples* (1983), sociologists Philip Blumstein and Pepper Schwartz report that although cohabiting couples represent only about 2 percent to 3.8 percent of all couples, their number is increasing. One bit of supporting evidence for increase is that among couples in which the male is under age 25, the percentage of cohabiting couples is 7.4 percent. In Sweden, a country that often leads in sexual trends, 12 percent of all couples are cohabitants.

Another example is the gay male or lesbian couple who live together as "domestic partners"—a relatively new term for people living in a committed relationship—and have all the characteristics of a "family." Many of these couples have children from previous heterosexual unions, through artificial insemination, or by adoption. Although accurate statistics are difficult to secure, primary relationships among gays and lesbians seem more common than the popular media lead us to believe. Research estimates the number of gay and lesbian couples to be 70 percent to more than 80 percent of the gay population (itself estimated variously at between 4 percent and 16 percent of the total population, depending on the definitions used and the studies cited). In summarizing these previous studies and their own research, Blumstein and Schwartz (1983) conclude, "'Couplehood,' either as a reality or as an aspiration, is as strong among gay people as it is among heterosexuals."

The communication principles that apply to the traditional nuclear family (the mother-father-child family) also apply to these relationships. In the following discussion, the term **primary relationship** denotes the relationship between the two principal parties—the husband and wife, the lovers, the domestic partners, for example—and the term **family** denotes the broader constellation that includes children, relatives, and assorted significant others. Here are a variety of definitions of "family" by the authors of works on family communication. Before reading the list, you may want to formulate your own definition and then compare it with those presented here.

"any number of persons who live in relationship with one another and are usually, but not always, united by marriage and kinship"

Family Talk: Interpersonal Communication in the Family (Beebe and Masterson 1986)

"networks of people who share their lives over long periods of time bound by ties of marriage, blood, or commitment, legal or otherwise, who consider themselves as family and who share a significant history and anticipated future of functioning in a family relationship"

Family Communication: Cohesion and Change (Galvin and Brommel 2000)

"a group of intimates, who generate a sense of home and group identity, complete with strong ties of loyalty and emotion, and an experience of a history and a future."

Communication in Family Relationships (Noller and Fitzpatrick 1993)

"an organized, relational transaction group, usually occupying a common living space over an extended time period, and possessing a confluence of interpersonal images that evolve through the exchange of meaning over time"

Communication in the Family (Pearson 1993)

"a multigenerational social system consisting of at least two interdependent people bound together by a common living space (at one time or another) and a common history, and who share some degree of emotional attachment to or involvement with one another"

Understanding Family Communication (Yerby, Buerkel-Rothfuss, and Bochner 1990

All primary relationships and families have several characteristics that further define this relationship type: defined roles, recognition of responsibilities, shared history and future, shared living space, and established rules.

Defined Roles

Primary relationship partners have a relatively clear perception of the roles each person is expected to play in relation to the other and to the relationship as a whole. Each acquired the rules of the culture and social group; each knows approximately what his or her obligations, duties, privileges, and responsibilities are. The partners' roles might include wage earner, cook, house cleaner, child care giver, social secretary, home decorator, plumber, carpenter, food shopper, money manager, and so on. At times, the roles may be shared, but even then it's generally assumed that one person has primary responsibility for certain tasks and the other person for others.

WEB EXPLORATION
To learn more about family roles, go to www.awl.com/devito.

Most heterosexual couples divide the roles rather traditionally, with the man as primary wage earner and maintenance person and the woman as primary cook, child rearer, and housekeeper. This is less true among the more highly educated and those in the higher socioeconomic classes, where changes in traditional role assignments are first seen. However, among gay male and lesbian couples, clear-cut, stereotypical male and female roles are not found. In her review of the research literature, psychologist Letitia Anne Peplau (1988) notes that scientific studies "have consistently debunked this myth. Most contemporary gay relationships do not conform to traditional 'masculine' and 'feminine' roles; instead, role flexibility and turn-taking are more common patterns. . . . In this sense, traditional heterosexual marriage is not the predominant model or script for current homosexual couples."

Recognition of Responsibilities

Family members see themselves as having certain obligations and responsibilities to each other. A single person does not have the same kinds of obligations to another as someone in a primary relationship. For example, individuals have an obligation to help each other financially. There are also emotional responsibilities: to offer comfort when our family members are distressed, to take pleasure in their pleasures, to feel their pain, to raise their spirits. Each person also has a temporal obligation to reserve some large block of time for the other. Time sharing seems important to all relationships, although each couple will define it differently.

Shared History and Future

Primary relationships have a shared history and the prospect of a shared future. For a relationship to become a primary one, there must be some history, some significant past interaction. This interaction enables the members to get to know each other, to understand each other a little better, and ideally to like and even love each other. Similarly, the individuals view the relationship as having a potential future.

Despite researchers' prediction that 50 percent of those couples now entering first marriages will divorce (the rate is higher for second marriages) and that 41 percent of all persons of marriageable age will experience divorce, most couples entering a relationship such as marriage view it—ideally, at least—as permanent.

Shared Living Space

In general American culture, persons in primary interpersonal relationships usually share the same living space. When living space is not shared, the situation is generally seen as an "abnormal" or temporary one both by the culture as a whole and by the individuals involved in the relationship. Even those who live apart for significant periods probably perceive a shared space as the ideal and, in fact, usually do share some special space at least part of the time. In some cultures, men and women don't share the same living space; the women may live with the children while the men live together in a communal arrangement (Harris 1993).

Although shared-living space is generally a goal of most primary relationships, the number of long-distance relationships is increasing. Further, although living together is a goal, this does not mean that long-distance relationships are necessarily less satisfying. After a thorough review of the research, one researcher concludes that "there is little, if any, decrease in relationship satisfaction, intimacy, and commitment as long as lovers are able to reunite with some frequency (approximately once a month)" (Rohlfing 1995, pp. 182–183).

Not surprisingly, research finds that lovers employ a variety of strategies to maintain long-distance relationships, acknowledging in their use of strategies that something extra has to be done to keep the relationships satisfying and together. Among these strategies are recognizing that long-distance relationships are common, establishing support systems while apart, and communicating in creative ways (for example, sending cards or videos) (Westefeld and Liddell 1982).

Family history (as opposed to the history of two people in a relationship) is an extremely important factor in influencing the way in which the family operates. For example, understanding the history of your parents' families may help explain the values, beliefs, and traditions considered important (or unimportant) in your home and perhaps the reasons for the differences and conflicts. Books on genealogy—the science of tracing your family history—can be found in any bookstore. More interesting sources are on the Internet. For example: http://members.aol.com/johnf14246/internet/html will provide you with a list of cultural mailing lists (Weitzman 1996); http://www.gensource.com/ifoundit/ is a search engine for finding online resources; and http://genealogy.emcee.com/ and http:www/gengateway.com/ will help you find hundreds of useful resources. The Mormon church's Web site (www.familysearch.org) contains links to 400 million names going back to 1500. Or you can go to any search engine such as Yahoo, WebCrawler, or Lycos and ask it to search genealogy [your last name] or genealogy [cultural identifiers, for example, nationality, religion]. What information about your family history would you like to know? Why?

Established Rules

Relying on the insights of family communication researchers Kathleen Galvin and Bernard Brommel (2000), we note the importance of family rules. You can view rules as concerning three main interpersonal communication issues (Satir 1983): (1) What can you talk about? Can you talk about the family finances? Grandpa's drinking? Your sister's lifestyle? (2) How can you talk about something? Can you joke about your brother's disability? Can you address directly questions of family history or family skeletons? (3) To whom can you talk? Can you talk openly to extended family members such as cousins and aunts and uncles? Can you talk to close neighbors about family health issues?

All families teach rules for communication. Some of these are explicit, such as "Never contradict the family in front of outsiders" or "Never talk finances with outsiders." Other rules are unspoken; you deduce them as you learn the communication style of your family. For example, if financial issues are always discussed in secret and in hushed tones, then you can infer that you shouldn't tell other more distant family members or neighbors about family finances.

These rules tell you which behaviors will be rewarded (and therefore what you should do) and which will be punished (and therefore what you should not do). Rules tell you what moves are permissible and what moves are not permissible. Rules also provide a kind of structure that defines the family as a cohesive unit and that distinguishes it from other similar families.

Not surprisingly, the rules a family develops are greatly influenced by the culture. For example, members of collectivist cultures are more likely to restrict family information from outsiders as a way of protecting the family than are members of individualist cultures. As already noted, this tendency to protect the family can create serious problems in cases of wife abuse. Many women will not report spousal abuse due to this desire to protect the family image and not let others know that things aren't perfect at home (Dresser 1996).

How do the characteristics discussed here operate in your own primary relationship and family?

◀◀ THINKING BACK

Family communication theorists argue that rules should be flexible so that special circumstances can be accommodated; there are situations that necessitate changing the family dinner time, vacation plans, or savings goals (Noller and Fitzpatrick 1993). Rules should be negotiable so that all members can participate in their modification and feel a part of family government.

THINKING AHEAD ▶▶

Do you want a relationship in which traditional sex roles are observed? A relationship in which you both retain your own identity and autonomy? A relationship in which you both share your feelings and engage in significant mutual self-disclosure?

TYPES OF RELATIONSHIPS

Based on responses from more than 1,000 couples to questions concerning their degree of sharing, their space needs, their conflicts, and the time they spend together, researchers have identified three basic types of primary relationships: traditionals, independents, and separates (Fitzpatrick 1983, 1988, 1991, Noller and Fitzpatrick 1993). At this point, you may wish to examine your own relational attitudes and style by taking the self-test "What Type of Relationship Do You Prefer?" If you have a relational partner, you might wish to have him or her also complete the test and then compare your results.

TEST YOURSELF *What Type of Relationship Do You Prefer?*

Respond to each of the following 16 statements by indicating the degree to which you agree with each. Circle *High* if you agree strongly, *Med* (medium) if you agree moderately, and *Low* if you feel little agreement. For now, don't be concerned with the fact that these terms appear in different positions in the columns to the right. Note that in some cases there are only two alternatives. When you agree with an alternative that appears twice, circle it both times.

The statements are from Mary Anne Fitzpatrick's *Relational Dimensions Instrument* (reprinted by permission of MaryAnne Fitzpatrick.)

	Col 1	Col 2	Col 3
Ideology of Traditionalism [the extent to which you believe in the traditional sex roles for couples]			
1. A woman should take her husband's last name when she marries.	High	Low	Med
2. Our wedding ceremony was (will be) very important to us.	High	Low	Med
Ideology of Uncertainty and Change [the extent to which you tolerate and welcome unpredictability and change]			
3. In marriage/close relationships, there should be no constraints or restrictions on individual freedom.	Low	High	Med

	Col 1	Col 2	Col 3
4. The ideal relationship is one marked by novelty, humor, and spontaneity.	Low	High	Med
Sharing [the extent to which you share your feelings for each other and engage in significant self-disclosure]			
5. We tell each other how much we love or care about each other.	High	Med	Low
6. My spouse/mate reassures and comforts me when I am feeling low.	High	Med	Low
Autonomy [the extent to which you each retain your own identity and autonomy]			
7. I have my own private work space (study, workshop, utility room, etc.).	Low	High	High
8. My spouse has his/her own private work space (workshop, utility, etc.).	Low	High	High
Undifferentiated Space [the extent to which you each have your own space and privacy]			
9. I feel free to interrupt my spouse/mate when he/she is concentrating on something if he/she is in my presence.	High	High	Low
10. I open my spouse/mate's personal mail without asking permission.	High	Med	Low
Temporal Regularity [the extent to which you spend time together]			
11. We eat our meals (i.e., the ones at home) at the same time every day.	High	Low	High
12. In our house, we keep a fairly regular daily time schedule.	High	Low	High
Conflict Avoidance [the extent to which you seek to avoid conflict and confrontation]			
13. If I can avoid arguing about some problems, they will disappear.	Med	Low	High
14. It is better to hide one's true feelings in order to avoid hurting your spouse/mate.	Med	Low	High
Assertiveness [the extent to which you assert your own rights]			
15. We are likely to argue in front of friends or in public places	Low	Med	Med
16. My spouse/mate tries to persuade me to do something I do not want to do.	Low	Med	Med

The responses noted in column 1 are characteristic of traditionals. The number of circled items in this column, then, indicates your agreement with and similarity to those considered traditionals. Responses noted in column 2 are characteristic of independents; those noted in column 3 are characteristic of separates. ■

Traditional couples share a basic belief system and philosophy of life. They see themselves as a blending of two persons into a single couple rather than as two separate individuals. They're interdependent and believe that an individual's independence must be sacrificed for the good of the relationship. Traditionals believe in mutual sharing and do little separately. This couple holds to the traditional sex roles, and there are seldom any role conflicts. There are few power struggles and few conflicts because each person knows and adheres to a specified role within the relationship. In their communications, traditionals are highly responsive to each other. Traditionals lean toward each other, smile, talk a lot, interrupt each other, and finish each other's sentences.

Independents stress their individuality. The relationship is important but never more important than each person's individual identity. Although independents spend a great deal of time together, they don't ritualize it, for example, with schedules. Each individual spends time with outside friends. Independents see themselves as relatively androgynous, as individuals who combine the traditionally feminine and the traditionally masculine roles and qualities. The communication between independents is responsive. They engage in conflict openly and without fear. Their disclosures are quite extensive and include high-risk and negative disclosures that are typically absent among traditionals.

Separates live together but view their relationship more as a matter of convenience than a result of their mutual love or closeness. They seem to have little desire to be together and, in fact, usually are together only at ritual functions, such as mealtime or holiday get-togethers. It's important to these separates that each has his or her own physical as well as psychological space. Separates share little; each seems to prefer to go his or her own way. Separates hold relatively traditional values and beliefs about sex roles, and each person tries to follow the behaviors normally assigned to each role. What best characterizes this type, however, is that each person sees himself or herself as a separate individual and not as a part of a "we."

How would you now describe your primary relationship? How would you describe your parents' relationship?

◀◀ THINKING BACK

In addition to these three pure types, there are also combinations. For example, in the *separate-traditional couple* one individual is a separate and one a traditional. Another common pattern is the *traditional-independent,* in which one individual believes in the traditional view of relationships and one in autonomy and independence.

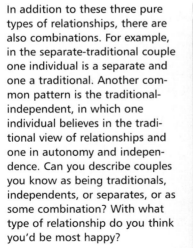

In addition to these three pure types of relationships, there are also combinations. For example, in the separate-traditional couple one individual is a separate and one a traditional. Another common pattern is the traditional-independent, in which one individual believes in the traditional view of relationships and one in autonomy and independence. Can you describe couples you know as being traditionals, independents, or separates, or as some combination? With what type of relationship do you think you'd be most happy?

ASK THE RESEARCHER

Resolving Relationship Difficulties

I'm planning on getting married at the end of this semester. My fiancé and I are at opposite ends of the patterns you describe. He very clearly falls into what you describe as the traditional pattern, whereas I score very high on the independent pattern. Will this create problems in our marriage?

Every relationship experiences difficulties. How you resolve those difficulties is the key. The particular mixed couple type you're part of is an interesting one that we've studied in our work. This Traditional husband/Independent wife pairing demonstrates a commitment to a strong relationship although each sees companionship and sharing in different ways. The Independent wife is willing to argue and discuss a variety of issues, is not afraid of expressing feelings, and is less bound to conventional gender roles than other wives. Her more Traditional spouse is able to express his concerns but believes they should only fight about major issues. This husband wants a close relationship although he's more conventional than she about gender roles. Clearly, both sides have to understand the way the other approaches relationship differences. She may need to moderate her need for total expressivity, and he may need to engage in more bargaining and negotiation. Being sensitive to one another's preferences for conflict management should go a long way toward helping this marriage succeed.

—Mary Anne Fitzpatrick (Ph.D., Temple University) is currently dean of social sciences at the University of Wisconsin, where she also conducts research and teaches in the area of interpersonal communication in social and personal relationships.

COMMUNICATION IN PRIMARY RELATIONSHIPS AND FAMILIES

In this final section we look at communication within the primary relationship and the family. First, we identify four general communication patterns, and second, we look at a program for improving family communication.

THINKING AHEAD ▸▸
How would you describe the communication that takes place in your own primary relationship and family?

Communication Patterns

Another way to gain insight into primary relationships is to focus on communication patterns rather than on attitudes and beliefs, as in the previous discussion. Four general communication patterns are identified here; each interpersonal relationship may then be viewed as a variation on one of these basic patterns.

The Equality Pattern The equality pattern probably exists more in theory than in practice, but it's a good starting point for looking at communication in primary relationships. It exists more among same-sex couples than opposite-sex couples, however (Huston and Schwartz 1995). In the equality pattern, each person shares equally in the communication transactions; the roles played by each are equal. Thus, each person is accorded a similar degree of credibility; each is equally open to the ideas, opinions, and beliefs of the other; each engages in self-disclosure on a more or less equal basis. The communication is open, honest, direct, and free of the power plays that characterize so many other interpersonal relationships. There is no leader or follower, no opinion giver or opinion seeker; rather, both parties play these roles equally. Because of this basic equality, the communication exchanges themselves, over a substantial period, are equal. For example, the number of questions asked, the depth and frequency of self-disclosures, and the nonverbal behaviors of touching and eye gaze would all be about the same for both people.

Both parties share equally in the decision-making processes—the insignificant ones, such as which movie to attend, as well as the significant ones, such as where to send the child to school, whether to attend religious services, and what house to buy. Conflicts in equality relationships may occur with some frequency, but they're not seen as threatening to the individuals or to the relationship. They're viewed, rather, as exchanges of ideas, opinions, and values. These conflicts are content rather than relational in nature (Unit 19), and the couple has few power struggles within the relationship domain.

Equal relationships are also equitable. According to equity theory, family or relationship satisfaction will be highest when there is equity, when the rewards are distributed in proportion to the costs one pays into the relationship (Unit 16). Dissatisfaction over inequities can lead to a "balancing of the scales" reaction. For example, an underbenefitted partner may seek outside affairs as a way to get more relationship benefits—more love, more consideration, more support (Walster, Walster, and Traupmann 1978, Noller and Fitzpatrick 1993).

The Balanced Split Pattern In the balanced split pattern, an equality relationship is maintained, but each person has authority over different domains. Each person is seen as an expert or a decision-maker in different areas. For example, in the traditional nuclear family, the husband maintains high credibility in business matters and perhaps in politics. The wife maintains high credibility in such matters as child care and cooking. These sex roles are, in many cultures, breaking down although they still define lots of families throughout the world (Hatfield and Rapson 1996).

Conflict is generally viewed as nonthreatening by these individuals because each has specified areas of expertise. Consequently, the outcome of the conflict is almost predetermined.

The Unbalanced Split Pattern In the unbalanced split relationship, one person dominates; one person is seen as an expert in more than half the areas of mutual communication. In many unions, this expertise takes the form of control. Thus, in the unbalanced split, one person is more or less regularly in control of the relationship. In some cases, this person is the more intelligent or more knowledgeable, but in many cases he or she is the more physically attractive or the higher wage earner. The less attractive or lower-income partner compensates by giving in to the other person, allowing the other to win the arguments or to have his or her way in decision making.

The person in control makes more assertions, tells the other person what should or will be done, gives opinions freely, plays power games to maintain control, and seldom asks for opinions in return. The noncontrolling person, conversely, asks questions, seeks opinions, and looks to the other for decision-making leadership.

The Monopoly Pattern In a monopoly relationship, one person is seen as the authority. This person lectures rather than communicates. Rarely does this person ask questions to seek advice, and he or she always reserves the right to have the final say. In this type of couple, the arguments are few because both individuals already know who is boss and who will win the argument should one arise. When the authority is challenged, there are arguments and bitter conflicts. One reason the conflicts are so bitter is that these individuals have had no rehearsal for adequate conflict resolution. They don't know how to argue or how to disagree agreeably, so their arguments frequently take the form of hurting the other person.

The controlling person tells the partner what is and what is not to be. The controlling person talks more frequently and goes off the topic of conversation more than

ASK THE RESEARCHER

Improving Family Communication

My family rarely communicates, except to argue. Now that I am taking a course in interpersonal communication, I want to put some of this knowledge to work. Can you give me some suggestions for encouraging better family communication?

Not all arguments are bad! It's not that you disagree; it's how you disagree that causes trouble. If arguments lead to fairer, more equitable outcomes that enhance the quality of life within the family, they have value. However, if they demean members, unfairly dominate those with good ideas, or are used to reinforce the family "pecking order" of who is really in charge, changes should be sought.

Talk with your family members about how they argue and ask if there are other ways to resolve differences. Tell one another how you feel when through arguments you are "put down" unfairly. Ask those that argue unfairly to consider your right to be heard. Maybe your family needs to create some new rules to govern how you argue. For example: only one person speaks at a time; no interruptions until a person finishes his or her comment; everyone will get a chance to speak on an issue; no shouting or "hogging" the time available; etc.

For more information see K. M. Galvin and B. J. Brommel, *Family Communication: Cohesion and Change* (New York: Longman, 2000), and V. Escuerdo, L. E. Rogers, and E. Gutierrez, "Patterns of Relational Controls and Nonverbal Affect in Clinic and Nonclinic Couples," *Journal of Social and Personal Relationships* 14 (1997): 5–29.

—Bernard J. Brommel (Ph.D., Indiana University) is a professor of communication, Northeastern Illinois University, and teaches courses in interpersonal and family communication. With K. M. Galvin, he wrote the first textbook in the field of family communication. He was for 19 years a member of the Board of the Lakeview Mental Health Center in Chicago and has a private practice in individual and marital counseling.

does the noncontrolling partner (Palmer 1989). The noncontrolling person looks to the other to give permission, to voice opinion leadership, and to make decisions, almost as a child looks to an all-knowing, all-powerful parent.

Communication Enhancement

There seems little doubt that effective communication is at the heart of effective interpersonal and family relationships. Without effective communication such relationships are likely to be a lot less meaningful and satisfying than they could be. Interpersonal communication (and, as a result, primary and family relationships) can be improved and strengthened by applying the same principles that improve communication in other contexts.

General principles of effective communication, applied to primary and family relationships, can be spelled out with the help of the acronym POSITIVE: positiveness, openness, supportiveness, interest, truth, involvement, value, and equality. You might find it interesting to first read "How to Talk to Your Kids About Drugs" (p.363) and consider if and how it incorporates the eight qualities we discuss here.

Positiveness Positiveness in conversation (see Unit 14) entails a positive attitude toward the communication act and the expression of positiveness toward the other person, as in complimenting. In relationship effectiveness, it also includes a positiveness toward the relationship, toward the prospect of continued "couplehood." It includes not only being positive toward your partner but also being positive about your partner when interacting with third parties.

Positiveness should not be confused with perfection. Whether influenced by the media, by a self-commitment to have a relationship better than one's parents', or by a

ETHICS IN INTERPERSONAL COMMUNICATION

Vote online at http://www.awl.com/devito

Keeping Secrets

In *Secrets* (1983), ethicist Sissela Bok identifies three types of situations in which she argues it would be unethical to reveal the secrets of another person. These conditions aren't always easy to identify in any given instance, but they do provide excellent starting points for asking whether or not it's ethical to reveal what we know about another person. Of course, for any situation, there may be legitimate exceptions.

First, it's unethical to reveal information that you have promised to keep secret. When you promise to keep information hidden, you take on an ethical responsibility.

Second, it's unethical to talk about another person when you know the information to be false. When you try to deceive listeners by saying things about another person that you know to be false, your communications are unethical.

Third, it's unethical to invade the privacy to which everyone has a right, to reveal information that no one else has a right to know. This is especially unethical when such disclosures can hurt the individual involved.

What would you do? *As Bok suggests, consider the case of an 18-year-old student with whom you're fairly friendly. He confides to you that he intends to commit suicide. Using these three guidelines, how would you evaluate the ethics involved in revealing or not revealing this secret? What ethical justification might be offered for revealing such a secret? If you were this friend, what would you do in this situation?*

mistaken belief that other relationships are a lot better than one's own, many people look for and expect perfection. Because this quest sets up unrealistic expectations, it is almost sure to result in dissatisfaction and disappointment with existing relationships and, in fact, with any relationship that's likely to come along. Psychologist John DeCecco (1988) puts this in perspective when he argues that relationships should be characterized by reasonableness: "reasonableness of need and expectation, avoiding the wasteful pursuit of the extravagant fantasy that every desire will be fulfilled, so that the relationship does not consume its partners or leave them chronically dissatisfied."

Openness Openness entails a variety of attitudes and behaviors. It includes an openness to listen to the other person—whether you want to or not. It means you're open to listening to the anxieties and worries of your partner, even when you honestly believe these are minor issues and will go away in the morning. It means that you're open to listening to these even when you really want to watch the ballgame or work on some work-related project.

Openness entails a willingness to experience the feelings of your partner as your partner feels them, a willingness to see the world as your partner sees it. It's a willingness to empathize with your partner, to feel what your partner feels as your partner feels. It does not mean that you should simply take on the feelings of your partner or even to agree with them, but only that you understand them as your partner experiences them.

Openness recognizes that throughout any significant relationship, there will be numerous and significant changes in each of the individuals and in the relationship. Because persons in relationships are interconnected, with each having an impact on the other, changes in one person may demand changes in the other person. Frequently asked-for changes include, for example, giving more attention, complimenting more often, and expressing feelings more openly (Noller 1982). Your willingness to be responsive to such changes, to be adaptable and flexible, is likely to enhance relationship satisfaction (Noller and Fitzpatrick 1993). Openness thus entails a willingness to consider new ideas, new ways of seeing your partner and your relationship, and new ways of interacting.

How To Talk To Your Kids About Drugs.

It's never too early to start.

The best thing about this subject is that you don't have to do it well. You simply have to try.

If you try, your kids will get the message.

That you care about them.

That you understand something about the conflicts they face.

That you're there when they need you.

The alternative is to ignore the subject. Which means your kids are going to be listening to others who have strong opinions about the subject. Including those who use drugs. And those who sell them.

Accept Rebellion.

At the heart of it, drugs, alcohol, wild hairstyles, trendy clothes, ear-splitting music, outrageous language are different ways of expressing teenage rebellion.

That's not all bad. Part of growing up is to create a separate identity, apart from parents — a process which ultimately leads to feelings of self worth. A step along that path is rebellion of one kind or another — which is to say rejecting parental values, and staking out new ones.

You did it. They're doing it. And that's the way it is.

The problem comes when kids choose a path of rebellion that hurts them, destroys their self worth, and can ultimately kill them.

That's the reality of drugs.

Don't get discouraged.

When you talk to your kids about drugs, it may seem as though nothing is getting through.

Don't you believe it.

The very fact you say it gives special weight to whatever you say.

But whether or not your kids let on they've heard you, whether or not they play back your words weeks or months later, keep trying.

Start anywhere.

"Have you heard about any kids using drugs?"

"What kind of drugs?"

"How do you feel about that?"

"Why do you think kids get involved with drugs?"

"How do other kids deal with peer pressure to use drugs? Which approaches make sense to you?"

"Have you talked about any of this in school?"

However you get into the subject, it's important to state exactly how strongly you feel about it.

Not in threatening tones. But in matter-of-fact, unmistakably clear language:

"Drugs are a way of hurting yourself."

"Drugs take all the promise of being young and destroy it."

"I love you too much to see you throw your life down the drain."

Some do's and don'ts.

The do's are as simple as speaking from the heart.

The biggest don't is don't do all the talking. If you listen to your kids – really listen and read between the lines – you'll learn a lot about what they think. About drugs. About themselves. About the world. And about you. They'll also feel heard and that, too, is a step along the path towards self esteem.

There are other do's and don'ts: Don't threaten. Don't badger them. Don't put your kid on the spot by asking directly if he or she has ever tried drugs. They'll probably lie, which undermines your whole conversation.

If you suspect your child is on drugs – there are all sorts of symptoms – that's a different matter. Then you've got to confront the subject directly.

In the meantime, just talk to them.

It's okay if you don't know much about drugs.

Your kids *do*.

But they need to know how you feel about the subject.

And whether you care.

For more information on how to talk with your kids about drugs, ask for a free copy of "Keeping Youth Drug-Free." Call 1-800-729-6686.

Partnership for a Drug-Free America®

Supportiveness As explained in the discussion of interpersonal effectiveness (Unit 8), supportiveness entails a variety of behaviors such as being descriptive rather than evaluative, and recognizing that you don't know everything. In relationship communication, being supportive also includes encouraging the other person to be the best he or she can be. It entails empowering your partner by raising his or her self-esteem, by sharing the skills you have that your partner needs to control his or her own destiny, and by offering criticism that is constructive rather than simple but discouraging fault-finding.

Interest The more interested you are in your partner, the more likely your partner will be interested in you. Sharing joint activities, learning to appreciate the job your partner does outside the home as well as inside, will enable you to share more of your lives with each other and thereby get to know and understand each other a lot better. Developing shared interests—learning new hobbies together, learning to appreciate new music as a couple, or even something as simple as going to the movies once a week to share the experience together may help each person learn about the other—their likes and dislikes, their values and interests, their emotions and motivations. In doing so, you're likely to become a more interesting person yourself, which contributes further to communication enhancement. After all, it's a lot easier and more rewarding to communicate with interesting rather than uninteresting people.

Children (or even pets) are a good example of a joint interest that partners come to experience as a couple. As they share child rearing and its accompanying joys and problems, they often grow closer as a couple. Through this experience they come to know each other better because they see each other in a new set of circumstances.

TRY IT!
To learn more about truthfulness in relationships, go to www.awl.com/devito.

Truthfulness Being honest and truthful does not mean revealing every thought and every desire you have. Nor is it expecting that your partner reveal everything he or she is thinking. After all, everyone has a right to some privacy. At times, it may be expedient to omit, for example, past indiscretions, certain fears, and perceived personal inadequacies if these disclosures may lead to negative perceptions or damage the relationship in some way. As already stressed, in any decision concerning self-disclosure, the possible effects on the relationship should be considered (Unit 4). Total self-disclosure, in fact, may not always be effective (Noller and Fitzpatrick 1993). But effectiveness is not the only consideration that needs to be recognized. It's also necessary to consider the ethical issues involved, specifically the other person's right to know about behaviors and thoughts that may influence the choices he or she will make.

Most relationships would profit from greater self-disclosure of present feelings rather than details of past sexual experiences or past psychological problems. The truthful sharing of present feelings also helps a great deal in enabling each person to empathize with the other; each comes to understand better the other's point of view when these self-disclosures are made.

Truthfulness as a quality of effective relationship communication means that what you do reveal will be an honest reflection of what you feel rather than, for example, an attempt to manipulate your partner's feelings to achieve a particular and perhaps selfish goal.

Involvement Involvement means an active participation in the relationship. Simply being there is not sufficient. Simply going through the motions is not sufficient. Relationship involvement calls for active participation in the other person's life and goals—but not to the point of intrusion; after all, most mature people want some independence. It includes active participation in the relationship, taking responsibility for its maintenance, satisfaction, and growth. In conflict resolution, as already mentioned (Unit 19), withdrawal and silence are generally unfair conflict strategies. Actively listening to your partners complaints, actively searching for solutions to problems and differences, and actively working to incorporate these solutions into your everyday lives are all part of relationship involvement.

Value When you fall in love or develop a close friendship, you probably do so, in part at least, because you see value and worth in the other person. You're attracted to the person because of some inner qualities you feel this person has. Sometimes this is lost over the years and you may eventually come to take the other person for granted, a situation that can seriously damage an interpersonal relationship. It's often helpful to renew and review your reasons for establishing the relationship in the first place and perhaps to focus on the values that originally brought you together. Very likely these qualities have not changed; what may have changed instead is that they're no longer as salient as they once were. Your task is to bring these again to the forefront and to learn to appreciate them all over again.

Equality Earlier we noted that the theory of equity argues that relationships are generally most satisfying when each person perceives them to be reasonably equitable (Unit 16). Each person wants and has a right to expect a fair share of the profits. This means that each person has a right to expect to receive benefits in proportion to the costs he or she pays into the relationship.

An interesting perspective on equality can be gained from looking at interpersonal and relationship conflict. Conflict is inevitable; it's an essential part of every meaningful interpersonal relationship. Perhaps the most general rule to follow is to fight fair. Winning at all costs, beating down the other person, and getting one's own way have little value in a primary or family relationship, largely because these are unfair and unequal exercises of power. Instead, cooperation, compromise, and mutual understanding—the strategies of equality—are more productive substitutes. If you enter into conflict with a person you love with the idea that you must win and the other must lose, the conflict has to hurt at least one partner, very often both. In these situations, the loser gets hurt and frequently retaliates, so no one truly wins in any meaningful sense. However, if you enter a conflict as equal cooperating partners, with the aim of resolving it by reaching some kind of mutual understanding, neither party need be hurt, and both parties may benefit from the clash of ideas or desires, from the airing of differences, and from the search for reasonable solutions. Equality entails a sharing of power and decision making in conflict resolution as well as in any significant relationship undertaking. As a quality of positive relationship communication, equality relies on and comes close to the equality communication pattern discussed earlier in this unit.

REVIEWING KEY TERMS AND CONCEPTS IN PRIMARY AND FAMILY RELATIONSHIPS

This unit looked at primary relationships and families and considered their nature, types, communication patterns, and ways to improve such communication.

Characteristics of Primary Relationships and Families

What characteristics define primary relationships and families?

- *Defined roles:* members understand the roles each of them serves.
- *Recognition of responsibilities:* members realize that each person has certain responsibilities to the relationship.
- *Shared history and future:* members have an interactional past and an anticipated future together.
- *Shared living space:* generally, members live together.
- *Established rules:* the relationship is rule governed, rather than random or unpredictable.

Types of Primary Relationships and Families

How can the various types of families be classified? How do families differ from each other?

- *Traditionals* see themselves as a blending of two people into a single couple.
- *Independents* see themselves as primarily separate individuals, an individuality that is more important than the relationship or the connection between the individuals.

- *Separates* see their relationship as a matter of convenience rather than of mutual love or connection.

Communication in Primary Relationships and Families
What are the major communication patterns that can be identified? How can family communication be improved?

- Among the communication patterns are *equality* (each person shares equally in the communication transactions and decision making), *balanced split* (each person has authority over different but relatively equal domains), *unbalanced split* (one person maintains authority and decision-making power over a wider range of issues than the other), and *monopoly* (one person dominates and controls the relationship and the decisions made).
- Communication enhancement can be achieved by using communication that is POSITIVE:

  Positiveness. Stress the positive aspects of the relationship; look for positives even among negatives.

  Openness. Be open to experiencing the world as your partner does; be open to the inevitable changes in the relationship and in the other person.,

  Supportiveness. Be supportive, encouraging, and empowering of your partner.

  Interest. Become interested in your partner by sharing activities, learning about his or her "outside" life.

  Truth. Be honest and truthful but not necessarily totally revealing.

  Involvement. Participate actively in the relationship—its problems and its rewards.

  Value. Remember the values that helped create the rela tionship and develop new values that relationship changes have inspired.

  Equality. Strive for equity, making sure your partner gets a fair share of the rewards, even when in conflict.

APPLYING KEY TERMS AND CONCEPTS IN PRIMARY AND FAMILY RELATIONSHIPS

1. How would you define "family"? What types of relationships would be included in your definition? What types would be excluded?
2. Of the characteristics of primary relationships and families discussed in this unit (defined roles, recognition of responsibilities, shared history and future, shared living space, and established rules), which is the most important in keeping a relationship or family together? Which one—when absent—will contribute most to the breakup of the relationship?
3. What communication pattern (equality, balanced split, unbalanced split, or monopoly) characterizes your primary relationship? How effective is it in keeping the relationship together? How personally satisfying is it?
4. Although studies show there is no disadvantage in a child's growing up in a gay home (Goleman 1992), the major argument made against granting adoption rights to gay men and lesbians is that the child will suffer. How do you account for this?
5. What roles do you play in your family, primary, and friendship relationships? How satisfied are you with these roles?
6. What suggestion would you give one of your friends for improving his or her primary or family communication?
7. If you looked at the family from an evolutionary-Darwinian point of view, one researcher notes, you'd have to conclude that families are "inherently unstable" and that it's necessity, not choice, that keeps them together. If the family members had better opportunities elsewhere, they would leave immediately (Goleman 1995a). What do you think of this position?
8. Can you describe couples you know as being traditionals, independents, or separates? In what type of relationship do you feel most comfortable?
9. What communication rules does your own family follow? What happens when these rules are broken?
10. How would you go about finding answers to the following questions?
    - Do persons who are high in self-disclosure make better primary relationship partners than those who are low in self-disclosure?
    - Are couples with children happier than couples without children?
    - Will primary relationships involving people who entered with unrealistically low expectations last longer than those involving people with realistic or unrealistically high expectations?
    - Do couples who live together stay together longer than couples who live separately? Is one group significantly happier than the other?
    - In what ways are primary relationships among heterosexuals and homosexuals different? In what ways are they the same?

EXPERIENCING KEY TERMS AND CONCEPTS IN PRIMARY AND FAMILY RELATIONSHIPS

Go to www.awl.com/devito
Exercise No. 28, "The Television Relationship," may be used to illustrate any of a number of family communication issues. Exercise No. 1, "Analyzing an Interaction," can be used to focus on family communication or, if already used, can be returned to as a summary of the entire course or to illustrate the more sophisticated analysis that is possible now rather than at the beginning of the semester. Exercise No. 23, "Relationship Repair from Advice Columnists," may be used to illustrate family problems and solutions. Exercise No. 25, "Power Plays," will illustrate how power may be used unfairly in the family.

UNIT 22

INTERPERSONAL COMMUNICATION AND RELATIONSHIPS IN THE WORKPLACE

Working Girl (1988)

WEAR YOUR LEARNING LIKE YOUR WATCH, IN A PRIVATE POCKET, AND DO NOT PULL IT OUT AND STRIKE IT MERELY TO SHOW THAT YOU HAVE ONE.

--LORD CHESTERFIELD

IN WORKING GIRL a secretary (Melanie Griffith), pretending to be an executive, puts together a huge business deal with the help of a colleague (Harrison Ford) who falls in love with her. With only minor problems along the way, the deal goes through, establishing her as a top executive with a secretary of her own. She also gets the last laugh on her former and ill-tempered boss (Sigourney Weaver). It's an interesting but not very realistic view of today's workplace. In this unit, a more balanced view of the workplace, we focus on the role of interpersonal communication in getting the job, communication on the job, and the nature of workplace relationships.

THINKING AHEAD ▸▸
How can you maximize your potential in the job interview?

WEB EXPLORATION
To learn more about employment interviews , go to www.awl.com/devito.

COMMUNICATING TO JOIN THE WORKPLACE: THE EMPLOYMENT INTERVIEW

An **interview** is a form of interpersonal communication in which two people interact, largely through a question-and-answer format, to achieve specific goals. While interviews usually involve two people, some involve more. At job fairs, for example, where many people apply for the few available jobs, interviewers may talk with several persons at once. Similarly, therapy frequently involves entire families, groups of coworkers, or other related individuals.

Although most interviewing is done face-to-face, much interviewing is now taking place via computer—through e-mail and in chat groups. For example, you can use e-mail or IRC groups to conduct an informative interview with people living in different parts of the world. The Internet enables employers to interview candidates in different parts of the world for the price of a few local phone calls. It also enables candidates to explore employment opportunities from their own desk. With advanced hardware and software enabling audio and video exchanges over the Internet, the computer-mediated interview will very closely resemble the traditional face-to-face situation.

The interview is different from other forms of communication because it usually proceeds through questions and answers. Both parties in the interview can ask and answer questions, but most often the interviewer asks and the interviewee answers. The interview has specific goals that guide and structure its content and format. In an employment interview, for example, the interviewer's goal is to find an applicant who can fulfill the tasks of the position. The interviewee's goal is to get the job, if it

People demonstrating apprehension during a job interview will be perceived less positively than will those demonstrating confidence and composure. How might you learn to better display confidence?

seems desirable. These goals guide the behaviors of both parties, are relatively specific, and are usually clear to both parties.

Perhaps of most immediate concern to college students, though significant for all working people, is the employment, or selection, interview. In such an interview, a great deal of information and persuasion will be exchanged. The interviewer will learn about you, your work experience, college record, interests, talents—and, if clever enough, some of your weaknesses and liabilities. You'll be informed about the nature of the company and the position for which you're interviewing, its benefits, its advantages—and, if you're clever enough, some of its disadvantages and problems.

For a variety of reasons—because the employment interview is so crucial in determining your future and because it's a relatively infrequent and unfamiliar experience—you may feel apprehension . You may, therefore, want to take the accompanying self-test to examine your apprehension in this situation.

TEST YOURSELF *How Apprehensive Are You in Employment Interviews?*

This questionnaire is composed of five questions concerning your feelings about communicating in the job interview setting. Indicate, in the spaces provided, the degree to which each statement adequately describes your feelings about the employment interview. Use the following scale: 1 = strongly agree, 2 = agree, 3 = undecided, 4 = disagree, 5 = strongly disagree.

_______ 1. While participating in a job interview with a potential employer, I am not nervous.
_______ 2. Ordinarily, I am very tense and nervous in job interviews.
_______ 3. I have no fear of speaking up in job interviews.
_______ 4. I'm afraid to speak up in job interviews.
_______ 5. Ordinarily, I am very calm and relaxed in job interviews.

In computing your score, follow these steps:

1. Reverse your scores for items 2 and 4 as follows: if you said 2 reverse it to 4, and if you said 4 reverse it to 2.
2. Add the scores from all 5 items; be sure to use the reverse scores for items 2 and 4 and the original scores for 1, 3, and 5.

The higher your score, the greater your apprehension. Since this test is still under development, specific meanings for specific scores are not possible. A score of 25 (the highest possible score) would, however, indicate an extremely apprehensive individual while a score of 5 (the lowest possible score) would indicate an extremely unapprehensive individual. How does your score compare with those of your peers? What score do you think would ensure optimum performance at the job interview?

Your apprehension will probably differ somewhat depending on the type of job interview, your responsibilities, the need and desire you have for the job, and so on. What factors would make you especially apprehensive? Do these answers give you clues as to how to lessen your apprehension?

Source: This test was developed by Joe Ayres, Debbie M. Ayres, and Diane Sharp, "A Progress Report on the Development of an Instrument to Measure Communication Apprehension in Employment Interviews," *Communication Research Reports* 10 (1993): 87–94. ■

Prepare Yourself

Before going into a job interview, prepare yourself. Interestingly enough, if you're apprehensive about the employment interview, you're more likely to avoid thinking about it and preparing for it (Ayres, Keereetaweep, Chen, and Edwards 1998). This is exactly what you don't want to do, especially if you're apprehensive. Instead, do your homework researching at least four areas: the field, the position, the company, and current events (Taub 1997). First, research the career field you're entering and its current trends. With this information you'll be able to demonstrate that you're up-to-date and committed to the area you want this company to pay you to work in.

Second, research the specific position you're applying for so you'll be able to show how your skills and talents mesh with the position. A good way to do this is to visit the company's Web site. Most large corporations and many small firms maintain Web sites and frequently include detailed job descriptions. Prepare yourself to demonstrate your ability to perform each of the tasks noted in the job description.

Third, research the company or organization—its history, mission, and current directions. If it's a publishing company, familiarize yourself with their books and software products. If it's an advertising agency, familiarize yourself with their major clients and major advertising campaigns. A good way to do this is to call and ask the company to send you any company brochures, newsletters, or perhaps a quarterly or annual report. Be sure to visit their Web site; not only will it provide you with lots of useful information about this company but it will show the interviewer that you make use of the latest technology. With extensive knowledge of the company, you'll be able to show your interest in and focus on this specific company.

Fourth, research what is going on in the world in general and in the business world in particular. This will help you demonstrate your breadth of knowledge and that you're a knowledgeable individual who continues to learn. Reading a good newspaper daily or a news magazine weekly should help you in mastering current events.

With the employment interview, both you and the company are trying to fill a need. You want a job that will help build your career, and the company wants an effective employee who will be an asset to the company. View the interview as an opportunity to engage in a joint effort to each gain something beneficial. If you approach the interview in this cooperative frame of mind, you're much less likely to become defensive and much more likely to be perceived as an appealing potential colleague.

The most important element you can prepare is your résumé. The résumé is a summary of essential information about your experience, education, and abilities. Often, a job applicant may respond to a job listing and submit a résumé. If the employer thinks the applicant's résumé is promising, the candidate is asked in for an interview. Because of the importance of the résumé and its close association with the interview, a sample one-page résumé and some guidelines to assist you in preparing your own are provided here. A variety of computer programs are available to help you in preparing your résumé; most offer an extensive array of templates that you fill in (or customize if you wish) with your specific data.

Prepare Answers and Questions

It's often helpful to anticipate the questions you'll be asked. If the interview is at all important to you, you'll probably think about it for some time. If you rehearse the interview's predicted course, you're likely to walk into the interview feeling much more in control of the situation. Try also to predict the questions you'll be asked. Table 22.1 identifies some of the frequently asked questions you may wish to consider.

Try being specific when answering questions and be prepared to give specific examples that testify as to your abilities—from your work, school, or extracurricular

❶ Your name, address, phone and fax number, and e-mail are generally centered at the top of the résumé.

❷ For some people, employment objectives may be more general than indicated here, for example," to secure a management trainee position with an international investment bank." If you do have more specific objectives, put them down. Don't imply that you'll take just anything,but also don't appear too specific or demanding.

❸ List work experience in chronological order, beginning with your latest position and working back. Depending on your work experience, you may have to pare down what you write. Or, you may have little or nothing to write, so you will have to search through your employment history for some relevant experience. Often the dates of the various positions are included. If you have little or no paid work experience or large gaps in employment history due, say, to time off raising a family, include volunteer work or other unpaid work that requires skills important to the job, for example, coordinator of a little league team or treasurer of the PTA.

❶ Ramona Morales
57-12 Horace Harding Expressway #15D
Corona, NY 11368
(718) 555-0005
rmorales@ifindit.com

❷ Objective

To secure a position with a college textbook publisher in marketing and sales

❸ Employment Experience

Bookstore Assistant, Queens College Bookstore
1998–present

- Maintained shelf stock
- Managed inventory data base
- Placed orders with textbook publishers
- Assisted with front desk operations including client interaction, operating cash register, typing, and filing

Front Desk Employee, Queens College Library
1989–1995

- Responsible for periodical library
- Checked books in and out at front desk
- Acted as liaison for interlibrary loan books
- Offered general information about college library, the online catalog system, interlibrary loan, and the Internet terminals

Retail sales and management, luggage department, Macy's Department Store, Queens Center

❹ Education

Queens College, BA expected 1999
Major: Communication (Emphasis on interpersonal communication and public relations)
Minor: Marketing
12 Credits in Computer Science
LaGuardia Community College, AA, 1997
Major: Business

❺ Activities

- Vice President, Debate Club, Queens College, 1998–1999
- Member, Championship Debate Team, Eastern Division, 1997–1999
- Literacy Volunteer for Spanish-speaking grade school students in English at PS 150, 1995
- Class Treasurer, LaGuardia Community College, 1996–1997
- Member, Young Business Person's Association

❻ Skills and Competencies

- Apple Macintosh (MS Word, MacWrite)
- IBM (Word, WordPerfect)
- Working knowledge of Microsoft Excel and Lotus 1-2-3
- Knowledge of HTML language inventory software
- Bilingual in English and Spanish, capable in French
- Excellent interpersonal and public speaking skills

❼ References available upon request

❽

❹ Provide more information than simply your educational degree. For example, include your major and your minor and perhaps sequences of courses in communication or management or some other field which will further establish your suitability for the job. List honors or awards if they're relevant to your education or job experience. If the awards are primarily educational (for example, Dean's List), list them under the Education heading; if job-related, list them under the Work Experience heading.

❺ Identify those activities that are relevant to the job skills you want to demonstrate (for example, debating) and also those that attest to the personal qualities you want to stress (for example, reliability and trustworthiness as shown in being treasurer).

❻ Highlight your special skills. Do you have some foreign language ability? Do you have experience with business or statistical software? If you do, put it down. Such competencies are relevant to many jobs.

❼ Some interview experts recommend you include on your résumé the names of references, people who can attest to your abilities and character. If you do this, then include these names with addresses, phone number, and e-mail address at the end of the résumé under a heading labeled "References." Usually, however, you mention in your cover letter that references are available on request.

❽ Make sure your résumé creates the impression you want to make. Typographical errors, incorrect spelling, poorly spaced headings and entries, and generally sloppy work will make a negative impression.

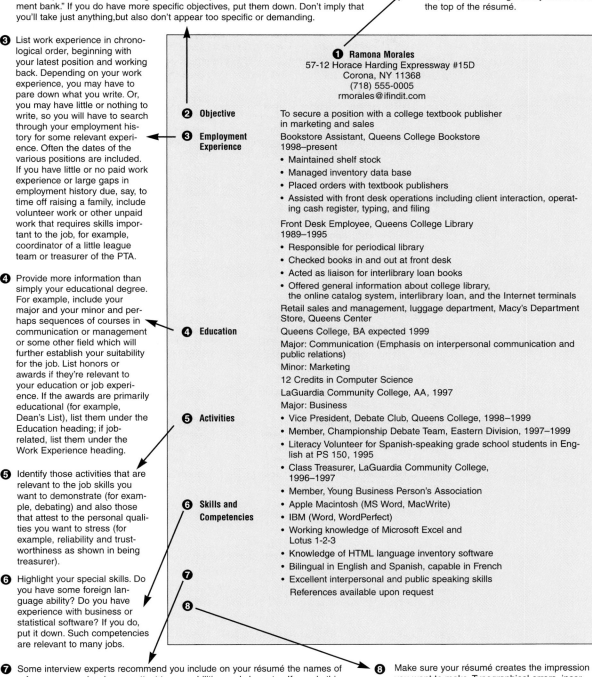

TABLE 22.1 Common Interview Questions

These questions, commonly asked in employment interviews, are organized around the major topics on the résumé. They're drawn from a variety of interviewing experts (Stewart and Cash 1984; Skopec 1986; Sincoff and Goyer 1984; Zima 1983; Seidman 1991). Jandt and Nemnich (1995) provide suggestions specifically for Internet interviews. You may find it helpful to rehearse with this list before going into the interview.

Question Areas	Examples	Suggestions
Objectives and Career Goals	Why did you decide to work in this field? What made you apply to Datacomm? If you took a job with us, where do you see yourself in five years? What benefits do you want to get out of this job? What are your salary requirements?	Be positive (and as specific as you can be) about the company. Demonstrate your knowledge of the company. Take a long-range view; no firm wants to hire someone who will be looking for another job in six months. Be prepared to state a salary range that you're seeking.
Employment	Tell me about your previous work experience. What did you do exactly? Did you enjoy working at Happy Publications? Why did you leave? How does this previous experience relate to the work you'd be doing here at Datacomm? What kinds of problems did you encounter at your last position? How did you solve them?	Again, be positive; never knock a previous job. If you do, the interviewer will think you may be criticizing them in the near future. Especially avoid criticizing specific people with whom you worked. When asked about problems be ready to present a specific case with your positive and constructive solution.
Education	What do you think of the education you got at Queens College? Has it prepared you for a career at Datacomm? Why did you major in communication? What kinds of courses did you take? What courses did you like the most? Did you do an internship? What were your responsibilities?	Be positive about your educational experience. Try to relate your educational experience to the job for which you're interviewing. Demonstrate competence but at the same time the willingness to continue your education (either formally or informally).
Skills	I see here you have a speaking and writing knowledge of Spanish. Could you talk with someone on the phone in Spanish or write letters in Spanish to our customers? Do you know any other languages? How much do you know about computers?	Before going into the interview, review your competencies. Explain your skills in as much detail as needed to establish their relevance to the job and your own specific competencies.

activities (Taub 1997). For example, if the interviewer asks you to identify your best quality, an ineffective response would be to give an abstract answer such as "I'm an effective communicator and I enjoy it." A more preferred response would be to say: "I'm an effective communicator. I led focus groups and brainstorming sessions, and I represented my department several times at general meetings. All turned out successfully and I really enjoyed the experience as well."

In responding, emphasize your positive qualities (you're dependable, creative, and team oriented, for example). At the same time, emphasize your knowledge and skills (you can speak Chinese, lead work groups, or use Quark XPress, for example).

Even though the interviewer will ask most of the questions, you also will want to ask questions. In addition to rehearsing some answers to predicted questions, think of some open-ended questions that will reveal the information you need.

Make an Effective Presentation of Self

Arrive on time—in interview situations, this means 10 to 15 minutes early. This will allow you time to relax, get accustomed to the general surroundings, and perhaps fill out any required forms. It also gives you a cushion should something delay you on the way.

A great number of jobs are won or lost solely on physical appearance, so also give attention to physical preparation. Dress in a way that shows you care enough about the interview to make a good impression. At the same time, dress comfortably so that you're not fidgeting throughout the interview. Perhaps the most specific advice that can be given is to avoid extremes—in hairstyle, makeup, jewelry, perfume, or cologne. Remember that the casual-dress Friday, popular at many organizations, does not apply to people interviewing for jobs. If in doubt, dress up: wear a tie, dress shoes, dress, or skirt; avoid sneakers and jeans.

Be sure you know the name of the company, the job title, and the interviewer's name. Although you'll have much on your mind, the interviewer's name is not one of the things you can afford to forget or mispronounce.

Bring with you the appropriate materials, whatever they may be. At the very least, bring a pen and paper, an extra copy or two of your résumé and, if appropriate, a business card. If you're applying for a job in which you have experience, you might bring samples of your previous work.

In presenting yourself, try not to be too casual or too formal. When there is doubt, choose increased formality. Slouching back in the chair, smoking, and chewing gum or candy are obvious behaviors to avoid when you're trying to impress an interviewer.

Acknowledge Cultural Rules and Customs

Each culture—and each organization is much like a culture—has its own rules for communicating (Barna 1994, Ruben 1985, Spitzberg 1991). These rules—whether in the interview situation or in friendly conversation—prescribe appropriate and inappropriate behavior, rewards and punishments, and what will help you get the job and what won't. For example, the general advice given in Table 22.2 (under "positiveness") is to emphasize your positive qualities, to highlight your abilities and positive qualities, and to minimize any negative characteristics or failings. But in some cultures—especially collectivist cultures such as China, Korea, and Japan, interviewees are expected to show modesty (Copeland and Griggs 1985). Should you stress your own competencies too much, you may be seen as arrogant, brash, and unfit to work in an organization where teamwork and cooperation are emphasized.

In collectivist cultures, great deference is to be shown to the interviewer, who represents the company. If you don't treat the interviewer with great respect, you may appear as disrespecting the entire company. On the other hand, in individualist cultures, such as the United States, too much deference may make you appear unassertive, unsure of yourself, and unable to assume a position of authority.

Demonstrate Effective Interpersonal Communication

Throughout the interview, be certain you demonstrate the interpersonal communication skills covered in this book. Put into practice all the skills you've learned. Table 22.2 shows the ten characteristics of interpersonal effectiveness, discussed at length in Unit 8, specifically applied to the interview situation.

Follow Up

Much as you would write a thank-you note to the person you interviewed for information and discussed earlier, you would also follow up the employment interview with a thank-you note to the interviewer. In this brief, professional

TABLE 22.2 Some Dos and Don'ts of Interpersonal Communication in the Interview

Here are a few dos and don'ts that may prove useful. What other dos and don'ts would you suggest job interviewees observe?

Characteristic	Do	Don't
Openness	Answer questions as fully as appropriate. Give enough detail to answer the question.	Give one-word answers that may signal a lack of interest or knowledge or, at the other extreme, ramble or go off on tangents.
Empathy	See the questions from the interviewer's point of view. Focus your eye contact and orient your body toward the interviewer. Lean forward as appropriate.	Focus your attention away from the interviewer or the interview situation.
Supportiveness	Assume the questions are legitimate requests for information.	Perceive questions as personal attacks or act defensively when asked a difficult question.
Positiveness	Emphasize your positive qualities and your interest in the position and in the company.	Criticize yourself or emphasize your negative qualities. Criticize your previous employer or your education.
Equality	Approach disagreements as attempts to understand the job and the interviewer's position.	Projecting an image that would lead the interviewer to see you as someone who feels inferior and who could not handle serious responsibilities or as someone who might antagonize others by appearing superior.
Confidence	Project a confident self, someone willing and able to tackle the tasks the job requires.	Appearing overly confident or cocky or overly shy, as someone who would not be able to function on a team or in group situations.
Immediacy	Connect yourself with the interviewer throughout the interview by, for example, using the interviewer's name, focusing clearly on the interviewer's remarks, and expressing responsibility for your thoughts and feelings.	Distance yourself from the interviewer, forget the interviewer's name (or mispronounce it), or fail to respond directly to the interviewer's questions.
Interaction management	Ensure the interviewer's satisfaction by being positive, complimentary, and generally cooperative.	Appear defensive, cocky, lacking in assertiveness, extremely introverted, or overly aggressive.
Expressiveness	Let your nonverbal behaviors (especially facial expression and vocal variety) reflect your verbal messages and your general enthusiasm.	Fidget, move about excessively, or use self-adaptors, self-touching gestures that communicate a lack of confidence and comfort. Talk in a monotone or look bored or unenthusiastic.
Other-orientation	Focus on and express interest in the interviewer and in the company. Express agreement and ask for clarification as appropriate.	Argue or engage in unnecessary criticism.

letter, thank the interviewer for his or her time and consideration. You also have an opportunity to resell yourself—to mention qualities you possess and wish to emphasize but may have been too modest to discuss at the time. Reiterate your interest in the job and the company. If you didn't get the job, you might ask to be kept in mind for future openings. Such letters help you stand out in the interviewer's mind, since not many interviewees write letters of thanks. It's a kind of pat on the back to the interviewer and says, in effect, that the interview was an effective one.

What specifically can you do to prepare yourself for your next job interview?

◀◀ THINKING BACK

? ASK THE RESEARCHER

Negotiating the Job Offer

I'm entering the job market and have completed screening interviews. I've been invited to visit several organizations and want to negotiate the best deal in my first job. What issues should I consider, and how should I engage in an job negotiation?

In negotiating a job offer, focus on four aspects of communication: managing information, introducing multiple issues, packaging alternatives, and understanding your BATNA. In managing information, pose questions about particular needs and don't just follow the interviewer's questions. Make sure the information you're given is accurate and provides a realistic preview of the actual job. Introducing multiple issues into the bargaining mix enhances the prospects of reaching a mutually satisfactory agreement. Issues such as job requirements, starting date, promotion opportunities, relocation, training programs, medical benefits, and office support are critical aspects of a job and should be brought up in the interview in addition to starting salary. Both parties can then package issues by trading off options and compensating for relative costs. Finally, go into the job negotiation with consideration of your "best alternative to a negotiated agreement" (BATNA). If you have unique skills in a tight marketplace or have multiple job offers, you hold a stronger BATNA and can make use of it in bargaining for higher wages and job benefits.

For further information see R. J. Lewicki, D. M. Saunders, and J. W. Minton, *Negotiation,* 3d ed. (Boston, MA: Irwin-McGraw Hill, 1999), and L. L. Putnam, "Bargaining," in *International Encyclopedia of Communication,* Vol. 1, ed. E. Barnouw (Philadelphia, PA: Oxford University Press, 1989), pp. 176–178.

—Linda L. Putnam (Ph.D., University of Minnesota) is a professor of speech communication at Texas A&M University and teaches courses in negotiation, conflict management, and organizational communication. She conducts research on public sector bargaining, managerial negotiation, and environmental conflict management and is the director of the Program on Conflict and Dispute Resolution at the George Bush School of Government and Public Service.

COMMUNICATING IN THE WORKPLACE

THINKING AHEAD ▸▸

How do people communicate in the workplace? What kinds of communication occur between managers and subordinates? Between coworkers?

It's useful to discuss communication in the workplace in terms of the direction in which it flows. Upward and downward (also called vertical) communication and lateral communication are the formal channels, those that can be found in an organization chart, for example, and which are officially sanctioned by the organization. In addition, we also need to look at the grapevine—the informal channel that no organization seems to be without. Last, we look at workplace groups.

Upward Communication

Upward communication refers to messages sent from the lower levels of the hierarchy to the upper levels—for example, line worker to manager, faculty member to dean. This type of communication is usually concerned with (1) job-related activities—that is, what is going on at the job, what was accomplished, what remains to be done, and similar issues; (2) job-related problems and unresolved questions; (3) ideas for change and suggestions for improvement; and (4) job-related feelings about the organization, about the work, about other workers, and similar issues.

Upward communication is vital to the maintenance and growth of the organization. It gives management necessary feedback on worker morale and possible sources of dissatisfaction. It gives subordinates a sense of belonging to and being a part of the organization. It also provides management with the opportunity to acquire new ideas from workers.

Downward Communication

Downward communication refers to messages sent from the higher levels of the hierarchy to the lower levels. Messages sent by managers to workers or from deans to faculty members are examples of downward communication. Orders are the most obvious example of downward communication: "Type this in duplicate," "Send these crates out by noon," "Write the advertisement copy," and so on. Along with these order-giving messages are the accompanying explanations of procedures, goals, and the like. Managers are also responsible for giving appraisals of workers and for motivating them, all in the name of productivity and for the good of the organization as a whole. It's interesting to note that subordinates who were more satisfied with their job reported better quality communication with their superiors (Callahan 1993).

A somewhat different form of downward communication concerns dealing with complaints. Complaints are essential sources of feedback; they tell you that at least one person (perhaps many) is dissatisfied with the way things are going and that something should be changed. If you wish to keep this channel of vital information open, try these suggestions for dealing with complaints.

- Let the person know that you're open to complaints and that you do view them as essential sources of information. Welcome complaints; stress that they're essential for improving the workplace environment. Be careful that you don't fall into the trap of seeing someone who voices a complaint as a complainer and as someone to avoid.
- Listen to complaints. Follow the suggestions for effective listening already discussed: listen supportively and with empathy. Give the person voicing the complaint your complete attention and avoid interrupting.
- Make sure you understand both the thoughts and the feelings that go with the complaint. Listen to both the complaint about working too hard and to the frustration the worker feels when he or she has to work overtime without advance notice. Respond to both the thoughts and feelings. Express your concern about the workload and the frustration that these demands create.

ASK THE RESEARCHER

Managing Emotions

People have told me I'm overly emotional, and it's made me anxious about my new job, which I'm starting next month. I want to appear the picture of the cool, totally in control individual. Any suggestions for controlling my emotions and projecting this confident image?

If your response is due to the situation (you feel anxious and over-emotional in new, highly evaluative settings), you can probably function more effectively by maintaining a "problem-focus." Keep your thoughts and plans focused on the job problems (what are the standards for productivity, when do we have staff meetings) and don't get trapped into an "emotion-focus" (my heart's pounding, I look like a fool). If your response is driven by your personality (you're just an anxious, nervous person), things are a little more complicated. The "problem-focus" is still an excellent strategy, but in this case, it can be much more difficult to ignore your emotional response because this is who you are. If you find that you cannot produce the smooth communication (even with a problem-focus), you might want to consider clinical help. No, you're not crazy or mentally ill, but your anxiety is clearly interfering with your skilled performance. Several effective treatments for social anxiety exist and may help you learn to cope more effectively.

—Melanie Booth-Butterfield (Ph.D.,University of Missouri) is a professor and chair of communication studies at West Virginia University. Her teaching concentrations include interpersonal communication, social issues associated with communication, and health communication; among her research interests are health communication, emotion and cognition, and related interpersonal communication topics. Steven Booth-Butterfield (Ed.D., West Virginia University) is the chief of the Health Communication Research Branch of the National Institute for Occupational Safety and Health. His teaching focuses on media effects, influence and persuasion, and health communication. His research areas include health communication, influence and persuasion, and emotion and cognition related to communication.

- Ask the person making the complaint what he or she would like you to do about it. Sometimes all a person wants is for someone to hear the complaint and to appreciate its legitimacy. At other times, the complaint is presented for you to do something specific. But before you assume that you know what a person really wants, ask. The very act of asking is a further affirmation that you welcome complaints and that you value the person's bringing this to your attention.

Lateral Communication

Lateral communication refers to messages between equals—manager to manager, worker to worker. Such messages may move within the same subdivision or department of the organization or across divisions. Lateral communication refers to the communication that takes place between two history professors at Arizona State University or between the psychologist at the University of Akron and the communicologist at Kent State.

Lateral communication facilitates the sharing of insights, methods, and problems. It helps the organization avoid some problems and solve others. Lateral communication also builds morale and worker satisfaction. Good relationships and meaningful communication between workers are among the main sources of worker satisfaction. More generally, lateral communication serves the purpose of coordinating the various activities of the organization and enabling the various divisions to pool insights and expertise.

Grapevine Communication

The types of communication discussed to this point follow the formal structure of the organization. **Grapevine messages** don't follow such formal lines. Rather, they seem to have a life of their own and are concerned primarily with personal and social matters rather than with the organization itself. Grapevine communication, however, can be and often is used to enhance a feeling of stability and to establish the credibility of the organization (Mishra 1990).

Grapevine communications grow along with the formal communications; the more active the formal communication system, the more active the informal system. Not surprisingly, the grapevine also grows as the size of the organization increases.

The grapevine seems most likely to be used when (1) there is great upheaval or change within the organization; (2) the information is new—no one likes to spread old and well-known information; (3) face-to-face communication is physically easy; and (4) workers "cluster in clique-groups along the vine" (Davis 1977, 1980). The grapevine is most active immediately after the happening that is to be communicated and is most likely to be activated when the news concerns one's intimates, friends, and associates. Although the grapevine is part of every large organization's informal communications, it's not used as frequently as folklore would have us believe (Baird 1977). It's unlikely to grow in climates that are stable and comfortable. Change, ambiguity, and organizational secrecy nourish the grapevine.

Workplace Groups

Groups and meetings of all kinds are everywhere in the workplace. Some are face-to-face; some are conducted via videophones, online through e-mail, or on a conference telephone call. Some meetings are designed to solve problems while others may be devoted to developing ideas or planning future activities. Although workplace

ETHICS IN INTERPERSONAL COMMUNICATION

Vote online at http://www.awl.com/devito

Interview Questions

Through the Equal Employment Opportunity Commission, the federal government has classified some interview questions as unlawful. As you review this brief discussion, ask yourself if unlawful questions are also unethical questions. Some of the more important areas in which unlawful (and unethical?) questions are frequently asked concern age, marital status, race, religion, nationality, citizenship, physical condition, and arrest and criminal records. For example, it's legal to ask applicants whether they meet the legal age requirements for the job and could provide proof of that. But it's unlawful to ask their exact age, even in indirect ways such as "When did you graduate from high school, Mary?" It's unlawful to ask about a person's marital status or about family matters that are unrelated to the job, for example, "Will you have trouble getting a baby sitter?" An interviewer may ask you, however, to identify a close relative or guardian if you're a minor, or any relative who currently works for the company.

Questions concerning your race, religion, national origin, affectional orientation, age, handicaps unrelated to job performance, or even arrest record are unlawful, as are questions that get at this same information in oblique ways. For example, requiring someone to provide a photograph along with a job application may be a way of discriminating against an applicant on the basis of sex, race, and age.

The interviewer may ask you what languages you're fluent in but may not ask what your native language is, what language you speak at home, or what language your parents speak. The interviewer may ask you if you are in this country legally but may not ask if you were born in this country or naturalized.

The interviewer may inquire into your physical condition only insofar as the job is concerned. For example, the interviewer may ask, "Do you have any physical problems that might prevent you from fulfilling your responsibilities at this job?" But the interviewer may not ask about any physical disabilities. The interviewer may ask you if you've been convicted of a felony but not if you've been arrested.

What would you do? *Sally has a Ph.D. in communication and has been teaching for the last ten years. Now she's applying for a new position as head of the department at a state college. At the job interview, one of the faculty members says: "I notice that you've taught courses in gay and lesbian studies. Are you a lesbian, an open lesbian?" Although this question is illegal, would you consider it unethical? If you were Sally, what would you do in this situation?*

groups and meetings are largely task oriented, lots of socializing goes on. The most common workplace groups are described below.

WEB EXPLORATION
To learn more about idea-generation groups, go to www.awl.com/devito.

Idea-Generation Groups Many small groups exist solely to generate ideas. They often follow a formula called **brainstorming,** a technique for bombarding a problem and generating as many ideas as possible (Beebe and Masterson 2000, Osborn 1957). In this system the process occurs in two phases: (1) the brainstorming period proper and (2) the evaluation period.

In brainstorming, a problem is selected that is amenable to many possible solutions. Each person contributes as many ideas as he or she can think of. All ideas are recorded in writing or on tape. During this idea-generating session, four general rules are followed: (1) no criticism is allowed, (2) quantity is desired (the more suggestions, the better), (3) combining and extending ideas is welcomed, and (4) the wilder the idea, the better.

At times the brainstorming session may break down, with members failing to contribute new ideas. At this point the moderator may prod the members with statements such as "Let's try to get a few more ideas before we close this session" or "Here's what we have so far. As I read the list of contributed suggestions, additional ideas may come to mind."

One of the most surprising facts about grapevines is that they're relatively accurate. Approximately 75 to 95 percent of grapevine information is correct (Davis 1980, Hellweg 1992). Even though many details are omitted, the stories are basically true. Do you find this true of your own workplace grapevine? Is the grapevine on campus similarly accurate?

After all the ideas are generated—a period lasting no longer than 15 or 20 minutes—the entire list of ideas is evaluated. The ones that are unworkable are thrown out; the ones that show promise are retained and evaluated further.

Focus Groups In the focus group the leader tries to discover the beliefs, attitudes, thoughts, and feelings that members have, so as to better guide decisions on changing the scent or redesigning the packaging or constructing advertisements for luxury cars. It's the leader's task to prod members to analyze their thoughts and feelings on a deeper level and to use the thoughts of one member to stimulate the thoughts of others.

Nominal Groups The **nominal group technique** is a method of problem solving that uses limited discussion and confidential voting to obtain a group decision (Kelly 1994). It's especially helpful when some members may be reluctant to voice their opinions in a regular problem-solving group or when the issue is controversial or sensitive. Generally, the procedure involves defining the problem and having each member write down his or her ideas or suggested solutions. Each member then states one idea from his or her list, which is recorded on a board or flip chart so everyone can see it. This process is repeated until all suggestions are stated and recorded.

Once recorded, the suggestions are rank ordered by each member. The rankings are then combined to get a group ranking, which is then written on the board. The highest ranking solution might then be selected to be tested, or perhaps several high ranking solutions may be put into operation.

Delphi Groups In the **Delphi method,** a group of experts is established, but there is no interaction among them; instead, they communicate by repeatedly responding to questionnaires (Tersine and Riggs 1980, Kelly 1994). The method is especially useful when you want to involve people who are geographically distant from each other and when you want all members to uphold the solution.

In this method, the problem is defined and each member contributes anonymously five ideas in writing. This stage used to be completed through questionnaires sent through traditional mail but is now more frequently done through e-mail, which greatly increases the speed with which this entire process can be accomplished. The ideas of all members are combined, written up, and distributed to all members, who may be asked to select the three or four best ideas from this composite list. From these responses another list is produced and distributed to all members, who may be asked to select the one or two best ideas. The process may be repeated any number of times, but usually three rounds are sufficient for achieving a fair degree of agreement. The best solutions are then identified and communicated to all members.

Quality Circles **Quality circles** are groups of workers (usually from about 6 to 12) whose task it is to investigate and make recommendations for improving the quality of some organizational function. The motivations for establishing quality circles are to improve quality and profitability and to improve worker morale (Gorden and Nevins 1993). The basic idea is that people who work on similar tasks will be better able to improve their departments or jobs by pooling their insights and working through problems they share.

Quality circle members investigate problems using any method they feel might be helpful, such as face-to-face problem-solving groups, nominal groups, Delphi methods. The group then reports its findings and its suggestions to those who can do something about it.

A somewhat similar type of group is the improvement group or what is often called "kaizen," a Japanese word that means "continual improvement" (Beebe and Masterson 2000). These groups are based on the assumption that every process or product in any organization can be improved. Such groups may be set up for a certain amount of time or may be permanent.

TRY IT!
To learn more about online groups, go to www.awl.com/devito.

Telephone or Online Groups More and more groups meet via some electronic channel, for example, telephone or Internet. In an early study of mediated versus face-to-face communication, it was found that telephone group conferences allowed members easy speaking access and promoted good attention and eager participation (Remp 1974). Telephone groups also felt less pressure to conform to group opinion and were more comfortable changing their positions. There was productive conflict but no hostility.

More recent research has focused on computer groups and compared them with face-to-face groups (Olaniran 1994, Kiesler and Sproull 1992, Harris 1995). Compared with face-to-face groups, computer groups:

- generated a greater number of unique ideas
- proposed more unconventional or risky decisions
- took longer to reach agreement
- engaged in more explicit and outspoken advocacy
- had more equal participation among members

One researcher has proposed that the student preference for computer-mediated over face-to-face communication was due to the fact that in mediated communication the students didn't have to worry about the rules for interpersonal communication, such as those for eye contact and body communication, and there were reduced concerns about shyness (Mendoza 1995). Research is just beginning to identify the differences between the various forms of communication and their computer counterparts. Similarly, the insights from these studies are just beginning to be incorporated into interpersonal communication courses and textbooks (cf. Harris 1995).

Here are some guidelines for making your own online communication more effective:

- Watch your spelling. If you have a spell-check program on the computer, use it.
- Remember that what you write can easily be made public. To paraphrase Sidney Biddle Barrows: "Never say anything on the [Internet] that you wouldn't want your mother to hear at your trial."
- Follow the rules of netiquette; for example, don't spam or flame.
- Clean up your writing—consider your choices for communicating mindfully.
- Follow the suggestions and guidelines for interpersonal communication generally.
- Be explicit about your good intentions; avoid the possibility of being misunderstood. If you think your sarcasm may not be interpreted as humor, for example, then use an emoticon that shows you smiling :-).

What kinds of relationships do you think you'll find profitable to pursue in the workplace? What kinds of relationships are you likely to avoid or discourage?

◀◀ THINKING BACK

COMMUNICATING IN WORKPLACE RELATIONSHIPS

THINKING AHEAD ▶▶

How does the workplace influence the kinds and quality of your interpersonal relationships?

The workplace is a context in which all forms of communication take place and, not surprisingly, all kinds of relationships may be seen. Here we discuss three kinds

ETHICS IN INTERPERSONAL COMMUNICATION

Vote online at http://www.awl.com/devito

On the Job

The various ethical issues and guidelines already offered are similar to those that would operate within a workplace environment (Johannesen 1995). These guides can be reviewed with the acronym ETHICS—empathy (Cheney and Tompkins 1987), talk rather than force, honesty (Krebs 1989), interaction management, confidentiality, and supportiveness.

Empathy. Workers in an organization have an ethical obligation to understand what others are feeling as well as thinking from their point of view. This is especially important when members from vastly different rungs of the organizational ladder communicate.

Talk. Decisions in an organization should be arrived at by talk rather than force, by persuasion rather than coercion.

Honesty. Organizational communication—whether from the highest levels of management or from the trainees in the mail room—should be honest and truthful.

Interaction management. Organizational communication and relationships should be satisfying and comfortable.

Confidentiality. Members have a right to expect that what they say in confidence will not be made public or even whispered about at the water cooler.

Supportiveness. A supportive and cooperative climate should characterize the interpersonal interactions throughout the organization.

What would you do? *You're managing a work team of three colleagues charged with redesigning the company Web site. The problem is that Jack doesn't do any work and misses most of the meetings. You spoke with Jack about it, and he confided that he's going through a divorce and child custody battles and really can't concentrate on the project. You feel sorry for Jack and have been carrying him for the last few months, but you realize now that you'll never be able to bring the project in on time if you don't get someone to replace Jack. In addition, you really don't want to get a negative appraisal because of Jack; in fact, you were counting on the raise that this project was going to get you. What would you do in this situation?*

of relationships that are especially important in the workplace: romantic, mentoring, and network relationships.

Workplace Romantic Relationships

Unlike television depictions where workers are always best friends who would do anything for each other and where the characters move in and out of interoffice romances with little difficulties—at least with no difficulties that can't be resolved in 24 minutes—real life is quite different. Opinions vary widely concerning workplace romances. Some organizations, on the assumption that romantic relationships are basically detrimental to the success of the workplace, have explicit rules prohibiting such relationships. In some organizations, workers can be fired for such relationships.

On the positive side, the work environment seems a perfect place to meet a potential romantic partner. After all, by virtue of the fact that you're working in the same office, you're probably both interested in the same field, have similar training and ambitions, and will spend considerable time together—all factors that foster the development of a successful interpersonal relationship.

Similarly, office romances can lead to greater work satisfaction. For example, if you're romantically attracted to another worker, it can make going to work, working together, and even working added hours more enjoyable and more satisfying. If the relationship is a good one and one that is mutually satisfying, the individuals are likely to develop empathy for each other and act in ways that are supportive, cooperative, and friendly; in short, the workers are more likely to act with all the characteristics of effective communication noted throughout this book.

However, even when the relationship is a good one for the two individuals, it may not be good for other workers. Seeing the loving couple every day in every way may generate office gossip that may prove destructive. Others may think the lovers are a team that has to be confronted as a pair, and that you can't criticize one without incurring the wrath of the other.

Workplace romantic relationships may cause problems for management when, for example, a promotion is to be made or relocation decisions are necessary. Can you legitimately ask one lover to move to Boston and the other to move to San Francisco? Will it prove difficult for management to promote one lover who then becomes the supervisor of the other?

The workplace also puts pressure on the individuals. Most organizations, at least in the United States, are highly competitive; one person's success often means another's failure. In this environment, the normal self-disclosures (which often reveal weaknesses, doubts, and misgivings) that regularly accompany increased intimacy may actually prove a liability in this kind of competitive context.

When the romance goes bad or when it's one-sided, there are even more disadvantages. One obvious problem is that it can be stressful for the former partners to see each other regularly and perhaps to work together. Other workers may feel they have to take sides, being supportive of one partner and critical of the other. This can easily cause friction throughout the organization. Another and perhaps more serious issue is the potential for charges of sexual harassment, especially if the romance is between a supervisor and a worker. Whether the charges are legitimate, or the result of an unhappy love affair and unrelated to the organization, management will find itself in the middle, facing lawsuits and time and money lost from investigating and ultimately acting on the charges.

The generally negative attitude of management toward such relationships and the problems in dealing with the normal stress of both work and romance seem to outweigh the positive benefits that could be derived from such relationships, so workers are generally advised not to romance their colleagues. Friendships seem the much safer course.

Mentoring Relationships

A **mentoring relationship** is one in which an experienced individual helps to train one who is less experienced. An accomplished teacher, for example, might mentor one who is newly arrived or who has never taught before. The mentor guides the new person through the organization maze, teaches the strategies and techniques for success, and otherwise communicates his or her accumulated knowledge and experience to this "mentee."

The mentoring relationship provides an ideal learning environment. It's usually a one-on-one relationship between expert and novice, a relationship that is supportive and trusting. There's a mutual and open sharing of information and thoughts about the job. The relationship enables the novice to try out new skills under the guidance of an expert, to ask questions, and to obtain the feedback so necessary in learning complex skills. It's a relationship that is perhaps best characterized as one in which the experienced and powerful mentor empowers the novice, giving the novice the tools and techniques for gaining the same power the mentor now holds.

The mentoring relationship has been found to be one of the three primary paths for career achievement among African American men and women (Bridges 1996). In another study (of middle-level managers), those who had mentors and participated in mentoring relationships were found to get more promotions and higher salaries than those who didn't have mentors (Scandura 1992).

At the same time, the mentor benefits from clarifying his or her thoughts, seeing the job from the perspective of a newcomer, and considering and formulating answers to a variety of questions. Much as a teacher learns from teaching, a mentor learns from mentoring.

Networking Relationships

In the popular mind, **networking** is often viewed simply as a technique for securing a job. But it's actually a much broader process that can be viewed as one of using other people to help you solve your problems, or at least offer insights that bear on your problem—for example, how to publish your manuscript, where to look for low-cost auto insurance, how to find an affordable apartment, or how to empty your cache.

Networking comes in at least two forms: informal and formal. Informal networking is what we do every day when we find ourselves in a new situation or unable to answer questions. Thus, for example, if you're new at a school, you might ask someone in your class where to eat or shop for new clothes or who's the best teacher for interpersonal communication. In the same way, when you enter a new work environment, you might ask more experienced workers how to perform certain tasks or whom you should avoid or approach when you have questions.

Formal networking is the same thing except that it's a lot more systematic and strategic. It's the establishment of connections with people who can help you—answer questions, get you a job, help you get promoted, help you relocate or accomplish any task you want to accomplish.

At the most obvious level, you can network with people you already know. If you review the list of people in your acquaintance, you'll probably discover that you know a great number of people with very specialized knowledge who can be of assistance to you in a wide variety of ways. In some cultures, Brazil is one example, friendships are established in part because of potential networking connections (Rector and Neiva 1996). You can also network with people who know people you know. Thus, you may contact a friend's friend to find out if the firm he or she works for is hiring. Or you may contact people you have no connection with. Perhaps you've read something the person wrote or you've heard the person's name raised in connection with an area in which you're interested and you want to get more information. With e-mail addresses so readily available, it's now quite common to e-mail individuals who have particular expertise and ask them questions you might have.

The great value of networking, of course, is that it provides you with access to a wealth of specialized information. At the same time, it often makes accessing that information a lot easier than if you had to find it all by yourself.

In networking, it's often recommended that you try to establish relationships that are mutually beneficial. After all, much as others are useful sources of information for you, you're likely to be a useful source of information for others. If you can provide others with helpful information, it's more likely that they will provide helpful information for you. In this way, a mutually satisfying and productive network is established.

Some networking experts advise you to develop files and directories of potentially useful sources that you can contact for needed information. For example, if you're a freelance artist, you might develop a list of people who might be in positions to offer you work or who might lead you to others who might offer such work. Authors, editors, art directors, administrative assistants, people in advertising, and a host of others might eventually provide useful leads for such work. Creating a directory of such people and keeping in contact with them on a fairly regular basis can often simplify your obtaining freelance work.

Formal networking requires that you take an active part in locating and establishing these connections. Be proactive; initiate contacts rather than wait for them to come to you. Of course, this can be overdone; you don't want to rely on people to do the work you can easily do yourself. Yet if you're also willing to help others, there is nothing wrong in asking these same people to help you. If you're respectful of their time and expertise, it's likely that your networking attempts will be responded to favorably. Following up your requests with thank-you notes will help you establish networks that can be ongoing, productive relationships rather than one-shot affairs.

What kinds of workplace communication have you taken part in? In what ways could you have been more effective?

◂◂ THINKING BACK

REVIEWING KEY TERMS AND CONCEPTS IN INTERPERSONAL COMMUNICATION IN THE WORKPLACE

In this unit we looked at interpersonal communication in the workplace and considered the employment interview, the patterns of communication that are common in organizations, and three workplace relationships: romantic, mentoring, and network.

Communicating to Join the Workplace: The Employment Interview

What are some of the dos and don'ts for effective job interview?

- Prepare yourself by researching the career field, the specific position, the company, and what is going on in the world related to that organization and position.
- Prepare answers to anticipated questions, and prepare questions you want to ask.
- Make an effective presentation of self by following the general characteristics of effective interpersonal communication discussed throughout the text.
- Acknowledge and avoid violating the cultural rules and customs of the organization.
- Demonstrate effective interpersonal communication throughout the interview.
- Follow up the interview with a renewed expression of interest and thanks.

Communicating in the Workplace

How are messages sent and received in the workplace? What are the most common workplace groups?

- **Upward communication** refers to messages sent from the lower levels of the hierarchy to the upper levels.

- **Downward communication** refers to messages sent from the upper levels of the hierarchy (for example, management) to the lower levels.
- **Lateral communication** refers to messages sent from equal to equal—manager to manager, worker to worker.
- **Grapevine** communication refers to messages that don't follow the formal structure of the organization; instead, they can be sent from anyone to anyone.
- **Workplace groups** include:
  Idea-generation groups: designed to develop new ideas or ways of looking at problems.
  Focus groups: interviewed in depth to discover what people are thinking.
  Nominal groups: problem-solving groups that rely on limited discussion and confidential voting in order to obtain a group decision.
  Delphi groups: a collection of experts who repeatedly respond to questionnaires without any face-to-face interaction.
  Quality circles: workers who investigate and make recommendations for improving the quality of some organizational function.
  Telephone or online groups: similar in function to face-to-face groups but they "meet" through some electronic connection.

Communicating in Workplace Relationships

What types of relationships occur in the workplace, and what influence does the workplace have on such relationships?

- Romantic relationships in the workplace, although having a variety of benefits, are often frowned upon and often entail a variety of problems that would not arise in other contexts.
- Mentoring relationships help you learn the ropes of the organization through the experience and knowledge of someone who has gone through the processes you'll be going through.
- Networking enables you to expand your area of expertise and enable you to secure information bearing on a wide variety of problems you want to solve and questions you want to answer.

APPLYING KEY TERMS AND CONCEPTS IN INTERPERSONAL COMMUNICATION IN THE WORKPLACE

1. How many employment interviews do you estimate you'll be involved in throughout your professional life? How important will these be to your eventual professional success?
2. Visit www.monster.com, a huge database of jobs that you can access by keyword, location, or industry. Of what values can this Web site and similar ones be to seeking employment?
3. Visit the Web site of a corporation you might be interested in working for. (Most corporations have Web addresses of the form www.nameofcorporation.com, or you can locate such addresses through any of the many search engines.) What can you learn about the corporation that might prove of value in your employment interview?
4. How would you describe the communication that takes place within your workplace? How does it differ from family communication?
5. With which type of communication (upward, downward, or lateral) are you most comfortable and most effective? What specific communication skills do you have that will prove of value in each of these types of workplace communication?
6. How active are you in grapevine communication on your job? Are you as often a source as you are a receiver? What accounts for your status?
7. Has information overload entered your life? In what way? What are you doing about it?
8. What are your feelings about romantic relationships in the workplace? Altercast—put yourself into both the position of the worker who sees great opportunities for relationships and the manager who focuses on making sure the company makes money.
9. In what ways might you serve as a mentor? What values might you gain from mentoring those less experienced than you?
10. How would you go about finding answers to such questions as these?
    - What communication problems do managers and workers identify as most significant in hindering productivity? In reducing morale?
    - What communication strategies work best to increase worker morale?
    - Do popular workers receive more grapevine messages than less popular workers?
    - Do college students with mentors earn higher grades? Do they get higher starting salaries?
    - Do men and women differ in their networking behavior?

EXPERIENCING KEY TERMS AND CONCEPTS IN INTERPERSONAL COMMUNICATION IN THE WORKPLACE

Go to www.awl.com/devito

Exercise No. 29, "Practicing Interviewing Skills," will prove useful for reviewing the principles of the employment interview and allowing for interviewing practice. Exercise No. 30, "Confronting Workplace Communication Difficulties," illustrates some potential communication problems and asks for possible solutions. This exercise may also be used to summarize the wide variety of skills covered throughout the course.

GLOSSARY OF INTERPERSONAL COMMUNICATION CONCEPTS AND SKILLS

In the film *Alice in Wonderland* (1951), based on the works of Lewis Carroll, we hear Humpty Dumpty tell Alice, "When I use a word it means just what I choose it to mean; neither more nor less." Of course, if everyone used Humpty Dumpty's system, communication would be impossible. The meaning of a word is in both the speaker and the listener, and although their meanings are never identical, we assume that both speaker and listener have some common reference for the words used. Here, then, is the jargon of interpersonal communication, a glossary of words and meaning, concepts and skills, that should provide a basis for understanding and talking about communication.

Listed here are definitions of the technical terms of interpersonal communication—the words that are peculiar or unique to this discipline—and, where appropriate, the corresponding skills (*in italics*). These definitions and statements of skills should make new or difficult terms a bit easier to understand and should help to place the skill in context. All boldface terms within the definitions appear as separate entries in the glossary.

acculturation. The process by which your culture is modified or changed through contact with or exposure to another culture.

active listening. The process by which a listener expresses his or her understanding of the speaker's total message, including the verbal and nonverbal, the thoughts and feelings.

adaptors. Nonverbal behaviors that serve some kind of need—for example, scratching one's head. *Avoid adaptors that interfere with effective communication and reveal your discomfort or anxiety.*

adjustment. The principle of verbal interaction that claims that effective communication depends on the extent to which communicators share the same system of signals.

affect displays. Movements of the facial area that convey emotional meaning such as anger, fear, and surprise.

affinity-seeking strategies. Behaviors designed to increase interpersonal attractiveness.

affirmation. The communication of support and approval.

allness. The illogical assumption that all can be known or said about a given person, issue, object, or event.

alter-adaptors. Body movements you make in response to your current interactions, for example, crossing your arms over your chest when someone unpleasant approaches or moving closer to someone you like.

altercasting. Placing the speaker in a specific role for a specific purpose and asking that he or she assume the perspective of this specific role, for example, "as a professor of communication, what would you say is . . ."

ambiguity. The condition in which a message may be interpreted as having more than one meaning.

apprehension. See **communication apprehension**.

argot. The **cant** and **jargon** of a particular class, generally an underworld or a criminal class, which is difficult and sometimes impossible for outsiders to understand.

argumentativeness. A willingness to argue for a point of view, to speak one's mind. Distinguished from **verbal aggressiveness.**

assertiveness. A willingness to stand up for your rights but with respect for the rights of others.

assimilation. A process of message distortion in which messages are reworked to conform to your own attitudes, prejudices, needs, and values. See **cultural assimilation.**

attention. The process of responding to a stimulus or stimuli; usually some consciousness of responding is implied.

attitude. A predisposition to respond for or against an object, person, or position.

attraction theory. The theory that people develop relationships on the basis of attractiveness, proximity, and similarity.

attractiveness. The degree of physical attractiveness or pleasantness in personality.

attribution. The processes involved in assigning causation or motivation to a person's behavior. .

avoidance. An unproductive **interpersonal conflict** strategy in which you take mental or physical flight from the actual conflict. .

back-channeling cues. Responses a listener makes to a speaker (while the speaker is speaking) but which do not ask for the speaking role: for example, interjecting "I understand" or "You said what?" .

barriers to intercultural communication. Those physical or psychological factors that prevent or hinder effective communication, such as ignoring differences between yourself and the culturally different, ignoring differences among the culturally different, ignoring differences in meaning, violating cultural rules and customs, and evaluating differences negatively.

behavioral synchrony. The similarity in the behavior, usually nonverbal (for example, postural stance or facial expressions) of two persons, generally, taken as an indicator of liking.

belief. Confidence in the existence or truth of something; conviction.

beltlining. An unproductive **interpersonal conflict** strategy in which one hits at the level at which the other person cannot withstand the blow.

blame. An unproductive **interpersonal conflict** strategy in which we attribute the cause of the conflict to the other person or devote our energies to discovering who is the cause and avoid talking about the issues causing the conflict.

boundary markers. Markers that set boundaries around or divide one person's territory from another's—for example, a fence.

brainstorming. An idea-generating strategy groups use to produce as many ideas as possible by following four basic rules: strive for quantity, avoid negative evaluation, suggest ideas as wild as possible, combine ideas that are generated.

breadth. The number of topics about which individuals in a relationship communicate.

cant. The conversational language of a special group (usually, a lower-social-class group), generally understood only by members of that group. Also see **argot**.

censorship. Restrictions imposed on one's right to produce, distribute, or receive various communications.

central markers. Markers or items that are placed in a territory to reserve it for a specific person—for example, the sweater thrown over a library chair to signal that the chair is taken.

certainty. An attitude of closed-mindedness that creates defensiveness among communicators. *Opposed to* **provisionalism.**

channel. The vehicle or medium through which signals are sent—for example, the vocal-auditory channel.

cherishing behaviors. Small behaviors you enjoy receiving from others, especially from your relational partner—for example, a kiss before leaving for work.

chronemics. The study of the communicative nature of time, how a person's or culture's treatment of time reveals something about the person or culture; often divided into psychological and cultural time.

civil inattention. Polite ignoring of others (after a brief sign of awareness) so as not to invade their privacy.

cliché. An expression whose overuse calls attention to itself.

closed-mindedness. An unwillingness to receive certain communication messages.

code. A set of symbols used to translate a message from one form to another.

collectivist culture. A culture in which the group's goals rather than the individual's are given greater importance and in which, for example, benevolence, tradition, and conformity are given special emphasis. *Opposed to* **individualist culture**.

color communication. The use of color to communicate different meanings; each culture seems to define the meanings colors communicate somewhat differently.

communication. (1) The process or act of communicating; (2) the actual message or messages sent and received; (3) the study of the processes involved in the sending and receiving of messages. (The term **communicology** is suggested for the third definition.)

communication apprehension. Fear or anxiety of communicating and usually identified as either **trait apprehension** or **state apprehension.**

communicology. The study of communication, particularly the subsection concerned with human communication.

competence. "Language competence" is a speaker's ability to use the language; it is a knowledge of the elements and rules of the language. "Communication competence" generally refers to both the knowledge of communication and also to the ability to engage in communication effectively.

complementarity. A principle of **attraction** holding that you are attracted by qualities you do not possess or you wish to possess and to people who are opposite or different from yourself. *Opposed to* **similarity.**

complementary relationship. A relationship in which the behavior of one person serves as the stimulus for the complementary behavior of the other; in complementary relationships, behavioral differences are maximized.

compliance-gaining strategies. Behaviors designed to gain the agreement of others, to persuade others to do as you wish.

compliance-resisting strategies. Behaviors directed at resisting the persuasive attempts of others. .

confidence. A quality of interpersonal effectiveness; a comfortable, at-ease feeling in interpersonal communication situations.

confirmation. A communication pattern that acknowledges another person's presence and indicates an acceptance of this person, this person's definition of self, and the relationship as defined or viewed by this other person. *Opposed to* **rejection** and **disconfirmation.**

conflict. A disagreement or difference of opinion; a form of competition in which one person tries to bring a rival to surrender; a situation in which one person's behaviors are directed at preventing something or at interfering with or harming another individual. *See also* **interpersonal conflict.**

congruence. A condition in which both verbal and nonverbal behaviors reinforce each other.

connotation. The feeling or emotional aspect of meaning, generally viewed as consisting of the evaluative (for example, good-bad), potency (strong-weak), and activity (fast-slow) dimensions. *Opposed to* **denotation.**

consistency. A process that influences you to maintain balance in your **perception** of messages or people; a process that makes you see what you expect to see and to be uncomfortable when your perceptions run contrary to expectations.

content and relationship dimensions. Two aspects to which messages may refer: the world external to both speaker and listener (content) and the connections existing between the individuals who are interacting (relationship).

context. The physical, psychological, social, cultural, and temporal environment in which communication takes place.

conversation. Two-person communication usually following five stages: opening, feedforward, business, feedback, and closing.

conversational management. The management of the way in which messages are exchanged in **conversation**.

conversational maxims. Principles that are followed in **conversation** to ensure that the goal of the conversation is achieved.

conversational turns. The process of passing the speaker and listener roles during conversation.

cooperation. An interpersonal process by which individuals work together for a common end; the pooling of efforts to produce a mutually desired outcome.

credibility. The degree to which you see a person to be believable; competence, character, and charisma (dynamism) are its major dimensions.

critical thinking. The process of logically evaluating reasons and evidence and reaching a judgment on the basis of this analysis.

cultural assimilation. The process by which a person's culture is given up and he or she takes on the values and beliefs of another culture as when, for example, an immigrant gives up his or her native culture to become a member of this new adopted culture.

cultural display. Signs that communicate one's cultural identification, for example, clothing or religious jewelry.

cultural rules. Rules that are specific to a given culture.

cultural time. The meanings given to the ways time is treated in a particular culture.

date. An **extensional device** used to emphasize the notion of constant change and symbolized by a subscript: for example, John Smith_{1986} is not John Smith_{1996}.

decoder. Something that takes a message in one form (for example, sound waves) and translates it into another form (for example, nerve impulses) from which meaning can be formulated. In human communication, the decoder is the auditory mechanism; in electronic communication, the decoder is, for example, the telephone earpiece. *Decoding* is the process of extracting a message from a code—for example, translating speech sounds into nerve impulses. *See also* **encoder.**

defensiveness. An attitude of an individual or an atmosphere in a group characterized by threats, fear, and domination; messages evidencing evaluation, control, strategy, neutrality, superiority, and certainty are thought to lead to defensiveness. *Opposed to* **supportiveness.**

delayed reaction. A reaction that is consciously delayed while the situation is analyzed and possible choices for communication are evaluated.

Delphi method. A small-group technique in which a group of experts is established but there's no interaction among them; instead they communicate by repeatedly responding to questionnaires.

denial. One of the obstacles to the expression of emotion; the process by which you deny your emotions to yourself or to others.

denotation. The objective or descriptive meaning of a word; the meaning you'd find in a dictionary. *Opposed to* **connotation.**

depenetration. A reversal of **penetration;** a condition in which the **breadth** and **depth** of a relationship decrease.

depth. The degree to which the inner personality—the inner core of an individual—is penetrated in interpersonal interaction.

determinism, principle of. The principle of verbal interaction that holds that all verbalizations are to some extent purposeful, that there is a reason for every verbalization.

dialogue. A form of **communication** in which each person is both speaker and listener; communication characterized by involvement, concern, and respect for the other person. *Opposed to* **monologue.**

direct speech. Speech in which the speaker's intentions are stated clearly and directly. .

disclaimer. Statement that asks the listener to receive what you say without its reflecting negatively on you.

disconfirmation. The process by which one ignores or denies the right of the individual even to define himself or herself. *Opposed to* **rejection** and **confirmation.**

downward communication. Communication sent from the higher levels of the hierarchy to the lower levels—for example, messages sent by managers to workers, or from deans to faculty members.

dyadic coalition. A two-person group formed from some larger group to achieve a particular goal.

dyadic communication. Two-person communication.

dyadic consciousness. An awareness on the part of the participants that an interpersonal relationship or pairing exists between them; distinguished from situations in which two individuals are together but do not see themselves as a unit or twosome.

dyadic effect. The tendency for the behaviors of one person to stimulate similar behaviors in the other interactant; often used to refer to the tendency of one person's self-disclosures to prompt the other to also self-disclose.

dyadic primacy. The significance or centrality of the two-person group, even when there are many more people interacting.

ear markers. Markers that identify an item as belonging to a specific person—for example, a nameplate on a desk or initials on a briefcase.

effect. The outcome or consequence of an action or behavior; communication is assumed always to have some effect.

emblems. Nonverbal behaviors that directly translate words or phrases—for example, the signs for "OK" and "peace."

emotional communication. The expression of feelings—for example, feelings of guilt, happiness, or sorrow.

empathy. The feeling of another person's feeling; the capacity to feel or perceive something as does another person.

encoder. Something that takes a message in one form (for example, nerve impulses) and translates it into another form (for example, sound waves). In human communication, the encoder is the speaking mechanism; in electronic communication, the encoder is, for example, the telephone mouthpiece. *Encoding* is the process of putting a message into a code—for example, translating nerve impulses into speech sounds. *See also* **decoder.**

enculturation. The process by which culture is transmitted from one generation to another.

E-prime. A form of the language that omits the verb "to be" except when used as an auxiliary or in statements of existence. Designed to eliminate the tendency toward **projection.**

equality. An attitude that recognizes that each individual in a communication interaction is equal, that no one is superior to any other; encourages supportiveness. .

equilibrium theory. A theory of **proxemics** holding that intimacy and physical closeness are positively related; as a relationship becomes more intimate, the individuals will maintain shorter distances between themselves.

equity theory. A theory claming that the two people in a relationship experience relational satisfaction when there is an equal distribution of rewards and costs between them.

etc. (et cetera). An **extensional device** used to emphasize the notion of infinite complexity; because you can never know all about anything, any statement about the world or an event must end with an explicit or implicit "etc."

ethics. The branch of philosophy that deals with the rightness or wrongness of actions; the study of moral values; in communication, the morality of message behavior.

ethnocentrism. The tendency to see others and their behaviors through your own cultural filters, often as distortions of your own behaviors; the tendency to evaluate the values and beliefs of your own culture more positively than those of another culture.

euphemism. A polite word or phrase used to substitute for some taboo or less polite term or phrase.

evaluating. A process whereby a value is placed on some person, object, or event.

excuse. An explanation designed to lessen the negative consequences of something done or said.

expectancy violations theory. A theory of **proxemics** holding that people have a certain expectancy for space relationships. When that is violated (a person stands too close to you, or a romantic partner maintains abnormally large distances from you), the relationship comes into clearer focus and you wonder why this "normal distance" is being violated.

experiential limitation. The limit on an individual's ability to communicate, as set by the nature and extent of that individual's experiences.

expressiveness. A quality of interpersonal effectiveness; genuine involvement in speaking and listening, conveyed verbally and nonverbally.

extensional devices. Linguistic devices proposed by Alfred Korzybski to make language a more accurate means for talking about the world. The extensional devices include **etc., date, index, hyphen,** and **quotes**.

extensional orientation. A point of view in which primary consideration is given to the world of experience and only secondary consideration is given to labels. *Opposed to* **intensional orientation.**

facial feedback hypothesis. The hypothesis or theory that your facial expressions can produce physiological and emotional effects.

facial management techniques. Techniques used to mask certain emotions and to emphasize others, for example, intensifying your expression of happiness to make a friend feel good about a promotion.

fact-inference confusion. A misevaluation in which one makes an inference, regards it as a fact, and acts upon it as if it were a fact.

factual statement. A statement made by the observer after observation and limited to what is observed. *Opposed to* **inferential statement.**

family. A group of people who consider themselves related and connected to one another and for whom the actions of one have consequences for others.

feedback. Information that is given back to the source. Feedback may come from the source's own messages (as when you hear what you're saying) or from the receiver(s) in the form of applause, yawning, puzzled looks, questions, letters to the editor of a newspaper, increased or decreased subscriptions to a magazine. *See also* **negative feedback, positive feedback.**

feedforward. Information that is sent prior to the regular messages, telling the listener something about what is to follow; messages that are prefatory to more central messages.

feminine culture. A culture in which both men and women are encouraged to be modest, oriented to maintaining the quality of life, and tender. Feminine cultures emphasize the quality of life and so socialize their people to be modest and to emphasize close interpersonal relationships. *Opposed to* **masculine culture**.

flexibility. The ability to adjust communication strategies and skills on the basis of the unique situation.

focus group. An in-depth interview of a small group which aims to discover what people think about an issue or product.

force. An unproductive **conflict** strategy in which you try to win an argument by physically overpowering the other person either by threat or by actual behavior.

free information. Information that is revealed implicitly and that may be used as a basis for opening or pursuing conversations.

friendship. An interpersonal relationship between two persons that is mutually productive, established and maintained through perceived mutual free choice, and characterized by mutual positive regard.

General Semantics. The study of the relationships among language, thought, and behavior.

gossip. Oral or written **communication** about someone not present, some third party, usually about matters that are private to this third party.

grapevine messages. Messages that do not follow any formal organizational structures; office-related gossip.

gunnysacking. An unproductive **conflict** strategy of storing up grievances—as if in a gunnysack—and holding them in readiness to dump on the person with whom one is in conflict.

halo effect. The tendency to generalize a person's virtue or expertise from one area to other areas.

haptics. Technical term for the study of touch or **tactile communication.**

heterosexist language. Language that denigrates lesbians and gay men.

high-context culture. A culture in which much of the information in communication messages is left implied; it's "understood," it's considered to be in the context or in the person rather than explicitly coded in the verbal messages. **Collectivist cultures** are generally high context. *Opposed to* **low-context culture.**

home field advantage. The increased power that comes from being in your own territory.

home territories. Territories for which individuals have a sense of intimacy and over which they exercise control—for example, a teacher's office.

hyphen. An **extensional device** used to illustrate that what may be separated verbally may not be separable on the event level or on the nonverbal level; although you may talk about body and mind as if they were separable, in reality they're better referred to as body-mind.

illustrators. Nonverbal behaviors that accompany and literally illustrate verbal messages—for example, upward movements of the head and hand that accompany the verbal "It's up there."

I-messages. Messages in which the speaker accepts responsibility for personal thoughts and behaviors; messages in which the speaker's point of view is stated explicitly. *Opposed to* **you-messages.**

immediacy. A quality of interpersonal effectiveness; a sense of contact and togetherness; a feeling of interest and liking for the other person.

implicit personality theory. A theory of personality, complete with rules about what characteristics go with what other characteristics, that you maintain and through which you perceive others.

inclusion. The principle of verbal interaction holding that all members should be a part of (included in) the interaction.

index. An extensional device used to emphasize the assumption that no two things are the same; symbolized by a subscript—for example, even though two people may both be politicians, $\text{politician}_{1\ [\text{Smith}]}$ is not $\text{politician}_{2\ [\text{Jones}]}$.

indirect speech. Speech that hides the speaker's true intentions; speech in which requests and observations are made indirectly.

indiscrimination. A misevaluation caused by categorizing people, events, or objects into a particular class and responding to them only as members of the class; a failure to recognize that each individual is unique. .

individualist culture. A culture in which the individual's rather than the group's goals and preferences are given greater importance. *Opposed to* **collectivist culture.**

inevitability. A principle of communication holding that communication cannot be avoided; all behavior in an interactional setting is communication.

inferential statement. A statement that can be made by anyone, is not limited to what is observed, and can be made at any time. See also **factual statement.**

informal time terms. Terms that are approximate rather than exact, for example, "soon," "early," and "in a while."

information overload. A condition in which the amount or complexity of information is too great to be dealt with effectively by an individual, group, or organization.

in-group talk. Talk about a subject or in a vocabulary that some group members understand and others do not; has the effect of excluding those who don't understand.

insulation. A reaction to **territorial encroachment** in which you erect some sort of barrier between yourself and the invaders, for example, a stone wall around your property, an unlisted phone number, or "caller ID"—all of which allow you to separate yourself from would-be invaders.

intensional orientation. A point of view in which primary consideration is given to the way things are labeled and only secondary consideration (if any) to the world of experience. *Opposed to* **extensional orientation.**

interaction management. A quality of interpersonal effectiveness in which the interaction is controlled and managed to the satisfaction of both parties; effectively managing conversational turns, fluency, and message consistency.

intercultural communication. Communication that takes place between persons of different cultures or persons who have different cultural beliefs, values, or ways of behaving.

interpersonal communication. Communication between two persons or among a small group of persons and distinguished from public or mass communication; communication of a personal nature and distinguished from impersonal communication; communication between or among connected persons or those involved in a close relationship.

interpersonal conflict. A disagreement between two connected persons.

interpersonal effectiveness. The ability to accomplish one's interpersonal goals; interpersonal communication that is satisfying to both individuals.

interpersonal perception. The **perception** of people; the processes through which you interpret and evaluate people and their behavior.

interview. A question and answer form of communication.

intimacy claims. Obligations incurred by virtue of being in a close and intimate relationship.

intimacy. The closest interpersonal relationship; usually used to denote a close primary relationship.

intimate distance. The closest distance in **proxemics**, ranging from touching to 18 inches.

intrapersonal communication. Communication with oneself.

irreversibility. A principle of communication holding that communication cannot be reversed; once something has been communicated, it cannot be uncommunicated.

jargon. The technical language of any specialized group, often a professional class, which is unintelligible to individuals not belonging to the group; shop talk. This glossary is an example of the jargon of a part of the communication field.

johari window. A diagram of the four selves (open, blind, hidden, and unknown).

kinesics. The study of the communicative dimensions of facial and bodily movements.

language. The rules of syntax, semantics, and phonology by which sentences are created and understood; **a language** refers to the sentences that can be created in any language, for example, English, Bantu, or Italian.

language relativity. See **linguistic relativity hypothesis.**

lateral communication. Communication between equals—manager to manager, worker to worker.

leave-taking cues. Verbal and nonverbal signals that indicate a desire to terminate a conversation.

leveling. A process of message distortion in which the number of details in a message is reduced as the messages gets repeated from one person to another.

linguistic relativity hypothesis. The theory that the language you speak influences your perceptions of the world and your behaviors and that therefore people speaking widely differing languages will perceive and behave differently as a result of the language differences.

listening. An active process of receiving aural stimuli consisting of five stages: receiving, understanding, remembering, evaluating, and responding.

loving. An interpersonal process in which you feel a closeness, a caring, a warmth, and an excitement for another person.

low-context culture. A culture in which most of the information in communication is explicitly stated in the verbal message, rather than left implied or assumed to be "understood." Low-context cultures are usually **individualistic cultures**. *Opposed to* **high-context culture**.

Machiavellianism. The belief that people can be manipulated easily; often used to refer to the techniques or tactics one person uses to control another.

manipulation. An unproductive **conflict** strategy that avoids open conflict; instead, attempts are made to divert the conflict by being especially charming and getting the other person into a noncombative frame of mind.

manner maxim. A principle of conversation that holds that speakers cooperate by being clear and by organizing their thoughts into some meaningful and coherent pattern.

markers. Devices that signify that a certain territory belongs to a particular person. *See also* **boundary markers, central markers,** and **ear markers.**

masculine culture. A culture in which men are viewed as assertive, oriented to material success, and strong; women on the other hand are viewed as modest, focused on the quality of life, and tender. Masculine cultures emphasize success and so socialize their people to be assertive, ambitious, and competitive. *Opposed to* **feminine culture**.

matching hypothesis. An assumption that you date and mate people who are similar to yourself—who match you—in physical attractiveness.

meaningfulness. A principle of **perception** that assumes that the behavior of people is sensible, stems from some logical antecedent, and is therefore meaningful rather than meaningless.

mentoring relationship. A relationship in which an experienced individual helps to train one who is less experienced: for example, an accomplished teacher might mentor one who is newly arrived or who has never taught before.

mere exposure hypothesis. The theory that repeated or prolonged exposure to a stimulus may result in a change in attitude toward the stimulus object, generally in the direction of increased positiveness.

messages. Signals or combinations of signals that serve as **stimuli** for a receiver.

metacommunication. Communication about communication.

metalanguage. Language that refers to language. See **metamessage.**

metamessage. A message that makes reference to another message: for example, the statements "Did I make myself clear?" or "That's a lie" are metamessages because they refer to other messages.

micromomentary expressions. Extremely brief movements that are not consciously controlled or recognized and that are thought to be indicative of your true emotional state.

mindfulness and mindlessness. States of relative awareness. In a mindful state, you are aware of the logic and rationality of your behaviors and the logical connections existing among elements. In a mindless state, you're unaware of this logic and rationality.

mixed messages. Messages that communicate two different and often contradictory meanings: for example, a message that asks for two different (often incompatible) responses such as "leave me alone" and "show me more attention." Often, one meaning (usually the socially acceptable meaning) is communicated verbally and the other (usually the less socially acceptable meaning) nonverbally.

model. A representation of an object or process.

monochronic. A view of time in which things are done sequentially; one thing is scheduled at a time. *Opposed to* **polychronic.**

monologue. A form of **communication** in which one person speaks and the other listens; there's no real interaction among participants. *Opposed to* **dialogue.**

negative feedback. Feedback that serves a corrective function by informing the source that his or her message is not being received in the way intended. Looks of boredom, shouts of disagreement, letters critical of newspaper policy, and teachers' instructions on how better to approach a problem would be examples of negative feedback and would (ideally) serve to redirect the speaker's behavior.

networking. Connecting with people who can help you accomplish a goal or help you find information related to your goal, for example, finding a job.

neutrality. A response pattern lacking in personal involvement; encourages defensiveness;. *Opposed to* **empathy.**

noise. Anything that interferes with your receiving a message as the source intended the message to be received. Noise is present in communication to the extent that the message received is not the message sent.

nominal group technique. A method of problem solving that uses limited discussion and confidential voting to obtain a group decision; especially helpful when some members may be reluctant to voice their opinions in a regular problem-solving group or when the issue is controversial or sensitive.

nonallness. A point of view holding that you can never know all about anything and that what you know, say, or hear is only a part of what there is to know, say, or hear.

nonnegotiation. An unproductive **conflict** strategy in which the individual refuses to discuss the conflict or to listen to the other person.

nonverbal communication. Communication without words; communication by means of space, gestures, facial expressions, touching, vocal variation, and silence, for example.

nonverbal dominance. Nonverbal behavior that allows one person to achieve psychological dominance over another.

object language. Language used to communicate about objects, events, and relations in the world (rather than about words as in **metalanguage**).

object-adaptors. Movements that involve your manipulation of some object: for example, punching holes in a styrofoam coffee cup, clicking a ball point pen, or chewing on a pencil.

olfactory communication. Communication by smell.

openness. A quality of interpersonal effectiveness encompassing (1) a willingness to interact openly with others, to self-disclose as appropriate; (2) a willingness to react honestly to incoming stimuli; and (3) a willingness to own one's feelings and thoughts.

opinion. A tentative conclusion concerning some object, person, or event.

other-talk. Talk about the listener or some third party. *Opposed to* **self-talk**.

other-orientation. A quality of interpersonal effective ness involving attentiveness, interest, and concern for the other person.

outing. The process whereby a person's affectional orientation is made public by another person without the gay man or lesbian's consent.

owning feelings. The process by which you take responsibility for your own feelings instead of attributing them to others.

paralanguage. The vocal (but nonverbal) aspect of speech. Paralanguage consists of voice qualities (for example, pitch range, resonance, tempo), vocal characterizers (laughing or crying, yelling or whispering), vocal qualifiers (intensity, pitch height), and vocal segregates ("uh-uh," meaning "no," or "sh" meaning "silence").

passive listening. Listening that is attentive and supportive but occurs without talking and without directing the speaker in any nonverbal way; also used negatively to refer to inattentive and uninvolved listening.

pause. A silent period in the normally fluent stream of speech. Pauses are of two types: filled pauses (interruptions in speech that are filled with such vocalizations as "er" or "um") and unfilled pauses (silences of unusually long duration).

perception. The process by which you become aware of objects and events through your senses.

perception checking. The process of verifying your understanding of some message, situation, or feeling.

perceptual accentuation. A process that leads you to see what you expect or want to see—for example, seeing people you like as better looking and smarter than people you don't like.

personal distance. The second-closest distance in **proxemics**, ranging from 18 inches to 4 feet.

personal rejection. An unproductive **conflict** strategy in which you withhold love and affection and seek to win the argument by getting the other person to break down under this withdrawal.

persuasion. The process of influencing attitudes and behavior.

phatic communion. Communication that is primarily social; communication designed to open the channels of communication rather than to communicate something about the external world; "Hello" and "How are you?" in everyday interaction are examples.

pitch. The highness or lowness of the vocal tone.

polarization. A form of fallacious reasoning by which only two extremes are considered; also referred to as "black-or-white" and "either-or" thinking or two-valued orientation.

polychronic. A view of time in which several things may be scheduled or engaged in at the same time. *Opposed to* **monochronic time orientation**.

positive feedback. Feedback that supports or reinforces the continuation of behavior along the same lines in which it is already proceeding—for example, applause during a speech encourages the speaker to continue speaking this way.

positiveness. A characteristic of effective communication involving positive attitudes toward oneself and toward the interpersonal interaction and to expressing these attitudes (as in complimenting) to others along with acceptance and approval.

power. The ability to influence or control the behavior of another person; A has power over B when A can influence or control B's behavior; an inevitable part of interpersonal relationships.

power plays. Consistent patterns of behavior in which one person tries to control the behavior of another.

pragmatic implication. An assumption that is logical (and therefore appears true) but is actually not necessarily true.

pragmatics. In interpersonal communication, an approach that focuses on communication behaviors and effects and on communication effectiveness.

primacy-recency. Primacy refers to giving more importance to that which occurs first; recency refers to giving more importance to that which occurs last (that is, most recently).

primary affect displays. The communication of the six primary emotions: happiness, surprise, fear, anger, sadness, and disgust/contempt.

primary relationship. The relationship between two people that they consider their most (or one of their most) important: for example, the relationship between husband and wife or domestic partners.

primary territories. Areas that you consider your exclusive preserve, such as your room or office.

process. Ongoing activity; communication is referred to as a process to emphasize that it's always changing, always in motion.

projection. A psychological process whereby you attribute characteristics or feelings of your own to others; often used to refer to the process whereby you attribute your faults to others.

pronouncements. Statements made to sound authoritative and that therefore imply that the speaker is in a position of authority and that the listener is in a childlike or learner role.

protection theory. A theory of **proxemics** holding that people establish a body-buffer zone to protect themselves from unwanted closeness, touching, or attack.

provisionalism. An attitude of open-mindedness that leads to the development of a supportive relationship and atmosphere; opposed to **certainty.**

proxemics. The study of the communicative function of space; the study of how people unconsciously structure their space—the distance between people in their interactions, the organization of space in homes and offices, and even the design of cities.

proximity. As a principle of **perception,** the tendency to perceive people or events that are physically close as belonging together or representing some unit; physical closeness—one of the qualities influencing interpersonal attraction.

psychological time. The importance you place on past, present, or future time.

public distance. The farthest distance in **proxemics,** ranging from 12 feet to more than 25 feet.

public territories. Areas that are open to all people—for example, restaurants or parks.

punctuation. The breaking up of continuous communication sequences into short sequences with identifiable beginnings and endings or stimuli and responses.

pupil dilation. The extent to which the pupil of the eye is expanded; generally large pupils indicate positive reactions.

pupillometrics. The study of communication through changes in the size of the pupils of the eyes.

Pygmalion effect. The condition in which you make a prediction of success, act as if it is true, and thereby make it come true (for example, acting toward students as if they'll be successful influences them to become successful); a type of **self-fulfilling prophecy.**

quality circles. Small groups of workers (usually about 6 to 12) whose task is to investigate and make recommendations for improving the quality of some organizational function.

quality maxim. A principle of **conversation** that holds that speakers cooperate by saying what they think is true and by not saying what they think is false.

quantity maxim. A principle of **conversation** that holds that speakers cooperate by being only as informative as necessary to communicate their intended meanings.

quotes. An **extensional device** to emphasize that a word or phrase is being used in a special sense and should therefore be given special attention.

racist language. Language that denigrates, demeans, or is derogatory toward members of a particular race.

rate. The speed with which you speak, generally measured in words per minute.

receiver. Any person or thing that takes in messages. Receivers may be individuals listening to or reading a message, a group of persons hearing a speech, a scattered television audience, or machines that store information.

reconciliation strategies. Behaviors designed to repair a broken relationship.

regulators. Nonverbal behaviors that regulate, monitor, or control the communications of another person.

rejection. A response to an individual that acknowledges another person but expresses disagreement. *Opposed to* **confirmation** *and* **disconfirmation**.

relation maxim. A principle of **cooperation** in **conversation** that holds that speakers communicate by talking about what is relevant and by not talking about what isn't.

relationship communication. Communication between or among intimates or those in close relationships; used by some theorists as synonymous with interpersonal communication.

relationship deterioration. The stage of a relationship during which the connecting bonds between the partners weaken and the partners begin drifting apart.

relationship development. The initial or beginning stage of a relationship; the stage at which two people begin to form an interpersonal relationship.

relationship dialectics theory. A theory that describes relationships along a series of opposites representing competing desires or motivations, such as the desire for autonomy and the desire to belong to someone, for novelty and predictability, and for closedness and openness.

relationship dissolution. The termination or end of an interpersonal relationship.

relationship maintenance. A stage of relationship stability in which the relationship does not progress or deteriorate significantly; a continuation as opposed to a dissolution (or an intensification) of a relationship.

relationship messages. Messages that comment on the relationship between the speakers rather than on matters external to them.

relationship repair. A relationship stage in which one or both parties seek to improve the relationship.

resemblance. As a principle of **perception**, the tendency to perceive people or events that are similar in appearance as belonging together.

response. Any bit of overt or covert behavior.

role. The part an individual plays in a group; an individual's function or expected behavior.

rules theory. A theory that describes relationships as interactions governed by a series of rules that a couple agrees to follow. When the rules are followed, the relationship is maintained; when they are broken, the relationship experiences difficulty.

schemata. Ways of organizing perceptions; mental templates or structures that help you organize the millions of items of information you come into contact with every day as well as those you already have in memory; general ideas about people (for Pat and Chris, for Japanese, for Baptists, for New Yorkers), for yourself (your qualities, abilities, liabilities), or social roles (what's a police officer, professor, or multimillionaire CEO like).

script. A type of schema; an organized body of information about some action, event, or procedure; a general idea of how some event should play out or unfold, the rules governing the events, and their sequence.

secondary territories. Areas that do not belong to you but that you've occupied and are therefore associated with you—for example, the seat you normally take in class.

selective exposure. A principle that states that listeners actively seek out information that supports their opinions and actively avoid information that contradicts their existing opinions, beliefs, attitudes, and values.

self-acceptance. Being satisfied with yourself, your virtues and vices, your abilities and limitations.

self-adaptors. Movements that usually satisfy a physical need, especially to make you more comfortable: for example, scratching your head to relieve an itch, moistening your lips because they feel dry, or pushing your hair out of your eyes.

self-attribution. A process through which you seek to account for and understand the reasons and motivations for your own behaviors.

self-awareness. The degree to which you know yourself.

self-concept. Your self-image; the view your have of who you are.

self-disclosure. The process of revealing something about yourself to another; usually used to refer to information that you'd normally keep hidden.

self-esteem. The value you place on yourself; your self-evaluation; usually used to refer to the positive value placed on oneself.

self-fulfilling prophecy. The situation in which you make a prediction or prophecy and fulfill it yourself—for example, expecting a person to be hostile, you act in a hostile manner toward this person, and in doing so elicit hostile behavior in the person, thus confirming your prophecy that the person is hostile.

self-monitoring. The manipulation of the image you present to others in interpersonal interactions so as to give the most favorable impression of yourself.

self-serving bias. A bias that operates in the self-attribution process and leads you to take credit for the positive consequences and to deny responsibility for the negative consequences of your behaviors.

self-talk. Talk about yourself. *Opposed to* **other-talk**.

semantics. The area of language study concerned with meaning.

sexist language. Language derogatory to one sex, generally women.

sexual harassment. Unsolicited and unwanted verbal or nonverbal sexual messages.

sharpening. A process of message distortion in which the details of messages, when repeated, are crystallized and heightened.

shyness. The condition of discomfort and uneasiness in interpersonal situations.

signal and noise, relativity of. The principle of verbal interaction that holds that what is signal (meaningful) and what is noise (interference) is relative to the communication analyst, the participants, and the context.

signal reaction. A conditioned response to a signal; a response to some signal that is immediate rather than delayed. *Opposed to* **delayed reaction.**

silence. The absence of vocal communication; often misunderstood to refer to the absence of communication.

silencers. A tactic (such as crying) that literally silences your opponent—an unproductive **conflict** strategy.

similarity. A principle of **attraction** holding that you're attracted to qualities similar to those you yourself possess and to people who are similar to yourself; opposed to **complementarity.**

slang. The language used by special groups that is not considered proper by the general society; language made up of the **argot, cant,** and **jargon** of various groups and known by the general public.

social comparison processes. The processes by which you compare yourself (for example, your abilities, opinions, and values) with others and then assess and evaluate yourself on the basis of the comparison; one of the sources of **self-concept**.

social distance. The third farthest distance in **proxemics**, ranging from 4 feet to 12 feet; the distance at which business is usually conducted.

social exchange theory. A theory hypothesizing that you develop profitable relationships (those in which your rewards are greater than your costs) and that you avoid or terminate unprofitable relationships (those in which your costs exceed your rewards).

social penetration theory. A theory concerned with relationship development from the superficial to the intimate levels (**depth**) and from few to many areas of interpersonal interaction (**breadth**). *See also* **depenetration.**

source. Any person or thing that creates messages: for example, an individual speaking, writing, or gesturing, or a computer solving a problem.

speech. Messages conveyed via a vocal-auditory channel.

spontaneity. The communication pattern in which you say what you're thinking without attempting to develop strategies for control; encourages **supportiveness;** opposed to **strategy.**

stability. The principle of **perception** that refers to the fact that your perceptions of things and of people are relatively consistent with your previous conceptions.

state apprehension. Communication apprehension for specific types of communication situations—for example, public speaking or interview situations. *Opposed to* **trait apprehension.**

static evaluation. An orientation that fails to recognize that the world is constantly changing; an attitude that sees people and events as fixed rather than as ever changing.

status. The relative level one occupies in a hierarchy; status always involves a comparison, and thus your status is only relative to the status of another. In the United States, occupation, financial position, age, and educational level are significant determinants of social status.

stereotype. In communication, a fixed impression of a group of people through which we then perceive specific individuals; stereotypes are most often negative (Martians are stupid, uneducated, and dirty) but may also be positive (Venusians are scientific, industrious, and helpful).

stimuli. Any external or internal changes that impinge on or arouse an organism. (*Stimulus* is the singular form of this term.)

stimulus-response models of communication. Models of communication that assume that the process of communication is linear, beginning with a stimulus that then leads to a response.

strategy. The use of some plan for control of other members of a communication interaction that guides your communications; often encourages **defensiveness;** opposed to **spontaneity.**

subjectivity. The principle of **perception** that refers to the fact that your perceptions are not objective but are influenced by your wants and needs, expectations and predictions.

superiority. A point of view or attitude that assumes that others are not equal to yourself; encourages **defensiveness;** opposed to **equality.**

supportiveness. An attitude of an individual or an atmosphere in a group that is characterized by openness, absence of fear, and a genuine feeling of equality. *Opposed to* **defensiveness.**

symmetrical relationship. A relation between two or more persons in which one person's behavior serves as a stimulus for the same type of behavior in the other person(s), for example, a relationship in which anger in one person encourages anger in another person or in which a critical comment by one person leads the other person to respond in kind.

taboo. Forbidden; culturally censored. Taboo language is language that is frowned upon by "polite society." Topics and specific words may be considered taboo—for example, death, sex, certain forms of illness and various words denoting sexual activities and excretory functions.

tactile communication. Communication by touch; communication received by the skin.

temporal communication. The messages that your time orientation and treatment of time communicates.

territorial encroachment. The trespassing on, use of, or appropriation of one person's territory by another.

territoriality. A possessive or ownership reaction to an area of space or to particular objects.

theory. A general statement or principle applicable to a number of related phenomena.

touch avoidance. The tendency to avoid touching and being touched by others.

trait apprehension. Communication apprehension generally; a fear of communication situations regardless of their specific form. *Opposed to* **state apprehension.**

transactional. A point of view that sees communication as an on-going process in which all elements are interdependent and influence each other.

uncertainty reduction theory. Applied to interpersonal relationships, the theory holds that as relationships develop, uncertainty is reduced; relationship development is seen as a process of reducing uncertainty about one another.

universal of interpersonal communication. A feature of communication common to all interpersonal communication acts.

unproductive conflict strategies. Ways of engaging in conflict that generally prove counterproductive, for example, avoidance, force, blame, silencers, gunnysacking, manipulation, personal rejection, and fighting below the belt.

upward communication. Communication sent from the lower levels of the hierarchy to the upper levels—for example, line worker to manager, faculty member to dean.

value. Relative worth of an object; a quality that makes something desirable or undesirable; ideals or customs about which we have emotional responses, whether positive or negative.

verbal aggressiveness. A method of winning an argument by attacking the other person's **self-concept.** Avoid inflicting psychological pain on the other person to win an argument.

visual dominance. The use of your eyes to maintain a superior or dominant position: for example, when making an especially important point, you might look intently at the other person. .

voice qualities. Aspects of **paralanguage**—specifically, pitch range, vocal lip control, glottis control, pitch control, articulation control, rhythm control, resonance, and tempo.

volume. The relative loudness of the voice.

you-messages. Messages in which you deny responsibility for your own thoughts and behaviors; messages that attribute your **perception** to another person; messages of blame. *Opposed to* **I-messages.**

BIBLIOGRAPHY

The old-fashioned image of the librarian captured so cleverly in the film *The Music Man* is long gone. Today's librarians are a techno-savvy group on the cutting edge of technology and available to help you locate just the right source material, whether it's in print, in some CD-ROM database, or on the Internet. Here are the sources used in the preparation of this book.

Adams, R. G. (1987). Patterns of Network Change: A Longitudinal Study of Friendships of Elderly Women. *The Gerontologist* 27:222–227.

Albert, Rosita, and Gayle L. Nelson (1993). Hispanic/Anglo American Differences in Attributions to Paralinguistic Behavior. *International Journal of Intercultural Relations* 17 (Winter): 19–40.

Albert, S. M., and M. Moss (1990). Consensus and the Domain of Personal Relationships Among Older Adults. *Journal of Social and Personal Relationships* 7:353–369.

Alberti, Robert E., ed. (1977). *Assertiveness: Innovations, Applications, Issues.* San Luis Obispo, CA: Impact.

Alessandra, Tony (1986). How to Listen Effectively. *Speaking of Success* (Video Tape Series). San Diego, CA: Levitz Sommer Productions.

Allen, Mike, John Bourhis, Tara Emmers-Sommer, and Erin Sahlstein (1998). Reducing Dating Anxiety: A Meta-analysis. *Communication Reports* 11 (Winter): 49–55.

Altman, Irwin (1975). *The Environment and Social Behavior.* Monterey, CA: Brooks/Cole.

Altman, Irwin, and Dalmas Taylor (1973). *Social Penetration: The Development of Interpersonal Relationships.* New York: Holt, Rinehart and Winston.

Amato, Paul R. (1994). The Impact of Divorce on Men and Women in India and the United States. *Journal of Comparative Family Studies* 25 (Summer): 207–221.

Andersen, Peter (1991). Explaining Intercultural Differences in Nonverbal Communication. In *Intercultural Communication: A Reader,* 6th ed., ed. Larry A. Samovar and Richard E. Porter. Belmont, CA: Wadsworth, pp. 286–296.

Andersen, Peter A., and Ken Leibowitz (1978). The Development and Nature of the Construct Touch Avoidance. *Environmental Psychology and Nonverbal Behavior* 3:89–106. Reprinted in DeVito and Hecht (1990).

Angier, Natalie (1995a). Powerhouse of Senses: Smell, at Last, Gets Its Due, *New York Times* (February 14): C1, C6.

Angier, Natalie (1995b). Scientists Mull Role of Empathy in Man and Beast. *New York Times* (May 9): C1, C6.

Angier, Natalie (1995c). New View of Family: Unstable but Wealth Helps. *New York Times* (August 29): C1, C5.

Ardrey, Robert (1966). *The Territorial Imperative.* New York: Atheneum.

Argyle, Michael (1988). *Bodily Communication.* 2d ed. New York: Methuen.

Argyle, Michael, and J. Dean (1965). Eye Contact, Distance and Affiliation. *Sociometry* 28:289–304.

Argyle, Michael, and Monika Henderson (1984). The Rules of Friendship. *Journal of Social and Personal Relationships* 1 (June): 211–237.

Argyle, Michael, and Monika Henderson (1985). *The Anatomy of Relationships: And the Rules and Skills Needed to Manage Them Successfully.* London: Heinemann.

Argyle, Michael, and R. Ingham (1972). Gaze, Mutual Gaze, and Distance. *Semiotica* 1:32–49.

Aronson, Elliot, Timothy D. Wilson, and Robin M. Akert (1999). *Social Psychology.* 3d ed. New York: Longman.

Aronson, J., J. Cohen, and P. Nail (1998). Self-affirmation Theory: An Update and Appraisal. In *Cognitive Dissonance Theory: Revival with Revisions and Controversies*, ed. E. Harmon-Jones and J. S. Mills. Washington, DC: American Psychological Association.

Asch, Solomon (1946). Forming Impressions of Personality. *Journal of Abnormal and Social Psychology* 41:258–290.

Ashcraft, Mark H. (1998). *Fundamentals of Cognition.* New York: Longman.

Aspinwall, L. G., and S. E. Taylor (1993). Effects of Social Comparison Direction, Threat, and Self-esteem on Affect, Evaluation, and Expected Success. *Journal of Personality and Social Psychology* 64:708–722.

Aune, R. Kelly, and Toshiyuki Kikuchi (1993). Effects of Language Intensity Similarity on Perceptions of Credibility, Relational Attributions, and Persuasion. *Journal of Language and Social Psychology* 12 (September): 224–238.

Auter, Philip J., and Roy L. Moore (1993). Buying from a Friend: A Content Analysis of Two Teleshopping Programs. *Journalism Quarterly* 70 (Summer): 425–436.

Authier, Jerry, and Kay Gustafson (1982). Microtraining: Focusing on Specific Skills. In *Interpersonal Helping Skills: A Guide to Training Methods, Programs, and Resources,* ed. Eldon K. Marshall, P. David Kurtz, and Associates. San Francisco: Jossey-Bass, pp. 93–130.

Axtell, Roger E. (1990). *Do's and Taboos of Hosting International Visitors.* New York: Wiley.

Axtell, Roger E. (1993). *Do's and Taboos Around the World.* 3d ed. New York: Wiley.

Ayres, Joe (1983). Strategies to Maintain Relationships: Their Identification and Perceived Usage. *Communication Quarterly* 31:62–67.

Ayres, Joe, and Tim Hopf (1993). *Coping with Speech Anxiety.* Norwood, NJ: Ablex Publishing Company.

Ayres, Joe, and Tim Hopf (1995). An Assessment of the Role of Communication Apprehension in Communicating with the Terminally Ill. *Communication Research Reports* 12 (Fall): 227–234.

Ayres, Joe, Debbie M. Ayres, Gary Grudzinskas, Tim Hopf, Erin Kelly, and A. Kathleen Wilcox (1995). A Component Analysis of Performance Visualization. *Communication Reports* 8 (Summer): 185–192.

Ayres, Joe, Tanichya Keereetaweep, Pao-En Chen, and Patricia A. Edwards (1998). Communication apprehension and employment interviews. *Communication Education* 47 (January): 1–17.

Ayres, Joe, Tim Hopf, and Debbie M. Ayres (1994). An Examination of Whether Imaging Ability Enhances the Effectiveness of an Intervention Designed to Reduce Speech Anxiety. *Communication Education* 43 (July): 252–258.

Bach, George R., and Peter Wyden (1968). *The Intimacy Enemy.* New York: Avon.

Baird, John E., Jr. (1977). *The Dynamics of Organizational Communication.* New York: Harper and Row.

Banks, Stephen P., Dayle M. Altendorf, John O. Greene, and Michael J. Cody (1987). An Examination of Relationship Disengagement: Perceptions, Breakup Strategies, and Outcomes. *Western Journal of Speech Communication* 51 (Winter): 19–41.

Barker, Larry, R. Edwards, C. Gaines, K. Gladney, and F. Holley (1980). An Investigation of Proportional Time Spent in Various Communication Activities by College Students. *Journal of Applied Communication Research* 8:101–109.

Barker, Larry L. (1990). *Communication.* 5th ed. Englewood Cliffs, NJ: Prentice-Hall.

Barker, Randolph T., et al. (1992). An Investigation of Perceived Managerial Listening Ability. *Journal of Business and Technical Communication* 6 (October): 438–457.

Barna, LaRay M. (1994). Stumbling Blocks in Intercultural Communication. In *Intercultural Communication: A Reader,* 4th ed., ed. Larry A. Samovar and Richard E. Porter. Belmont, CA: Wadsworth, pp. 337–346.

Barnlund, Dean (1989). *Communicative Styles of Japanese and Americans: Images and Realities.* Belmont,CA: Wadsworth.

Barnlund, Dean C. (1975). Communicative Styles in Two Cultures: Japan and the United States. In *Organization of Behavior in Face-to-Face Interaction,* ed. A. Kendon, R. M. Harris, and M. R. Key. The Hague: Mouton.

Baron, Robert (1990). Countering the Effects of Destructive Criticism: The Relative Efficacy of Four Interventions. *Journal of Applied Psychology* 75 (3): 235–245.

Bartholomew, Kim (1990). Avoidance of Intimacy: An Attachment Perspective. *Journal of Social and Personal Relationships* 7:147–178.

Basso, K. H. (1972). To Give Up on Words: Silence in Apache Culture. In *Language and Social Context,* ed. Pier Paolo Giglioli. New York: Penguin.

Bateson, Gregory (1972). *Steps to an Ecology of Mind.* New York: Ballantine.

Battaglia, Dina M., Francis D. Richard, Darcee L. Datteri, and Charles G. Lord (1998). Breaking Up Is (Relatively) Easy to Do: A Script for the Dissolution of Close Relationships. *Journal of Social and Personal Relationships* 15 (December): 829–845.

Bavelas, Janet Beavin (1990). Can One Not Communicate? Behaving and Communicating: A Reply to Motley. *Western Journal of Speech Communication* 54 (Fall): 593–602.

Baxter, Leslie A. (1983). Relationship Disengagement: An Examination of the Reversal Hypothesis. *Western Journal of Speech Communication* 47:85–98.

Baxter, Leslie A. (1986). Gender Differences in the Heterosexual Relationship Rules Embedded in Break-up Accounts. *Journal of Social and Personal Relationships* 3:289–306.

Baxter, Leslie A. (1988). A Dialectical Perspective on Communication Strategies in Relationship Development. In *Handbook of Personal Relationships,* ed. Steve W. Duck. New York: Wiley.

Baxter, Leslie A. (1990). Dialectical Contradictions in Relationship Development. *Journal of Social and Personal Relationships* 7 (February): 69–88.

Baxter, Leslie A., and C. Bullis (1986). Turning Points in Developing Romantic Relationships. *Human Communication Research* 12 (Summer): 469–493.

Baxter, Leslie A., and Eric P. Simon (1993). Relationship Maintenance Strategies and Dialectical Contradictions in Personal Relationships. *Journal of Social and Personal Relationships* 10 (May): 225–242.

Baxter, Leslie A., and W. W. Wilmot (1984). Secret Tests: Social Strategies for Acquiring Information About the State of the Relationship. *Human Communication Research* 11:171–201.

Beach, Wayne A. (1990). On (Not) Observing Behavior Interactionally. *Western Journal of Speech Communication* 54 (Fall): 603–612.

Beatty, M. (1988). Situational and Predispositional Correlates of Public Speaking Anxiety. *Communication Education* 37:28–39.

Beck, A. T. (1988). *Love Is Never Enough.* New York: Harper and Row.

Becker, Samuel L., and Churchill L. Roberts (1992). *Discovering Mass Communication.* 3d ed. New York: HarperCollins.

Beebe, Steven A., and John T. Masterson (1986). *Family Talk: Interpersonal Communication in the Family.* New York: Random House.

Beebe, Steven A., and John T. Masterson (2000). *Communication in Small Groups: Principles and Practices.* 6th ed. New York: Longman.

Bell, Andrew (1996). Personal communication, November.

Bell, Robert A., and N. L. Buerkel-Rothfuss (1990). S(he) Loves Me, S(he) Loves Me Not: Predictors of Relational Information-Seeking in Courtship and Beyond. *Communication Quarterly* 38:64–82.

Bennett, Mark (1990). Children's Understanding of the Mitigating Function of Disclaimers. *Journal of Social Psychology* 130 (February): 29–37.

Berg, John H., and Richard L. Archer (1983). The Disclosure-Liking Relationship. *Human Communication Research* 10:269–281.

Berger, Charles R., and James J. Bradac (1982). *Language and Social Knowledge: Uncertainty in Interpersonal Relations.* London: Edward Arnold.

Berger, Charles R., and Richard J. Calabrese (1975). Some Explorations in Initial Interaction and Beyond: Toward a Theory of Interpersonal Communication. *Human Communication Research* 1 (Winter): 99–112.

Berger, P. L., and T. Luckmann (1980). *The Social Construction of Reality.* New York: Irvington.

Berman, J. J., V. Murphy-Berman, and P. Singh (1985). Cross-Cultural Similarities and Differences in Perceptions of Fairness. *Journal of Cross-Cultural Psychology* 16:55–67.

Bernstein, W. M., W. G. Stephan, and M. H. Davis (1979). Explaining Attributions for Achievement: A Path Analytic Approach. *Journal of Personality and Social Psychology* 37:1810–1821.

Berry, John W., Ype H. Poortinga, Marshall H. Segall, and Pierre R. Dasen (1992). *Cross-Cultural Psychology: Research and Applications.* Cambridge: Cambridge University Press.

Berscheid, E., and H. T. Reis (1998). Attraction and close relationships. In *The Handbook of Social Psychology*, 4th ed., Vol. 2, ed. D. Gilbert, S. Fiske, and G. Lindzey. New York: Freeman, pp. 193–281.

Berscheid, Ellen (1985). Interpersonal Attraction. In *Handbook of Social Psychology,* ed. G. Lindzey and E. Aronson. New York: Random House, pp. 413–484.

Bierhoff, Hans W., and Renate Klein (1991). Dimensionen der Liebe: Entwicklung einer Deutschsprachigen Skala zur Erfassung von Liebesstilen. *Zeitschrift for Differentielle und Diagnostische Psychologie* 12 (March): 53–71.

Bippus, Amy, and John A. Daly (1999). What Do People Think Causes Stage Fright? Naive Attributions About the Reasons for Public Speaking Anxiety. *Communication Education* 48 (January): 63–72.

Bishop, Jerry E. (1993). New Research Suggests That Romance Begins by Falling Nose Over Heels in Love. *Wall Street Journal* (April 7): B1.

Blieszner, Rosemary, and Rebecca G. Adams (1992). *Adult Friendship.* Thousand Oaks, CA: Sage.

Blood, Robert O., Jr. (1973). Resolving Family Conflicts. In *Conflict Resolution Through Communication,* ed. Fred E. Jandt. New York: Harper and Row, pp. 221–239.

Blumstein, Philip, and Pepper Schwartz (1983). *American Couples: Money, Work, Sex.* New York: Morrow.

Bochner, Arthur (1984). The Functions of Human Communication in Interpersonal Bonding. In *Handbook of Rhetorical and Communication Theory,* ed. C. C. Arnold and J. W. Bowers (1984). Boston: Allyn and Bacon, pp. 544–621.

Bochner, Arthur, and Clifford Kelly (1974). Interpersonal Competence: Rationale, Philosophy, and Implementation of a Conceptual Framework. *Communication Education* 23:279–301.

Bochner, Stephen (1994). Cross-Cultural Differences in the Self-concept: A Test of Hofstede's Individualism/Collectivism Distinction. *Journal of Cross Cultural Psychology* 25 (June): 273–283.

Bochner, Stephen, and Beryl Hesketh (1994). Power Distance, Individualism/Collectivism, and Job-related Attitudes in a Culturally Diverse Work Group. *Journal of Cross Cultural Psychology* 25 (June): 233–257.

Bok, Sissela (1978). *Lying: Moral Choice in Public and Private Life.* New York: Pantheon.

Bok, Sissela (1983). *Secrets.* New York: Vintage.

Booth-Butterfield, Melanie (1998). Measurement of Communication Flexibility: Working Adults vs. College Students. *Communication Research Reports* 15 (Fall): 365–369.

Borden, George A. (1991). *Cultural Orientation: An Approach to Understanding Intercultural Communication.* Englewood Cliffs, NJ: Prentice-Hall.

Bosmajian, Haig (1974). *The Language of Oppression.* Washington, DC: Public Affairs Press.

Boster, Franklin J., et al. (1999). The Impact of Guilt and Type of Compliance-Gaining Message on Compliance. *Communication Monographs* 66 (June): 168–177.

Bravo, Ellen, and Ellen Cassedy (1992). *The 9 to 5 Guide to Combating Sexual Harassment.* New York: Wiley.

Breidenstein-Cutspec, Patricia, and Elizabeth Goering (1989). Exploring Cultural Diversity: A Network Analysis of the Communicative Correlates of Shyness Within the Black Culture. *Communication Research Reports* 6 (June): 37–46.

Bremner, John B. (1980). *Words on Words: A Dictionary for Writers and Others Who Care About Words.* New York: Columbia University Press.

Bresnahan, Mary I., and Deborah H. Cai (1996). Gender and Agression in the Recognition of Interruption. *Discourse Processes* 21 (March/April): 171–189.

Bridges, Carl R. (1996). The Characteristics of Career Achievement Perceived by African American College Administrators. *Journal of Black Studies* 26 (July): 748–767.

Briton, Nancy J., and Judith A. Hall (1995). Beliefs About Female and Male Nonverbal Communication. *Sex Roles* 32 (January): 79–90.

Briton, Nancy J., and Judith A. Hall (1995). Gender-Based Expectancies and Observer Judgments of Smiling. *Journal of Nonverbal Behavior* 19 (Spring): 49–65.

Brody, Jane F. (1994). Notions of Beauty Transcend Culture, New Study Suggests. *New York Times* (March 21): A14.

Brougher, Toni (1982). *A Way with Words.* Chicago: Nelson-Hall.

Brown, Penelope (1980). How and Why Are Women More Polite: Some Evidence from a Mayan Community. In *Women and Language in Literature and Society,* ed. Sally McConnell-Ginet, Ruth Borker, and Mellie Furman. New York: Praeger, pp. 111–136.

Brown, Penelope, and S. C. Levinson (1987). *Politeness: Some Universals of Language Usage.* Cambridge: Cambridge University Press.

Brownell, Judi (1987). Listening: The Toughest Management Skill. *Cornell Hotel and Restaurant Administration Quarterly* 27:64–71.

Bugental, J., and S. Zelen (1950). Investigations into the "Self-Concept." I. The W-A-Y Technique. *Journal of Personality* 18:483–498.

Bull, R., and N. Rumsey (1988). *The Social Psychology of Facial Appearance.* New York: Springer-Verlag.

Buller, David B., and R. Kelly Aune (1992). The Effects of Speech Rate Similarity on Compliance: Application of Communication Accommodation Theory. *Western Journal of Communication* 56 (Winter): 37–53.

Buller, David B., Beth A. LePoire, R. Kelly Aune, and Sylvie Eloy (1992). Social Perceptions as Mediators of the Effect of Speech Rate Similarity on Compliance. *Human Communication Research* 19 (December): 286–311.

Bumby, Kurt M., and David J. Hansen (1997). Intimacy Deficits, Fear of Intimacy, and Loneliness Among Sexual Offenders. *Criminal Justice and Behavior* 24 (September): 315–331.

Burgoon, Judee K. (1991). Relational Message Interpretations of Touch, Conversational Distance, and Posture. *Journal of Nonverbal Behavior* 15 (Winter): 233–259.

Burgoon, Judee K., and Jerold L. Hale (1988). Nonverbal Expectancy Violations: Model Elaboration and Application to Immediacy Behaviors. *Communication Monographs* 55:58–79.

Burgoon, Judee K., David B. Buller, and W. Gill Woodall (1995). *Nonverbal Communication: The Unspoken Dialogue.* 2d ed. New York: McGraw-Hill.

Burgoon, Michael (1971). The Relationship Between Willingness to Manipulate Others and Success in Two Different Types of Basic Speech Communication Courses. *Communication Education* 20:178–183.

Burns, D. D. (1980). *Feeling Good.* New York: New American Library.

Buss, David M., and David P. Schmitt (1993). Sexual Strategies Theory: An Evolutionary Perspective on Human Mating. *Psychological Review* 100 (April): 204–232.

Butler, Pamela E. (1981). *Talking to Yourself: Learning the Language of Self-Support.* New York: Harper and Row.

Cabello, B., and R. Terrell (1994). Making Students Feel Like Family: How Teachers Create Warm and Caring Classroom Climates. *Journal of Classroom Interaction* 29:17–23.

Camden, Carl, Michael T. Motley, and Ann Wilson (1984). White Lies in Interpersonal Communication: A Taxonomy and Preliminary Investigation of Social Motivations. *Western Journal of Speech Communication* 48:309–325.

Canary, D. J., and L. Stafford (1994). Maintaining Relationships Through Strategic and Routine Interaction. In *Communication and Relational Maintenance,* ed. D. J. Canary and L. Stafford. New York: Academic Press.

Canary, Daniel J., William R. Cupach, and Susan J. Messman (1995). *Relationship Conflict: Conflict in Parent-Child, Friendship, and Romantic Relationships.* Thousand Oaks, CA: Sage.

Canary, Daniel J., and Kimberley S. Hause (1993). Is There Any Reason to Research Sex Differences in Communication? *Communication Quarterly* 41 (Spring): 129–144.

Canary, Daniel J., and Laura Stafford (1994). *Communication and Relational Maintenance.* Orlando, Fla.: Academic Press.

Canary, Daniel J., Laura Stafford, Kimberley S. Hause, and Lise A. Wallace (1993). An Inductive Analysis of Relational Maintenance Strategies: Comparisons Among Lovers, Relatives, Friends, and Others. *Communication Research Reports* 10 (June): 5–14.

Cappella, Joseph N. (1993). The Facial Feedback Hypothesis in Human Interaction: Review and Speculation. *Journal of Language and Social Psychology* 12 (March–June): 13–29.

Carducci, Bernardo J., with Philip G. Zimbardo (1996). Are You Shy? *Psychology Today* 28 (November–December): 34–41, 64–70, 78–82.

Carlock, C. Jesse, ed. (1999). *Enhancing Self-Esteem.* 3d ed. Philadelphia, PA: Accelerated Development, Inc.

Carroll, D. W. (1994). *Psychology of Language.* 2d ed. Pacific Grove, CA: Brooks/Cole.

Carroll, John B., ed. (1956). *Language, Thought, and Reality: Selected Writings of Benjamin Lee Whorf.* New York: Wiley.

Chadwick-Jones, J. K. (1976). *Social Exchange Theory: Its Structure and Influence in Social Psychology.* New York: Academic Press.

Chaney, Robert H., Carolyne A. Givens, Melanie F. Aoki, and Michael L. Gombiner (1989). Pupillary Responses in Recognizing Awareness in Persons with Profound Mental Retardation. *Perceptual and Motor Skills* 69 (October): 523–528.

Chang, Hui-Ching, and G. Richard Holt (1996). The Changing Chinese Interpersonal World: Popular Themes in Interpersonal Communication Books in Modern Taiwan. *Communication Quarterly* 44 (Winter): 85–106.

Chanowitz, B., and E. Langer (1981). Premature Cognitive Commitment. *Journal of Personality and Social Psychology* 41:1051–1063.

Chen, Guo-Ming (1992). Differences in Self-Disclosure Patterns Among Americans versus Chinese: A Comparative Study. Paper presented at the annual meeting of the Eastern Communication Association, Portland, Me.

Chen, Ling (1993). Chinese and North Americans: An Epistemological Exploration of Intercultural Communication. *Howard Journal of Communications* 4 (Summer): 342–357.

Cheney, George, and Phillip K. Tompkins (1987). Coming to Terms with Organizational Identification and Commitment. *Central States Speech Journal* 38 (Spring): 1–15.

Chesebro, Joseph L., and James C. McCroskey (1998). The Relationship of Teacher Clarity and Teacher Immediacy with Students' Experiences of State Receiver Apprehension. *Communication Quarterly* 46 (Fall): 446–456.

Christie, Richard (1970). Scale Construction. In *Studies in Machiavellianism,* ed. R. Christie and F. L. Geis. New York: Academic Press, pp. 35–52.

Clark, Ruth Anne (1991). *Studying Interpersonal Communication: The Research Experience.* Thousand Oaks, CA: Sage.

Clement, Donald A., and Kenneth D. Frandsen (1976). On Conceptual and Empirical Treatments of Feedback in Human Communication. *Communication Monographs* 43:11–28.

Cline, M. G. (1956). The Influence of Social Context on the Perception of Faces. *Journal of Personality* 2:142–185.

Cody, Michael J. (1982). A Typology of Disengagement Strategies and an Examination of the Role Intimacy, Reactions to Inequity, and Relational Problems Play in Strategy Selection. *Communication Monographs* 49:148–170.

Collier, Mary Jane (1991). Conflict Competence Within African, Mexican, and Anglo American Friendships. In *Cross-Cultural Interpersonal Communication,* ed. Stella Ting-Toomey and Felipe Korzenny. Thousand Oaks, CA: Sage, pp. 132–154.

Collins, James E., and Leslie F. Clark (1989). Responsibility and Rumination: The Trouble with Understanding the Dissolution of a Relationship. *Social Cognition* 7 (Summer): 152–173.

Collins, Nancy L., and Lynn Carol Miller (1994). Self-Disclosure and Liking: A Meta-Analytic Review. *Psychological Bulletin* 116 (November): 457–475.

Cooley, Charles Horton (1922). *Human Nature and the Social Order.* Rev. ed. New York: Scribner's.

Coon, Christine A., and Paula J. Schwanenflugel (1996). Evaluation of Interruption Behavior by Naive Encoders. *Discourse Processes* 22 (July/August): 1–24.

Copeland, Lennie, and Lewis Griggs (1985). *Going International: How to Make Friends and Deal Effectively in the Global Marketplace.* New York: Random House.

Counts, D. A., J. K. Brown, and J. C. Campbell (1992). *Sanctions and Sanctuary: Cultural Perspectives on the Beating of Wives.* Boulder, CO: Westview Press.

Crohn, Joel (1995). *Mixed Matches: How to Create Successful Interracial, Interethnic, and Interfaith Relationships.* New York: Fawcett Columbine.

Cross, E. E., and L. Madson (1997). Models of the Self: Self-Construals and Gender. *Psychological Bulletin* 122:5–37.

Crusco, April H., and Christopher G. Wetzel (1984). The Midas Touch: The Effects of Interpersonal Touch on Restaurant Tipping. *Personality and Social Psychology Bulletin* 10 (December): 512–517.

Dainton, M., and L. Stafford (1993). Routine Maintenance Behaviors: A Comparison of Relationship Type, Partner Similarity, and Sex Differences. *Journal of Social and Personal Relationships* 10:255–272.

Davis, Flora (1973). *Inside Intuition.* New York: New American Library.

Davis, Keith (1977). The Care and Cultivation of the Corporate Grapevine. In *Readings in Interpersonal and Organizational Communication,* 3d ed., ed. R. Huseman, C. Logue, and D. Freshley. Boston: Holbrook, pp. 131–136.

Davis, Keith (1980). Management Communication and the Grapevine. In *Intercom: Readings in Organizational Communication,* ed. S. Ferguson and S. D. Ferguson. Rochelle Park, NJ: Hayden Books, pp. 55–66.

Davis, Murray S. (1973). *Intimate Relations.* New York: Free Press.

Deal, James E., and Karen Smith Wampler (1986). Dating Violence: The Primacy of Previous Experience. *Journal of Social and Personal Relationships* 3:457–471.

Deaux, K., and M. LaFrance (1998). Gender. In *The Handbook of Social Psychology*, 4th ed., Vol. 1, ed. D. Gilbert, S. Fiske, and G. Lindzey. New York: Freeman, pp. 788–828.

deBono, Edward (1987). *The Six Thinking Hats.* New York: Penguin.

DeCecco, John (1988). Obligation versus Aspiration. In *Gay Relationships,* ed. John DeCecco. New York: Harrington Park Press.

DeFrancisco, Victoria (1991). The Sound of Silence: How Men Silence Women in Marital Relations. *Discourse and Society* 2:413–423.

Delia, Jesse G. (1977). Constructivism and the Study of Human Communication. *Quarterly Journal of Speech* 63:66–83.

Delia, Jesse G., Barbara J. O'Keefe, and Daniel J. O'Keefe (1982). The Constructivist Approach to Communication. In *Human Communication Theory: Comparative Essays,* ed. Frank E. X. Dance. New York: Harper and Row, pp. 147–191.

Derlega, V. J., B. A. Winstead, P. T. P. Wong, and S. Hunter (1985). Gender Effects in an Initial Encounter: A Case Where Men Exceed Women in Disclosure. *Journal of Social and Personal Relationships* 2:25–44.

Derlega, Valerian J., Barbara A. Winstead, Paul T. P. Wong, and Michael Greenspan (1987). Self-Disclosure and Relationship Development: An Attributional Analysis. In *Interpersonal Processes: New Directions in Communication Research,* ed. Michael E. Roloff and Gerald R. Miller. Thousand Oaks, CA: Sage, pp. 172–187.

DeVito, Joseph A., ed. (1981). *Communication: Concepts and Processes.* 3d ed. Englewood Cliffs, NJ: Prentice Hall.

DeVito, Joseph A. (1989). *The Nonverbal Communication Workbook.* Prospect Heights, IL: Waveland Press.

DeVito, Joseph A., and Michael L. Hecht, eds. (1990). *The Nonverbal Communication Reader.* Prospect Heights, IL: Waveland Press.

Dillard, James Price, ed. (1990). *Seeking Compliance: The Production of Interpersonal Influence Messages.* Scottsdale, AZ: Gorsuch Scarisbrick.

Dindia, Kathryn (1987). The Effects of Sex of Subject and Partner on Interruptions. *Human Communication Research* 13:345–371.

Dindia, Kathryn, and Leslie A. Baxter (1987). Strategies for Maintaining and Repairing Marital Relationships. *Journal of Social and Personal Relationships* 4:143–158.

Dindia, Kathryn, and Mary Anne Fitzpatrick (1985). Marital Communication: Three Approaches Compared. In *Understanding Personal Relationships: An Interdisciplinary Approach,* ed. Steve Duck and Daniel Perlman. Thousand Oaks, CA: Sage, pp. 137–158.

Dion, K. K., and K. L. Dion (1996). Cultural Perspectives on Romantic Love. *Personal Relationships* 3:5–17.

Dion, K., E. Berscheid, and E. Walster (1972). What Is Beautiful Is Good. *Journal of Personality and Social Psychology* 24:285–290.

Dion, Karen K., and Kenneth L. Dion (1993a). Individualistic and Collectivist Perspectives on Gender and the Cultural Context of Love and Intimacy. *Journal of Social Issues* 49 (Fall): 53–69.

Dion, Kenneth L., and Karen K. Dion (1993b). Gender and Ethnocultural Comparisons in Styles of Love. *Psychology of Women Quarterly* 17 (December): 464–473.

Dolgin, Kim G., Leslie Meyer, and Janet Schwartz (1991). Effects of Gender, Target's Gender, Topic, and Self-Esteem on Disclosure to Best and Midling Friends. *Sex Roles* 25 (September): 311–329.

Donohue, William A., with Robert Kolt (1992). *Managing Interpersonal Conflict.* Thousand Oaks, CA: Sage.

Dosey, M., and M. Meisels (1976). Personal Space and Self-Protection. *Journal of Personality and Social Psychology* 38:959–965.

Douglas, William (1994). The Acquaintanceship Process: An Examination of Uncertainty, Information Seeking, and Social Attraction during Initial Conversation. *Communication Research* 21 (April): 154–176.

Drass, Kriss A. (1986). The Effect of Gender Identity on Conversation. *Social Psychology Quarterly* 49 (December): 294–301.

Dresser, Norine (1996). *Multicultural Manners: New Rules of Etiquette for a Changing Society.* New York: Wiley.

Dreyfuss, Henry (1971). *Symbol Sourcebook.* New York: McGraw–Hill.

Drummond, Kent, and Robert Hopper (1993). Acknowledgment Tokens in Series. *Communication Reports* 6 (Winter): 47–53.

Duck, Steve (1986). *Human Relationships.* Thousand Oaks, CA: Sage.

Duncan, Barry L., and Joseph W. Rock (1991). *Overcoming Relationship Impasses: Ways to Initiate Change When Your Partner Won't Help.* New York: Plenum Press/Insight Books.

Duncan, S. D., Jr. (1972). Some Signals and Rules for Taking Speaking Turns in Conversation. *Journal of Personality and Social Psychology* 23:283–292.

Duran, R. L., and L. Kelly (1988). The Influence of Communicative Competence on Perceived Task, Social, and Physical Attraction. *Communication Quarterly* 36:41–49.

Eder, D., and J. L. Enke (1991). The Structure of Gossip: Opportunities and Constraints on Collective Expression Among Adolescents. *American Sociological Review* 56:494–508.

Ehrenhaus, Peter (1988). Silence and Symbolic Expression. *Communication Monographs* 55 (March): 41–57.

Ekman, Paul (1985). *Telling Lies: Clues to Deceit in the Marketplace, Politics, and Marriage.* New York: W. W. Norton.

Ekman, Paul, and Wallace V. Friesen (1969). The Repertoire of Nonverbal Behavior: Categories, Origins, Usage, and Coding. *Semiotica* 1:49–98.

Ekman, Paul, and Wallace V. Friesen (1978). *The Facial Action Coding System.* Palo Alto, CA: Consulting Psychologists Press.

Ekman, Paul, Wallace V. Friesen, and Phoebe Ellsworth (1972). *Emotion in the Human Face: Guidelines for Research and an Integration of Findings.* New York: Pergamon Press.

Ellis, Albert (1988). *How to Stubbornly Refuse to Make Yourself Miserable About Anything, Yes Anything.* Secaucus, NJ: Lyle Stuart.

Ellis, Albert, and Robert A. Harper (1975). *A New Guide to Rational Living.* Hollywood, CA: Wilshire Books.

Elmes, Michael B., and Gary Gemmill (1990). The Psychodynamics of Mindlessness and Dissent in Small Groups. *Small Group Research* 21 (February): 28–44.

Esten, Geri, and Lynn Willmott (1993). Double-Bind Message: The Effects of Attitude Towards Disability in Therapy. *Women and Therapy* 14:29–41.

Exline, R. V., S. L. Ellyson, and B. Long (1975). Visual Behavior as an Aspect of Power Role Relationships. In *Nonverbal Communication of Aggression,* ed. P. Pliner, L. Krames, and T. Alloway. New York: Plenum Press.

Farrell, M. P., and S. D. Rosenberg (1981). *Men at Midlife.* Westport, CT: Auburn House.

Feeley, Thomas H., and Mark A. deTurck (1995). Global Cue Usage in Behavioral Lie Detection. *Communication Quarterly* 43 (Fall): 420–430.

Fengler, A. P. (1974). Romantic Love in Courtship: Divergent Paths of Male and Female Students. *Journal of Comparative Family Studies* 5:134–139.

Fernald, C. D. (1995). When in London . . . : Differences in Disability Language Preferences Among English-Speaking Countries. *Mental Retardation* 33 (April): 99–103.

Festinger, L., S. Schachter, and K. W. Back (1950). *Social Pressures in Informal Groups: A Study of Human Factors in Housing.* New York: Harper and Row.

Fischer, C. S., and S. J. Oliker (1983). A Research Note on Friendship, Gender, and the Life Cycle. *Social Forces* 62:124–133.

Fisher, Donna (1995). *People Power: 12 Power Principles to Enrich Your Business, Career, and Personal Networks.* Austin, TX: Bard and Stephen.

Fishman, Joshua (1960). A Systematization of the Whorfian Hypothesis. *Behavioral Science* 5:323–339.

Fitzpatrick, Mary Anne (1983). Predicting Couples' Communication from Couples' Self-Reports. In *Communication Yearbook 7,* ed. R. N. Bostrom. Thousand Oaks, CA: Sage, pp. 49–82.

Fitzpatrick, Mary Anne (1988). *Between Husbands and Wives: Communication in Marriage.* Thousand Oaks, CA: Sage.

Fitzpatrick, Mary Anne (1991). Sex Differences in Marital Conflict: Social Psychophysiological versus Cognitive Explanations. *Text* 11:341–364.

Floyd, James J. (1985). *Listening: A Practical Approach.* Glenview, IL: Scott, Foresman.

Fox, M., M. Gibbs, and D. Auerbach (1985). Age and Gender Dimensions of Friendship. *Psychology of Women Quarterly* 9:489–501.

Fraser, Bruce (1990). Perspectives on Politeness. *Journal of Pragmatics* 14 (April): 219–236.

Frazier, P. A., and S. W. Cook (1993). Correlates of Distress Following Heterosexual Relationship Dissolution. *Journal of Social and Personal Relationships* 10:55–67.

Freedman, Jonathan (1978). *Happy People: What Happiness Is, Who Has It, and Why.* New York: Ballantine.

French, J. R. P., Jr., and B. Raven (1968). The Bases of Social Power. In *Group Dynamics: Research and Theory,* 3d ed., ed. Dorwin Cartwright and Alvin Zander. New York: Harper and Row, pp. 259–269.

Frentz, Thomas (1976). A General Approach to Episodic Structure. Paper presented at the Western Speech Association Convention, San Francisco. Cited in Reardon (1987).

Friedman, Joel, Marcia Mobilia Boumil, and Barbara Ewert Taylor (1992). *Sexual Harassment.* Deerfield Beach, FL: Health Communications, Inc.

Fuller, Linda K. (1995). *Media-Mediated Relationships: Straight and Gay, Mainstream and Alternative Perspectives.* New York: Harrington Park Press.

Furlow, F. Bryant (1996). The Smell of Love. *Psychology Today* 29 (March/April): 38–45.

Furnham, Adrian, and Stephen Bochner (1986). *Culture Shock: Psychological Reactions to Unfamiliar Environments.* New York: Methuen.

Galvin, Kathleen, and Bernard J. Brommel (2000). *Family Communication: Cohesion and Change.* 5th ed. Glenview, IL: Scott, Foresman.

Gangestad, S., and M. Snyder (1985). To Carve Nature at Its Joints: On the Existence of Discrete Classes in Personality. *Psychological Review* 92:317–349.

Gao, Ge, and William B. Gudykunst (1995). Attributional Confidence, Perceived Similarity, and Network Involvement in Chinese and American Romantic Relationships. *Communication Quarterly* 43 (Fall): 431–445.

Gelles, R., and C. Cornell (1985). *Intimate Violence in Families.* Thousand Oaks, CA: Sage.

Gergen, K. J., M. S. Greenberg, and R. H. Willis (1980). *Social Exchange: Advances in Theory and Research.* New York: Plenum Press.

Gibb, Jack (1961). Defensive Communication. *Journal of Communication* 11:141–148.

Giles, Howard, Anthony Mulac, James J. Bradac, and Patricia Johnson (1987). Speech Accommodation Theory: The First Decade and Beyond. In *Communication Yearbook 10,* ed. Margaret L. McLaughlin. Thousand Oaks, CA: Sage, pp. 13–48.

Glucksberg, Sam, and Joseph H. Danks (1975). *Experimental Psycholinguistics: An Introduction.* Hillsdale, NJ: Lawrence Erlbaum.

Goffman, Erving (1967). *Interaction Ritual: Essays on Face-to-Face Behavior.* New York: Pantheon.

Goffman, Erving (1971). *Relations in Public: Microstudies of the Public Order.* New York: Harper Colophon.

Goleman, Daniel (1992). Studies Find No Disadvantage in Growing Up in a Gay Home. *New York Times* (December 2): C14.

Goleman, Daniel (1995a). *Emotional Intelligence.* New York: Bantam.

Goleman, Daniel (1995b). For Man and Beast, Language of Love Shares Many Traits. *New York Times* (February 14): C1, C9.

Gonzalez, Alexander, and Philip G. Zimbardo (1985). Time in Perspective. *Psychology Today* 19:20–26. Reprinted in DeVito and Hecht (1990).

Goodwin, Robin, and Iona Lee (1994). Taboo Topics Among Chinese and English Friends: A Cross-Cultural Comparison. *Journal of Cross Cultural Psychology* 25 (September): 325–338.

Gorden, William I., and Randi J. Nevins (1993). *We Mean Business: Building Communication Competence in Business and Professions.* New York: Longman.

Gordon, Thomas (1975). *P.E.T.: Parent Effectiveness Training.* New York: New American Library.

Gottman, John (1993). *What Predicts Divorce: The Relationships Between Marital Processes and Marital Outcomes.* Hillsdale, NJ: Lawrence Erlbaum Associates.

Gottman, John (1994). *Why Marriages Succeed or Fail.* New York: Simon and Schuster.

Gottman, John M., James Coan, Sybil Carrere, and Catherine Swanson (1998). Predicting Marital Happiness and Stability from Newlywed Interactions. *Journal of Marriage and the Family* 60 (February): 5–22.

Gould, Stephen Jay (1995). No More "Wretched Refuse." *New York Times* (June 7): A27.

Graham, E. E. (1994). Interpersonal Communication Motives Scale. In *Communication Research Measures: A Sourcebook,* ed. R. B. Rubin, P. Palmgreen, and H. E. Sypher. New York: Guilford, pp. 211–216.

Graham, E. E., C. A. Barbato, and E. M. Perse (1993). The Interpersonal Communication Motives Model. *Communication Quarterly* 41:172–186.

Graham, Jean Ann, and Michael Argyle (1975). The Effects of Different Patterns of Gaze, Combined with Different Facial Expressions, on Impression Formation. *Journal of Movement Studies* 1 (December): 178–182.

Graham, Jean Ann, Pio Ricci Bitti, and Michael Argyle (1975). A Cross-Cultural Study of the Communication of Emotion by Facial and Gestural Cues. *Journal of Human Movement Studies* 1 (June): 68–77.

Grant, August E., and K. Kendall Guthrie (1991). Television Shopping: A Media System Dependency Perspective. *Communication Research* 18 (December): 773–798.

Greif, Esther Blank (1980). Sex Differences in Parent-Child Conversations. *Women's Studies International Quarterly* 3:253–258.

Grice, H. P. (1975). Logic and Conversation. In *Syntax and Semantics,* Vol. 3, *Speech Acts,* ed. P. Cole and J. L. Morgan. New York: Seminar Press, pp. 41–58.

Griffin, Em (2000). *A First Look at Communication Theory.* 3d ed. New York: McGraw-Hill.

Griffin, Em, and Glenn G. Sparks (1990). Friends Forever: A Longitudinal Exploration of Intimacy in Same-Sex Friends and Platonic Pairs. *Journal of Social and Personal Relationships* 7:29–46.

Gross, Larry (1991). The Contested Closet: The Ethics and Politics of Outing. *Critical Studies in Mass Communication* 8 (September): 352–388.

Gu, Yueguo (1990). Polite Phenomena in Modern Chinese. *Journal of Pragmatics* 14 (April): 237–257.

Gudykunst, W., and T. Nishida (1984). Individual and Cultural Influence on Uncertainty Reduction. *Communication Monographs* 51:23–36.

Gudykunst, W., S. Yang, and T. Nishida (1985). A Cross-Cultural Test of Uncertainty Reduction Theory: Comparisons of Acquaintance, Friend, and Dating Relationships in Japan, Korea, and the United States. *Human Communication Research* 11:407–454.

Gudykunst, W. B., ed. (1983). *Intercultural Communication Theory: Current Perspectives.* Thousand Oaks, CA: Sage.

Gudykunst, W. B. (1989). Culture and the Development of Interpersonal Relationships. In *Communication Yearbook 12,* ed. J. A. Anderson. Thousand Oaks, CA: Sage, pp. 315–354.

Gudykunst, W. B., and Y. Y. Kim (1992). *Communicating with Strangers: An Approach to Intercultural Communication.* 2d ed. New York: Random House.

Gudykunst, William B. (1994). *Bridging Differences: Effective Intergroup Communication.* 2d ed. Thousand Oaks, CA: Sage.

Gudykunst, William B., and Stella Ting-Toomey, with Elizabeth Chua (1988). *Culture and Interpersonal Communication.* Thousand Oaks, CA: Sage.

Guerrero, L. K., S. V. Eloy, and A. I. Wabnik (1993). Linking Maintenance Strategies to Relationship Development and Disengagement: A Reconceptualization. *Journal of Social and Personal Relationships* 10:273–282.

Guerrero, Laura, Joseph A. DeVito, and Michael L. Hecht, eds. (1999). *The Nonverbal Communication Reader: Classic and Contemporary Readings.* Prospect Heights, IL: Waveland Press.

Guerrero, Laura K. (1997). Nonverbal Involvement Across Interactions with Same-Sex Friends, Opposite-Sex Friends, and Romantic Partners: Consistency or Change? *Journal of Social and Personal Relationships* 14 (February): 31–58.

Guerrero, Laura K., and Peter A. Andersen (1991). The Waxing and Waning of Relational Intimacy: Touch as a Function of Relational Stage, Gender and Touch Avoidance. *Journal of Social and Personal Relationships* 8 (May): 147–165.

Guerrero, Laura K., and Peter A. Andersen (1994). Patterns of Matching and Initiation: Touch Behavior and Touch Avoidance Across Romantic Relationship Stages. *Journal of Nonverbal Behavior* 18 (Summer): 137–153.

Haferkamp, Claudia J. (1991/1992). Orientations to Conflict: Gender, Attributes, Resolution Strategies, and Self-Monitoring. *Current Psychology: Research and Reviews* 10 (Winter): 227–240.

Haga, Yasushi (1988). Traits de Langage et Caractere Japonais. *Cahiers de Sociologie Economique et Culturelle* 9 (June): 105–109.

Hall, Edward T. (1959). *The Silent Language.* Garden City, NY: Doubleday.

Hall, Edward T. (1963). System for the Notation of Proxemic Behavior. *American Anthropologist* 65:1003–1026.

Hall, Edward T. (1966). *The Hidden Dimension.* Garden City, NY: Doubleday.

Hall, Edward T. (1976). *Beyond Culture.* Garden City, NY: Anchor Press.

Hall, Edward T., and Mildred Reed Hall (1987). *Hidden Differences: Doing Business with the Japanese.* New York: Anchor Books.

Hall, J. A. (1984). *Nonverbal Sex Differences.* Baltimore: Johns Hopkins University Press.

Hall, Joan Kelly (1993). Tengo una Bomba: The Paralinguistic and Linguistic Conventions of the Oral Practice *Chismeando. Research on Language and Social Interaction* 26:55–83.

Han, Sang-pil, and Shavitt, Sharon (1994). Persuasion and Culture: Advertising Appeals in Individualistic and Collectivistic Societies. *Journal of Experimental Social Psychology* 30 (July): 326–350.

Haney, William (1973). *Communication and Organizational Behavior: Text and Cases.* 3d ed. Homewood, IL: Irwin.

Harrell, W. Andrew (1990). Husband's Masculinity, Wife's Power, and Marital Conflict. *Social Behavior and Personality* 18:207–215.

Harris, Judy (1995). Educational Telecomputing Projects: Interpersonal Exchanges. *Computing Teacher* 22 (March): 60–64.

Harris, Marvin (1993). *Culture, People, Nature: An Introduction to General Anthropology.* 6th ed. New York: Longman.

Hart, Fiona (1990). The Construction of Masculinity in Men's Friendships: Misogyny, Heterosexism and Homophobia. *Resources for Feminist Research* 19 (September/December): 60–67.

Hart, R. P., and D. M. Burks (1972). Rhetorical Sensitivity and Social Interaction. *Communication Monographs* 39:75–91.

Hart, R. P., R. E. Carlson, and W. F. Eadie (1980). Attitudes Toward Communication and the Assessment of Rhetorical Sensitivity. *Communication Monographs* 47:1–22.

Harvey, John H., Rodney Flanary, and Melinda Morgan (1986). Vivid Memories of Vivid Loves Gone By. *Journal of Social and Personal Relationships* 3:359–373.

Hasart, Julie K., and Kevin L. Hutchinson (1993). The Effects of Eyeglasses on Perceptions of Interpersonal Attraction. *Journal of Social Behavior and Personality* 8:521–528.

Hasegawa, Tomohiro, and William B. Gudykunst (1998). Silence in Japan and the United States. *Journal of Cross Cultural Psychology* 29 (September): 668–684.

Hatfield, Elaine, and Richard L. Rapson (1992). Similarity and Attraction in Close Relationships. *Communication Monographs* 59:209–212.

Hatfield, Elaine, and Richard L. Rapson (1996). *Love and Sex: Cross Cultural Perspectives.* Boston: Allyn and Bacon.

Hayakawa, S. I., and A. R. Hayakawa (1989). *Language in Thought and Action.* 5th ed. New York: Harcourt Brace Jovanovich.

Hays, Robert B. (1989). The Day-to-Day Functioning of Close Versus Casual Friendships. *Journal of Social and Personal Relationships* 6:21–37.

Heasley, John B. "Sean," Charles E. Babbitt, and Harold J. Burback (1995). The Role of Social Context in Students' Anticipatory Reaction to a "Fighting Word." *Sociological Focus* 27 (August): 281–283.

Hecht, Michael L., Mary Jane Collier, and Sidney Ribeau (1993). *African American Communication: Ethnic Identity and Cultural Interpretation.* Thousand Oaks, CA: Sage.

Heiskell, Thomas L., and Joseph F. Rychiak (1986). The Therapeutic Relationship: Inexperienced Therapists' Affective Preference and Empathic Communication. *Journal of Social and Personal Relationships* 3:267–274.

Hellweg, Susan A. (1992). Organizational Grapevines. In *Readings in Organizational Communication,* ed. Kevin L. Hutchinson. Dubuque, IA: William. C. Brown, pp. 159–172.

Henderson, M., and A. Furnham (1982). Similarity and Attraction: The Relationship Between Personality, Beliefs, Skills, Needs, and Friendship Choice. *Journal of Adolescence* 5:111–123.

Hendrick, Clyde, and Susan Hendrick (1990). A Relationship-Specific Version of the Love Attitudes Scale. In *Handbook of Replication Research in the Behavioral and Social Sciences* (special issue), ed. J. W. Heulip, *Journal of Social Behavior and Personality* 5:239–254.

Hendrick, Clyde, Susan Hendrick, Franklin H. Foote, and Michelle J. Slapion-Foote (1984). Do Men and Women Love Differently? *Journal of Social and Personal Relationships* 1:177–195.

Henley, Nancy M. (1977). *Body Politics: Power, Sex, and Nonverbal Communication.* Englewood Cliffs, NJ: Prentice Hall.

Hensley, Wayne E. (1996). A Theory of the Valenced Other: The Intersection of the Looking-Glass-Self and Social Penetration. *Social Behavior and Personality* 24:293–308.

Hess, Eckhard H. (1975). *The Tell-Tale Eye.* New York: Van Nostrand Reinhold.

Hess, John A. (1993). Assimilating Newcomers Into an Organization: A Cultural Perspective. *Journal of Applied Communication Research* 21 (May): 189–210.

Hess, Eckhard H., Allan L. Seltzer, and John M. Schlien (1965). Pupil Response of Hetero- and Homosexual Males to Pictures of Men and Women: A Pilot Study. *Journal of Abnormal Psychology* 70:165–168.

Hess, Ursula, Arvid Kappas, Gregory J. McHugo, John T. Lanzetta, et al. (1992). The Facilitative Effect of Facial Expression on the Self-Generation of Emotion. *International Journal of Psychophysiology* 12 (May): 251–265.

Hewitt, John, and Randall Stokes (1975). Disclaimers. *American Sociological Review* 40:1–11.

Hofstede, Geert (1983). National Culture Revisited. *Behavior Science Research* 18:285–305.

Hofstede, Geert (1997). *Cultures and Organizations: Software of the Mind.* New York: McGraw-Hill.

Hoft, Nancy L. (1995). *International Technical Communication: How to Export Information About High Technology.* New York: Wiley.

Hoijer, Harry, ed. (1954). *Language in Culture.* Chicago: University of Chicago

Holden, Janice M. (1991). The Most Frequent Personality Priority Pairings in Marriage and Marriage Counseling. *Individual Psychology Journal of Adlerian Theory, Research, and Practice* 47 (September): 392–398.

Holmes, Janet (1986). Compliments and Compliment Responses in New Zealand English. *Anthropological Linguistics* 28:485–508.

Holmes, Janet (1995). *Women, Men and Politeness.* New York: Longman.

Honeycutt, James (1986). A Model of Marital Functioning Based on an Attraction Paradigm and Social Penetration Dimensions. *Journal of Marriage and the Family* 48 (August): 51–59.

Hopper, Robert, Mark L. Knapp, and Lorel Scott (1981). Couples' Personal Idioms: Exploring Intimate Talk. *Journal of Communication* 31:23–33.

Hosman, Lawrence A. (1989). The Evaluative Consequences of Hedges, Hesitations, and Intensifiers: Powerful and Powerless Speech Styles. *Human Communication Research* 15:383–406.

How Americans Communicate. http://www.natcom.org/Research/Roper/how_Americans_communicate.htm.

Huston, Michelle, and Pepper Schwartz (1995). The Relationships of Lesbians and Gay Men. In Wood, Julia T. and Steve Duck (1995). *Under-Studied Relationships: Off the Beaten Track.* Thousand Oaks, CA: Sage, pp. 89–121.

Ikemi, Akira, and Shinya Kubota (1996). Humanistic Psychology in Japanese Corporations: Listening and the Small Steps of Change. *Journal of Humanistic Psychology* 36 (Winter): 104–121.

Infante, Dominic A. (1988). *Arguing Constructively.* Prospect Heights, IL: Waveland Press.

Infante, Dominic A., Teresa A. Chandler, and Jill E. Rudd (1989). Test of an Argumentative Skill Deficiency Model of Interspousal Violence. *Communication Monographs* 56 (June): 163–177.

Infante, Dominic A., Karen C. Hartley, Matthew M. Martin, Mary Anne Higgins, Stephen D. Bruning, and Gyeongho Hur (1992). Initiating and Reciprocating Verbal Aggression: Effects on Credibility and Credited Valid Arguments. *Communication Studies* 43 (Fall): 182–190.

Infante, Dominic A., and Andrew Rancer (1982). A Conceptualization and Measure of Argumentativeness. *Journal of Personality Assessment* 46:72–80.

Infante, Dominic A., Andrew S. Rancer, and Felecia F. Jordan (1996). Affirming and Nonaffirming Style, Dyad Sex, and the Perception of Argumentation and Verbal Aggression in an Interpersonal Dispute. *Human Communication Research* 22 (March): 315–334.

Infante, Dominic A., Andrew S. Rancer, and Deanna F. Womack (1996). *Building Communication Theory.* 3d ed. Prospect Heights, IL: Waveland Press.

Infante, Dominic A., Bruce L. Riddle, Cary L. Horvath, and S. A. Tumlin (1992). Verbal Aggressiveness: Messages and Reasons. *Communication Quarterly* 40 (Spring): 116–126.

Infante, Dominic A., Teresa Chandler Sabourin, Jill E. Rudd, and Elizabeth A. Shannon (1990). Verbal Aggression in Violent and Nonviolent Marital Disputes. *Communication Quarterly* 38 (Fall): 361–371.

Infante, Dominic A., and C. J. Wigley (1986). Verbal Aggressiveness: An Interpersonal Model and Measure. *Communication Monographs* 53:61–69.

Insel, Paul M., and Lenore F. Jacobson, eds. (1975). *What Do You Expect? An Inquiry into Self-Fulfilling Prophecies.* Menlo Park, CA: Cummings.

Iverson, Jana M., and Susan Goldin-Meadow, eds. (1998). *The Nature and Functions of Gesture in Children's Communication.* San Francisco: Jossey-Bass.

Ivy, Diana K., and Phil Backlund (2000). *Exploring Gender-Speak: Personal Effectiveness in Gender Communication.* 2d ed. New York: McGraw-Hill.

Jackson, Linda A., and Kelly S. Ervin (1992). Height Stereotypes of Women and Men: The Liabilities of Shortness for Both Sexes. *Journal of Social Psychology* 132 (August): 433–445.

Jaksa, James A., and Michael S. Pritchard (1994). *Communication Ethics: Methods of Analysis.* 2d ed. Belmont, CA: Wadsworth.

James, David L. (1995). *The Executive Guide to Asia-Pacific Communications.* New York: Kodansha International.

Jandt, Fred E. (1995). *Intercultural Communication.* Thousand Oaks, CA: Sage.

Jandt, Fred E., and Mary B. Nemnich (1995). *Using the Internet in Your Job Search.* Indianapolis, IN: Jist Works, Inc.

Janus, Samuel S., and Cynthia L. Janus (1993). *The Janus Report on Sexual Behavior.* New York: Wiley.

Jaworski, Adam (1993). *The Power of Silence: Social and Pragmatic Perspectives.* Thousand Oaks, CA: Sage.

Johannesen, Richard L. (1996). *Ethics in Human Communication.* 4th ed. Prospect Heights, IL: Waveland Press.

Johansson, Warren, and William A. Percy (1994). *Outing: Shattering the Conspiracy of Silence.* New York: Harrington Park Press.

Johnson, C. E. (1987). An Introduction to Powerful and Powerless Talk in the Classroom. *Communication Education* 36:167–172.

Johnson, F. L., and E. J. Aries (1983). The Talk of Women Friends. *Women's Studies International Forum* 6:353–361.

Johnson, Frank A., and Anthony J. Marsella (1978). Differential Attitudes Toward Verbal Behavior in Students of Japanese and European Ancestry. *Genetic Psychology Monographs* 97 (February): 43–76.

Jones, E. E., et al. (1984). *Social Stigma: The Psychology of Marked Relationships.* New York: W. H. Freeman.

Jones, Stanley (1986). Sex Differences in Touch Communication. *Western Journal of Speech Communication* 50:227–241.

Jones, Stanley, and A. Elaine Yarbrough (1985). A Naturalistic Study of the Meanings of Touch. *Communication Monographs* 52:19–56. A version of this paper appears in DeVito and Hecht (1990).

Jourard, Sidney M. (1968). *Disclosing Man to Himself.* New York: Van Nostrand Reinhold.

Jourard, Sidney M. (1971a). *Self-Disclosure.* New York: Wiley.

Jourard, Sidney M. (1971b). *The Transparent Self.* Rev. ed. New York: Van Nostrand Reinhold.

Kanner, Bernice (1989). Color Schemes. *New York Magazine* (April 3): 22–23.

Kapoor, Suraj, Arnold Wolfe, and Janet Blue (1995). Universal Values Structure and Individualism-Collectivism: A U.S. Test. *Communication Research Reports* 12 (Spring): 112–123.

Kassing, Jeffrey W. (1997). Development of the Intercultural Willingness to Communicate Scale. *Communication Research Reports* 14 (Fall): 399–407.

Kearney, P., T. G. Plax, V. P. Richmond, and J. C. McCroskey (1984). Power in the Classroom IV: Alternatives to Discipline. In *Communication Yearbook 8,* ed. R. N. Bostrom. Thousand Oaks, CA: Sage, pp. 724–746.

Kearney, P., T. G. Plax, V. P. Richmond, and J. C. McCroskey (1985). Power in the Classroom III: Teacher Communication Techniques and Messages. *Communication Education* 34:19–28.

Keating, Caroline F., Alan Mazur, and Marshall H. Segall (1977). Facial Gestures Which Influence the Perception of Status. *Sociometry* 40 (December): 374–378.

Kelly, P. Keith (1994). *Team Decision-Making Techniques.* Irvine, CA: Richard Chang Associates.

Kennedy, C. W., and C. T. Camden (1988). A New Look at Interruptions. *Western Journal of Speech Communication* 47:45–58.

Keyes, Ken, Jr., and Penny Keyes (1987). *Gathering Power Through Insight and Love.* St. Mary, KY: Living Love.

Keyes, Ralph (1980). *The Height of Your Life.* New York: Warner Books.

Kiesler, Sara, and Lee Sproull (1992). Group Decision Making and Communication Technology. Special Issue: Group Decision Making. *Organizational Behavior and Human Decision Processes* 52 (June): 96–123.

Kim, Min-Sun, and William F. Sharkey (1995). Independent and Interdependent Construals of Self: Explaining Cultural Patterns of Interpersonal Communication in Multi-Cultural Organizational Settings. *Communication Quarterly* 43 (Winter): 20–38.

Kim, Sung Hee, and Richard H. Smith (1993). Revenge and Conflict Escalation. *Negotiation Journal* 9 (January): 37–43.

Kim, Young Yun (1991). Intercultural Communication Competence. In *Cross-Cultural Interpersonal Communication,* ed. Stella Ting-Toomey and Felipe Korzenny. Thousand Oaks, CA: Sage, pp. 259–275.

Kirkpatrick, C., and T. Caplow (1945). Courtship in a Group of Minnesota Students. *American Journal of Sociology* 51:114–125.

Kivik, Piibi Kai (1998). What Silence Says: Communicative Style and Identity. *Trames* 2(1): 66–90.

Kleinfield, N. R. (1992). The Smell of Money. *New York Times* (October 25): 1, 8.

Kleinke, Chris L. (1986). *Meeting and Understanding People.* New York: W. H. Freeman.

Klineberg, O., and W. F. Hull (1979). *At a Foreign University: An International Study of Adaptation and Coping.* New York: Praeger.

Knapp, Mark L. (1984). *Interpersonal Communication and Human Relationships.* Boston: Allyn and Bacon.

Knapp, Mark L., Donald Ellis, and Barbara A. Williams (1980). Perceptions of Communication Behavior Associated with Relationship Terms. *Communication Monographs* 47:262–278.

Knapp, Mark L., and Judith Hall (1992). *Nonverbal Behavior in Human Interaction.* 3d ed. New York: Holt, Rinehart and Winston.

Knapp, Mark L., and Eric H. Taylor (1994). Commitment and Its Communication in Romantic Relationships. In *Perspectives on Close Relationships,* ed. Ann L. Weber and John H. Harvey. Boston: Allyn and Bacon, pp. 153–175.

Knapp, Mark L., and Anita Vangelisti (1992). *Interpersonal Communication and Human Relationships.* 2d ed. Boston: Allyn and Bacon.

Kochman, Thomas (1981). *Black and White: Styles in Conflict.* Chicago: University of Chicago Press.

Komarovsky, M. (1964). *Blue Collar Marriage.* New York: Random House.

Korzybski, A. (1933). *Science and Sanity.* Lakeville, CT: The International Non-Aristotelian Library.

Krebs, Gary L. (1989). *Organizational Communication.* 2d ed. New York: Longman.

Kurdek, Lawrence A. (1994). Areas of Conflict for Gay, Lesbian, and Heterosexual Couples: What Couples Argue About Influences Relationship Satisfaction. *Journal of Marriage and the Family* 56 (November): 923–934.

Kurdek, Lawrence A. (1995). Developmental Changes in Relationship Quality in Gay and Lesbian Cohabiting Couples. *Developmental Psychology* 31 (January): 86–93.

Laing, Milli (1993). Gossip: Does It Play a Role in the Socialization of Nurses? *Journal of Nursing Scholarship* 25 (Spring): 37–43.

Langer, Ellen J. (1989). *Mindfulness.* Reading, MA: Addison-Wesley.

Lanzetta, J. T., J. Cartwright-Smith, and R. E. Kleck (1976). Effects of Nonverbal Dissimulations on Emotional Experience and Autonomic Arousal. *Journal of Personality and Social Psychology* 33:354–370.

Laroche, Christiane, and Gaston Rene deGrace (1997). Factors of Satisfaction Associated with Happiness in Adults. *Canadian Journal of Counselling* 31 (October): 275–286.

Larsen, Randy J., Margaret Kasimatis, and Kurt Frey (1992). Facilitating the Furrowed Brow: An Unobtrusive Test of the Facial Feedback Hypothesis Applied to Unpleasant Affect. *Cognition and Emotion* 6 (September): 321–338.

Lea, Martin, and Russell Spears (1995). Love at First Byte? Building Personal Relationships over Computer Networks. In *Under-Studied Relationships: Off the Beaten Track,* ed. Julia T. Wood and Steve Duck. Thousand Oaks, CA: Sage, pp. 197–233.

Leaper, Campbell, Mary Carson, Carilyn Baker, Heithre Holliday, et al. (1995). Self-Disclosure and Listener Verbal Support in Same-Gender and Cross-Gender Friends' Conversations. *Sex Roles* 33:387–404.

Leaper, Campbell, and Heithre Holliday (1995). Gossip in Same-Gender and Cross-Gender Friends' Conversations. *Personal Relationships* 2 (September): 237–246.

Leathers, Dale G. (1990). *Successful Nonverbal Communication: Principles and Applications.* New York: Macmillan.

Lederer, William J. (1984). *Creating a Good Relationship.* New York: W. W. Norton.

Lederer, William J., and D. D. Jackson (1968). *The Mirages of Marriage.* New York: W. W. Norton.

Lee, Fiona (1993). Being Polite and Keeping MUM: How Bad News Is Communicated in Organizational Hierarchies. *Journal of Applied Social Psychology* 23 (July): 1124–1149.

Lee, John Alan (1976). *The Colors of Love.* New York: Bantam.

Leon, Joseph J., Joseph L. Philbrick, Fernando Parra, Emma Escobedo, et al. (1994). Love Styles Among University Students in Mexico. *Psychological Reports* 74 (February): 307–310.

Leung, K. (1987). Some Determinants of Reactions to Procedural Models for Conflict Resolution: A Cross-National Study. *Journal of Personality and Social Psychology* 53:898–908.

Leung, Kwok (1988). Some Determinants of Conflict Avoidance. *Journal of Cross Cultural Psychology* 19 (March): 125–136.

Lever, Janet (1995). The 1995 Advocate Survey of Sexuality and Relationships: The Women, Lesbian Sex Survey. *The Advocate* 687/688 (August 22): 22–30.

LeVine, R., and K. Bartlett (1984). Pace of Life, Punctuality, and Coronary Heart Disease in Six Countries. *Journal of Cross-Cultural Psychology* 15:233–255.

LeVine, R., S. Sato, T. Hashimoto, and J. Verma (1994). Love and Marriage in Eleven Cultures. Unpublished manuscript. California State University, Fresno, cited in Hatfield and Rapson (1996).

Lewis, David (1989). *The Secret Language of Success.* New York: Carroll and Graf.

Lindeman, Marjaana, Tuija Karakka, and Liisa Keltikangas-Jaervinen (1997). Age and Gender Differences in Adolescents' Reactions to Conflict Situations: Aggression, Prosociality, and Withdrawl. *Journal of Youth and Adolescence* 26:339–351.

Littlejohn, Stephen W. (1999). *Theories of Human Communication.* 6th ed. Belmont, CA: Wadsworth.

Lu, Luo, and Jian Bin Shih (1997). Sources of Happiness: A Qualitative Approach. *Journal of Social Psychology* 137 (April): 181–188.

Luft, Joseph (1969). *Of Human Interaction.* Palo Alto, CA: Mayfield Publishing Co.

Luft, Joseph (1984). *Group Processes: An Introduction to Group Dynamics.* 3d ed. Palo Alto, CA: Mayfield Publishing Co.

Lujansky, H., and G. Mikula (1983). Can Equity Theory Explain the Quality and Stability of Romantic Relationships? *British Journal of Social Psychology* 22:101–112.

Lukens, J. (1978). Ethnocentric Speech. *Ethnic Groups* 2:35–53.

Lurie, Alison (1983). *The Language of Clothes.* New York: Vintage.

Lustig, Myron W., and Jolene Koester (1999). *Intercultural Competence: Interpersonal Communication Across Cultures.* 3d ed. New York: Longman.

Ma, Karen (1996). *The Modern Madame Butterfly: Fantasy and Reality in Japanese Cross-Cultural Relationships.* Rutland, VT: Charles E. Tuttle.

Ma, Ringo (1992). The Role of Unofficial Intermediaries in Interpersonal Conflicts in the Chinese Culture. *Communication Quarterly* 40 (Summer): 269–278.

MacLachlan, James (1979). What People Really Think of Fast Talkers. *Psychology Today* 13:113–117.

Maggio, Rosalie (1997). *Talking About People: A Guide to Fair and Accurate Language.* Phoenix, AZ: Oryx Press.

Main, Frank, and Ronald Oliver (1988). Complementary, Symmetrical, and Parallel Personality Priorities as Indicators of Marital Adjustment. *Individual Psychology Journal of Adlerian Theory, Research, and Practice* 44 (September): 324–332.

Malandro, Loretta A., Larry Barker, and Deborah Ann Barker (1989). *Nonverbal Communication.* 2d ed. New York: Random House.

Malinowski, Bronislaw (1923). The Problem of Meaning in Primitive Languages. In *The Meaning of Meaning,* ed. C. K. Ogden and I. A. Richards. New York: Harcourt Brace Jovanovich, pp. 296–336.

Manes, Joan, and Nessa Wolfson (1981). The Compliment Formula. In *Conversational Routine,* ed. Florian Coulmas. The Hague: Mouton, pp. 115–132.

Mao, LuMing Robert (1994). Beyond Politeness Theory: "Face" Revisited and Renewed. *Journal of Pragmatics* 21 (May): 451–486.

Markway, Barbara G., Cheryl N. Carmin, C. Alex Pollard, and Teresa Flynn (1992). *Dying of Embarrassment: Help for Social Anxiety and Phobia.* Oakland, CA: New Harbinger Publications.

Marsh, Peter (1988). *Eye to Eye: How People Interact.* Topside, MA: Salem House.

Marshall, Evan (1983). *Eye Language: Understanding the Eloquent Eye.* New York: New Trend.

Marshall, Linda L., and Patricia Rose (1987). Gender, Stress, and Violence in the Adult Relationships of a Sample of College Students. *Journal of Social and Personal Relationships* 4:229–316.

Marston, Peter J., Michael L. Hecht, and Tia Robers (1987). True Love Ways: The Subjective Experience and Communication of Romantic Love. *Journal of Personal and Social Relationships* 4:387–407.

Martin, Matthew M., and Carolyn M. Anderson (1995). Roommate Similarity: Are Roommates Who Are Similar in Their Communication Traits More Satisfied? *Communication Research Reports* 12 (Spring): 46–52.

Marwell, G., and D. R. Schmitt (1967). Dimensions of Compliance-Gaining Behavior: An Empirical Analysis. *Sociometry* 39:350–364.

Marwell, Gerald ,and David R. Schmitt (1990). An Introduction. In *Seeking Compliance: The Production of Interpersonal Influence Messages,* ed. James Price Dillard. Scottsdale, AZ.: Gorsuch Scarisbrick, pp. 3–5.

Masheter, Carol, and Linda M. Harris (1986). From Divorce to Friendship: A Study of Dialective Relationship Development. *Journal of Social and Personal Relationships* 3:177–189.

Maslow, Abraham, and N. L. Mintz (1956). Effects of Esthetic Surroundings: I. Initial Effects of Three Esthetic Conditions upon Perceiving Energy and Well-Being in Faces. *Journal of Psychology* 41:247–254.

Matsumoto, David (1991). Cultural Influences on Facial Expressions of Emotion. *Southern Communication Journal* 56 (Winter): 128–137.

Matsumoto, David (1994). *People: Psychology from a Cultural Perspective.* Pacific Grove, CA: Brooks/Cole.

Matsumoto, David (1996). *Culture and Psychology.* Pacific Grove, CA: Brooks/Cole.

Matsumoto, David, and T. Kudoh (1993). American-Japanese Cultural Differences in Attributions of Personality Based on Smiles. *Journal of Nonverbal Behavior* 17:231–243.

Maynard, Harry E. (1963). How to Become a Better Premise Detective. *Public Relations Journal* 19:20–22.

McBroom, William H., and Fred W. Reed (1992). Toward a Reconceptualization of Attitude-Behavior Consistency. Special Issue. Theoretical Advances in Social Psychology. *Social Psychology Quarterly* 55 (June): 205–216.

McCarthy, B., and S. W. Duck (1976). Friendship Duration and Responses to Attitudinal Agreement-Disagreement. *British Journal of Clinical and Social Psychology* 15:377–386.

McCroskey, James, and Lawrence Wheeless (1976). *Introduction to Human Communication.* Boston: Allyn and Bacon.

McCroskey, James C. (1997). *Introduction to Rhetorical Communication.* 7th ed. Englewood Cliffs, NJ: Prentice Hall.

McCroskey, James C., S. Booth-Butterfield, and S. K. Payne (1989). The Impact of Communication Apprehension on College Student Retention and Success. *Communication Quarterly* 37:100–107.

McCroskey, James C., and John Daly, eds. (1987). *Personality and Interpersonal Communication.* Thousand Oaks, CA: Sage.

McCroskey, James C., and Virginia P. Richmond (1990). Willingness to Communicate: Differing Cultural Perspectives. *Southern Communication Journal* 56 (Fall): 72–77.

McGill, Michael E. (1985). *The McGill Report on Male Intimacy.* New York: Harper and Row.

McLaughlin, Margaret L. (1984). *Conversation: How Talk Is Organized.* Thousand Oaks, CA: Sage.

McLaughlin, Margaret L., Michael L. Cody, and C. S. Robey (1980). Situational Influences on the Selection of Strategies to Resist Compliance-Gaining Attempts. *Human Communication Research* 1:14–36.

McLean, Paula A., and Brian D. Jones (1992). Machiavellianism and Business Education. *Psychological Reports* 71 (August): 57–58.

McLoyd, Vonnie C., and Leon Wilson (1992). Telling Them Like It Is: The Role of Economic and Environmental Factors in Single Mothers' Discussions with Their Children. *American Journal of Community Psychology* 20 (August): 419–444.

Meeks, Brenda S., Susan S. Hendrick, and Clyde Hendrick (1998). Communication, Love and Relationship Satisfaction. *Journal of Social and Personal Relationships* 15 (December): 755–773.

Mendoza, Louis (1995). Ethos, Ethnicity, and the Electronic Classroom: A Study in Contrasting Educational Environments. Paper presented at the 46th Annual Meeting of the Conferences on College Composition and Communication. Washington, D. C. (March 23–25).

Merton, Robert K. (1957). *Social Theory and Social Structure.* New York: Free Press.

Messick, R. M., and K. S. Cook, eds. (1983). *Equity Theory: Psychological and Sociological Perspectives.* New York: Praeger.

Metts, Sandra (1989). An Exploratory Investigation of Deception in Close Relationships. *Journal of Social and Personal Relationships* 6 (May): 159–179.

Metz, Michael E., B. R. Rosser, and Nancy Strapko (1994). Differences in Conflict Resolution Styles Among Heterosexual, Gay, and Lesbian Couples. *Journal of Sex Research* 31:293–308.

Meyer, Janet R. (1994). Effect of Situational Features on the Likelihood of Addressing Face Needs in Requests. *Southern Communication Journal* 59 (Spring): 240–254.

Midooka, Kiyoshi (1990). Characteristics of Japanese Style Communication. *Media, Culture and Society* 12 (October): 477–489.

Miller, George A., and David McNeill (1969). Psycholinguistics. In *The Handbook of Social Psychology,* 2d ed., Vol. 3, ed. Gardner Lindzey and Elliot Aronson. Reading, MA: Addison-Wesley, pp. 666–794.

Miller, Gerald R. (1978). The Current State of Theory and Research in Interpersonal Communication. *Human Communication Research* 4:164–178.

Miller, Gerald R., and Judee Burgoon (1990). In DeVito and Hecht (1990), pp. 340–357.

Miller, Gerald R., and Malcolm R. Parks (1982). Communication in Dissolving Relationships. In *Personal Relationships 4. Dissolving Personal Relationships,* ed. Steve Duck. New York: Academic Press, pp. 127–154.

Miller, J. G. (1984). Culture and the Development of Everyday Social Explanation. *Journal of Personality and Social Psychology* 46:961–978.

Miller, Mark J. and Charles T. Wilcox (1986). Measuring Perceived Hassles and Uplifts Among the Elderly. *Journal of Human Behavior and Learning* 3:38–46.

Mintz, N. L. (1956). Effects of Esthetic Surroundings: II. Prolonged and Repeated Experience in a Beautiful and Ugly Room. *Journal of Psychology* 41:459–466.

Mishra, Jitendra M. (1990). Managing the Grapevine. *Public Personnel Management* 19 (Summer): 213–228.

Moghaddam, Fathali M., Donald M. Taylor, and Stephen C. Wright (1993). *Social Psychology in Cross-Cultural Perspective.* New York: W. H. Freeman.

Mole, John (1990). *When in Rome . . . A Business Guide to Cultures and Customs in 12 European Nations.* New York: American Management Association.

Molloy, John (1981). *Molloy's Live for Success.* New York: Bantam.

Molloy, John (1988). *The New Dress for Success.* New York: P. H. Wyden.

Molloy, John (1996). *The New Woman's Dress for Success Book.* Chicago: Follet.

Montgomery, Barbara M. (1981). The Form and Function of Quality Communication in Marriage. *Family Relations* 30:21–30.

Moon, Dreama G. (1966). Concepts of "Culture": Implications for Intercultural Communication Research. *Communication Quarterly* 44 (Winter): 70–84.

Moore, Alexis, John T. Masterson, Diane M. Christophel, and Kathleen A. Shea (1996). College Teacher Immediacy and Student Ratings of Instruction. *Communication Education* 45 (January): 29–39.

Moreland, R. L., and R. Beach (1992). Exposure Effects in the Classroom: The Development of Affinity Among Students. *Journal of Experimental Social Psychology* 28 (May): 255–176.

Morrill, Calvin (1992). Vengeance Among Executives. *Virginia Review of Sociology* 1:51–76.

Morris, Desmond (1977). *Manwatching: A Field Guide to Human Behavior.* New York: Abrams.

Morrow, Gregory D., Eddie M. Clark, and Karla F. Brock (1995). Individual and Partner Love Styles: Implications for the Quality of Romantic Involvements. *Journal of Social and Personal Relationships* 12 (August): 363–387.

Motley, Michael T. (1990a). On Whether One Can(not) not Communicate: An Examination via Traditional Communication Postulates. *Western Journal of Speech Communication* 54 (Winter): 1–20.

Motley, Michael T. (1990b). Communication as Interaction: A Reply to Beach and Bavelas. *Western Journal of Speech Communication* 54 (Fall): 613–623.

Murstein, Bernard I., Joseph R. Merighi, and Stuart A. Vyse (1991). Love Styles in the United States and France: A Cross-Cultural Comparison. *Journal of Social and Clinical Psychology* 10 (Spring): 37–46.

Myers, Scott A. (1995). Student Perceptions of Teacher Affinity-Seeking and Classroom Climate. *Communication Research Reports* 12 (Fall): 192–199.

Naifeh, Steven, and Gregory White Smith (1984). *Why Can't Men Open Up? Overcoming Men's Fear of Intimacy.* New York: Clarkson N. Potter.

Neimeyer, Robert A., and Greg J. Neimeyer (1983). Structural Similarity in the Acquaintance Process. *Journal of Social and Clinical Psychology* 1:146–154.

Neimeyer, Robert A., and Kelly A. Mitchell (1988). Similarity and Attraction: A Longitudinal Study. *Journal of Social and Personal Relationships* 5 (May): 131–148.

Neugarten, Bernice (1979). Time, Age, and the Life Cycle. *American Journal of Psychiatry* 136:887–894.

Neuliep, James W., and James C. McCroskey (1997). The Development of a U.S. and Generalized Ethnocentrism Scale. *Communication Research Reports* 14 (Fall): 385–398.

Nicotera, Anne Maydan, and Andrew S. Rancer (1994). The Influence of Sex on Self-Perceptions and Social Stereotyping of Aggressive Communication Predispositions. *Western Journal of Communication* 58 (Fall): 283–307.

Noble, Barbara Presley (1994). The Gender Wars: Talking Peace. *New York Times* (August 14): 21.

Noelle-Neumann, E. (1973). Return to the Concept of Powerful Mass Media. In *Studies in Broadcasting: An International Annual of Broadcasting Science,* ed. H. Eguchi and K. Sata. Tokyo: Nippon Hoso Kyokai, pp. 67–112.

Noelle-Neumann, E. (1980). Mass Media and Social Change in Developed Societies. In *Mass Communication Review Yearbook,* Vol. 1, ed. G. C. Wilhoit and H. de Bock. Thousand Oaks, CA: Sage, pp. 657–678.

Noelle-Neumann, Elisabeth (1991). The Theory of Public Opinion: The Concept of the Spiral of Silence. *Communication Yearbook/14,* ed. James A. Anderson. Thousand Oaks, CA: Sage, pp. 256–287.

Noller, Patricia (1982). Couple Communication and Marital Satisfaction. *Australian Journal of Sex, Marriage, and Family* 3:69–75.

Noller, Patricia, and Mary Anne Fitzpatrick (1993). *Communication in Family Relationships.* Englewood Cliffs, NJ: Prentice Hall.

Norton, Robert, and Barbara Warnick (1976). Assertiveness as a Communication Construct. *Human Communication Research* 3:62–66.

Notarius, Clifford I., and Lisa R. Herrick (1988). Listener Response Strategies to a Distressed Other. *Journal of Social and Personal Relationships* 5:97–108.

Oberg, K. (1960). Cultural Shock: Adjustment to New Cultural Environments. *Practical Anthropology* 7:177–182.

O'Hair, D., M. J. Cody, and M. L. McLaughlin (1981). Prepared Lies, Spontaneous Lies, Machiavellianism, and Nonverbal Communication. *Human Communication Research* 7:325–339.

O'Hair, Mary John, Michael J. Cody, and Dan O'Hair (1991). The Impact of Situational Dimensions on Compliance-Resisting Strategies: A Comparison of Methods. *Communication Quarterly* 39 (Summer): 226–240.

Olaniran, Bolanle A. (1994). Group Performance in Computer-Mediated and Face-to-Face Communication Media. *Management Communication Quarterly* 7 (February): 256–281.

Osborn, Alex (1957). *Applied Imagination,* rev. ed. New York: Scribners.

Palmer, M. T. (1989). Controlling Conversations: Turns, Topics, and Interpersonal Control. *Communication Monographs* 56:1–18.

Papa, Michael J., and Elizabeth J. Natalle (1989). Gender, Strategy Selection, and Discussion Satisfaction in Interpersonal Conflict. *Western Journal of Speech Communication* 53:260–272.

Parker, Rhonda G., and Roxanne Parrott (1995). Patterns of Self-Disclosure Across Social Support Networks: Elderly, Middle-Aged, and Young Adults. *International Journal of Aging and Human Development* 41:281–297.

Parks, Malcolm R. (1995). Webs of Influence in Interpersonal Relationships. In *Communication and Social Influence Processes,* ed. C. R. Berger and M. E. Burgoon. East Lansing: Michigan State University Press, pp. 155–178.

Parks, Malcolm R., and Kory Floyd (1996). Making Friends in Cyberspace. *Journal of Communication* 46 (Winter): 80–97.

Parlee, Mary Brown (1979). The Friendship Bond. *Psychology Today* 13 (October): 43–54, 113.

Pearson, Judy C. (1993). *Communication in the Family.* 2d ed. New York: HarperCollins.

Pearson, Judy C., and Brian H. Spitzberg (1990). *Interpersonal Communication: Concepts, Components, and Contexts.* 2d ed. Dubuque, IA: William C. Brown.

Pearson, Judy C., Lynn H. Turner, and William Todd-Mancillas (1991). *Gender and Communication.* 2d ed. Dubuque, IA: William C. Brown.

Pearson, Judy C., Richard West, and Lynn H. Turner (1995). *Gender and Communication.* 3d ed. Dubuque, IA: William C. Brown.

Penfield, Joyce, ed. (1987). *Women and Language in Transition.* Albany: State University of New York Press.

Pennebacker, James W. (1991). *Opening Up: The Healing Power of Confiding in Others.* New York: Morrow.

Peplau, Letitia Anne (1988). Research on Homosexual Couples: An Overview. In *Gay Relationships,* ed. John DeCecco. New York: Harrington Park Press, pp. 33–40.

Petrocelli, William, and Barbara Kate Repa (1992). *Sexual Harassment on the Job.* Berkeley, CA: Nolo Press.

Phlegar, Phyllis (1995). *Love Online: A Practical Guide to Digital Dating.* Reading, MA: Addison-Welsey.

Pilkington, Constance, and Steven P. Woods (1999). Risk in Intimacy as a Chronically Accessible Schema. *Journal of Social and Personal Relationships* 16 (1999): 263–263.

Pilkington, Constance J., and Deborah R. Richardson (1988). Perceptions of Risk in Intimacy. *Journal of Social and Personal Relationships* 5:503–508.

Pinker, Steven (1994). *The Language Instinct: How the Mind Creates Language.* New York: William Morrow.

Piot, Charles D. (1993). Secrecy, Ambiguity, and the Everyday in Kabre Culture. *American Anthropologist* 95 (June): 353–370.

Pollack, Andrew (1995). A Cyberspace Front in a Multicultural War. *New York Times* (August 7): D1, D4.

Pollack, Andrew (1996). Happy in the East (^—^) or smiling:—) in the West. *New York Times* (August 12): D5.

Porter, R. H., and J. D. Moore (1981). Human Kin Recognition by Olfactory Cues. *Physiology and Behavior* 27:493–495.

Potter, Ellen F., and Sue V. Rosser (1992). Factors in Life Science Textbooks That May Deter Girls' Interest in Science. *Journal of Research in Science Teaching* 29 (September): 669–686.

Prins, K. S., B. P. Buunk, and N. W. Van Yperen (1994). Equity, Normative Disapproval, and Extramarital Sex. *Journal of Social and Personal Relationships* 10 (February): 39–53.

Prosky, Phoebe S. (1992). Complementary and Symmetrical Couples. *Family Therapy* 19:215–221.

Prusank, Diane T., Robert L. Duran, and Dena A. DeLillo (1993). Interpersonal Relationships in Women's Magazines: Dating and Relating in the 1970s and 1980s. *Journal of Social and Personal Relationships* 10 (August): 307–320.

Purnell, Rosentene B. (1982). Teaching Them to Curse: A Study of Certain Types of Inherent Racial Bias in Language Pedagogy and Practices. *Phylon* 43 (September): 231–241.

Rabinowitz, Fredric E. (1991). The Male-to-Male Embrace: Breaking the Touch Taboo in a Men's Therapy Group. *Journal of Counseling and Development* 69 (July–August): 574–576.

Radford, Mark H, Leon Mann, Yasuyuki Ohta, and Yoshibumi Nakane (1993). Differences Between Australian and Japanese Students in Decisional Self-Esteem, Decisional Stress, and Coping Styles. *Journal of Cross-Cultural Psychology* 24 (September): 284–297.

Rancer, Andrew S. (1998). Argumentativeness. In *Communication and Personality: Trait Perspectives,* ed. James C. McCroskey, John A. Daly, Matthew M. Martin, and Michael J. Beatty. Cresskill, NJ: Hampton Press, pp. 149–170.

Rancer, Andrew S., Roberta L. Kosberg, and Robert A. Baukus (1992). Beliefs About Arguing as Predictors of Trait Argumentativeness: Implications for Training in Argument and Conflict Management. *Communication Education* 41 (October): 375–387.

Rankin, Paul (1929). Listening Ability. *Proceedings of the Ohio State Educational Conference's Ninth Annual Session.*

Rappaport, Herbert, Kathy Enrich, and Arnold Wilson (1985). Relation Between Ego Identity and Temporal Perspective. *Journal of Personality and Social Psychology* 48 (June): 1609–1620.

Raven, B., C. Centers, and A. Rodrigues (1975). The Bases of Conjugal Power. In *Power in Families,* ed. R. E. Cromwell and D. H. Olson. New York: Halsted Press, pp. 217–234.

Rawlins, William K. (1983). Negotiating Close Friendship: The Dialectic of Conjunctive Freedoms. *Human Communication Research* 9 (Spring): 255–266.

Reardon, Kathleen K. (1987). *Where Minds Meet: Interpersonal Communication.* Belmont, CA: Wadsworth.

Rector, M., and E. Neiva (1996). Communication and Personal Relationships in Brazil. In *Communication in Personal Relationships Across Cultures,* ed. W. B. Gudykunst, S. Ting-Toomey, and T. Nishida. Thousand Oaks, CA: Sage, pp. 156–173.

Regan, Pamela C., Elizabeth R. Kocan, and Teresa Whitlock (1998). Ain't Love Grand! A Prototype Analysis of the Concept of Romantic Love. *Journal of Social and Personal Relationships* 15 (June): 411–420.

Reik, Theodore (1944). *A Psychologist Looks at Love.* New York: Rinehart.

Reisman, John (1979). *Anatomy of Friendship.* Lexington, MA: Lewis.

Reisman, John M. (1981). Adult Friendships. In *Personal Relationships. 2: Developing Personal Relationships,* ed. Steve Duck and Robin Gilmour. New York: Academic Press, pp. 205–230.

Remp, Richard (1974). The Efficacy of Electronic Group Meetings. *Policy Sciences* 5 (March): 101–115.

Rezabeck, Landra L., and John J. Cochenour (1995). Emoticons: Visual Cues for Computer-Mediated Communication. In *Imagery and Visual Literacy: Selected Readings from the Annual Conference of the International Visual Literacy Association* (Tempe, Arizona, October 12–16). Eric Document No. ED380096.

Rich, Andrea L. (1974). *Interracial Communication.* New York: Harper and Row.

Richards, I. A. (1951). Communication Between Men: The Meaning of Language. In *Cybernetics, Transactions of the Eighth Conference,* ed. Heinz von Foerster.

Richmond, Virginia P., and James C. McCroskey (1996). *Communication: Apprehension, Avoidance, and Effectiveness.* 4th ed. Scottsdale, AZ: Gorsuch Scarisbrick.

Richmond, Virginia P., and J. C. McCroskey (1984). Power in the Classroom II: Power and Learning. *Communication Education* 33:125–136.

Richmond, Virginia P., and J. C. McCroskey (1989). *Communication: Apprehension, Avoidance, and Effectiveness.* 2d ed. Scottsdale, AZ: Gorsuch Scarisbrick.

Richmond, Virginia P., L. M. Davis, K. Saylor, and J. C. McCroskey (1984). Power Strategies in Organizations: Communication Techniques and Messages. *Human Communication Research* 11:85–108.

Riggio, Ronald E. (1987). *The Charisma Quotient.* New York: Dodd, Mead.

Rockwell, Patricia, David B. Buller, and Judee K. Burgoon (1997). The Voice of Deceit: Refining and Expanding Vocal Cues to Deception. *Communication Research Reports* 14 (Fall): 451–459.

Roeher Institute (1995). *Harm's Way: The Many Faces of Violence and Abuse Against Persons with Disabilities.* North York (Ontario): Roeher Institute.

Roger, Derek, and Willfried Nesshoever (1987). Individual Differences in Dyadic Conversational Strategies: A Further Study. *British Journal of Social Psychology* 26 (September): 247–255.

Rogers, Carl (1970). *Carl Rogers on Encounter Groups.* New York: Harrow Books.

Rogers, Carl, and Richard Farson (1981). Active Listening. In J. DeVito (1981), pp. 137–147.

Rogers, Everett M. (1983). *Diffusion of Innovations.* 3d ed. New York: Free Press.

Rogers, Everett M., and Rekha Agarwala-Rogers (1976). *Communication in Organizations.* New York: Free Press.

Rogers, L. E., and R. V. Farace (1975). Analysis of Relational Communication in Dyads: New Measurement Procedures. *Human Communication Research* 1:222–239.

Rogers-Millar, Edna, and Frank E. Millar (1979). Domineeringness and Dominance: A Transactional View. *Human Communication Research* (Spring): 238–246.

Rohlfing, Mary E. (1995). "Doesn't Anybody Stay in One Place Anymore?" An Exploration of the Under-Studied Phenomenon of Long-Distance Relationships. In *Under-Studied Relationships: Off the Beaten Track,* ed. Julia T. Wood and Steve Duck. Thousand Oaks, CA: Sage, pp. 173–196.

Rokach, Ami (1997). Relations of Perceived Causes and the Experience of Loneliness. *Psychological Reports* 80 (June): 1067–1074.

Rokach, Ami (1998). The Relation of Cultural Background to the Causes of Loneliness. *Journal of Social and Clinical Psychology* 17 (Spring): 75–88.

Rokach, Ami, and Heather Brock (1995). The Effects of Gender, Marital Status, and the Chronicity and Immediacy of Loneliness. *Journal of Social Behavior and Personality* 19 (December): 833–848.

Rokach, Ami, and Heather Brock (1997). The Causes of Loneliness. *Psychology: A Journal of Human Behavior* 33:1–11.

Roloff, Michael E., Gaylen D. Paulson, and Jennifer Vollbrecht (1998). The Interpretation of Coercive Communication: The Effects of Mode of Influence, Powerful Speech, and Speaker Authority. *International Journal of Conflict Management* 9 (April): 139–161.

Rosen, Emanuel (1998). Think Like a Shrink. *Psychology Today* (October): 54–59.

Rosenbaum, M. E. (1986). The Repulsion Hypothesis. On the Nondevelopment of Relationships. *Journal of Personality and Social Psychology* 51:1156–1166.

Rosenfeld, Lawrence (1979). Self-Disclosure Avoidance: Why I Am Afraid to Tell You Who I Am. *Communication Monographs* 46:63–74.

Rosengren, Annika, et al. (1993). Stressful Life Events, Social Support, and Mortality in Men Born in 1933. *British Medical Journal* (October 19). Cited in Goleman (1995a).

Rosenthal, Robert, and L. Jacobson (1968). *Pygmalion in the Classroom.* New York: Holt, Rinehart and Winston.

Rosnow, Ralph L. (1977). Gossip and Marketplace Psychology. *Journal of Communication* 27 (Winter): 158–163.

Rothblum, Esther D., and Lynne A. Bond (1996). *Preventing Heterosexism and Homophobia.* Thousand Oaks, CA: Sage.

Rowatt, Wade C., Michael R. Cunningham, and Perri B. Druen (1999). Lying to Get a Date: The Effect of Facial Physical Attractiveness on the Willingness to Deceive Prospective Dating Partners. *Journal of Social and Personal Relationships* 16: 209–223.

Rowland-Morin, Pamela A., and J. Gregory Carroll (1990). Verbal Communication Skills and Patient Satisfaction: A Study of Doctor-Patient Interviews. *Evaluation and the Health Professions* 13:168–185.

Ruben, Brent D. (1985). Human Communication and Cross-Cultural Effectiveness. In *Intercultural Communication: A Reader,* 4th ed., ed. Larry A. Samovar and Richard E. Porter. Belmont, CA: Wadsworth, pp. 338–346.

Rubenstein, Carin (1993). Fighting Sexual Harassment in Schools. *New York Times* (June 10): C8.

Rubin, Alan, Elizabeth Pearse, and Robert Powell (1985). Loneliness, Parasocial Interaction, and Local Television News Viewing. *Human Communication Research* 12:155–180

Rubin, D. C., E. Groth, and D. J. Goldsmith (1984). Olfactory Cues of Autobiographical Memory. *American Journal of Psychology* 97:493–507.

Rubin, Rebecca, and Michael McHugh (1987). Development of Parasocial Interaction Relationships. *Journal of Broadcasting and Electronic Media* 31:279–292.

Rubin, Rebecca B., C. Fernandez-Collado, and R. Hernandez-Sampieri (1992). A Cross-Cultural Examination of Interpersonal Communication Motives in Mexico and the United States. *International Journal of Intercultural Relations* 16:145–157.

Rubin, Rebecca B., and Elizabeth E. Graham. (1988). Communication Correlates of College Success: An Exploratory Investigation. *Communication Education* 37:14–27.

Rubin, Rebecca B., and M. M. Martin (1994). Development of a Measure of Interpersonal Communication Competence. *Communication Research Reports* 11:33–44.

Rubin, Rebecca B., and Randi J. Nevins (1988). *The Road Trip: An Interpersonal Adventure.* Prospect Heights, IL: Waveland Press.

Rubin, Rebecca B., Elizabeth M. Pearse, and Carole A. Barbato (1988). Conceptualization and Measurement of Interpersonal Communication Motives. *Human Communication Research* 14:602–628.

Rubin, Rebecca B., and Alan M. Rubin (1992). Antecedents of Interpersonal Communication Motivation. *Communication Quarterly* 40:3, 5, 317.

Rubin, Zick (1973). *Liking and Loving: An Invitation to Social Psychology.* New York: Holt, Rinehart and Winston.

Rundquist, Suellen (1992). Indirectness: A Gender Study of Fluting Grice's Maxims. *Journal of Pragmatics* 18 (November): 431–449.

Rusbult, Caryl E., and Bram P. Buunk (1993). Commitment Processes in Close Relationships: An Interdependence Analysis. *Journal of Social and Personal Relationships* 10 (May): 175–204.

Sabatelli, Ronald M., and John Pearce (1986). Exploring Marital Expectations. *Journal of Social and Personal Relationships* 3:307–321.

Sabath, Ann Marie (1999). *International Business Etiquette: Asia and the Pacific Rim.* Franklin Lakes, NJ: Career Press.

Salminen, Simo, and Timo Glad (1992). The Role of Gender in Helping Behavior. *Journal of Social Psychology* 132 (February): 131–133.

Samovar, Larry A., and Richard E. Porter, eds. (1991). *Communication Between Cultures.* Belmont, CA: Wadsworth.

Samter, Wendy, and William R. Cupach (1998). Friendly Fire: Topics Variations in Conflict Among Same- and Cross-Sex Friends. *Communication Studies* 49 (Summer): 121–138.

Sanders, Judith A., Richard L. Wiseman, and S. Irene Matz (1991). Uncertainty Reduction in Acquaintance Relationships in Ghana and the United States. In *Cross-Cultural Interpersonal,* ed. Stella Ting-Toomey and Felipe Korzenny. Thousand Oaks, CA: Sage, pp. 79–98.

Sapadin, Linda A. (1988). Friendship and Gender: Perspectives of Professional Men and Women. *Journal of Social and Personal Relationships* 5:387–403.

Sapir, Edward (1929). *Language: An Introduction to the Study of Speech.* New York: Harcourt, Brace and World.

Sarwer, David B., Seth C. Kalichman, Jennifer R. Johnson, Jamie Early, et al. (1993). Sexual Aggression and Love Styles: An Exploratory Study, *Achives of Sexual Behavior* 22 (June): 265–275.

Satir, Virginia (1983). *Conjoint Family Therapy.* 3d ed. Palo Alto, CA: Science and Behavior Books.

Scandura, T. (1992). Mentorship and Career Mobility: An Empirical Investigation. *Journal of Organizational Behavior* 13:169–174.

Schafer, R. B., and P. M. Keith (1980). Equity and Depression Among Married Couples. *Social Psychology Quarterly* 43:430–435.

Schegloff, E. (1982). Discourses as an Interactional Achievement: Some Uses of "uh huh" and Other Things That Come Between Sentences. In *Georgetown University Roundtable on Language and Linguistics,* ed. Deborah Tannen. Washington, D.C.: Georgetown University Press, pp. 71–93.

Schmidt, Tracy O., and Randolph R. Cornelius (1987). Self-Disclosure in Everyday Life. *Journal of Social and Personal Relationships* 4:365–373.

Schoeneman, T. J., and E. E. Rubanowitz (1985). Attributions in the Advice Columns: Actors and Observers, Causes and Reasons. *Personality and Social Psychology Bulletin* 11:315–325.

Schutz, Astrid (1999). It Was Your Fault! Self-Serving Biases in Autobiographical Accounts of Conflicts in Married Couples. *Journal of Social and Personal Relationships* 16:193–208.

Schwartz, Marilyn, and the Task Force on Bias-Free Language of the Association of American University Presses (1995). *Guidelines for Bias-Free Writing.* Bloomington: Indiana University Press.

Seidman, I. E. (1991). *Interviewing as Qualitative Research: A Guide for Researchers in Education and the Social Sciences.* New York: Teachers College.

Sergios, Paul A., and James Cody (1985). Physical Attractiveness and Social Assertiveness Skills in Male Homosexual Dating Behavior and Partner Selection. *Journal of Social Psychology* 125 (August): 505–514.

Shaffer, David R., et al. (1996). When Boy Meets Girl (Revisited): Gender, Gender Role Orientation, and Prospect of Future Interaction as Determinants of Self-Disclosure Among Same- and Opposite-Sex Acquaintances. *Personality and Social Psychology Bulletin* 22 (May): 495–506.

Shannon, J. (1987). Don't Smile When You Say That. *Executive Female* 10:33, 43. Reprinted in DeVito and Hecht (1990), pp. 115–117.

Sharkey, William F., and Laura Stafford (1990). Turn-Taking Resources Employed by Congenitally Blind Conversers. *Communication Studies* 41 (Summer): 161–182.

Sheppard, James A., and Alan J. Strathman (1989). Attractiveness and Height: The Role of Stature in Dating Preferences, Frequency of Dating, and Perceptions of Attractiveness. *Personality and Social Psychology* 15 (December): 617–627.

Shibazaki, Kozue, and Kelly A. Brennan (1998). When Birds of Different Features Flock Together: A Preliminary Comparison of Intra-Ethnic and Inter-Ethnic Dating Relationships. *Journal of Social and Personal Relationships* 15 (April): 248–256.

Shuter, Robert (1990). The Centrality of Culture. *Southern Communication Journal* 55 (Spring): 237–249.

Siavelis, Rita L., and Leanne K. Lamke (1992). Instrumentalness and Expressiveness: Predictors of Heterosexual Relationship Satisfaction. *Sex Roles* 26 (February): 149–159.

Siegert, John R., and Glen H. Stamp (1994). "Our First Big Fight" as a Milestone in the Development of Close Relationships. *Communication Monographs* 61 (December): 345–360.

Signorile, Michelangelo (1993). *Queer in America: Sex, the Media, and the Closets of Power.* New York: Random House.

Simpson, Jeffry A. (1987). The Dissolution of Romantic Relationships: Factors Involved in Relationship Stability and Emotional Distress. *Journal of Personality and Social Psychology* 53 (October): 683–692.

Sincoff, Michael Z., and Robert S. Goyer (1984). *Interviewing.* New York: Macmillan.

Singelis, T. M. (1994). The Measurement of Independent and Interdependent Self-Construals. *Personality and Social Psychology Bulletin* 20:580–591.

Skopec, Eric William (1986). *Situational Interviewing.* Prospect Heights, IL: Waveland Press.

Slade, Margot (1995). We Forgot to Write a Headlline. But It's Not Our Fault. *New York Times* (February 19): 5.

Snyder, C. R. (1984). Excuses, Excuses. *Psychology Today* 18:50–55.

Snyder, C. R., Raymond L. Higgins, and Rita J. Stucky (1983). *Excuses: Masquerades in Search of Grace.* New York: Wiley.

Snyder, Mark (1987). *Public Appearances, Private Realities.* New York: W. H. Freeman.

Solomon, Denise Haunani, and Jennifer Anne Samp (1998). Power and Problem Appraisal: Perceptual Foundations of the Chilling Effect in Dating Relationships. *Journal of Social and Personal Relationships* 15 (April): 191–209.

Sorenson, Paula S., Katherine Hawkins, and Ritch L. Sorenson (1995). Gender, Psychological Type and Conflict Style Preference. *Management Communication Quarterly* 9 (August): 115–126.

Spencer, Ted (1993). A New Approach to Assessing Self-Disclosure in Conversation. Paper presented at the Annual Convention of the Western Speech Communication Association, Albuquerque, New Mexico.

Spencer, Ted (1994). Transforming Relationships Through Everyday Talk. In *The Dynamics of Relationships: Vol. 4. Understanding Relationships,* ed. Steve Duck. Thousand Oaks, CA: Sage.

Spitzberg, Brian H. (1991). Intercultural Communication Competence. In *Intercultural Communication: A Reader,* ed. Larry A. Samovar and Richard E. Porter. Belmont, CA: Wadsworth, pp. 353–365.

Spitzberg, Brian H., and William R. Cupach (1984). *Interpersonal Communication Competence.* Thousand Oaks, CA: Sage.

Spitzberg, Brian H., and William R. Cupach (1989). *Handbook of Interpersonal Competence Research.* New York: Springer-Verlag.

Spitzberg, Brian H., and Michael L. Hecht (1984). A Component Model of Relational Competence. *Human Communication Research* 10:575–599.

Sprecher, S., and P. Schwartz (1994). Equity and Balance in the Exchange of Contributions in Close Relationships. In *Entitlement and the Affectional Bond: Justice in Close Relationships,* ed. M. J. Lerner and G. Mikula. New York: Plenum, pp. 11–42.

Sprecher, Susan (1987). The Effects of Self-Disclosure Given and Received on Affection for an Intimate Partner and Stability of the Relationship. *Journal of Social and Personal Relationships* 4:115–127.

Sprecher, Susan, and Sandra Metts (1989). Development of the "Romantic Beliefs Scale" and Examination of the Effects of Gender and Gender-Role Orientation. *Journal of Social and Personal Relationships* 6:387–411.

Staines, Graham L., Kathleen J. Pottick, and Deborah A. Fudge (1986). Wives' Employment and Husbands' Attitudes Toward Work and Life. *Journal of Applied Psychology* 71:118–128.

Steil, Lyman K., Larry L. Barker, and Kittie W. Watson (1983). *Effective Listening: Key to Your Success.* Reading, MA: Addison-Wesley.

Steiner, Claude (1981). *The Other Side of Power.* New York: Grove.

Steinfatt, Thomas M. (1987). Personality and Communication: Classic Approaches. In *Personality and Interpersonal Communication,* ed. James C. McCroskey and John A. Daly. Thousand Oaks, CA: Sage, pp. 42–126.

Stephan, Walter G., and Cookie White Stephan (1985). Intergroup Anxiety. *Journal of Social Issues* 41:157–175.

Stephens, Gregory K., and Charles R. Greer (1995). Doing Business in Mexico: Understanding Cultural Differences. *Organizational Dynamics* 24 (Summer): 39–55.

Stern, John A. (1992). The Eye Blink: Affective and Cognitive Influences. In *Anxiety: Recent Developments in Cognitive, Psychophysiological, and Health Research,* ed. Donald G. Forgays, Tytus Sosnowski, and Kazimierz Wrzesniewski. Washington, DC: Hemisphere Publishing, pp. 109–128.

Sternberg, Robert J. (1986). A Triangular Theory of Love. *Psychological Review* 93:119–135.

Sternberg, Robert J. (1988). *The Triangle of Love: Intimacy, Passion, Commitment.* New York: Basic Books.

Stewart, Charles J., and William B. Cash Jr. (1988). *Interviewing: Principles and Practices.* 4th ed. Dubuque, IA: William C. Brown.

Strecker, Ivo (1993). Cultural Variations in the Concept of "Face." *Multilingua* 12:119–141.

Sunnafrank, Michael (1989). Uncertainty in Interpersonal Relationships: A Predicted Outcome Value Interpretation of Gudykunst's Research Program. In *Communication Yearbook 12,* ed. J. A. Anderson. Thousand Oaks, CA: Sage, pp. 355–370.

Sutter, Deirdre L., and Matthew M. Martin (1998). Verbal Aggression During Disengagement of Dating Relationships. *Communication Research Reports* 15 (Summer): 318–326.

Szapocznik, Jose (1995). Research on Disclosure of HIV Status: Cultural Evolution Finds an Ally in Science. *Health Psychology* 14 (January): 4–5.

Tannen, Deborah (1990). *You Just Don't Understand: Women and Men in Conversation.* New York: Morrow.

Tannen, Deborah (1994a). *Gender and Discourse.* New York: Oxford University Press.

Tannen, Deborah (1994b). *Talking from 9 to 5.* New York: Morrow.

Taraban, Carolyn Beth, and Clyde Hendrick (1995). Personality Perceptions Associated with Six Styles of Love. *Journal of Social and Personal Relationships* 12 (August): 453–461.

Taub, Marci (1997). *Interviews.* Princeton, NJ: Princeton Review.

Taylor, D. M., and V. Jaggi (1974). Ethnocentrism and Causal Attribution in a South Indian Context. *Journal of Cross Cultural Psychology* 5:162–171.

Tersine, Richard J., and Walter E. Riggs (1980). The Delphi Technique: A Long-Range Planning Tool. In *Intercom: Readings in Organizational Communication,* ed. Stewart Ferguson and Sherry Devereaux Ferguson. Rochelle Park, NJ: Hayden Books, pp. 363–373.

Thelen, Mark H., Michelle D. Sherman, and Tiffany S. Borst (1998). Fear of Intimacy and Attachment Among Rape Survivors. *Behavior Modification* 22 (January): 108–116.

Thibaut, J. W., and H. H. Kelley (1959). *The Social Psychology of Groups.* New York: Wiley. Reissued (1986). New Brunswick, NJ: Transaction Books.

Thompson, Catherine A., and Donald W. Klopf (1991). An Analysis of Social Style Among Disparate Cultures. *Communication Research Reports* 8 (June/December): 65–72.

Thompson, Catherine A., Donald W. Klopf, and Satoshi Ishii (1991). A Comparison of Social Style Between Japanese and Americans. *Communication Research Reports* 8 (June/December): 165–172.

Ting-Toomey, Stella (1985). Toward a Theory of Conflict and Culture. *International and Intercultural Communication Annual* 9:71–86.

Ting-Toomey, Stella (1986). Conflict Communication Styles in Black and White Subjective Cultures. In *Interethnic Communication: Current Research,* ed. Young Yun Kim. Thousand Oaks, CA: Sage, pp. 75–88.

Tolhuizen, James H. (1986). Perceiving Communication Indicators of Evolutionary Changes in Friendship. *Southern Speech Communication Journal* 52:69–91.

Tolhuizen, James H. (1989). Communication Strategies for Intensifying Dating Relationships: Identification, Use, and Structure. *Journal of Social and Personal Relationships* 6 (November): 413–434.

Trager, George L. (1958). Paralanguage: A First Approximation. *Studies in Linguistics* 13:1–12.

Trager, George L. (1961). The Typology of Paralanguage. *Anthropological Linguistics* 3:17–21.

Trower, P. (1981). Social Skill Disorder. In *Personal Relationships* 3, ed. S. Duck and R. Gilmour. New York: Academic Press, pp. 97–110.

Tschann, J. M. (1988). Self-Disclosure in Adult Friendship: Gender and Marital Status Differences. *Journal of Social and Personal Relationships* 5:65–81.

Ueleke, William, et al. (1983). Inequity Resolving Behavior as a Response to Inequity in a Hypothetical Marital Relationship. *A Quarterly Journal of Human Behavior* 20:4–8.

VanHyning, Memory (1993). *Crossed Signals: How to Say No to Sexual Harassment.* Los Angeles: Infotrends Press.

Van Kijk, Teun A. (1992). Discourse and the Denial of Racism. *Discourse and Society* 3 (January): 87–118.

Varonis, Evangeline Marlos, and Susan M. Gass (1985). Miscommunication in Native/Nonnative Conversation. *Language in Society* 14 (September): 327–343.

Veenendall, Thomas L., and Marjorie C. Feinstein (1995). *Let's Talk About Relationships: Cases in Study.* Prospect Heights, IL: Waveland Press.

Victor, David (1992). *International Business Communication.* New York: HarperCollins.

Von Hassell, Malve (1993). Issei Women: Silences and Fields of Power. *Feminist Studies* 19 (Fall): 549–569.

Walster, E., G. W. Walster, and E. Berscheid (1978). *Equity: Theory and Research.* Boston: Allyn and Bacon.

Walster, Elaine, G. W. Walster, and J. Traupman (1978). Equity and Premarital Sex. *Journal of Personality and Social Psychology* 36:82–92.

Watzlawick, Paul (1977). *How Real Is Real? Confusion, Disinformation, Communication: An Anecdotal Introduction to Communications Theory.* New York: Vintage.

Watzlawick, Paul (1978). *The Language of Change: Elements of Therapeutic Communication.* New York: Basic Books.

Watzlawick, Paul, Janet Helmick Beavin, and Don D. Jackson (1967). *Pragmatics of Human Communication: A Study of Interactional Patterns, Pathologies, and Paradoxes.* New York: W. W. Norton.

Weigel, Daniel J., and Deborah S. Ballard-Reisch (1999). Using Paired Data to Test Models of Relational Maintenance and Marital Quality. *Journal of Social and Personal Relationships* 16 (1999): 175–191.

Weinberg, Harry L. (1959). *Levels of Knowing and Existence.* New York: Harper and Row.

Weiner, Bernard, J. Amirkhan, V. S. Folkes, and J. A. Verette (1987). An Attributional Analysis of Excuse Giving: Studies of a Naive Theory of Emotion. *Journal of Personality and Social Psychology* 52:316–324.

Weinstein, Eugene A., and Paul Deutschberger (1963). Some Dimensions of Altercasting. *Sociometry* 26:454–466.

Weitzman, Jennifer (1996). Drawing a Family History Out of Cyberspace. *New York Times* (June 13): C2.

Wertz, Dorothy C., James R. Sorenson, and Timothy C. Heeren (1988). Can't Get No (Dis) Satisfaction: Professional Satisfaction with Professional-Client Encounters. *Work and Occupations* 15 (February): 36–54.

West, Candace, and Don H. Zimmerman (1977). Women's Place in Everyday Talk: Reflections on Parent-Child Interaction. *Social Problems* 24 (June): 521–529.

Westefeld, J. S., and D. Liddell (1982). Coping with Long-Distance Relationships. *Journal of College Student Personnel* 23:550–551.

Westwood, R. I., F. F. Tang, and P. S. Kirkbride (1992). Chinese Conflict Behavior: Cultural Antecedents and Behavioral Consequences. *Organizational Development Journal* 10 (Summer): 13–19.

Wetzel, Patricia J. (1988). Are "Powerless" Communication Strategies the Japanese Norm? *Language in Society* 17:555–564.

Wheeless, Lawrence R., and Janis Grotz (1977). The Measurement of Trust and Its Relationship to Self-Disclosure. *Human Communication Research* 3:250–257.

Wiederman, Michael W., and Catherine Hind (1999). Extradyadic Involvement During Dating. *Journal of Social and Personal Relationships* 16 (1999):265–274.

Wiemann, John M. (1977). Explication and Test of a Model of Communicative Competence. *Human Communication Research* 3:195–213.

Wilkins, Brenda M., and Peter A. Andersen (1991). Gender Differences and Similarities in Management Communication: A Meta-Analysis. *Management Communication Quarterly* 5 (August): 6–35.

Wilmot, William W. (1995). *Relational Communication.* New York: McGraw-Hill.

Wilson, A. P., and Thomas G. Bishard (1994). "Psst." Here's the Dirt on Gossip. *American School Board Journal* 181 (December): 27–29.

Winhahl, Sven, and Benno Signitzer, with Jean T. Olson (1992). *Using Communication Theory: An Introduction to Planned Communication.* Thousand Oaks, CA: Sage.

Winquist, Lynn A., Cynthia D. Mohr, and David A. Kenny (1998). The Female Positivity Effect in the Perception of Others. *Journal of Research in Personality* 32 (September): 370–388.

Winstead, Barbara A., Valerian J. Derlega, Melinda J. Montgomery, and Constance Pilkington (1995). The Quality of Friendships at Work and Job Satisfaction. *Journal of Social and Personal Relationships* 12 (May): 199–215.

Wolfson, Nessa (1988). The Bulge: A Theory of Speech Behaviour and Social Distance. In *Second Language Discourse: A Textbook of Current Research,* ed. J. Fine. Norwood, N.J: Ablex.

Wolpe, Joseph (1957). *Psychotherapy by Reciprocal Inhibition.* Stanford, CA: Stanford University Press.

Won-Doornink, Myong-Jin (1991). Self-Disclosure and Reciprocity in South Korean and U.S. Male Dyads. In *Cross-Cultural Interpersonal Communication,* ed. Stella Ting-Toomey and Felipe Korzenny. Thousand Oaks, CA: Sage, pp. 116–131.

Wood, Julia T. (1994). *Gendered Lives: Communication, Gender, and Culture.* Belmont, CA: Wadsworth.

Wright, J. W., and L. A. Hosman (1983). Language Style and Sex Bias in the Courtroom: The Effects of Male and Female Use of Hedges and Intensifiers on Impression Formation. *Southern Speech Communication Journal* 48:137–152.

Wright, John W. (1995). *The Universal Almanac 1995.* Kansas City, MO: Andrews and McMeel.

Wright, Paul H. (1978). Toward a Theory of Friendship Based on a Conception of Self. *Human Communication Research* 4:196–207.

Wright, Paul H. (1984). Self-Referent Motivation and the Intrinsic Quality of Friendship. *Journal of Social and Personal Relationships* 1:115–130.

Wright, Paul H. (1988). Interpreting Research on Gender Differences in Friendship: A Case for Moderation and a Plea for Caution. *Journal of Social and Personal Relationships* 5:367–373.

Yerby, Janet, Nancy Buerkel-Rothfuss, and Arthur P. Bochner (1990). *Understanding Family Communication.* Scottsdale, AZ: Gorsuch Scarisbrick.

Yun, Hum (1976). The Korean Personality and Treatment Considerations. *Social Casework* 57:173–178.

Zajonc, Robert B. (1968). Attitudinal Effects of Mere Exposure. *Journal of Personality and Social Psychology Monograph* Suppl. 9, no. 2, pt. 2.

Zima, Joseph P. (1983). *Interviewing: Key to Effective Management.* Chicago: Science Research Associates.

Zimbardo, Philip A. (1977). *Shyness: What It Is and What to Do About It.* Reading, MA: Addison-Wesley.

Zimmer, Troy A. (1986). Premarital Anxieties. *Journal of Social and Personal Relationships* 3:149–159.

Zimmerman, Don H., and Candace West (1975). Sex Roles, Interruptions and Silences in Conversations. In *Language and Sex: Differences and Dominance,* ed. B. Thorne and N. Henley. Rowley, MA: Newbury House.

Zuckerman, M., R. Klorman, D. T. Larrance, and N. H. Spiegel (1981). Facial, Autonomic, and Subjective Components of Emotion: The Facial Feedback Hypothesis versus the Externalizer-Internalizer Distinction. *Journal of Personality and Social Psychology* 41:929–944.

Zunin, Leonard M., and Natalie B. Zunin (1972). *Contact: The First Four Minutes.* Los Angeles: Nash.

PHOTO CREDITS

CHAPTER 1
1: Everett Collection, Inc.; 07: NeoSoft Inc.; 11: David R. Frazier Photolibrary/Photo Researchers, Inc.; 19: Michael Newman/PhotoEdit

CHAPTER 2
23: Kobal Collection; 30: Index Stock Imagery, Inc.; 36: Mary Kate Denny/PhotoEdit;

CHAPTER 3
39: Everett Collection, Inc.; 48: Esbin-Anderson/The Image Works; 49: Terry Williams/The Image Bank

CHAPTER 4
59: Kobal Collection; 66: Richard Hutchings/Photo Researchers, Inc.; 71: SuperStock, Inc.

CHAPTER 5
78: Everett Collection, Inc.; 81: Stewart Cohen/Stone; 85: Frank Micelotta/AP/Wide World Photos

CHAPTER 6
109: Paul Conklin/PhotoEdit; 92: Everett Collection, Inc.; 97: John Coletti/Stock Boston

CHAPTER 7
113: Kobal Collection; 121: Loren Santow/Stone; 125: Kobal Collection

CHAPTER 8
131: Demmie Todd/Everett Collection, Inc.; 140: Josh Mitchell/Index Stock Imagery, Inc.; 144: Mark Burnett/Stock Boston

CHAPTER 9
151: Everett Collection, Inc.; 157: Photofest; 160: Joseph Schuyler/Stock Boston

CHAPTER 10
164: Everett Collection, Inc.; 169: Gary A. Conner/Index Stock Imagery, Inc.; 173: Walter Hodges/Stone

CHAPTER 11
177: Everett Collection, Inc.; 179: Jonathan Daniel/Allsport Photography (USA), Inc.; 184: Jeff Greenberg/PhotoEdit

CHAPTER 12
193: Kobal Collection; 199: M. Siluk/The Image Works; 202: Myrleen Ferguson/PhotoEdit

CHAPTER 13
212: Kobal Collection; 221: E. Agostin/Liaison Agency, Inc.; 225: Robert Frerck/Odyssey Productions; 228: Ian Jones/FSP/Liaison Agency, Inc.

CHAPTER 14
231: Everett Collection, Inc.; 236: V. Hazaticonos/Explorer/Photo Researchers, Inc.; 238: David R. Frazier Photolibrary, Inc.

CHAPTER 15
248: Everett Collection, Inc.; 255: Rick Gerharter/Impact Visuals Photo & Graphics, Inc.; 262: Gary A. Conner/PhotoEdit

CHAPTER 16
264: Everett Collection, Inc.; 268: David Joel/Stone; 276: Joseph Nettis/Photo Researchers, Inc.

CHAPTER 17
283: Everett Collection, Inc.; 286: Jim Whitmer Photography; 290: Photofest

CHAPTER 18
295: Everett Collection, Inc.; 299: Walter Hodges/Stone; 304: Gary Conner/PhotoEdit

CHAPTER 19
312: Archive Photos; 326: Index Stock Imagery, Inc.; 329: David R. Frazier Photolibrary, Inc.

CHAPTER 20
334: Everett Collection, Inc.; 338: Dee Snider/The Image Works; 343: Esbin-Anderson/The Image Works;

CHAPTER 21
350: Everett Collection, Inc.; 355: SuperStock, Inc.; 358: Bruce Ayres/Stone

CHAPTER 22
367: Everett Collection, Inc.; 368: D. Young-Wolff/PhotoEdit; 379: Bachmann/The Image Works;

INDEX

Note: The letters *f* and *t* indicate material in figures and tables, respectively.

C

T